Canadian Cataloguing in Publication Data

Rosen, L.S. (Lawrence Sydney), 1935-
   Accounting: A Decision Approach

Includes index.
ISBN 0-13-001389-7

1. Accounting. I. Title

HF5635.R67 1986   657'.044   C85-099644-9

Prentice-Hall Inc., Englewood Cliffs, *New Jersey*
Prentice-Hall International, Inc., *London*
Prentice-Hall of Australia, Pty., Ltd., *Sydney*
Prentice-Hall of India Pvt., Ltd., *New Delhi*
Prentice-Hall of Japan Inc., *Tokyo*
Prentice-Hall of Southeast Asia (Pte.) Ltd., *Singapore*
Editora Prentice-Hall do Brasil Ltda., *Rio de Janeiro*
Prentice-Hall Hispanoamericana, S.A., *Mexico*

Production Editors: Peter Scargall, Sharyn Rosart
Design: Robert Garbutt Productions
Cover Graphic: J. Hunter
Manufacturing Buyer: Sheldon Fischer
Composition: York Typographers Inc.

ISBN 0-13-001389-7

2 3 4 5 THB 90 89 88 87

Printed in Canada by T.H. Best Printing Company Ltd.

Accounting

A Decision Approach

L.S. ROSEN

York University

Prentice-Hall Canada Series in Accounting

Prentice-Hall Canada Inc.
Scarborough, Ontario

Contents

7   Revenue Recognition   *201*

8   Financial Accounting Concepts   *234*

16   Statement of Changes in Financial Position   *508*

Preface

Accounting education is currently in the midst of a major evolutionary change. The focus in teaching has shifted from an emphasis on detailed procedures toward a greater understanding of concepts, and more importantly, onwards to the way concepts are *applied* in a variety of Canadian businesses. This book attempts to blend a combination of procedures, concepts and application skills into a foundation for financial accounting. Considerable attention has been given to balancing the educational process, so that students not only learn a reasonable number of concepts and procedures but also receive adequate practice in *applying* the concepts. Without such practice, students can too easily resort to a mere memorization of principles or concepts without realizing the most important message—that different concepts apply in each of several situations. Students must comprehend that the "basics" of accounting are not debits and credits, but adaptability and usefulness. Different concepts and procedures have to be fitted to the many, varied circumstances that can be encountered in Canada, and this process requires practice. Students should not complete an introductory accounting course carrying with them the unwarranted belief that one set of basic procedures, rules, or concepts would be applied in such vastly different industries as mining, fishing, logging, oil and gas, banking, computer software, farming, retailing and manufacturing.

Forty years ago, when the body of knowledge of financial accounting was much smaller than it is today, accounting instructors had sufficient time to teach all of the procedures, concepts and applications. As the scope of financial accounting has broadened, however, and the subject has grown in complexity, classroom choices have become essential. Should an introductory accounting course concentrate *primarily* on illustrating a wide range of rules and procedures? If it does, concepts and applications will largely have to be learned by students *after* the course has been completed, and without an instructor's guidance. Learning is a process of risk-taking, in which the student makes mistakes and corrects them: clearly, a decision to teach only procedures—without applications—has severe limitations as an educational approach.

Can the primary emphasis in the classroom be placed on teaching a combination of procedures and concepts? Ten years ago, many Canadian accounting instructors felt that such an approach was ideal for the classroom. Hindsight is now telling us that a combination of procedures and concepts has some serious drawbacks, including undesired student memorization. Educational focus has to be on a broader mixture of knowledge, comprehension, analysis, evaluation and synthesis. The skills needed to interpret or prepare financial statements require development. Consequently, the application of problem diagnosis, analysis, evaluation and judgment has to be given considerable attention, on a chapter by chapter basis. Otherwise, students may find it difficult to grasp a decision approach.

This book is designed to allow instructors considerable flexibility in introducing application skills. Each chapter has four categories of discussion and assignment materials: Questions, Exercises, Problems and Exploration Materials and Cases. Virtually all of the Questions and Exercises are intended to help students build knowledge and comprehension skills. The Problem category should encourage them to develop diagnostic and judgmental skills in a variety of situations. The Exploration Materials and Cases vary in complexity and in the depth of analytical skills that are needed to resolve them. Instructors can, therefore, adapt the level of complexity from chapter to chapter in accordance with their students' abilities and needs.

The illustrations in each chapter have been chosen to dispel any student beliefs that accounting has "right answers" in many or most situations. The need for adaptability, and for tailoring accounting to circumstances is demonstrated in each chapter by referring to different industries, size of companies, types of ownership (private, public, and unincorporated), and similar variables. Naturally, accounting treatment tends to differ because corporate laws, facts, and objectives of accounting vary from company to company. Initially, some students may become frustrated because they do not find right answers. However, reinforcement by the instructor of the book's themes will enable them to adjust to the adaptable nature of financial accounting.

Chapters 1 to 4 devote much space to the bookkeeping cycle, and accounting in traditional teaching settings—such as large, public retailing organizations. Chapter 5 provides an antidote to the emphasis on accrual accounting in the previous chapters. Contrasts between cash and accrual accounting and decision situations are stressed. Chapters 6, 7 and 8, and their appendices, constitute the core of the book and its decision approach. Chapter 6 points out that, where legal constraints are minimal and facts are not clear, objectives of accounting greatly affect how one accounts and reports. Chapter 7 builds on Chapter 6 by illustrating how different objectives and facts can affect accounting for revenue. Chapter 8 provides two sets of key accounting concepts that are referred to extensively in the remaining chapters. Where possible, instructors should allocate considerable time to Chapters 3 to 8 inclusive because the essence of financial accounting is presented in these chapters. The appendices to Chapters 7 and 8 can be assigned whenever the instructor believes that most students are ready to grasp the decision orientation.

Chapters 9 through 17 concentrate on the application of the first eight chapters to a variety of assets and liabilities. These chapters are devoted to imparting to the student a decision orientation for the common situations that are encountered by readers of financial statements.

This book is a blend of the procedural-conceptual, preparer-user, and memorization-application approaches. Its organization is consistent with first and second courses in most disciplines. Students often need to see the broad scope of the subject before they can tackle small, tricky portions of it. Coverage of a broad scope is especially helpful in a course that is taken by non-business students. A course that blends viewpoints and skills is just as likely to provide a solid foundation for accounting majors, who should avoid the temptation to believe that accounting consists primarily of rules and pronouncements.

In recent years, pressure from the public and the government has forced accountants to focus on what the public expects, and not on what accountants have traditionally provided. Financial statements and accounting methods will undergo significant changes by the time today's students become managers. To be ready for greater responsibility and change, students have to improve their decision making, procedural and conceptual skills—and not just one or two of the three.

Suggestions for improving the book are welcome.

L.S. ROSEN
Toronto
January 1986

Acknowledgments

The process of seeking more efficient and effective ways of teaching the essence of accounting is endless. We must follow the nature of learning, and devise new teaching methods, test them in the classroom, and thereby improve accounting education through a trial and error approach. In view of the evolutionary nature of accounting, instructors have no other choice but to seek improvements.

Much of what is contained in this book is the result of classroom experimentation over many years—trying a link between concepts and applications, or between procedures and applications, and finding that some portions help students, but others do not; then trying something else, retaining what is useful and amending the other portions. Given this background to the book, the main acknowledgment has to be to the students who endured the process and provided helpful comments. The next major group of contributors are my colleagues at the Clarkson Gordon Foundation, York University and several other Canadian universities.

The following reviewers for Prentice-Hall Canada Inc. provided many helpful comments:

Harry D. Elmslie   *Lakehead University*
Michael Gibbins   *University of Alberta*
Taylor Gilbert   *University of Toronto*
Veronica Hanton   *Certified General Accountants Association of Ontario*
John Hughes   *Memorial University*
Howard Liebman   *Concordia University*

C.A. Prentice   *University of Calgary*
W.A. Tilleman   *University of Calgary*
James Torcov   *Seneca College*
Nora Wilson   *Humber College*
M. Woltersdorf   *Northern Alberta Institute of Technology*

Several enthusiastic people at Prentice-Hall Canada Inc. gave strong advice: Yolanda De Rooy, Shelley Duke, John Fleming, Elynor Kagan, Lu Mitchell, Cliff Newman, Sharyn Rosart and Marta Tomins. I would also like to acknowledge the wise counselling that I received from the late Frank Hintenberger. Frank, John Fleming and Cliff Newman were among the pioneers in trying to improve accounting education in Canada.

Although many of my colleagues have made contributions to the themes and illustrations, I particularly would like to mention Howard Armitage, Tom Beechy, Joe Bolla, Glenn Bowman, Jylan Khalil, Bill King, J.A. Milburn, Gord Richardson, Seymour Trachimovsky, Raymonde Vachon, Charlie Vincent and John Waterhouse.

A major acknowledgment has to be given to Teresa Colavecchia, my secretary at York University. Typing a manuscript and making helpful suggestions is a major task, and Teresa always meets the deadlines efficiently and cheerfully.

CHAPTER 1

Purposes of Financial Accounting

Chapter Themes

1. There are many different ways of recording and communicating (reporting) accounting figures and information. Learning has to focus on which of the multiple ways fits each of many possible situations, and why particular ways may be inappropriate in some or many situations.

2. Considerable judgment and variations of opinion exist in accounting. Although the teaching of judgment creates some classroom uncertainty and anxiety, it is necessary to impart a sense of the variety of solutions that may be required for particular problems. Otherwise, the course can become a bookkeeping exercise and create serious misconceptions about the practical nature of accounting. Experience has shown that authors of accounting books must stress that there is *not* one, right answer to most accounting situations.

3. From time to time we must pause and ask: What uses can be made of the accounting reports and data that we are preparing? Can we provide more useful reports? If so, at what cost and risk to those who are preparing the reports?

4. Accounting has experienced a knowledge explosion in recent years. To avoid learning obsolete or soon-to-be-outdated accounting, we have to focus on understanding general principles, and give less attention to memorizing current rules.

5. Many myths about accounting such as "precision", "true" methods, there is "only one way of accounting", and "accuracy" must be dispelled before worthwhile learning can occur.

A Fable or Reality?

Douglas Grant owns a tailor shop (called Grant's Tailors) that specializes in making made-to-measure clothing for women and men. He keeps a variety of fabrics in his store so that he can try to please as many potential customers as possible. Mr. Grant's employees try to help a potential customer choose an appropriate weight, color, and pattern of fabric. Then a tailor must prepare the clothes to suit the customer's height, weight, and shape. Many of Mr. Grant's customers buy only made-to-measure clothes. A few, however, sometimes also buy factory-made clothes that are hung on racks at a store across the street. The factory-made clothes have to be modified slightly, after being purchased, to meet the customer's needs.

Mr. Grant's clothes are more expensive than those in the store across the street (called Classic Clothes) because Mr. Grant must pay tailors for the many hours that it takes to fit the clothes to each person. A factory process that assembles many suits of the same size and shape at the same time uses machines more extensively than Mr. Grant's tailors are able to do. Costs per garment are therefore lower at Classic Clothes than at Grant's Tailors. (See Illustration 1-1.)

ILLUSTRATION 1-1

Grant's Tailors	*Classic Clothes*
•	•
•	•
•	•
Made-to-measure clothing (more expensive than Classic Clothes)	Standard sizes, shapes, and fabrics made
•	•
•	•
•	•
Made mainly by people, for one customer	Mainly made by machines, for "average person"

Some customers are able to buy well-fitting clothes in the fabric that they like at Classic Clothes. This would occur when their tastes and body shape fit the average that the designers at the factory had in mind. But most customers would likely have to sacrifice something—color, cloth pattern, or the fit they desire—in order to get a lower price than Grant's Tailors would charge.

Mr. Grant was surprised to learn one day that his accountant saw many similarities between the operations of Grant's Tailors and Classic Clothes and the practice of accounting. That is, sometimes the accountant prepared accounting figures and reports for a broad, general group of readers (called a general purpose report), and sometimes the figures were assembled a different way for the needs of one particular reader (called a special, or specific purpose, report). The general-purpose report may prove useful to one particular reader who seeks general information, but it might also be far less informative for this reader than would a specific, or special-purpose, report.

To illustrate one difference between general and specific-purpose reports, the accountant pointed to the automobile Grant's Tailors uses to deliver clothes to customers. The car cost Mr. Grant $12,000 about six months ago. In its present used condition, however, it can be sold for about $9,000 (or less). The cost of the same make of car today, in new condition, would be about $12,500, because the manufacturer raised its selling price two months ago.

Three different figures exist for the same car: $12,500, $12,000, and $9,000. (More figures for the same car will be mentioned in later chapters.) The most commonly used one for a general-purpose report prepared in accordance with what are called *generally accepted accounting principles*, GAAP, would be the $12,000.[1] The $9,000 could be used in a special-purpose report for a bank manager to tell her how much the car could be sold for *if* Mr. Grant had to sell it to repay a loan made by the bank to Mr. Grant. The $12,500 could also be used in a different special-purpose report for, say, Mr. Grant to tell him how much money he would need to buy a second car, for business purposes. Special-purpose reports may or may not use GAAP.

Users of General Purpose Reports

Who would use the general purpose report? The following people or groups or organizations tend to use them:

1. Department of National Revenue—Taxation (often called Revenue Canada). They require financial figures and reports (called *financial statements*) when calculating the amount of income tax that a taxpayer company has to pay. Often, (but certainly not always) taxation legislation requires the use of figures that would be in general purpose reports.

---

[1]Later in the book, a figure of less than $12,000 will be used to signify that the automobile is now in used condition.

2. Creditors (people who may loan or have loaned money to the company) could use financial statements to try to determine (a) whether and when the loan may be repaid by the company, and (b) what *collateral* or security (such as an automobile or house) could be offered, in the event the loan is not repaid on time and the creditor—perhaps a banker—has to seize the collateral. The seized collateral would then be sold, perhaps at an auction, and the amount received on sale (called *proceeds*) would be used to repay the loan. It is important to remember, however, that figures in special purpose reports could be more useful to creditors than figures in general purpose reports. Much more will be said about this in later chapters.

3. Owners of the company and prospective owners would want to look at the company's general purpose financial statements to obtain a rough indication of how the company is progressing. (Special purpose reports might also be needed to give more than just a rough indication of a company's current status and recent results.) For example, the owners may want to decide whether they ought to sell the company, expand it, and so forth. Portions of the company's financial statements—to be described shortly—may help in these decisions. Much more will be said about users and uses of accounting in later chapters.

In addition to these users of general purpose reports, we could mention (1) union negotiators (who would try to ascertain whether the company can afford to pay more wages), (2) politicians and government policy makers (who may wish to learn how successful are particular industries—perhaps clothing manufacturers—and whether they need government loans or subsidies to survive), and (3) the general public and media (who want to evaluate corporate and government policies). As the themes of this book unfold, we frequently will be discussing entitlement, or access, to financial statements and financial information. The term *accountability* has been given to this interesting topic of how much information corporations (such as Air Canada or Eaton's) and governments ought to provide to the general public. How much privacy are these organizations entitled to? How much information are we entitled to? At what point do we reach a reasonable compromise about entitlements?

Accounting is Evolving

Surprisingly, accountants do not know a great deal about precisely who uses financial statements and for what purposes. Accountants have been able to form only general impressions. For example, they know that some people do not understand financial statements and tend to believe the figures more than they ought to. These people are frequently referred to as *naive investors*. Accountants also know that other readers are *sophisticated* and read financial statements with great care, comparing them to many other sources of information. Sophisticated investors evaluate the financial information for credibility, and believe only what makes sense to them, based on what they have previously read and heard about the company. Naturally, there are individuals and groups of people whose understanding of accounting and financial statements falls somewhere between the naive and the sophisticated. A prime purpose of this book is to assist you to become part of the sophisticated group. To accomplish this goal you have to learn to be both a *preparer* and a *user* of financial statements. When you know how both preparer and user think, you will better grasp what financial statements are saying.

There are many reasons why accountants do not have a better understanding of precisely who uses, and how they use, one of their main products, general-purpose financial statements. One is that users themselves may not know in exact terms how to make use of the financial figures. Most of us do not know for certain why we decided to buy one item instead of another, or chose to do one thing instead of another. Thus, asking users, such as creditors or owners, how they use accounting reports is often not worthwhile. Their answers are often vague. A second reason is that accounting methods evolve when changes in laws, people's attitudes, education levels, and similar factors occur. Like many subjects, accounting has been rocked by a knowledge explosion in the past ten years. Change is inevitable.

The message is therefore quite clear. We must grasp how and why accounting is changing. Above all, we must ascertain the main components that are causing change. Otherwise, our accounting knowledge could become obsolete very quickly. We must learn to sharpen our skills of analysis, judgment, diagnosis, assessment, and evaluation. These are skills that we can use for future years. The challenge for us is to sharpen our skills without becoming frustrated with the uncertainty and change. In summary, unfortunately for newcomers to the subject, there are serious dangers to learning a body of knowledge that is considered basic, only to find later that it is not basic, but is obsolete.

Financial Reporting Approaches

We have briefly discussed general-purpose financial statements, but they will be introduced in detail in this chapter and in the next few chapters. Now we will preview what is to come. At the beginning of most courses, the pieces in the puzzle, or parts, cannot be fully displayed. A general picture, however, can be provided—with this caution: Do not be concerned if you do not understand all the ramifications. We will return to the themes many times. This chapter merely gives us some direction to follow through the course of the book.

So far we have learned that:

1. There are two main classes of *financial accounting* reports: general purpose and special purpose. (Note that we added the word *financial* as a modifier of accounting. Financial, roughly-speaking, means accounting primarily for those *outside* the company, such as owners, creditors, and Revenue Canada. Another type of accounting is *management accounting*; it is designed for managers *inside* the company to enable them to make decisions such as how much to manufacture and at what price to sell. More will be said about this later. This book is virtually restricted to financial accounting.)

2. In the early portions of this book, the main focus will be on general purpose reports. It is important to note that a business organization will have *only one* general-purpose financial report per period of time—per month, per quarter, per year. To have more than one general purpose report for the same time period probably would be regarded as unethical and could be illegal.

This leads us to a consideration that we must always bear in mind as we study general purpose reports—and financial accounting in general. The preparers of these reports (usually accountants and their employers) may not have the same goals or objectives as the users, or readers, such as Revenue Canada or a creditor. Thus, recalling our discussion of Grant's Tailors and Classic Clothes, the general-purpose report may not suit the user's needs. (See Illustration 1-2.)

ILLUSTRATION 1-2

PREPARERS

Such as:

    Accountants
    Business managers

USERS

Such as:

    Revenue Canada
    Creditors
    Owners of the
      business
    Union officials

(Do these two groups want the financial statements to show the same figures, and accomplish the same goals? Is there harmony or conflict between the preparers and users?)

One area of difference between preparers and users was illustrated in the example of the car owned by Grant's Tailors. Which figure should be reported by the preparers of the financial statements to the users? The preparers may want to report the original cost of $12,000, whereas the users may want to know about the $9,000 current selling price, or perhaps the cost of replacement of $12,500. Hence, we could have two markedly different approaches. We will see both harmony and conflict many times throughout the chapters in this book. Which is "right"? Obviously both points of view have merit. Which "wins" when there is a conflict? We will see examples on each side as the course progresses. To understand financial statements we must keep our eyes open to see whether the preparer or the user approach has "won" on each important matter.

It is only natural to want "right" answers. This desire can be dangerous in accounting, however, if we do not remember that what is sensible or appropriate (*not* "right") from a preparer viewpoint may be useless from a particular user viewpoint. This book tries to blend preparer and user thinking into all topics. We will consider differing viewpoints and try not to be biased toward one position through a lack of awareness of other views.

Financial Statements

The general purpose financial statements that were alluded to are:

1. A *balance sheet* (which is prepared as at a particular time, such as the close of business on December 31, 19—1);

2. An *income statement* (which is usually prepared for a period of time, such as the calendar year ending on December 31, 19—1);

3. A *statement of changes in financial position* (which is prepared for the same period of time as that of an income statement); and

4. A *statement of retained income,* or *retained earnings* (which is also prepared for the same period of time as that of an income statement).

In order to prepare the foregoing financial statements (and others that you will learn about later), *measurement,* or *quantification,* is necessary. Generally speaking, accountants concentrate their efforts on measuring, in *dollars,* transactions that have already occurred. They usually avoid attempting to measure the worth of people, because of the lack of agreement on what would be a suitable figure. Exceptions may occur when financial statements of a sports organization (e.g., hockey, baseball, soccer) are being prepared. The sports teams may have paid $X to acquire rights to the person and therefore could record this cost (as we could have for the $12,000 car).

Accountants report information that is not in the foregoing four financial statements on an appended page entitled "notes to financial statements". This process is often called *disclosure.* Some people would say that disclosure also includes all items of information that are within the four financial statements. An example of disclosure that is not in "notes" would be to use the $12,000 cost of the car owned by Grant's Tailors as the primary figure and also to provide the current selling price in brackets:

Automobile, at cost (estimated selling
price $9,000) $12,000

(Some of the disclosure, i.e., the $9,000, could also be in a separate, special-purpose report for one particular user. Sometimes there is overlap between *disclosure* in a general-purpose report, and *measurement* in a special-purpose report.)

A note to the financial statements might read as follows:

Note 1: The current replacement cost of the automobile, in new condition, would be approximately $12,500.

A precise definition of *disclosure* is not important at this point. What is important is that financial reporting be recognized as including both measurement and disclosure. Sometimes an event can be very important but it is not capable of measurement as of the date that the financial statements are being prepared. An example would be a major lawsuit against the business that has yet to be settled in court. Existence of the lawsuit would be shown in notes to the financial statements:

Note 7:   Several lawsuits have been filed or are pending against the company as a result of an aircraft accident in October 19—1. The company carries insurance for claims in excess of $10,000,000. Ultimate liability to the company, if any, is not known at this time.

Balance Sheet

Some courses consist primarily of memorization, others of drill at mechanical exercises, and so forth. The accounting in this book is a combination of memorization and exercise drills, as well as analytical, diagnostic, judgmental, and abstract reasoning. Memorization is used at first to learn the terminology, e.g., the term *financial accounting* or a formula/algorithm. Memorization will eventually give way to a process of reasoning. At some point, problem solving, thinking, and creativity skills need attention.[2]

Our first major formula is:

$$\text{ASSETS} = \text{LIABILITIES} + \text{OWNER'S EQUITY}$$
$$(\text{or OWNER'S INVESTMENT})$$

This can be restated as:

$$\text{ASSETS} - \text{LIABILITIES} = \text{OWNER'S EQUITY}$$

You will gradually grasp the full significance of this equation. Roughly speaking, *assets* are items that we own (e.g., a house) or have the use of (e.g., a car that has money owing on it). A creditor or a mortgage company may hold what is termed a *lien*, or a mortgage, on our house, but we legally own it. With a car that has money owing on it, however, some creditors may not allow us to register the car in only our own name. They may attach an *agreement-for-sale* lien instead of a mortgage lien on our car. The agreement-for-sale lien allows us to use the car, but not fully own it until the creditor is paid in full.

A *liability* is money that we owe. For example, the mortgage or the agreement for sale owed by us is a liability to us. The owner's equity is what is left over after sub-

[2]This book attempts to integrate into accounting education some of the thoughts of the following writers: W.G. Perry, Jr., *Forms of Intellectual and Ethical Development in the College Years* (New York: Holt, Rinehart and Winston, Inc., 1970); *Taxonomy of Educational Objectives*, Benjamin S. Bloom, ed. (London: Longman Inc., 1954); and Edward de Bono, *de Bono's Thinking Course* (London: British Broadcasting Corporation, 1982).

tracting the liability from the assets. This residual is our ownership interest in, say, a house:

Asset - house	$100,000
Liability - mortgage on house	(70,000)
Owner's equity	$ 30,000

Similarly, we may have just bought an automobile costing $10,000 by paying $2,500 cash and agreeing to pay $7,500 plus interest over the next three years. Accountants would show this as:

Asset		*Liability and Owner's Equity*	
Automobile, at cost	$10,000	Liability:	
		Contract payable	$ 7,500
		Owner's equity	2,500
	$10,000		$10,000

Observe that the page has been split vertically into two sections to show that assets in total ($10,000) do indeed equal the total ($10,000) of the liabilities plus the owner's equity in the automobile. This process of dual recording is called the *double entry* system. Over the next few chapters, we will study this system in more detail. The double-entry system proves invaluable in catching some types of errors that accountants and bookkeepers may make.

Note that the owner's equity is treated much like a liability. We may ask: Whose car is this? Unlike the house in the mortgage example,[3] until all payments of $7,500 are made on the car, it is legally owned by the liability holder—perhaps a creditor such as the Royal Bank of Canada or Canada Trustco. In reality, however, there are two owners: The Royal Bank may own three quarters ($7,500) and we would own the remaining one quarter ($2,500). On *our* balance sheet, the $2,500 would be shown as "owner's equity".

Large business corporations have many assets and liabilities. Similar ones are usually grouped together for purposes of preparing a balance sheet. That is, all automobiles would tend to be added together and only the total reported, unless the preparer believed that greater detail were important.

PERSONAL BALANCE SHEET

Suppose that we "own" the following: cash, wages owing to us from a part-time job (called *accounts receivable*), a car that we just bought for $8,000 (on which we owe $6,000), books, a new watch (which we purchased by using our credit card), and clothes. If we attach dollar figures, based on *what we paid* for these items, our personal balance sheet would appear as in Illustration 1-3.

---

[3] Legally, we own a house that has a mortgage liability attached to it. The mortgage is simply a registered claim on our house.

ILLUSTRATION 1-3

PERSONAL BALANCE SHEET

		Accounts						Owners'
	Cash	receivable	Car	Books	Watch	Clothes	= Liabilities +	Equity
	+2,000							$+2,000
		+600						+ 600
			+8,000				+6,000	+2,000
				+300				+ 300
					+200		+ 200	
						+800		+ 800
	+2,000	+600	+8,000	+300	+200	+800		
			$11,900				=	$6,200 + $5,700

This information would normally be reported in a general-purpose balance sheet as follows:

YOUR NAME
Balance Sheet
September 15, 19—0

Cash	$ 2,000	Liabilities:		
Accounts receivable	600	Owing for car★	$ 6,000	
Books	300	Owing on credit card★	200	
Watch	200		6,200	
Clothes	800			
Automobile	8,000			
		Owner's Equity:		
		Your name	5,700	
	$11,900		$11,900	

★These would be called *accounts payable* by most accountants.

USES OF THE BALANCE SHEET

Of what use is the balance sheet? We chose original cost (what we paid) figures for the books, watch, clothes, and car. Thus, it is unlikely that these assets could be sold for their original, or *historic cost*. As a result, we could *not* say that we are "worth" the owner's equity of $5,700. However, we do get the following pieces of information from the balance sheet:

1. The *type* of assets owned. (Are they cash, or *illiquid* ones such as the clothes? *Illiquid* means not easily turned into cash.)

2. Liabilities owed. (To whom do we owe money? When must these amounts be paid?)

3. A general indication of the size of the organization (you).

Even though the $5,700 is not a precise measure of our wealth, the above information can help a potential creditor, such as a banker, decide whether to lend us money to purchase another asset. He then knows what liabilities would or could have priority over his potential loan, and have to be paid shortly. He also could tell which assets he can request as collateral for the loan (in addition to the one that would be acquired if the loan were granted). Above all, he knows that, with $5,700 of equity, we are not wealthy, and that any loan would be risky (i.e., he may not get back the money that he loaned to us).

How Much Disclosure?

An obvious question to ask at this point is how much measurement and disclosure should there be in a general-purpose financial statement? There are no simple answers to this question. The preparer vs. user harmony/conflict issue lies at the heart of the matter. In order for us to grapple with this issue, *judgment* has to be acquired. In the same way that a physician-surgeon must decide whether to prescribe medicine, or surgery, or do nothing, the accountant has to decide upon:

1. Measurement?   2. Disclosure?   3. Show neither?

Such issues can only be decided by having criteria or guidelines based on how people may behave, what costs and benefits are involved, what laws exist, and so forth. Illustration 1-4 gives some introductory guidance on how preparer viewpoints can differ from those of users.

ILLUSTRATION 1-4

One Possible Preparer Viewpoint	One Possible User Viewpoint
• Wants to prepare financial reports as economically as possible • Wants to avoid being sued for preparing a misleading financial statement • Wants to avoid providing information that can be used by a competitor to the disadvantage of the company • Wants to avoid giving too much information that invites questions from unions, Revenue Canada and other government agencies	• Wants the information free-of-charge • Will sue the preparer if the financial statements are misleading • Wants information that other people have not received, especially from other sources • Wants a financial statement tailored to his particular need

Succeeding chapters will modify the material in Illustration 1-4 as we look at specific preparers and specific users, and at subdivisions within the general purpose report category. It is important that we note that there could be many different degrees of quantity/quality and of disclosure/measurement in financial statements of business oganizations. Sometimes, disclosing/measuring as little as possible makes sense. Other times, disclosing/measuring as much as possible is wise. Somewhere between the two extremes is usually appropriate. We have to learn "what fits where". Thus, we see that there are no universally correct answers to disclosure/measurement questions. We have to avoid settling on a simple, universally applicable approach such as "always disclose everything". The cost of disclosing "everything" could well exceed any benefits.

COMPLEX BALANCE SHEET

An organization's balance sheet changes over time. This can be illustrated by assuming that the following activities occur:

September 1, 19—1: Two people, *A* and *B*, decide to commence a business—the "A and B Co." that imports electronic goods and sells them to retail stores. They open a bank account and deposit $100,000.

September 5, 19—1: They import, at a cost of $80,000, the goods that are to be resold, and undertake to pay the exporter within ten days. (Goods held for resale are called *inventory*.)

September 6, 19—1: They buy a used delivery truck for $10,000 by paying $4,000 cash and promising to pay the remainder at $1,000 per month for six months, commencing September 25, 19—1. The truck will be available for use by "A and B" on September 29, 19—1. It requires some repairs that take about three weeks to complete.

September 15, 19—1: They pay the $80,000 owing to the exporter.

September 18, 19—1: They pay a $3,000 deposit for some warehouse space in which to store the inventory. The space will be ready for occupancy on October 1, 19—1, and the $3,000 will be used to pay the rent for October, November, and December. (A payment in advance is called *prepaid;* in this instance, the $3,000 is *prepaid rent,* which is an asset.)[4]

September 25, 19—1: The $1,000 cash payment is made for the truck.

September 29, 19—1: Truck is picked up by "A and B". They pay $2,200 for the repairs that they requested.

September 30, 19—1: More inventory, costing $30,000, is ordered for delivery in October 19—1.

If a balance sheet were prepared as of September 1, 19—1, it would be a simple one:

[4]Commencing October 1, some of the asset disappears as time passes. By December 31, all of the $3,000 asset will have vanished.

"A AND B CO."
BALANCE SHEET
September 1, 19—1

Assets

Cash	$100,000

Owners' Equity

A	$ 50,000
B	50,000
	$100,000

In preparing the balance sheet, we have assumed that each of A and B contributed $50,000 to start the business. Notice also that we have used an alternative or vertical form of balance-sheet presentation. Previously, we showed the horizontal form, which had the assets on the left-hand side of a split page, with the liabilities and owners' equity being on the right-hand side. Both forms will be used in this book and both are seen in practice in Canada.

An aside may be of interest. Those of you who have driven a car in England (or have watched U.K. television shows) can probably guess what horizontal form the balance sheet takes in the U.K.: the assets are on the right and the liabilities/owners' equity are on the left.

What would the balance sheet of "A and B" look like at September 30, 19—1? What about at September 6, or September 18? Illustration 1-5 follows each transaction noting its impact on the balance sheet equation: assets = liabilities + owners' equity.

A closer look at the transactions reveals:

September 5: An asset (inventory) is acquired by increasing a liability.

September 6: An asset (truck) is acquired by reducing another asset (cash) and by assuming, or increasing, a liability.

September 15: A liability is reduced by reducing an asset (cash).

September 18: An asset (prepaid rent) is obtained by reducing another.
September 25: A liability is reduced by reducing an asset (cash).
September 29: An asset (truck) is increased by reducing another asset (cash).

September 30: An asset (inventory $30,000) is ordered, for which a liability eventually will be incurred. (Usually, accountants do not record this transaction until one of the parties to the transaction, i.e., the exporter or "A and B", acts to fulfil a legally binding contract. Often, this would occur when the goods are delivered, in October, and "A and B" agree to pay. An agreement in which neither party has performed what is required is an *executory contract*. [Exceptions to this approach to recording will be noted much later in the book.] As of September 30, no cash has been exchanged, nor promise to pay has been undertaken, and no goods have been shipped or delivered. Thus, the transaction has not been recorded in Illustration 1-5.)

ILLUSTRATION 1-5

		Assets				= Liabilities	+ Owner's Equity
	Cash	Inventory	Prepaid Rent	Truck			
September 1	$100,000						$100,000
5		$80,000				$80,000	
	100,000 +	80,000			=	80,000 +	100,000
6	(4,000)			$10,000		6,000	
	96,000 +	80,000	+	10,000 =		86,000 +	100,000
15	(80,000)					(80,000)	
	16,000 +	80,000	+	10,000 =		6,000 +	100,000
18	(3,000)		$3,000				
	13,000 +	80,000 +	3,000 +	10,000 =		6,000 +	100,000
25	(1,000)					(1,000)	
	12,000 +	80,000 +	3,000 +	10,000 =		5,000 +	100,000
29	(2,200)			2,200			
	9,800 +	80,000 +	3,000 +	12,200 =		5,000 +	100,000
30		Nil				Nil	
Balance at September 30	$ 9,800	$80,000	$3,000	$12,200		$ 5,000	$100,000

"A and B Co."
Balance Sheet
September 30, 19—1

Assets		*Liability and Owners' Equity*		
Cash	$ 9,800	Liability:		
Inventory	80,000	Accounts payable		$ 5,000
Prepaid rent	3,000			
Truck	12,200	Owners' equity:		
		A	$50,000	
		B	50,000	100,000
	$105,000			$105,000

Interpreting Illustration 1-5

In the month of September, 19—1, all that *A* and *B* have done is to *switch assets and liabilities.* Their owners' equity has remained unchanged at $100,000. In the next few chapters, we will see the owners' equity change as a result of these four transactions:

1. Having the owners, *A* and *B*, put more of their own money into the "A and B Co.";
   OR

2. Having the owners take out money from the "A and B Co." OR

3. Having "A and B" sell an asset, such as inventory, for more than they paid for the asset; OR

4. Having "A and B" sell an asset for less than they paid for it.

Transactions 1 and 3 *increase* owners' equity, whereas 2 and 4 *decrease* it.

A and *B* no doubt would be more interested in increasing owners' equity than in seeing it decrease. The two owners may judge their success in terms of transactions 3 and 4. As neither 3 nor 4 occurred in Illustration 1-5, the balance sheet as of September 30, 19—1 is not of great importance. (There are some liquidity [cash] implications that will be discussed in Chapter 3.) Subsequent balance sheets will, however, incorporate the effects of transactions 3 and 4.

For example, *if*, on October 1, 19—1, "A and B" sold the inventory that cost them $80,000 for $99,000 cash, this transaction would be handled as in Illustration 1-6.

ILLUSTRATION 1-6

	Cash	Inventory	Prepaid Rent	Truck	= Liabilities +	Owners' Equity
		Assets			= Liabilities +	Owners' Equity
September 30	$ 9,800 +	$80,000 +	$3,000 +	$12,200 =	$5,000 +	$100,000
October 1	99,000	(80,000)				19,000
	$108,800 +	0 +	$3,000 +	$12,200 =	$5,000 +	$119,000

"A and B Co."
Balance Sheet
October 1, 19—1

Cash	$108,800	Liability:		
Prepaid rent	3,000	Accounts payable		$ 5,000
Truck	12,200			
		Owners' Equity		
		A	$59,500	
		B	59,500	119,000
	$124,000			$124,000

The sale for $99,000 of inventory that cost $80,000 resulted in an increase in assets of $19,000. The balance sheet equation, assets = liabilities + owners' equity, raises the question: To whom does the $19,000 belong—to creditors (liability holders, such as the Royal Bank) *or* to owners' equity "A and B"?

Obviously, "A and B" do not owe the $19,000 to any creditor. It is already reported what they owe, which is a liability of $5,000. Therefore, the $19,000 must belong to "A and B". In preparing the balance sheet at October 1, 19—1 it has been assumed that one half ($9,500) of the $19,000 belongs to each of the owners, of *A* and *B*.

In subsequent chapters, changes in owners' equity between two balance-sheet dates will be reported in two of the financial statements that we mentioned earlier: an income statement, and a statement of retained earnings. When we have access to these financial statements, we can say more about uses of them by creditors, Revenue Canada, and the owners of the business.

Summary

The main themes of this chapter are:

1. A business transaction can be accounted for in different ways, often using a combination of measurement and disclosure.

2. To understand financial statements, we must understand the thought processes of both preparers and users. The viewpoint of the preparer can differ significantly from that of various users.

3. Both general purpose and special purpose financial reports exist. A company may have only *one* general purpose financial report per period.

4. The balance sheet equation is:
   ASSETS = LIABILITIES + OWNERS' EQUITY

5. Owners' equity will change as a result of two main types of transactions: (a) the owners make additional asset investments or withdraw assets (usually cash), and (b) assets are sold for more or less than what they cost. The latter, (b), is shown on income statements, which are described in the next three chapters.

6. In learning accounting, it is important to avoid looking for "all-purpose right answers". Considerable judgment and tailoring are required in accounting, and it is essential to learn what procedures make sense in different, yet similar, situations.

Appendices

1-A: Illustrative Financial Statements
1-B: Some Accounting Bodies in Canada

Appendix 1-A reprints the actual financial statements of a company operating in Canada. The appendix should be referred to from time to time as we proceed through the course. Appendix 1-B describes some of the groups of accountants who practise in Canada.

APPENDIX 1-A
Illustrative Financial Statements

This appendix reproduces the 1984 financial statements of Fiberglas Canada Inc. as they appeared in their 1984 Annual Report. These financial statements ought to be referred to from time to time as we proceed through subsequent chapters—to ensure that we are fitting all of the pieces together; and, by the end of Chapter 17, we will be able to fully understand financial statements.

The Fiberglas Canada Inc. statements are not being reproduced because they display model accounting treatment, or have some peculiarity. They are typical of what we will see in Canada—financial statements tailored to fit the company's circumstances. Terminology may differ somewhat from what we will use in this book. This is something we will become accustomed to, and reason through. Observe that the "Notes to Consolidated Financial Statements" are almost as lengthy as the formal statements. This indicates that a single number in the financial statements cannot capture all that is important.

FIBERGLAS
CANADA INC

CONSOLIDATED BALANCE SHEET—ASSETS

(See accompanying notes to consolidated financial statements)

December 31

(thousands of dollars)

	1984	1983
Current:		
Cash and short-term investments	$ 27,714	$ 24,811
Accounts receivable	30,675	22,227
Inventories *(note 2)*	352	27,675
Deposits and prepaid expenses	7,320	531
Deferred income taxes	66,061	2,837
Total current assets	66,061	78,081
Fixed:		
Land	8,750	8,605
Buildings	66,523	61,013
Machinery and equipment	140,894	134,809
Office furniture and equipment	7,229	4,632
	223,396	209,059
Less accumulated depreciation	105,119	97,083
Total fixed assets	118,277	111,976
Other:		
Debenture issue expenses	222	322
Manufacturing rights	250	250
Loans receivable *(note 3)*	1,802	1,560
Long-term investment *(note 4)*	25,000	
Total other assets	27,274	2,132
	$211,612	$192,189

On behalf of the Board:

Director

Director

GROSS SALES BY GROUP ($ Millions)

☐ INSULATION
■ TR&C

CONSOLIDATED BALANCE SHEET—LIABILITIES

(thousands of dollars)

	1984	1983
Current:		
Bank and short-term indebtedness	$ 5,592	
Accounts payable and accrued charges	32,059	$ 24,121
Dividends payable	139	8,425
Income and other taxes payable	14,984	950
Current provision for rebuilding furnaces	1,184	1,696
Total current liabilities	**53,958**	35,192
Non-current:		
Series A debentures *(note 5)*	25,000	25,000
Deferred income taxes	13,474	19,965
Deferred provision for rebuilding furnaces	6,362	5,445
Obligation under capital leases	2,469	1,027
Total non-current liabilities	**47,305**	51,437
Shareholders' equity:		
Capital stock *(note 6)*	2,739	5,239
Retained earnings	107,610	100,321
Total shareholders' equity	**110,349**	105,560
	$211,612	$192,189

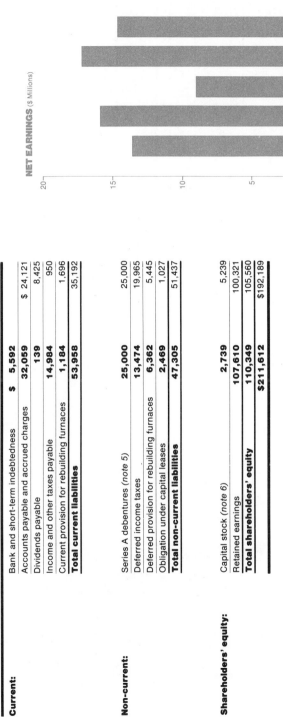

NET EARNINGS ($ Millions)

CONSOLIDATED STATEMENT OF EARNINGS

(See accompanying notes to consolidated financial statements)

(thousands of dollars, except per share data)

	For the year ended December 31	
	1984	1983
Gross sales	**$343,526**	$312,796
Costs, excluding amounts shown below	**295,813**	261,261
Depreciation	**12,795**	12,501
Research and development expenses	**7,259**	6,385
Interest on Series A debentures	**4,250**	4,250
Dividend income	**(1,568)**	(608)
Net interest expense (income)	**507**	100
Amortization	**100**	100
Loss on disposal of fixed assets	**232**	112
	319,388	284,001
Earnings before income taxes and extraordinary charge	**24,138**	28,795
Income taxes (note 7)	**8,534**	11,563
Earnings before extraordinary charge	**15,604**	17,232
Extraordinary charge (note 8)	**831**	
Net earnings for the year	**$ 14,773**	$ 17,232
Earnings per share:		
Before extraordinary charge	**$7.46**	$8.24
Net earnings for the year	**$7.06**	$8.24

CONSOLIDATED STATEMENT OF RETAINED EARNINGS

(See accompanying notes to consolidated financial statements)

(thousands of dollars)

	For the year ended December 31	
	1984	1983
Balance, beginning of year	**$100,321**	$ 91,514
Net earnings for the year	**14,773**	17,232
	115,094	108,746
Dividends (note 6)	**7,484**	8,425
Balance, end of year	**$107,610**	$100,321

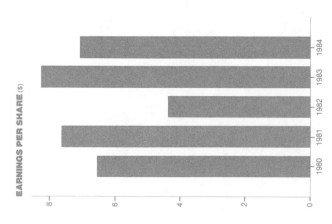

EARNINGS PER SHARE ($)

CONSOLIDATED STATEMENT OF CHANGES
IN FINANCIAL POSITION

(See accompanying notes to consolidated financial statements)

For the year ended December 31

(thousands of dollars)

	1984	1983
Sources of cash:		
Operations—		
Earnings before extraordinary charge	$15,604	$17,232
Add (deduct) non-cash items:		
Depreciation and amortization	12,895	12,601
Loss on disposal of fixed assets	232	112
Net (decrease) increase in deferred income taxes	(10,721)	4,506
Provision for rebuilding furnaces	4,495	1,497
	22,505	35,948
Effect on cash of changes in:		
Accounts receivable	(5,487)	687
Inventories	(2,887)	(1,385)
Deposits and prepaid expenses	179	273
Loans receivable	(242)	(571)
Accounts payable and accrued charges	7,972	4,945
Income and other taxes payable	14,393	(10,422)
Total cash provided from operations	**36,433**	**29,475**
Proceeds of share issue		672
Total cash provided	**36,433**	**30,147**
Uses of cash:		
Additions to fixed assets, net of investment tax credits (1984—$1,630; 1983—$285)	15,910	9,749
Dividends paid	15,770	180
Expenditures for rebuilding furnaces	3,405	3,625
Long-term investment	25,000	
Extraordinary charge—		
Expenditures relating to plant closure	730	
Business acquisition *(note 9)*	3,521	
Redemption of preference shares	2,500	
Total cash used	**66,836**	**13,554**
(Decrease) increase in cash and short-term financing	(30,403)	16,593
Balance, beginning of year	24,811	8,218
Balance, end of year	**$ (5,592)**	**$24,811**

OPERATING PROFIT BY GROUP ($ Millions)

☐ INSULATION
■ TR & C

NOTES TO CONSOLIDATED FINANCIAL STATEMENTS

December 31, 1984

1. Summary of significant accounting policies

The consolidated financial statements have been prepared by management in accordance with accounting principles generally accepted in Canada consistently applied. These consolidated financial statements are, in management's opinion, properly prepared within reasonable limits of materiality and within the framework of the accounting policies summarized below:

Basis of consolidation—
The consolidated financial statements include the accounts of the wholly-owned subsidiaries.

Inventories—
Inventories of in-process and finished goods are stated at the lower of cost, determined on the average cost method, and estimated realizable value less an allowance for gross margins and costs to complete and sell. Raw materials and supplies are stated at the lower of cost, determined on the first-in, first-out method, and replacement cost.

Fixed assets and depreciation—
Fixed assets are stated at cost less accumulated depreciation. Cost and accumulated depreciation for fixed assets sold or disposed of are eliminated from the respective accounts with the resulting gain or loss reflected in earnings. Government assistance in the form of investment tax credits, research and development allowances and capital grants is applied as a reduction of the cost of the related assets.

Fixed assets under lease are capitalized and the related lease obligations recorded as liabilities in instances where the terms of the leases transfer to the corporation substantially all the benefits and risks incident to ownership of the assets. The leased assets so capitalized are included in the consolidated balance sheet at a net book value of $3,106,000 at December 31, 1984 (1983—$1,738,000).

Fixed assets are depreciated on the straight-line method over their estimated useful lives at the following rates:

Buildings	2½%–10%
Machinery and equipment	10%–25%
Office furniture and equipment	10%–25%

Manufacturing rights—
The corporation's original manufacturing rights are carried at cost.

Income taxes—
Deferred income taxes are recorded on timing differences between reported and taxable earnings. These differences relate principally to depreciation of fixed assets, the provision for rebuilding furnaces and investment tax credits to be claimed in future years.

Provision for rebuilding furnaces—
The corporation's glass melting furnaces and related equipment periodically require substantial rebuilding which, depending on the nature of the process, normally occurs from three to eight years after a furnace has been placed in production. The estimated future costs of such rebuilds are charged to earnings on a straight-line basis over the estimated period to the next rebuild date and are accumulated as a provision for rebuilding furnaces. The actual costs of rebuilds are charged against the accumulated provision as incurred.

Research and development—
Research and development costs are expensed as incurred. If there were to be reasonable assurance of future recovery of the development costs, these costs would be deferred to future periods.

Pension costs—
Pension plans are reviewed at least every three years and any experience deficiencies which arise are amortized over the next five-year period. Past service pension costs are amortized over a maximum fifteen-year period. The most recent actuarial valuations did not reveal any unfunded liabilities. The pension costs for 1984 were $4,074,000 (1983—$3,820,000).

Foreign exchange—
Revenues and expenses denominated in foreign currency are translated at the prevailing rates of exchange on the dates of the transactions. Amounts receivable or payable in foreign currencies are translated at the year-end rates. All translation gains and losses are reflected in earnings.

2. Inventories

(thousands of dollars)	1984	1983
Raw materials and supplies	$10,741	$ 9,718
In-process and finished goods	19,934	17,957
	$30,675	$27,675

3. Loans receivable

Loans receivable includes advances aggregating $1,164,000 to certain employees of the corporation for the purchase of homes in connection with relocation moves.

Also included are advances aggregating $638,000 to certain officers and shareholders of the corporation to enable them to purchase the Class B, Series II shares referred to in note 6. These advances are to be repaid over a maximum period of ten years.

4. Long-term investment

On March 30, 1984 the corporation acquired 2,500,000 8.3% Cumulative Preference Shares, Series C of Precambrian Shield Resources Ltd. for $25,000,000. These shares are to be redeemed on April 1, 1987.

5. Series A debentures

The $25,000,000 Series A debentures bear interest at 17% per annum and mature on March 19, 1987. The trust indenture securing the debentures contains covenants restricting the payment of dividends. At December 31, 1984, approximately $30,500,000 of retained earnings was unrestricted under such covenants.

6. Capital stock and dividends

The authorized and issued shares are summarized below:

			December 31	
	Authorized	Issued	**1984**	1983
			(thousands of dollars)	
Preference				$2,500
Class A, voting	5,000,000	2,039,000	**$2,039**	$2,039
Class B, non-voting—	100,000			
Series I		28,000	**28**	28
Series II, redeemable		11,100	**672**	672
	5,100,000	2,078,100	**$2,739**	$2,739

All shares are without par value.

The corporation redeemed and cancelled all of the issued 4½% non-cumulative $100 redeemable preference shares on December 14, 1984 at stated value.

The corporation declared dividends as follows:

(thousands of dollars)	**1984**	1983
Preference shares	**$ 107**	$ 112
Class A shares	**7,239**	8,156
Class B shares		
Series I	**99**	112
Series II	**39**	45
	$7,484	$8,425

7. Effective income tax rate

A reconciliation between the combined Canadian federal and provincial statutory income tax rate and the effective tax rate applied in the consolidated statement of earnings is as follows:

	1984	1983
Combined Canadian federal and provincial statutory income tax rate	**48.85%**	49.31%
Manufacturing and processing profits deduction	**(5.35)**	(5.34)
Investment tax credit on scientific research	**(3.13)**	(2.25)
Inventory allowance	**(1.34)**	(1.03)
Non-taxable dividend income	**(2.82)**	(0.53)
Miscellaneous	**(0.85)**	(0.53)
Effective rate	**35.36%**	40.16%

8. Extraordinary charge

On March 31, 1984, the corporation terminated manufacturing operations at Moncton, New Brunswick. The net cost of closure amounted to $831,000 after the related income tax reduction of $612,000.

9. Business acquisition

On December 4, 1984, the corporation purchased for cash certain assets of a manufacturing operation in the Province of Quebec. The purchase price was allocated as follows:

Fixed assets	$3,300,000
Inventories	221,000
	$3,521,000

10. Segmented information

The corporation's operations consist of the following two business segments as determined by the Board of Directors:

(a) Insulation—

The insulation group manufactures thermal insulation for residential, commercial and industrial buildings, including mobile homes, as well as for vehicles, major home appliances, furnaces and air-conditioning equipment. This group also manufactures roof insulation and acoustic products, as well as insulation for piping, tanks, equipment, pre-engineered buildings, sound screens for office interiors, marine and cold storage applications and insulation for air ducts.

(b) Textiles, reinforcements and chemicals ("TR&C")—

The TR&C group produces a variety of materials in two major product categories: glass fibre materials and thermosetting polyester resins. These materials are sold primarily to the glass fibre reinforced plastics ("FRP") industry. The remaining sales of glass fibre materials are made principally to weavers who produce fabrics for use in the manufacture of such products as filter bags, glass fibre radial and belted bias tires, insect screening, non-combustible materials and electrical insulations.

The FRP industry uses the corporation's glass fibre materials and polyester resins to manufacture a wide range of products including boat hulls, automotive bodies and components, commercial trailer bodies, railcar doors, hopper car covers, tanks, pipe and processing equipment for the pulp and paper and chemical industries, and electrical components.

The results of operations of, and expenditures on fixed assets used in, the two segments for the years ended December 31, 1984 and 1983 and the identifiable assets of the segments as at those dates are as follows:

(thousands of dollars)	1984		
	Insulation	TR&C	Total
Gross sales	$248,978	$ 94,548	$343,526
Costs, excluding depreciation	210,257	77,875	288,132
Depreciation	10,426	1,485	11,911
Operating profits	28,295	15,188	43,483
Extraordinary charge	831		831
	$ 27,464	$ 15,188	42,652
Interest, income taxes and other corporate expenses			27,879
Net earnings for the year			$ 14,773
Additions to fixed assets	$ 15,713	$ 2,376	
Identifiable assets	$128,808	$ 37,505	$166,313
Corporate assets			45,299
Total assets			$211,612

(thousands of dollars)	1983		
	Insulation	TR&C	Total
Gross sales	$235,114	$ 77,682	$312,796
Costs, excluding depreciation	190,300	64,157	254,457
Depreciation	10,179	1,532	11,711
Operating profits	$ 34,635	$ 11,993	46,628
Interest, income taxes and other corporate expenses			29,396
Net earnings for the year			$ 17,232
Additions to fixed assets	$ 7,311	$ 586	
Identifiable assets	$120,607	$ 33,526	$154,133
Corporate assets			38,056
Total assets			$192,189

11. Commitments

Outstanding capital expenditure commitments amounted to approximately $10,965,000 at December 31, 1984 (1983—$15,110,000).

12. Related party transactions

The corporation enters into transactions with a major shareholder. In 1984, these transactions included sales of approximately $5,174,000 (1983—$306,000) and purchases of goods and services of approximately $7,429,000 (1983—$5,469,000). The corporation and such

AUDITORS' REPORT

To the Shareholders of
Fiberglas Canada Inc.

We have examined the consolidated balance sheet of Fiberglas Canada Inc. as at December 31, 1984 and the consolidated statements of earnings, retained earnings and changes in financial position for the year then ended. Our examination was made in accordance with generally accepted auditing standards, and accordingly included such tests and other procedures as we considered necessary in the circumstances.

In our opinion, these consolidated financial statements present fairly the financial position of the corporation as at December 31, 1984 and the results of its operations and the changes in its financial position for the year then ended in accordance with generally accepted accounting principles applied on a basis consistent with that of the preceding year.

Chartered Accountants

Toronto, Canada
January 25, 1985.

shareholder have also entered into arrangements for the exchange of technical services know-how and the use of patents. The net amount payable by the corporation to the shareholder under these arrangements was $1,730,000 in 1984 (1983—$1,556,000).

APPENDIX 1-B
Some Accounting Bodies in Canada

The three main groups of accountants in Canada, in alphabetical order, are:

Certified General Accountants Association of Canada (CGAC)

The Canadian Institute of Chartered Accountants (CICA)

The Society of Management Accountants of Canada (SMAC)

Each of these groups has provincial (or equivalent) representation (for example, the Certified General Accountants Association of British Columbia) because legislation (if any) affecting accountants is provincially regulated, often by individual acts of incorporation.

The CGAC members, through their provincial organizations, are called CGAs (Certified General Accountants) or FCGAs (indicating the honorary fellowship designation granted for service to the organization and the community). The CICA members are also members of one or more provincial institutes/orders, and are designated as CAs (Chartered Accountants) or FCAs. The SMAC members, through their provincial organizations, use the designation CMA or RIA. The honorary or fellowship designation of SMAC is FSMAC. The dual designation CMA and RIA exists because some provincial governments have approved the change to CMA (Certified Management Accountant), whereas others have not and continue with the RIA (Registered Industrial Accountant) designation.

Legislation affecting accountants differs considerably from province to province. Some provinces, e.g., Ontario, essentially permit only CAs to do audits. See Appendix 1-A, and note the wording of an auditor's report, especially: "…present fairly…in accordance with generally accepted accounting principles…". (The auditor is *not* saying that the financial statements are "fair" or "tell the truth". The emphasis is on generally accepted accounting principles—GAAP. An auditor does not actively look for fraud.)

Other provinces allow any person to perform an audit. The person's credibility as an auditor may be low, however, and lending credibility to the financial statements is the prime responsibility of an auditor.

Accountants may perform their services as public accountants, or as accountants internal to a company or government, or as teachers, or in many other capacities. Many people obtain an accounting designation (CA, CMA or CGA) primarily to receive an introduction to business practice. With this training, they may move on to a variety of duties and challenges.

Accountants may undertake a variety of responsibilities. Auditors may do what are called "attest" audits, as in Appendix 1-A, or "value for money" audits of government departments and agencies. Most public accountants offer income tax advice. Accountants employed by companies prepare budgets as well as financial statements, investigate whether the business should expand, and perform many other duties.

Besides the three professional accounting bodies mentioned so far, there are several groups to which accountants may belong. The Canadian Academic Accounting

Association (CAAA) has opened its membership to those interested in education and research, and includes CMA, RIA, CGA, and CA members plus many of those teaching accounting at universities. Some other groups are: the Financial Executives Institute and the Institute of Internal Auditors.

In essence, people who started their careers as accountants can be found in many positions. Accountants have to become familiar with all aspects of a business; thus, the training is invaluable.

QUESTIONS

1-1 List some myths or misconceptions that tend to exist about financial accounting.

1-2 What are the differences between financial and management accounting?

1-3 Who are the prime users of general purpose financial accounting figures and financial statements?

1-4 What does GAAP mean?

1-5 What are some reasons why accountants do not know more about who uses their financial statements and for which specific purposes?

1-6 Why might preparers and users have different opinions about how to account for a particular financial transaction or activity?

1-7 Why might accountants choose to report an activity as a note to the financial statements instead of as an asset or liability?

1-8 If owners' equity amounts to $100,000, and assets equal $120,000, how much are the liabilities?

1-9 What might a creditor use a balance sheet for?

1-10 What is meant by the term "accountability"?

EXERCISES

(Note: The Exercise category in the book is for those assignments that can be answered primarily by referring to the material in the most recent chapter.)

E1-1 Replace the ? in each line (A to E are separate parts of the question) with a dollar amount.

	Assets	*Liabilities*	*Owners' Equity*
A.	$1,000,000	$ 600,000	$?
B.	?	200,000	300,000
C.	500,000	?	400,000
D.	2,000,000	?	2,000,000
E.	3,000,000	3,500,000	?

E1-2 Prepare a balance sheet after *each* of the transactions that follows:

January 2, 19—6: Ms. Chester and Ms. Field are partners. Each contributes $100,000 cash to start a new business.

January 6, 19—6: The partners buy inventory that costs $120,000 by paying $30,000 cash and promising to pay the balance by January 20, 19—6.

January 12, 19—6: The partners rent space in a shopping centre, commencing January 29, 19—6. They pay $4,000 cash in advance.

January 20, 19—6: The $90,000 owing for the inventory is paid in cash.

January 28, 19—6: A truck costing $16,000 is acquired for $4,000 cash and a promise to pay the balance at $1,000 cash per month.

E1-3 Refer to **E1-2**. Instead of preparing a balance sheet after each transaction, prepare only the one as of the close of business on January 28, 19—6.

E1-4 Prepare a balance sheet after each of the transactions that follow:

September 1, 19—7: Mr. Horse and Mr. Radish are partners. Each contributes $50,000 cash to the partnership on this date, and signs an agreement to provide another $50,000 each on October 1, 19—7.

September 8, 19—7: The partners consider buying an automobile that would cost $12,000.

September 12, 19—7: Inventory costing $70,000 is acquired by paying $40,000 cash and agreeing to pay the balance before month end.

September 15, 19—7: The partners each contribute $20,000 cash to the business.

September 20, 19—7: $10,000 cash is paid to rent a store, commencing October 1, 19—7.

September 25, 19—7: $30,000 cash is paid for the inventory bought on September 12.

September 28, 19—7: Inventory costing $38,000 is sold for $10,000 cash plus $39,000 that is due on October 15. (The $39,000 is called an accounts receivable on September 28, until cash is received by the seller.)

September 30, 19—7: An automobile costing $13,000 is acquired by paying $4,000 cash and by signing an agreement for sale. The agreement is to pay the additional $9,000 at $3,000 per month commencing October 30, 19—7.

E1-5 Refer to **E1-4**. Instead of preparing a balance sheet after each transaction, prepare a schedule such as that shown for Illustration 1-3 [or 1-5] in the chapter.

E1-6 Refer to **E1-4**. Instead of preparing a balance sheet after each transaction, prepare a balance sheet as of the close of business on September 30, 19—7.

E1-7 Use the following schedule to mark an "X" in the appropriate columns to indicate what has happened:

	No Effect	Assets		Liabilities		Owners' Equity	
Date		Increase	Decrease	Increase	Decrease	Increase	Decrease
19—1:							
October 1		X				X	

The transactions are:

October 1: The business commences by depositing $100,000 in a bank account. The sum represents ownership interest in a partnership of Mr. D. and Ms. M. (Each person pays $50,000 to the partnership, which opens a bank account.)

October 2: An agreement is signed to commence renting retail store space in a shopping mall effective October 31, 19—1. Monthly rent is set at $2,000.

October 3: A deposit of $10,000 cash is made for inventory to be delivered October 17, 19—1 to the home of one of the partners (for storage until the store opens on November 1, 19—1).

October 4: Furniture and fixtures are purchased on account for $22,000, and are to be delivered by October 31, 19—1.

October 6: An additional $20,000 each is contributed by the two partners, and deposited in a bank.

October 7: A sum of $4,000 is paid for rent for the period October 31 to December 31, 19—1.

October 10: Office supplies that will be used over the next several months are purchased on account for $8,200.

October 17: Inventory costing $62,500 is received. An additional $18,000 in cash is paid on this date (i.e., in addition to the $10,000 deposit for this inventory that was paid on October 3). The balance of $34,500 is due on account on or before October 31, 19—1.

October 20: The $8,200 that is due for the purchase of office supplies is paid on this date.

October 28: The $34,500 balance due for the purchase of inventory is paid on this date.

October 29: The furniture and fixtures ordered on October 4 are delivered to the rented store (which is now available at no cost for October 29, 30 and 31).

October 30: A sum of $10,000 is paid on the amount due for the purchase of furniture and fixtures.

October 31: Each partner withdraws $5,000 from the partnership's bank account.

E1-8 Use the schedule provided at the beginning of **E1-7** to indicate the effect of the following transactions:

September 1: Three partners commence a business on September 1, 19—2 by having each contribute $25,000, and putting the total into a bank account in the partnership's name.

September 2: One of the partners, Ms. A, contributes inventory worth $10,000 in order to increase her share of, or percentage of, ownership of the partnership.

September 4: Office and sales space is rented for ten months, commencing October 1, 19—2, at a cost of $3,000 per month. A sum of $5,000 is paid as a deposit.

September 6: A contract is signed to acquire land on December 1, 19—2 for $120,000. A cheque for $15,000 is issued in accordance with the terms of the contract.

September 8: An architect is hired to design a building that is to be constructed on the land. The architect's fee is $15,000.

September 15: Inventory costing $60,000 is acquired by paying $9,000 and promising to pay $21,000 before the end of September and $30,000 before the end of October. The inventory will be stored by the seller until the partnership's rented space is available.

September 20: Another $10,000 is paid in accordance with the contract to acquire the land.

September 24: A contract is signed to acquire some furniture and equipment for $38,800. The furniture and equipment will be stored by the seller until the rented space is available, around October 1, 19—2.

September 28: A payment of $21,000 is made for the inventory purchased on September 15.

September 29: Each partner contributes another $10,000, and the $30,000 is placed in the partnership's bank account.

September 30: A sum of $20,000 is paid to a contractor to prepare the rented store for use.

September 30: More inventory, costing $69,500, is ordered for delivery on October 17, 19—2.

PROBLEMS

(Note: The Problems category in this book is for assignments that require some additional thought beyond the illustrations in the chapter, and may draw upon materials from previous chapters.)

P1-1 Prepare a schedule, similar to those shown for illustrations 1-3 and 1-5 in the chapter, for the following: (Explain your answers when the method of recording is not obvious.)

September 1, 19—8: Mr. Salt and Mr. Pepper form a partnership to sell imported goods. Each contributes $100,000 cash to the partnership's bank account.

September 5, 19—8: The partners order some goods, which will cost $120,000, for delivery to them later in September.

September 8, 19—8: Inventory costing $40,000 is acquired by paying cash of $15,000 and agreeing to pay the balance before month end.

September 10, 19—8: A customer gives the partners $10,000 cash as a deposit for inventory to be delivered to him in October. (Inventory cost to partnership is $60,000; selling price to customer is $99,950.)

September 15, 19—8: Each of the partners withdraws $5,000 in cash of his investment made on September 1, 19—8. The $5,000 is used for personal, non-partnership needs such as food.

September 22, 19—8: The goods ordered on September 5, 19—8 arrive. The partners pay $65,000 cash and agree to pay the balance in one month.

September 25, 19—8: The balance owing for the goods acquired on September 8, 19—8 is paid.

September 28, 19—8: Inventory costing $70,000 is sold for $118,900. Cash of $65,000 was received, and the balance is due in cash before the end of October 19—8.

September 30, 19—8: A truck costing $18,000 is bought by paying $10,000 cash and agreeing to pay the balance later.

P1-2 Refer to **P1-1**. Instead of using a schedule, prepare only a balance sheet as of the close of business on September 30, 19—8.

P1-3 Prepare a balance sheet for an "equal" partnership (i.e., the two partners, Ms. D. and Ms. E., have equal amounts of owners' equity) as of October 31, 19—8. (Provide full explanations and details to support your figures.) The following transactions and activities occurred in October 19—8:

October 1: The partnership commenced. Each partner contributed assets worth $100,000. Ms. D. provided inventory valued at $100,000, and Ms. E. provided cash of $100,000.

October 3: A deposit of $10,000 was provided to the owner of a store that the partnership would rent for $4,000 per month commencing November 1.

October 5: Ms. D. contributed a truck to the partnership. It was valued at $14,000. Ms. E. wrote a cheque to the partnership for $14,000, to maintain an equal partner's capital balance with Ms. D.

October 8: The truck that Ms. D. brought into the partnership was sold for $14,000, of which $8,000 was received in cash.

October 14: The partnership received a cheque for $18,500 for inventory to be delivered to the customer on November 5, 19—8. The inventory cost the partnership $11,000. The cheque for $18,500 was deposited in the bank.

October 15: A postdated cheque for $15,900 was received for an order to be shipped by the partnership on November 3, 19—8. The cheque was dated November 1, 19—8 and was deposited in the bank on this date.

October 17: A new truck, to handle deliveries, was ordered at a cost of $22,000. A cheque for $8,000 was given to the seller and a liability was incurred for the balance of $14,000. The truck will be ready for use before October 31, 19—8.

October 20: A cheque for $18,000 was issued to an insurance company, to cover insurance for 36 months commencing November 1, 19—8.

October 25: Inventory costing $30,000 was purchased on account.

October 28: The inventory purchase on October 25 was paid by issuing a cheque.

October 31: A cheque for $6,000 was received for the balance owing on sale of the truck on October 8.

P1-4 Refer to **P1-3**. Prepare a schedule similar to Illustration 1-3 or 1-5, and enter each of the applicable transactions mentioned in Problem 3. If the transaction does not have to be entered for the period October 1-31, 19—8, explain your reasoning.

P1-5 Prepare a balance sheet at November 30, 19—9 from the following list of total sums of assets, liabilities and owners' equity as of the close of business on November 30, 19—9. The company is owned by two partners, F and G, who share all owners' equity equally. Replace the ? with your computation of the owners' equity sum for each person.

Automobile	18,300
Owners' equity	?
Accounts payable	7,920
Cash	47,200
Inventory	65,770
Prepaid rent	3,000
Money received for inventory to be delivered in December (called "unearned revenue")	15,290
Accounts receivable	20,100
Furniture	16,440
Note that is payable to the seller of the automobile (called "note payable")	7,600

EXPLORATION MATERIALS AND CASES

(Note: This category includes less directive material designed to encourage the development of judgmental, diagnostic, analytical and similar skills.)

MC1-1 The following conversation occurs in a university snack bar:

Arts Student (A):   I hear you are taking an accounting course. Tell me, how do you stay awake during lectures?

Business Student (B):   At least I'll get a job when I graduate....Besides, there's more to it than I thought at first.

A: Sure..., like what?

B: It hadn't occurred to me before that there were many different ways of accounting for the same thing, like the worth of a car. Somehow I thought accounting had rigid rules that had to be followed.

A: Is that why you signed up for the course?

B: No, I thought that it would be practical.

A: Why are you surprised that there are different ways of accounting? Not all businesses are the same, are they? Not all people are the same.

B: No, they aren't. But I thought that the government forced everybody to follow the same accounting rules—like for speed limits, and temperature readings, and....

A: Oh yeah? That sure hadn't occurred to me before. Our courses aren't like that.... Hmmm... I've always wondered where people get their strange ideas from.

B: Maybe from math and science classes....

A: Science??? Are you crazy? Think of a tree. It can be looked at lots of different ways: its size, species, what feeds it, how it reproduces, leaf colour at different times of the year, and so on. A logger, an artist, a forest warden, an environmentalist, and many others can look at a tree dozens of different ways.... Why should accountants be so unobservant? Even the worth of a tree changes as it grows....

B: I see your point.... I wonder where I did get my idea about rigid accounting rules from?

Required:

A. Evaluate A's remarks. (To what extent do you believe what he says? Why?)
B. Where might B have obtained his impressions about rigidity in accounting?
C. What might B do to rid himself of the misconception?
D. List several different viewpoints that exist for considering the worth of a car. In which respects does each differ?

MC1-2

THE SHEEPHERDERS*
An Accounting Game
Part I

In the high mountains of Chetele, two sheepherders, Deyonne and Batonne sit arguing their relative positions in life, an argument which has been going on for years. Deyonne says that he has 400 sheep while Batonne has only 360 sheep. Therefore, Deyonne is much better off. Batonne, on the other hand, argues that he has 30 acres of land while Deyonne has only 20 acres; then too, Deyonne's land was inherited while Batonne had given 35 sheep for 20 acres of land 10 years ago, and this year he gave 40 sheep for 10 acres of land. Batonne also makes the observation that, of Deyonne's sheep, 35 belong to another man and he merely keeps them. Deyonne counters that he has a large one-room cabin that he built himself. He claims that he has been offered three acres of land for the cabin. Besides these things, he has a plow, which was a gift from a friend and is worth a couple of goats; two carts which were given him in trade for a poor acre of land; and an ox which he had acquired for five sheep.

Batonne goes on to say that his wife has orders for five coats to be made of homespun wool, and that she will receive 25 goats for them. His wife has 10 goats already, three of which have been received in exchange for one sheep just last year. She has an ox which she acquired in a trade for three sheep. She also has one cart which cost her two sheep. Batonne's two-room cabin, even though smaller in dimensions than Deyonne's, should bring him two choice acres of land in a trade. Deyonne is reminded by Batonne that he owes Tyrone three sheep for bringing up his lunch each day last year.

Required:

By studying the situation carefully, see what solution you may be able to offer these men. Specify any assumptions which you find it necessary to make.

*Reprinted with permission from Marvin L. Carlson and J. Warren Higgins, "A Games Approach To Introducing Accounting" in J.D. Edwards, *Accounting Education: Problems and Prospects* (American Accounting Association, 1974).

CHAPTER 2

Financial Statements: Measuring Capital and Income

Chapter Themes

1. In the 1980s, many organizations are using computers to do their required bookkeeping. Although this chapter illustrates a manual bookkeeping method, the basic concepts and techniques that are set forth are essentially the same as those that are followed in computer bookkeeping systems.

2. To gain maximum benefit from the chapter, it is necessary to think not only in terms of the balance-sheet equation (assets = liabilities + owner's equity), but also in terms of how each transaction may be evaluated by different readers of financial statements: a creditor, an owner of the business, a prospective creditor.

3. In general purpose financial statements, considerable attention is given to separating *capital* invested by owners of the business from *income*, or what the invested capital earns. Income is similar to interest that we earn on our bank balance. We can withdraw and spend the interest that the bank has provided to us. When we also spend the original capital dollars deposited in our bank account, however, we are likely to receive less interest income in the future. The amount of interest that we receive can vary with economic business conditions—and the same concept applies for business income. The causes of variations in income are of concern to businesspersons. Accounting reports attempt to assist owners and other businesspeople in measuring income.

Capital and Income

Much of Chapter 1 focussed on transactions that altered specific assets and liabilities but left the *original owners' equity* (also often referred to as *capital,* or *capital investment*) constant. Illustration 1-6, unlike the previous illustrations, showed one way of bringing about a change in owners' equity—by selling inventory for a sum in excess of what it cost. The chapter noted that owners' equity might increase or decrease as a result of four kinds of transactions. We will now reclassify these four into what are called *capital transactions* and *income transactions,* resulting in three basic types:

1. The owners invested some, or more, of their personal assets in the business, or withdrew assets from the business to use for a personal transaction. This type of change in owners' equity is called a *capital transaction.* It merely increases or decreases owners' equity through transactions with the owners, usually by directly increasing or decreasing cash assets. (See Illustration 2-1.)

ILLUSTRATION 2-1

Capital Transactions

Transaction	Assets	= Liabilities	+	Owners' Equity
Initial investment by owners to commence the business	$100,000			$100,000
Additional investment by owners	+50,000			+50,000
Withdrawal by owners of *dollars previously invested*	−25,000			−25,000
Current balance of original owners' equity	$125,000	0		$125,000

2. The managers of the business sold an asset such as inventory (or rendered a service, such as a lawyer who gave legal advice) for an amount in excess of the cost of buying and disposing of the inventory. This results in *income,* or a *profit.* If the sale is for an amount below cost, a *loss* occurs. This rendering of services or selling of assets is an *income transaction.* For a profit-seeking business (i.e., in contrast to an organization such as a hospital whose goal is good health care at a reasonable cost), the creation of income is the essence or purpose of the business. The higher the income the more successful the business. In view of the broad interest in the size of income by both preparers and users, accountants assemble income transactions on a separate *income statement.* This involves the use of *revenue* and *expense* accounts, which are subdivisions or parts of *owners' equity.* They are illustrated later in this chapter.

3. The owners of the organization (or their representatives, who may be called the *board of directors*) could decide to pay out the income in cash. In Illustration 1-6, inventory costing $80,000 was sold for $99,000, resulting in an income (ignoring all other matters) of $19,000. If $19,000 in cash were paid to the owners, the cash asset would be reduced by $19,000, and the owners' equity would be reduced by $19,000. This distribution of income (or return *on* capital) is a *capital transaction*. Later, we will refer to this transaction as a *dividend* to, or withdrawal by, the owners. It differs from transaction type 1; (which was also a capital transaction) in that type 1 does *not* include payments out of income transactions. Type 3 is restricted to *withdrawals of income*.

The distinctions in the three different transactions become clearer when we think in terms of a savings account at a bank. If we put $90 in the account when we open it, then add another $20 the next day, and withdraw $10 the next day, we have a net balance of $100. All of these are type 1 *capital* transactions, as shown in Illustration 2-1. If the bank credits us for $10 interest on our $100 of capital (or owners' equity) this would be a type 2 *income* transaction. The owners' equity would now be $110. If we withdrew the $10 in cash, we would be paying ourselves a dividend, a type 3 transaction. Accountants do not use terms such as type 1 and type 2. We have to keep the three distinctive types clearly in mind, however, as we study the following chapters.

As we proceed, we will learn that the income figure can be "manipulated" upward or downward by choosing one accounting method instead of another. Thus, the capital-versus-income distinction might become less useful. Nevertheless, some people, such as lawyers and bankers, attach great importance to the distinction between capital and income. This means that we have to give it considerable attention.

In an important sense, *income* is one possible measure of success. If we compare an organization's income this year to that of previous years, we obtain a general impression of success trends for this one organization. Yet such comparisons can be dangerous, if the nature of this organization's business operations has changed since last year. For example, income may have increased this year because the organization bought one of its competitors. If so, more *capital* may well have been invested to obtain the higher *income*.

Newspapers frequently report the income of various Canadian companies—especially of banks, and of large companies such as Air Canada and The Canada Development Corporation. As the course progresses, we will see that such an income number is very rough, and often means less than people think.

Many accountants and businesspeople try to compare the income of one business organization to that of another (i.e., between company or inter-company comparisons). In some situations, especially when the organizations are small, e.g., corner grocery stores, such a comparison can be useful in assessing progress. For larger organizations, which are in different lines of business (e.g., mining, oil and gas, real estate, department stores), comparisons of the income of one company to that of another can often be meaningless or dangerous. We will encounter many reasons why inter-company income comparisons have to be interpreted with care.

In summary, year-to-year income comparisons for the *same* company can be informative whereas same-year income comparisons among several companies are potentially dangerous. Much more will be said on this topic in subsequent chapters.

Now that we have given a few reasons why income is important, it is time to proceed to illustrations of how it might be computed.

INCOME ILLUSTRATION

Suppose that on September 1, 19—2 Ms. *J* and Mr. *K* form a business, known as JK Grocery Market, by opening a bank account in which they each deposit $50,000, for a total of $100,000. During September, the following occurs:

September 2: A store is rented for $800 per month. The first month's rent of $800, plus a rental deposit of $1,000, is paid.

September 3: Store shelves, refrigerators, a cash register, and similar furnishings are rented for $1,100 a month. A cheque is issued for $1,100 for September's rent.

September 4: Inventory of $50,000 is acquired by paying $30,000 cash and by promising to pay the remainder of $20,000 before the end of the month.

September 10: $2,000 cash is paid to local newspapers for advertising the opening of the store.

September 20: Sales of inventory to date amount to $11,499 cash. The cost of the inventory that was sold (i.e., this inventory was acquired on September 4) amounts to $7,800.

September 24: More inventory is purchased for $32,000 cash.

September 26: $20,000 cash is paid for the inventory bought on September 4.

September 29: $4,880 cash is paid out in wages to employees and for other expenses for the month of September.

September 30: Sales from September 20 until today amount to $18,501 in cash. The cost of the inventory that was sold (most accountants refer to this as *cost of goods sold*) totals $10,400.

We will use a format similar to Illustration 1-5 to record the transactions for JK Grocery Market. This is to illustrate the effects on the balance sheet equation (assets = liabilities + owners' equity); it is *not* how bookkeepers actually record the transactions. The transactions are shown in Illustration 2-2.

Before we explain each of the transactions, it is useful to remember that revenue and expenses are *subdivisions of owners' equity:*

Revenue increases owners' equity;
Expense decreases owners' equity.

It is very important that we do *not* confuse revenue and expense with the type of asset or liability that each may take. That is, revenue is earned by selling a good or providing a service but may be received as an asset in the form of additional cash (or perhaps as a promise to pay by the customer, which is an *account receivable*). Similarly, expenses may result in a reduction of cash. Cash is the asset whereas revenue

ILLUSTRATION 2-2

JK GROCERY MARKET

	Assets			− Liabilities =	Owners' Equity (O.E.)		
	Cash	Inventory	Deposit		Expense Reduces O.E.	Revenue Increases O.E.	Initial Investment
September 1	$100,000						$100,000
2	(1,800)		$1,000		$ 800		
	98,200		1,000		800		100,000
3	(1,100)				1,100		
	97,100		1,000		1,900		100,000
4	(30,000)	$50,000		$20,000			
	67,100	50,000	1,000	20,000	1,900		100,000
10	(2,000)				2,000		
	65,100	50,000	1,000	20,000	3,900		100,000
20	11,499					$11,499	
		(7,800)			7,800		
	76,599	42,200	1,000	20,000	11,700	11,499	100,000
24	(32,000)	32,000					
	44,599	74,200	1,000	20,000	11,700	11,499	100,000
26	(20,000)			(20,000)			
	24,599	74,200	1,000	0	11,700	11,499	100,000
29	(4,880)				4,880		
	19,719	74,200	1,000		16,580	11,499	100,000
30	18,501					18,501	
		(10,400)			10,400		
	38,220	63,800	1,000		26,980	30,000	100,000
						(26,980)	
Income						3,020	3,020
	$ 38,220 +	$63,800 +	$1,000	=			$103,020

and expense are owners' equity. All transactions are recorded in this "double entry" form.

The explanation of each transaction is:

September 1: The owners put some cash in a bank account. Whose cash is it? The owners'. In order to separate initial *capital investment* from the income (revenue *less* expenses), we have placed the $100,000 under the "initial investment" column in Illustration 2-2. (The full reasoning for this will be provided later in the book.)

September 2: In the process of earning income (through getting more revenue than expenses), it is necessary to incur some expenses in order to generate the revenue. In a sense, expenses are assets that have worn out, or have been used up in generating revenue. At the beginning of September, the $800 represents an asset, called *prepaid expenses*. Through time, however, the asset becomes an expense, a reduction of owners' equity. By September 30, the entire $800 will have become an expense. (We have set up Illustration 2-2 from the viewpoint of those who want financial statements as of September 30. Generally, accountants would choose a month-end date, but they do not have to. For example, later in the book, we mention income tax consequences. It may be advantageous for income tax purposes to prepare financial statements for a year ending January 3.) The $800 has had the effect, *for accounting purposes*, of reducing owners' equity. In reality, of course, the $800 has helped to generate the revenue that we have shown for September 20 and 30. The other $1,000 of the September 2 transaction is merely switching the form of the asset from cash to a deposit with the landlord. Presumably, the $1,000 will be returned to JK Grocery Market when the store is vacated. The $1,000 is like an account receivable, but is not yet due; therefore, we show it as a "deposit"—an asset.

September 3: This transaction is like the $800 on September 2. By September 30, the entire $1,100 will have become an expense. Therefore, for convenience, we will record the $1,100 using a September 30 viewpoint.

September 4: This transaction involves only the assets and liabilities. An asset—inventory (goods held for resale)—is acquired by giving up another asset—cash—and taking on a liability of $20,000.

September 10: Advertising is incurred for the purpose of generating revenue. Some types of advertising (such as advertisements in the "yellow pages" or in souvenir magazines) have a longer life, i.e., life as an asset, than do other types (such as flyers handed out to shoppers in a mall). At this stage, we will treat advertising as an expense because we cannot determine from the facts in the situation what asset life, if any, it may have. That is, advertising is unlike rent, which we know has a life extending to September 30.

As a general rule, most types of advertising are expensed by accountants; but there are exceptions when we know that the advertising will help to generate revenue over several months. For example, the cost of building and installing neon advertising signs at the entrance to a shopping mall could be treated as a long-lasting asset, much as an automobile is. (We may call the neon sign something other than advertising; this topic receives more coverage in later chapters.)

September 20: In effect, two transactions occur on this date. An asset, cash, amounting to $11,499, is received by selling some inventory. If we ignore the cost of the inventory just for a moment, we can say that the asset increase of $11,499 belongs to the owners. Thus, we increased revenue, which is a part of owners' equity. We must remember, however, that one of the costs of generating this revenue is the sum that was paid for the inventory sold. Consequently, we have to acknowledge, through a second transaction, the disappearance of the $7,800 cost that was incurred for the inventory. We do this by reducing the inventory asset by $7,800 and by increasing an expense (usually called cost of goods sold) by $7,800. When we subtract the $7,800 from the $11,499, we get a $3,699 net increase in owners' equity. The $3,699 is a portion of income; it usually is called *gross profit*, or *gross margin*, or *gross income*. The word *gross* means that not all the expenses of generating the $11,499 of revenue have been included in the $3,699 (i.e., the $3,699 ignores rent, advertising, and similar expenses that have to be incurred to operate the business).

The term *cost of goods sold* is simply a shorter version of "the *cost* to us *of* the *goods* that we *sold*". Some accountants use the term *cost of sales*.

September 24: The managers of the market have exchanged an inventory asset for a cash asset.

September 26: A liability of $20,000 has been eliminated by paying cash.

September 29: One of the expenses of generating revenue is payments to employees, and for incidentals: heat, lights, telephone. Expenses are incurred by using up the cash asset.

September 30: This is a repetition of the September 20 transaction, except that the amounts involved are higher.

Observe in Illustration 2-2 how we have "closed out", or transferred, the revenue and expense totals at September 30 to an *income* figure. The income ($3,020), in turn, is "closed out" to the "initial investment" column—a step that is not strictly correct. Later, we will encounter some situations (for proprietorships and partnerships), which will be explained, where it is conventional to total to the one figure ($103,020). This figure will *not* be called "initial investment". For corporations or limited companies we have to separate the *income* ($3,020) from any *capital* investment because such separation is required by law, i.e., corporations law. The separation helps us keep track of what we invested versus what we earned on the investment.

Financial Statements

The information in Illustration 2-2 can be used to prepare financial statements for JK Grocery Market. The information is not really in a convenient form for us to prepare financial statements easily, however. Therefore, accountants assemble the transaction data another way, which will be explained in Chapter 3.

By using the data in Illustration 2-2 and the accompanying explanations, we can derive the following figures to prepare an income statement:

Revenue: $11,499 + $18,501		= $30,000
Expenses:		
Cost of goods sold	$7,800 + $10,400 = $18,200	
Rent on store	800	
Rent on equipment	1,100	
Advertising	2,000	
Wages and other	4,880	26,980
Income		$ 3,020

The figures needed to prepare a balance sheet at September 30 can be picked up from the bottom line of Illustration 2-2. JK Grocery Market, formed by Ms. *J* and Mr. *K*, is technically known as a *partnership*. This means that two or more people have combined their resources to form the business, *and* that they have *not* incorporated as a limited company. (Limited companies or corporations are explained in considerable detail later in the book.) The reason that we raise this distinction is that partnerships and proprietorships tend to present the owners' equity section of a balance sheet differently than do corporations or limited companies. (A *proprietorship* is a one owner business that is not incorporated.) A corporation has to register with a provincial or the federal government, file certain documents, and comply with laws affecting corporations. Some of these laws concern the owners' equity section of their balance sheet.

We will now illustrate the different owners' equity presentations for proprietorship/partnerships and for limited companies/corporations. As JK Grocery Market is a partnership, its financial statements can be demonstrated first, in Illustration 2-3.

ILLUSTRATION 2-3

JK GROCERY MARKET
Balance Sheet
September 30, 19—2

Assets

Cash	$ 38,220
Inventory	63,800
Deposit	1,000
	$103,020

Owners' Equity

Partners' capital, per accompanying statement:

Ms. *J*	$ 51,510
Mr. *K*	51,510
	$103,020

Observe in Illustration 2-3 that the owners' equity refers to an accompanying statement, often called *Statement of Partners' Capital*. The net capital figure for each partner ($51,510) combines their initial capital investment ($50,000) and their 50 percent share ($1,510) of September's income. That is, it does *not* permit the complete separation of income and capital as was stressed at the beginning of this chapter. We find out about September's income by looking at the income statement. But, as we will discover over the next few chapters, as the months pass, it will become more difficult to separate capital investment from income earned in *prior* periods on this investment. The Statement of Partners' Capital, shown in Illustration 2-4, is prepared for the same time period as that used for the partnership's income statement, which is shown in Illustration 2-5. (For convenience, we have assumed that each partner is entitled to 50 percent of income.)

ILLUSTRATION 2-4

JK GROCERY MARKET
Statement of Partners' Capital
For the month ended September 30, 19—2

	Ms. *J*	Mr. *K*	Total
Initial investment, September 1	$50,000	$50,000	$100,000
Income for September	1,510	1,510	3,020
Balance, September 30	$51,510	$51,510	$103,020

ILLUSTRATION 2-5

JK GROCERY MARKET
Income Statement
For the month ended September 30, 19—2

Revenue (or sales revenue)		$30,000
Cost of goods sold		18,200
Gross profit		$11,800
Expenses:		
Wages and other	$4,880	
Advertising	2,000	
Rentals on equipment	1,100	
Store rent	800	8,780
Income		$ 3,020

Some aspects of illustrations 2-3, 2-4, and 2-5 merit additional comment:

1. Note that each statement provides *three* pieces of information in the heading: (a) the name of the business, (b) a title of the statement, and (c) a date (for the balance sheet) or period of time (for the income statement and statement of partners' capital).

2. The income statement contains a line "gross profit", which is revenue less cost of goods sold. The gross-profit figure helps readers to grasp quickly how much is left over (after paying for the inventory) to meet the usual monthly expenses and to provide for a profit (income). Some of the expenses (such as rents of $1,100 and $800) may not change in amount even though the volume of sales revenue may have increased or decreased. Expenses that do not change are called *fixed*. However, the cost of goods sold tends to change in relation to sales revenue; it is called a *variable* expense.

   People, such as creditors, may wish to compare the gross profit from month to month, to ascertain any business trends. For example, if gross profit is increasing, and the JK Grocery Market has many fixed expenses, then income ought to be increasing. (More gross profit less no *additional* variable expenses = more income.) There are other uses for the gross-profit computation than the one just stated; they will be mentioned in later chapters. Keep in mind that financial-statement disclosure methods (such as whether or not to show a gross profit line) have to be tailored to the needs of the users/readers and the preparers. If nobody wants to make use of the amount of gross profit for JK Grocery Market, then it should *not* be shown. This theme was stressed in Chapter 1, and continues throughout the book. "One right way" of disclosure does not exist.

3. One of the expenses is called "Wages and other". The word "other" is uninformative, and could prevent us from determining trends affecting wages over the coming months. That is, the figure for "Wages and other" could increase in October and November, but we would not know whether "Wages" OR "other" was the cause of the increase. (On the other hand, we may not care to track down causes of expense changes, in which case the combined title "Wages and other" is adequate.)

The point of the previous paragraph is that although there are some conventional practices in accounting, much thinking about users and uses of financial statements must occur *before* we account. Otherwise, our financial statements could be inappropriate for both preparers and users. It is possible to be misled when reading this and some of the following chapters. Accounting is not rigid and rule-bound. To be a good accountant (preparer), we have to understand user needs. Similarly, users have to understand which alternatives have been chosen by accountants. Otherwise, financial statements can easily be misinterpreted.

Whether we use one, or two, or more lines on a financial statement (to combine or separate expenses, such as "Wages and other") can only be decided by preparer desires, user needs, and any applicable laws. This book therefore has to *concentrate on much more than giving numeric illustrations*. It has to explain:

1. Why accountants follow particular practices and procedures;
2. When alternatives are available; and
3. What the benefits and limitations are of each alternative method of measurement or disclosure.

In summary, although it may be annoying, we have to provide many "commercial messages". The reasons for them will become apparent.

Limited Company or Corporation

We mentioned that two of several reasons for having different financial-statement disclosure for a partnership and for a limited-liability company could be: (1) corporations are governed by the provincial *or* federal law under which they are incorporated (whereas a partnership is governed by a provincial *Partnership Act*, which does not regulate accounting); and (2) creditors', owners' or other users' desires or needs. Corporations' law states that capital should be separated from income. Briefly, one of the reasons for this law is that several frauds occurred many years ago. The repayment of *capital* contribution to investors was called *income*.

For example, a shady character, Mr. *Z*, could collect $1,000 from investors and promise to pay them $500 a month as *income* on their $1,000 investment. The investors would be led to think that, in total, they had a sum of $1,500 ($1,000 plus $500) at the end of the first month. On this date, Mr. *Z* would give the investors back one half of their $1,000 capital, *but* he would call it *income* (*not* a return of one half of their capital). The word would spread in the community that Mr. *Z* had a super investment opportunity, and more people would be only too willing to give $1,000 to him. At the end of the second month, the new investors would receive their $500, and the original investors would receive another $500 (for a total of $1,000). The procedure would therefore be much like a chain-letter fraud. More and more investors would give money to Mr. *Z* as others told of their windfall.

Whenever he felt that the time was appropriate, Mr. *Z* would disappear with the investors' money. Laws eventually were passed to prevent some of these fraud schemes from being repeated. The separation of capital and income is fundamental in corporate accounting because corporations ask for money from the public, who are strangers (whereas a partnership usually involves friends).

A corporation employs a "retained earnings" or "retained income" statement instead of a Statement of Partners' Capital. The "retained earnings" statement does *not* include any capital contribution by the owners. Its format is:

Beginning balance—January 1, 19—7	$ 900,000
Income for 19—7	200,000
	1,100,000
Dividends	70,000
Closing balance—December 31, 19—7	$1,030,000

The beginning balance of $900,000 represents income that arose in previous periods, less any losses and any dividends paid in previous periods. If we refer to the previous example of our bank account:

1. The $900,000 would represent interest (income) credited by the bank to us, less any cash withdrawals of the *interest* (income), up to the beginning of the current year, 19—7. Any withdrawals of our original capital investment deposited with the bank would *not* appear in the "retained earnings" statement.

2. The $200,000 represents income for the year ended December 31, 19—7.

3. The $70,000 represents a cash withdrawal of $70,000 of the $200,000 (or perhaps $900,000), leaving a net of $130,000, which, when added to the $900,000, gives $1,030,000.

The capital contributions are shown on the balance sheet as part of owners' equity. *If* JK Grocery Market were not a partnership but a limited liability company, or corporation, its statement of retained earnings and balance sheet would appear as in illustrations 2-6 and 2-7. *If* JK Grocery Market were incorporated, by law it would have to use a title such as the following on its financial statements:

JK Grocery Market *Limited*,
JK Grocery Market *Corporation* or
JK Grocery Market, *Inc.*

Other possible terms are *Incorporated* and *Ltd.* or any description that is prescribed or permitted by the particular act or legislation under which the business is incorporated.

In Illustration 2-7, the $100,000 is designated "common shares". That is, pieces of paper called *share certificates* would be issued to the owners of JK Grocery Market Limited. (For example, each owner may receive share certificates for 25,000 shares at an issue price of $2 per share.) This process is briefly described later in the book. The separation of the $100,000 (capital) from the $3,020 (income) is clear in Illustration 2-7, but was unavailable in Illustration 2-3 (for the partnership).

ILLUSTRATION 2-6

JK GROCERY MARKET LIMITED
Statement of Retained Earnings
For the month ended September 30, 19—2

Balance, September 1, 19—2	$ —
Income for September	3,020
Balance, September 30, 19—2	$3,020

ILLUSTRATION 2-7

JK GROCERY MARKET LIMITED
Balance Sheet
September 30, 19—2

Assets

Cash	$ 38,220
Inventory	63,800
Deposit	1,000
	$103,020

Owners' Equity

Common shares; issued 50,000 shares	$100,000
Retained earnings, per accompanying statement	3,020
	$103,020

If the preparer and user are in agreement, we could, of course, recast Illustration 2-4 to separate capital from income. Illustration 2-8 shows one possible way.

ILLUSTRATION 2-8

JK GROCERY MARKET
Statement of Partners' Capital
For the month ended September 30, 19—2

	Capital Investment			Retained Income		
	Ms. *J*	Mr. *K*	Total	Ms. *J*	Mr. *K*	Total
Balance, September 1	$50,000	$50,000	$100,000	—	—	—
Additional capital contributions	—	—	—			
Income				$1,510	$1,510	$3,020
Balance, September 30	$50,000	$50,000	$100,000	$1,510	$1,510	$3,020

The owners' equity section of the partnership balance sheet could be recast, using the information in Illustration 2-8, as follows:

Capital investment	$100,000
Retained income	3,020
	$103,020

In summary, Illustration 2-4 is more commonly seen than is Illustration 2-8. This does not mean that Illustration 2-8 is wrong. If the need exists for information on both capital inflows and outflows, and for income transactions, Illustration 2-8 can be more informative than Illustration 2-4. Other reasons for the separation (or combining) of capital and income will become apparent.

A Practice Problem

Accounting, like any other subject, involves a new terminology. Practice is required in order to feel comfortable with it.

This section of the chapter provides a somewhat different illustration to that given earlier for JK Grocery Market. This example is (1) for the *second* financial period (instead of the first), (2) a *limited-liability* company (instead of a partnership), and (3) a *service* business (instead of a retail merchandiser).

Try to solve this problem before looking at one possible solution, which follows. If you have difficulty, then look up only the pertinent point, and go back to doing the problem on your own.

Question

The balance sheet of Nancy's Hairstylists Limited is as follows after the company's first period of operations:

NANCY'S HAIRSTYLISTS LIMITED
Balance Sheet
August 31, 19—7

Assets

Cash	$ 1,300
Accounts receivable	1,330
Deposit on equipment	6,120
Deposits on leases	4,000
	$12,750

Liabilities and Owners' Equity

Liabilities:

Accounts payable		$ 970
Bank loan payable		1,000
		1,970

Owners' equity:

Common shares. Authorized 50,000 shares;		
issued 10,000 shares	$10,000	
Retained earnings	780	10,780
		$12,750

During September the following transactions occur:

September 3: Paid rent on building for September	$ 750
September 5: Paid rent on equipment for September	475
September 7: Bought hairdressing supplies on account (supplies will be used up by September 30)	320
September 15: Hairdressing services provided September 1-15:	
—for cash	7,300
—on account	1,150
September 16: Wages paid to employees (i.e., paid with cash for period September 1 to 15 inclusive)	3,260
September 18: Advertising incurred, on account (i.e., payable)	290
September 19: Owner invests additional capital in the business and receives 5,000 common shares	5,000
September 22: Accounts receivable collected	1,530
September 25: Accounts payable paid	970
September 27: Cash dividend paid on common shares	500
September 29: Wages paid to employees (for September 16 to 30 inclusive)	3,020
September 30: Hairdressing services provided September 16-30:	
—for cash	7,030
—on account	920
September 30: Hairdressing supplies for October bought for cash	480

September 30: Heat, light, telephone, and other expenses for
September paid   635

September 30: Paid the bank interest (expense) owing on
the bank loan for the month of September   120

Prepare the following financial statements:

A. Balance Sheet as at September 30, 19—7

B. Income Statement and Statement of Retained Income (its usual title is Statement of Retained Earnings or Retained Earnings Statement) for the month of September 19—7.

Show all calculations.

A tabulation that is useful for preparing the financial statements is shown in Illustration 2-9.

ANALYSIS OF ILLUSTRATION 2-9

A good review of the balance sheet equation (assets = liabilities + owners' equity) can be obtained by carefully examining the use of brackets around numbers in Illustration 2-9. The brackets generally represent a subtraction. For example, on September 3, cash is reduced by $750 and the number is therefore in brackets. The $750 also has the effect of reducing owners' equity, however (i.e., assets must equal owners' equity plus liabilities). The $750 under expense is *not* in brackets because the entire "expense" column is being totalled for the month—to be subtracted at the bottom of the page. (See the brackets around $8,870 in the revenue column at the bottom of the page.)

The dividend on September 27 is similar to the September 3 transaction in that cash is reduced, and so is owners' equity, by $500. The three columns "expense", "revenue", and "dividends" are netted together, eventually, in arriving at the closing September 30 retained-earnings number $7,810. Thus, the $500 in the "dividends" column for September 27 is *not* in brackets.

Except for the "expense" and "dividends" columns, the remainder of Illustration 2-9 conveniently adheres to the "assets — liabilities = owners' equity" equation. The opening balances are entered so as to permit easier computation of the month-end balance of assets, liabilities, retained earnings, and common shares. The transactions that may be different from those in Illustration 2-2 are:

September 19: The $5,000 is put in the "common shares" owner's equity column (as well as in cash). This is because the corporate law, such as the *Canada Business Corporations Act,* or CBCA, that allows the company to exist, requires the owners' equity to be divided between common shares and retained earnings. (See the discussion "Capital and Income" at the beginning of this chapter.)

September 27: The dividend of $500, which is paid to the owner in cash, can be thought of as a reduction of the $780 *income* earned last month, which is shown as the opening balance of retained earnings. As described earlier, the $500 is similar to withdrawing cash from our bank account in an amount equal to or less than the interest income that was earned on our bank balance. Corporate law

ILLUSTRATION 2-9

NANCY'S HAIRSTYLISTS LIMITED

September	Assets					−	Liabilities		=	Owners' Equity (O.E.)				
	Cash	Accounts Receivable	Supplies	Deposit on Equipment	Deposit on Leases		Bank Loan	Accounts Payable		Expense (Reduces O.E.)	Revenue (Increases O.E.)	Dividends (Reduces O.E.)	Retained Earnings	Common Shares
Opening Balance	$1,300	$1,330		$6,120	$4,000		$1,000	$970					$780	$10,000
3rd	(750)									$750				
5th	(475)									475				
7th								320		320				
15th	7,300	1,150									$8,450			
16th	(3,260)									3,260				
18th								290		290				
19th	5,000													5,000
22nd	1,530	(1,530)												
25th	(970)							(970)						
27th	(500)											$500		
29th	(3,020)	920								3,020				
30th	7,030										7,950			
30th	(480)		$480											
30th	(635)									635				
30th	(120)									120				
										8,870	16,400	500		
											(8,870)	(500)		
											7,530		7,530	
	$11,950	+$1,870	+$480	+$6,120	+$4,000		−$1,000	−$610					$7,810	+$15,000

requires that dividends be shown separately on financial statements.

September 30: Because the hairdressing supplies are to be used in October, they are shown as an asset as of the end of September.

September 30: The bank has required the company to pay $120 in interest on the $1,000 loan owing to the bank. The $120 was paid in cash; therefore, the loan liability remains unchanged at $1,000.

If a sum had been paid to reduce the bank loan, however, both the asset (cash) and the liability (bank loan) would have to be reduced. We need to watch for entries recording payments made to cover *both* interest, e.g., the $120, and some of the *principal*—$1,000 in this example. A mortgage on a house is a good example of where you have to pay the mortgage company a "blended" monthly sum that includes both principal and interest. The interest is an expense but the mortgage principal repayment would be a reduction of a liability.

Concerning the owners' equity columns, an actual limited company would close out the revenue and expense categories into "retained earnings" *once a year*. The dividend category would also be closed into retained earnings at *the end* of the *financial year*. For practice, we have conducted closings at the ends of August and of September. The income for September (ignoring income tax) is $7,530 (as computed in Illustration 2-9).

Financial Statements

NANCY'S HAIRSTYLISTS LIMITED
Balance Sheet
September 30, 19—7

Assets

Cash	$11,950
Accounts receivable	1,870
Supplies	480
Deposit on equipment	6,120
Deposit on lease	4,000
	$24,420

Liabilities and Owners' Equity

Liabilities:

Accounts payable		$ 610
Bank loan payable		1,000
		1,610

Owners' Equity:

Common shares. Authorized 50,000 shares; issued 15,000 shares (5,000 for cash in September 19—7)	$15,000	
Retained earnings	7,810	22,810
		$24,420

NANCY'S HAIRSTYLISTS LIMITED
Statement of Retained Earnings
For the month of September 19—7

Balance, August 31, 19—7	$ 780
Add net income for September	7,530
	8,310
Deduct dividends paid	500
Balance, September 30, 19—7	$7,810

NANCY'S HAIRSTYLISTS LIMITED
Income Statement
For the month of September 19—7

Revenue		$16,400
Expenses:		
Wages	$6,280	
Rent of building	750	
Heat, light, telephone, and other	635	
Equipment rental	475	
Supplies	320	
Advertising	290	
Interest	120	8,870
Net income		$ 7,530

COMMENTARY ON FINANCIAL STATEMENTS

As stated earlier in this chapter, preparation of the financial statements is difficult when we do not have a separate column in Illustration 2-9 for expenses. Preparation of the income statement was particularly awkward because all of the expenses were grouped together. This difficulty is overcome by having books of account, which are described in Chapter 3.

Financial-statement presentation is largely a matter of personal taste. Nevertheless, many (but not all) accountants follow these conventions:

1. On the asset side of the balance sheet, the most liquid asset, cash, is listed first. The other assets then follow *roughly* in order of when they become cash (e.g., accounts receivable) or save us having to pay cash (e.g., "deposit on equipment" reduces the final cash payment at a later date). A similar liquidity ordering approach is used for liabilities based on when they are due for cash payment.

2. Expenses on the income statement *tend to* be shown in order of their dollar magnitude, unless a law or accounting pronouncement (such as GAAP) requires different treatment.

3. The disclosure within the owners' equity section of a limited-liability company is usually dictated by corporate law. For instance, the statement shows that 5,000 shares were issued for cash during September. These corporate-law requirements are mentioned later in this book.

4. Unlike Illustration 2-2, there is no gross profit line on the income statement in Illustration 2-9. All the expenses are listed in one column, primarily because the company offers a service, and does not sell a product at a gross profit.

Now that we have dealt with the technical aspects of the company's financial statements, we may ask: Is the company in good financial condition? Interpreting financial statements is often difficult and involved; so, give the topic much attention throughout this book. Some vital points to keep in mind are:

1. The balance sheet is as of an *instant* of time, e.g., the close of business on September 30, 19—7. The asset-and-liability situation could look much different a minute before or a minute after September 30, 19—7. Hence, we should not jump to conclusions.

2. Many alternatives exist in accounting. As the book progresses, it is possible to lose track of the vast number of alternatives. We have to be careful that we base all analyses on whichever alternative the company actually followed.

What do the financial statements tell us?

1. Almost one half of the assets are cash. Yet, the company has a small bank loan. Why? Is the cash needed soon to pay for equipment, for which the company has made a deposit? If not, why doesn't the company repay the bank? (Maybe it did repay early in October; the balance sheet as at September 30 would not show this.)

2. Who owes the $1,870? It is to be hoped that the customers are worthy of credit— and that the asset is legitimate.

3. The month of September was very profitable. Income of $7,530 was earned on a capital investment of only $15,000. Is the company certain that all the "bills" (called *invoices*) for September were paid, or recorded?

4. Why is income tax, that would be payable on the income for September, not shown on the financial statements? (This book discusses income taxes, and unpaid invoices, in later chapters.)

Summary

The chapter commenced by stressing the importance of trying to separate *capital* from *income*. If Canadian citizens are to maintain or improve their standard of living, huge sums of capital have to be assembled to build steel mills, factories, and power plants as well as to develop mines and oil-and-gas resources. Investors will place their savings, or capital, into a company only if they expect to get their capital repaid *plus* receive income on their capital investment.

Income can be computed in different ways, as we will see in later chapters. One way of measuring income was partially explained in this chapter. Separation of income from capital becomes very important when cash is paid to investors. Investors want to know whether they are receiving a dividend from income earned by the company, or are merely being repaid a portion of their original investment. If they are being repaid a portion of their capital investment, any continuing cash payments will exhaust their investment. Payments out of income could continue for many years.

Brief attention was given to the interpretation of financial statements; succeeding chapters will deal with this in great detail. Many alternatives exist in accounting; thus financial-statement interpretation is complex.

QUESTIONS

2-1 Distinguish a capital transaction from an income transaction. Give examples of each.

2-2 Give examples of situations where there is a withdrawal of income and a withdrawal of capital.

2-3 List some interpretation problems that may be encountered in comparing the income figures of two different companies.

2-4 What is the difference in balance sheet presentation between a partnership and a limited company, or corporation?

2-5 What uses may be made of income statements? Be specific.

2-6 Explain why the generation of revenue increases owners' equity.

2-7 What does the line "gross profit" or "gross margin" signify? Who might find the figure useful?

2-8 How does an accountant determine the number of different expense categories or lines that are needed on an income statement?

EXERCISES

(Note: The Exercises category includes assignments that can be answered primarily by referring to material in the most recent chapters.)

E2-1 Use a design that is similar to Illustration 2-2 to display the undernoted transactions and activities. Then, prepare a Balance Sheet at January 31, and a Statement of Partners'

Capital, and an Income Statement for January for Kagan and Rosart, who are equal partners. (Note that you may need different categories of assets than is shown in Illustration 2-2.)

January 2: Each partner contributes $125,000 in cash to the partnership, and the $250,000 is deposited in a bank account opened in the name of the partnership, Kagan and Rosart.

January 3: Store space is rented for $1,200 per month, commencing immediately. A cheque for $2,400 is issued.

January 4: Display facilities, equipment and cash registers are rented for $1,450 per month. A cheque for $4,350 is issued for January, February and March.

January 5: Inventory of $70,000 is acquired by paying $20,000 cash and undertaking to pay the balance before the end of January.

January 6: Advertising agreements are made with local newspapers, at a cost of $3,000. It is expected that $2,000 of the advertising will appear in January and the balance in February. A cheque for $3,000 is issued.

January 7: Two employees are hired, and are to be paid on an hourly wage basis.

January 9: Additional inventory is purchased for $30,000 cash.

January 15: The employees are paid $600, less various deductions. (This transaction can be recorded as a reduction in cash of $600. Further comments on payroll accounting and payroll deductions are made in Chapter 12.)

January 19: Light and heat expenses for January have been estimated at $450 by the owner of the store building. A cheque is issued for this sum. (Once per year the owner adjusts the amount due for overpayments or underpayments.)

January 25: Miscellaneous expenses of $920 are paid in cash.

January 30: The employees are paid another $600, which is the balance of their wages for January.

January 31: Sales for January amount to $60,650. The cost of the inventory that was sold amounts to $40,500.

E2-2 Y and Z formed a partnership on September 1, 19—9. Prepare a balance sheet at September 30, 19—9, and an income statement for September 19—9, from the following totals as of September 30, 19—9. (Note that the partners' capital accounts are as of the *beginning* of the month, and therefore exclude the revenue and expense effects for September.)

Revenue	205,700
Cash	3,100
Mr. Y, partner's capital, September 1, 19—9	80,000
Ms. Z, partner's capital, September 1, 19—9	80,000
Accounts payable	12,800
Automobile	20,000
Accounts receivable	38,900
Inventory	52,000
Cost of goods sold	99,200
Rent expense	18,000
Advertising expense	17,700
Prepaid expense	2,300
Wages expense	39,800
Bank loan payable	40,000
Land	120,000
Miscellaneous expense	13,900
Miscellaneous payable	6,400

E2-3 Use the following schedule to mark an "X" in the appropriate columns, to indicate what has happened:

		Assets		Liabilities		Owners' Equity	
Date	No Effect	Increase	Decrease	Increase	Decrease	Increase	Decrease
19—8:							
October 1		X				X	

October 1: $200,000 in cash is deposited in a bank, to commence a business.

October 3: Inventory costing $85,000 is purchased for $20,000 cash, and the balance is due within 21 days.

October 5: A store is rented for three years commencing today. A cheque for $5,000 is issued. Rent for October is $1,100. Each month thereafter, the rent will be $1,200.

October 7: Some equipment costing $20,000 is ordered for delivery in November.

October 9: Advertising in the newspapers for October is expected to cost $1,600. A cheque is issued for $1,000; the balance is due within two weeks.

October 11: Inventory costing $19,000 is sold on account for $27,900.

October 15: An automobile is purchased for $16,000 cash. It is to be delivered within two weeks.

October 17: Employees' wages for the first half of October amount to $2,100. (Assume that the $2,100 is paid in cash. Payroll accounting is described later, in Chapter 12.)

October 19: A customer gives us a cheque for $10,000 for inventory to be delivered in November. The cheque is deposited in the company's bank account.

October 21: The additional $600 owing for the advertising is paid.

October 23: The automobile purchased on October 15 is delivered.

October 25: A bank loan is arranged for $50,000. The bank will be putting the $50,000 in the company's bank account on October 31.

October 27: Cash of $27,900 is collected for the inventory that was sold on October 11.

October 29: A cheque for $20,000 is issued for inventory purchased on October 3.

October 30: Miscellaneous expenses of $1,650 are paid in cash.

October 31: The bank places the $50,000, arranged on October 25, in the company's bank account.

E2-4 Use the following schedule to indicate whether the undernoted 19—9 transactions increase, decrease, or have no effect on income in November 19—9.

		Income	
	No Effect	Increase	Decrease
November 1	X		

November 1: A customer telephones to ask the price of an inventory item and is told that it is $14,000.

November 3: Inventory is sold for $30,000.

November 4: The inventory that was sold on November 3 cost the company $17,600.

November 5: More inventory is purchased, for $21,500.

November 7: Advertising expenses are incurred, costing $1,000.

November 9: A deposit of $12,000 is received from a customer, who wants inventory delivered in December.

November 11: Wages of $4,500 are paid to employees.

November 15: A cheque for $1,600 is issued for November's rent.

November 17: A cheque for $1,600 is issued for the December's rent.

November 19: Miscellaneous expenses of $1,210 are paid in cash.

November 21: A deposit of $10,000 is paid to a supplier of inventory.

November 25: Heat and light invoices are received for November, totalling $1,390, and are paid in cash.

November 30: Interest of $105 is received on the company's bank balance for the month of November.

E2-5 Prepare a balance sheet at January 31, 19—8, and an income statement for January 19—8 from the following totals as of January 31, 19—8:

L. Mitchell, proprietor's balance, January 1, 19—8	$85,000
Wages expense	3,100
Furniture and equipment	16,800
Inventory	41,000
Bank loan payable	20,000
Land	40,000
Miscellaneous expense	890
Revenue	28,000
Accounts receivable	17,500
Accounts payable	29,950
Delivery expense	950
Cash	2,000
Automobile	19,500
Advertising expense	1,010
Prepaid expense	3,200
Cost of goods sold	17,000

E2-6 Replace the ? with dollar figures in each of the separate situations A through H.

	Balance as of the end of the month			Totals for the month		
	Assets	Liabilities	Owners' equity	Owners' equity at beginning of month	Revenue	Expense
A.	$2,700	$1,200	?	$1,000	$4,500	$4,000
B.	5,000	?	?	2,000	6,000	4,800
C.	6,000	?	5,000	?	7,000	5,600
D.	?	2,000	?	2,500	5,400	3,600
E.	?	1,500	6,000	2,000	9,200	?
F.	10,000	?	7,500	3,000	?	6,800
G.	?	2,000	9,000	?	9,900	6,500
H.	8,000	?	4,200	3,000	4,000	?

PROBLEMS

(Note: The Problems category is for assignments that may require some additional thought beyond the material in the chapter, and may draw upon material from previous chapters.)

P2-1 Use a design that is similar to Illustration 2-2 to display the undernoted transactions and activities. Then, prepare a balance sheet at September 30, and an income statement and statement of proprietor's capital for September. (Note that you may need different categories of assets from those that are shown in Illustration 2-2.)

September 1: C. Newman commences his recreation business by placing $50,000 in his newly opened proprietorship bank account.

September 3: Mr. Newman orders sailing equipment that will be sold in his store. He gives a $10,000 deposit to the supplier.

September 5: Store space is rented at a cost of $1,100 for September, and $1,200 per month thereafter. A cheque for $5,000 is issued.

September 7: Inventory costing $45,000 arrives. Mr. Newman pays another $10,000 and agrees to pay the balance before October 31.

September 9: Mr. Newman decides to use sailing equipment costing $6,200 for his personal use.

September 11: Miscellaneous expenses of $1,475 are incurred, and are paid by cheque.

September 13: Inventory costing $21,000 is sold for $37,200. The buyers pay $18,000 cash, and promise to pay the remainder within one month.

September 15: Mr. Newman issues a personal cheque for $20,000 to increase his equity in the proprietorship.

September 17: Mr. Newman negotiates a $40,000 bank loan for the proprietorship. The sum is placed in the proprietorship's bank account.

September 19: An automobile costing $21,000 is ordered for delivery in a week or two. A deposit cheque of $10,000 is given to the automobile dealer.

September 21: Furniture and display equipment is ordered at a cost of $35,000. A cheque for $35,000 is issued. Delivery is promised by the end of September.

September 25: Inventory costing $15,000 is sold for $24,200.

September 29: Wages of $7,100 are paid in cash. (Assume that the $7,100 is paid in cash. Payroll accounting is covered later, in Chapter 12.)

September 30: Interest expense of $180 is paid to the bank.

P2-2 Indicate into which category each of the following transactions fits best:

Category:

A. No effect on assets, liabilities or owner's equity (including revenue and expenses.)
B. Increases one or more assets and increases owners' equity.
C. Increases one or more assets and increases liabilities.
D. Increases one asset and decreases another asset.
E. Decreases one or more assets and decreases a liability.
F. Increases both an expense and a liability.
G. Increases an expense and decreases one or more assets.
H. Increases one or more assets and increases revenue.
I. Other (If this category is used, the reasons should be given.)

November 1: M. Tomins deposits $20,000 in a bank account to open her proprietorship business, Telephone Answering, Wake Up and Reminder Service.

November 2: Customers pay $2,000 for service for the month of November.

November 3: A contract is signed to rent an office for $350 per month.

November 4: Advertising of $275 is paid by cheque.

November 6: Equipment of $1,750 is purchased on account. Delivery is to occur before the end of the month.

November 8: Miscellaneous expenses of $895 are paid by cheque.

November 10: A cheque for $1,500 is received from a customer for service in December and the following five months.

November 12: A cheque for $1,000 is issued for rent of office space. A sum of $325 is being charged for November; and, $350 per month applies to December and succeeding months.

November 14: A cheque is issued for the equipment that was purchased on November 6.

November 20: An invoice for November's rental of telephone equipment arrives in the mail, and requires payment of $1,050 by December 10.

November 22: An insurance company has sent the proprietorship an invoice for $1,800 to cover insurance for the three year period commencing November 1. A cheque is issued for $1,800.

November 24: Ms. Tomins arranges a bank loan of $20,000 for the proprietorship. The bank deposits the $20,000 in the proprietorship's bank account.

November 27: The equipment ordered on November 6 arrives.

November 29: Interest of $24 is paid on the bank loan.

November 30: Interest of $62 is received for money deposited in the proprietorship's savings account at the bank.

P2-3 Analyze the undernoted financial statements and explain what the statements do and do not tell us.

FLEMING CORPORATION
Balance Sheets
December 31

Assets

	(in thousands)	
	19—9	19—8
Current:		
Cash	$ 5	$ 30
Accounts receivable	710	670
Inventory	890	810
Prepaid expenses	45	40
	1,650	1,550
Long-lived:		
Land	450	450
Building and equipment	10,465	8,970
Accumulated depreciation	(3,080)	(2,210)
	7,835	7,210
	$9,485	$8,760

Liabilities and Owners' Equity

Current liabilities:		
Accounts payable	$ 920	$ 725
Bank loan payable	410	—
Other liabilities	330	310
	1,660	1,035
Owners' equity:		
Common shares	2,000	2,000
Retained earnings	5,825	5,725
	7,825	7,725
	$9,485	$8,760

FLEMING CORPORATION
Income Statement
Year ended December 31

	(in thousands)	
	19—9	19—8
Revenue	$5,690	$6,705
Cost of goods sold	3,670	4,015
Gross profit	2,020	2,690
Expenses:		
Selling expenses	530	525
Administrative expenses	300	305
Interest expense	140	80
Depreciation expense	870	910
	1,840	1,820
Income before income tax	180	870
Income tax	80	420
Net income	$ 100	$ 450

FLEMING CORPORATION
Retained Earnings Statement
Year ended December 31

	(in thousands)	
	19—9	19—8
Balance, beginning of year	$5,725	$5,375
Net income	100	450
	5,825	5,825
Dividends	—	100
Balance, end of year	$5,825	$5,725

P2-4 Rod Strong made a contract with a farmer to purchase a quantity of Christmas trees, which Rod trucked to the city and offered for sale on a rented lot. By December 20th he had sold half of his trees.

Rod often bargains with his customers over the selling price of a tree. Thus prices tend to drop toward Christmas day in order to clear all the trees off the lot. The tree inventory is financed by a loan from the bank.

A friend asked Rod how much profit he had made on the trees already sold. Rod threw up his hands, explaining: "I don't know. My accountant looks after all my bookkeeping and she tells me that it is pointless to determine profit until Christmas day."

Required:

A. Assume the role of Rod's accountant. Explain why you have told Rod to wait until Christmas day to determine profit.

B. As Rod's accountant, what information can you give Rod at this time (December 20) to aid in evaluating his position and success?

C. Assume the bank has just called (December 20) and wants a report on how Rod is doing. What accounting information can be given to the banker?

D. What value would you assign to the inventory of trees on December 26th? On January 15 of the following year?

P2-5 The following account balances are taken from the records of the Mintz Company, a sole proprietorship, as of December 31, 19—8.

Cash	$18,000
H. Mintz, capital (January 1, 19—8)	45,000
Sales	72,000
Cost of goods sold	52,000
Prepaid insurance	1,000
Advances from customers	3,000
Patents	8,000
Insurance expense	2,000
Interest revenue	500
Interest expense	900
Prepaid interest	200
Interest payable	600
Accounts receivable	10,000
Inventory	9,000
Rent expense	6,000
Advertising expense	5,000
Notes payable (due in 3 years)	8,000
Buildings and equipment (ignore depreciation)	26,000
Notes receivable	10,000
Accounts payable	19,000

Required:

A. Prepare an income statement and a balance sheet. Title and date the statements as appropriate, and, insofar as the information permits, separate assets and liabilities into current and non-current classifications.

B. Assume the role of a short-term creditor, indicate the information that you would use from the statements in deciding whether to loan the company money. Why? What additional information would you require?

P2-6 The following data is for A. Milburn, a proprietorship. Compute sales revenue, cost of goods sold, expenses (ignore depreciation), and income for the year ended October 31, 19—9:

	October 31	
	19—9	19—8
Cash	$ 8,000	$10,000
Accounts receivable	37,000	40,000
Inventory	37,800	30,000
Accounts payable	9,200	8,500

Additional Information:

1. Cash received from customers during the year: $82,000.
2. Payments made to suppliers for inventory purchased during the year: $69,900.
3. All sales are made on account, and all purchases of inventory are made on account.
4. All expenses are paid in cash.

P2-7 **A.** Replace the ? with figures that balance the financial statements for Bolla Corporation.
B. If you were a banker, would you loan large sums of money to this company? Why?

	As of December 31, in thousands		
	19—7	19—8	19—9
Current assets:			
Cash	$?	$?	$ 1,520
Short-term investment	1,800	—	—
Receivables	1,965	2,110	1,990
Inventory	1,270	1,490	?
	5,205	5,450	?
Long-lived assets:			
Land	700	?	700
Building and equipment	6,360	6,480	?
Accumulated depreciation	(2,210)	(?)	(3,005)
	?	?	4,310
	$?	$?	$9,560
Current Liabilities:			
Accounts payable	895	905	550
Bank loan payable	620	?	?
	?	1,110	?
Owners' equity:			
Common shares	4,000	4,000	4,000
Retained earnings	?	4,860	5,010
	?	?	?
	$?	$?	$9,560

	Year ended December 31, in thousands		
	19—7	19—8	19—9
Income statement:			
Sales revenue	$?	$9,940	$?
Cost of goods sold	5,070	?	5,860
Gross profit	3,820	?	4,370
Expenses:			
Selling	1,215	1,305	1,360
Administrative	975	?	1,090
Depreciation	510	490	?
Interest	?	95	60
	?	2,970	3,020
Income before income taxes	?	970	?
Income taxes	440	?	650
Net income	$ 490	$ 520	$?
Retained earnings statement:			
Balance, beginning of year	$4,250	$?	$4,860
Net income	490	520	?
	4,740	5,060	?
Dividends	200	?	?
Balance, end of year	$?	$4,860	$5,010

EXPLORATION MATERIALS AND CASES

(Note: This category includes less directive material designed to encourage the development of judgmental, diagnostic, analytical and similar skills.)

MC2-1   **THE SHEEPHERDERS★**
An Accounting Game
Part II

A year has elapsed since you solved Part I of the Sheepherders Game. After studying your solution to Part I, Deyonne and Batonne grudgingly accepted your opinion as to their relative wealths at the end of last year. The passage of time has not diminished their penchant for argument, however. Now they're arguing about who had the largest income for the year just ended.

Deyonne points out that the number of sheep which he personally owns at year end exceeds his personal holdings at the beginning of the year by 80, whereas Batonne's increase was only 20. Batonne replies that his increase would have been 60 had he not traded 40 sheep during the year for 10 acres of additional land. Besides, Batonne

---

★Reprinted with permission from Marvin L. Carlson and J. Warren Higgins, "A Games Approach To Introducing Accounting" in J.D. Edwards, *Accounting Education: Problems and Prospects* (American Accounting Association, 1974)

points out that he exchanged 18 sheep during the year for food and clothing items; whereas Deyonne exchanged only seven for such purposes. The food and clothing has been pretty much used up by the end of the year.

Batonne is happy because his wife made five coats during the year (fulfilling the orders she had at the beginning of the year) and received 25 goats for them. She managed to obtain orders for another five coats (again for 25 goats)—orders on which she has not begun to work. Deyonne points out that he took to making his own lunches this year; therefore he does not owe Tyrone anything now. Deyonne was very unhappy one day last year when he discovered that his ox had died of a mysterious illness. Both men are thankful, however, that none of the other animals died or was lost.

Except for the matters reported above, each man's holdings at the end of the current year are the same as his holdings at the end of last year.

Required:

What solution can you offer the two men as to who had the greater income for the year?

MC2-2 Refer to Appendix 1-A, Fiberglas Canada Inc.'s financial statements:

A. What seems to have caused the net earnings for the year to have dropped from $17,232,000 in 1983 to $14,773,000 in 1984 in a period when gross sales rose?

B. Capital stock (or common shares) at the end of 1984 is $2,739,000, whereas total shareholders' equity (or owners' equity) is $110,349,000. What accounts for the difference? How did the difference arise?

C. As of December 31, 1983, the company had $24,811,000 of cash and short-term investments. At the end of 1984, this asset had vanished. What are the likely reasons for its disappearance?

D. Do the auditors say that they have checked for frauds and have not found any? What are the auditors telling us? Explain thoroughly.

CHAPTER 3

The Bookkeeping Cycle

Chapter Themes

1. Much of this chapter explains the bookkeeping, or accounting, cycle. The cycle refers to the steps that bookkeepers take while keeping a set of "books of account", and in preparing financial statements. Those new to this cycle will have to practise if they wish to become proficient in the bookkeeping aspects of accounting. To obtain a *user's view* of accounting, we need to understand the logic underlying the steps, but not necessarily all the details at this time. It will gradually all fall into place. We should not expect *instant* understanding.

2. Appendix 3-A provides a brief illustration of specialized bookkeeper's journals, which are designed to simplify the recording process. In practice, companies tend to invent whatever suits their needs and would not necessarily follow the designs illustrated in this appendix.

BOOKKEEPING CYCLE

The final product of an accountant's effort is the report, or set of financial statements. Some of the financial statements have already been illustrated. Others will be introduced later. It is obvious that the method of recording that we have used to date in this book is cumbersome. Over many centuries—but mainly since the fifteenth century—bookkeepers (or accounting technicians) have devised methods of recording that help to eliminate some types of errors and permit easier preparation of financial statements.

Bookkeepers use:

1. Journals (and journal entries),
2. Ledgers,
3. Trial balances, and
4. Work sheets, and similar technical tools.

One cycle from transaction (e.g., opening a bank account) to financial statement involves employing the following steps in the *manual* bookkeeping cycle:

1. *Original* transaction, or accountable event, occurs;
2. *Original* transaction is entered in a *journal* (sometimes called a book of original entry) by making a journal entry;
3. Journal entry is posted to each *ledger* account that is affected;
4. A *trial balance* is taken of the totals in the ledger accounts, to ensure that the books are in balance; (Some types of "posting" errors will be discovered by taking a trial balance. An explanation follows shortly.)
5. *Adjusting* journal entries are entered in a journal;
6. These *adjusting* journal entries are posted to the affected ledger accounts;
7. An *adjusted* trial balance is prepared to ensure that the books are in balance;
8. *Closing* journal entries are entered in a journal;
9. These *closing* journal entries are posted to the affected ledger accounts;
10. An *after-closing* trial balance is prepared to ensure that the books are in balance; and
11. Financial statements are prepared.

There are variations of the 11 steps. For instance, some accountants may take step 11 after step 7, and renumber 8, 9, and 10 to 9, 10, and 11. Observe that three steps repeat: journal — ledger — trial balance (2-3-4, 5-6-7, 8-9-10) for three types of journal entries: *original, adjusting,* and *closing.* In the JK Grocery Market (in Chapter 2), we were using original transaction entries. Adjusting journal entries will be shown when we make the illustrations more complicated — in Chapter 4. Closing entries will be explained shortly.

Journal entries involve the use of *debits* and *credits.* Illustration 3-1 and the explanations that follow must be studied carefully to grasp the meaning of "debit" and "credit". (The term debit is often shortened to "Dr." and credit to "Cr.")

ILLUSTRATION 3-1

Debit	Credit
Increases an asset	Decreases an asset
Decreases a liability	Increases a liability
Decreases owners' equity	Increases owners' equity
Increases an expense	Decreases an expense
Decreases revenue	Increases revenue

Some typical journal entries are:

1. To start a business by depositing $30,000 in a bank:

| Debit: Cash | $30,000 | |
| Credit: Owners' equity (or capital) | | $30,000 |

Observe that, relative to the debit, we have indented the credit "owners' equity" and its amount of $30,000. At this point we may ask: "If a debit *increases* cash, why does the bank *credit* the account when money is deposited?" The reason is that the bank book, or bank statement, is a *part of the bank's books* of account (its liabilities to its customers). From the *bank's* point of view, it has made the following journal entry:

Debit: Cash	$30,000	
Credit: Name		$30,000
(Accounts-payable liability)		

The bank credits the depositor for its accounts-payable liability. When money is withdrawn, the bank *debits* that account to reduce or decrease its accounts-payable liability.

Communication with others, especially with accounting instructors and markers, is greatly aided by following this accounting convention of indenting *both* the name of the *ledger* account being credited ("owners' equity") and the amount being credited ($30,000). *All credits should be handled this way* from this point forward. Note also that the debits come first and that the credits are underneath. (The only exception to this convention occurs when specialized journals, or computers, are used. See Appendix 3-A.)

2. To buy an asset, such as inventory costing $19,000, by paying $10,000 cash and promising to pay the $9,000 in a month:

Debit: Inventory (asset +)	$19,000	
Credits: Cash (asset −)		$10,000
Accounts payable (liability +)		9,000

Three ledger accounts — one debit to "inventory", and two credits: to "cash" and to "accounts payable" — are needed to ensure that the *debits equal the credits.*

Note that cash has been *credited* to reduce it. Illustration 3-1 points out that credits decrease, or reduce, an asset. Thus, be sure to *not* confuse the balance-sheet equation (assets = liabilities + owners' equity) with debits = credits. Debits, for example, are not assets. A debit increases an asset; but, a debit can also *decrease* a liability or owners' equity.

We have added information in brackets in the journal entry for illustrative purposes only, e.g., inventory (asset +). The "asset +" would be deleted in actual practice.

3. To reduce the accounts payable, by paying cash:

| Debit: Accounts payable (liability −) | $ 9,000 | |
| Credit: Cash (asset −) | | $ 9,000 |

4. To sell inventory costing $8,500 for $12,999, of which $4,000 was received in cash:

    A. Revenue journal entry:

Debit: Cash (asset +)	$ 4,000	
Debit: Accounts receivable (asset +)	8,999	
Credit: Revenue (revenue +)		$12,999

    B. Cost of goods sold (expense) journal entry:

Debit: Cost of goods sold (expense +)	$ 8,500	
Credit: Inventory (asset −)		$ 8,500

The journal entries just shown (1 to 4) are in abbreviated form. In actuality, in manual (as opposed to, say, computerized) bookkeeping systems, journal entries have *six* parts:

1. Date of transaction, e.g., September 11, 19—6;
2. Ledger account(s) being debited, e.g., "cost of goods sold";
3. Ledger account(s) being credited, e.g., "inventory";
4. Amount of each debit, e.g., $8,500;
5. Amount of each credit, e.g., $8,500; and
6. An explanation.

In a manual system, complete journal entry form for entry 4A, (assuming a September 11, 19—6 date), would be:

September 11, 19—6 Cash (asset +)	4,000	
Accounts receivable (asset +)	8,999	
Revenue (revenue +)		12,999

    To record earning of revenue by
    selling goods for $4,000 cash plus
    an account receivable for the
    balance.

Note that we delete (1) the words "debit" and "credit", and (2) the dollar signs, when we use conventional manual journal-entry form. Computer systems may have other deletions such as the explanations, and would tend to group similar transactions into one composite tabulation or journal entry. Computer systems may also use numbers in place of account titles. The amount of stress placed on explanations, dollar signs, and similar "form" issues varies. This book supplies little comment on bookkeeping form.

JOURNALS AND LEDGERS

The bookkeeping cycle mentions journals and ledgers (journal — ledger — trial balance) three times for the three different types of journal entries (original, adjusting, and closing). In a manual system, a journal may look like that in Illustration 3-2, and a ledger like that in Illustration 3-3.

For convenience, in this book, we will use one of the two ledger forms shown in Illustration 3-4. Usually these abbreviated forms are called "T" accounts. The bal-

ILLUSTRATION 3-2

Manual General Journal

General Journal

Date	Ledger Accounts and Explanation	Ledg. Acct.	Debit	Credit
19—2 September 1	Cash	1	100,000 —	
	Owners' capital — Ms. J	71		50,000 —
	Owners' capital — Mr. K	72		50,000 —
September 2	(next journal entry placed here)			

ILLUSTRATION 3-3

Ledger Accounts

Cash   Account No. 1

Date	Explanation	Journal Page	Debit	Credit	Balance	
19—2 September 1		GJ1	100,000 —		100,000 —	Dr.

Owners' capital — Ms. J   Account No. 71

Date	Explanation	Journal Page	Debit	Credit	Balance	
19—2 September 1		GJ1		50,000 —	50,000 —	Cr.

Owners' capital — Mr. K   Account No. 72

Date	Explanation	Journal Page	Debit	Credit	Balance	
19—2 September 1		GJ1		50,000 —	50,000 —	Cr.

ance column is deleted because it is easier to understand debits and credits when there are only two columns. In practice, manual systems would have ledgers like that in Illustration 3-3.

ILLUSTRATION 3-4

Illustrated Ledger Forms

Cash

Date	Debit	Credit
19—2: September 1	100,000	

OR

Cash

19—2: September 1	100,000	

A ledger account would exist for *each* asset, liability, owners' equity, revenue, and expense account. Large businesses may have thousands of ledger accounts for each type of, say, expense. The more separate expense accounts that we have, the easier it is to trace the reasons for expense increases or decreases from period to period. When we know the cause, we can try to prevent a further increase, or whatever makes sense.

For example, suppose that we have one ledger account called "heat and light", and that the total debit amount for the current year is $11,000, whereas last year it was $8,900. What caused the increase of $2,100 ($11,000 less $8,900)? Heat only? Light only? Both? If there were separate ledger accounts for each of "heat" and "light", we would have the answer simply by looking at two accounts in the ledger. (A ledger is just a looseleaflike book with separate pages for each ledger account.)

Observe in Illustration 3-2 that a "ledger account" number column exists. This number, e.g., the "1", would be entered into the column when the *posting* (or entering) is made to the ledger account, e.g., cash. Similarly, in Illustration 3-3, the page number of the *general journal*, i.e., GJ1, is entered into each ledger account at the time of posting. (There are several types of journals; in this book we mainly use general journals, which are able to handle all types of journal entries and not just specialized transactions.) The cross referencing between the journal and ledgers allows bookkeepers to check for errors and investigate each journal entry in the ledger.

The steps in the bookkeeping cycle seem to require us to prepare a trial balance after each posting (to the ledgers) process occurs, which may be daily, weekly, monthly, etc. The *trial balance* (literally, we "try" to balance) as of September 1, 19—2 for the information in illustrations 3-2 and 3-3 would show:

JK GROCERY MARKET
Trial Balance
September 1, 19—2

Ledger Account	Debit	Credit
Cash	$100,000.00	
Owners' capital - Ms. *J*		$ 50,000.00
Owners' capital - Mr. *K*		50,000.00
	$100,000.00	$100,000.00

Notice, in the trial balance, that we (generally) do not indent the credits when we list the ledger account title. We have a debit and a credit column, and we total each to see whether they equal each other. If they do, we have probably posted all journal entries. We may, however, have posted to the wrong ledger account. The trial-balance step in the bookkeeping cycle only helps us to catch errors such as failing to post one part of a journal entry, and posting a debit as a credit, or vice versa.

REVIEW EXERCISE

A new exercise will help bring several of the steps in the bookkeeping cycle together. Adjusting journal entries will not be needed, but closing journal entries will be explained at the end of this review exercise. The steps to be followed are:

1. Journalize those transactions that require a journal entry;
2. Post to ledger "T" accounts;
3. Prepare a trial balance;
4. Prepare financial statements;
5. Journalize closing entries;
6. Post the closing entries to the ledger accounts; and
7. Prepare an after-closing trial balance.

The following occurred in October 19—4:

1. October 1, 19—4: A company called Donamar Corporation is incorporated under

federal corporate legislation (called the *Canada Business Corporations Act*) by its owner.

2. October 2, 19—4: The owner of Donamar Corporation opens a bank account in the company's name and deposits $200,000. Common shares are issued to the owner to reflect his $200,000 equity.

3. October 4, 19—4: The owner hires a manager of the business and promises to pay him $2,000 per month at the end of each month.

4. October 6, 19—4: The manager orders $60,000 of inventory, for delivery on October 10, 19—4.

5. October 7, 19—4: Rent of $600 cash is paid for store space for October 19—4.

6. October 9, 19—4: A cash register and shelving is rented for $800 a month.
   Only $590 is paid for the month of October because the equipment is not being used for a full month.

7. October 11, 19—4: The inventory ordered on October 6 arrives today. Its cost turns out to be $57,800. $20,000 cash is paid today; the balance is due in 14 days.

8. October 17, 19—4: Inventory costing $39,500 is sold for $50,000. The terms are a cash down-payment of $10,000, and the balance of $40,000 is due periodically, but no later than November 15, 19—4.

9. October 21, 19—4: A $20 telephone bill for October is paid in cash.

10. October 25, 19—4: The accounts payable of $37,800 for inventory bought on October 11 is paid today.

11. October 28, 19—4: $10,000 cash is received from the person who bought the goods on October 17, 19—4.

12. October 31, 19—4: $2,000 in cash is paid to the manager of the business.

Using manual bookkeeping procedures, we would make the following general journal entries for Donamar Corporation for October 19—4:

1. October 1: No journal entry is required. There is nothing to quantify, i.e., record in dollars.

2. Cash (in bank) (asset +)   200,000

        Common Shares (owners' equity +)   200,000

   (to record receipt of cash and issuance of shares)

3. No journal entry is required at this point because: (1) the manager has not yet completed his part of the contract (by doing the work of a manager), and (2) the $2,000 may only be an estimate, subject to change when the work is actually performed. Accountants record only when they have somewhat reliable numbers, and the work has been performed.

4. No journal entry; same reasoning as for October 4, that is, the goods have not been delivered, and the price may change. Accountants tend to record when the amounts are capable of being estimated within reasonable limits, and the

contract is being or has been performed. (There are exceptions, which are explained later.)

5. Rent expense (expense +)	600	
Cash (asset −)		600

(to record payment for October's rent on the store)

6. Rent expense (expense +)	590	
Cash (asset −)		590

(to record rental on equipment and shelving)

7. Inventory (asset +)	57,800	
Cash (asset −)		20,000
Accounts payable (liability +)		37,800

(to record purchase of inventory and partial payment)

8A. Cash (asset +)	10,000	
Accounts receivable (asset +)	40,000	
Revenue (revenue +)		50,000

(to record revenue, cash receipt and receivable)

8B. Cost of goods sold (expense +)	39,500	
Inventory (asset −)		39,500

(to record as an expense the cost of the inventory that was sold today)

9. Telephone expense (expense +)	20	
Cash (asset −)		20

(to record payment of telephone bill— invoice)

10. Accounts payable (liability −)	37,800	
Cash (asset −)		37,800

(to record cash payment)

11. Cash (asset +)	10,000	
Accounts receivable (asset −)		10,000

(to record collection of cash)

12. Wages expense (expense +)	2,000	
Cash (asset −)		2,000

(to record payment of wages to manager)

The next two steps are to post each debit and credit of each journal entry to the appropriate ledger account. (See Illustration 3-5.) Then we prepare a trial balance.

ILLUSTRATION 3-5

Ledger Accounts (actually T accounts):

	Cash		
October 2	200,000	October 7	600
October 17	10,000	October 9	590
October 28	10,000	October 11	20,000
		October 21	20
		October 25	37,800
		October 31	2,000
Net amount	158,990		

	Accounts Receivable		
October 17	40,000	October 28	10,000
	30,000		

	Inventory		
October 11	57,800	October 17	39,500
	18,300		

	Accounts Payable		
October 25	37,800	October 11	37,800
	0		

	Common Shares		
		October 2	200,000
			200,000

	Revenue		
		October 17	50,000
			50,000

	Cost of Goods Sold		
October 17	39,500		
	39,500		

	Wages Expense		
October 31	2,000		
	2,000		

	Telephone Expense		
October 21	20		
	20		

	Rent Expense		
October 7	600		
October 9	590		
	1,190		

The trial balance becomes the focal point of our attention when we wish to prepare financial statements. For instance, in preparing the income statement we look at the lines pertaining to the two "subdivisions" of owners' equity called revenue and expense. Note that these two "subdivisions" are listed toward the bottom of the trial balance. Note also that we clearly label the expense ledger accounts as *expense* and not merely call them "rent", for example. (Cost of goods sold is an exception, but it is the conventional title used by most accountants. We know that the ledger account *may* have been called "the cost of goods that were sold, expense" or "expensed goods

DONAMAR CORPORATION
Trial Balance
October 31, 19—4

Cash	158,990	
Accounts receivable	30,000	
Inventory	18,300	
Common shares		200,000
Revenue		50,000
Cost of goods sold	39,500	
Wages expense	2,000	
Telephone expense	20	
Rent expense	1,190	
	250,000	250,000

that have been sold".) Revenue is similarly labelled clearly. The word "sales" may be used in place of revenue. The point is that we want ledger account titles that distinguish between assets and expenses, and between liabilities and revenue. If we do not have explicit titles, it is difficult to use the trial balance to help us to prepare financial statements.

Finally, note that we have *not* listed "accounts payable" on the trial balance. The reason is that it had a zero balance at October 31, 19—4, the date of the trial balance. We want the trial balance to be a handy reference when we prepare financial statements, and not be cluttered with zero balance ledger accounts.

Normally, we commence financial-statement preparation with the income statement. It would appear as follows:

DONAMAR CORPORATION
Income Statement
Month Ended October 31, 19—4

Revenue		$50,000
Cost of goods sold		39,500
Gross profit		10,500
Expenses:		
Wages	$2,000	
Rent	1,190	
Telephone	20	3,210
Income*		$ 7,290

*In later chapters, this figure for corporations will be called "income before income taxes". We will ignore income-tax effects until later in the book.

Rather than repeat the word "expense", we have used a heading "expenses", and have indented all the ledger accounts under the heading. Also, we have employed a second column of figures to the left of the others. These two format modifications are merely a matter of style to permit easier reading of the financial statement. If we knew that it wasn't important to separate rent and telephone expenses, we could group these two ledger accounts. The income statement would then show "rent and telephone" as $1,210. Financial statement presentation requires judgment — and knowledge of preparer and user desires.

Because Donamar is a corporation, or limited company, it is necessary to prepare a "retained earnings" or "retained income" statement (rather than a statement of partners' capital).

DONAMAR CORPORATION
Retained Earnings Statement
Month Ended October 31, 19—4

Balance, October 1, 19—4	$ Nil
Income	7,290
Balance, October 31, 19—4	$7,290

The retained earnings statement shows the continuity in the retained-earnings figure. *If* any dividends, i.e., a form of withdrawal of the income, had been declared and paid to the owner, the journal entry would be:

Debit:	Retained earnings (owners' equity −)	xxx	
Credit:	Cash (asset −)		xxx
	(to record cash payment of portion		
	of October's income)		

The debit amount would then reduce the retained earnings. For example, *if* the dividend were $1,000 for Donamar, the retained earnings would be as follows:

Balance, October 1, 19—4	$ Nil
Income	7,290
	7,290
Dividend	1,000
Balance, October 31, 19—4	$6,290

As no dividend was, in fact, declared and paid, the retained earnings remains at $7,290 and, knowing this amount, we can proceed to prepare the balance sheet. The design of the balance sheet, like that for the other *general-purpose financial statements*, is a matter of:

1. Complying with any applicable laws governing corporations; plus
2. Considering the desires of the issuer company's owners and managers (preparer's viewpoint); plus
3. Deciding the extent to which the needs of the users/readers will be catered to.

Financial statement preparation and interpretation is not a simple task. Applicable laws, conventions or traditions, and accountants' "rules" will be discussed. Surprisingly, there are *relatively few* laws and rules; mainly, it is a matter of judgment. We have to understand how people behave. To be a competent interpreter of financial statements, we have to understand the thinking of the preparers. Although Donamar's balance sheet is easy to prepare, those of larger organizations can be quite complex and difficult to fully comprehend.

DONAMAR CORPORATION
Balance Sheet
October 31, 19—4

Assets		*Owners' Equity*	
Cash	$158,990	Common shares	$200,000
Accounts receivable	30,000	Retained earnings	7,290
Inventory	18,300		
	$207,290		$207,290

Statement Analysis

What do the financial statements of Donamar Corporation tell us? The balance sheet tells us that the assets are relatively *liquid*, meaning that they are cash or will be turned into cash shortly, i.e., the accounts receivable will be collected in cash in a few weeks. Also, some of the inventory will be sold for cash and the remainder for accounts receivable, which will eventually become cash. Note that the inventory is shown at its *cost* to Donamar, and when sold will likely generate more cash than $18,300. Assets that are likely to be turned into cash within the coming year (to October 31, 19—5) are called *current assets*. Thus, all Donamar's assets are current, as opposed to non-current ones such as buildings, trucks, machinery, and similar *long-lived* assets.

Liquidity and *profitability* are two characteristics of a company that we have to track closely. Liquidity information is available from the balance sheet. Profitability has to be assessed by looking at the income statement. (Other sources of liquidity and profitability data could be notes to financial statements and the Statement of Changes in Financial Position, both of which are described in more detail later, especially in chapters 5 and 16.)

Is Donamar profitable? The income for one month is $7,290. *If* the next eleven months generate a similar income per month, over $85,000 will have been earned by investing $200,000. The $85,000/$200,000 equals 42.5 percent. Is this good? We need some basis for comparison. A bank may pay 10 percent interest on the $200,000. Compared to what the bank pays, Donamar is very profitable. But, the investment in the bank is safer than is the investment in Donamar, which could be lost if sales drop off and expenses rise. The likelihood of losing one's investment (of $200,000) is called *risk*. In general, the riskier the investment, the higher the percent of "income divided by investment" ought to be. Much more will be said about profitability in this book. Overall, though, we cannot decide whether liquidity and profitability are good or bad unless we have a *basis for comparison*. The comparison may be made with alternate forms of investment, or with a prior period—how was November's income, compared with October's? To be useful, financial statements must try to help make the comparisons that the users require.

The Canadian economy needs huge *capital investments* to produce the goods and services that we require to maintain or improve our standard of living. People will not invest unless they receive adequate information. Financial statements are merely one source of information about a company's activities that investors would want to read.

CLOSING JOURNAL ENTRIES

Closing journal entries, for a corporation, are entries that close out *revenue* and *expenses* to retained earnings. A closing entry would also be made for dividends *if* they were entered in a separate ledger account. We noted earlier that, in preparing the retained-earnings statement for Donamar, the journal entry for a dividend could be:

| Debit: | Retained earnings (owners' equity −) | xxx | |
| Credit: | Cash (asset −) | | xxx |

An alternative entry would be:

| Debit: | Dividends (owners' equity −) | xxx | |
| Credit: | Cash (asset −) | | xxx |

The "dividends" ledger account (as explained in Chapter 2) is really just a *temporary* account, which is a subdivision of retained earnings. The balance sheet shows only the ending, or closing, retained earnings. To arrive at the closing balance we have to "close out" dividends, if any, to retained earnings, by the following journal entry:

| Debit: | Retained earnings (owners' equity −) | xxx | |
| Credit: | Dividends (owners' equity +) | | xxx |

The dividends account therefore has a closing balance of zero (debit xxx; credit xxx), *after* we make the closing entry.

We also noted that we set up "expense" and "revenue" accounts as subdivisions of retained earnings, to make preparation of the income statement easier. They also have to be closed out to prepare the balance sheet.

One important caution, mentioned in Chapter 2, should again be noted. In practice, Canadian companies close out their revenue, expense, and dividend accounts *once per year.* We will close them out monthly in some of our illustrations for practice.

The closing entry for Donamar's revenue and expense accounts is:

October 31:

Debit:	Revenue (revenue −)	50,000	
Credits:	Cost of goods sold (expense −)		39,500
	Wages expense (expense −)		2,000
	Rent expense (expense −)		1,190
	Telephone expense (expense −)		20
	Retained earnings (owners' equity +)		7,290

(to close revenue and expense accounts
to retained earnings)

Note that we have *debited* revenue to reduce the closing ledger balance to zero. Similarly, we have *credited* each expense account to reduce each expense ledger account to zero. The balancing debit or credit (in this case, a credit, or income, of $7,290) is recorded to retained earnings.

When we post the closing journal entry, the ledger accounts for revenue, expense, and retained earnings are per Illustration 3-6.

ILLUSTRATION 3-6

Retained Earnings				Revenue			
		October 31	7,290			October 17	50,000
						Subtotal	50,000
				October 31	50,000		
							0

Cost of Goods Sold				Wages Expense			
October 17	39,500			October 31	2,000		
Subtotal	39,500			Subtotal	2,000		
		October 31	39,500			October 31	2,000
	0				0		

Telephone Expense				Rent Expense			
October 21	20			October 7	600		
				October 9	590		
Subtotal	20			Subtotal	1,190		
		October 31	20			October 31	1,190
	0				0		

The revenue and expense ledger accounts, once closed to a zero balance, are then available for postings in the next month. For example, if revenue of $10,000 were earned on November 2, 19—4, the posted ledger account would appear as:

Revenue			
		October 17	50,000
		Subtotal	50,000
October 31	50,000		
		November 1	
		November 2	10,000

Thus, by looking at the ledger account, we would know that November's revenue total (if there were no other November credit) would be $10,000. We could then easily prepare November's income statement by referring to the $10,000. In real situations, however, where revenue and expense accounts are closed annually, we would arrive at November's revenue by subtracting the subtotal at the end of October from the amount at the end of November.

AFTER-CLOSING TRIAL BALANCE

The asset, liability, and owners' equity accounts are permanent accounts and are not closed out. The reason is that the balance sheet at any point in time shows the *net* cumulative effect since the business was commenced. Each balance sheet account's net balance can be the result of many debits and credits over many months.

The after-closing trial balance at October 31, 19—4 shows the same asset, liability, and owners' equity ledger account balances as the balance sheet at October 31, 19—4.

DONAMAR CORPORATION
After-Closing Trial Balance
October 31, 19—4

Cash	158,990	
Accounts receivable	30,000	
Inventory	18,300	
Common shares		200,000
Retained earnings		7,290
	207,290	207,290

PARTNERSHIPS AND PROPRIETORSHIPS

The closing process for partnerships and proprietorships is similar to that of corporations. Instead of using the retained earnings account to close out revenue and expense ledger accounts, the closing would be to the partners' accounts. To illustrate:

Debit:	Revenue (revenue −)	100	
Credits:	Expense (expense −)		80
	Partner A, capital (owners' equity +)		10
	Partner B, capital (owners' equity +)		10

An alternative method, using an intermediate step, would be to first close to a ledger account called "income summary" (or something similar), and then to the partners' capital accounts:

Debit:	Revenue (revenue −)	100	
Credits:	Expense (expense −)		80
	Income summary (owners' equity +)		20
Debit:	Income summary (owners' equity −)	20	
Credits:	Partner A, capital (owners' equity +)		10
	Partner B, capital (owners' equity +)		10

(The two-step "income summary" approach could also be used for corporations.)

Summary

Much of the chapter explained the bookkeeping cycle (except for adjusting journal entries) and the terminology associated with *general-purpose* financial statements. The end product of an accountant's efforts is generally a set of financial statements. The bookkeeping cycle helps in preparing the end product. Notes to accompany the financial statements also have to be assembled, and are outside of the bookkeeping cycle. Precisely what an accountant discloses in financial statements is a result of his considering the requirements of laws, what preparers desire, what users require, and similar considerations.

Although it is difficult to comprehend fully the bookkeeping cycle, it is important to remember that there is much more to accounting than just the cycle. Communicating effectively with readers of financial statements is a challenge. Interpreting financial statements is a greater challenge.

We need to bear in mind that some accountants prepare financial statements so that they disclose only the bare minimum required by law and by accepted practice: Much more will be said about this. The amount of disclosure and type of measurement has a direct effect on the usefulness of the financial statements. Thus, we must be sure that we are interpreting the financial statements in concert with the preparer's aims. That many alternative methods of accounting exist will become apparent as we study the following chapters.

The next chapter explains adjusting journal entries. It is vital that the differences between original transaction journal entries and closing journal entries be fully understood before proceeding to Chapter 4. After Chapter 4, we spend most of our time studying the subject of accounting data from both an accountant's viewpoint and the position of the user.

Specialized Journals

Saving time is the principal thought underlying specialized journals — in posting, and in searching the accounting records at a later date. Many transactions occur day after day, such as:

Sales: debit cash, or accounts receivable,
          credit sales revenue

Payments of accounts payable: debit accounts payable
                          credit cash

Collections of accounts receivable: debit cash
                              credit accounts receivable

Specialized journals collect these repeating transactions in separate columns (or computer coding categories). For example, a sales journal may look like this:

Sales Journal

Date	*(Any reference details)*	Accounts receivable Customer Name or Number	Debit Amount	Cash *(Debit)*	Sales *(Credit +)*
October 3	Invoice 12302	J. Smith	120.00		120.00
7	Invoice 12303	S. Jones	199.95		199.95
14	Cash Sale			190.00	190.00
27	Invoice 12304	T. Colavecchia	300.00		300.00
Totals			619.95	190.00	809.95

A bookkeeper merely has to make one posting to the general ledger for each of the column totals:

$619.95 to accounts receivable, as a debit,
$190.00 to cash, as a debit, and
$809.95 to sales, as a credit.

The individual details of who owes the money (J. Smith, etc.) are posted to separate *subsidiary ledger* accounts for each customer. (Subsidiary ledgers are discussed in chapters 9, 10, and 11.)

Specialized journals could also exist for:

Purchases,
Cash receipts,
Cash disbursements,
Payroll, and

for any other frequent transactions.

Purchases Journal

Date	Reference	Inventory (debit)		Accounts Payable (credit)	
		Inventory Code No.	Amount	Customer Name or Number	Amount Credited

Cash Receipts Journal

Date	Reference	Cash (debit)	Other Accounts (credit)			Accounts Receivable (credit)		
			Account Title	Ledger No.	Amount	Customer	Ledger No.	Amount

Cash Disbursements Journal

Date	Reference	Cash (credit)	Office Expense (debit)	Other Accounts (debit)★		
				Name or Reference	Ledger No.	Amount

★If many accounts payable exist, a separate column would be set aside for them, much like the accounts-receivable columns in the cash-receipts journal.

QUESTIONS

3-1 Name and explain the several parts of the bookkeeping or accounting cycle.

3-2 A debit _____ (increases or decreases) an asset, and _____ a revenue and liability.

3-3 Why does your bank book show a *credit* when you deposit money in the bank?

3-4 What are the differences between journals and ledgers?

3-5 Describe the process that we ought to use to decide the number of ledger accounts to employ in a company.

3-6 What is the purpose of a trial balance?

3-7 What does the *gross profit* figure tell us?

3-8 What is the main purpose of closing journal entries?

3-9 Illustrate how the owners' equity section of a balance sheet differs among a proprietorship, a partnership, and a limited company.

3-10 What are the purposes of, or reasons for, specialized journals?

EXERCISES

E3-1 Provide journal entries for each of the undernoted activities and transactions of an ongoing company. If no journal entry is required, explain your reasoning:

October 1: Inventory costing $22,400 is sold on account for $39,800.

October 3: A customer pays us $12,990 for inventory that is to be delivered in November. The inventory cost us $5,900.

October 5: A new building is purchased for $875,000. Cash of $300,000 is paid, and a mortgage is signed by us for the balance of $575,000.

October 7: An order for $19,200 is received for inventory to be delivered on November 3. The inventory cost us $11,800.

October 9: Miscellaneous expenses of $1,230 are paid in cash.

October 11: Rent, heat and light are paid in cash for October and amount to $1,100, $92 and $65 respectively. (Heat and light are estimates made by the utility companies.)

October 13: Inventory costing $14,900 is sold on account for $21,850.

October 15: Additional inventory is purchased on account for $26,500.

October 17: Equipment is purchased on account for $220,000.

October 19: Cash is received for the inventory that was sold on account on October 1.

October 21: Wages of $6,200 are paid. (Assume that the $6,200 is paid in cash. Payroll accounting is described later, in Chapter 12.)

October 23: A bank loan of $20,000 is arranged, and the bank deposits the money in our account.

October 25: The inventory purchased on October 15 is paid for in cash.

October 27: A dividend of $1,500 is paid in cash.

October 29: Interest on the bank loan is paid in cash, $110.

October 31: An invoice for $300 is received in the mail for supplies to be delivered on November 1.

E3-2 The trial balance of Waterhouse Corporation at October 31, 19—8 shows:

	Debits	Credits
Cash	$ 5,200	$
Accounts receivable	46,700	
Inventory	89,740	
Short-term investment certificate	4,860	
Land	80,000	
Building	372,500	
Equipment	269,750	
Mortgage payable		173,200
Accounts payable		18,990
Bank loan payable		50,000
Common shares		400,000
Retained earnings		226,560
	$868,750	$868,750

During November 19—8, the following transactions and activities occurred:

November 1: Inventory costing $32,000 is sold on account for $51,900.

November 3: $12,850 of the accounts receivable are collected in cash.

November 5: Additional inventory is purchased on account for $21,700.

November 7: Accounts payable of $10,000 are paid in cash.

November 9: Inventory costing $20,000 is sold for $33,310 cash.

November 11: Wages of $2,350 for the first half of November are paid. (Assume that the $2,350 is paid in cash. Payroll accounting is described later, in Chapter 12.)

November 13: $14,000 of the bank loan is paid.

November 15: Additional equipment costing $19,900 is purchased on account.

November 17: The short term investment of $4,860 is exchanged for cash. Interest revenue of $140 is also received in cash.

November 19: Additional common shares of $100,000 are issued for cash.

November 21: November's telephone expense of $65 is paid in cash.

November 23: A one-year insurance policy commencing December 1, 19—8 is paid for in cash, $1,800.

November 25: Miscellaneous expenses of $1,265 are paid in cash.

November 27: An advertising invoice (bill) for $2,260 is received in the mail. The sum represents November advertising expense and is due for payment before December 15.

November 28: Heat and light invoices for November of $180 and $85 respectively are paid in cash.

November 29: Salary expense for the remainder of November is paid in cash, $2,690.

November 30: Interest expense of $105 is paid on November's bank loan.

November 30: A dividend of $1,000 is declared, and paid in cash.

Required:

A. Prepare journal entries to record each of November's transactions.

B. Post the journal entries in A to their respective ledger accounts. (T accounts, such as in Illustration 3-4, may be used.)

C. Prepare a trial balance as of November 30, 19—8.

D. On the basis of the trial balance in C, prepare a balance sheet at November 30, 19—8, and an income statement for November 19—8.

E. Prepare closing journal entries (i.e., one or more) as at November 30, 19—8.

F. Post the closing journal entries to their respective ledger accounts.

G. Prepare an after closing trial balance as at November 30, 19—8.

E3-3 Specialized journals. Refer to Appendix 3-A, and enter the following transactions that belong in a specialized *sales journal* for December 19—8:

December 1: Invoice C 1359 for a cash sale to R. Inkpen for $199.89.

December 3: Invoice A 76420 for a sale on account to A. McPhee of $485.50.

December 5: Collected $150.00 from a previous sale on account to J. Fleming.

December 7: Invoice A 76421 for a sale of $500.00 to E. Kagan. Cash of $100.00 was paid, and the balance is due on account.

December 9: Invoice C 1360 for a cash deposit of $1,000 on inventory that is to be delivered January 15, 19—9 to P. Aitch.

December 11: Invoice A 76422 for a sale on account of $149.99 to S. Rosart.

E3-4 The trial balance of Wayne Enterprises, a proprietorship, at September 30, 19—9 shows:

	Debits	*Credits*
Cash	$ 8,750	$
Accounts receivable	69,750	
Inventory	70,000	
Marketable security	10,000	
Rental deposit	5,000	
Land	18,500	
Accounts payable		21,550
Bank loan payable		50,000
P. Wayne, owner's capital		110,450
	$182,000	$182,000

During October 19—9, the following transactions and activities occurred:

October 1: Inventory costing $26,000 is sold on account for $42,770.

October 3: The owner withdraws $5,000 cash.

October 5: $35,000 cash is collected on account.

October 7: $14,200 of accounts payable are paid.

October 9: An invoice of $2,290 is received for October's advertising materials and radio commercials.

October 11: $1,400 is paid for October's rent.

October 13: Additional inventory costing $13,500 is purchased on account.

October 15: Inventory costing $15,000 is sold for $24,200 cash.

October 17: $20,000 is paid on the bank loan.

October 19: A delivery company's invoice for $255 is received for sales made on October 1 and 15. A cheque is issued.

October 21: Wages of $2,120 for the first half of October are paid. (Assume that the $2,120 is paid in cash. Payroll accounting is described later, in Chapter 12.)

October 23: The telephone company's invoice for charges for October arrives in the mail, and amounts to $75. The amount is due by November 10.

October 25: Accounts receivable of $32,000 are collected in cash.

October 27: $3,600 is paid for insurance for the one year period commencing November 1, 19—9.

October 29: Interest of $100 is received on the marketable security.

October 30: Equipment costing $20,000 is purchased by paying cash of $8,000 and undertaking to pay the balance by November 30, 19—9.

October 31: Interest of $330 is paid on the bank loan.

Required:

A. Prepare journal entries to record each of October's transactions.

B. Post the journal entries in A to their respective ledger accounts. (T accounts, such as in Illustration 3-4, may be used.)

C. Prepare a trial balance as of October 31, 19—9.

D. On the basis of the trial balance in C, prepare a balance sheet at October 31, 19—9 and an income statement for October 19—9.

E. Prepare closing journal entries (i.e., one or more) as at October 31, 19—9.

F. Post the closing journal entries to their respective ledger accounts.

G. Prepare an after closing trial balance as at October 31, 19—9.

E3-5 Indicate why each of the undernoted events should or should not be recorded as a transaction in January 19—9. Where applicable, provide the journal entry that would be made in January 19—9:

January 3: An order is received for $10,000, for inventory to be delivered by us on February 10, 19—9.

January 7: $20,000 is paid for equipment that will be delivered on February 10, 19—9.

January 11: $12,000 is paid for inventory that will be received in late February 19—9.

January 15: An order is placed over the telephone for inventory costing $8,500 that is to be delivered to us in mid February 19—9.

January 19: A pledge is signed to pay $10 per kilometre to a charity that is sponsoring a children's road race on January 25. The team of children that is being sponsored could run as much as 50 kilometres. The charity will inform us of their actual travel distance in late January.

January 25: A cheque is received for $7,500 for inventory that is to be delivered in February. The cost of the inventory to us is $4,890.

E3-6 Use the following schedule to indicate what has occurred in December for each of the undernoted transactions:

Date	No Income Statement Effect	Revenue		Expenses	
		Increased	Decreased	Increased	Decreased
December 1	X				

Transactions:

December 1: A truck is purchased for $40,000 cash.

December 3: An order is received for $14,000 of inventory that is to be delivered tomorrow. The cost of the inventory is $8,950.

December 5: A deposit of $9,000 is received for inventory that is to be delivered in January.

December 7: Wages of $3,120 are paid. (Assume that the $3,120 is paid in cash. Payroll accounting is described later, in Chapter 12.)

December 9: A bank loan of $20,000 is negotiated.

December 11: A cheque is issued for $3,000 to pay for advertising for December.

December 13: A cheque for $17,500 is issued for inventory that will be shipped to us in January.

December 15: Interest is paid on a bank loan that was arranged in November.

December 17: The proprietor withdraws $3,000.

December 19: The telephone company sends an invoice for $60 for December's telephone charge (which excludes long distance charges).

December 21: Miscellaneous expenses of $1,375 are paid in cash.

December 23: A regular customer telephones and asks about the possible purchase of inventory costing us $17,200, that usually sells for $29,900.

December 29: Interest of $310 is earned on an investment certificate purchased from a trust company on November 30.

December 31: Wages of $3,490 are paid.

PROBLEMS

P3-1 The income statement for Vincent Enterprises Limited (VEL) shows the following for the month of October 19—8:

Revenue		$148,600
Cost of goods sold		101,200
Gross profit		47,400
Expenses:		
Selling	$18,300	
Administrative	10,250	
Interest	125	28,675
Income before income tax		$ 18,725

On reviewing the income statement, the new president of VEL became upset with the figure of $18,725, and asked the company's accountant two questions: Is that all we earned in October? Where did you get these figures from? The two then entered into the following conversation:

President (P): I sold $50,000 myself. How could sales be only $148,600, which is $25,000 below September's sales revenue?

Accountant (A): But you sold that $50,000 of inventory on October 30. By the time the paperwork was done and the goods were shipped, it was November 1. We will show that sales revenue and cost of goods sold in November.

P: Why? The sales were in October. They agreed to buy the inventory in October...Also, I received a cheque for $22,700 from another customer. Are those sales included in October, or where are they?

A: The $22,700 is not a sale yet. You received a cheque, but the customer wants us to deliver the inventory at a later date, to be decided by him. We'll include the $22,700 in revenue whenever the inventory is shipped from our warehouse. We've always done it that way.

P: What did you do with the $17,100 of inventory that was returned by that company that is now bankrupt?

A: We received some inventory from them on October 10. But, the inventory was worth only $9,000. So, we reversed the sale (which had been made in September) in October, by debiting sales revenue and crediting cost of goods sold. The cost of goods sold figure for this sale had been $11,500 in September. Since the inventory that we recovered was worth only $9,000, we charged selling expense for the difference of $2,500 ($11,500 – $9,000).

Required:

Evaluate the accountant's responses to the president's questions. Explain in which respect you agree and disagree with the accountant.

P3-2 For each of situations A to D noted below, provide as much data as you are able to about the nature of the business, and industry, of the organization:

	A	B	C	D
Revenue – sales	$100,000			
– interest		$100,000		
– rentals			$100,000	
– donations				$100,000
Cost of goods sold	65,000			
Gross profit	35,000			
Expenses:				
Selling	8,500	1,000	30,000	—
Administration	2,200	20,000	3,000	18,000
Interest	300	15,000	5,000	—
Grants	—	—	—	70,000
Maintenance	—	—	15,000	—
Operating	—	45,000	22,000	—
	11,000	81,000	75,000	88,000
Net	24,000	19,000	25,000	12,000

P3-3 The trial balance of Jackson Corporation at October 31, 19—9 shows:

Cash	14,200
Accounts receivable	65,900
Inventory	88,600
Prepaid expense	3,200
Land	70,000
Accounts payable	57,250
Bank loan payable	35,000
Note payable on land	30,000
Common shares	100,000
Retained earnings	19,650

During November 19—9 the following transactions and activities occurred:

November 1: Accounts receivable of $36,000 are collected in cash.

November 3: A payment of $15,000 is made to reduce the bank loan.

November 5: Inventory costing $25,000 is sold on account for $42,700.

November 7: Rent for November is paid in cash, $1,600.

November 9: Miscellaneous expenses of $975 are paid in cash.

November 11: Additional inventory costing $18,500 is purchased on account.

November 13: Accounts payable of $30,000 are paid.

November 15: A cheque for $1,875 is issued to an insurance company. A sum of $75 is for November's insurance, and the balance of $1,800 applies to the period commencing December 1.

November 17: A cheque for $10,000 is received from a customer who wants inventory delivered in December.

November 19: A cheque for $8,000 is issued as a down payment on an automobile to be delivered in 10 days. The full cost of the automobile is $19,500.

November 21: Inventory costing $3,000, that was sold on November 5 on account for $4,600, is returned by the customer.

November 23: Wages of $6,950 are paid. (Assume that the $6,950 is paid in cash. Payroll accounting is described later, in Chapter 12.)

November 25: Accounts receivable of $13,500 is collected in cash.

November 27: The balance owing on the automobile is paid in cash.

November 28: The automobile is delivered.

November 29: Interest on the bank loan of $220 is paid in cash.

November 30: Heat, light and telephone invoices of $120, $85 and $70 respectively are paid in cash.

Required:

A. Prepare journal entries to record each of November's transactions.

B. Post the journal entries in A to their respective ledger accounts. (T accounts, such as in Illustration 3-4, may be used.)

C. Prepare a trial balance as of November 30.

D. On the basis of the trial balance in C, prepare a balance sheet at November 30, and an income statement for November.

E. Prepare closing journal entries (i.e., one or more) as at November 30.

F. Post the closing journal entries to their respective ledger accounts.

G. Prepare an after closing trial balance as at November 30.

H. Analyze the financial statements that you prepared in D. Do you believe that the income statement has been "comprehensively" prepared? What might be missing?

P3-4 Parkwood Limited (PL) operates a new automobile dealership, which sells new and used automobiles, leases new automobiles, and repairs mechanical and body parts of various automobiles. New automobiles are purchased from the manufacturer, and readied for sale to customers at the dealership's one location. The inventory of new automobiles is financed at current interest rates by the manufacturer. Most of the used automobiles are accepted as trade-ins when new automobiles are purchased. The used automobiles usually have to be repaired. Typically, a bank loan is used to finance the inventory of used automobiles and those that are leased.

The mechanical and body shops employ several repair persons. Customers are usually invoiced, and have to pay for their repairs, before they are given the keys to their automobile. Most invoices include charges for labor, parts, general overhead (i.e., other expenses incurred in operating the repair shops) and a profit element.

The leasing operation of PL usually leases the automobiles for two, three or four years at a monthly rate. At the end of the lease PL has to sell the automobile through its used automobile department, or by other means.

PL has a small office staff that handles advertising, purchasing, accounting, and general administration. The company is owned by the Parkwood family, but is managed by four experienced people who are in charge of each major department.

From the above description and your general knowledge of automobile dealerships, indicate for each of the undernoted activities (A to J):

1. Whether (a) an income, or (b) an expense or (c) both result *in the current month*, and

2. The *reasons* for your choice in 1.

Transactions or activities in the current month:

A. An automobile accepted as a trade-in is repaired at a cost of $490, in order to ready it for sale.

B. Interest of $6,200 is paid to a bank for financing needed on leased and used automobiles.

C. Wages of the office staff are paid.

D. A new automobile is sold for a 20 percent down payment, and a promise to pay the remainder over four years.

E. A customer has engine repairs on his automobile and is invoiced $395. Cost of the repairs (parts and labor and other items) is about $280.

F. Spare parts are purchased from the automobile manufacturer.

G. During the month, equipment, buildings and other assets are being used in the process of generating revenue from sales of new and used automobiles, from leasing, and from repairing automobiles.

H. Several customers are driving automobiles that have been leased from PL.

I. Insurance on the company's building, automobiles and other assets is paid.

J. Telephone, heat and light invoices are received on the last day of the month. They will be paid next month.

P3-5 A junior bookkeeper made several errors, which are noted below. For the period in which the errors were made (i.e., January), indicate whether they would cause a misstatement of:

1. the balance sheet only, or

2. the income statement only, or

3. both the balance sheet and the income statement. Explain your response.

Errors in January:

A. Recorded as a sale in January, inventory that will be delivered in February. The selling price is $11,500 and the cost is $7,850.

B. Recorded collection of an account receivable on February 1 even though the cheque was received in the mail on January 30.

C. Ignored the fact that a bank loan had been granted, and the funds were deposited in our account on January 29.

D. Ignored an invoice from the telephone company that was received on January 28 and listed January's expenses.

E. Recorded a cash disbursement as rent expense instead of repairs expense.

F. Failed to record the purchase of a new automobile on account.

G. Failed to record the sale of inventory that was shipped directly from the manufacturer's plant to the customer (instead of having it pass through our warehouse).

H. Recorded a payment on an insurance policy as insurance expense instead of prepaid insurance.

I. Did not record interest earned on the company's bank account in January.

J. Did not record a $10,000 deposit received from a customer who wants inventory delivered in February.

P3-6 How might the income statements of each of the following types of businesses differ from the other businesses that are mentioned below:

1. A real estate company that owns several large shopping centres and office buildings.
2. A construction company that builds shopping centres and office buildings over a two or three-year period.
3. A wheat farmer.
4. An oil and gas exploration company, which has producing wells.
5. A fish canning company.
6. A forest products company that owns timber, logging companies and lumber mills.
7. A bank.
8. A department store.

EXPLORATION MATERIALS AND CASES

MC3-1 Recently you have been approached by a man carrying a very large shoebox, who asked if you would straighten out his accounts. He explained to you that he incorporated a company, Imperial Soil Limited (ISL) one month ago and since that time he has been doing a booming business. Unfortunately, he has been so busy that he has neglected the accounting function of his business. Now, because of a mysterious shortage of cash, ISL must acquire outside financing in order to continue its day-to-day operations. Someone told him that accounting information would be useful in securing a loan. For this reason, he has asked you to prepare a set of financial statements for the one-month period during which his company has been in operation. You agreed to accept this engagement whereupon he turned over to you the large shoebox that contained his accounting records for the past month.

A review of the contents of the shoebox (cheques, invoices, scratch pieces of paper, etc.) indicated that the following transactions had taken place:

September 1: Peter Moss, the stranger with the shoebox, incorporated ISL to operate as an enriched soil supplier.

September 1: Moss contributed land originally costing $25,000 (current value $50,000), a tractor originally costing $10,000 (replacement cost $5,000) and $35,000 cash in exchange for 100,000 common shares in the company.

September 2: Paid $10,000 cash for a prefabricated building with an estimated life of 5 years.

September 3: Received a bill from a firm of lawyers in the amount of $5,000—$4,000 of which related to Moss's divorce and $1,000 to incorporating ISL.

September 4: Bought office equipment for $8,000 cash.

September 5: Purchased on account $10,000 worth of sales invoices specially printed with Imperial Soil Limited letterhead.

September 6: Received first shipment of enriched soil costing $15,000 of which $10,000 was paid immediately in cash to the farmer.

September 8: Paid $5,000 cash for supplies bought on credit.

September 10: Placed following ad in the *Toronto Sun:* "Enriched soil is good for plants and is cheap to use". This ad was syndicated across Canada and cost the company $1,500 on account.

September 13: Hired two employees at a rate of $10 each per day.

September 15: Paid lawyer's bill.

September 20: Received $5,000 cash on deposit from a customer for enriched soil to be delivered April 15th.

September 22: Paid $5,000 cash for invoices bought on account on Sept. 5.

September 25: Sold a batch of enriched soil for $6,000 of which $1,000 was received in cash.

September 27: Paid the two employees for the previous two weeks' work.

September 29: Sold one quarter of land for $30,000 on credit.

September 30: A piece of paper bearing the date September 30th had the following scratches:

Supplies inventory at month end	$ 9,900
Enriched soil inventory	$13,000

Required:

A. Assume the role of an accounting advisor:
   1. What are the needs of the users of ISL's financial statements?
   2. Which financial statements would you recommend be prepared for ISL? Explain your reasoning.
   3. Design a record keeping system for ISL. Explain your reasoning.

B. Assume the role of a bookkeeper:
   1. Prepare journal entries to record the transactions of the first month of operations. Indicate any assumptions you have made.
   2. Post the journal entries to T accounts.
   3. Prepare an income statement and balance sheet.

C. Assume the role of a business advisor:
   1. Explain to Mr. Moss why ISL is experiencing a shortage of cash despite profitable operations.
   2. What additional information would you supply, by way of a special report, to assist creditors in deciding whether to make a loan to ISL?
   3. What important operating decisions is Moss likely to make? Can accounting assist? How?

MC3-2 J. Benny had been actively employed as an appliance and furniture salesman for Interiors Limited. Unfortunately, Interiors Limited went into bankruptcy and J. Benny was forced to seek a livelihood elsewhere. He decided that his experience in the appliance business could be best put to use by creating his own company.

The following data relates to the company's first month of activity:

December 31, 19—3: J. Benny started, as a sole proprietorship, a retail appliance store called Bargain Benny's Basement and contributed $25,000 in cash as his initial investment.

December 31, 19—3: The company purchased a building that cost $15,000 and land that cost $10,000, paying $5,000 in cash and obtaining a $20,000 first mortgage at 12 percent interest per annum. Repayment of $1,000 principal and interest is due January 31, 19—4. The balance of principal is to be paid in equal instalments of $1,000 per year commencing January 31, 19—5.

January 4, 19—4: Purchased $5,000 of store equipment and $2,000 of office supplies on credit.

January 7, 19—4: Paid $10,000 in cash for appliances to stock the store.

January 15, 19—4: J. Benny purchased a boat for his own use for $5,000 cash.

January 15, 19—4: Sold $5,000 of appliances for $7,000 on credit.

January 21, 19—4: Customers paid $5,000 of amounts outstanding.
January 30, 19—4: J. Benny withdrew $500 from the company.
January 31, 19—4: Paid principal and interest on the mortgage.
January 31, 19—4: Paid the following bills pertaining to the month of January in cash:

Salaries	$2,500
Telephone	200
Heat	350
Water	50
Taxes	400
	$3,500

Required:

A. For what purposes will Benny require financial accounting?

B. What are some of the accounting problems facing Bargain Benny's Basement? How would you resolve them?

C. Prepare journal entries to record the transactions of the first month of operations. Indicate any assumptions that you have made.

D. Post the journal entries to T accounts.

E. Prepare an income statement and balance sheet.

F. Assume that J. Benny has approached you with the offer to become his partner. What factors would you consider? Specifically, how would you use the income statement and balance sheet? What additional information would you require?

MC3-3 Tywand Co. Ltd. (TCL) has just completed its first year of operation. It is a closely held company and the owners do not take an active part in the management of the company.

The company presently operates a gift shop. However, this is only the beginning of its planned activities. When it was created, the owners envisaged it becoming involved in the importing and manufacture of merchandise for sale in both their own and other gift shops.

All operating decisions were left up to Cathy Richardson, a seasoned merchandiser and buyer. Ms. Richardson had several years' experience with a large retailer, Conception Bay Co. Ltd., and had learned that the key to success is volume purchasing.

Ms. Richardson was intrigued by the glamor of buying merchandise and promoting the store. However, she was not fond of accounting. She had taken a few accounting courses in high school and university but found them dull and preoccupied with debits and credits.

For this reason, she has asked you to look after the accounting for TCL. Through a series of interviews you determine the company had the following major financial events in its first year of operations:

1. The owners purchased 1,000 common shares at a price of $100 per share.

2. The company leased a store in a major shopping centre. Monthly rent was $3,000. During the year, rent payments of $36,000 were made. The space being rented was twice as big as the company required at the time, because TCL was expected to grow quickly.

3. The company purchased furniture and fixtures for the store at a cost of $60,000. The company paid $40,000 and gave a one-year note on the balance. The estimated useful life of the furniture and fixtures was 15 years.

4. In the course of the year, the company purchased merchandise at a cost of $340,000, which it intended to resell. Ms. Richardson's main method of purchasing was to order large quantities from suppliers in order to obtain volume discounts. The company paid $210,000 cash for the merchandise; as of year end the balance was owed.

5. The company had sales of $300,000. Sales were made for both cash and credit. As of the year end, the company had outstanding receivables from customers of $100,000.

6. The company paid salaries of $40,000.

7. The company had incurred and paid other operating costs of $15,000.

8. As of the year end, the company had $170,000 of merchandise still on hand.

Before you have had an opportunity to prepare TCL's financial statements, you receive a telephone call from the company's bank manager requesting a meeting with you and Ms. Richardson in two days. You inform Ms. Richardson of this meeting and she replies: Oh good, the bank probably wants to give us some more money because of our excellent performance in the first year of operation.

Ms. Richardson then instructs you to prepare an income statement as soon as possible. She wants to send it to the owners of the company to assure them that the company is performing well. In addition, she is eager to receive her bonus, which is based on income.

Required:

A. Prepare journal entries to reflect the financial events of the company's first year of operations.

B. Prepare an income statement.

C. What other information do you feel the owners require to assess the performance of the company?

D. Why do you think the bank manager requested the meeting? What information would you present to the bank manager during your meeting?

E. Prepare a balance sheet and an analysis of the cash account. Indicate the sources of cash and how it was used.

F. What would you recommend that the company do?

6. Cash Flow Analysis

CHAPTER 4

Accrual Accounting
and Adjusting Entries

Chapter Themes

1. The illustrations in the first three chapters were somewhat simplified, or artificial. For example, it was assumed (except for inventory) that cash payments for expenses would be made every month, and that there was no overlap from one month to the next. This chapter focusses on the normal situation where cash receipts and cash disbursements precede or follow the earning of revenues and incurring of expenses. Under such circumstances, bookkeepers have to make adjusting entries and tend to use *accrual accounting*.

2. We must not assume, however, that accrual accounting is the "true way" of accounting under all circumstances. (A major theme of this book is the downplaying of a search for the "true way", and the emphasizing of the need to tailor accounting to fit the current situation.) Accrual accounting definitely has sensible applications. But, there are times when cash-basis reports can prove far more helpful to particular users. Various non-accrual accounting reports will be illustrated.

3. We must avoid simply memorizing the different types of adjusting journal entries, and try to understand why each type has to be made. Merely memorizing adjusting entries can be misleading.

4. Statement interpretation is important. What do accrual-based statements tell us that cash-basis ones do not? Keep this in mind as you read the chapter.

ARTIFICIAL ILLUSTRATIONS

A cash-basis approach to accounting consists of tracking receipts and disbursements of cash, instead of comparing revenues with expenses. The first three chapters provided illustrations of how the changes in cash also tend to reflect income (revenue less expenses). Such illustrations are artificial because cash tends to be in advance of, or follow, the financial period in which revenue is earned and expenses are incurred. Succeeding chapters address the topics of earning revenue and incurring expenses. This chapter is primarily concerned with explaining how adjusting journal entries should be made. But, special attention has to be given to ensure that *undue* respect for accrual accounting is avoided. Accrual accounting has its place of importance. However, it also has some severe limitations for judgments that must be made in some situations.

Suppose that we have been asked to recommend whether our employer (say, a bank) should loan money to Waterhouse Enterprises Limited (WEL). WEL commenced business a few weeks ago and engaged in the following transactions in 19—8:

October 1: The company was incorporated.

October 2: The owners invested $200,000 in exchange for common shares.

October 4: A building was acquired for $220,000 by paying $80,000 and assuming a mortgage of $140,000. Furniture and equipment were bought for $25,000 cash.

October 7: Inventory costing $65,000 was acquired by paying cash.

October 12: An insurance policy for one year to September 30, 19—9 was paid in cash ($12,000).

October 17: The lawyer who incorporated the company was paid $2,000 cash.

October 20: Stationery and various office supplies were bought for $2,100 cash.

October 22: Employees were paid $6,000 for the period to October 20.

October 25: Various licences and incidentals costing $3,000 were paid in cash.

October 31: During October, inventory costing $30,000 was sold for $21,000 cash plus accounts receivable of $25,000.

If we try to judge the "success" of WEL by looking at the cash transactions during October, we would not find it very useful. A cash-basis report would show the following:

	Cash Receipts	Cash Disbursements
Common shares	$200,000	
Building		$ 80,000
Furniture and equipment		25,000
Inventory		65,000
Insurance policy		12,000
Lawyer, for incorporation		2,000
Stationery and similar		2,100
Employees' wages		6,000
Licences		3,000
Sales of inventory	21,000	
	221,000	$195,100
	195,100	
Net increase in cash	$ 25,900	

If we look at the "net increase in cash" sum of $25,900, we might think that, because the receipts are more than the disbursements, WEL has been successful. This conclusion *could* be completely unwarranted for several reasons:

1. The $200,000 was placed in the company to get it started, and has little to do with "success in October". Presumably the $200,000 will benefit many future months.

2. Although sales were $46,000 ($21,000 plus $25,000) in October, only $21,000 was collected in cash. If the $25,000 is likely to be received in November, why is it not included as part of October's success?

3. The cash expenditures on building, furniture and equipment, inventory, stationery, licences, and the insurance policy are assets that have a life well beyond October 31.

4. The cost of incorporation presumably is of use to the company over its entire life.

5. Several expenses that were probably incurred in October were not paid in cash that month. Some likely October expenses are: employees' wages for October 21 to 31, telephone, lights, heat, advertising, income taxes deducted from employees' wages, and similar.

What may be more useful than the cash-basis report could be the *accrual*-basis report, which ignores cash flows (receipts less disbursements) and concentrates on:

1. When the service was provided, or when the product was sold to the customer, and

2. When the expense was incurred in the process of earning the revenue.

That is, an attempt is made under accrual accounting to *match* revenue and expenses (*not* match cash receipts to disbursements) in each financial period.

ACCRUAL ACCOUNTING

In accounting, there are four types of accrual adjusting entry situations that are frequently seen, and a few others that are less common. The four are:

1. Cash disbursements come *before* the expenses are incurred.

2. Cash disbursements come *after* the expenses have been incurred.

3. Cash receipts come *before* the revenue is considered to be earned.

4. Cash receipts come *after* the revenue has been earned.

These four can also be viewed another way:

1. Cash disbursements before   =   Expense/asset
                                                 (or asset becomes an expense)

2. Cash disbursements after   =   Expense/liability situation
                                                 (or debit expense, credit liability)

3. Cash receipts before   =   Liability/revenue situation
                                                 (or liability becomes revenue)

4. Cash receipts after   =   Asset/revenue situation
                                                 (or debit asset, credit revenue)

Type 1:   *Expense/Asset* (or asset becomes an expense) This type of situation is common because cash disbursements are made to acquire buildings, inventory, insurance policies, licences and similar assets that have a life of more than one financial period. Accountants attempt to measure income *by matching up revenues earned with the expenses that were incurred to earn that revenue.* At the date of acquisition, the building or inventory is an asset. But, as the building is used, or the inventory is sold, the asset becomes an expense.

For example, suppose that $12,000 is paid on January 1, 19—7 for an insurance policy that provides coverage for three years to December 31, 19—9. The *original* transaction journal entry would be:

January 1, 19—7:   Prepaid insurance (asset +)   12,000
                      Cash (asset −)   12,000

That is, the asset "prepaid insurance" is debited, and the asset "cash" is credited. For extra emphasis the terms "asset +" and "asset −" have been added to signify increases and decreases. Observe that the term "prepaid" is used to designate the existence of an asset, i.e., prepaid, or paid in advance. As time passes, the asset becomes an expense. At December 31, 19—7, for instance, one third of the $12,000 has become an expense and two thirds (for 19—8 and 19—9) is still an asset.

The accountant or bookkeeper would recognize the decrease in the asset as of December 31, 19—7 by making the following *adjusting* journal entry:

December 31, 19—7: Insurance expense (expense +)   4,000
                      Prepaid insurance (asset −)   4,000

When are *adjusting* entries made? They are made *whenever it is necessary to prepare financial statements*. That is, income cannot be measured unless the cash-basis figures are converted to a complete accrual basis by making adjusting journal entries. In this illustration, we have assumed that financial statements will be prepared once per year, as of December 31.

The process of moving from an asset to an expense over time can be also illustrated by ledger accounts:

At January 1, 19—7:

(For simplicity 1-1-—7 means month-day-year.)

Prepaid Insurance	
1-1-—7 12,000	

At December 31, 19—7, *after* the adjusting and closing entries have been posted:

Prepaid Insurance		Insurance Expense	
1-1-—7 12,000		1-1-—7 0	
	12-31-—7 4,000	12-31-—7 4,000	
			Closing
1-1-—8			entry 4,000
Subtotal 8,000			
		1-1-—8 0	

At December 31, 19—8, *after* the following adjusting entry for 19—8 has been posted:

December 31, 19—8: Insurance expense (expense +)   4,000
                        Prepaid insurance (asset −)   4,000

Prepaid Insurance		Insurance Expense	
1-1-—7 12,000		1-1-—7 0	
	12-31-—7 4,000	12-31-—7 4,000	
	12-31-—8 4,000		Closing
			entry 4,000
1-1-—9			
Subtotal 4,000		1-1-—8 0	
		12-31-—8 4,000	
			Closing
			entry 4,000
		1-1-—9 0	

At December 31, 19—9, after the following adjusting entry for 19—9 has been posted:

December 31, 19—9: Insurance expense (expense +)   4,000
                        Prepaid insurance (asset −)   4,000

Prepaid Insurance				Insurance Expense			
1-1-—17	12,000			1-1-—7	0		
				12-31-—7	4,000		
		12-31-—7	4,000			Closing	
		12-31-—8	4,000			entry	4,000
				1-1-—8	0		
		12-31-—9	4,000	12-31-—8	4,000		
						Closing	
12-31-—9						entry	4,000
Subtotal	0			1-1-—9	0		
				12-31-—9	4,000		
						Closing	
						entry	4,000
				12-31-—9			
				After			
				Closing	0		

99 Accrual Accounting and Adjusting Entries

In summary, the asset "prepaid insurance" (sometimes called "unexpired insurance") turns into an expense as time passes. Each year, the expense account is closed to retained earnings (assuming that we are dealing with a limited company) so that the next year starts fresh. Overall, each year of 19—7 to 19—9 inclusive has been debited, or *charged*, which is an alternative name for debited, with $4,000 of expense. Insurance expense is thereby matched with the revenue that is generated each year.

Type 2 *Expense/Liability* (or debit an expense, credit a liability, which will be paid in the next financial period) This situation is also quite common because few people pay cash on the spot for purchases and services rendered. Some examples of expenses that sometimes are paid after the service or product has been rendered are: employees' wages and fringe benefits (such as pensions and medical coverage), heat and light, perhaps property taxes, and bank service charges.

It is very important to distinguish these Type 2 *accruals* (accountants do *not* call them Type 2) from original transaction entries. For instance, if an invoice, or "bill", is submitted before the end of a year, the following *original transaction* entry may be made:

Debit:	Heat and light expense (expense +)	1,250	
Credit:	Accounts payable (liability +)		1,250

But, when the invoice is not submitted until, say, February 19—7, but pertains to December 19—6, an *adjusting* journal entry is needed as of December 31, 19—6 to record *your best estimate* of the expense in 19—6:

Debit:	Heat and light expense (expense +)	1,200	
Credit:	Accrued liability (liability +)		1,200
	(or the credit might also be directly to accounts payable)		

In essence, the distinction between an original transaction entry and an adjusting entry situation for these expense/liability transactions is one of "as of what date the entry is made". When the person rendering the service or supplying the product has not yet sent an invoice, and the accountant has to estimate the expense, an adjusting journal entry would be made at the last moment—such as of December 31, 19—6. (Note that it may be January 24, 19—7, or later, when the accountant makes the adjusting journal entry *as of* December 31, 19—6. That is, some hindsight would be available because the accounting journals and revenue/expense accounts have not been closed out for the year.)

In the *next* financial period, the liability would have to be paid, which requires an original transaction journal entry. Suppose that we credited the accrued liability for $1,200, but when the utility company's invoice arrived, it was for $1,250. When we pay the invoice the original transaction journal entry would be:

February 19—7:	Accounts payable (liability −)	1,200	
	Heat and light expense (expense +)	50	
	Cash (asset −)		1,250

Note that the $50 difference between actual ($1,250) and estimated ($1,200) becomes an expense for 19—7, and not for 19—6. This is simply the result of the estimation process needed at December 31, 19—6. Also, this difference is just another example of why accounting figures should not be viewed as being "the truth" or 100 percent "accurate".

Type 3 *Liability/Revenue* (or liability becomes revenue) This type of transaction is less common than the previous two. In a sense, it is the opposite of the expense/asset (Type 1) situation. This liability/revenue transaction tends to occur when a customer pays in advance, usually because the supplier demands payment in advance before providing the service. Other examples would be when we pay rent or a newspaper/magazine subscription in advance. The receiver of the money has to record the *original* transaction as follows:

March 1, 19—8:	Cash (asset +)	1,600	
	Unearned rent (liability +)		1,600
	To record receipt of rent for March and April 19—8		

An alternative ledger title for the credit may be "rent received in advance".

If we require an income statement for March 19—8, the *adjusting* entry at March 31, 19—8 would be:

March 31, 19—8:	Unearned rent (liability −)	800	
	Rent revenue (revenue +)		800

The same adjusting entry would be made at April 30, 19—8 to recognize that the entire $1,600 has now been earned.

The ledger accounts would look as follows, *assuming* that the revenue and expense ledger accounts are closed at the end of each *month*, which is not usual practice.

Unearned Rent				Rent Revenue		
		3-1-—8	1,600		3-1—8	0
3-31-—8	800				3-31—8	800
				Closing entry 3-31-—8	800	
		4-1-—8	800		4-1—8	0
4-30—8	800				4-30—8	800
				Closing entry 4-30—8	800	
		5-1-—8	0		5-1—8	0

In summary, the $1,600 liability to provide rental accommodation for March and April diminished day-by-day throughout March and April. Technically, we could have recorded an adjusting journal entry at the end of each day, i.e., debit unearned rent and credit rent revenue. But, we did not because we did not need financial statements at the end of each day. When we want an income statement for each month, however, the adjusting journal entry would be made at the end of each month. Adjusting journal entries correct what is in the ledger account in order to permit the measurement of income for a financial period.

Type 4 *Asset/Revenue* (or debit asset, credit revenue) In a sense, this type of transaction is the opposite of Type 2 (expense/liability). That is, at the end of a financial period, we have to recognize that a service or product has been provided. An asset and revenue therefore ought to be recorded in order to allow us to compute income by matching revenue and expense.

As in Type 2, it is necessary to distinguish adjusting entries from original transaction entries. To illustrate, suppose that we have a bank account and that the bank records interest on our balance in the account every October 31 and April 30. Suppose also that our financial year end is December 31, 19—8. As of December 31, we would have earned interest on our account balance during November and December 19—8 of, say, $50. But this interest would not be recorded in our bank passbook until the following April 30 (19—9), when it would be included as part of, say, $300.

The *adjusting* entry that you would record on December 31, 19—8 would be:

Debit: Accounts receivable (or accrued   50
         interest receivable) (asset +)
Credit: Interest revenue (revenue +)   50

On April 30, 19—9 when the bank "credited" (from its point of view) the interest for the period October 31, 19—8 to April 30, 19—9 *our original* transaction entry would be:

April 30, 19—9:   Cash (asset +)   300
        Accounts receivable (or accrued
        interest receivable) (asset −)   50
        Interest revenue (revenue +)   250

This journal entry has the effect of cancelling the $50 receivable set up in 19—8 and recording 19—9 revenue of $250. The $300 has been placed in the years to which it belongs: $50 in 19—8 and $250 in 19—9.

In contrast, what would happen if our financial year ended on October 31, 19—8 instead of on December 31, 19—8? On October 31, 19—8, we would make the following *original transaction* journal entry:

Debit: Cash (asset +)   xx
Credit: Interest revenue (revenue +)   xx

It is worthwhile to note that bookkeepers must use some hindsight when making adjusting journal entries and in preparing financial statements. A company with an October 31, 19—8 year-end may not complete the financial statements for October 31, 19—8 until December 15, or later. This hindsight helps to reduce the amount of estimating that is necessary in measuring income. It may, however, do little to cut down on the number of adjusting entries that are needed.

SOME COMPLICATIONS — COMPUTERS

In addition to making accruals for interest and similar incidental revenue, bookkeepers usually have to watch for delayed invoicing of accounts receivable. Computer systems may prepare invoices (bills) for customers on a routine or automatic basis, and thus may not be set up for "rush" orders, where the customer needs immediate shipment. If our financial year ends on October 31, 19—8, and the inventory is shipped in a rush on October 31, the revenue, and income effect, should be recorded as of October 31, 19—8. Yet, the computerized invoices may be dated November 1 or 2, which would be in the next financial year, ended October 31, 19—9. If so, the bookkeeper would have to make the following *adjusting* journal entry on October 31, 19—8:

Debit: Accounts receivable (asset +)   10,000
Credit: Revenue (revenue +)   10,000

Then, when the computer *automatically* makes the *same* entry on November 1 or 2, 19—8 (that is, records it a *second* time, but as an *original* transaction entry), a correction would be needed. The "correcting" entry (called a "reversing" entry by some) would cancel the original transaction entry of November 1 or 2.

For example, on November 1 or 2 the computer automatically would make this entry:

Debit: Accounts receivable (asset +)   10,000
Credit: Revenue (revenue +)   10,000

Because this records the $10,000 a second time, the bookkeeper would have to cancel the second entry by the following entry:

Debit: Revenue (revenue −)   10,000
Credit: Accounts receivable (asset −)   10,000

Both entries in November can be considered to be original transaction entries. They cancel each other.

A PRACTICE PROBLEM — JOURNAL ENTRIES

The point of this problem is to provide practice in making adjusting journal entries. A series of *unrelated* situations are provided. For *each* situation, you are required to give the journal entry at December 31, 19—7, which is the *year* end of each of the companies.

1. On September 1, 19—7, the company bought a one-year insurance policy and paid $2,400.

2. Wages earned by employees totalled $65,900 for the last 10 days of 19—7. This sum was paid in January 19—8.

3. Customers paid $12,000 on November 1, 19—7 for a service contract, e.g., maintenance, that extends from November 1, 19—7 to October 31, 19—8.

4. The company received $20,000 in cash on December 10, 19—7 for goods to be delivered in January 19—8.

5. At December 31, 19—7, interest of $925 had "accrued" (i.e., was owing but would not be paid until later) on the company's interest-bearing bank account balance for November and December.

To gain maximum benefit, try to make the journal entries before reading beyond this paragraph. To ensure that you pause, we will refer to the origin of the phrase "debits go on the side nearest the window". In the May 1981 issue of *Accountancy* (page 39), M.G. Bacchus writes: "In the days before electric light, articled clerks arranged their desks to maximize the natural light. As most clerks were right handed, the shadows cast by their hands on the ledgers were less if the windows were on the left. Debits also go on the left: and so the phrase was born."

Response to #1: The typical style to use in doing adjusting journal entries is to ask yourself three questions:

1. What *is* now in the ledger accounts?

2. What *should be* in the ledger accounts?

3. What is needed to go from "is" to "should be"?

On September 1, 19—7, the following original transaction journal entry probably was made: (It is not the only possibility: See Appendix 4-A.)

Debit:	Prepaid insurance (asset +)	2,400	
Credit:	Cash (asset −)		2,400

At December 31, 19—7, *before* any adjusting journal entries are made, the ledger accounts would show:

Prepaid Insurance		Insurance Expense	
9-1--7　2,400		0	

By December 31, 19—7 (simply through the passage of time), one third (4/12) of the prepaid insurance asset has become an expense. Therefore, we have to lower the debit balance from $2,400 to $1,600, and this is done by *crediting* prepaid insurance for $800. What is debited? We now have an insurance expense of $800; thus, we must show this in the expense ledger account. Our *adjusting* journal entry therefore is:

Debit:	Insurance expense (expense +)	800	
Credit:	Prepaid insurance (asset −)		800

After posting the *adjusting* entry, the ledger accounts would show:

Prepaid Insurance			Insurance Expense		
9-1--7	2,400				
		12-31--7　800	12-31--7	800	
Subtotal	1,600		Subtotal	800	

The effect of the adjusting journal entry is to help us match revenue earned in 19—7 with expenses incurred in earning this revenue. One such expense is insurance of $800. The remaining $1,600 becomes an expense in 19—8.

Response to #2:　When we ask ourselves the three questions noted in #1, it is clear that the expense account would show zero, and not the needed $65,900. Also, the liability ledger account re employees would show zero. We, therefore, have to increase from zero to $65,900 by this *adjusting* journal entry at December 31, 19—7:

Debit:	Wages expense (expense +)	65,900	
Credit:	Wages payable (liability +)		65,900

Response to #3:　We must always be careful to distinguish situations in which we *pay* money from those in which we *receive* money. Note that the question says "customers paid us", which means that we received the $12,000. "Possibly" we made the following *original* transaction journal entry on November 1, 19—7:

Debit:	Cash (asset +)	12,000	
Credit:	Unearned revenue (liability +)		12,000

By December 31, 19—7, the company's liability ought to have dropped to $10,000 (for services to be performed in the first 10 months of 19—8). We decrease a liability by debiting it. What is to be credited? The $2,000 is earned in 19—7 and therefore becomes revenue. The *adjusting* entry at December 31 is:

Debit:	Unearned revenue (liability −)	2,000
Credit:	Revenue (revenue +)	2,000

The ledger account would show:

Unearned Revenue			Revenue	
	11-1-—7 12,000			12-31-—7 2,000
12-31-—7 2,000				
	Subtotal 10,000			Subtotal 2,000

Note that the $12,000 has split into revenue of $2,000 and a liability of $10,000 as of December 31, 19—7, *before* we close the revenue account.

Response to #4: On December 10, 19—7, the following *original* transaction journal entry would have been made:

Debit:	Cash (asset +)	20,000
Credit:	Unearned revenue (liability +)	20,000

What has changed as of December 31, 19—7? Nothing has. The company still has an obligation to deliver the goods in January. Thus, *no* adjusting entry is needed at December 31, 19—7. The ledger account "unearned revenue" is correct as it stands.

Response to #5: As of December 31, 19—7, the interest revenue account would *not* show the $925 as having been earned. Therefore, the revenue would have to be accrued by way of an adjusting journal entry:

Debit:	Accounts receivable (or interest receivable) (asset +)	925
Credit:	Revenue (revenue +)	925

OTHER ASSET/EXPENSE ADJUSTMENTS

The typical business encounters several variations of the asset/expense adjusting journal entry. Two common ones are:

1. Depreciation expense, and

2. Bad-debt expense.

Usually, each of these two has the complication of another ledger account called a *contra*, or *contra asset*, account.

Suppose that we buy a machine that will last for three years and will then have to be scrapped for zero cash. Over the three years, the asset becomes an expense. From what has been stated to this point in the book, we would expect the adjusting journal entry to be:

Debit:	Expense (expense +)	xx	
Credit:	Asset (asset −)		xx

Instead, most companies choose to use a third ledger account, so as to *separate* the original cost of the asset from what is called the arbitrary *allocation* of the cost over its useful life. There are several reasons for the separation. Two are:

1. Income tax. (This will be explained in a later chapter. Broadly speaking, the separation is helpful to the company in complying with tax regulations.)

2. Information benefits. The separation of the original cost from the amount that has been depreciated is useful to some people who believe that the expensed portion is a "rough guess". Thus, these people want two accounts—one for the cost, and one for the so-called "rough guesses". If the two were merged into one account, the net figure would not be helpful to these people.

Instead of the "debit expense, credit asset" entry, the following *adjusting* journal entry would be made:

Debit:	Depreciation expense (expense +)	xx	
Credit:	Accumulated depreciation		
	—machine (asset −)		xx

Thus, if the machine cost $15,000 on January 1, 19—1 and had a life of three years, with no scrap value, the adjusting journal entry at the end of *each* of the three years would be:

Debit:	Depreciation expense (expense +)	5,000	
Credit:	Accumulated depreciation		
	—machine (asset −)		5,000

The ledger accounts and the balance sheet position at the end of *each* year would be:

End of first year:

Depreciation Expense		Accumulated Depreciation—machine	
12-31-—1 5,000	Close to retained earnings 5,000		12-31-—1 5,000
0			

Balance sheet:

	Assets		
Machine		$15,000	
	Accumulated depreciation	5,000	$10,000

Note that the contra asset, i.e., accumulated depreciation, is shown on the asset side, and is deducted in a separate column, with the net of $10,000 shown separately.

End of second year:

Depreciation Expense		Accumulated Depreciation—machine	
0		12-31--1	5,000
12-31--2 5,000		12-31--2	5,000
			10,000

Balance sheet:

Assets

Machine	$15,000	
Accumulated depreciation	10,000	$5,000

It is important to distinguish the "depreciation expense" ledger account from the "accumulated depreciation" account. The latter is a balance sheet account that continues to build up or be cumulative—as do all balance sheet accounts. The depreciation expense account would be closed each year to "retained earnings" (assuming that we are accounting for a limited company), or to capital (assuming the existence of a sole proprietorship or partnership).

End of third year:

Depreciation Expense		Accumulated Depreciation—machine	
0		12-31--1	5,000
12-31--3 5,000		12-31--2	5,000
		12-31--3	5,000
			15,000

There usually would be no need to report the machine on the balance sheet at the end of the third year because the net would be zero, i.e., asset $15,000 less accumulated depreciation of $15,000.

A similar approach would be used for bad debts; but there are some complications that have to be described in a later chapter. Suppose that of $200,000 of accounts receivable, $3,200 may never be collected. If so, the adjusting entry would be:

Debit:	Bad debt expense (expense +)	$3,200	
Credit:	Allowance for bad debts, or		
	doubtful receivables (asset −)		$3,200

This entry would help in the process of matching to revenues those costs of earning that sum of revenue. Bad debt expense is really an adjustment to revenue, but is typically called an expense.

Balance sheet:

Assets

Accounts receivable	$200,000	
Allowance for bad debts	3,200	196,800
or		
Accounts receivable		196,800

Most companies would tend to use the latter treatment, i.e., one figure, on the balance sheet, even though they would have the two ledger accounts. Presumably, the net method is used more frequently in practice because readers of financial statements have not demanded both figures. As stated earlier, preparers of financial statements have considerable freedom in choosing financial reporting methods.

A Comprehensive Problem

Douglas Limited (DL) was incorporated on January 10, 19—8. During the year, the following (grouped and simplified) transactions and events occurred:

January 19: $400,000 was invested in DL, in exchange for common shares.

February 15:   A building was rented for $2,000 per month. A deposit of $25,000 was made, and occupancy commenced March 1, 19—8.

February 22:   Inventory of $250,000 is purchased for cash.

March 7:   Equipment was purchased for $36,000 cash. (The expected life of the equipment is three years, and the salvage value at the end of this time likely will be zero.)

May 29:   A customer paid DL $100,000 cash for goods that are to be delivered each month commencing in June 19—8. For each month, the retail price of shipments is required to be set at $10,000.

Periodically, throughout the year, the following expenses were paid in cash:

Office	$ 32,000
Wages	107,000
Interest	2,100
Selling	41,800

(Journal entries would be made throughout the year. As a shortcut in this illustration, we will group the payments.)

Also, the following revenues were earned in cash during the year (excluding those mentioned for the May 29 transaction):

Sale of inventory	$460,500
Interest revenue	10,200

In total (including the May 29 contract and transaction — i.e., including the $70,000 of previously unearned revenue that was later earned in 19—8) the *cost* of the inventory that was sold during 19—8 amounted to $210,000.

As of December 31, 19—8, the following expenses had been incurred, and are to be paid in 19—9:

Wages	$ 3,500
Selling	1,650

In addition, $870 of interest revenue had been earned late in 19—8 but will not be received in cash until 19—9.

Required: Prepare a set of books (of account) for Douglas Limited, and prepare a balance sheet at December 31, 19—8, and an income statement for the period from date of incorporation, January 10, 19—8 to December 31, 19—8. (In other words, proceed through the accounting/bookkeeping cycle, and prepare original, adjusting, and closing journal entries, post them to the ledger accounts, and prepare the financial statements.)

RESPONSE TO COMPREHENSIVE PROBLEM

To obtain maximum learning benefit from the problem, attempt it before reading the response that follows:

Original Transaction Entries

January 19:	Cash (asset +)	400,000	
	Common shares (equity +)		400,000
February 15:	Prepaid rent (asset +)	25,000	
	Cash (asset −)		25,000
February 22:	Inventory (asset +)	250,000	
	Cash (asset −)		250,000
March 7:	Equipment (asset +)	36,000	
	Cash (asset −)		36,000
May 29:	Cash (asset +)	100,000	
	Unearned revenue (liability +)		100,000
Debit:	Office expense (expense +)	32,000	
	Wages expense (expense +)	107,000	
	Interest expense (expense +)	2,100	
	Selling expense (expense +)	41,800	
Credit:	Cash (asset −)		182,900
	(The above is called a *compound* journal entry because it has more than one debit or credit.)		
Debit:	Cash (asset +)	470,700	
Credit:	Revenue (from inventory sales) (revenue +)		460,500
	Interest revenue (revenue +)		10,200
Debit:	Cost of goods sold (expense +)	210,000	
Credit:	Inventory (asset −)		210,000
	(Some accountants might consider this to be an adjusting journal entry as of December 31.)		

Adjusting Journal Entries

December 31: Wages expense (expense +)   3,500
              Selling expense (expense +)   1,650
                Accounts payable (or accrued
                liabilities) (liability +)   5,150

December 31: Accounts receivable (or accrued interest
                receivable) (asset +)   870
                Interest revenue (revenue +)   870

December 31: Rent expense (expense +)   20,000
                Prepaid rent (asset −)   20,000
              (to record expiry of 10 months at $2,000
              per month)

December 31: Depreciation expense—equipment
                (expense +)   10,000
                Accumulated depreciation—
                equipment (asset −)   10,000
              (to record depreciation expense at an
              assumed rate of $1,000 per month)

December 31: Unearned revenue (liability −)   70,000
                Revenue (revenue +)   70,000
              (to record the earning of 7 month's reve-
              nue at $10,000 per month)

Ledger Accounts—After Adjusting Entries

Cash				
1-19	400,000	2-15	25,000	
5-29	100,000	2-2	250,000	
19—8	470,700	3-7	36,000	
		19—8	182,900	
Subtotal	476,800			

Accounts Receivable		
12-31	870	

Inventory			
2-22	250,000	19—8	210,000
Subtotal	40,000		

Prepaid Rent			
2-15	25,000	12-31	20,000
Subtotal	5,000		

Equipment		
3-7	36,000	

Accumulated
Depreciation—equipment
	12-31	10,000

Accounts Payable
	12-31	5,150

Common Shares
	1-19	400,000

Revenue
	19—8	460,500
	12-31	70,000
	Subtotal	530,500

Cost of Goods Sold
19—8	210,000	

Office Expense
19—8	32,000	

Interest Expense
19—8	2,100	

Selling Expense
19—8	41,800	
12-31	1,650	
Subtotal	43,450	

Depreciation Expense
12-31	10,000	

Retained Earnings
	0

Unearned Revenue
12-31	70,000	5-29	100,000
		Subtotal	30,000

Interest Revenue
		19—8	10,200
		12-31	870
		Subtotal	11,070

Wages Expense
19—8	107,000	
12-31	3,500	
	110,500	

Rent Expense
12-31	20,000	

The *adjusted* trial balance at December 31, 19—8 is:

Cash	476,800	
Accounts receivable	870	
Inventory	40,000	
Prepaid rent	5,000	
Equipment	36,000	
Accumulated depreciation—equipment		10,000
Accounts payable		5,150
Unearned revenue		30,000
Common shares		400,000
Revenue		530,500
Interest revenue		11,070
Cost of goods sold	210,000	
Office expense	32,000	
Wages expense	110,500	
Interest expense	2,100	
Selling expense	43,450	
Rent expense	20,000	
Depreciation expense	10,000	
	986,720	986,720

FINANCIAL STATEMENTS

The adjusted trial balance can then be used to help in preparing the financial statements. Typically, an accountant/bookkeeper would start with the income statement, then a statement of retained income (or retained earnings), and finally with the balance sheet.

DOUGLAS LIMITED
Income Statement
From the date of incorporation,
January 10, 19—8, to December 31, 19—8

Revenue:		
Sales of inventory		$530,500
Interest		11,070
		541,570
Expenses:		
Cost of goods sold	$210,000	
Wages	110,500	
Selling	43,450	
Office	32,000	
Rent	20,000	
Depreciation	10,000	
Interest	2,100	428,050
Net income		$113,520

The net income figure excludes any applicable income tax. Some accountants/ bookkeepers may prefer a different type of income statement. (One form is not "right" and the other "wrong". The statements are supposed to be vehicles of communication. What one person understands easily, another person may find confusing. A preparer of financial statements tries to tailor the statement style, or format, to the situation.) The following income statement emphasizes the gross profit that the company makes on its sales of inventory. This gross profit has to cover the company's operating expenses such as wages, selling, office, and so forth. Most retailers (sellers of inventory) like to keep a close watch on gross profit, and will calculate percentages of gross profit to sales and compare them from period to period.

DOUGLAS LIMITED
Income Statement
From the date of incorporation,
January 10, 19—8, to December 31, 19—8

Revenue		$530,500
Cost of goods sold		210,000
Gross profit		320,500
Expenses:		
Wages	$110,500	
Selling	43,450	
Office	32,000	
Rent	20,000	
Depreciation	10,000	
Interest	2,100	
	218,050	
Less interest revenue	11,070	206,980
Net income		$113,520

DOUGLAS LIMITED
Statement of Retained Earnings
From the date of incorporation
January 10, 19—8, to December 31, 19—8

Net income for the period, and balance as of December 31, 19—8	$113,520

The statement of retained earnings is brief because: (1) there were no dividends, and (2) there is a zero opening balance of retained earnings.

DOUGLAS LIMITED
Balance Sheet
December 31, 19—8

Assets

Current assets:		
Cash		$476,800
Accounts receivable		870
Inventory		40,000
Prepaid rent		5,000
		$522,670
Long-lived assets:		
Equipment, at cost	$36,000	
Accumulated depreciation	10,000	26,000
		$548,670

Liabilities and Owners' Equity

Current liabilities:		
Accounts payable		$ 5,150
Unearned revenue		30,000
		35,150
Owners' equity:		
Common shares	$400,000	
Retained earnings	113,520	513,520
		$548,670

Note that the balance-sheet equation is met—assets equal liabilities and owners' equity.

CLASSIFIED BALANCE SHEETS

The balance sheet has been prepared in what is called a "classified" style, or format. That is, so-called similar assets and liabilities have been grouped together. Note that the assets have been split into "current" and "long-lived". Current assets are those that are generally turned into cash within a one-year period, or within one operating cycle of the company. (An operating cycle may extend beyond one year when the manufacturing process takes over twelve months, or the selling of inventory and collection of receivables is lengthy. An example is a cheese producer who has to age the cheese for several months or years before offering it for sale.)

The balance-sheet order for current assets is to start with cash and then proceed in the order in which the asset would be turned into cash. Usually, accounts receivable would be next to cash, and inventory would follow the receivable because it has to be sold before a receivable would be owing from the customer. Prepaid expenses are not usually turned into cash, but save the company from having to pay cash. Thus, conventional practice includes prepaid expenses among the current assets. The total of the current assets ($522,670) gives us a rough indication of the cash that may become available to pay liabilities. We say "rough" because inventory, for example, is recorded at cost, not at its cash value when sold.

A long-lived asset is one that provides a benefit over more than one year—with the benefit usually extending over several years. The long-lived category usually includes assets that are not for sale, but are intended for use in the business to help generate revenue. The equipment, for instance, may be used to move the inventory within a warehouse, or to deliver inventory to a customer. Long-lived assets can also include the cost of assets that may be sold in a year or two from now. An example would be an investment in common shares of another company, i.e., the Royal Bank of Canada, that DL will sell in a few years when it needs the cash for expansion.

The current liability section of the balance sheet is organized much like the current asset side. That is, the top item would be the first to require cash to defray the liability. Unearned revenue is like prepaid expenses in that the cash "original" transaction has already occurred. Unearned revenue usually is defrayed by delivering inventory or a service to the customer. As inventory (or the service that usually requires a cash outlay) is *current* in classification, it is logical to call the unearned revenue a *current* item.

A major theme of this book is that there are many ways of accounting and reporting. Thus, to understand the subject we have to look for differences in accounting treatment and attempt to learn why they occur. The balance-sheet format that was just illustrated makes sense for a company that sells large dollar-amounts of inventory. (In this example, the reader's eye starts at the top of the balance sheet and notes the cash, inventory, and receivables balances first.)

Does the statement presentation, however, make sense for a utility company that provides electricity or telephone service? Utilities tend to have most of their assets in the long-lived category. They sell power or telephone services that the long-lived assets provide over many years. It is therefore fairly common in utility companies to see the long-lived assets at the top of the balance sheet and the current assets below. Quite often the long-lived assets represent 80% to 90%+ of total assets.

In some types of organizations, it is not unusual to see "unclassified" balance sheets. There is no magic in the idea underlying the definition of "current" as being "one year or the operating cycle of the company—if the operating cycle extends beyond one year." After all, the balance sheet is at an instant of time. One day later, the situation may have changed in a significant way. Cash, for example, is being generated or paid daily. Real-estate companies, which tend to have an "inventory" of apartments or offices for rent over a long period of time, are often unenthusiastic about classifying (or segmenting) their balance sheets. Should apartments for rent be inventory or be long-lived assets? It is possible to argue on behalf of each. For example, if the apartments will be offered for sale in a year, they could be inventory. When they are to be rented for a long period of time, however, and are therefore being exposed to wear and tear, they would be long-lived assets.

CLOSING ENTRY AND CLOSING PROCESS

Some adjusted ledger balances (i.e., those ledger accounts such as revenue, expense, and dividends, which are subdivisions of the retained-earnings account) have to be closed as of December 31, 19—8 so that the new year can start with a zero balance. The following journal entry is needed as of December 31, 19—8:

Debit:	Revenue	530,500	
	Interest revenue	11,070	
Credit:	Cost of goods sold		210,000
	Office expense		32,000
	Wages expense		110,500
	Interest expense		2,100
	Selling expense		43,450
	Rent expense		20,000
	Depreciation expense		10,000
	Retained earnings		113,520

Notice that the credit to "retained earnings" represents the net income for the year. (In effect, the entry is the *opposite* to original transaction and adjusting journal entries—revenue is debited and expense is credited—in order to reduce these ledger balances to zero.)

The closed ledger accounts would appear as follows:

Revenue			
	19—8	460,500	
	12-31	70,000	
	Subtotal	530,500	
Closing	530,500		
		0	

Interest Revenue			
	19—8	10,200	
	12-31	870	
	Subtotal	11,070	
Closing	11,070		
		0	

Cost of Goods Sold		
19—8	210,000	
		Closing 210,000
0		

Office Expense		
19—8	32,000	
		Closing 32,000
0		

Wages Expense		
19—8	107,000	
12-31	3,500	
	110,500	
		Closing 110,500
	0	

	Interest Expense		
19—8	2,100		
		Closing	2,100
	0		

	Selling Expense		
19—8	41,800		
12-31	1,650		
Subtotal	43,450		
		Closing	43,450
	0		

	Rent Expense		
12-31	20,000		
		Closing	20,000
	0		

	Depreciation Expense		
12-31	10,000		
		Closing	10,000
	0		

Retained Earnings		
	Closing	
	entry	113,520

Those ledger accounts that are still open, i.e., the balance sheet accounts, are the basis for the *after-closing* trial balance:

DOUGLAS LIMITED
After Closing Trial Balance
December 31, 19—8

Cash	476,800	
Accounts receivable	870	
Inventory	40,000	
Prepaid rent	5,000	
Equipment	36,000	
Accumulated depreciation		10,000
Accounts payable		5,150
Unearned revenue		30,000
Common shares		400,000
Retained earnings		113,520
	558,670	558,670

Note that the total of $558,670 does not agree with the total assets (or total liabilities and owners' equity) on the balance sheet. The reason in this particular case is that the accumulated depreciation has been placed on a different side, so-to-speak. In the balance sheet, the $10,000 of accumulated depreciation has been deducted from the asset, equipment.

In summary, we have responded to the requirements of the comprehensive problem, Douglas Limited. We have also discussed several related issues. It is important that we fully comprehend this problem before proceeding. We must also relate the information in this problem to that in previous chapters.

INTERPRETING THE FINANCIAL STATEMENTS

Has Douglas Limited been successful? *Without some basis for comparison,* that is difficult to determine. When the company has been operating for a few years, or periods, it is then possible to compare year to year, and month to month. Then, better judgments can be made. As succeeding chapters will discuss at some length, however, it is difficult to compare one company with another. The many differences in accounting often make interpretation difficult. There are a few features about DL's financial statements, however, that are worth noting, even though we are not certain what they mean. A review of the financial statements indicates the following:

1. Why has the management of DL not invested some of the cash in short-term certificates that pay interest revenue? (Perhaps the company made such an investment on January 2, 19—9. A balance sheet, prepared as of a particular instant of time, does not tell us what happened one day later.)

2. Is more inventory needed to help generate income in 19—9? The $40,000 at December 31 may be low in relation to $210,000 of cost of goods sold in 19—8. If sales are relatively steady from month to month, much of the inventory could be used up in a little over two months. ($210,000 divided by twelve months is $17,500 per month of cost of goods sold in 19—8. Will 19—9 be similar?)

3. The gross profit is quite good. The sum of $320,500 divided by $530,500 is slightly over 60 percent. (This sounds good; but, we have to know more, such as how much the expenses are, and how much has to be invested to own the business.)

4. Why is DL paying interest expense of $2,100 when it has so much cash on hand? (We do not know; we need to ask management.)

5. The interest-revenue figure on the income statement tells us that management must be investing some of its idle cash. (Thus, we have more insight than was stated in point (1) above regarding what the cash figure on the balance sheet told us.)

6. Overall, DL's results for 19—8 look very good. The owners have invested $400,000 and made net income (profits) of $113,520—ignoring income taxes. This is a *rate of return* (or rate of "interest") of 28.38 percent ($113,520/$400,000).

Other observations about DL's financial statements are possible. Our purpose at this point is to keep in mind that financial statements are vehicles of communication, and we always have to look at what they seem to be telling us.

More Complex Situations

Appendix A to this chapter covers situations where adjusting entries have to be made to correct bookkeeping errors, or are for other complications. Studying the Appendix will make sure that we *understand*, and that we have not merely memorized.

Work Sheet Methods

Appendix B explains the procedure that one may follow when *work sheets*, or spread sheets, are used in a *manual* bookkeeping system. Work sheets are not in the same category (i.e., are they permanent records and documents?) as are journals and ledgers. They are part of the bookkeeper's tool kit, however, and therefore merit a few remarks.

In recent years, a variety of computer "spread sheets" have appeared on the market for use with micro home and office computers. Some of these "spread sheets" bear similarities to manual work sheets (sometimes called *working papers).* Computer "spread sheets" tend to be discussed in specialized courses.

DIVIDENDS

In both statute law, i.e., written law passed by parliaments, and common law, i.e., interpretations of written law, including accepted practice, directors of the company, who are appointed by the owners, decide when a dividend will be declared and when it will be paid in cash. Typically, in large companies, the dividend is declared as of one date and is paid on another date, perhaps two months later. (Often, a third date exists; but this will be described in a later chapter.) Once a dividend has been approved by the board of directors, a liability exists. The declaration of a dividend ought therefore to be an *original* transaction journal entry.

It is sometimes necessary, however, to make an *adjusting* journal entry for a dividend because the original transaction journal entry was not made. For example, suppose that a company's year end is December 31, and that the board of directors met on November 28, 19—8 and declared a dividend, which is to be paid on January 10, 19—9. A liability (to pay the shareholders or owners) exists as of November 28, 19—8, and an *original* transaction journal entry ought to have been made. If it were not made, *one* of the following *adjusting* journal entries would have to be made as of December 31, 19—8:

Debit: Dividends (equity −)   xxx
Credit: Dividend payable (or accounts
             payable) (liability +)   xxx

The dividend account would then be closed to retained earnings by debiting "retained earnings" and crediting "dividends" or "dividends payable."

OR

Debit: Retained earnings (equity −)   xxx
Credit: Dividend payable (or accounts
             payable) (liability +)   xxx

Both of these "adjusting" entries could be called "owners' equity/liability", which *could* be regarded as a *fifth* category of adjusting journal entry.

Summary

This chapter rounds out our understanding of the accounting/bookkeeping cycle. Whenever a financial statement has to be prepared, it is necessary that adjusting entries be recognized. That is, the ledger account balances have to be transformed from a cash (or modified cash) basis to a full accrual basis so that *accounting income* can be computed.

Four types of adjusting journal entries are common:

1. Expense/Asset,
2. Expense/Liability,
3. Liability/Revenue, and
4. Asset/Revenue.

The basic approach in making adjusting entries is: (1) Ask yourself what *should be* in the balance sheet and income statement accounts. (2) Then, look to see what the accounts show. Finally, (3) by way of debits and credits, move from "what is" to "what should be". The appendices to this chapter elaborate on the bookkeeping process.

APPENDIX 4-A
Adjusting and Correcting Journal Entries

INTERNAL CONTROL

In order to protect a company against fraud and error, its accountants set up a system of internal control. Such a system attempts to divide up warehouse, plant, and office-work procedures so that a person acting alone is less likely to cause serious errors and fraud.

Often internal control can be strengthened by selecting one accounting procedure over another. Consider a situation where a company pays $3,600 in advance for thirty-six months of insurance. The transaction may be recorded in at least two ways:

1. Prepaid (or unexpired) insurance (asset +)	$3,600	
Cash (asset −)		$3,600
2. Insurance expense (expense +)	$3,600	
Cash (asset −)		$3,600

Entry 1 is preferred when internal control is an important objective of accounting. As a matter of convenience, companies usually have far greater controls placed on a balance sheet account than on an income statement account, and the prepaid insurance account would be analysed and controlled more carefully than an expense account. Consequently, internal control is usually strengthened when the offsetting debits or credits to cash receipts and payments are made to balance-sheet accounts rather than income statement accounts.

UNDERSTANDING ADJUSTMENTS

There may be a temptation to memorize without understanding, particularly with adjusting journal entries. In order to minimize this temptation, an additional exercise is provided to aid in understanding. Some of the original entries that follow are unusual and may be contrary to a good system of internal control; but we are using them to help our understanding of adjusting journal entries, which are needed to measure income. This should be carefully noted as we proceed.

The theme of adjusting and correcting entries is quite easy. Adjusting entries amend each of the ledger accounts from its current balance before adjustment to the required amount at statement-preparation dates. Error can be avoided by asking: What is the current balance before adjustment?

Asset/Expense Example

To illustrate, refer to the two journal entries that we may have made for the thirty-six-month $3,600 insurance purchase. The adjusting entry after one month, assuming the original debit was to prepaid insurance, would be:

Insurance expense (expense +)	$100	
Prepaid insurance (asset −)		$100

In contrast, if the original debit of $3,600 was to insurance expense, the adjusting entry at the end of the first month would be:

Prepaid insurance (asset +)	$3,500	
Insurance expense (expense −)		$3,500

The variations can be depicted by the following three examples:

If the original transaction entry is:	The adjusting entry would be:
January 1, 19—1:	**January 31, 19—1:**

1. Prepaid insurance
   (asset +) $3,600
   Cash (asset −) $3,600
	1. Insurance expense
	   (expense +) $ 100
	   Prepaid insurance
	   (asset −) $ 100

2. Insurance expense
   (expense +) $3,600
   Cash (asset −) $3,600
	2. Prepaid insurance
	   (asset +) $3,500
	   Insurance expense
	   (expense −) $3,500

3. Insurance expense
   (expense +) $ 100
   Prepaid insurance
   (asset +)   3,500
   Cash (asset −) $3,600
	3. No entry required.

In (3) above, we ask ourselves the basic questions:

A. What are the balances in the accounts before adjustment?

B. What should the balances be after adjustment?

C. How do I get from A to B?

At the end of January, the figures for (3) are:

Account	What *is now* before adjustment	What *ought to be* after adjustment	Adjustment needed
Insurance expense	$ 100 Debit	$ 100 Debit	None
Prepaid insurance	$3,500 Debit	$3,500 Debit	None

Liability/Revenue Example

Suppose that we were given the following facts and asked for adjusting journal entries on January 31, 19—1 for a magazine publisher: "$72,000 was received on January 1, 19—1 for magazine subscriptions extending to the next thirty-six months; the magazine is published monthly at mid-month."

Clearly, it is not possible to provide an adjusting entry without first making an assumption about the original transaction journal entry. The variations are:

If the original transaction entry is:	Then, the adjusting entry would be:
January 1:	**January 31:**

1. Cash (asset +) $72,000
    Unearned revenue
        (liability +) $72,000
	1. Unearned revenue
	        (liability −) $2,000
	    Revenue
	        (revenue +) $2,000

2. Cash (asset +) $72,000
    Revenue
        (revenue +) $72,000
	2. Revenue
	        (revenue −) $70,000
	    Unearned revenue
	        (liability +) $70,000

3. Cash (asset +) $72,000
    Revenue
        (revenue +) $ 2,000
    Unearned revenue
        (liability +)   70,000
	3. No entry needed

The ability of students to recognize that different original transaction entries require different adjusting entries distinguishes those who understand the accounting cycle and adjustments from those who memorize one way of handling adjustments. A complete answer should be worded somewhat as follows: If the original transaction entry was _____ then the adjusting journal entry would be _____."

Using (2) for illustrative purposes:

Revenue		Unearned Revenue	
Balance before adjustment	$72,000	Balance before adjustment	$ 0
Balance needed after adjustment	2,000	Balance needed after adjustment	70,000

Adjusting entry needed:

Revenue (revenue −)	70,000	
Unearned revenue (liability +)		70,000

Note that on February 28, assuming that the correct adjustments were made on January 31, all of (1), (2) and (3) would require the same adjusting entry:

Unearned revenue (liability −)	$ 2,000	
Revenue (revenue +)		$2,000

Adjusting entries can affect, in addition to the above two examples, expense/liability, expense/asset contra, and some other combinations of accounts. Sometimes complex adjusting entries are required. For instance, suppose that a fixed asset costing $60,000 and having a life of five years (with zero salvage value at the end of five years) is inadvertently charged to a "maintenance expense" account on January 1, 19—2. The adjusting (and correcting) journal entry at January 31, 19—2 (assuming that depreciation is recorded monthly) would have to be:

Asset (asset +)	$60,000	
Depreciation expense (expense +)	1,000	
Maintenance expense (expense −)		$60,000
Accumulated depreciation (asset −,		
or asset contra +)		1,000

The journal entry could be split into two parts: (a) debiting the fixed asset and crediting the expense in order to correct the error, and (b) recognizing depreciation on the newly recorded asset. Part (b) can easily be missed unless we consider the consequences of all previous adjusting entries.

Summary

Before preparing an adjusting entry, we must know: (1) what is currently showing as the account balance and, (2) what should or ought to be in the account. The remainder of one's effort is addition or subtraction as long as the double entry mechanism and related accounts are kept in mind. For example, an expense generally decreases only when an asset increases, a liability decreases, or another expense increases. Adjusting entries *rarely affect cash.* Most often, in fact, the purpose of the adjusting entry is to move away from cash accounting to accrual-basis accounting.

APPENDIX 4-B
Work Sheets and Working Papers

Work sheets are particularly useful in manual bookkeeping systems when monthly financial statements are being prepared. The preparation of monthly financial statements involves the use of *month-end* adjusting journal entries—ones that usually would not be recorded in the journals and ledgers because they could prove to be a nuisance or might even have to be reversed. For example, an adjusting entry such as "debit wage expense, credit wages payable" that is made at the end of the first month of a new year probably would have to be reversed at the start of the next month. Why? One important reason is that an expense *could* become overstated when the cash was paid.

To illustrate, suppose that $1,480 is owing to employees on January 31, 19—9, and the following adjusting journal entry is made:

Debit:	Wage expense (expense +)	1,480	
Credit:	Wages payable (liability +)		1,480

Suppose also that the sum is paid on February 3, 19—9 and perhaps is recorded in a special "cash disbursements" journal through an office *routine procedure*, i.e., a procedure performed by a junior clerk, that results in this entry:

Debit:	Wage expense (expense +)	1,480	
Credit:	Cash (asset −)		1,480

The latter entry would result in the wage expense for 19—9 being overstated by $1,480.

Some accountants employ a procedure called *reversing entries* to help eliminate possible duplication. That is, on *February 1, 19—9,* i.e., *after* the financial statements as of January 31, 19—9 have been prepared, they would make the following reversing entry (to reverse the effect of the January 31, 19—9 adjusting entry):

Debit:	Wages payable (liability −)	1,480	
Credit:	Wage expense (expense −)		1,480

The reversing entry cancels both the expense and liability. Thus, there is *no* duplication on February 3, 19—9 when the following entry is made:

Debit:	Wage expense (expense +)	1,480	
Credit:	Cash (asset −)		1,480

The need to make reversing entries *every month* can be eliminated by using a work sheet. Adjusting journal entries are recorded at month end *only on the work sheet* and *not* in the company's journals and ledgers. (At the year end, adjusting journal entries would be recorded in the ledgers.)

A work sheet consists of columns on a large sheet of paper. See Illustration 4-B-1, which has the information that we used in preparing the financial statements for Douglas Limited (earlier in Chapter 4). Typically, the columns may be labelled:

Column 1 Unadjusted trial balance—debits
2 Unadjusted trial balance—credits
3 Adjusting entry—debits
4 Adjusting entry—credits
5 Adjusted trial balance—debits
6 Adjusted trial balance—credits
7 Income statement—debits
8 Income statement—credits
9 Retained earnings—debits
10 Retained earnings—credits
11 Balance sheet—debits
12 Balance sheet—credits

The bookkeeper would therefore perform the steps of the bookkeeping cycle by moving from column 1 to 2 to 3/4, and so on. That is, the unadjusted ledger-account balances would be entered in columns 1 and 2. Then, the adjusting entries would be recorded in columns 3 and 4. Next, the rows would be *added across* (or subtracted across) and the totals entered in columns 5 and 6, which contain the adjusted trial-balance.

The adjusted trial balance would form the basis for preparing the financial statements. Those balances in columns 5 and 6 that pertain to revenues and expenses would be recorded in, i.e., moved across to, columns 7 and 8. The net income from 7/8 and the retained-earnings ledger accounts from columns 5 and 6, i.e., the opening balance of retained earnings, and dividends, would be placed in columns 9 and 10. Finally, the *closing* balance of retained earnings from 9/10 plus the balance-sheet ledger accounts from 5/6 would be placed in columns 11 and 12. The financial statements would therefore be prepared by using the figures in columns 6 through 12.

Carefully study columns 6 through 12 at the bottom of the work sheet. Note how the income figure is transferred to column 10, and how closing retained earnings is transferred to 12.

Note that, by totalling the columns, some types of errors may be found. If the total of column 11 does not equal that of column 12, we have to go back to 5/6 to ensure that they equal each other (5 = 6). If they do, the error probably is in cross-adding in columns 7 through 12.

(In Illustration 4-B-1, the figures in columns 1 and 2 have been derived from the ledger account balances shown earlier in this chapter. The figures are those *before* adjustment.)

ILLUSTRATION 4-B-1

WORK SHEET
DOUGLAS LIMITED
December 31, 19—8

Account Titles	Unadjusted Trial Balance		Adjusting Journal Entries		Adjusted Trial Balance		Income Statement		Retained Earnings		Balance Sheet	
	(1)	(2)	(3)	(4)	(5)	(6)	(7)	(8)	(9)	(10)	(11)	(12)
	Dr.	Cr.	Dr.	Cr.	Dr.	Cr.	Dr.	Cr.	Dr.	Cr.	Dr.	Cr.
Cash	476,800				476,800						476,800	
Accounts receivable			(b) 870		870						870	
Inventory	40,000				40,000						40,000	
Prepaid rent	25,000			(c) 20,000	5,000						5,000	
Equipment	36,000				36,000						36,000	
Accum. depreciation —equipment				(d) 10,000		10,000						10,000
Accounts payable				(a) 5,150		5,150						5,150
Unearned revenue		100,000	(e) 70,000			30,000						30,000
Common shares		400,000				400,000						400,000
Retained earnings —opening		0				0				0		
Revenue		460,500		(e) 70,000		530,500		530,500				
Interest Revenue		10,200		(b) 870		11,070		11,070				
Cost of goods sold	210,000				210,000		210,000					
Office expense	32,000				32,000		32,000					
Wages expense	107,000		(a) 3,500		110,500		110,500					
Interest expense	2,100				2,100		2,100					
Selling expense	41,800		(a) 1,650		43,450		43,450					
Rent expense			(c) 20,000		20,000		20,000					
Depreciation expense			(d) 10,000		10,000		10,000					
Net income							113,520			113,520		
Retained earnings —closing								113,520	113,520			113,520
	970,700	970,700	106,020	106,020	986,720	986,720	541,570	541,570	113,520	113,520	558,670	558,670

QUESTIONS

4-1 Is accrual basis accounting the only sensible method of accounting for most businesses and situations?

4-2 When an expense is debited, what different *types* of accounts are credited?

4-3 When revenue is credited, what different *types* of accounts are debited?

4-4 How do adjusting journal entries differ from original transaction, and closing, journal entries? (What are the purposes of adjusting journal entries?)

4-5 What are current assets and current liabilities? Define each, and indicate their significance.

4-6 What are the four most common types of adjusting journal entries?

4-7 What is internal control?

4-8 What are work sheets or working papers? What is their purpose?

EXERCISES

E4-1 Give adjusting journal entries at October 31, 19—9 for each of the undernoted *independent* situations. Assume that the company prepares monthly financial statements.

1. A cheque for $7,200 is issued on October 1, 19—9 to pay for insurance for the 36 months commencing October 19—9. The $7,200 is debited to prepaid insurance.

2. An automobile costing $18,000 is acquired on October 1, 19—9. Its life is expected to be five years with no scrap value. The $18,000 is debited to an automobile asset account.

3. Wages due for the last five days of October amount to $3,620. No journal entry has been made for these wages, which will be paid in November.

4. A tenant gave us a cheque for $3,300 on October 15 for one of our buildings that is being rented. The $3,300 covers a three month period commencing October 15, and was credited to unearned rent.

5. At October 31, 19—9, it appears as though an account receivable of $620 will not be collected. The debtor went bankrupt suddenly, in late October.

E4-2 The trial balance of Armitage Corporation at November 30, 19—8 is as follows:

Cash	15,000	
Accounts receivable	65,000	
Inventory	50,000	
Prepaid expenses	20,000	
Land	50,000	
Building and equipment	200,000	
Accumulated depreciation		60,000
Accounts payable		37,500
Bank loan payable		32,000
Unearned revenue		8,000
Common shares		100,000
Retained earnings		162,500
	400,000	400,000

During December 19—8, the following transactions occurred:

1. Inventory costing $22,000 was sold on account for $99,900.
2. Salary expenses of $21,250 were paid in cash.
3. Accounts receivable of $89,700 were collected in cash.
4. Accounts payable of $32,800 were paid in cash.
5. Various selling expenses of $7,600 and office expenses of $4,350 were paid in cash.
6. A cheque for $12,500 was received from a customer who wants inventory delivered in January.
7. A $5,000 payment was made on the bank loan.

At December 31, 19—8, the following adjusting journal entries are required:

1. $4,200 of prepaid expense have now expired.
2. Depreciation expense for December amounts to $1,900.
3. Wages for December, that have not yet been paid, amount to $4,175.
4. Bank interest of $65 is owing at the end of December.
5. Unearned revenue of $6,400 became earned in December.

Required:

A. Prepare original transaction journal entries for December 19—8.
B. Prepare adjusting journal entries at December 31, 19—8.
C. Post the journal entries in A and B to the applicable ledger accounts.
D. Prepare an adjusted trial balance at December 31, 19—8.
E. Prepare a balance sheet at December 31, 19—8, and an income statement for December 19—8.
F. Prepare closing journal entries as at December 31, 19—8.

E4-3 (Accounting or Bookkeeping Cycle Review.) Mark Lawrence decided to open a grocery store, "Corner Store", with an investment of $200,000 in proprietor's capital as of February 15, 19—3. The following transactions occurred in the period to March 31, 19—3:

February 16: A cheque for $5,000 was issued to the owner of the building that Corner Store is renting. Monthly rental is $1,000 for March and subsequent months, and $500 for February.

February 18: Inventory of $46,000 is purchased for cash.

February 20: Display counters, cash registers, freezers and similar equipment are purchased on account for $88,000.

February 22: Advertising signs are purchased for cash of $5,000.

February 24: Two employees are hired at a wage rate of $10 per hour. Others are told that they will be hired in March.

February 26: The display counters are installed at a cost of $820. A cheque is issued.

February 28: The store is opened for business. $315 of inventory is given away as store opening advertising.

March 2: Heat and light invoices of $110 are paid in cash.

March 4: Employee wages of $1,390 are paid in cash.

March 6: Insurance costing $4,800 is paid in cash. The insurance policy is for two years commencing March 1, 19—3.

March 7: A delivery automobile is purchased for $12,000 cash.

March 9: To date, inventory costing $30,000 has been sold for $44,900 cash.

March 11: Additional inventory costing $43,500 is purchased on account.

March 13: A rich customer gives us a $10,000 deposit for groceries that are to be delivered on a daily basis to a local home for disadvantaged people. Corner Store is required to keep track of what is delivered, and to request additional funds when needed.

March 15: Advertising invoices totalling $320 are paid in cash.

March 17: Miscellaneous expenses of $195 are paid in cash.

March 19: Inventory costing $2,960 is sold on account for $4,100.

March 21: Employee wages of $11,200 are paid in cash.

March 23: Accounts payable of $40,000 are paid in cash.

March 25: An invoice for $1,700 is received from a janitorial service. The sum will be paid in April.

March 27: Mr. Lawrence withdraws $210 of groceries for his personal use. Retail price would be $290.

March 29: Miscellaneous expenses of $395 are paid.

March 30: Arrangements are made for a bank loan up to $50,000 on a "when needed" basis.

March 31: Interest on the company's bank account balance amounts to $295. Also, inventory costing $40,000 is sold for $58,700 cash.

In addition to what has already been noted above, the following adjusting entries are needed:

1. Depreciation for the period to March 31 amounts to $830.
2. The deposit from the rich customer (March 13) amounts to $1,790 at the close of business on March 31. The cost of the inventory sold amounts to $6,100.
3. Wages owing to employees amount to $8,150 at the close of business on March 31.
4. Unpaid miscellaneous expense invoices amount to $425 at the close of business on March 31.
5. Rent for March, and similar expenses.

Required:

A. Prepare journal entries for the original transactions that occur in the period to March 31.

B. Post the journal entries in A to their appropriate ledger accounts. (T accounts may be used.)

C. Prepare a trial balance as of March 31, 19—3.

D. Prepare adjusting journal entries as of March 31, 19—3.

E. Post the adjusting entries to their appropriate ledger accounts.

F. Prepare an adjusted trial balance as of March 31, 19—3.

G. Prepare a balance sheet as of March 31, 19—3, and an income statement and statement of proprietor's capital for the period to March 31, 19—3.

H. Prepare closing journal entries as of March 31, 19—3.

I. Post the journal entries in H to their appropriate ledger accounts.

J. Prepare an after closing trial balance.

E4-4 In each of the following *independent* situations, prepare any necessary journal entries that would be required either to adjust the company's books or to bring them up to date in order to prepare financial statements at December 31, 19—8. Assume that closing journal entries have not yet been made, and that no previous adjusting journal entries have been made for these transactions.

1. A one year insurance policy was purchased on October 15, 19—8 and the $1,800 cost was charged to prepaid insurance.

2. The employees are owed $3,390 for wages for the last few days of December.

3. Depreciation for the year amounts to $10,550.

4. The allowance for bad debts account has a credit balance of $295. It is believed that a figure of $1,700 would be more appropriate.

5. A company that is renting one of our buildings paid us $12,000 rent for the year commencing September 16, 19—8. The $12,000 was credited to unearned revenue.

6. Inventory costing $20,000 was sold to a customer for $32,000. The inventory was shipped from our warehouse on December 31, 19—8. However, in error, it was not invoiced to the customer until January 3, 19—9.

7. A used automobile costing $10,000 with a life of five years and zero scrap value was debited, in error, to equipment repairs on November 1, 19—8.

8. A cheque for $995 was charged to selling expense when it ought to have been charged to administrative expense.

E4-5 Replace the ? with figures that balance the transaction, and explain your reasoning, for each of the following *independent* situations:

	Transactions During Year	Balance, Beginning of Year	Balance, End of Year
Situation A:			
Accounts receivable for sales on account		?	40,500
Allowance for bad debts		?	7,200
Bad debts expense	3,100		
Cash collected on accounts receivable	100,000		
Accounts receivable credited, because they are uncollectible	0		
Sales on account	110,000		
Situation B:			
Accounts payable		20,200	?
Cash paid on accounts payable	60,000		
Purchases of inventory	68,500		
Cost of goods sold	66,200		
Inventory		?	27,700
Situation C:			
Unearned revenue		?	15,000
Additional deposits, to increase unearned revenue	13,300		
Revenue earned during year	16,000		

E4-6 The following information is for Reverse Limited. Construct the after closing trial balance of Reverse Limited as of December 31, 19—7, (i.e., the beginning of the current year). Show all calculations.

	Trial Balance at December 31, 19—8	
Cash	10,000	
Accounts receivable	30,000	
Inventory	28,000	
Prepaid insurance	8,000	
Land	60,000	
Building and equipment	300,000	
Accumulated depreciation		68,000
Accounts payable		21,000
Unearned revenue		6,000
Common shares		100,000
Retained earnings		241,000
	436,000	436,000

During the year, the following transactions occurred:

1. Inventory costing $70,000 was sold for $124,700. Sales on account were $95,000, cash sales were $23,700, and $6,000 came from unearned revenue.
2. Inventory purchases amounted to $67,300, all of which were on account.
3. Expenses other than cost of goods sold amounted to $26,850 of which $15,400 were on account, $4,000 was from prepaid insurance and the remainder of $7,450 was for cash.
4. Depreciation expense for the period was $8,300.
5. Cash collections of accounts receivable amounted to $77,950.
6. Cash payments of accounts payable amounted to $46,830.
7. Cash deposits for future delivery (unearned revenue) amounted to $4,800.
8. A small parcel of land costing $20,000 was purchased for cash.

PROBLEMS

P4-1 Prepare *adjusting* journal entries at September 30, 19—9 for each of the following independent situations. Assume that September 30, 19—9 is the year end of the company. State all of the important assumptions that you make, and explain all of your journal entries thoroughly.

1. On September 1, 19—9 the company paid $2,400 for one year's insurance coverage.
2. A fixed asset costing $12,000 with a life of 10 years was acquired September 15, 19—9 and inadvertently charged to maintenance expense.
3. Casual laborers earned $3,625 in September 19—9, but were not paid until October 4, 19—9.
4. $10,000 was received from customers on September 16, 19—9 for goods to be delivered in September and early October 19—9. By September 30, 19—9 goods priced at $9,750 had been delivered to customers.
5. During September, accounts receivable of $2,698 were written off as uncollectible accounts receivable.

P4-2 Compute the *beginning*-of-period balance of accounts receivable from the following information:

Accounts receivable—closing balance	$ 39,855
Revenue for period	100,000
Unearned revenue—beginning balance	22,100
—closing balance	19,730
Allowance for doubtful accounts:	
—beginning balance	2,620
—closing balance	2,965
Bad debt expense for period	3,825
Cash receipts:	
Unearned revenue	10,000
Accounts receivable	89,575

P4-3 Compute the *end*-of-period balance of accounts payable from the following information:

Accounts payable—opening balance	$ 29,443
Purchases of inventory	?
Inventory—opening balance	24,190
—closing balance	25,175
Payments on accounts payable	89,110
Cost of goods sold	100,000
Inventory spoiled and scrapped (charged to administrative expense)	2,000

P4-4 The bookkeeper for Richardson Grocery Stores Limited (RGSL) prepared the following financial statement for the month of September:

Revenue—cash sales		$120,000
Borrowings from bank		30,000
		150,000
Expenses:		
Purchases of inventory for cash	$62,900	
Purchase of equipment for cash	21,000	
Payment for one year insurance policy	2,400	
Wages paid in cash	12,950	
Miscellaneous expenses paid in cash	9,760	
Payment for accounts payable	10,500	119,510
Net		$ 30,490

Required:

A. Of what possible use is the financial statement that the bookkeeper prepared? Explain your response.

B. What are the limitations of the bookkeeper's financial statement? Explain your response.

C. Under which conditions and situations is accrual accounting appropriate? Explain your response.

P4-5 The trial balances of Babiak Corporation before and after adjustment as of November 30, 19—8 are as follows:

	Before Adjusting Entries	After Adjusting Entries
Cash	10,000	10,000
Accounts receivable	100,000	100,000
Interest receivable	—	2,000
Inventory	110,000	110,000
Prepaid expenses	20,000	12,000
Land	70,000	70,000
Building and equipment	300,000	300,000
Accumulated depreciation	60,000	80,000
Accounts payable	50,000	59,000
Unearned revenue	30,000	18,000
Common shares	200,000	200,000
Retained earnings	250,000	250,000
Revenue	100,000	112,000
Cost of goods sold	65,000	65,000
Expenses	16,000	53,000
Miscellaneous income	1,000	3,000

Required:
Provide the adjusting journal entries that occurred as of November 30, 19—8, and explain why each would have been made.

P4-6 Prentice Limited made the following adjusting journal entries at December 31, 19—8:
1. Prepaid rent was decreased by $2,000.
2. Interest revenue was increased by $1,250 to recognize interest that was earned in December but which will not be paid until January.
3. Depreciation expense of $8,600 was recorded.
4. Unearned revenue was decreased by $3,125.
5. A liability for unpaid wages of $6,190 was recorded.
   The *adjusted* trial balance at December 31, 19—8 shows the following income statement ledger account balances:

Sales revenue	200,000
Cost of goods sold	140,000
Wages expense	30,000
Rent expense	5,000
Depreciation expense	8,800
Interest revenue	3,000
Other expense	3,200

Required:
A. Provide the *unadjusted* trial balance at December 31, 19—8 for the above income statement ledger accounts. Show all calculations.
B. Provide the adjusting journal entries that were made at December 31, 19—8.

P4-7 For each of the undernoted unrelated transactions, provide an example of a transaction that has the *opposite* effect on the particular *balance sheet* ledger account that has been affected by the first transaction. Give the journal entry for the opposite balance sheet effect. Wherever possible, choose an example of a transaction that affects both the balance sheet and the income statement.

Example: The first transaction is a sale of inventory on account. The opposite effect would occur if the inventory is returned because it became damaged in transport to the customer. That is, sales would be debited, and accounts receivable would be credited.

Transactions:

1. A deposit of $10,000 is received from a customer who wishes to have inventory delivered in the next financial period.
2. A cheque for $9,000 is issued to pay for an insurance policy that is in effect for the next two years.
3. A truck is purchased for $40,000 cash.
4. Inventory is acquired on account for $70,000.
5. A bank loan for $50,000 is obtained at current rates of interest.
6. A sum of $20,000 is deposited in the company's savings account at a bank.

EXPLORATION MATERIALS AND CASES

MC4-1 Captain Smith recently incorporated a company, Toronto Tours Limited (TTL), to provide tours between Toronto harbor and Niagara-on-the-Lake. In the mid-1920s these trips had been very popular. However, in recent times, trips of this nature were not being offered. Captain Smith was confident that these tours would again become successful. He observed more tourists coming to Toronto and more people interested in the Shaw Festival at Niagara-on-the-Lake. In addition to providing tours, he intended to charter his boat on a per hour basis to special groups. During the month of September the company engaged in the following transactions:

September 1: TTL was incorporated and Captain Smith contributed $35,000 in cash in exchange for 10,000 common shares in the company.

September 2: Signed a five year lease for a boat house calling for a monthly rent of $200. Paid $400 in cash. Bought a boat at an auction for $25,000 (replacement cost $40,000). Paid $20,000 in cash and signed a 12 percent promissory note payable in two years for the remainder.

September 6: Purchased the following items on credit:
fuel - $5,000
life preservers - $200

September 7: Paid $1,000 in cash for a liquor licence.

September 12: Paid for fuel previously purchased on credit.

September 14: Paid $5,000 in cash for wood to be used in the construction of Mr. Smith's cottage.

September 28: Received $1,000 as a deposit from a customer wishing to charter the boat on October 4.

September 29: Declared a dividend of $1,000 payable on October 2.

September 1-30: A summary of charters for the month is as follows:

Charters made to customers who paid cash $6,000.

Charters made to customers on credit $2,000.

September 1-30: Collected a total of $500 on charters made to customers on credit.

September 30: Paid the crew's salary of $600 in cash. This $600 represented $500 for the month of September and $100 for the first four days of October.

Additional information:

1. A review of the accounts receivable ledger indicates that $200 is likely to be uncollectible.
2. The value of fuel in the storage tanks at the end of the month is $3,000.
3. During September, Captain Smith stood on a busy street corner handling out coupons for free trips of Toronto harbor in the month of October.
4. On October 6, Captain Smith received an invoice in the amount of $500 from his lawyer for incorporating the company.

Required:

A. Assume the role of the controller of TTL.
1. What are the accounting problems or issues?
2. Which financial statements would you prepare? Why?
3. Prepare journal entries for the above transactions, and explain why you believe that each is appropriate.
4. Prepare an income statement and balance sheet.

B. Assume the role of a banker.
1. What questions would you raise with Captain Smith in assessing the company's financial statements?
2. Would you make a loan to the company? Why?

MC4-2 Good Boy Limited (GBL) was incorporated several years ago by Mr. Oaster. Since its incorporation, the company has been moderately successful. Its operations consist of three retail appliance stores located in Southwestern Ontario. The company's fiscal year end is August 31.

The success of the appliance business is directly related to the state of the economy. More specifically, appliance sales improve as the number of new homes being built increases, the unemployment rate decreases and disposable incomes increase.

Mr. Oaster has been in the appliance business for thirty-five years and he loves it. He would like to expand GBL's operations. At present, he is the president and only shareholder of the company. Unfortunately, his wife would prefer that he retire and move to Florida with their two dogs. Mr. Oaster has managed to appease his wife by promising that he will retire within three years. However, before he retires he would like to see his company grow to be one of the largest retail operations in Ontario. However, growth requires capital and Mr. Oaster has little personal savings. Therefore, the only options that appear to be available are to sell additional shares or borrow money from a creditor.

Recently, Mr. Oaster has had offers from individuals who are interested in purchasing the property upon which his stores are situated. In addition he has been approached by large retail operations wishing to acquire his appliance operations. Both of these courses of action were rejected by Mr. Oaster.

In order that he might better assess his company's future, Mr. Oaster would like a set of financial statements prepared. He has provided you with the following unadjusted trial balance and additional information as at August 31, 19—7:

	Debit	Credit
Cash	$ 1,000	$
Accounts receivable	150,000	
Inventory	200,000	
Unexpired insurance	5,000	
Property, plant and equipment	200,000	
Accumulated depreciation		60,000
Accounts payable		150,000
Notes payable (bearing interest at 12%)		200,000
Common shares		30,000
Retained earnings		55,000
Sales		510,000
Cost of goods sold	240,000	
Salaries expense	80,000	
Office expenses	32,000	
Heat, light and power expense	10,000	
Selling expense	75,000	
Interest expense	12,000	
	$1,005,000	$1,005,000

Additional data:

1. A review of the accounts receivable ledger indicates that $12,000 is likely to be uncollectible.
2. At year-end, unexpired insurance is $1,400.
3. Salaries payable at August 31 total $1,500.
4. Interest on the 12 percent notes payable at August 31 is $4,000. The notes payable are due on December 31, 19—7.
5. Estimated electricity expense for August is $800.
6. A physical count of inventory at year end revealed that merchandise costing $185,000 was on hand.

Required:

A. Assume the role of an accounting advisor to GBL, and
   1. Prepare the adjusting journal entries at August 31, 19—7 that you feel are appropriate.
   2. Prepare a balance sheet and an income statement together with the notes to the financial statements that you feel are appropriate.
   3. What would you recommend that Mr. Oaster do? Why?

B. Assume the role of a potential creditor. What additional information do you require? Would you loan money to the company? Why?

C. Assume the role of a potential investor. What additional information do you require? Would you invest in the company? Why?

CHAPTER 5

Measuring Income and Liquidity

Chapter Themes

1. Businesses must strike a balance between being profitable (high income) and being liquid enough (adequate cash) to be able to pay their liabilities, thereby avoiding bankruptcy. Liquidity and profitability implications of large dollar-transactions have to be evaluated carefully, and accounting figures can help in the evaluation.

2. A form of bankruptcy can occur in profitable companies. Lack of profitability and possible bankruptcy are not the same.

3. The role of auditors in financial reporting is limited, and auditors do not actively seek out fraud or "unfairness" in financial statements. What is fair to one person may be regarded as unfair by some other people. "Fair" is usually interpreted with reference to generally accepted accounting principles—that is, "fair per GAAP".

4. Liquidity can be measured in several, different ways. We have to be alert to which method makes the most sense under different situations.

Income and Liquidity

People studying business, and taking business courses (such as accounting) often tend to look for "right" answers to various issues. Further study, however, shows them that there are few, if any, "right" answers, and that trade-offs must occur. These trade-offs are no different from those in our personal life: Do I want to work overtime and get paid more, or do I want more leisure time?

One of the many trade-offs in business is maintaining a sensible balance between profitability and liquidity. Profitability refers to the amount of income that the business generates. The previous chapters mentioned that there is more than one way to compute income; we will, however, focus primarily on one particular way in the *first* major portion of this book.

Similarly, "liquidity" can be measured or defined in many different ways. These differences will become apparent as we proceed. Our concern with liquidity is as vital as our concern with income versus capital. Investors do not want to invest in a company that may go bankrupt because it could become too *illiquid* and not able to pay its liabilities. (If large liabilities are not paid, the creditors can apply to the courts to force a company into bankruptcy.)

The major recession in Canada in the early 1980s clearly pointed to the need for Canadian businesses to give greater attention to liquidity. Many owners of small businesses, farmers, and others lost their companies or farms because they failed to manage liquidity adequately. This chapter only introduces the topic so that we may add to our understanding in succeeding chapters, especially in Chapter 16.

An illustration will help to convey the importance of maintaining a balance between liquidity and profitability. Company *X* Limited and Company *Y* Limited are in the same line of business; both sell women's shoes and both have one retail store in a shopping mall. Their balance sheets are shown in Illustration 5-1.

ILLUSTRATION 5-1
Balance Sheets of Two Retail Shoe Stores

COMPANY X LIMITED
Balance Sheet
September 30, 19—7

Assets		*Owners' Equity*	
Cash	$ 900	Common shares	$1,000
Inventory	100		
	$1,000		$1,000

COMPANY Y LIMITED
Balance Sheet
September 30, 19—7

Assets		*Liabilities and Owners' Equity*	
Cash	$ 100	Liability:	
Inventory	2,900	Accounts payable	$2,000
		Owners' equity:	
		Common shares	1,000
	$3,000		$3,000

Which company, X or Y, is likely to be the more profitable in the coming months? Both have invested \$1,000. Shoe styles change, and the inventory may become out-of-date *(obsolete)* before it is sold. Or, the retail selling prices of shoes may drop. But, *if* we disregard possible *obsolescence* of styles of shoes and falling retail prices, the more profitable company in the short term likely will be Y, which has the higher inventory. Presumably the inventory will be sold at a price in excess of its cost. (Remember, inventory is shown at the *cost* of purchasing it under the income-measurement basis that we described in the earlier chapters of this book, which is the basis commonly used in Canada.)

Ideally, the cash received by Company Y on the sale of its inventory will allow it to pay off the \$2,000 of accounts payable. (The payable was probably incurred to buy the inventory.) Company Y may continue the process of buying shoes from the manufacturer and selling them to people for many months. But, sooner or later, an economic recession will occur, and people will buy fewer pairs of shoes. Inventory is not like cash; it is somewhat illiquid. Large quantities may have to be sold for well below cost, resulting in losses. Worse still, the cash proceeds on sale of the inventory may not be enough to pay the accounts payable.

Company Y could go bankrupt. Why? Its owners or managers took a chance and put nearly all their assets into inventory—in the hope of generating more and more income. The company could become fairly illiquid; and, if it was not able to pay its debts (accounts payable), it could be forced into bankruptcy.

Company X, on the other hand, has no creditors but has plenty of cash. The cash may very well be in a type of bank account that does not earn interest income. Company X would not likely be very profitable because it has very little inventory to sell, to generate a gross profit. Many people coming into X's retail store would probably not find the size and design of shoe that they desire. (They may go to buy from Y.)

The Company X and Company Y illustrations are somewhat extreme. Company X has sacrificed profitability in order to have liquidity. In contrast, Company Y has sacrificed liquidity to try for more profitability. A sensible trade-off between liquidity and profitability has to be struck. Exactly what this balance, or asset mix (of inventory versus cash) is at any time is a function of many factors, such as (1) economic conditions (2) susceptibility of the inventory to spoilage or obsolescence, and (3) willingness of creditors to wait extra weeks for their cash.

In accounting, we have to be aware that creditors may want to use financial statements in assessing the liquidity of past financial periods in deciding whether or not to grant extra credit to debtors (such as Company Y). In circumstances such as the above, *general-purpose* financial statements can help creditors; but often the general-purpose statements have limitations. Comprehending what those limitations are takes up much of this book. It is too easy to misinterpret general-purpose financial statements.

A creditor who really wants to know whether he will delay his demand for payment (perhaps, thereby not forcing a company into bankruptcy) would benefit from a special-purpose report. It would contain such information as when the company expects to receive and pay cash, on a month-by-month basis. Such reports are described in other courses, primarily in management accounting. One possible special-purpose report for a creditor, however, is shown in Illustration 5-2.

ILLUSTRATION 5-2

COMPANY Z
Schedule of Cash Receipts and Disbursements

19—8

	January to March	*April to June*	*July to September*	*October to December*
Cash at beginning of quarter	$ 5,500	$ 2,100	$ 1,050	$ 6,800
Add:				
Cash sales	12,400	10,200	16,850	20,100
Collections of receivables	20,100	15,700	16,800	18,600
Interest received	200	100	200	400
Other	1,100	900	1,200	1,500
	39,300	29,000	36,100	47,400
Deduct:				
Expenses paid	19,600	10,950	12,650	16,000
Payment of payables	14,100	12,300	11,750	18,000
Interest paid	2,000	3,700	3,700	400
Repayment of bank loan	—	—	—	10,000
Other payments	1,500	1,000	1,200	1,200
	37,200	27,950	29,300	45,600
Cash at end of quarter	$ 2,100	$ 1,050	$ 6,800	$ 1,800

The special-purpose report in Illustration 5-2 is prepared on a *cash* basis (rather than on the accrual basis described in Chapter 4), and could be for a *future* period (instead of for the past, which is usually used in such reports). Special-purpose reports, other than the one in Illustration 5-2, may be audited (to be discussed shortly) or not, and be based on generally accepted accounting principles (GAAP) or not. By their nature such special purpose reports are specifically tailored to fit the situation and needs of the users of the report.

Bankruptcy and Losses

Bankruptcy legislation and practices are quite complex. Nevertheless, some comments have to be made about this subject because the newspapers frequently contain references to bankruptcy, and from time to time we encounter bankrupt firms. The two basic situations that exist might be called 1. private, and 2. public bankruptcy.

A *private* circumstance arises when a creditor (such as a mortgage company) has loaned money to a company, and the company has signed documentation that details procedures that will be followed if mortgage payments are not made when due. Generally, the documentation calls for appointment of a *receiver* and manager (and sometimes an agent). The receiver's task is to assess whether the creditor would be better off by *liquidating* (selling) the company's assets, or by continuing to operate the company. The latter would occur if the company is basically sound, but has encountered temporary liquidity problems, i.e., a shortage of cash and potential creditors. The receiver manages the business until the company is healthy, or has been liquidated. Sometimes, the receiver has to seek support from a provincial Supreme Court if owners of the company do not cooperate with the receiver/manager.

A *public* bankruptcy is one that is governed by the provisions of the *Bankruptcy Act*. There are three main variations of a public bankruptcy: 1. an assignment; 2. a petition, and 3. a proposal. An *assignment* occurs when a person/company admits to being bankrupt, i.e., unable to pay debts as they come due. They then turn their assets over to creditors, in accordance with the provisions in the *Bankruptcy Act*. A *trustee in bankruptcy* (often a chartered accountant) is then appointed to try to resolve the problems and arrange for payments to creditors.

A *petition* is a request to the court, by a creditor, to have a firm declared bankrupt. The usual situation is that the creditors are owed more than $1,000 and the company does not make its payments, in spite of having been requested to do so on several occasions. The court will decide whether evidence exists to have the company declared bankrupt. If so, a trustee in bankruptcy will be appointed. The trustee would perform essentially the same function as for an assignment.

A *proposal* to creditors would be made by the company, in order to try to head off a possible petition by creditors. The proposal might offer creditors one of a variety of possibilities, such as full payment, if they delay their demands for six months, or a year. A preliminary proposal may be drafted by what is called an *interim receiver*—who is quite different from a receiver. The interim receiver tries to ascertain what payments can be made to creditors, and at what times, so that the company can continue to operate successfully. A trustee in bankruptcy would be appointed by the court to administer the conditions set forth in the proposal. The existence of a trustee provides a degree of assurance that, to the extent possible, cash liquidity will be monitored.

Bankruptcy legislation tends to provide for three different types of creditors, each having different rights: 1. secured, 2. preferred, and 3. unsecured. A *secured* creditor is someone who lends money but also registers a legal claim against a particular asset or specified assets. A mortgage company would hold a mortgage against property, and therefore be called a secured creditor. In the event of a private bankruptcy, a trustee could be empowered to sell the specified property, and pay off the mortgage company with the proceeds of sale. If any funds are left over they would be used to pay off the other creditors. If there are insufficient funds to pay the mortgage in full, the mortgage company becomes an unsecured creditor. For example, the property could be sold for $120,000 and the mortgage liability could be for $135,000. The mortgage company gets the $120,000, and becomes an unsecured creditor for $15,000. (The mortgage company probably then would petition to the court to have the company declared bankrupt.)

Preferred creditors are named in bankruptcy legislation, and tend to be restricted to employees, governments, landlords and those having a claim that is ranked secondary to secured creditors, but is in advance of unsecured creditors. That is, secured creditors tend to get paid first, followed by preferred, then by unsecured. If any money is left over after selling the company's assets and paying all creditors, the funds would go to shareholders.

Unsecured creditors are those not fitting the secured and preferred categories. Accounts payable would tend to be owing to unsecured creditors. These people would not have registered any specific, legal claim against an asset. They hope that, in the event of a private bankruptcy, the assets would sell for a high enough figure that all creditors would be paid in full.

In summary, it is important in a bankruptcy whether a person is a secured, preferred or unsecured creditor. Most banks tend to take steps, when they loan money, to become secured creditors. To be useful to creditors, financial statements therefore ought to indicate whether secured creditors (and secured assets) exist. This may be done through a note to the financial statements.

It is important to distinguish between bankruptcy and profitability. A profitable company (one with income) can become bankrupt. In contrast, a company that incurs losses for a few years may avoid becoming bankrupt.

Suppose, for instance, that a company is profitable, but is unable to make payments on its mortgage liability because it lacks cash. (Maybe the company is a farm and many of its assets consist of a growing crop that is not yet matured and ready for sale; or, sales for a retail store could be slow and many of the assets in the form of an inventory of Christmas merchandise, equipment or buildings.) The secured mortgage creditor could legally seize any "secured assets"—such as farm property and equipment, or the building in which the store is located—and eventually sell them at an auction so as to pay off the mortgage. Obviously, lacking the building and equipment that was sold at the auction, the retail store quite likely would now become unprofitable and go bankrupt because it would not be able to readily display its merchandise for sale. It may try renting a store and equipment, but potential landlords may want cash payment—something that the store does not have.

In contrast, a company that has a considerable common-share investment and plenty of cash could incur small losses for several years. Its balance sheet may look like Illustration 5-3. As long as it is able to pay its debts as they come due, creditors could not force the company into bankruptcy. The secret of survival is a combination of liquidity *and* having a solid shareholders' equity investment to withstand adversity. Many small businesses that go bankrupt have insufficient shareholders' investment to withstand unforeseen problems, such as a recession or management mistakes.

In Illustration 5-3, observe two points. First, an accumulation of losses (that is, *negative* retained earnings) is shown on the right-hand side of the balance sheet as a deduction from the common shares investment, and is called a *deficit*. The net shareholders' equity is therefore $134,800. Second, accountants often try to compute subtotals for categories of balance-sheet accounts. In the case of shareholders' equity, we have used two rows of figures on the right-hand side of the balance sheet. By doing this, we permit the reader to see quickly that both "common shares" and "deficit" are part of shareholders' equity.

ILLUSTRATION 5-3

Company Having Losses To Date

NAME
Balance Sheet
Date

Assets		*Liabilities and Owners' Equity*		
Cash	$ 64,000	Liabilities:		
Accounts receivable	26,000	Accounts payable		$ 25,200
Inventory	70,000	Shareholders' equity:		
		Common shares	$200,000	
		Deficit	(65,200)	134,800
	$160,000			$160,000

Role of Auditors

We noted previously that the standard of living of Canadians is dependent upon many factors. One is having what is called a "capital market" system that permits the accumulation of the large sums needed to "harvest" forests, and oil and gas ventures, and to build Canadian factories, mines, and other industries. Individual Canadians somehow must be allowed to safely acquire an ownership interest in large businesses. They must be able to invest their savings in the common shares of certain Canadian companies without taking needless risks (of loss of their capital investment).

The measurement and separation of income from capital investment, and the disclosure of changes in a corporation's liquidity (cash and near-cash assets) prove helpful in informing investors about the status of their investment in common shares of businesses. Most investors learn about capital, income, and liquidity changes by examining a company's financial statements.

Who is responsible for preparing a corporation's financial statements? Generally, *officers* (president, vice-presidents, controllers) prepare the statements and the *board of directors* approves the release of the financial statements to the public.

The board of directors, in accordance with corporate law, is voted into its position of power once a year by the common or voting shareholders (owners) of the limited company, or corporation. The board of directors then appoints or hires officers to operate the company on a daily basis. The board of directors may meet only once a month, or less, to check on the actions of the officers, who are often referred to as *management.*

In effect, therefore, management prepares financial statements on the results of actions that it has taken. The managers and board of directors are "stewards" that are reporting to shareholders, in accordance with corporate law. This type of financial accounting is often called *stewardship reporting.* (This subject will be dealt with in later chapters.)

As management and the board of directors are responsible totally for stewardship reporting, there are opportunities for misinformation, if not collusion. As we mentioned previously, accountants have devised a system of measurement and disclosure called "generally accepted accounting principles", (GAAP), in order to discourage this type of unprofessional conduct. The main problem with Canadian GAAP, as it exists in the l980s, is that many alternatives exist for reporting seemingly *identical* transactions. For example, Company *A* could choose one of the possible GAAP accounting methods that results in *double* the profit as is shown by Company *B* for the very *same* transaction. (This point will become clearer in succeeding chapters.)

Can auditors prevent a company's management from presenting a less-than-"fair" picture of the state of a company? Before we try to answer, it is first necessary to explain what auditors do, and to note that many Canadian firms do not have auditors.

Canadian corporate law states that under some circumstances (to be discussed shortly) auditors are to be appointed annually. *In theory*, according to corporate law, shareholders or owners appoint the auditors at each annual meeting of shareholders. That is, corporate law requires that an annual meeting of shareholders be held and that the shareholders receive financial statements for the year just completed. The shareholders are also required to choose auditors for the coming or current year.

Often, for large corporations with many shareholders, the board of directors or management suggests that a particular auditor be appointed. Few people tend to attend the shareholders' annual meeting. Therefore, *in practice*, management, or the board of directors, tends to choose the auditor that it prefers. This point is very important for it explains many aspects of financial reporting.

The auditor's job is to examine the financial statements that have been *prepared by management*. Auditors who are members of the provincial Institutes/Ordre of Chartered Accountants, (CA), are required to audit in accordance with what are called GAAS—generally accepted auditing standards. Generally speaking, GAAS sets out broad steps that the auditor ought to follow in checking the company's accounting system and its financial statements.

Corporate law in Canada tends to separate companies that are owned by a few friends or family members (*private* companies) from those where the general public—unrelated people/strangers—are the owners (*public* companies). Private companies *may* not need auditors when the owners and management are the same people. There are situations where outsiders, however, such as creditors, may not be willing to loan funds to private companies unless they see a set of audited financial statements. Fortunately, most bankers for small businesses tend to be willing to accept unaudited statements; but they often prefer to see them prepared in accordance with Canadian GAAP. (Each country tends to have its own version of GAAP. There are many differences, for example, between Canadian GAAP and U.S. GAAP.)

Private companies that are large may be required to have an audit. The definition of "large" differs from province to province, and from the federal legislation, e.g., *Canada Business Corporations Act*. This *Act* defines large in terms of a company with $10 million of revenue per year, or assets in excess of $5 million. Sometimes, these large companies can avoid having an audit if all shareholders agree in writing that it is not needed, *and* the government approves the company's request to avoid an audit.

Public companies generally have to have a GAAP audit. The level of competence of the auditor, however, differs from province to province. Some provinces require auditors to be licensed; others do not. The picture is continually changing or is under review. Therefore, it is not possible to be more specific.

The point is that an audit may *not* provide the necessary protection, for these reasons:

1. There can be vast differences in who may audit, and how competent the auditors are.

2. Generally-speaking, auditors do not check the books (invoices or "bills", journals, ledgers) in a way that is certain to uncover fraud.

3. Usually, the auditor's role is restricted to saying whether:

   A. GAAP has been consistently applied from this year to prior ones, and

   B. the financial statements are "fair in accordance with GAAP".

This second clause is very important. The auditor is *not* saying that the financial statements are "fair", or that they "fairly" depict the company's financial position (balance sheet) and results of operations (income statement).

The phrase "in accordance with GAAP" simply means that the managers/board of directors have prepared the financial statements using GAAP principles and policies. However, GAAP may permit *any one* of six or more methods for recording the effects of one specific transaction. This can result in quite different income figures for the financial period. All that the auditor says is: Yes, the company has used a method that is on the list of acceptable Canadian GAAP.

The auditor is *not* saying that the GAAP selected is the best one under the circumstances. It is management and/or the board of directors, not the auditor, who chooses the GAAP. The auditor's reference to "fair" is always qualified or softened by the phrase "in accordance with generally accepted accounting principles".

In summary:

1. Not all companies are required to have an audit.

2. Often, in practice, the auditor is appointed by management, not by the owners (shareholders).

3. The competence of auditors can vary from province to province.

4. Management prepares its own financial statements, using the GAAP that it prefers. (Management must, however, apply GAAP consistently from year to year, or describe what departures from consistency have occurred.) For some situations, accounting principles other than GAAP may be selected, and what is called "a disclosed basis of accounting" may be used. (This is described later.)

5. Auditors do not actively seek out fraud. Nor do they have the power to force a company to choose the best GAAP for its circumstances.

6. Auditors are required under most (but not all) corporate legislation to state whether the financial statements are prepared "fairly in accordance with GAAP". This is quite different from saying that the financial statements are "fair". Financial statements are used by many different groups. What is fair to one group may not be fair to another group.

This section on the "Role of Auditors" is vital in indicating why we have to place much stress on *variability* and differences in accounting. There is *no* "one basic way of accounting": Financial statements will be *badly misinterpreted* if we believe that such is the case. (Appendix 1-A shows an auditors' report.)

We have purposely fitted the discussion of bankruptcy, liquidity, and auditors into the early chapters of the book. These discussions highlight some of the realities of financial accounting. Our grasp of these realities has to be fitted to Canadian laws and business practices.

Problem: Liquidity Evaluated

This problem attempts to attach numbers to the preceding discussions about liquidity and profitability. It can also serve as another practice problem in journalizing, posting to ledgers, and preparing financial statements. Suppose that the following occurred:

December 19—7:   Blanche Corporation was incorporated. The sum of $10,000 was placed in the company's bank account, and the owners received common shares.

December 31, 19—7:   First year end of the company; no other transactions occurred in 19—7. The balance sheet shows cash of $10,000 and common shares of $10,000.

During the calendar year 19—8, the following transactions occurred:

1. Machinery and equipment were purchased for $9,000. The sum of $6,000 was paid in 19—8 and the balance is due in 19—9.

2. Inventory costing $9,900 was acquired in 19—8. Cash of $3,800 was paid and the balance is due in 19—9.

3. Inventory costing $7,900 was sold for $15,000. Cash of $3,000 was received in 19—8, and the balance is due in 19—9.

4. Selling expenses of $1,600 and administrative (office) expenses of $1,500 were paid in cash in 19—8.

5. Depreciation expense of $3,000 was recorded in 19—8.

The ledger accounts would show:

Cash			
19—7	10,000	19—8 (a)	6,000
19—8 (c)	3,000	19—8 (b)	3,800
		19—8 (d)	1,600
		19—8 (d)	1,500
Subtotal	100		

Accounts Receivable			
19—8 (c)	12,000		
Subtotal	12,000		

Inventory			
19—8 (b)	9,900	19—8 (c)	7,900
Subtotal	2,000		

Machinery and Equipment		
19—8 (a)	9,000	

Accumulated Depreciation – Machinery and Equipment		
	19—8 (e)	3,000

Accounts Payable		
	19—8 (a)	3,000
	19—8 (b)	6,100
	Subtotal	9,100

Common Shares		
	19—7	10,000

Retained Earnings

Sales Revenue		
	19—8 (c)	15,000

Cost of Goods Sold		
19—8 (c)	7,900	

Selling Expense		
19—8 (d)	1,600	

Administrative Expense		
19—8 (d)	1,500	

Depreciation Expense		
19—8 (e)	3,000	

The financial statements are:

BLANCHE CORPORATION
Balance Sheet
December 31, 19—8

Assets

Current assets:		
Cash		$ 100
Accounts receivable		12,000
Inventory		2,000
		14,100
Long-lived assets:		
Machinery and equipment	$ 9,000	
Accumulated depreciation	3,000	6,000
		$20,100

Liabilities and Owners' Equity

Current liabilities:		
Accounts payable		$ 9,100
Owners' equity:		
Common shares	$10,000	
Retained earnings	1,000	11,000
		$20,100

BLANCHE CORPORATION
Income Statement
Year ended December 31, 19—8

Sales revenue		$15,000
Cost of goods sold		7,900
Gross profit		7,100
Expenses:		
Selling	$ 1,600	
Administrative	1,500	
Depreciation	3,000	6,100
Net income		$ 1,000

BLANCHE CORPORATION
Statement of Retained Earnings
Year ended December 31, 19—8

Balance, December 31, 19—7	$ 0
Add net income for 19—8	1,000
Balance, December 31, 19—8	$ 1,000

What has happened to the company from November 31, 19—7 to December 31, 19—8?

1. The cash has dropped from $10,000 (on incorporation) to $100. (Is the company in danger of going bankrupt?) What happened to the cash?

2. The company has a net profit of $1,000 on an investment of $10,000. This is equivalent to 10 percent ($1,000 divided by $10,000). The 10 percent is referred to technically as a *"return on investment* of 10 percent". The income or, return *on* capital, is $1,000, and the investment is $10,000. (See Chapter 2, "Capital and Income".) Note that this is *not* saying the same as: I received $1,000 cash interest on my bank balance of $10,000. Why?

    A. The common shares are *not* cash, nor is retained earnings equal to cash. (The "owners' equity" is the balancing figure in the balance-sheet equation. The actual equity, if the company were sold or liquidated, could be much higher or lower than $10,000.)

    B. Individual assets may be sold for much more, or much less, than the sums shown on a balance sheet. Thus, the income figure of $1,000 is not a cash figure.

What, then, does the 10 percent figure tell us? Have we sacrificed liquidity in order to improve the profitability and return on investment?

There are no simple answers to the questions posed above. We can, however, perform more analyses than have been illustrated so far in this book. Our aim is to try to "guess" intelligently, based on the *past,* whether Blanche Corporation is in reasonable financial shape. Is it likely to be able to pay its debts next year *if:*

1. the sales and expenses in 19—9 are similar to those in 19—8?, and

2. the due dates of receivables and payables are spread fairly evenly throughout 19—9?

In brief, when we think about "paying debts when they are due", we are referring to the liquidity aspect of a business. There are *several* ways of evaluating liquidity. At this point, we will initially look at *just two* measures of liquidity:

1. Cash

2. Cash and near cash, i.e., cash and receivables less payables that will likely affect the cash balance in the near future.

ANALYSIS OF THE CASH LEDGER ACCOUNT

The measurement of changes in liquidity may be illustrated in different ways. We need to proceed slowly through the cash transactions. We will start with an analysis of the cash ledger account, and then try to prove the figure through subsequent analysis. Next, we will link the results to our discussions of liquidity and bankruptcy.

A statement of cash consumed by operations for the Blanche Corporation example would look like this:

BLANCHE CORPORATION
Statement of Cash Funds Consumed by Operations
Year ended December 31, 19—8

Receipts:
  Cash collections from customers:
  (i.e., sales revenue of $15,000
    less   closing   accounts
    receivable
    of $12,000) $3,000(c)★
Disbursements:
  Cash payments for
    selling expenses $1,600 (d)★
  Cash payments for
    administrative expenses $1,500 (d)★
  Cash payments to suppliers
    of goods:
    Purchased on account:
      Cost of goods sold $7,900
      Add closing inventory   2,000
    Total purchased   9,900
    Sum still unpaid (closing
      accounts payable)   6,100   3,800 (b)★   6,900
Cash funds consumed by operations $3,900

★These are cross references to the journal entries in the cash ledger account.

Now that we have ascertained the figure for cash consumed by operations, we may take another step, and prepare a statement that shows why cash decreased by $9,900.

BLANCHE CORPORATION
Statement of Cash Funds Flow
Year ended December 31, 19—8

Uses of cash:
  Consumed by operations $3,900
  Downpayment made on machinery and equipment (cost of $9,000) 6,000 (a)★
Net decrease in cash funds ($10,000 − $100) $9,900

★See coding in cash ledger account.
  (This type of statement receives much greater attention in Chapter 16.)

One of the statement's purposes is to help us to monitor changes during a period, and thereby assist in the prediction of possible unfavorable liquidity trends. We must now work toward finding sensible applications for the statements of "cash from operations" and "cash funds flow".

CASH LIQUIDITY

If the income statement in 19—9 is exactly the same as it was in 19—8, what effect will there be on the cash ledger account? When we answer this question, we will be able, for the most part, to evaluate the company's liquidity status and prospects.

To reach an "answer", however, we have to make a few assumptions: that the 1. accounts receivable, 2. accounts payable, and 3. inventory balances at December 31, 19—9 will be the same as at December 31, 19—8. (If the assumptions are not reasonable, we can make the necessary alterations to our "answer" later in our analysis.)

Once we make the above assumptions, we, *in effect*, are saying that 1. revenue, 2. cost of goods sold, 3. selling expense, and 4. administrative expense are received in, or paid by, *cash*. It is *extremely important* that we fully understand this principle. We will give two illustrations to help us to increase our understanding of the relationship between cash and accrual accounting.

1. Revenue:

Accounts receivable, December 31, 19—8	$12,000
Accounts receivable, December 31, 19—9	
(assumed to the same)	12,000
Revenue (assumed to be the same as 19—8)	15,000

Under the foregoing, how much cash would be received?

There are many ways of computing the amount of cash that would be received. Two are:

		Cash Received
Method (i):	All of the accounts receivable at December 31, 19—8 are collected in cash.	$12,000
	If the accounts receivable at December 31, 19—9 is $12,000, then $12,000 of the $15,000 19—9 revenue would be sold on account. This means that only $3,000 of the $15,000 would be received in cash.	3,000
	Total cash received in 19—9	$15,000

		Cash Received
Method (ii):	None of the accounts receivable at December 31, 19—8 is collected in 19—9. (This is unrealistic, but it is a way of doing the arithmetic.)	0
	If none of the accounts receivable is collected, and the ending balance equals the opening balance, it follows that all of the 19—9 revenue was received in cash.	15,000
	Total cash received in 19—9	$15,000

2. *Cost of goods sold:*

This computation is more difficult than revenue because we have to deal with three ledger accounts: cost of goods sold, inventory, and accounts payable. (We are assuming for simplicity that accounts payable is used solely for inventory that is purchased on account.) Again, there are *many* methods of ascertaining how much cash would have to be disbursed if inventory and accounts payable balances are unchanged during the year, and cost of goods sold is $7,900.

		Cash Paid
Method A:	We could assume that none of the opening (December 31, 19—8) accounts payable is paid. If so, all inventory must have been acquired for cash.	
	But, how much was acquired for cash? If the beginning and ending inventory balance is unchanged, then the amount of inventory acquired must be equal to cost of goods sold.	
	Hence, cash paid must be	7,900
	Total cash paid for cost of goods sold	$7,900

		Cash Paid
Method B:	We could assume that $6,000 of the opening (December 31, 19—8) accounts payable is paid. This would leave $3,100 unpaid.★ (Note that the $6,000 is a random figure.)	$6,000
	If the inventory balance is unchanged during the year, then $7,900 of inventory must have been purchased, because $7,900, at cost, was sold.	
	How much of the $7,900 required a cash payment?	
	We know that the ending balance of accounts payable is in the ledger account after the $6,000 is paid. To get to $9,100★ from $3,100★ another $6,000 must have been credited to accounts payable. Thus, of the $7,900 of inventory that was bought, only $1,900 must have been bought for cash	1,900
		$7,900

★In this illustration, assume that no payments were made on the $3,000 of accounts payable that relate to machinery and equipment. Alternatively, assume that the whole sum of accounts payable relates to inventory only.

Method (B) seems, on first impression, to be needlessly confusing. Why use (B) when you can use (A)? It illustrates a point: When account balances *change* during the year, which is usually the case, we will not be able to use Method (A).

Method (B) becomes easier to understand if we use journal entries and ledger accounts:

a. Accounts payable   6,000
   Cash   6,000

b. Cost of goods sold   7,900
   Inventory   7,900

c. Inventory   7,900
   ?   ?

Entry (b) seems somewhat out of place. That is, we are selling inventory that we do not have. Assume, however, that entries (b) and (c) occur simultaneously. To find out what goes in the credit in (c) to replace the ?, let us look at the ledger accounts.

Inventory			
12-31—8	2,000		
		(b)	7,900
(c)	7,900		
Assumed			
12-31-—9	2,000		

Accounts Payable			
		12-31—8	9,100
(a)	6,000		
		Subtotal	3,100
		(c)	6,000
		Assumed	
		12-31-—9	9,100

Cost of Goods Sold		
(b)	7,900	
Assumed		
for 19—9	7,900	

Cash			
★	(a)	6,000	
	(c)	1,900	
	Subtotal	7,900	

*Ignore opening balance of $100; it is not relevant to our analysis.

To balance, the credits for entry (c) would have to be:
Accounts payable $6,000
Cash   1,900
                   $7,900

That is, for:

Accounts payable $6,000 + $3,100 equals the required sum of $9,100.
Cash $1,900 is needed to balance entry (c).

Hence, entry (c) is:

Inventory	7,900	
Accounts payable		6,000
Cash		1,900

Overall, the *effect on cash* was to reduce it by $7,900, i.e., entry (a) amounts to $6,000 and the cash effect in entry (b) is $1,900.

3. Selling and administrative expenses:

In view of the assumptions that we made in designing the Blanche Corporation illustration, *all* the selling and administrative expenses would have to have been paid in cash. That is, the non-cash current assets and liabilities (accounts receivable, inventory, and accounts payable) were *assumed* by us to relate strictly to the revenue and cost of goods sold transactions. Thus, through a process of elimination, we must assume that the selling expense of $1,600 and the administrative expense of $1,500 were *paid in cash*. Hence, cash was reduced by a total of $3,100.

4. Depreciation expense:

Unlike the revenue, cost of goods sold, and selling/administrative expenses, depreciation expense does not involve cash. The journal entry (debit depreciation expense, credit asset or asset contra account called "accumulated depreciation") is *made to measure income*, in accrual accounting. Such non-cash entries as this (and we will see many more of them) tend to *obscure liquidity changes*.

5. Overall effect:

It is important to recall that we are trying to evaluate the evolving *liquidity position* of Blanche Corporation as 19—9 unfolds. To simplify matters, we have made the assumption that 19—9's income statement transactions will be the same as that of 19—8. Under this *simplifying assumption*, we have calculated that the effect of the 19—9 income transactions on cash will be:

	Decrease Cash	Increase Cash
Revenue		$15,000
Cost of goods sold	$ 7,900	
Selling and administrative expense	3,100	
Depreciation expense	0	
	11,000	15,000
		11,000
Net increase in cash		$ 4,000

The difference between net income of $1,000 and the increase in cash of $4,000 is depreciation expense of $3,000. In a simple illustration such as this, the difference may be obvious; we will find that this is not always the case. Yet, we will see that the *procedure* to relate accrual income to cash will be the *same as we have just outlined;* and we understand more about the *differences between cash effects and accrual income.* Confusion between cash effects and accrual income lies at the heart of much needless controversy in accounting circles.

Overall, what is the significance of an expected increase in cash of $4,000 in 19—9 as compared with a 19—9 income figure of $1,000? As a generalization, we can say that Blanche Corporation will generate $4,000 to help the company improve its *cash liquidity* position by the end of 19—9. Thus, the company will *not* be as illiquid as the $100 cash balance at December 31, 19—8 would seem to indicate.

From a practical point of view, it is important to note in the foregoing illustration that expected changes in net income *should not* be used in forecasting future liquidity. *Accrual income is not cash.* Often, but not always, income trends may well be a very poor predictor of cash-balance trends. The two concepts—cash and accrual income— *must be kept separate* in our minds at all times. Cash changes are used in judging liquidity. Accrual net-income is a profitability measure. Successful managers of businesses keep their eye on both liquidity and profitability.

6. An alternative computation:

Many people who use financial statements in making their assessments about a company's liquidity and profitability employ a short-cut method of computing expected liquidity changes. Instead of working with likely cash receipts and cash disbursements, they work with the non-cash items to arrive at the same answer.

The income statement "equation" is:

Revenue less expenses	= Net income	(a)

An expansion of this is:

Revenue less (cash expenses plus non-cash expenses)	= Net income	(b)

By moving the non-cash expenses to the right-hand side, we get:

Revenue★ − cash expenses	= Net income + non-cash expenses	(c)

★Assumed to be received in cash.

In the foregoing examples, we worked with the *left*-hand side of equation (c). Because so many transactions are involved on the left-hand side, however, some analysts prefer to work with the right-hand side, which has fewer computations. Thus, they would calculate the cash increase of $4,000 by adding net income and non-cash expenses, such as depreciation (see page 149):

Net Income	$1,000
Depreciation	3,000
	$4,000

The figure of $4,000 for Blanche Corporation for 19—9 (or 19—8) is called *funds from operations*. This is an important term to remember. We should also remember that the "net income plus depreciation" approach to calculating *funds from operations* is no more than a computation method. Neither net income, nor depreciation, involve a flow of funds. We must not confuse the method of calculation with the flow of cash, or funds. Such confusion is serious because liquidity and profitability get mixed up, leading to additional confusion of cash and accrual-income accounting.

NEAR-CASH LIQUIDITY

One of the major, repeating themes of this book is that we must focus on "what fits where". All-purpose "truths" do not exist in the majority of accounting situations. We have to know which techniques or procedures are available to us, and which one makes the most sense for a particular situation. For instance, when does cash accounting usefully apply, and when ought we to use accrual accounting?

Our present theme is that liquidity can be measured in different ways. If a creditor is demanding cash today, *cash* liquidity (rather than near-cash liquidity) is important. In contrast, if we are looking at longer-run liquidity, short-term receivables and payables, i.e., those which involve cash receipts and payments in the next 30-60-90 days, are close in time to cash. Hence, we can use a "near-cash" liquidity concept, which may include a net pool of funds represented by "cash plus current receivables, less current payables".

The liquidity-pool approach has the benefit of offsetting the effects of temporary delays in the receipt or payment of cash. That is, on December 31, 19—8, a company's cash balance may be $1,000. A receivable of $150,000 may be collected on January 2, 19—9, however. Which is the better measure of liquidity when receivables and payables balances are fluctuating rapidly? A liquidity pool that includes "cash plus current receivables less current payables" does *not* change when a receivable is collected or cash is paid. Thus, given the *facts* of the situation, and our *objective* or purpose of looking at longer-term liquidity, the near-cash liquidity pool concept seems useful to us.

For example, suppose that the following exists at December 31, 19—8:

Cash	$ 1,000
Accounts receivable	150,000
Accounts payable	(60,000)
Near-cash liquidity-pool balance	$ 91,000

If, on January 2, 19—9, the receivable is collected in full, the pool is made up of:

Cash	$151,000
Accounts payable	(60,000)
Near-cash liquidity-pool balance	$ 91,000

Over the three day period, near-cash liquidity has not changed but cash has changed dramatically.

Let us return to the Blanche Corporation example. The question posed after reading the company's financial statements for 19—8 was: Is the company in danger of going bankrupt? Our general response was: It depends on what is likely to happen in 19—9. Will revenue, cost of goods sold, selling and administrative expenses in 19—9 be similar to those in 19—8?

Suppose that our answer is: Yes, 19—9, will be the same as 19—8 even to the point of having the same end-of-year balances for receivables, inventory, and payables. We saw, from the computations under "cash liquidity", that cash improved by $4,000. Blanche Corporation would therefore *not* go bankrupt—unless it used the $4,000 and more dollars, which it may have borrowed, to buy something relatively illiquid, such as a building (which took months to re-sell, and may have resulted in a large loss on sale).

In evaluating the liquidity prospects for Blanche Corporation, does a cash liquidity or a near-cash liquidity concept make the more sense? *Either makes sense* in the unusual situation that was posed—where receivables, inventory, and payables balances are *unchanged* in the 19—9 year. Both liquidity pools:

1. Cash, and

2. Cash plus receivables, less payables
   would increase by $4,000.

Funds from operations for 19—8 and 19—9 are also $4,000, using the assumptions that we made for Blanche Corporation. But, what happens when we relax the assumptions and consider the usual situation where the amounts of receivables, inventories, and payables change during a period? In general, what happens is:

1. Funds from operations (as we have calculated it using either of the two methods that were previously shown) would *not* be the same as the change in cash.

2. Accordingly, some type of near-cash concept of liquidity would tend to make more sense because, owing to the fluctuating balances, cash changes would differ from funds from operations. And, "funds from operations" tends to be more useful to us because it can provide a longer-term perspective *whenever the past also tends to occur in the future.*

As we have seen from previous illustrations, the change in cash is subject to wide variation simply because a cash receipt or cash disbursement has been delayed a day or two. For a *longer-term viewpoint,* we thus have to smooth out these minor variations by using one of the near-cash definitions of liquidity, such as one that gives us the same, or roughly the same, result that we get when we compute funds from operations.

To illustrate, assume the following for Gibbins Corporation:

Balance Sheet

	June 30 19—8	June 30 19—7
Assets		
Current:		
Cash	$ 8,200	$ 200
Accounts receivable	3,180	5,920
Inventory	4,200	6,850
	15,580	12,970
Long-lived:		
Equipment	20,000	20,000
Accumulated depreciation	4,500	3,000
	15,500	17,000
	$31,080	$29,970
Liabilities and Owners' Equity		
Current:		
Accounts payable	$ 4,800	$ 2,340
Owners' equity:		
Common shares	20,000	20,000
Retained earnings	6,280	7,630
	26,280	27,630
	$31,080	$29,970

Income Statement
Year ended June 30, 19—8

Revenue		$20,000
Cost of goods sold		12,950
Gross profit		7,050
Expenses:		
Selling	$4,100	
Administrative	2,800	
Depreciation	1,500	8,400
Loss for the year		$ 1,350

The cash balance in Gibbins Corporation has increased significantly during the 19—8 year from $200 to $8,200. (Incidentally, note that we used the term "19—8 year" because the year *ended* in 19—8. This is normal, practical terminology.) Does this increase indicate that the corporation is quite liquid, and that there is no need to be concerned with possible bankruptcy?

When we look at the income statement, we see not a profit but a loss for the year. Why are we getting these mixed signals—a cash liquidity signal that indicates a strong position and a profitability signal that indicates a weak position? The reasons for the difference are:

1. Liquidity and profitability are two, *different* concepts, or measurements.

2. The *cash* measure of liquidity is an extreme in this particular situation, where the receivables, inventory, and payables balances have changed significantly during the year.

When we adopt a *different one* of the near-cash definitions of liquidity, i.e., one that includes inventory, we get a picture closer to that conveyed by the profitability result:

	June 30, 19—8	June 30, 19—7
Cash	$ 8,200	$ 200
Accounts receivable	3,180	5,920
Inventory	4,200	6,850
	15,580	12,970
Less accounts payable	4,800	2,340
Liquidity pool (near-cash accounts)	$10,780	$10,630

That is, Gibbins Corporation has had a *marginal improvement* of $150 ($10,780 less $10,630) in near-cash liquidity. (One of the near-cash liquidity definitions was chosen because it offset the temporary effects on cash from early, or late, receipt or payment of receivables and payables—including payables relating to inventory.)

How does the $150 compare to funds generated from operations? Using what may be called the "backward" way of computing *funds from operations,* we arrive at:

Loss for the year	$(1,350)
Add depreciation (i.e., depreciation expense caused the company to have a loss, but did not affect the amounts making up near-cash liquidity)	1,500
Funds from operations	$ 150

Note that we get the same result when we use the "forward" approach:

	−	+
Revenue		$20,000
Cost of goods sold	$12,950	
Selling	4,100	
Administrative	2,800	19,850
Funds from operations		$ 150

The reason that funds from operations and our selected near-cash definition of liquidity show the *same* result, i.e., a plus figure of $150, is that:

Except for depreciation expense, all the transactions that affected the income statement also affected the accounts included in our selected near-cash definition of funds. For instance, revenue increased as a result of debits to cash or to receivables. Cost of goods sold increased through debits or credits to inventory, accounts payable, and cash. Selling and administrative expense increased by decreasing cash.

Examples in later chapters will show how funds from operations are *not* the same as the change in near-cash liquidity. This occurs because cash and similar current accounts are affected by buying more equipment, or by selling common shares, or by paying dividends, or by engaging in other transactions that affect the *non*-current accounts on the balance sheet.

Given the foregoing, what is our conclusion about the prospects for Gibbins Corporation? The company generated a loss in 19—8, but only some good forecasting will tell us whether or not this situation will continue. If a loss continues but *funds from operations still give a positive number,* the company could survive for many years—until it has to replace its long-lived equipment. In the future, it may not have the cash *or* the ability to borrow. (A creditor looks at the longer-term prospects of a company before lending money. As of 19—8, the lack of profitability of Gibbins Corporation is a concern, and may very well discourage many potential creditors and investors.)

Summary

Both liquidity and profitability have to be monitored in companies. There are several different concepts of both liquidity and profitability. Much of this chapter has looked at a few of the liquidity measures. At this point in the book, we have reached some tentative conclusions:

1. Cash is a useful measure of *immediate* liquidity, but has potentially severe limitations caused by fluctuating payments and receipts affecting payables and receivables.

2. Funds from operations is a useful indication of the near-cash that is available over several months, perhaps to spend on non-current assets. This measure would *not*, however, be very useful in predicting liquidity trends if the future bears little relation to the past. (This is because we usually calculate funds from operations after the period has been completed.)

3. A company having a net loss but positive funds from operations could continue in existence for many years. (That is, the net loss is being caused by non-cash depreciation; hence, near-cash is still being generated by operating the company.)

4. We cannot allow ourselves to think only in terms of accrual income—a subject that tends to absorb much time in introductory financial accounting. Liquidity is especially vital in small businesses; but it is a major concern of all organizations when the economy turns to a recession, or interest rates become high, requiring greater cash to pay interest on bank loans.

QUESTIONS

5-1 Explain the term liquidity.

5-2 Why is it necessary that small companies maintain a reasonable balance between liquidity and profitability?

5-3 Explain the term bankruptcy.

5-4 Illustrate a special purpose report titled Schedule of Cash Receipts and Disbursements.

5-5 Distinguish the following terms in the *Bankruptcy Act:* an assignment, a petition and a proposal.

5-6 Distinguish the three types of creditors: secured, preferred and unsecured.

5-7 What is the role and what are the responsibilities of auditors?

5-8 Explain the term "fair...in accordance with GAAP."

5-9 Distinguish cash from accrual accounting and explain when each would be appropriate for readers of financial information.

5-10 Explain *funds from operations*. How is it computed?

EXERCISES

E5-1 Assume that a company went bankrupt and the secured creditor and receiver sold the assets for $700,000. The following classes of creditors existed at the date of bankruptcy:

Unsecured	800,000
Preferred	90,000
Secured	500,000

How much would each class of creditor receive if:

A. The assets that are secured were sold for $600,000 (i.e., $100,000 higher than the secured liability) and other assets were sold for $100,000 (for a total of $700,000).

B. The assets that are secured were sold for $400,000 (i.e., $100,000 less than the secured liability).

E5-2 Compute funds from operations for each of the two situations that follow and explain your response:

	Situation A	Situation B
Revenue	$100,000	$100,000
Cost of goods sold	60,000	60,000
Gross profit	40,000	40,000
Expenses:		
Selling	18,000	18,000
Administrative	16,000	16,000
Depreciation	5,000	10,000
	39,000	44,000
Income (loss)	$ 1,000	$ (4,000)

E5-3 Prepare a Schedule of Cash Receipts and Disbursements from the following information:

Cash balance at the beginning of the period	$100,000
Cash balance at the end of the period	?
Interest received in cash	950
Repayment of a bank loan	10,000
Expenses paid in cash	16,200
Collection of accounts receivable	90,000
Payment of accounts payable	60,000
Purchase of equipment for cash	21,000
Cash sales	11,500
Interest paid in cash	3,700
Other cash payments	8,900
Purchase of inventory on account	17,800

E5-4 Explain the benefits and limitations of the following balance sheet presentation:

THORNTON CORPORATION
Balance Sheet
December 31, 19—8

Assets		Liabilities and Owners' Equity	
Current:		Current liabilities:	
Cash	$ 5,000	Accounts payable	$150,000
Accounts receivable	20,000	Other current	
Inventory	75,000	liabilities	40,000
	100,000		190,000
Land	100,000	Long term liability	60,000
Deficit	200,000	Owners' equity:	
		Common shares	150,000
	$400,000		$400,000

E5-5 (Review of Chapters 3, 4 and 5.) Replace the ? with figures that balance the transactions for each of the following *independent* situations. Explain your computations.

Situation A:

Accounts receivable for sales	
—beginning of period	$100,000
—end of period	90,000
Cash sales	68,500
Sales revenue (cash and on account)	500,000
Unearned revenue—beginning of period	15,000
—end of period	12,000
Cash collections of accounts receivable	?

Situation B:

Accounts payable for inventory purchases	
—beginning of period	$ 50,000
—end of period	60,000
Inventory—beginning of period	85,000
—end of period	90,000
Cost of goods sold	400,000
Purchases of inventory for cash	12,500
Cash payments on accounts payable	?

E5-6 Compute *cash consumed by operations* from the following information. Explain your response.

Cash sales	$ 12,200
Accounts receivable for sales	
—beginning of period	0
—end of period	25,000
Total sales	290,000
Accounts payable for inventory purchases	
—beginning of period	0
—end of period	14,000
Inventory—beginning of period	0
—end of period	52,000
Cost of goods sold	180,000
Cash purchases of inventory	0
Cash payments for selling expenses	43,000
Cash payments for administrative expenses	39,200

PROBLEMS

P5-1 For each of situations A to D noted below, compute the amount of cash that each class of creditor would receive, and explain your response. Where applicable indicate how much would be received by common shareholders on liquidation of the business.

	Situation			
	A	B	C	D
Cash received on liquidation of company's assets:				
Assets which are pledged to secured creditors	$ 600,000	$ 600,000	$ 600,000	$ 600,000
Assets which are not pledged to secured creditors	400,000	400,000	400,000	100,000
	1,000,000	1,000,000	1,000,000	700,000
Amount owing to each class of creditor:				
Secured	500,000	700,000	900,000	600,000
Preferred	100,000	100,000	350,000	50,000
Trustee's fees (which can be treated like a preferred creditor)	50,000	50,000	50,000	50,000
Unsecured creditors	250,000	250,000	250,000	250,000
	900,000	1,100,000	1,550,000	950,000
Capital contribution by common shareholders	500,000	500,000	500,000	500,000

P5-2 Replace the ? with figures that balance the transactions. Explain your computations.

Situation A:

Accounts receivable for sales	
—beginning of period	$120,000
—end of period	113,100
Allowance for bad debts	
—beginning of period	16,400
—end of period	17,100
Bad debts expense for the period	?
Accounts written off (debit allowance for bad debts;	
credit accounts receivable)	3,000
Cash sales	19,200
Sales revenue for period	500,000
Unearned revenue—beginning of period	30,000
—end of period	18,000
Cash collections of accounts receivable	?
Cash received and credited to unearned revenue	0

Situation B:

Accounts payable for inventory purchases	
—beginning of period	$?
—end of period	37,800
Inventory—beginning of period	80,000
—end of period	85,000
Cost of goods sold	495,000
Purchases of inventory for cash	11,000
Cash payments on accounts payable	483,200
Inventory withdrawal by owner (i.e., debit proprietor's capital)	2,000

P5-3 Compute "cash generated by operations" from the following information, and replace the ? with figures that balance the transactions:

Unearned revenue—beginning of period	$ 8,500
—end of period	7,000
Cash received and credited to unearned revenue	14,000
Cash sales	12,200
Cash collected from accounts receivable	?
Accounts receivable for sales	
—beginning of period	110,000
—end of period	135,000
Total sales revenue	800,000
Accounts payable for inventory purchases:	
—beginning of period	65,000
—end of period	77,000
Inventory—beginning of period	80,000
—end of period	86,000
Cost of goods sold	560,000
Cash purchases of inventory	15,000
Cash payments for selling expenses	120,000
Cash payments for administrative expenses	80,000
Sales on account	?

Unearned revenue at the beginning of the period that became earned during the period	?
Inventory purchases on account	?
Cash payments on accounts payable	?
Prepaid expenses for administrative expenses:	
—beginning of period	8,000
—end of period	5,200
Cash spent on additional prepaid expenses during the period (i.e., debit prepaid expense)	0
Administrative expenses for the period	?

P5-4 Compute accrual funds from operations for each of the undernoted *unrelated* situations and explain your responses.

	Situation			
Year ended December 31, 19—9	A	B	C	D
Net income (loss)	$150,000	$(72,500)	$(21,700)	$10,000
Depreciation expense	82,000	50,000	50,000	50,000
Bad debts expense (recovery, credited to expense)	11,200	2,100	—	(1,000)

P5-5 Eckel Sales Limited's balance sheet at December 31, 19—8 shows:

Assets		Liabilities and Owners' Equity	
Current assets:		Current liabilities:	
Cash	$ 2,000	Accounts payable	$320,000
Accounts receivable	240,000	Bank loan payable	200,000
Inventory	490,000	Other current	
Prepaid expenses	38,000	liabilities	45,700
	770,000		565,700
		Owners' equity:	
Automobile	19,500	Common shares	200,000
Accumulated		Retained earnings	15,000
depreciation	8,800		
	10,700		215,000
	$780,700		$780,700

The income statement for the year ended December 31, 19—8 shows:

Revenue		$980,000
Cost of goods sold		730,000
Gross profit		250,000
Expenses:		
Selling	$130,500	
Administrative	110,700	
Depreciation	20,000	261,200
Loss		$ 11,200

Required:

A. Is Eckel Sales' financial position liquid or illiquid? Explain your response.

B. Evaluate the general financial position of Eckel Sales.

P5-6 Prepare a Schedule of Cash Receipts and Disbursements for Hanna Corporation from the following information for the year ended October 31, 19—9:

Cash balance, beginning of year	$100,000
Cash balance, end of year	?
Cash sales	32,700
Collection of accounts receivable	217,200
Cash received from a bank loan	105,000
Interest received from bank	3,100
Cash received on sale of land	42,650
Cash expenses paid	106,200
Payment of accounts payable	97,850
Purchase of equipment for cash	86,900
Interest paid to bank	15,770
Purchase of inventory on account	165,200
Cash deposit paid	20,000

EXPLORATION MATERIALS AND CASES

MC5-1 In September 1985, the Canadian government commenced proceedings to wind up the operation of Canadian Commercial Bank (CCB). The CCB had encountered financial difficulties and came close to financial collapse earlier in 1985. The Canadian government intervened in early 1985 and guaranteed some of CCB's debt. However, as the year progressed CCB's financial position did not seem to improve. CCB became the first Canadian bank to fail in many years.

A condensation of the CCB's financial statement for its year ended October 31, 1984 follows:

CANADIAN COMMERCIAL BANK
Consolidated Statement of Assets and Liabilities
October 31, 1984 and 1983

Assets

	(in thousands)	
	1984	1983
Cash resources	$ 251,410	$ 80,150
Securities	272,082	196,248
Loans	2,415,927	2,006,231
Other	147,197	114,644
	$3,086,616	$2,397,273

Liabilities, Capital and Reserves

Liabilities:

	1984	1983
Deposits	$2,838,423	$2,173,958
Other	77,657	84,137
Debentures	49,000	33,800
	2,965,080	2,291,895

Capital and reserves:

	1984	1983
Appropriations for contingencies	16,596	23,947
Shareholders' equity:		
Capital stock	79,148	48,725
Contributed surplus	25,680	25,334
Retained earnings	112	7,372
	121,536	105,378
	$3,086,616	$2,397,273

CANADIAN COMMERCIAL BANK
Consolidated Statement of Income
Years ended October 31, 1984 and 1983

	(in thousands)	
	1984	1983
Interest income	$284,128	$221,587
Interest expense	256,883	191,419
Net interest income	27,245	30,168
Provision for loan losses	14,832	9,024
Net	12,413	21,144
Other income	21,698	24,040
Net interest and other income	34,111	45,184
Non-interest expenses	41,039	36,959
Net income (loss) before income taxes	(6,928)	8,225
Income taxes (recoverable)	(7,732)	1,720
Net income for the year	$ 804	$ 6,505

CANADIAN COMMERCIAL BANK
Consolidated Statement of Appropriations for Contingencies
Years ended October 31, 1984 and 1983

	(in thousands)	
	1984	1983
Balance at beginning of year	$ 23,947	$ 22,430
Changes during year:		
Loss experience	(25,183)	(14,507)
Included in income statement	14,832	9,024
Transfer from retained earnings	3,000	7,000
Balance at end of year	$ 16,596	$ 23,947

CANADIAN COMMERCIAL BANK
Consolidated Statement of Changes in Retained Earnings
Years ended October 31, 1984 and 1983

	(in thousands)	
	1984	1983
Balance at beginning of year	$ 7,372	$ 7,395
Net income for the year	804	6,505
Dividends paid	(4,065)	(2,894)
Transfer to appropriations for contingences, net of tax	(3,000)	(3,556)
Expenses of issuing capital stock	(999)	(78)
Balance at end of year	$ 112	$ 7,372

Required:

Analyze the financial statements of CCB and list indications where CCB appears to be, and does not appear to be, in financial difficulty. Explain your response.

MC5-2 Financial Statements of the Government of Canada: The financial statements prepared by the Government of Canada differ from those compiled in the private sector (such as those for Fiberglas, which are reproduced in Chapter 1). The balance sheet (called a Statement of Assets and Liabilities) shows liabilities, cash and receivables but does not show fixed assets or owners' equity. It is balanced by a large debit amount called "excess of recorded liabilities over net recorded assets". The income statement (called a Statement of Revenue and Expenditure) shows tax and other revenue received in cash during the year less cash expenditures for both expenses and fixed assets, and less some expense accruals. The bottom line is called budgetary deficit (not net income or loss). The Statement of Changes in Financial Position is in abbreviated form and mainly shows changes in long term liabilities. In addition, the activities of some government organizations such as CNR and Air Canada are excluded from the financial statements.

Student A: Who uses the financial statements of the Government of Canada?

Student B: I'm not sure. When the government wants to sell bonds in the world money markets it always tells people what its liabilities are, but no more than this; no financial statements are provided. I guess that some people are concerned about the amount of budgetary deficit and think that the government should try to balance expenditures to the amount of revenues that it collects.

A: Does the budgetary deficit mean the same thing as net income—that is, does it measure some form of success or failure?

B: Not really. Fixed assets are expensed; and there is no depreciation accounting. The deficit is not a loss, I think, because some of the cash expenditures are for fixed assets which last much longer than one year. Such expenditures could well exceed any depreciation expense in a year. Also, it's hard to know what the assets owned by the government are currently worth. Maybe the increase during the year in value of the fixed assets could exceed the budgetary deficit.

A: What else is different about the government situation to lead to reporting that differs from the private sector?

Student C: The amount of dollars involved is huge compared to that for most companies. Also, the government can borrow on the basis of its ability to tax individuals and companies. Investors will lend to a government as long as the government can repay the debt from tax receipts. It doesn't have to earn revenue from its fixed assets.

A: Is that why the government doesn't record fixed assets, depreciation, and owners' equity?

Student D: Possibly, I'm not sure. The government does not have to worry about disclosure constraints in Companies Acts, Securities Acts and various income tax legislation when it prepares financial statements. Governments have to be concerned with more than a profit motive. For instance, the health of citizens should not be viewed only in quantitative cost-benefits terms. Welfare programs are devised to aid people, not to show a profit.

Student E: But how do we know whether or not the government is peforming well? You imply that the financial statements are of little use in indicating a government's performance.

D: Should and can the government's financial statements be set up to permit people to judge performance? These are tough questions. For example, if the financial statements are organized to permit performance evaluation, will they be rendered useless for another judgment or purpose?

B: Can anyone judge performance from an annual financial statement? Government programs are set up to attain benefits over several years—not immediately. Besides, how do you measure the benefit of police protection, amateur sports programs, or aid to other countries?

A: I still do not understand what the government's financial statements are used for. How do you know whether the government might be near bankruptcy?

B: The budgetary deficit is a rough indication of the amount of new cash which the government must borrow in the bond market. If it can borrow it won't go bankrupt.

A: Rough indication? How rough? Revenues seem to be on a cash basis whereas expenses are on a part cash, part accrual basis, excluding expenditures on fixed assets. What does this tell you?

C: The government doesn't have to borrow all of the budgetary deficit from the bond market. It borrows some of its needs from its employees' pensions plans.

E: The more I hear the more I think that the government's financial statements need a major revision.

Student F: To accomplish what?

Required:

In your opinion, are the financial statements prepared by the Government of Canada sensible, given the probable users? Explain your reasoning. What do you recommend?

CHAPTER 6

Objectives of Accounting

Chapter Themes

1. It is *not possible* to account and prepare informative financial statements unless we know the purposes, or *objectives*, of accounting. Who is using the financial statements and for what purposes? There are situations where facts are clear, and only one possible way of accounting exists. In reality, however, facts often are not clear, and future outcomes are difficult to predict.

2. Sometimes we are *not* able to design the financial information and statements in a way that permits us to attain or pursue a particular objective. In addition to the situation where facts are clear, objectives are less important when we are *constrained*, or restricted, by some law, or by generally accepted accounting principles that are unduly rigid.

3. In Canada, the authority and power to decide whose objectives of accounting will be catered to, or given first priority, usually rests with those who prepare the financial statements. The preparers, ultimately, are the board of directors and management of the organization. Only in some situations would certain users of financial statements, such as potential investors, have most of their financial information needs or objectives met.

4. Given the foregoing, all financial information must be interpreted with special care. Financial statements that have been prepared with one, particular objective in mind might well be of little use for another objective. It is *vital* that we do not fall into the trap of believing that there is only one way of accounting, and that accounting numbers are accurate.

5. Many occupations or professions or people are subject to stereotyping. As Chapter 1 stated, students of introductory accounting have to bear the burden of having heard endless myths about "accuracy" and "truthful-

ness" of accounting figures and "why accounting is boring". Far more damaging from a learning point of view is the belief that "accounting has rules for everything"—that all one has to do is memorize the rules to learn accounting.

6. There are more sensible approaches to learning accounting. *First,* we must try to think out which of the alternative accounting treatments best serve a particular objective of accounting. *Second,* we will try to learn whether any accounting rule or constraint prevents choosing the best alternative. This chapter and Chapter 7 stress several alternatives for the recognition of revenue, that is, *when* (in which financial period) may we "credit" revenue on the income statement. Few, rigid accounting rules exist with respect to revenue recognition. Yet the timing and measurement of revenue often has the greatest effect on income for a financial period.

Who Uses Financial Statements?

Many different categories of people use financial information and statements for a variety of purposes. It is not possible to give an exhaustive list of users and uses. We can focus on a few major users and thereby illustrate a primary theme of how users' needs can differ markedly.

Pertinent to any coverage of users and uses is a recognition of the nature of Canada, and how it differs from that of the U.S.A. and the U.K. Many accountants have been trained in a large, American public-company setting. Some of these accountants are more familiar with merchandising and manufacturing businesses. Although there are such companies in Canada, the Canadian economy has some major differences from that of the U.S.A. Many Canadian companies are chiefly engaged in fishing, logging, mining, farming, oil and gas, and other resource ventures. A large number of Canadian businesses are small, private companies with one or two owners, who incorporated primarily to take advantage of income-tax law and legislation. Rules and concepts that may suit a large, American merchandising company could very well be misleading for a small, private oil-and-gas company in Canada. Resource companies tend to have serious measurement problems because they often do not know the extent of the oil, gas or minerals in the ground or ocean.

Accordingly, it seems worthwhile to issue a warning before we proceed: Remember that it is impossible to have rigid rules that apply to every situation. Different circumstances demand different responses, and the nature of accounting must be fundamentally adaptable. Laws, people's beliefs, the state of the economy, events in other countries, and many other factors affect accounting and financial statement presentation and people's decisions.

Owners of small private companies, and potential creditors of these companies, are two categories of preparers/users with quite different viewpoints. To compare and contrast these two categories will help us to understand why much time and effort has to be devoted to learning "what fits where", and why general rules usually cannot be provided.

AN ILLUSTRATION

The objectives of financial accounting of the owner of a small private company usually differ from the objectives of a potential creditor, e.g., a bank:

Owner: Wants to keep net income and income subject to income tax—called *taxable income*—as *low* as possible within the requirements of taxation law.

Potential Creditor: Wants some assurance that the loan will be repaid in full (original principal amount loaned plus interest), when it is due.

As we concluded in the previous chapter, *funds from operations* could prove useful in helping us to forecast the likelihood that a loan "could" (not "will") be repaid. That is, we are provided with a figure for "funds" that might be available to repay a loan. Funds from operations vary in amount as a result of the revenues and expenses that require cash receipts and payments within a short span of time. Thus, if the owner chooses—from among several accounting methods, *all* of which are GAAP—to record revenue in the *next* financial period (19—9), funds from operations in the current (19—8) financial period would be *lower* than they may otherwise have been.

	What Owner Chooses To Do in the Current Financial Period	*Income if Revenue Had Been Recorded in the Current Period*
Revenue	$100,000	$180,000
Cost of goods sold	75,000	135,000
Gross profit	25,000	45,000
Expenses	25,000	25,000
Income before income tax	$ 0	$ 20,000

The delay in recording $80,000 of revenue (and its accompanying $60,000 of cost of goods sold) has brought about zero income subject to income tax in 19—8. *If* the $80,000 revenue had been recorded in 19—8, however, $20,000 of taxable income would result. Hence, if the company were subjected to a tax rate of 25 percent, $5,000 of tax would be owing virtually immediately. The $5,000 would probably have to be borrowed from a bank, and interest would have to be paid, quite possibly for an entire year. At 15 percent interest per annum, $750[1] (15% x $5,000) would be saved by delaying revenue recognition over the company's year end. (Suppose that the company's financial year ends on December 31: the $750 saving would result if the $80,000 of

---

[1] The "saving" could be higher than $750 because of the cumulative effect of a delay, in making cash payments, that is permitted by income-taxation law.

revenue were recorded in January 19—9 instead of in December 19—8. This is because tax payments are based on the amount of the company's *annual* income. A delay would mean the $20,000 would be taxable income in 19—9 and not in 19—8.)

A delay in recording the $80,000 accomplishes the owner's objective of saving cash through postponing the payment of income tax. But does the delay jeopardize the owner's chances of getting a loan from the bank to help in expanding the business?

The banker may look at the "income before income tax" figure of zero and believe that the company is unsuccessful. He or she may not understand the company's tax-minimization objective of financial accounting, and might not appreciate the wise tax management that has been employed—*quite legally.* If the banker does understand that taxable income has been kept as low as possible, then he or she will automatically amend the funds from operations figure for 19—8, realizing that a loan could be very profitable for both the bank and the company. (An alternative to amending the funds from operations figure would involve preparing a special purpose report of expected future cash receipts and disbursements. See Chapter 5.)

Details of how a delay in revenue recognition could be accomplished are provided later in the chapter. What is important at this point is fully understanding that an accounting method may accomplish one objective—such as postponing income tax for a year or more—and prevent another, perhaps very legitimate, borrowing objective because the banker did not understand the owner's accounting method. (That is, from a business point of view, $80,000 of cash would be received from the customer, probably in 19—9. The only difference is *strictly* one of bookkeeping for the $80,000, i.e., recording it, in either 19—8 or 19—9.)

Objectives of Financial Accounting

People use accounting information in different ways; specific uses or applications are mentioned from place to place in the book whenever concrete illustrations are provided. To the degree that is practical, we want to avoid sweeping generalizations because they are counterproductive in trying to explain a major theme of this book—that accounting must be *tailored to the situation.* Nevertheless, there are times when generalizations have to be given, so that we do not lose sight of broad categories.

Whenever broad categories and generalizations have to be provided, we must not expect precise clarity. Insight into objectives will be gained from the material in subsequent chapters.

INTERNAL CONTROL

Illustration 6-1 sets forth some broad categories of objectives of *financial accounting.* The internal-control objective is discussed in greater detail in subsequent chapters, and primarily involves designing accounting systems and policies that help to catch certain types of errors and frauds. The double entry method of journal entries is an example of an internal-control mechanism because it can help to catch some errors in recording assets, liabilities, and equities.

ILLUSTRATION 6-1

Some Objectives of Financial Accounting

1. Internal Control. (The choice of accounting policies and practices that help to protect the organization against certain types of fraud and error.)

2. Special-Purpose Reports. (This includes a variety of financial reports that:

   A. May or may not be in accordance with GAAP;

   B. May pertain to the past, or to the future; and

   C. May or may not be audited.

   The reports are designed for whatever purpose is specified in the particular report, or is implied from the manner in which the report has been designed or constructed.)

3. General-Purpose Reports. (Each financial year, an incorporated company may issue only *one* general-purpose annual report, required by corporate law.)

   A. Preparer's choice, e.g., management of the company or a board of directors chooses the accounting procedures and disclosure:

      a. Income tax postponement;

      b. Compliance with minimum requirements of laws; or

      c. Bonus plan or evaluation of management by the company's board of directors is based on income-statement figures, e.g., gross profit, net income or other.

   B. User choice, e.g., creditors, prospective creditors or shareholders have their needs catered to in part, or more so than under preparer-choice and preparer-power situations:

      a. Evaluation of management by users outside of the organization—such as creditors. A set of financial statements that fits this category has more *information content* than for A (b).

      b. Cash flow prediction, i.e., some people attempt to ascertain the *current worth* or *value* of a business by estimating the cash flows—or funds from operations—that will be generated in the future. A financial statement based on this objective attempts to assist those who wish to predict.

What type of organization would have internal control as its *sole* objective of financial accounting? One may be an organization that is not concerned with having to pay income taxes, or attract debt or equity financing from shareholders and creditors. A charity would be one example of an entity that may want accounting systems primarily to keep track of its daily transactions. Another possibility would be those who operate on a tight budget, and try to keep a close watch on their expenses and any trends in expenses.

If we disregard "internal control" in the listing in Illustration 6-1, categories (2) and (3) together are often referred to as objectives of financial *reporting* because they involve some form of financial statements. A company may issue many different special purpose reports in a financial period. Only one general purpose annual report "ought" to be issued for a financial year, however. Incorporated companies would issue only one general-purpose annual financial statement per financial year because corporate legislation usually sets out this requirement in careful wording. Unincorporated companies are not closely regulated, however, and could issue more than one annual report, which could be confusing. (Large companies tend to issue quarterly general-purpose reports for each of the first three quarters of a year. These are usually unaudited, but follow GAAP.)

Many companies have *more* than one objective for their annual general-purpose report. The illustration earlier in this chapter could be viewed as a situation where there seemed to be more than one objective, but income-tax postponement was the most important. Often it is necessary to read a company's financial statement carefully in order to ascertain what objective of accounting the preparers would seem to be adopting. Sometimes, the objective may not be clear, and potential investors should therefore ask questions before considering an investment in the company.

It is important to discuss objectives of accounting because the *choice of objectives can have such a dramatic effect on the organization's income statement and balance sheet.* For purposes of illustration, three different situations will be considered. *First,* there are situations where GAAP may be clear and there *may* be only one way of accounting for the transaction, i.e., a GAAP constraint exists. Under such circumstances, objectives of accounting do not become relevant, and there is only one possible *effect* on the financial statements. (Generally, GAAP permits more than one method of accounting, but there are some situations when only one method is practical.) *Second,* there are situations where GAAP is unclear, unknown, evolving or permits many alternatives. Yet the facts of the situation are clear—say, someone has paid cash for a service and the "contract" with them is complete. Under these circumstances, there would seem to be only one credible way of accounting, i.e., debit cash, and credit revenue. As with the first situation, objectives of accounting are not relevant, and the *facts* speak for themselves. *Third,* there are many situations where the facts do not speak for themselves, perhaps because they will be known only through the passage of time, and no restrictive GAAP constraint exists. It is this third, quite common, category that especially raises the importance of objectives of financial reporting.[2]

We begin with a basic situation, and build on it. But which of these three, different situations is the "basic" one? We could start with the GAAP constraint, but this is not basic. Indeed, such a label is dangerous because it tends to reinforce the belief that accounting is just a set of rules. Accountants have to make many estimates and exercise judgment frequently. There is no rule in accounting except the existence of diversity—much of which arises because facts are unclear and constraints do not exist for the particular transaction. We must recognize that there are at least three types of situations, which differ from each other because (1) *objectives* of accounting, (2) *facts* of the situation, and (3) the existence (or absence) of tight *constraints* can vary.

Our thinking in a particular situation ought to progress *in this order:*

1. When constraints exist, e.g., GAAP is clear and there is only one "choice", then we account in accordance with the rule or constraint.

2. When there are no tight constraints, or many possible GAAP treatments, but the facts are clear and point toward one way of accounting, then we account in accordance with the facts.

---

[2] More than three situations exist; but only three will be covered at this time.

3. When there are no constraints and the facts are unclear or are unknown, then the objectives of accounting become important in resolving the accounting treatment. (Usually, a decision will be made on the basis of objectives and those facts that are available.)

There are more than just these three categories. Nevertheless, an understanding of the three will carry us a long way in grasping more complex situations. As stated in earlier chapters, we should not overemphasize today's constraints. They may not exist by the time a student graduates. Futhermore, the learning process may be hindered if we understand only today's constraints, or if we expect "all purpose" answers. An adaptable approach, then, may prepare us more effectively for working in the real world.

General-Purpose Reports—Preparer Viewpoint

TAX POSTPONEMENT

Most Canadian corporations fall into the private company category. As a result, the most common objective of accounting is income-tax postponement. The mechanics of this basis of accounting were briefly described near the beginning of this chapter. Much more will be added in subsequent chapters.

MINIMUM COMPLIANCE

The second preparer objective mentioned in Illustration 6-1 is "*compliance* with the minimum requirements of laws". The term "laws" has been used loosely, in Illustration 6-1, and could include more than corporate law. Many of the larger, non-private, i.e., public, companies would rank this "compliance" objective at or near the top of their list of objectives of financial accounting.

A so-called *public company* is one that obtains money from the "general public", i.e., strangers or people not previously acquaintances of the board of directors and shareholders of the company. The money could be obtained from a public creditor or from a new shareholder. A company does *not* become "public" by borrowing from a bank, life-insurance company or other established lending institution because such organizations are neither strangers nor are they viewed as "the public". Laws to protect investors and creditors (such as each province's securities act and regulations) are generally aimed at providing information so that the less sophisticated investor is made aware of controversial aspects of the business. Parliamentarians usually take the view that the banks are able to take care of themselves.

A public company would have to comply with the following "laws":

1. The corporations act under which the company is incorporated, e.g., *Canada Business Corporations Act* or a similar act of one of the provinces/territories.

2. The securities acts of the provinces in which public creditors and shareholders were offered the debt or shares.

3. GAAP, because the above legislation tends to require the appointment of auditors. (A large percentage of the auditors of public companies are chartered accountants, who are required to follow GAAP.)

In addition, many public companies are listed on one or more of the larger stock exchanges that exist in Canada, e.g., Alberta, Montreal, Toronto or Vancouver stock exchange. (See the financial section of most daily newspapers for details.) Each stock exchange has different "listing requirements", designed to protect investors to differing degrees. Complying with the requirements of a stock exchange are included in this "minimum compliance" category of objectives.

Several of the corporations and securities acts require the company to adhere to the CICA Handbook. (CICA refers to the Canadian Institute of Chartered Accountants.) The CICA Handbook contains only a small portion of Canadian GAAP. The stock exchanges may require quarterly (unaudited) reports in addition to the annual reports. Thus, compliance with GAAP and stock-exchange requirements is a much broader requirement than complying with a corporations act.

Which companies would tend to have "minimum compliance" as a prime objective of financial accounting? Perhaps those companies that do not have either tax postponement, 'income-based bonus plans' or 'user choice' as their main objective. As a generalization, we have said that tax postponement is favored by private companies. It is also possible to say, however, that tax postponement could be an important, but perhaps a secondary, objective in many public companies. For tax postponement to be a secondary objective in a private company, it is *probable* that users, e.g., potential creditors or potential investors, have been given some power and have demanded more than minimum compliance in the financial statements.

Again, as a generalization, which will be explained in greater detail in later chapters, users gain power when one or more of the following exist:

1. The company needs money and is trying to convince people to invest as creditors or shareholders. (Thus, the financial statements try to cast the company in a favorable light, perhaps by having a net income figure that increases year after year.)

2. Management is being evaluated, in part, on the basis of how the company performs. A company's performance, in turn, may be judged by net income, or more likely, by the amount that the price of the company's common shares increase, per the stock market quotations.

3. Existing investors or creditors in the company have been able to demand a certain quality of reporting. Sometimes creditors demand what are called *restrictive covenants* before they invest. These covenants are requirements such as "no dividend may be paid to common shareholders unless retained earnings exceeds $___, after the dividend has been paid". In order to not break the covenant, management may choose to speed up the recording of revenue and to delay recording expenses as much as possible. This would increase net income; but it would also increase income tax.

To summarize, if the company does not face a user power situation (because none of the above three or similar generalizations exist), its financial accounting could take the "cheapest approach possible"—minimum compliance. One example may be a small mining company. Such a company tends to have one ore body; and when all the metal (gold, silver or other) is mined, the company often ceases to exist. All the money needed to operate the mine over its lifetime is usually required at the beginning of the company's life. Once the mine shaft, camp, and related assets are in place, there is little or no need to ask the public for more funds. (The mine cannot expand unless it finds more ore, and the discovery of more ore at the same site is unlikely.) If anything, funds will be *given back* to the investors by way of dividends, after a few years of operation of the mine.

For a mine, the factor of greatest significance to shareholders, or owners, is the selling price of the metal. Metal prices tend to fluctuate widely over the years in the life of a mine. Thus, revenue and cash receipts cannot be predicted by looking at last year's financial statements. Accounting statements and reports therefore take on much less significance to owners who wish to try to *predict* cash flows. Accordingly, for many small mines with one ore body, a "minimum compliance" objective of accounting is logical.

BONUS/INCENTIVE PLAN

Management incentive or bonus plans may be based on several factors such as obtaining new orders from customers, saving money in the process of building a new factory, and so forth. In smaller companies, it is not uncommon for the owners of a business to reward their senior managers, e.g., president and any vice-presidents, or general manager, on the basis of any income that is generated. A bonus plan may state "senior management, as a group, will receive 10 percent of any income before income taxes that is in excess of $100,000". Incentive plans may specify a basis other than "income before income taxes", for example, "net income", "operating income" or other terms, which will be considered later in this book.

Even when no explicit bonus plan exists, management may believe that its performance is being evaluated by the board of directors, or owners, on the basis of how much net income the company generates. After all, in businesses, the objective of the organization is usually to make a profit, and this is often with "net income" —the so-called "bottom-line".

In accordance with corporate law, the owners or shareholders of a company appoint a board of directors to "direct the operations" of a company. In small companies, the owners and board of directors and managers may be the same few people. In larger companies, the board of directors appoints managers to handle the daily operations of the business, e.g., obtaining sales orders, producing goods, purchasing materials, handling personnel, and making various other operating decisions. The board of directors may also tend to delegate to senior management the choice of accounting principles, e.g., *when* to record revenue, and *when* to record expenses, etc. By delegating, the board of directors has given management the responsibility of preparing its own assessment of its stewardship. As a consequence, when such delegation has occurred, people who read the organization's financial statements have to give extra attention to the basis of accounting that was used.

Much of the remainder of this book is devoted to explaining alternative accounting methods, and in giving their effect on the income statement, balance sheet, and other financial data.

Observe that "tax postponement" and "bonus/incentive plan" could be opposing objectives of accounting. Owners may want to keep income taxes low (through keeping income before income taxes low) whereas managers may want income before income taxes to be high so that they receive a higher bonus.

Ideally, in bonus plans one would want to see the following type of relationship:

1. Effort by managers,

2. Accomplishments by company,

3. Accomplishments reflected by financial statements, and

4. Whether bonus is in relationship to management's efforts and accomplishments.

A major difficulty occurs in (3) because financial accounting (as we will see more and more in succeeding chapters) tends to lag in recording accomplishments. Also, effort expended today, e.g., to build a new assembly line, may not show up in revenues and net income for two or more years. Thus, a person has to be careful in using financial information to evaluate managers. Nevertheless, basing bonuses and assessments of management on net income is widespread. It should therefore not be surprising that managers would spend some time ensuring that their net-income report looks favorable to owners or directors of the company.

For a few situations, it is possible to accommodate both the "bonus/incentive plan" and the "tax postponement" objectives in one set of general-purpose financial statements. This is because of the way in which income-tax legislation is administered. In effect, there are two categories of transactions (when matters are viewed through the eyes of income-tax assessors):

Category 1: Tax Law Clear and One Method or Policy Exists.

Tax law and practice occasionally describe the bookkeeping treatment that must be used for tax purposes. Sometimes, for particular transactions, only one method of computation is permitted for tax purposes. Another method may be selected for the general-purpose financial statements. This leads to a difference between "accounting income before income taxes" and what is called "taxable income"—which is used in levying taxes. (The federal government, through Revenue Canada, requires persons and companies to calculate their taxes on the basis of "taxable income".)

Category 2: Income Taxes are Assessed on the Basis of the Method or Policy that Is Used in the Company's General-Purpose Financial Statements.

Where Revenue Canada does *not* require its own specific accounting method of calculating income taxes, a company will (within some limits) use its own method, and Revenue Canada will assess income taxes on this basis as long as the company uses a *consistent* method from year to year. In saying this, Revenue Canada is stating that they will look at the accounting policies and methods selected for the general-purpose financial statements. As a result, a company that wants to use the tax-postponement objective must carefully think out which one of several accounting methods should be used in the general-purpose financial statements.

Earlier in this chapter, an example of Category 2 was provided. Except for some special situations, Revenue Canada does not have a specific policy of requiring revenue to be recorded in one particular financial period. Undue postponement, however, is not realistic when the facts of the situation are clear. Generally speaking, Category 2 is the usual case.

Depreciation is an example of Category 1. Revenue Canada has its own rules and policies for calculating what they call *capital cost allowance*. Accounting depreciation used in the general-purpose financial statements can be different. Consequently, there may be a few situations where the only differences of opinion between owners (with their tax-postponement objective) and managers (who may have a bonus-plan objective) are entirely represented by Category 1 items. Then, both objectives of accounting can be accommodated by the one general-purpose financial statement. This is done by using a reconciling format, for income tax purposes, such as:

Income before income taxes, per the general-purpose financial statements	$300,500
Add: depreciation deducted in arriving at the $300,500 figure	50,000
Income before depreciation and income taxes	350,500
Deduct: Capital cost allowance (i.e., tax basis depreciation)	99,500
Taxable income (or income subject to taxation)	$251,000

Usually, however, differences of opinion between management and owners would arise in the Category 2 transactions. Compromises must therefore be struck. By law, the board of directors (owners) has the final decision in selecting accounting policies. But, they ought to be fair in their choices, otherwise management may seek employment elsewhere.

In summary, accounting is complex. Accountants can try to be neutral, and not favor one group over another. But often, power to decide accounting policies rests in one or more of several places within the preparer (owner, manager, or both) or the user groups. Who wins any possible power struggle can have a major effect on accounting statements.

General-Purpose Reports—User Viewpoint

EVALUATION OF MANAGEMENT BY OUTSIDERS

Users of financial statements sometimes are able to convince preparers through persuasion, or demand through written contracts, a higher level of response than would exist in the "minimum compliance" approach to financial accounting and reporting. The extent to which the additional disclosure or altered accounting policies help the users is not well documented or clear.

Broadly speaking, the objective of evaluation is supposedly to tell "outsiders" how well management has managed the company. In a small business, the owners are insiders, or preparers. In a large business, however, there are usually thousands of owners who have little or no say in how the company operates. They are outsiders, and have to rely on reports from management to learn what is happening in their company. (The managers are sometimes referred to as stewards and the term "stewardship accounting" is used in describing financial information that is given to outside owners.)

How much may outsiders learn about a company by reading general-purpose financial statements? We can assume that some benefits exist, otherwise financial accounting would not have grown in importance over the years. Yet three contingent issues require discussion:

1. Management prepares its *own* financial reports.

2. How does a reader separate good luck from good management?

3. How do readers take into account that good management today may not show up in improved income until next year or several years later? For example, the building of a new factory could lower production costs per unit of goods manufactured over a twenty-year period.

Owners of shares in large companies usually are trying to decide whether they ought to hold onto their shares, sell them or buy more. Many factors are important to their evaluation and decision: state of the economy; level of interest rates; consumers' beliefs about when to buy goods; type, quality, and profitability of the company's products; quality of the company's management; and other factors that affect the company's success.

What would you do if you were one of the senior managers of a company, and had the opportunity to pick from a list of methods of accounting, and knew that some of the methods would make your work "look better"? You might try to choose accounting methods that helped cover up your mistakes, *as long as you felt that people would believe your accounting and financial statements.* Within certain limits, managers tend to choose the accounting method that shows their work in the best light. Some owners are naive, and might believe that such financial statements are "accurate". However, other owners may be willing to question the methods of accounting. Still others could be sophisticated enough to try to replace figures in the financial statements with their own "best guesses" of what the figure would be if the company had accounted a different way.

It is not realistic to expect to be able to predict how a manager will behave. Much depends on the *facts* or assumptions about the situation, including the level of sophistication of the readers of the company's accounting reports. If the managers are trying to make themselves "look better", and they control the choice of accounting methods, then the accounting objective of "evaluation of management by outsiders" can be questioned as to its worthiness in the short term.

When readers take a longer term view, say over four or more years, a series of financial statements might be able to give a general impression about management. This might occur because management is required (by GAAP) to apply accounting methods on a *consistent basis.* That is, a different accounting policy cannot be chosen for every year. Generally speaking, in practice, management adopts the same method or policy for several years. This has the effect of reducing possible manipulation by management. But, as will become clear in subsequent chapters, management still has ample opportunity to cover up certain mistakes. Over the longer term, the effects of bad decisions tend to appear in the financial statements because economic conditions change, and income and balance sheet effects become harder to hide.

It is important to place the last few paragraphs in the context of the themes of this book. The paragraphs are not suggesting that the managements of large companies are unethical. Instead, the paragraphs are questioning the wisdom of those who believe that "evaluation of management by outsiders" is an important, attainable objective of accounting in many large companies. Corporate law allows management to prepare its own financial statements. Do we think that management would go out of its way to make itself appear incompetent? As long as the auditor's role is to ensure that *a* (not the so-called "best") GAAP method is being used, it is naive to think that auditors would question management's choice of a particular GAAP method of accounting. The parliamentarians and legislators of the land formulated corporate law. *If* the law is not helpful to owners of common shares, the people have to encourage the parliamentarians to change the law.

A second problem with the "evaluation of management" objective is the need to separate good luck from good management. Ideally, one would hope that good management would lead to greater profits, and an increase in the worth of a company. (The shareholder would therefore be able to sell his/her share at a profit because share prices ought to increase when profits get larger and larger.) Net income (profit) may increase purely due to good luck, however. For example, an unexpected increase may have occurred in the volume of sales of one of the company's products because a competitor had a prolonged labor strike. Profits could therefore increase in one financial year owing to a temporary situation.

In later chapters, examples will be provided to show how accountants try, in some situations, to separate what are called recurring from non-recurring (or extraordinary) transactions and events. The term *recurring* is used by accountants to refer to transactions that tend to occur frequently, each year. An example would be purchases and sales of inventory. (Recurring funds from operations are affected by purchases and sales of inventory. The amount of recurring funds from operations is therefore of interest to several groups of persons, as described in Chapter 5.) An example of a *non-recurring* transaction would be a fire that results in a loss, e.g., from not being insured. Non-recurring or extraordinary items are *not* the same as good luck vs. good management situations. That is, the prolonged labor strike at a competitor causes our company's sales to increase. We do not know how much the increase is, however, because we do not know with certainty what our sales *would* have been without the strike. Non-recurring gains and losses tend to be restricted to infrequent transactions whereas some good or bad luck could occur every year.

The third major problem with the "evaluation of management" objective of financial accounting concerns the delayed effects of management actions. Two different situations merit discussion: (1) where bad management decisions do not become evident in the financial statements for several years, and (2) where the income-statement effects of good management decisions are delayed. For instance, management can increase net income temporarily by reducing some types of costs, such as research, training, maintenance, and so forth. A person who looks at only the net income figure will conclude that management has saved money. Yet, the cost reductions may be detrimental to the company in the long run because: (1) the absence of research may prevent development of new products; (2) the neglect of training could cause employees to make mistakes or to be inefficient; and (3) inadequate maintenance could result in huge repair or replacement costs three or four years from now. A general-purpose financial statement is not likely to alert readers to "detrimental cost savings".

Many actions by management may appear, from an accounting point of view, to have serious shortcomings in the near term. Longer-term results, however, could be exceedingly beneficial. One example is the start up of a new product or division of a company. It is not unusual in a start-up situation to incur heavy "front end" costs. For instance, when commencing a new division, managers have to train people, get the machinery operating smoothly, advertise any new products frequently, waste some materials until quality of the product is high, and so on. These front-end costs eventually pay off because the product gains acceptance from the public, mainly owing to the "up front" efforts of people, advertising, quality controls, etc.

How then should accountants treat front-end costs? Are they assets or expenses? *If* they are assets, for how long are they an asset? It should not surprise us to find companies handling the situation in different ways. Management can use its judgment, and a reader may or may not know what alternative accounting treatment has been used. This affects the interpretations that readers of financial statements may make. Consequently, an objective of accounting such as "evaluation of management by outsiders" is difficult to achieve because several conclusions may be possible.

CASH-FLOW PREDICTION BY OUTSIDERS

In Illustration 6-1, the last category mentioned under "General-Purpose Reports" refers to attempts to establish a worth for a company by using, among other sources, a general-purpose financial statement. Other sources of information may include the company's public-relations documents that describe what quantities of the different products are currently being produced, and financial newpapers that report attempts to forecast the state of the economy, interest rates, and other factors that can affect a company's profits.

The ideas underlying this objective of financial accounting are similar to (but not the same as) placing money in a savings account at a bank or trust company. Suppose that we put $1,000 in a savings account that earns 10 percent interest per annum. Our so-called income (ignoring income taxes), or funds from operations, would be $100 per year (10% x $1,000). Our return on investment would be 10 percent ($100 divided by $1,000 expressed as a percentage).

What happens, however, when we invest $1,000 in a company's common shares? We probably have only a very rough idea whether our share of the funds from operations will be $50 per year, $100, $200 or more. Before we invest (or sell, once we have previously invested), however, we would try to ascertain what the annual funds from operations—or cash flow, if we can compute it—is likely to be. Then, we would have to decide whether the current price that someone would pay us for our shares is higher than what we think the company is worth. That is, suppose that we believe that our cash flow per annum is $100 and we want 10 percent as our return on investment:

Situation	Market Price of our Shares	Our Probable Action
A.	$1,100	We would sell our shares because we believe that they are worth only $1,000 ($100 divided by 10%).
B.	$ 900	We would hold on to our shares because we believe that they are worth $1,000, and eventually the market place will recognize this and the price will rise to $1,000.
C.	$1,000	We would hold on to our shares because we would be getting the income that we want.

The decision to sell or retain shares is often more complicated than what has just been described. Nevertheless, the basic idea is that when we invest in a company, we have to think in terms of what the company's funds or cash flow from operations is likely to be. What percentage would the company and market place be willing to "give back" to me when I want to cease investing.

To illustrate, suppose that we invested $2,000 in a company's common shares by buying 100 shares at $20 per share. Suppose also that one year later, we received a cash dividend of $100. Also, that one year later, the shares could be sold for $22 per share. Our return on investment would be:

$$\frac{\text{Dividend \& Increase in Share Price}}{\$2,000}$$

$$= \frac{\$100 + \$200 \, (\$2,200 - \$2,000)}{\$2,000} = \underline{\underline{15\%}}$$

The increase in share price from $20 to $22 per share could be a reflection of people's beliefs that future funds from operations, or cash flow, of the company are expected to increase. Any way we look at the situation, it is clear that investors have to try to forecast or predict cash flow/funds from operations. And, general-purpose financial statements may help investors *as long as they are designed with this objective in mind.* That is, a financial statement prepared to help postpone the payment of income taxes could very likely be useless for investors who want to predict.

It is important to understand who these "investors" are. They are not likely to be owners of a company that is small. Nor are they likely to be bankers to a small company. In a small company, the owners and bankers can get access to special-purpose reports, and do not have to rely on general-purpose reports. The cash flow prediction objective generally applies to large, publicly owned corporations—where (1) the shareholders have somehow been given some power to demand disclosures suited to their needs, or (2) the preparers have decided to cater to the outside users, possibly because the company is in need of cash and will have to sell shares or bonds/debt in the future. More will be said about this objective in succeeding chapters.

REVIEW

It is natural to seek out "like accounting for like situations", but the word "like" must be clearly defined. For instance, if two companies have the *same* objectives of accounting, and encounter the *same* facts (regarding quality, price, and quantity of purchases and sales), and are incorporated under the *same* legislation and constraints, it would be useful for comparative purposes if the two companies used the same accounting. However, when objectives, facts, and constraints differ, it would be misleading to try to impose one method of accounting. Dissimilar circumstances would, quite falsely, appear alike.

It is, therefore, important to understand that there are *several objectives of financial accounting,* and to comprehend *which accounting alternative makes sense for each of the objectives of accounting.* A search for one, all-purpose objective is considerably less effective than an understanding of the *relative* merits of different accounting for different situations. The following are some examples of objectives of accounting that may be helpful:

1. Many businesses that have one owner-manager have a sole objective of financial accounting—tax postponement.

2. Private businesses in which the owners do not participate in the daily operations may have a bonus plan for managers (possibly tied to income statement figures). The owners may also rank tax postponement high. Thus, two objectives exist, and one is probably ranked higher than the other. We would have to conduct further analysis to ascertain the order of importance of the objectives. When we know the ranking, we can choose accounting policies and proceed.

3. Public companies that do not have to borrow any more money from the general public, or sell more shares, could merely want to comply with the minimum requirements of law, which says that a financial-statement package (balance sheet, etc.) has to be sent to shareholders. The board of directors could therefore select accounting policies and methods that attempt to save taxes and also ease the task of reporting according to the minimum requirements of the law.

4. In some large public companies, users of financial statements may be catered to because the company chooses to do so, or because the users become entitled to it by contract. For instance, when shares are initially sold to the public, promises may be made in writing to the effect that particular information will be made available to shareholders. A second example may be where the managers own a few shares in the company and would like share prices to rise. They may believe (perhaps incorrectly; it depends on many factors) that greater disclosure and a higher-income figure will help share prices to rise. Many other illustrations could be provided. The point is, however, that there are situations where shareholders want to

evaluate management and predict cash flows. Sometimes the financial statements help the shareholders in one or more of these tasks; sometimes they do not. Because the company is publicly owned does not mean that shareholders have the power to demand particular methods of accounting. If one or a few shareholders had power to demand information, a competitor would merely have to buy a share in the company to have access to confidential information.

In this chapter, we have departed from many of the usual ways of thinking about accounting. We have set out what may be called an overview, and, as more examples are provided over the next few chapters, our understanding of this complex subject will increase.

When To Record Revenue

The term *revenue recognition* is used to characterize the thinking that eventually results in revenue appearing on an income statement. In short, *when* do we credit a revenue account? After our long discussion of objectives of financial accounting, we know that many ways exist. Much depends on the *facts* of the situation (e.g., how is the product manufactured/purchased? how is it sold? how and when is it paid for? and so on), and the *objectives* of accounting. In general, when the facts are clear and point to only one, credible way, then accountants follow whatever the facts dictate. When the facts are not clear or are not known with a reasonable degree of assurance, however, objectives of accounting come into effect and influence accounting.

The bulk of the discussion of revenue recognition is in the next chapter. An introduction is provided at this point to help us to understand the major importance of objectives of financial accounting *and* of adding to our understanding of how to tailor accounting to the situation.

We start with a clear set of facts. Suppose that we have our hair cut, and perhaps styled. The hairdresser/barber receives cash from us on completion of the cutting/styling. In this situation, revenue for the hairdresser/barber is recognized when the work is completed and we pay. Why? Because any alternative would not be credible/believable. That is:

1. The amount of revenue is 100 percent *known* because cash has been received. (The barber/hairdresser will not incur a bad debt owing to the cash not being collected. Also, we are not likely to receive a refund because we notice the next day that it is not to our satisfaction.)

2. The hairdresser/barber knows most, if not all, the costs that were incurred to cut/style our hair. (Some costs, such as for electricity, are not known for sure, but probably are not large and are not easily traceable to one customer. Rent of the hairdresser/barber shop/salon is another, similar cost. It is called a *period cost*, that is, it is incurred over a period of time rather than being traceable to one particular customer. Accountants generally do not try to match period costs to revenue from one customer because the process would be costly, and probably quite arbitrary.)

If the barber/hairdresser wanted to record the revenue next month (which say, would be in the next financial year) to help postpone the payment of income taxes, would such a delay make sense? Because Revenue Canada would attribute the revenue to the month in which the hair was cut and the cash was received, there is no point in considering objectives. The facts are too clear.

The design, construction, sale, and servicing of a new jet aircraft serves as an interesting *contrast* with the hairdresser/barber example. Suppose that the following major steps occurred in an aircraft-manufacturing company, e.g., building Boeing 767, or de Havilland Dash 8, over a period of time:

1. Idea for building a new aircraft gains acceptance in the company.

2. Designers complete a workable aircraft and construction plan, at much cost.

3. A prototype or single aircraft is built.

4. Governments approve the design for safety and air worthiness.

5. The aircraft flies successfully and receives all the necessary government approvals.

6. An order is received for twenty aircraft for delivery over the next two years. The selling price of the first ten aircraft is fixed by a contract.

7. Assembly commences on the first batch of new aircraft.

8. Two aircraft are completed and delivered to the airline that ordered the twenty.

9. The airline pays for the two aircraft that it received.

10. Some warranty and training costs are incurred by the manufacturer in order to service the airline's needs with respect to the aircraft.

In a situation such as the aircraft manufacturer, at what point or points does it make sense to say that revenue has been earned and should therefore appear on the income statement? We will develop some criteria in order to evaluate the so-called hardness or softness of the facts. For example, at different points in the process from point 1. (idea) to point 10. (after-delivery servicing), we could ask the following:

1. Can the amount of *revenue* be measured within a ''reasonable'' margin of error? (What is ''reasonable'' could depend upon various factors such as the objectives of accounting.)

2. Can the *costs* (such as cost of goods sold) involved in earning the revenue be measured within a reasonable margin of error?

3. Does the aircraft manufacturer have an *enforceable, legal contract* with a reliable (airline) buyer? That is, even though revenue can be measured, is cash likely to be received?

4. Do any commonplace or probable events stand in the way of the aircraft being built, in accordance with the contract? That is, even though the costs can be estimated, is it likely that an event, such as a strike, will prevent delivery on time as contractually agreed? This point queries whether there are any *significant uncertainties* that could interfere with the manufacturing and selling process.

Generally speaking, in the aircraft example, costs would not be known until several aircraft had been manufactured. This is because such complex situations are subject to what is called a "learning curve effect" where initial costs are much higher than they eventually will be—until employees learn to do their job efficiently. Revenue may be known quite precisely because the price could be set out in a contract. The airline may be on shaky financial grounds, or may have the right to cancel the order if specific conditions are not met, however. (For example, perhaps the aircraft manufacturer has guaranteed a low fuel-cost per passenger kilometre, and only time will tell whether the level will be achieved.)

Illustration 6-2 sets out what we know and do not know at various stages in the early life of the manufacturing and sale of a new aircraft. (Refer to points (1) to (10), described earlier.) Given the uncertainties up to, say, point (8), i.e., the facts are "soft", a company that had an income-tax postponement objective could wait until point (8) or possibly, later. Once we reach point (8), we would have to ascertain what costs and revenues are still subject to alteration, and whether the amounts involved are high enough to cause people to question the income figures. If the facts could lead us to more than one point of the (10), the final choice would be determined by objectives.

ILLUSTRATION 6-2

Ascertaining the Hardness or Softness of Measurements
—An Aircraft Manufacturer Example

	Point (3)	Point (6)	Point (8)	Point (10)
	Prototype Built?	Order Received for 20 Aircraft	Two Aircraft Are Completed	Warranty and Servicing Complete?
A. Revenue measurable?	no	generally yes	generally yes	yes
B. Costs measurable?	some are	not really	most are; some still to come	yes
C. Enforceable sales contract?	no	yes	yes	yes
D. Any significant uncertainties?	yes; much has to be done	yes; still much more to do	fewer than at earlier points	probably not

The aircraft manufacturer sets a policy for revenue recognition and tries to use it for *several* years. *Consistency* of application of accounting policies and methods helps readers of financial statements because they can watch for trends in the figures. The manufacturer might have two or more revenue recognition policies *if the facts differ.* For example, one type of aircraft may be sold on a basis that ensures immediate receipt of cash and no need for servicing after delivery. A second type of aircraft, however, may require much servicing and some modifications, and experience a delayed receipt of cash by the manufacturer.

Given the desire for consistency in revenue recognition, the company's management and board of directors would probably look ahead to try to forecast what will happen. Then, they will select one or more revenue-recognition policies to fit the facts that they expect to see and their objectives of accounting. Perhaps in five or six years, the facts and/or their objectives of financial accounting will change. If so, their accounting policies ought to change. Even though facts may change slowly over time (e.g., more and more costs may be incurred as a result of a warranty), a company is frequently *slower* to change its accounting policy.

As a *reader* of financial statements, we must always check to see what accounting policy a company is following, and whether the policy seems to make sense:

1. Given the objective of accounting *we* have in mind, and

2. Given the way the company conducts its business.

(Financial statements prepared in accordance with GAAP disclose accounting policies, such as revenue recognition, whenever they are unusual or not obvious.) Disclosure occurs in notes that accompany the financial statements. When what *we* seek differs from what the company has done, we will have to adjust the company's figures to our best guess of what we think they should be *for our purposes.*

Summary

This chapter sets out, at some length, a major theme— that accounting is adapted to fit the situation. We must see alternatives, seek new ways of resolving issues, and minimize prejudging or prejudice.

Let us step back for a moment and think about the need to tailor accounting to the situation. Judgment is called for in many situations in accounting. People's judgments differ. Accordingly, this book has been designed to include a number of opportunities that require the exercising of judgment. Our ability to evaluate situations will develop through practice.

Several objectives of general-purpose financial statements were provided in the chapter. A few generalizations about user and preparer power, ownership, size of company, need for funds, and similar factors were mentioned. Such generalizations are no more than aids to understanding. Our goal has to be to ascertain "what fits where"—what accounting method makes the most sense (not what is "right") after the pros and cons of each alternative are considered. In the first four chapters of this book, we acquired some facts about the basic accounting procedures that are followed by preparers. We have since considered the varied nature of situations in accounting in order to illustrate the importance of tempering facts with objectives of accounting and judgment.

QUESTIONS

6-1 In which respects would you agree or disagree with the following comment: Although there are a few situations in accounting where constraints or facts force us into one particular way of accounting, the most common situations in larger businesses require accountants to use their judgment. To exercise judgment, accountants have to know what they are trying to accomplish—their objectives of financial accounting and reporting.

6-2 Accounting has been described as adaptable. Do you agree? Explain your response.

6-3 What is meant by the "internal control" objective of financial accounting?

6-4 Is it possible for a company to have more than one special purpose financial statement for the same accounting period? Why?

6-5 Why can there be only one general purpose financial statement for each financial year of a limited company?

6-6 Is it possible to have only one basic objective of financial accounting and reporting?

6-7 If a company has chosen a tax objective of financial accounting, does this mean that it is not following GAAP?

6-8 Distinguish among the following objectives of a general purpose financial statement: tax postponement; minimum compliance; bonus/incentive plan.

6-9 What are the main differences between a public and a private company?

6-10 Give three reasons why it may be difficult for persons outside of the organization to use general purpose financial statements to evaluate management.

6-11 What are some of the difficulties in using general purpose financial statements to estimate the current market value of a company?

6-12 What is meant by *revenue recognition*?

EXERCISES

E6-1 You are an accounting adviser to Gordon's Garden Shop (GGS), a proprietorship. Gordon's financial year ends on December 31, to coincide with the calendar year that is used to assess taxes on individuals.

During the winter months, Gordon sells a variety of hobby items that people use during winter. Some of Gordon's customers are indifferent as to whether they receive the inventory items in December, or in January of the following financial year.

On December 27, 19—8, Gordon received a $10,000 cheque in the mail for hobby items that are needed by a local service club some time in the next few weeks. He has asked you whether he should send them the items before or after December 31.

You have learned that he will be sending the financial statements for the year ended December 31, 19—8 to his banker, who has loaned GGS $50,000. In addition, Gordon uses the financial statements for his personal purposes, and sends copies to Revenue Canada for taxation purposes.

What advice can you offer Gordon? Explain your response.

E6-2 Indicate when revenue would tend to be recognized in each of the unrelated factual situations noted below. Explain your reasoning.

1. A hairdresser cuts and styles a customer's hair, and receives cash payment.

2. A drug store sells merchandise for cash, or accepts a nationally-recognized credit card.

3. A newspaper charges customers as follows:
    A. Advertisers—as the advertising material appears in each day's newspaper, an invoice is sent to the advertiser.
    B. Purchasers of the newspaper—per week; or per copy, if the newspaper is purchased on a daily basis.

4. A used car lot accepts a 10 percent downpayment, and the balance is received over a 12-month period.

5. A life insurance company, which insures people on an annual basis as long as they pay their insurance premium each year.

6. A wheat farmer receives a sum from a government agency a few weeks after wheat is delivered to a grain elevator. Some months later, the farmer receives a large additional sum representing final settlement based on the price that the government agency received from buyers of the wheat.

7. A logging company sells logs to a customer. The price per unit is agreed upon, but the quantity will not be measured until the logs arrive at the customer's sawmill.

E6-3 Suppose that you were asked to choose revenue and expense recognition policies for Maple Leaf Publishers Limited (MLPL). You learn that their sole objective of financial accounting and reporting is income tax postponement. After reviewing the types of transactions that they are expected to encounter, you discover the following:

1. Much of MLPL's sales are books bought by retail bookstores. The retail bookstores are allowed to return up to 25 percent of their purchases for a period up to one year from the date of purchase.

2. Some of the bookstores are new and may not be able to survive economic downturns. Wherever possible, MLPL tries to sell to such stores on a cash only basis. However, it takes risks from time to time and issues credit to some of these bookstores.

3. Most of MLPL's sales are of books that it undertakes to publish itself. The company incurs the following types of *expenditures*:
    a. payments to printers and to binders,
    b. payments for advertising materials,
    c. salaries paid to editors, and other persons involved in producing the books,
    d. costs of operating the offices and warehouse,
    e. commissions paid to sales personnel,
    f. royalties paid to authors of the books (usually five, ten or fifteen percent of the price charged to the bookstores), and
    g. miscellaneous expenses (rentals, utilities, and similar) of operating a business.

4. Some of MLPL's sales are books that they import from other publishers, and sell on an agency basis. MLPL receives a discount of 40 to 60 percent on the net price at which the other publisher would normally sell in its home country. MLPL then markets the books on whatever basis makes the most sense in Canada. Usually, this means that it has to offer returns similar to (1) above.

Required:
How should each of the foregoing situations and activities be handled to help MLPL pursue its objective of accounting?

E6-4 Elmslie's Specialty Equipment Limited (ESEL) manufactures trucks and equipment according to customers' specifications. The following costs were incurred in November 19—8 in producing two specialty trucks.

Laborers	$ 64,500
Materials	100,000
Factory costs	45,500
Total inventory cost	$210,000

The trucks were sold on account for $248,000, with payment due in January 19—9.

Additional costs incurred in generating the sales revenue from the two specialty trucks:

Commission paid to salesperson	- December 19—8	$10,500
Delivery expenses	- December 19—8	1,250

The trucks were completed on November 28, 19—8. However, they were not shipped from ESEL's manufacturing plant to the customer until December 19—8.

Required:

Prepare a partial balance sheet at November 30, 19—8 and December 31, 19—8, and partial income statements for each of the months of November and December 19—8, assuming each of these two independent situations:
A: Revenue is recognized in November.   B: Revenue is recognized in December.
(Note: The partial financial statement shows only the effects of the transactions listed above.)

E6-5 Compute *taxable* income from the following information:

Revenue	$100,000
Cost of goods sold	55,000
Selling expenses	18,500
Administrative expenses	16,700
Interest expense	3,300
Depreciation expense	4,200
Capital cost allowance	6,000

$500

E6-6 The income statements of Tilleman Corporation for the years ended December 31, 19—6, 19—7 and 19—8 are as follows:

	(in thousands of dollars)		
	19—8	19—7	19—6
Revenue	$14,500	$13,000	$11,000
Cost of goods sold	8,150	7,080	5,400
Gross profit	6,350	5,920	5,600
Expenses:			
Selling	2,090	2,020	2,000
Administrative	1,460	1,400	1,390
Interest	320	300	280
Depreciation	600	550	500
	4,470	4,270	4,170
Income before income tax	$ 1,880	$ 1,650	$ 1,430

Required:

A. Suppose that you were asked to evaluate management's performance after reviewing the income statements for 19—6, 19—7 and 19—8. Provide your impressions, and explain your response.

B. What are some broad limitations of general purpose financial statements for those persons who desire to evaluate management's performance?

PROBLEMS

P6-1 Suppose that you are the general manager of a company, and a large portion of your take-home pay is based on a bonus of twenty percent of income before income taxes. How would you treat the following situations and transactions in 19—8, bearing in mind that your actions and methods would have to be credible? Explain your response.

A. One division in your company constructs medium-sized buildings on a contract basis. At the company's 19—8 year end, one-half of the construction on a major project was complete. It is expected that the division will make a $600,000 to $800,000 gross profit when the construction is completed in 19—9.

B. A large piece of equipment is repaired and improved at a cost of $40,000. The invoice from the repair shop does not clearly indicate what has been improved, and what has been repaired.

C. The company bought some land for $200,000 several years ago. The land is now worth about $700,000 and could be sold in 19—8. This land can be used to build a new factory. Or, the new factory could be built on land 20 kilometres away, which can be bought for $300,000.

D. A warehouse may be built on some land that can be acquired. Annual depreciation of the warehouse would be about $50,000. Alternatively, a warehouse building could be rented for $40,000 per year. If the building is constructed and owned, it is believed that its value will increase significantly in the future.

E. One assembly line will be productive for another 10 years if annual maintenance of $100,000 is incurred and paid. Without this maintenance the assembly line will have to be replaced in three to four years, at a cost of $2,000,000.

P6-2 The financial statements of Carter Real Estate Limited (CREL) for the year ended June 30, 19—9 are as follows:

Balance Sheet
June 30, 19—9
(In thousands of dollars)

Assets			*Liabilities and Owners' Equity*		
Current:			Current:		
Cash		$ 90	Accounts payable		$ 290
Accounts receivable		840	Bank loan		210
Inventory		190	Other liabilities		100
		1,120			600
Long-lived:					
Land		800			
Buildings	$8,150				
Appliances	620		Mortgages payable		5,550
	8,770		Owners' Equity:		
			Common		
			shares	$2,000	
Accumulated			Retained		
depreciation	1,290	7,480	earnings	1,250	3,250
		8,280			
		$9,400			$9,400

Income Statement
Year ended June 30, 19—9
(in thousands of dollars)

Revenue—rentals of buildings		$4,260
Expenses:		
Operating expenses	$1,565	
Real estate taxes	610	
Interest	820	
Utilities	170	
Depreciation	395	3,560
Income before income tax		700
Taxes on income		320
Net income		$ 380

CREL's main operations consist of renting office and apartment space to a variety of tenants. From time to time it will have a new apartment building constructed, finance it primarily through a debt issue, and then rent it for one or two-year periods, at market rates.

Required:

A. If you were asked to guess at CREL's objectives of financial accounting, which would you choose as being most important and why?

B. When would CREL recognize revenue? Why?

C. How profitable is CREL? Explain.

D. What are some limitations of conventional revenue recognition methods and policies for a company in the real estate rental industry? Explain.

P6-3 The balance sheet of Newton Mining Limited (NML) at December 31, 19—7 is:

NEWTON MINING LIMITED
Balance Sheet
December 31, 19—7

Assets

Current:

Cash		$ 499,500
Accounts receivable		5,500
Inventory		726,300
Prepaid expenses		31,700
		1,263,000

Long-lived:

Land	$ 600,000	
Buildings and equipment	1,756,200	
Mine under development	3,655,800	
Preproduction costs	1,100,000	7,122,000
		$8,385,000

Liabilities and Owners' Equity

Current liabilities:

Accounts payable		$ 262,500
Other current liabilities		122,500
		385,000

Owners' equity:

Common shares		8,000,000
		$8,385,000

As of December 31, 19—7, NML was still in the process of developing the ventilation system for its one mine. Some ore was extracted in 19—7 while the main shaft was being constructed, and the ore was refined into metal. The proceeds on sale of the metal had been credited to "mine under development". This procedure is conventional in many industries when the company is in its early stages, or not fully operational.

The common shares were sold to a small group of private investors. The developers of the mine believe that they now have sufficient funds to complete the mine. Several bank loans may be necessary to finance inventories and receivables. However, the amounts are not expected to be large, and the mine ought to be self-financing within a year or two.

The mining operations consist of blasting ore underground, bringing it to the surface through the main shaft, sending it through a concentrator to remove waste or excess rock, and then sending the concentrates to a smelter to be refined into metal. The process can take several months. Metal can either be sold in advance at agreed upon prices, or be sold at current prices after it has been refined.

Required:

A. In all probability, what would be the main objectives of financial accounting of NML?

B. What recommendations would you give to the owners about when revenue ought to be recognized?

C. What likely effect would the release of NML's financial statements for 19—8 or 19—9 have on the market value of NML? Explain.

P6-4 Mystery Books Limited (MBL) was recently sold to Mr. J. Williams, who decided to change the way the company's products were being marketed. Until recently, MBL acquired manuscripts from writers for a fixed fee, or on a royalty basis. The books were then marketed through the normal bookstore channels.

The new owner has decided to pay authors only on a royalty basis, for books that remain sold. That is, buyers have a right to return a percentage of the books that are shipped to them. Royalty payments would therefore be made on initial sales, less book returns.

The new marketing policy involves grouping books into different series, such as spy novels, murders, travel intrigue, and various combinations. People who wish to subscribe would then be sent a form each month telling them about this month's book in their series, and giving them an opportunity to receive it for review. They may either accept it or mail it back to MBL. Over the year, the subscribers have to accept at least six books, or pay the subscriber's minimum fee for six books. An option also exists whereby the subscriber can accept all 12 books in the series and receive a special discount. Whenever this 12-book option is chosen, no books may be returned, and full payment must be made within 90 days.

The new marketing policy commenced one month ago, and no useful data has been collected on returns. Approximately one quarter of the subscribers have selected the special discount option. Some books will still be sold directly to bookstores.

Mr. Williams does not intend to manage MBL. He has turned over all daily management matters to Mr. I. Band, who will receive a bonus based on income before income tax.

Required:

A. What are the most likely objectives of financial accounting for MBL?

B. What are the most appropriate revenue recognition policies for the different types of situations that MBL will encounter?

P6-5 Davis Real Estate Sales Limited (DRESL) has been in business for many years. Ownership of the company was recently acquired by H. Kennedy, a wealthy investor.

Up to and including the company's year end of December 31, 19—8, DRESL has been recognizing sales commission revenue whenever a real estate deal closed. A deal is considered closed when the buyer pays all sums due and is entitled to occupy the purchased property. DRESL's revenue arises from commissions that it earns by acting as a real estate agent in arranging sales of properties. A commission is usually three to six percent of the selling price of the property. The agency that locates the property and signs a sales agreement with the owner receives 50 percent of the commission. The agency that locates a buyer receives the other 50 percent. Salespersons are paid a pre-arranged commission by their employer agency, such as DRESL. Commissions are payable in cash when the deal closes.

You have been asked to comment on the suitability for DRESL of an idea that a person suggested to Mr. Kennedy. The person proposes that sales revenue should be recognized whenever the buyer and seller sign a standard real estate buy/sell contract. The real estate deal may actually close one to six months later. Sometimes, a deal does not close because a condition in the contract is not met. For those situations where the deal does not close, the revenue would have to be reversed.

Required:

A. Give the journal entry for commissions that would be made under the proposal:
   1. when the buy/sell contract is signed.
   2. when the deal closes.

B. For which objectives of accounting does it make sense to recognize revenue:
   1. when the buy/sell contract is signed.
   2. when the deal closes.

P6-6 What are the probable *differences* in effects on management's behavior if the managers receive a bonus based on:

1. Revenue in excess of a specified sum.

2. Gross profit.

3. Income before income tax.

4. Net income.

In answering, separately consider each of a retail grocery store, a professional organization such as a hospital, and a company that owns apartment buildings and rents them on an annual or multi-year basis.

EXPLORATION MATERIALS AND CASES

MC6-1 Tamboline Lumber Brokers Limited (TLBL) buys car loads of lumber from a sawmill and sells them to a variety of buyers such as lumber yards, construction companies, and other brokers. The lumber is often purchased on an estimated quantity basis. Also, it may require drying before it can become usable. Frequently, therefore, the lumber is measured several days after it has been purchased.

Often, the lumber is sold while it is in transit by rail car to a general destination, and before it has been measured on a final basis. Therefore, quantity adjustments have to be made to both the cost of goods sold and to revenue. Usually, the adjustments are for less than 10 percent of the revenue and cost of goods sold.

Required:

When would you recognize revenue in order to best accommodate the undernoted objectives of accounting? Consider each situation independently.

A. Income tax postponement objective.

B. Bonus/incentive program for sales staff and purchase staff.

C. Cash flow prediction objective.

MC6-2 Shifman, Shifman and Shifman (SSS) are chartered accountants who operate as a partnership. The firm has been in existence for several years and presently has five partners, three managers and a staff of about twenty-five. This year one of the partners, S. Shifman, is retiring and one of the managers, M. Mintz, will be admitted to the partnership. The partnership has a January 31 year end.

During the year, the firm moved its office in order to become more centrally located. Previously it was located 25 kilometres north of the city in a building which it owns. Now it is located 20 kilometres north of the city in an office which it rents from S. Shifman. The firm decided to retain the building which it owns because property values have increased dramatically since it was purchased twenty years ago. The original cost of the property was $100,000 and recently one of the tenants offered $600,000 for it.

Clients normally are billed at an hourly rate (differing rates exist for different levels of staff) at the completion of a job. Each staff member keeps track of the time he or she spends on a particular client and submits a weekly time report to the accounting office. Periodically, the accounting office summarizes these time reports by client, indicating the hours each staff member has spent to date on particular clients. At the completion of a job, the time spent by each employee is accumulated and extended at the employee's hourly rate. This rate includes a wage rate, a sum to cover cost of typists, stationery, office rental and an element of profit. The total sum of all employee time and cost is then calculated. The invoice sent to the client may be more than, less than, or equal to this total. When the invoice is sent, the firm records revenue.

Required:

One of the partners of SSS has approached you to provide an independent opinion on when to recognize revenue and how to record the accounting impact of the firm's move. Write a report outlining your recommendations. Your recommendations are particularly important to the firm because they will form the basis of determining how much capital M. Mintz must contribute on admission to the partnership.

CHAPTER 7

Revenue Recognition

Chapter Themes:

1. Small companies have to keep a close watch on cash receipts and disbursements because a weak cash liquidity position can lead to bankruptcy. *Accrual* accounting revenue recognition methods, i.e., ones that are not in synchronization with cash flow, may therefore be of less significance or perhaps be misleading to small companies that have to monitor their daily cash receipts and disbursements closely. Special-purpose reports that are used to try to forecast cash flows may help managers of small companies. Yet, for income tax purposes, general-purpose (accrual accounting) financial statements usually have to be prepared—and this requires the use of one or more revenue recognition policies, even for the smallest of companies that are required to pay taxes on the accrual basis.

2. Management of companies chooses revenue recognition policies and methods after giving careful consideration to the *facts* of the situation, *and* their *objectives* of financial accounting and reporting. GAAP allows many methods of recognizing revenue because of the existence of a large number of different objectives/facts situations. Legislation or constraints are relatively silent or non-existent with respect to revenue recognition methods. This may seem strange given the major importance of the revenue figure to a company's annual income statement. There are, however, *too many* different objectives/facts situations to provide a comprehensive listing of revenue recognition rules/constraints. Even if a list were provided, as business practices and laws change over time, rules could become awkward and may be more harmful than helpful. For example, a change in income tax law may make a particular method of accounting undesirable. Given the openness of the situation, we must focus on which of the methods makes the most sense under a particular set of objectives and facts.

3. Accounting policies (such as having two or three methods of recognizing revenue for different situations in a company) are usually set so that they may be applied for several years. That is, *consistent* application over several years helps readers to detect trend lines. The importance of *consistency* of revenue recognition policies and other accounting concepts is a major theme of Chapter 8. Chapter 7 therefore attempts to build up to Chapter 8 by stressing the need for accounting policies to be adapted to the specific objectives/facts situation.

An Application: One

Suppose that we have a rich aunt who wants to give us one of two small real estate companies that she owns. She wants us to make our choice based on a review of the annual income statements of the two companies. The income statements have been prepared in accordance with GAAP:

Real Estate Companies

Company A		Company B	
Revenue from tenants	$610,000	Revenue	$ 0
Expenses:		Expenses:	
Taxes on property	130,000	Taxes on property	40,000
Insurance	40,000	Insurance	3,000
Depreciation	60,000		
Office	42,000	Office	6,000
Advertising	67,000	Advertising	5,000
Other	98,000	Other	12,000
	$437,000		$66,000
Income before income taxes	173,000		
Taxes on income	63,000		
Net income	$110,000	Loss	$66,000

If we were not familiar with the flexibility within GAAP accounting, we would tend to pick Company *A*, which is showing a net income. We would probably feel that Company *B*'s net loss is not what we need at this time. Now that we know something about revenue recognition and GAAP, however, what questions would we ask our aunt? Here are some suggestions:

1. In which respects are the companies the same, and in which are they different? (That is, is it possible that the two companies are essentially the same, or are identical, and the *difference in income/loss is caused entirely by accounting policies and procedures*? For instance, one company, A, may be recognizing revenue in an earlier month or year than the other company, B. Suppose that our aunt says that although *both* companies are in the real estate business, Company A rents office buildings whereas Company B buys land from farmers, arranges to have the land rezoned to permit construction of houses and office buildings, and then sells the land to a company such as A.

2. How often does Company B sell the rezoned land? Suppose that our aunt says that it is difficult to be precise, but that a sale may occur only once every two or three years. This response should lead us to ask her whether a large net income might be expected in a few years. For example, is it possible that the net income over the next five years could look like this?

	Company A	Company B
First year	$110,000	$ (66,000)
Second year	110,000	(66,000)
Third year	110,000	532,000
Fourth year	110,000	(66,000)
Fifth year	110,000	566,000
	$550,000	$900,000

That is, we really should pick Company B—unless some other unspecified effects for Company B exceed $350,000 ($900,000 – $550,000) over the next five years.

The point of this illustration is twofold. First, it is to emphasize that assets held for resale, such as inventory, may be increasing in value. Yet, the *income statement would not indicate the increase* because revenue recognition may not have occurred *in accordance with the accounting policies followed by the company.* Second, the illustration shows that companies that appear to be in the same industry make their income in different ways. And, accounting policies *may not capture the differences* in ways that allow a reader to make useful comparisons among companies. In short, when we interpret the results of revenue recognition and other accounting policies, we have to understand the business that we are analysing and accounting for.

GAAP balance sheets *tend to* show the original cost of assets rather than their current worth. The land held by Company B would be shown on the balance sheet at original cost (amount paid to the farmer) plus some other costs (such as property taxes) that are described in later chapters. *If* a "sale" of the land to other companies meets the four criteria set forth in Chapter 6, such that

1. the amount of revenue can be measured within a reasonable margin of error, *and*

2. the costs of earning the revenue (that is, those costs that are capable of being traced to the revenue, such as cost of goods sold) can be measured in the way described in 1, *and*

3. an enforceable, legal contract exists (that is, in those situations where it is usual to sign contracts, which would *not* apply in the case of hairdressers/barbers), *and*

4. significant uncertainties do not exist,

then credible facts are in place, and point toward a recognition of revenue on the income statement. The criteria probably would not be in place until the third and the fifth years in Company *B*, however, when a buyer signs a contract to purchase the rezoned land.

In contrast, in Company *A* the criteria would be in place in every one of the five years *for the monthly rent. But,* the buildings being rented might increase in value over time (perhaps because of inflation). Yet, the increase in value of the building generally would not be recorded on the income statement until the building was sold and the four criteria were met.

Although one may think that accountants would credit *revenue* on sale of Company *A*'s building, they *do not* because the sale is of a long-lived asset—not of inventory held for resale. To illustrate, suppose that at the date of sale the building is shown in the ledger accounts at a cost of $10,000,000 with accumulated depreciation of $3,000,000. Suppose also that the building is sold for $9,200,000. The journal entry would be:

	Debit	Credit
Cash	$9,200,000	
Accumulated depreciation—building	3,000,000	
Building		$10,000,000
Gain on sale of building		2,200,000

In brief, in revenue recognition for a retail or merchandising organization it is important to remember:

Credit *revenue*—when inventory is sold
Credit *gain,* or debit *loss*—when a long-lived asset is sold

That is, if the building had been sold for $6,200,000, the journal entry would be:

Cash	$6,200,000	
Accumulated depreciation—building	3,000,000	
Loss on sale of building	800,000	
Building		$10,000,000

Note, however, that revenue would be credited on sale of a building if the company was in the construction business. That is, its inventory is buildings, or houses for sale. It is not, however, in business to sell its construction equipment. On sale of the construction equipment, a gain or loss would be recorded, as described above.

In total, for companies in the real estate business (and for others with similar facts), the income statements do not tell us about increases in asset values. On the balance sheets, inventories and long-lived assets would usually be shown at original cost. Income statements tell us only about the transactions that have been recorded as revenue, or as gains/losses—*in accordance with the company's policies.* When we discuss inventories in greater detail in later chapters, we will note that under GAAP, increases in the value of inventory do not appear on the income statement until the inventory is sold in accordance with the four criteria (or similar ones). Thus, we have to be careful how we use the figures that GAAP accounting produces. *Different people will interpret the four criteria in different ways,* leading to differences in income figures and balance sheets.

An Application: Two

Another illustration will help us to explore some deeper implications for accountants and managers of the choices that exist in accounting. Suppose that someone has offered us a share of ownership in a small company that sells food franchises. The company is called Scrumptious Canada Limited (SCL), and it has the Canadian distribution rights to a convenience food developed in the U.S.A.

SCL has analysed the Canadian market for its products and believes that it may be able to sell 1,000 or more franchises—which allow the *franchisee* to have exclusive rights to sell SCL's products in a particular region. The franchisee is required to pay SCL $50,000 for the franchise—either $50,000 now, or $10,000 per year for five years, with interest at 12 percent per annum on any unpaid balance. Also, the franchisee must pay a royalty of 4 percent on every dollar of sales. In exchange for the payments, the franchisee receives the "secret recipes" and other assistance in setting up the franchise and finding a suitable location.

Ignore what Canadian GAAP may say, and look at two possible ways of recording the sale of *one* franchise by SCL. At the date of sale, SCL may make either of two journal entries:

Method X			Method Y		
Cash	10,000		Cash	10,000	
Accounts receivable	40,000			Revenue	10,000
Revenue		50,000			

Suppose that we follow Method X in recognizing revenue, because we feel that the four criteria appear to have been met—and because we have confidence that the franchisee will be in business in five years and will make the necessary payments to SCL. What would happen if someone *who believed that we were following Method Y* saw our income statement, which showed Method X's method, after the sale of one franchise?

Revenue	$50,000
Expenses:	
(Details provided)	

The following incorrect conclusions may be drawn:

1. Five franchises were sold (instead of one).

2. $50,000 was received in cash (and not $10,000).

3. It is also possible, if the expenses were available on the above income statement, that a person may think that the cost of signing up a franchisee is only one fifth of what it is.

In a small company, the seriousness of any misunderstanding can be enormous. The manager of a small business may not understand what the accountant has done with accrual accounting and revenue recognition. The effect would be the same as if we were thinking that we had $50,000 in the bank instead of $10,000. Larger businesses have also been caught in this same revenue recognition trap and have lost hundreds of millions of dollars. They expanded operations based on revenue figures, instead of keeping track of cash flows, and the collectibility of their accounts receivable, i.e., $40,000 in our example. (For further details, see A. T. Demaree, "RCA After the Bath," *Fortune*, September 1972.)

After some recent, similar interpretation problems in Canada, Canadian GAAP has been tightened up. Interpretation and judgment still exist, however, and effects similar to the above could occur. The point of the two applications (provided in this chapter) is that the described variations occur throughout accounting, and not just for franchises and revenue recognition. Consequently, we cannot allow ourselves to seek out simple, all-purpose answers. We may find it easier, but it will not help us in the long run.

Revenue Recognition in General

The previous chapter stressed:

1. Organizations set revenue recognition policies so that the accounting method can be used for several years to aid readers in noting and analysing trends.

2. Accounting policies are set after carefully examining both *facts*, and expected *facts*, and *objectives* of accounting. Thus, it is possible to have more than one revenue recognition policy in a company because facts could differ for different types of sales of products.

3. "Facts" refers to criteria such as whether the revenue and expenses associated with a sale can be measured within a "reasonable" margin of error. What is reasonable depends on particulars of the situation, perhaps including the question of whether someone may try to sue for intentionally misstating accounting figures. (If there is a risk of being sued, a small margin of error is required.)

We have to be careful that, having noted the dangers of simplicity, we do not set out categories of simplified situations. We have to remember that many more *facts* and *objectives* of accounting situations exist that could lead to different, acceptable accounting treatment. We cannot assume that something we see in a company's financial statements is "wrong" just because it differs from what is considered in this book.

The common revenue recognition *situations* are:

1. Service is provided, and cash is received immediately, or shortly thereafter. (Barber/hairdresser example in Chapter 6.)

2. A contract exists setting forth the amount of revenue, and work is conducted over a long period of time, but expected costs are subject to close estimation. (An example would be a construction company that is building a large office tower for which the costs are reasonably predictable.)

3. A contract exists setting forth the amount of revenue, and work is done over a long period under conditions where costs are not easily estimated. (An example would be a construction company that is building a tunnel for a fixed price, but could lose money if bad weather causes delays or cave-ins or unexpected work conditions are encountered.)

4. A service or product is provided to the customer, but cash is due over more than one financial year. (An example would be the franchising illustration given earlier.)

5. A large portion of the service or product has been provided to the customer, but other services still have to be provided, and may prove costly. (An example would be where there are uncertainties about cost, such as when a warranty exists to replace the product if it does not work according to what is specified in the contract with the customer.)

6. The customer pays over a long period of time; uncertainty exists about cash receipts.

Situations (1) and (4) have already been illustrated at the end of Chapter 6 and at the beginning of this chapter. Situations (2) and (3) were briefly covered in Chapter 6, but another illustration involving a construction company should help in comparing and contrasting (2) and (3) with (1) and (4).

Situations (2) and (3): Percentage of Completion Versus Completed Contract Accounting

In construction companies, two common bases of accounting for revenue exist:

A. Recognizing revenue and related costs bit-by-bit as the work is progressing—called *percentage of completion* accounting (situation 2), and

B. Recognizing *all* revenue and related costs when the contract is, in effect, completed—called *completed contract* accounting (situation 3).

When the facts are clear, which tends to be infrequent in a risky business such as construction, each method would be used as follows:

Percentage of Completion—Used when the revenue figure is known within a reasonable margin of error, and the costs of completing the work are also known or can be estimated with little margin of error from what actually will happen.

Completed Contract—Used when either or both of revenue and expense are difficult to estimate within a reasonable margin of error.

The contrast between many merchandising/manufacturing companies and many construction companies is *extremely important.* In the typical merchandising (retail) and manufacturing company, revenue is recognized *when or after* the product has been "sold" (merchandising company) or the manufacturing process has been completed. In such companies, *most* of the costs tend to be known *as soon as* the goods have been purchased from suppliers, or have been manufactured. What is *not* known is the revenue. Thus, it is not until the customer appears, and agrees to buy, that we comply with the criterion of being able to measure revenue.

In contrast, many construction companies obtain their contracts by bidding for their work. Contracts tend to be awarded to the lowest bidder. Much of their work on contracts (except for what are called extras, which are usually billed at cost plus a profit) is done for a fixed revenue fee. The revenue is known early, but the costs usually are *not known* until the construction task is well underway. In short, in merchandising/manufacturing, the costs tend to be known before the revenue is. In construction companies that bid for their work, the revenue is known before costs are known or can even be reasonably estimated.

When the costs can be estimated as the work progresses, however, and the four criteria stated at the beginning of this chapter can be met, the percentage of completion basis can make sense. (We say "can" because when facts are unclear, objectives of accounting become important, and the board of directors may not want to use the percentage of completion method.)

To understand construction accounting, we have to contrast accrual accounting with cash basis accounting, as stressed in Chapter 5. Illustration 7-1 shows the journal entries for both the completed contract and percentage of completion methods. The figures are based on the following situation:

1. Assume, for simplicity, that the actual costs for the first, second, and third years of the construction contract turn out to be exactly the same as those forecast when the contract is awarded to us, because we made the lowest bid ($700).

	Forecast and Actual Costs	Amount Billed to Owner of Building by Us	Difference between Costs and Building
First year of contract	$200	$220	$ 20
Second year	300	340	40
Third year	100	140	40
Total	$600	$700	$100

ILLUSTRATION 7-1

Our Construction Company

Original Transaction Entries	Adjusting Journal Entries To Measure Income	
	Completed Contract Method	Percentage of Completion Method

First Year:

Original Transaction Entries		Completed Contract Method		Percentage of Completion Method	
Work in progress	200				
Cash, etc.	200				
Accounts receivable	220			Unearned revenue	233
Unearned revenue	220			Revenue	233
Cash	220				
Accounts receivable	220	No Journal Entry		Cost of contract	200
				Work in progress	200

Second Year:

Work in progress	300				
Cash, etc.	300				
Accounts receivable	340			Unearned revenue	350
Unearned revenue	340			Revenue	350
Cash	340				
Accounts receivable	340	No Journal Entry		Cost of contract	300
				Work in progress	300

Third Year:

Work in progress	100				
Cash, etc.	100				
Accounts receivable	140	Unearned revenue	700	Unearned revenue	117
Unearned revenue	140	Revenue	700	Revenue	117
Cash	140	Cost of contract	600		
Accounts receivable	140	Work in progress	600	Cost of contract	100
				Work in progress	100

2. Assume that our company makes the following journal entries:

A. As costs are incurred to construct the building:

Work in progress (this is a type of inventory account)	200	
Cash, accounts payable, etc.		200

(This entry charges all costs of construction to an asset account, to recognize the build-up of an inventory—building—for sale. Costs include labor, concrete, steel, equipment rentals, and any other expenditures for constructing a building.)

B. As the customer is invoiced for work that is done on the building:

Accounts receivable	220	
Unearned revenue		220

(It is *important* that we understand this entry. The contract allows us to send a bill to the customer every month, and to receive cash from the customer. The actual billing is a form of *cash basis* accounting and is not really associated with how we eventually recognize revenue—by way of either the percentage of completion or completed contract methods. Note that we have credited *unearned* revenue. We were able to bill $220 because the contract allowed us to do this.)

C. When the customer pays us in cash:

Cash	220	
Accounts receivable		220

The $220 is *not* revenue and the $200 is *not* the cost of goods sold. The $220 is *unearned* revenue (even though cash was received) and the $200 is *inventory* (even though cash was spent). The $20 ($220 – $200) is *not* a gross profit. One reason is that the contract may allow us to bill for only the completion of certain steps or segments in the construction process. And, of the costs of $200 incurred in the first year, perhaps only $187 relates to a completed segment; the other $13 could have been used to start another segment that will be completed in the second year of the contract—and billed at a later date.

We must be careful not to confuse the cash and accrual bases of accounting in this approach to revenue and cost recognition. The foregoing three journal entries (A, B, and C) are *original transaction* journal entries. (See relevant sections in Chapters 1 to 3.) When we recognize construction revenue, we are switching to accrual accounting and *adjusting* journal entries. The original transaction journal entries are the same, regardless of which method we use to measure income.

Under the *percentage of completion* method, annual income is typically arrived at by accountants from this formula:

$$\frac{\text{Costs incurred to date}}{\text{Expected total costs}} \times \text{Expected profit} = \text{Profit to Date}$$

To arrive at profit for any one year, we subtract profit recorded in previous years from "profit to date". Thus, for each of the years, we get:

First Year: $\dfrac{\text{Work in progress}}{\text{Total expected cost}} \quad \dfrac{\$200}{\$600} \quad \text{x} \quad \begin{matrix}\text{Expected profit} \\ (\$700 - \$600)\end{matrix} \quad = \quad \underline{\underline{\$33}}$

Second Year $\quad \dfrac{\$500}{\$600} \quad \text{x} \quad \$100 \quad = \quad \$83$

$\qquad\qquad$ *and* $\qquad \$83 - \$33 \text{ recorded last year} \qquad = \quad \underline{\underline{\$50}}$

Third Year $\quad \dfrac{\$600}{\$600} \quad \text{x} \quad \$100 \quad = \quad \$100$

$\qquad\qquad$ *and* $\qquad \$100 - \$83 \text{ recorded in previous years} \qquad = \quad \underline{\underline{\$17}}$

Under some situations (with different facts), accountants will depart from the foregoing formula. For example, suppose that construction is occurring in the Far North, and that the needed material can only be barged in when the water is not frozen, which is just a few weeks a year. Although all the necessary materials may be at the northern construction site (but they have not been used in construction), this does not mean that they should be included in the "costs incurred to date" portion of the formula. In all likelihood, most accountants would not include materials delivered to the construction site but not yet used.

When a loss is expected on a contract, the expected loss is *not* picked up in accordance with the formula. The entire loss would be recorded when it became measurable. That is, suppose in the first year that we realize that we made a mistake in bidding—we bid $500 for the job instead of $700. Our journal entries in the first year may be:

Unearned revenue	100	
Revenue		100
Cost of contract	200	
Work in progress		200

Returning to Illustration 7-1, what would the financial statements look like for the percentage of completion method in the first year?

Balance Sheet

(in part)

Assets

Work in progress	Nil
Revenue recorded in excess	
of billings	13

The "revenue recorded in excess of billings" acknowledges that higher billings are expected shortly because a high profit is anticipated on the contract. Thus, the $13 figure can be regarded as an asset in the sense that it will be billed/invoiced soon.

Income Statement

(in part)

Revenue	$233
Contract costs	200
Gross profit on contract	$ 33

Note: The company follows the percentage of completion basis for recording revenue on contracts that extend beyond two financial years for which costs and revenues can be closely approximated.

Under the *completed contract* method, all income statement effects are deferred until the contract is completed. This is, until the contract is in essence completed, we find ourselves unsure whether actual costs will closely approximate our cost estimates.

Some construction companies use both methods of recognizing revenue because they have different types of construction contracts, with different risks. Sometimes their customer may want alterations or additions to the original contract. These "extras" may be handled on a completed ("extra") contract basis whereas the original contract may be accounted for on a percentage of completion basis.

Tie-In to Objectives of Accounting

Illustration 7-2 sets out the general approach that companies follow when they wish to set accounting policies and methods in situations where there are few or no legal constraints. Much of the foregoing discussion of risks and measurement centred on the "fact" side only.

ILLUSTRATION 7-2

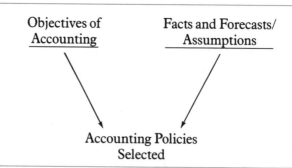

When the facts are subject to considerable interpretation, or are unknown, objectives of accounting become important. Suppose that we are paid in part through a bonus plan tied to accounting income. (See Chapter 6, "Bonus/Incentive Plan".) Which basis for recognizing revenue would we want to see in use? We would prefer percentage of completion because we would get our bonus each year, and not have to wait until the end of the contract. (Maybe we would no longer be with the company in two or three years.) Thus, we would try to measure the "expected profit" figure needed for the percentage of completion formula.

In contrast, suppose that we owned the company and wanted to postpone paying income taxes. We should try the completed contract method. This is one of the situations where Revenue Canada has its own rules, however. They will allow completed contract only when the contract will be completed in two financial years. Thus, for the three-year contract noted in Illustration 7-1, the percentage of completion method would have to be chosen for income tax purposes.

Another situation arises when management does not want to show wide swings in net income. Obviously, the percentage of completion basis of accounting would be used wherever possible.

Situation (5): Services Still To Be Provided

Sometimes, a manufacturer develops a new product, and, in order to sell it, has to offer an "extended warranty" for two or more years. (Some automobile manufacturers have five-year warranties against defective parts and labor.) As experience is gained in pinpointing design or manufacturing weaknesses, the warranty period and type of defect covered by the warranty can be reduced. In the first few years of a product's life, however, costs of servicing and manufacturing (including warranty costs) may be uncertain. What revenue recognition policy ought the company to adopt?

Some possibilities are to recognize revenue:

1. When someone buys the product;

2. When the warranty period expires; and

3. When someone buys the product; but, accrue a liability for possible costs of servicing the warranty. (Debit expense and credit "Estimated liability for warranty".)

Each of the three possibilities has pros and cons when we think about specific *facts* and *objectives* of accounting. For example:

1. When someone buys the product it may:
   - Be suitable when warranty costs are expected to be negligible. That is, most expenses and revenues would be known fairly closely. (Fact)
   - Not be suitable for a "tax postponement" objective because taxes may have to be paid in an earlier financial period. (Objective) (See the beginning of Chapter 6 for comments on tax deferral.)

2. When warranty period expires it may:
   - Not be very suitable if any defective components of the product are known early in the warranty period, after the customer has used it just a few times, and repair expenses are incurred. (Fact)
   - Not be suitable for a manager's income bonus plan objective if warranty costs are not expected to be high. That is, payment of the bonus would be delayed, perhaps "unfairly". (Objective)

3. When a person buys but expected warranty costs are accrued it:

- May be a reasonable compromise if the warranty-cost estimate proves to be close to actual. (Fact)
- Would not be suitable for income tax purposes. A specific income tax rule exists to prevent *estimates* of expected warranty costs from being expenses that are deductible for tax purposes. In computing income subject to income taxes (called taxable income), expenses can be claimed only when the work has been done and cash has been paid or is payable under accrual accounting. That is, tax would have to be paid on the revenue, but a warranty expense could not be claimed until perhaps the next financial year. (Objective)

The above discussion is important for managers who become involved in choosing accounting policies that meet their needs. In this book, we are being exposed to a variety of accounting methods and how they can affect readers. Choice (3) initially looks to be an interesting compromise; but, unless we ask what are the income tax implications, we could make a very poor choice.

The journal entries that would be used in each of the situations are:

1. When someone buys the product: (Assume selling price of $2,000 and inventory cost of $1,100.)

Accounts receivable	2,000	
Revenue		2,000
Cost of goods sold	1,100	
Inventory		1,100

2. When the warranty period expires:

   A. When customer receives delivery of product:

Inventory in customer's possession (Mr. *X*)	1,100	
Inventory		1,100

   B. When some warranty costs are paid:

Warranty expense	330	
Cash		330

   C. When the warranty period expires:

Accounts receivable, or cash	2,000	
Revenue		2,000
Cost of goods sold	1,100	
Inventory in customer's possession (Mr. *X*)		1,100

If the warranty expense is incurred in the same period as when the warranty expires, the gross profit on the sale would be $570 ($2,000 less $1,100 less $330). When the warranty expense is incurred in an earlier period , however, entry (2B) ought to be:

| Warranty costs prepaid (asset +) | 330 | |
| Cash | | 330 |

Then, when the warranty expires, (2C) would have this additional entry:

| Warranty expense (expense +) | 330 | |
| Warranty costs prepaid (asset −) | | 330 |

The effect of the second entry would be to put the expense of $330 in the same period as the revenue and cost of goods sold.

The journal entry under (2A) merits some comment. The point of (2A) is to ensure that revenue is *not* credited. We are, however, acknowledging that the inventory product is not in our warehouse, but is in the hands of the customer. This concept can appear in many different settings and companies.

3. When person buys; but accrue expected warranty costs:

A. When customer receives the product:

Accounts receivable	2,000	
Revenue		2,000
Cost of goods sold	1,100	
Inventory		1,100
Warranty expense	350	
Estimated liability for warranty		350

B. When the warranty costs are paid:

| Estimated liability for warranty | 330 | |
| Cash | | 330 |

C. When the warranty expires:

| Estimated liability for warranty | 20 | |
| Miscellaneous income | | 20 |

This entry in (3C) recognizes that the estimated costs of the warranty ($350) exceeded the actual costs ($330) by $20, and that the $20 remaining in the estimated liability account can be closed to an income statement account. (Alternatively, the $20 may be left in the liability account, and used for other warranties.)

The point of the illustration is that income may be affected in each of several years by using one of the three alternatives instead of another. For example, suppose that the date that the customer receives the product, the date that the warranty costs are incurred, and the date that the warranty expires are in three different financial years. Income and balance sheet effects could be immense if sales volume is high.

Situation (6): Cash Paid in Installments

Some years ago, a form of percentage of completion accounting was used when cash was paid over several financial periods. The accounting method operated as follows:

Selling Price	$5,000
Cost of goods sold	3,500
Gross profit	$1,500

Customer pays $100 per month for 50 months.
Gross profit per month = $1,500 divided by 50 = $30

Journal entries:

A. When the inventory is delivered to the customer:

Inventory in customer's possession	3,500	
Inventory		3,500

B. When a $100 payment is made, each month:

Cash	100	
Revenue		100
Cost of goods sold	70	
Inventory in customer's possession		70

This installment method of recognizing revenue eventually came to be regarded as being ultra cautious. That is, if the seller is so concerned about the ability of the customer to meet the monthly payments, why is the sale taking place? If the customer is basically trustworthy, the seller should be using the situation (1) method (debit asset; credit revenue) and making the conventional entry for possible "bad" debts:

Bad debts expense, or doubtful accounts expense	$xx	
Allowance for doubtful accounts		$xx

If the bad debt expense provision has to be large, the seller should not accept the sale/purchase.

More will be said about this type of method of accounting when we discuss interest on the unpaid balance of $5,000. Several different ways of journalizing the revenue and expenses exist.

REVENUE RECOGNITION REVIEW

Revenue recognition can be viewed as the anchor for the income statement. Whenever accountants record revenue, they try to match to that revenue the costs of earning the revenue. The basic income statement format is:

Revenue		$xxx
Less expenses:		
Ones that can be traced directly to the sale		
(e.g., cost of goods sold)	$xx	
Period costs (expenses that exist whether or not a sale		
takes place, e.g., heat and light in store)	xx	

If the period costs (incurred with the passage of time) are small, net income is heavily affected by when revenue is recognized. And, when revenue is recognized, the balance sheet is affected by changes in accounts receivable, inventory, unearned revenue, estimated liability for warranty, and similar accounts. The entire picture portrayed by financial statements can be deeply affected by revenue recognition.

Summary

Chapters 6, 7, and 8 form a package in which we focus our full attention on a primary theme of the book—that accounting has to be tailored to the specific situation. If objectives and facts and constraints are the same for two businesses, it would be convenient for readers if both companies were using the same accounting policies for revenue recognition, and for recording expenses. In an actual accounting situation, however, two different methods are probably in use. The consequences on income and balance sheet figures could be significant.

In a computer age, it is even easier to accept numbers as being fully representative of a situation, and then proceed to use them for all kinds of analyses. Computers can do many analyses for us at little cost. The accounting figures, however, must be thoroughly understood, just as they have to be in manual accounting.

As minor shareholders of a large company, we may not have the power to demand or receive information that better helps us to interpret accounting data. But, when we are in a responsible position with a stock broker or underwriter, bank, trust company or similar institution, we can ask "the right questions". There is no alternative. We have to know what assumptions went into the preparation of the figures. What accounting policies, such as revenue recognition, were used?

Chapter 8 delves further into the assumptions that some accountants make in the process of preparing journal entries. Together, Chapters 6, 7, and 8 get to the heart of accounting and what it is all about. Much of Chapter 9 and beyond explain the bookkeeping (Chapters 1 to 4) and the conceptual foundation (Chapters 6 to 8) of the subject.

APPENDIX 7-A
A Problem Solving Technique

Appendix 7-A introduces the process of how to tailor accounting to the specific environmental factors that affect a company or other organization, e.g., a charity or an educational institution. Specialists perform particular steps in solving problems.

Often, the specialists are not fully aware of the steps that they go through. As non-specialists, we have to condition ourselves to undertake *each* of the steps until we are comfortable, and able to develop problem-solving techniques and styles of our own.

Appendix 7-A illustrates a commonly used problem solving technique—one that may be used well beyond accounting: in buying an automobile, renting an apartment, and in choosing university courses. The process commences with knowing what are our objectives and purposes. Next, we have to have a good grasp of what is the problem that we are trying to solve. Without having a good comprehension of (1) objectives and related factors, and (2) the precise nature of the problem, subsequent analysis is likely to be meaningless.

As we know that accounting must be adaptable in nature, it is never too early to link up different procedures, such as revenue recognition, with the specific situations in which they make sense. The longer we wait, the greater are the chances that we fall into the trap that particular accounting procedures apply in all of the different types of companies and organizations.

INTRODUCTION

Chapters 5, 6, and 7 have been emphasizing the importance of avoiding the belief that there is one right answer to accounting problems. These chapters have also stressed the need to tailor accounting policies, procedures, and practices to fit each specific situation. Several important factors may vary in business situations, and we must be alert to their presence and their effect on accounting. A *few* of the more important factors are:

1. The *objectives*—goals or prime pursuits of the organization. (Profit seeking? Best possible health care, e.g., hospital care?)

2. The *ownership* of the organization. (Private company? A public one? Unincorporated? The existence of different ownership could result in quite different objectives for each of the companies.)

3. Factors that are *critical* to the *success* or *failure* of the organization. (Each organization's success is a result of doing particular jobs very well, such as better than competitors; or, as a minimum, meeting the needs of customers. What is critical could be product quality, cash control, location of the stores, etc. Sometimes, accounting plays an important role in monitoring what is critical; sometimes it does not. We cannot impose accounting when it does not fit the situation.)

4. *Decisions* that have to be made in order to pursue the goals or objectives of the organization. (Where may accounting play an important role in decisions? What type of information is of greatest help to those who are entitled to the accounting information?)

5. *Problem situations* that stand in the way of being able to pursue the goals and objectives of accounting, and require decisions to resolve them. (Where may accounting help?)

6. *Management* of the organization may be either professional employees or be the owners. (Owners need little motivation to work hard for their company. Professional managers, however, may have to be motivated with income-based bonus plans.)

Given the existence of these important factors, and given that they vary from organizational situation to organizational situation, it becomes essential that we begin to develop a way of analysing these different situations. We can begin with what may be called a "generic problem-solving technique"—one that we may use in a variety of situations—to help us in tailoring accounting to the specific problem situation. As we gain experience, the generic technique can be replaced by ones that we design to fit the specific problem situation that we are facing.

PROBLEM SOLVING STEPS

The major steps in the generic technique are as follows:

1. Identify the goals and objectives of the *organization* (not of accounting, see Chapter 6) under examination, *if* they are provided in the question/problem situation. (Some questions may be testing memory skills rather than problem solving skills. Therefore, they may not provide any information about an organization's goals and objectives.)

2. Ascertain the factors that are critical to the success or failure of the organization. (Does it have to borrow funds in order to survive? If so, does a prospective creditor want a cash transaction statement, such as is noted in Chapter 5?)

3. Identify the decisions that have to be taken to ensure that the organization is able to pursue its goals and objectives efficiently. (For example, what decisions are needed to maintain liquidity and profitability, as discussed in Chapter 5?)

4. Locate any problem situations that are currently preventing the organization from efficiently and effectively pursuing its goals. (For instance, the managers may not be adequately motivated; therefore, the owners of a company may want to introduce a bonus plan. For the plan to be effective, accounting measurements must be made in a way that appears to be fair to the managers.)

5. Rank the problem situations in order of their importance to the organization, and its goals and objectives. (Criteria are needed to rank, and these are derived from the objectives, critical success and failure factors, urgency of the situation, and similar matters. For example, it may be necessary to solve a liquidity problem *first*, before changing revenue recognition methods to make them more suitable for a bonus plan.)

6. Generate possible solutions for each of the problem situations that you have identified. (For most situations in accounting, there is *not* one right answer. We usually have to make a choice from possible solutions, none of which are completely to our liking.)

7. Identify the pros and cons of *each* of the alternative possible solutions. (The pros and cons have to be from the point of view of the organization's goals and objectives, and similar factors. Pros and cons include the desirability and feasibility of the alternatives, plus the costs and effectiveness of each alternative.)

8. Choose one of the alternative solutions, and identify why you believe that it is the most suitable of those that are available. (That is, make a decision by choosing one alternative instead of the others, and justify your choice.)

9. Explain how you would implement your chosen approach so that it eliminates or minimizes the undesired effects of the problem(s) that you have identified in 4.

It is important that *all* steps (1 to 9) be taken. If one is missed, the chances are high that our discussion of the situation will be inadequate. Our advice may therefore be worthless to the people who we are trying to help in the organization.

AN ILLUSTRATION

The foregoing problem-solving technique can be illustrated by using some of the material in chapters 5, 6, and 7. It is important to recognize that we are displaying only one possible way of approaching the problem situation.

This is *not* the only way, and it should therefore *not* be used as a model answer for all non-memory problems that are provided in the remaining chapters of this book. However, it is a beginning.

Straw Construction Limited

Straw Construction Limited (SCL) was incorporated under federal corporate legislation many years ago. Until this year, 19—8, the company was owned and managed by Mr. Little, who submitted all the bids required to obtain construction contracts. (Such contracts usually are awarded to the lowest bidder.) Mr. Little arranged all of the accounting policies and procedures for SCL to aid in the postponement of income taxes.

In January 19—8 all of the voting common shares of SCL were purchased by Mr. A. Wolff. Mr. Wolff's experience has been in the demolition business, and he does not feel qualified to manage SCL. Mr. Wolff therefore hired Mr. Brick to manage SCL. Mr. Brick is to be paid a salary plus 10 percent of the annual net income of SCL. Mr. Brick is very experienced in making construction bids, and in managing construction projects. Mr. Wolff was very fortunate in being able to obtain the services of Mr. Brick.

You have been hired in early 19—8 by Mr. Wolff and Mr. Brick in their capacities as owner and manager of SCL. They would like you to choose new financial accounting policies that would be fair to both Mr. Wolff and Mr. Brick, given their different circumstances. You investigate the business activities of SCL and discover the following:

1. Mr. Little employed the completed contract basis of revenue recognition wherever possible. (Revenue Canada allows its use for contracts that do *not* extend

beyond two financial years. When a contract requires work in three or more financial years, percentage of completion would normally have to be used.) He did not want to have his ledgers any different from what would be used to calculate taxable income. As a result, he sometimes had to use percentage of completion when Revenue Canada required it.

2. Mr. Little would not include in revenue any amount that the buyer of the property could legitimately holdback. A holdback is warranted when adequate inspection still must occur, or the terms of the contract still have to be fulfilled. (Revenue Canada allows companies to postpone the recording of revenue, or taxable income, if cash payment is being held back for an extended period in accordance with the terms of a contract.) Generally, these holdbacks were not really merited for accounting purposes because the construction work had already been performed satisfactorily. The holdback existed just in case cracks developed in concrete, or similar defects appeared—and because the contract permitted a holdback.

3. Mr. Little depreciated assets such as equipment in accordance with the procedures permitted by Revenue Canada. Generally, this meant that depreciation expense was higher in the early years of the equipment's life than was merited through its usage.

Required:

Prepare a report to Mr. Wolff and Mr. Brick recommending appropriate financial accounting policies and procedures. Provide your reasoning in support of your recommendations.

One Possible Response to Straw Construction Limited (SCL)

We ought to commence our analysis with the objectives or goals of SCL. The owner obviously wants to make as much net income as possible. If the 10 percent bonus figure is sufficiently motivating to Mr. Brick, he too would want to see as high a net income as possible. Thus, there is agreement about the objectives of the *organization*. (Agreement is important, because too much energy can be lost if people in an organization do not agree about the purposes of their activities and efforts.) Notice that although the objectives of the *organization* are to maximize net income over the longer term, a major objective of *accounting* in the short run could be to postpone the payment of income tax.

Next, we look at factors that are critical to the success or failure of SCL. In a construction business the critical factors are:

1. The skill of the person(s) who submits the bid for new work or contracts. If the bid is too high, someone else will be awarded the contract. If the bid is too low, we will win the contract but lose money. Therefore, we have to find the "just right" figure for a bid.

2. The skills of the person(s) who manages the construction work, to ensure that the costs incurred are close to those that were estimated in compiling the bid figure.

3. Interest rates—which might escalate, and cost SCL an additional amount on the funds that it has to borrow to pay for materials and labor incurred during the construction period.

4. Strikes, work slow downs, and labor unrest.

5. Unfavorable economic conditions that could bankrupt the company if they continue for long, and few companies want to build new plants or expand.

The important decisions that have to be made centre on having good information for managers, so that they can bid and carry out their duties and responsibilities. Much of this is in the realm of engineering—which deals with quantities of concrete and steel and similar commodities that are needed in construction projects. Accountants can help by keeping track of cash requirements, and by ensuring that the key person, Mr. Brick, is sufficiently motivated through an effective reward system.

Mr. Wolff has to make a choice between the *two* objectives of accounting that *now* exist in SCL—income tax postponement, and measurements to assist in the computation of the income-based bonus plan. The choice should be obvious—he needs a good manager for SCL because he cannot do the job himself. Therefore, he has the problem of ensuring that Mr. Brick is sufficiently motivated, and agrees with the basis of calculating the bonus. The basis of calculation is largely an accounting matter.

In terms of ranking the problems, the bonus plan comes first. Cash control would come second. Income tax postponement would come third, but it is closely related to cash control. (The more that income tax is postponed the more that cash is saved.)

SCL's income is affected *most* by the revenue recognition policies that have been chosen. (This is important because of the revenue's size.) Mr. Brick would be upset if completed contract accounting were used regardless of the situation. (Who wants a bonus two years from now, instead of today, after you have worked hard to earn the bonus?)

What alternative solutions might we offer? We could try to separate *types* of contracts i.e., pin down the *facts*, into (1) those that are susceptible to reasonable measurement of expected profit during the construction period, and (2) those where measurement of expected profit cannot be reasonably made until the contract is completed. (The last stage of a contract may be critical in some situations, because we may not know how well an asset functions until it has been completed.) Measurement would have to be made by other than Mr. Brick and his assistants. Otherwise, the net income and effects of the bonus plan could be manipulated by Mr. Brick.

The contracts would seem to break down into these additional categories:

1. Susceptible to reasonable measurement of expected profit during the period of the contract:
   A. Work performed in two or less financial years of SCL.
   B. Work performed in three or more financial years of SCL.

2. Not susceptible to reasonable measurement of expected profit during the period of the contract:
   A. Work performed in two or less financial years of SCL.
   B. Work performed in three or more financial years of SCL.

For category (1A) we could use percentage of completion in calculating the bonus, and completed contract in calculating income subject to taxation. That is, Revenue Canada allows us to use a different method of revenue recognition in 1A than we use in our ledgers. For category (1B) we could use percentage of completion for both the tax and the bonus objectives.

For category (2A) we could try to arrive at a percentage of completion figure for purposes of computing a bonus. However, when we identify the pros and cons of this alternative, the cons of having to guess at the expected profit are likely to outweigh the pros. Hence, we would probably recommend the completed contract method. (We might also recommend the opposite if we felt that Mr. Brick might be upset and regard the approach as unfair.) Category (2B) is troublesome because Revenue Canada *may* insist on taxing some of the revenue, and related expenses, even though expected profit estimates may be uncertain, or arbitrary. But, because of delays in assessing taxes, their insistence could come two or more years *after* the contract has been completed. However, if Revenue Canada *is likely* to insist, then the same figures as are used for computing taxes could be used for the bonus plan. On the other hand, Revenue Canada *may* allow postponement until the contract is completed. If so, completed contract accounting could be used. Of the four categories, this is the most difficult one on which to reach a conclusion. It also is the one that allows us to demonstrate our imaginative and creative skills. Quite obviously, there is no easy solution or right answer. We therefore choose an approach—such as using a rough-and-ready percentage of completion—and justify it in terms of our prime objective with respect to the bonus plan. That is, we ranked the bonus plan as more critical to the success of SCL than other objectives. Thus, in the event of a "tie" after considering our pros and cons and alternatives, we would tend to pick the alternative that favors the bonus plan.

A similar procedure would be followed for the holdback and for depreciation. That is, the holdback *may* be excluded for tax purposes, but the bonus would be calculated after treating the holdback as revenue. As well, depreciation for purposes of the bonus *could* be different from what is used for tax purposes. (A later chapter explains how these differences are handled.)

Summary

Procedures and techniques of accounting have to be fitted to the overall business or organizational setting. Business owners and managers have to make decisions to keep their company on track, pursuing its goals and objectives. Where might financial accounting help? We have to proceed through steps (1) to (9). If we leave out a step, we get much the same results as when we leave out a step in the bookkeeping/accounting cycle. As with the material in Chapters 1 to 4, the more we practice, the better our understanding. We have to avoid the temptation to look for a right answer, and deal with competing alternative solutions. Which makes the most sense?

QUESTIONS

7-1 "Accountants should have only one method of recognizing revenue. Then, it would be easier to compare several companies to determine which is more successful." Do you agree with this comment? Explain.

7-2 "Many of the problems of revenue recognition would not exist if assets were recorded at their current worth, instead of at original cost." Do you agree?

7-3 Why would a company not credit revenue when it sold the factory building that it had been using for 20 years?

7-4 How restrictive are the GAAP constraints that may apply to revenue recognition? (Does GAAP severely limit a company's choice of revenue recognition methods?)

7-5 Compare and contrast the following sets of companies, with respect to their probable revenue recognition methods:

A. A corner grocery store and a real estate company that receives commissions on sales of property (such as the building in which the grocery store is located.)
B. A construction company that builds office complexes, and a construction company that has to build facilities under severe weather conditions in the arctic.
C. A cable television company that receives a monthly payment from subscribers, and a company that offers annual service contracts on television sets (i.e., the customers pay a fixed fee, and receive free service whenever the television breaks down).

7-6 What are the major differences in income measurement between a construction company that receives a fixed fee for its work, and one that receives payment for all costs that are incurred, plus a profit based on incurred costs?

7-7 Under which circumstances is it sensible for a company to recognize revenue in accordance with:

A. the completed contract method?
B. the percentage of completion method?

7-8 When the facts category is unclear or unknown, objectives of financial accounting play an important role in the selection of accounting policies. Give some examples of unclear facts, or situations where assumptions have to be made, that pertain to revenue recognition.

7-9 Why is revenue recognition of major significance in the income measurement process?

7-10 What is meant by "factors that are critical to the success or failure of an organization"? Give some illustrations, and explain how they might affect revenue recognition policies and methods.

7-11 List the major generic steps that usually have to be followed in solving business problems. Explain the importance of each step. What might happen if some steps are not followed?

7-12 What effect on the choice of revenue recognition policies might occur as a result of an organization's structure? Explain with reference to an unincorporated company, a private company and a publicly-owned company.

EXERCISES

E7-1 Boritz Construction Corporation (BCC) builds shopping centres and office towers on a fixed fee basis. It obtains all of its work by competitive building.

Suppose that the following cash receipts and construction costs were incurred for contract 90-03:

	Invoiced to Owner of Building and Received in Cash by BCC	Construction Costs Incurred
19—7	$ 300,000	$250,000
19—8	300,000	250,000
19—9	400,000	300,000
	$1,000,000	$800,000

Suppose, also, that the amounts shown above are the same as was forecast by BCC. The contract was started in 19—7 and completed in 19—9.

Required:

A. Give the journal entries that would be made in *each* of the three years (19—7, 19—8, 19—9) assuming that the following revenue recognition methods are being used:
   1. Completed contract
   2. Percentage of completion

B. Compute the income in *each* year, and explain how this would be reported on the income statement, assuming that the following revenue recognition methods are being used:
   1. Completed contract
   2. Percentage of completion

E7-2 Gristle Burgers Limited (GBL) has 40 different locations that sell its fast food line. During 19—9 GBL sold two of its outlets that were not profitable. Costs and proceeds of sale were:

	Asset Cost	Accumulated Depreciation	Proceeds of Sale
Outlet Location 22	$195,000	$ 62,000	$140,000
Outlet Location 36	570,000	195,000	300,000

Required:

A. Give separate journal entries to record the sale of each of the two outlets, 22 and 36.

B. How and where would the sales be reported on the financial statements of GBL?

E7-3 King Corporation (KC) encountered the following situation in 19—9:

January: Inventory costing $1,000 is ordered by a customer at a retail price of $1,499.
February: The inventory is shipped to the customer.
June: $130 of warranty costs are incurred on the inventory shipped in February. The warranty expires at the end of July.
September: A cheque for $1,300 arrives from the customer who received the inventory in

February. An allowance for bad debts of $199 is thought necessary for the additional sum that is owing.

Required:

For the circumstances described above provide journal entries by month for 19—9 in each of the following unrelated situations:

A. Revenue is recognized when an order is shipped.

B. Revenue is recognized when some warranty costs are paid.

C. Revenue is recognized when the warranty period expires.

D. Revenue is recognized when cash is received.

E7-4 Rusty's Used Cars Limited (RUCL) uses the installment basis of recognizing revenue on the sale of its used cars. Some of the customers have questionable credit ratings and may never make the final payments. As a result, the cars may have to be repossessed, and sold to another customer.

The data for one of the cars sold by RUCL is:

Cost	$6,000
Selling price (in November 19—8)	8,000
Cash down payment made	2,000
Monthly payments (ignoring interest on selling price)	200/month

Required:

Provide journal entries to record the sale of the automobile, and the cash receipt of one month's $200 payment.

E7-5 Newton Publishing Corporation (NPC) is engaged in publishing textbooks for the university and college market. The company's financial year ends on December 31. NPC ships books to university bookstores in accordance with the bookstores' estimate of expected sales. NPC allows the bookstores to return 50 percent of the dollar value of what was shipped to them in the previous twelve months.

During 19—8 Brennan University purchased and returned the following:

January to August: purchased $250,000 of inventory at invoice price; inventory cost is $110,000.

September: Brennan University pays NPC $250,000.

November: returned $100,000 at invoice price; inventory cost is $41,000. No further returns are expected of inventory that was sold to Brennan University in January to August. NPC issues a cheque for $100,000 to Brennan University.

December: purchased $150,000 at invoice price; inventory cost is $62,000.

In February 19—9 Brennan University paid NPC $150,000. In April 19—9 Brennan University returned $30,000 at retail, and $12,000 at inventory cost, of the books that were sold to them by NPC in December 19—8. No further returns are expected from the December 19—8 sale.

Required:

A. Prepare journal entries for NPC for 19—8 and 19—9 for its transactions with Brennan University. Assume each of the following different revenue recognition points:

1. date of shipment

2. date of cash collection of an invoice

3. expiry of the date for which books may be returned (i.e., 12 months).

B. Prepare income statements for NPC for 19—8 and 19—9 for each of the three different revenue recognition points.

C. Which of the three revenue recognition points seems reasonable to you, assuming that you are:
1. the owner of NPC
2. the general manager, who receives a bonus based on income before income taxes of NPC
3. the company's banker.

E7-6 Compute the effect on income for each of 19—7, 19—8 and 19—9 if Carter Corporation (CC) had changed its method of recording revenue on long term construction contracts from the completed contract to the percentage of completion method. During this period there were two contracts in process:

	Invoiced to Owner of Building and Received in Cash by CC	Construction Costs Incurred
Contract #1234:		
19—7	$ 600,000	$ 500,000
19—8	600,000	500,000
19—9	800,000	600,000
	$2,000,000	$1,600,000
Contract #1236:		
19—7	$ 300,000	$ 400,000
19—8	300,000	300,000
19—9	400,000	200,000
	$1,000,000	$ 900,000

Assume that the above receipts and costs were exactly as was estimated at the beginning of the contract.

PROBLEMS

P7-1 Milburn Silver Mines Limited (MSML) sells its silver on two different bases: when ore is refined and when a reliable buyer seeks delivery. That is, some metal is sold at fixed prices months in advance of production. This ensures that the company has a sale, and that enough cash receipts are forthcoming to provide some stability for the mine's operations. The remaining product is then sold at market prices that exist at the time that a sale contract may be arranged, which could be up to several months after the metal is refined.

The basic mining process at MSML consists of (1) blasting out the rock and ore underground, (2) bringing the ore to the surface, (3) sending the ore through a concentrator, to separate unrefined metal concentrates from waste, and (4) sending the unrefined concentrates to a metal refinery. This process could take from three to ten months, and is dependent on factors such as weather, strikes and backlog at the refinery. Silver metal is measured in ounces and traded on this basis.

During 19—8 the following occurred:

Inventories of ore, concentrates and metal as of January 1, 19—8 were nil.	
Ore blasted and brought to surface	1,000,000,000 kilograms
Ore refined into metal	800,000,000 kilograms
Silver metal recovered from 800,000,000 kilograms of ore	6,000,000 ounces
Cost of recovering 6,000,000 ounces of silver	$5.10 per ounce
Selling price for 4,000,000 ounces of silver sold in advance	$8.20 per ounce
Selling price of 1,000,000 ounces of silver sold after being refined	$8.60 per ounce
Silver inventory on hand at December 31, 19—8	1,000,000 ounces

Required:

A. Prepare journal entries for 19—8 for cost of goods sold and revenue, and prepare the gross profit section of MSML's income statement for 19—8, assuming:

1. *All* revenue is recognized at the completion of the refining process, using the prices that apply to metal that has been sold in advance.
2. Revenue is recognized on two different bases:
   a. on completion of the refining process, for metal sold in advance at fixed prices,
   b. on delivery of the metal, for situations where the metal is sold after it has been refined.

B. For each of the situations set forth in (A) provide the current asset section of MSML's balance sheet at October 31, 19—8 assuming both of these factors:

1. the 4,000,000 ounces of silver sold in advance were refined and delivered prior to October 31, 19—8,
2. the 1,000,000 ounces of silver sold for $8.60 per ounce were contracted for, and delivered, in December 19—8. (Refining occurred in October 19—8.)

P7-2 The president of Lanfranconi Construction Limited (LCL) has recently decided to account for some of the company's new construction contracts on a completed contract basis. Until this year, 19—8, all contracts were accounted for on the percentage of completion basis. However, in 19—8, the riskiness of some of the types of contracts that LCL chose to bid on was intentionally increased, in the hope of generating some higher profits.

At December 31, 19—8 LCL had incurred the following costs and had generated the following receipts and receivables on the two contracts for which it had decided to use completed contract accounting:

Accounts receivable (for invoices rendered on the contracts in December)	$1,200,000
Cash received from previously rendered invoices	8,800,000
Costs incurred to date on the two contracts	9,450,000

The two contracts are expected to be completed in late 19—9.

The accountant for LCL offered two alternative presentation methods for the December 31, 19—8 financial statements for the contracts to be accounted for under the completed contract method:

Method A:

Current assets:	
Accounts receivable	1,200,000
Current liabilities:	
Amounts billed on contracts in progress in excess of	
related costs of $9,450,000	550,000

Method B:

Current assets:	
Accounts receivable	1,200,000
Costs of contracts in progress	9,450,000
Current liabilities:	
Amounts billed under contracts in progress	10,000,000

Canadian GAAP does not set forth a preference for either method. Corporate law does not comment on this situation.

Required:

A. Which method of presentation (A or B) would you prefer if your objective of financial accounting is minimum compliance with corporate law?

B. For which objectives of financial accounting would method B be preferable to method A?

P7-3 King Electronics Limited (KEL) was incorporated many years ago by William King. KEL sells a variety of electronic equipment that it imports from Asian countries. It also sells service contracts of two and three year duration. The service contracts contain fixed fees per year, and cover the cost of all labor and parts that could be incurred in repairing electronic items sold by KEL. A customer who purchases a service contract would normally not have to pay any sum in excess of the service contract fee, unless the component became damaged through an accident.

Until this year, 19—8, KEL had been operated by professional managers, because Mr. King was too busy to spend the time to improve the company's share of the market. In January 19—8 the company was sold to Ms. Growth, who terminated the professional managers and decided that KEL would be owner-managed.

In the financial statements to the year ended December 31, 19—7 KEL followed these accounting policies:

1. Revenue from the service contracts was recorded on a monthly basis at one-twelfth of the annual fixed fee. Expenses of servicing the contracts (such as labor and spare parts) were recorded as they were incurred in repairing a customer's component or equipment.

2. Revenue was recognized at the time of shipment of equipment or components, regardless of the terms of sale or credit rating of a customer. That is, some customers were allowed to pay over extended periods, such as eight to ten months. Sometimes, equipment was shipped to customers who had a questionable credit rating.

3. Expenses were recorded as they were incurred. The professional managers often had considerable freedom in deciding what would be expensed, and what would be capitalized as an asset. In general, the accounting policies had been chosen to recognize that the professional managers were receiving a bonus based on income before income tax. As a result, whenever judgment had to be exercised about a particular transaction, earlier revenue recognition was selected over later recognition.

Ms. Growth has approached you to assist her in reviewing the accounting policies in light of the departure of the professional managers. Her prime concern is avoiding the premature payment of income tax. She believes that she can explain any necessary changes in policies to KEL's banker.

During 19—8, the following volume is expected:

Delivery of electronic equipment:	
to governments	$2,600,000
to large companies	3,200,000
on extended credit	1,300,000
to customers with borderline credit ratings	150,000
Service contracts	1,800,000

Required:

Advise Ms. Growth, giving a thorough explanation of your recommendations.

P7-4 Colavecchia Enterprises Limited (CEL) was incorporated several years ago. The company operates two large retail stores. One sells sports clothes, the other sells sports equipment. CEL maintains separate income statements for each of the two stores. Three senior managers in each of the stores receive a bonus based on the profitability of their store. For income tax purposes the results of the two stores are combined into one income statement.

During the year ended January 31, 19—9 the following transactions occurred:

1. Sales by the clothing store amounted to $4,620,000 cash. Cost of goods sold was $2,965,000.

2. Sales by the sports equipment store amounted to $2,770,000 cash. Cost of goods sold was $1,305,000.

3. Sales returned by customers for cash were:

	Selling Price	Cost
Clothing store	$420,000	$272,500
Sports equipment	295,000	135,000

4. In the year ended January 31, 19—9 CEL decided to bid for sales to sports clubs and various charities. Discounts of 10 or 15 percent were offered on merchandise purchased in high volume. During the year, sales from these sources amounted to $2,016,000. The merchandise that was sold would normally have been on this basis:

	Selling Price	Cost
Clothing store	$ 940,000	$ 560,000
Sports equipment	1,300,000	590,000
	$2,240,000	$1,150,000

Required:

A. Prepare journal entries to record the sales, cost of sales, and returns for the 19—9 fiscal year.

B. Prepare the sales, cost of goods sold and gross profit section of the income statements for CEL, and for each of the two stores, for 19—9. Explain your computations.

C. Explain the pros and cons of CEL's bonus plan. Review the bonus plan from each of the owners', as well as from the managers' viewpoints, commenting on how different revenue recognition methods may affect the amount and timing of the bonuses.

P7-5 DeRooy Automotive Limited (DAL) operates an automobile repair service. The company has three different types of customers:

1. Those who bring in their cars on a periodic basis for engine repairs.

2. Those who subscribe to the coupon service. This allows people to buy prepaid repair services at a 10 percent discount. That is, they can buy discount coupons by paying cash. The coupons may not be used for 30 days from the date of purchase. This is to prevent people from buying discount coupons only when they know that they face an immediate and costly repair bill. The coupons are then valid for a period of up to five years. DAL can earn interest on the cash paid for the coupons.

3. Multiple automobile customers, such as taxi companies. Such customers are given a 10 percent discount on all repairs, and further lump sum discounts when annual repairs exceed specified sums, such as $50,000 or $100,000 or more.

The prime users of DAL's financial statements are Revenue Canada and the company's banker. The banker understands that DAL does not wish to pay income taxes earlier than is necessary. Consequently, there is no need to recognize revenue as soon as is possible, given the nature of the sales arrangements.

Required:

Select appropriate revenue recognition policies for DAL's transactions, and explain your reasoning.

P7-6 For each of the undernoted, independent situations, set forth feasible revenue recognition policies and methods that the company might use. For *each* method or policy indicate the circumstances (objectives of accounting and facts) where its use would seem to be sensible.

A. *Magazine publisher* Subscribers pay on a subscription basis of one, two or three years. The subscription rate is $60 for one year, $105 for two years, and $135 for three years. Advertisers pay every time one of their advertisements appears.

B. *Muffler repair shop* The shop warrants that it will replace the muffler or tail pipe free of charge "for as long as you own the car". On average, a new muffler or tail pipe should last for three to four years, unless large amounts of salt are used on roadways, to melt ice.

C. *Bus company* Most of the passengers buy batches of 10 or 20 tickets in advance, and use them periodically. Some passengers buy a monthly pass. Others pay cash.

D. *Soft drinks company* By law, the company is required to pay customers 5 cents for each soft drink can that they return to a "returned container" depot.

E. *Automobile insurance company* The company charges its insured customers a fee per year. Sometimes the company spreads its risk by selling a portion of the insurance coverage to another company (called a reinsurance company). For example, a customer may be insured for $1,000,000; but the insurance company may hold only $400,000 of the insurance risk.

F. *Credit card company* The company may buy credit card invoices from various stores for 95 cents or 96 cents on the dollar. The credit card holder may pay an annual fee of $24. Also, the card holder would have to pay interest on any monthly balance that remains unpaid 20 days after it is invoiced to the credit card holder by the company.

P7-7 Computer Software Limited (CSL) prepares software programs for a variety of clients. During February to May 19—8, CSL prepared a computer program at a cost of $195,500. The program was delivered to the client in June 19—8, and was invoiced to them at $375,000. However, the program did not operate successfully for some types of transactions. In July and August 19—8, $87,900 of warranty costs were incurred in correcting the program and ensuring that it worked in accordance with the contract between CSL and the client. In late August 19—8 the client agreed that the program met the terms of the contract, and paid the $375,000 to CSL.

Required:

A. Prepare journal entries on an appropriate monthly basis to record CSL's transactions assuming the following independent situations:
   1. Revenue is recognized when the program is delivered to the client for the first time, and no warranty costs are accrued.
   2. Revenue is recognized when the program is delivered to the client for the first time, and estimated warranty costs of $50,000 are accrued.

B. If most of CSL's contracts incur substantial warranty costs, what revenue recognition policy would you recommend for CSL? Why?

P7-8 Davis Forest Products Limited (DFPL) sells its products in Canada, the U.S. and Europe. In early 19—7 DFPL sold $1,650,000 of lumber products to a company in Europe. The terms of sale required a cash deposit of $200,000 and the balance within 120 days. Unfortunately, the European company went bankrupt before the remaining $1,450,000 was paid.

DFPL recently decided to introduce a "retention of title" clause in its standard sales agreement. Such a clause ensures that DFPL retains legal title to its products until full payment is received from the customer. Thus, trustees in bankruptcy have to treat the lumber products as a secured asset owned by DFPL.

Until the introduction of the "retention of title" clause, DFPL was recognizing revenue when the lumber was shipped to Europe.

Required:

Discuss the impact of the introduction of the "retention of title" clause on the company's revenue recognition policy. Is the policy still appropriate? Why?

EXPLORATION MATERIALS AND CASES

MC7-1 Gilbert Mutual Fund Limited (GMFL) is an open-ended mutual fund incorporated under federal legislation. As an open-ended fund, it may issue and redeem its common ownership shares at any time. Shareholders of GMFL buy and sell shares at the estimated current fair market value of the fund's assets less liabilities. All share transactions are made between the shareholder and the fund, rather than between two or more shareholders.

GMFL's assets are invested in the shares and bonds of other companies, primarily those companies that issue a large dollar volume of shares and bonds. Generally, with large issues, a quoted market price exists, thereby helping GMFL establish the fair market value of its mutual fund shares.

GMFL's primary sources of revenue are the dividends and interest received on its invested share and bond assets. Operating expenses and income taxes are paid out of this revenue, leaving a net income figure before gains and losses on disposal of shares and bonds. Normally, dividends paid by GMFL are equal to 100 percent of its net income.

The share and bond assets owned by GMFL are traded only when the managers believe that the timing is appropriate. As a result, there can be considerable differences in amounts between the cost of the shares and bonds paid by GMFL, and the current selling price of these assets.

The two main users of GMFL's financial statements are Revenue Canada, and the shareholders/prospective shareholders. Revenue Canada taxes GMFL on dividend and interest income less operating expenses, plus or minus gains and losses on sales of share and bond assets. The shareholders desire to know the current market value of their mutual fund shares in case they would like to redeem their shares or buy more.

Required:

Discuss how GMFL might set up general purpose and special purpose financial statements to accommodate the different objectives of accounting. How would revenue recognition be handled in each of the reports?

MC7-2 Brooks Real Estate Limited (BREL) owns several apartment and office complexes. Many of the buildings are financed by short-term mortgages that represent 60 percent of the value of the land and buildings at the date that the mortgage is arranged.

BREL is owned by about 40 investors who are friends of the founder, L. Brooks. The company is managed by a professional manager, Mr. Quick. Most of Mr. Quick's time is spend ensuring that monthly rents are collected from the tenants, and that repairs are carried out satisfactorily.

This year has been difficult for the company, because interest rates and operating expenses have risen, and governments have restricted the amount of annual rent increases that may be charged to tenants. The year end of the company is in two months, and Mr. Quick has been trying to find ways to increase the company's income. He believes that the investors might vote to dismiss him if profits are too low.

He has proposed that two apartment buildings be sold before the company's year end. Large gains are expected on sale of these buildings. He would use the proceeds on sale of the buildings to buy two other apartment projects that would have similar annual rental revenues.

Required:

A. Discuss the pros and cons of Mr. Quick's proposal.

B. Are accounting policies, or GAAP, heavily influencing Mr. Quick's thinking? Explain.

CHAPTER 8

Financial Accounting Concepts

focus our minds on the "relative state"—and not seek out a non-existent all-purpose approach. Under a specific set of circumstances, one particular accounting treatment makes more sense than the alternatives. This same treatment could be misleading, however, under a different set of circumstances.

KEY ACCOUNTING CONCEPTS

Some basic ideas or concepts followed by accountants have been mentioned from place to place to this point in the book. Examples are consistency, cost, and matching. Our understanding of the subject of financial accounting is aided when we are able to set out comprehensive lists of concepts that accountants follow. As we know, one all-purpose list does *not* exist because of the vast number of possible combinations of *objectives* and *facts* and legal *constraints* (companies legislation, for example). Judgment plays an important role in accounting measurement and disclosure. Good communication between preparer-accountant and the user ensures that the reader of the financial statements knows what criteria the preparer used in making judgments, and what the final decisions were that impacted on the figures on the financial statements. These criteria (such as consistency and cost) are used extensively by accountants when written GAAP constraints (such as those set forth in the CICA Handbook) are minimal or non-existent. For instance, throughout our discussions of revenue recognition, few rules were mentioned. We have to work continuously at improving our professional judgment because the business world is continually changing. We need to be aware of the effects of our judgment on income and balance sheet numbers. Much of chapters 6, 7, and 8 are devoted to giving the background that is needed to practise professional judgment in financial accounting.

In some sense, a listing of key concepts, and their definitions, has to be *specific to one particular objective* of accounting. That is, a set of concepts exists for the "income tax postponement" objective, a different set exists for "compliance with minimum requirements of corporate laws and GAAP", and a different set exists for a "cash flow prediction" objective. We are going to illustrate only the last two objectives—to stress the point that there is *more than one* set of concepts. We cannot allow ourselves to lock into only one set—thereby restricting our thinking to the point where we (1) misinterpret financial statements and (2) misunderstand the need for an adaptive approach to accounting and financial reporting.

Minimum Compliance Objective

The concepts that follow were originally formulated over fifty years ago. Although we have included them under the minimum compliance category, some accountants claim that these concepts have wider application. (A few accountants use only these concepts. Therefore, we have to be careful when interpreting a company's financial statement because they may have been prepared strictly on the basis of this somewhat restrictive listing.)

1. Entity	7. Revenue Recognition/Realization
2. Unit of Measure	8. Consistency/Comparability
3. Arm's-Length Status	9. Continuity/Going Concern
4. Cost	10. Disclosure (versus Measurement)
5. Objectivity	11. Materiality
6. Matching	12. Conservatism

These concepts will be referred to frequently in the book. At first, they may seem abstract; but we will see how thay can be an aid to our understanding of minimum compliance.

ENTITY

An entity may be defined in several ways. For our purposes, the entity is "whatever we are accounting for". That is: Who wants the information, about what (entity), and in order to make which decisions? It is very easy in accounting to account for more, or less, than what is needed by someone to make an intelligent decision. Therefore, we have to make clear to ourselves, and to readers of financial statements, exactly what "entity" the financial statements purport to represent. In financial accounting, the entity can be (a) a limited-liability company or corporation, (b) a proprietorship (one owner, unincorporated business), (c) a partnership (two or more owners of an unincorporated business), (d) a co-operative (sharing of profits by several people), (e) a charitable institution, (f) an employees' union, (g) a division of a corporation (e.g., Chevrolet division) or many similar forms of organization.

How many entities might we want to account for? Suppose that we have the following sources of income:

1. A bank account that bears interest,
2. 100 common shares of the Royal Bank of Canada,
3. a part-time job at a local store,
4. 50 percent ownership in a small partnership that sells used books.

First, we should determine how many entities exist: bank account = 1; Royal Bank shares = 2; part-time job = 3; partnership = 4; and all of them together = 5. For how many would we want a separate set of books? It depends upon the decisions that we want to make, and how complex is the business.

For income tax purposes, we would need entity (5)—the "all of them together" situation—because all of the first four entities generate taxable income. We may want records for (2)—to determine what dividends we have received over the years and, by comparing this to current information including selling price, to decide whether we wish to sell or hold the shares. We also may wish to have a set of books for (4)—the partnership—to help in dividing the income among the partners. The information prepared for entity (5) clearly would be confusing for the decisions affecting (2) and (4).

The more complex the organization is, the more attention we have to give to defining the entity. To illustrate, suppose that we own a building that has our retail food store on the ground floor, four rental apartments on the second and third floors, and our apartment on the fourth floor. We work in the store. At the end of the first year of owning the building and store, an accountant friend prepares the following income statement:

Year ended April 1, 19—6

Revenue from sales and rents		$308,500
Cost of food sold		200,100
Gross profit		108,400
Expenses:		
Heat, light, water	$ 6,350	
Depreciation	10,600	
Taxes and licences	13,800	
Part-time clerks	6,900	
Repairs	3,200	
Other	4,150	45,000
Income		$ 63,400

Of what use is this income statement? Count the "errors" in it.

1. For income tax purposes, a December 31 (calendar year) year end would be useful because people pay income taxes on a calendar year basis.

2. The figures are a mixture of apartment rentals and food sales and expenses. The two entities (food and apartments) are different. Is one entity more profitable than the other? The building may be worth keeping *if* the food store can be sold to others who would pay rent for the space that is occupied.

3. Do the expenses include heat, taxes, and the like for the apartment that we live in? Personal expenses should not be mixed with business expenses. The personal expenses are not deductible for income tax purposes, and may confuse us when we want to calculate the profitability of the store and the separate apartments.

4. The profitability of the food store cannot be calculated unless:
   A. Revenue from the stores is kept separate,
   B. The store is charged a "rental" for the space that it occupies, and
   C. The store is charged reasonable wages for the work that we do.

5. The income statement does not show income taxes. (This is *normal for unincorporated businesses*, however, and is not a "mistake". The owners, not the business, attract income taxes in unincorporated businesses. All proprietorship and part-

nership income is viewed by Revenue Canada as automatically being "distributed" to the owners.)

In summary, we have to know what it is that we are accounting for before we can prepare financial statements. If we are careful, we can get by with only one set of books, if we have enough separate ledger accounts to enable us to prepare separate financial statements for (a) the store, (b) the apartments, (c) for income tax purposes, and (d) for personal items (apartment, and assumed wages from the store).

UNIT OF MEASURE

Accountants usually use *dollars* (or the currency of the country) to measure. There are some benefits to measuring in dollars but there are also some serious shortcomings. One beneficial feature is that a common denominator exists in which to express a diverse group of assets and liabilities, e.g., trucks, supplies, accounts receivable. Another feature is that most business people think in terms of dollars.

The two chief shortcomings are potentially very serious ones: many assets and liabilities cannot easily be expressed in terms of dollars, and what the dollar will buy varies from year to year as a result of price inflation/deflation. How helpful is a set of financial statements when a buyer and a seller meet to decide whether to sell a company? It depends upon many factors. The buyer is acquiring a future whereas the financial statements are based on units of measure of the past. Will the past repeat? The financial statements do not measure people, and customer loyalty, and the potential of being in a particular location—factors that are difficult to express in dollars.

Over time, the changing purchasing power of the dollar (as a result of inflation) takes on greater significance. For instance, suppose that a company owns five automobiles of the same model and manufacturer, but that they were acquired in five different years. The "cost" figure on the balance sheet may show:

19—1	$10,000
19—2	10,800
19—3	12,000
19—4	13,200
19—5	14,100
	$60,100

Possibly, at the date of purchase, the five automobiles were the same. But the cost has increased each year because it took more dollars to buy the same quality and quantity of goods. (In Chapter 17, more will be said about how accountants may handle inflation and changing prices.)

The measuring unit—the dollar—has a major impact on how we account and how we ought to interpret financial statements. Companies that are *not* greatly affected by inflation/deflation, e.g., accountants, and lawyers' partnerships, and the factors that cannot be measured in dollars, e.g., the changing worth of people, have financial statements that are easier to understand and use. Accountants and lawyers may need their financial statements only for distributing profits among partners, and for income tax purposes. For other organizations and situations, the limitations of using the dollar measuring unit can be severe.

ARM'S-LENGTH STATUS

The concept of "arm's length" arises frequently in business, and is especially important in income tax legislation. The basic idea is that we are not able to deal at arm's length with those who are associated with us through blood, marriage, adoption, etc. For example, as the operator of a proprietorship, you cannot deal with yourself, as an employee, in setting an arm's-length (or fairly-bargained) salary level. The amount would be meaningless. Thus, accountants *either* do not record a phony figure for the proprietor's salary on the income statement of the proprietorship, *or* they clearly say what it is: Salary of proprietor—$xxx. On seeing the latter, the reader should realize that the figure may not represent "fair market value".

Although the concept of arm's-length seems clear, in reality it can be complex. Accountants try to avoid recording transactions that may appear to be arm's-length, bargained, figures when they really are non-arm's-length, or *related party, transactions*. To illustrate, we look to a topic that we just discussed: revenue recognition. Suppose that we have Canadian rights to sell a particular line of "fast foods". We decide to sell franchises to various interested businesspersons. One potential buyer is a company that is *50 percent owned* by a close relative. Would this be an arm's-length transaction? Should any revenue be recorded? If so, would it be recorded in full or just for the one-half owned by the "third" person (called a third party)—i.e., our relative's "partner"? To respond to these questions, we have to know more facts about the selling price, payment terms, and similar information that tells us whether the contract is the same as would be signed for an arm's-length sale. It may well be quite complex.

Similarly, consider an automobile dealership. Typically, a dealer will sell the automobiles manufactured by one company, e.g., Ford. Do the manufacturer and the dealer operate on an arm's-length basis? Many of the dealer's business decisions reflect policies set by the manufacturer. Usually, the dealer is not really free to refuse to stock a new model. But, what is the accounting effect? This situation is fairly clear to most readers of financial statements. They know that the success of the dealer is heavily dependent upon maintaining good relations with the manufacturer. Probably all that is needed on the financial statements is some indication of the relationship. Perhaps it would suffice to see, on the balance sheet, a major liability, "Owing to Ford of Canada".

In contrast, what if the manufacturing company is heavily dependent on one of the major department stores for 80 percent of its sales? Our company might make an Eaton's, or the Bay's, brand name under some year-to-year contract. Should the financial statements report: (a) the nature of the relationship? (b) the dollar amounts involved? (c) both? or (d) nothing? Again, we know that there is *not* one right answer. If the sole user of the financial statements is Revenue Canada, the matter is not relevant. They are interested in taxable income. We need not follow GAAP. Suppose that the financial statements are also being used by our banker or other creditors, however. These people would like to know that our company is economically dependent upon one large customer. If we lose the contract, we could go bankrupt quickly. Thus, in Canada, GAAP requires the use of an *economic dependence* note to the financial statements, reporting the existence of dependence (but *not* also giving the dollar amount). At some future date, GAAP may also call for the disclosure of dollar effects. The thinking underlying "existence note only" disclosure is that the note ought to be sufficient to encourage readers to ask questions of management about the relationship.

COST

Early in the book, we stressed that many assets are *usually* recorded at their original cost. Some exceptions were noted, however, and more will be discussed in subsequent chapters. For example, accounts receivable is recorded at cost plus a profit. (Technically, receivables ought to be reported at net realizable value, or the amount of cash that will be received.)

Why would accountants—following a minimum compliance objective of accounting—adopt concepts such as cost, arm's-length, unit-of-measure, and similar ideas? It is clear that accountants do not like the idea of changing value figures. There is considerable overlap in all the concepts, and that overlap favors systematic stability in the measurements. Some reasons in favor of stability are: (1) maybe the numbers will be more believable than others for some objectives, e.g., income taxation, (2) maybe accountants will be less subject to criticism if they avoid value changes in assets, caused by changing economic conditions, and (3) maybe accountants do not have the expertise to value some assets, e.g., people. Regardless of the original motives of accountants, it is clear that the way in which accountants exercise their duties has a *major impact* on what the resulting income statements and balance sheets tell us. These minimum compliance concepts definitely have a common thread of "stable, original costs".

What is "cost"? This is one of the most difficult questions that accountants must answer. They need to ask the question: Why do you want to know? The cost of an asset for income tax purposes may well differ from the cost figure that would be useful in deciding what to charge a customer, or whether it costs too much to keep manufacturing a particular product. The cost figure has to be tailored to the situation—as was described in Chapter 1.

Although we will proceed to give *one* definition of cost for a minimum compliance objective, what should not be forgotten is that this is *only one* of several possible definitions. Subsequent chapters will keep refining the definition, and will add other definitions. It is wise to prepare ourselves mentally for the following sum up: The cost that I use in any situation has to be specifically tailored by me to suit the particular situation that I face. In short, we have to think like a made-to-measure tailor does.

Accountants often become involved in giving "expert witness" testimony in court cases which can range from criminal cases about cost, e.g., predatory pricing, to disputes about contracts, where the contract uses the word "cost" as if it has only one possible definition and interpretation. Many businesspeople, lawyers, and financial writers look only for a simple definition of cost (and of revenue). Cost calculated for one purpose could be totally inappropriate for another purpose.

For a minimum compliance objective, under GAAP, it is best to try to keep the accounting process as simple as possible—and therefore as inexpensive as possible. Nevertheless, cost usually is defined to recognize two points: (A) cost should include all expenditures made to ready the item for resale (inventory) or use (long-lived asset, such as a machine), and (B) cost is the lowest cash cost, and *excludes* interest expense incurred to finance the asset. Unfortunately, there are circumstances where (A) and (B) conflict with each other—such as when a large factory, financed temporarily by borrowings from a bank, is still being built, and no products are available for sale. Two illustrations are helpful in clarifying (A) and (B).

Suppose that we own a grocery store in Canada, and buy our grapefruit and oranges from California and Florida. We pay (1) the U.S. grower in U.S. funds; (2) the bank to exchange our Canadian dollars for U.S. dollars; (3) the trucking company that brings the produce to our warehouse; (4) the person who unloads the truck; (5) the driver who delivers from the warehouse to our retail stores; (6) the person who places the produce on the shelves, so that the customers can buy; (7) store cashiers; and (8) store janitors. Which of these costs should be included as the cost of inventory?

Point (A) says that we should include costs from (1) through (6), because these are the costs of bringing the inventory to the point where it is *available to earn revenue.* (Thus (1) through (6) are assets, until the inventory is sold.) We exclude (7) and (8) because these are *period expenses* not traceable to particular revenue. (Period expenses go directly to the income statement.) On practical grounds, we may treat items (4) through (6) as period expenses if these people are paid a monthly salary, or if we cannot be bothered to try to keep track of such costs. Perhaps we cannot keep track of the cost of shelving particular orders. Judgment is used, and different people will exercise judgment in different ways.

Point (B) focusses on another fundamental difference in accounting that has serious effects on the balance sheet and on income statement figures. In an operating company, interest paid to a bank or other creditor usually is an *expense* on the income statement. Dividends paid to common shareholders are not expenses but are distributions of income, and appear on the retained income or retained earnings statement. When the company is just starting up, e.g., the factory is being built, however, does it make the most sense to debit (charge) interest paid to finance the construction:

1. To the income statement—even though there is no revenue? or

2. To the asset (factory building)—thereby increasing the cost of the asset to a higher figure *than would exist if the construction had been financed entirely by selling common shares?*

Generally, accountants have elected to follow the second option when the asset is still under construction. When another division of the company is operating, or the asset is available for sale, however, interest is usually expensed. (Expensing interest is advantageous in reducing taxable income.) Cheese and liquor that have to be aged are examples of goods not currently available for sale. Interest could therefore be added to the inventory cost (balance sheet asset) and not be expensed, as long as the product is still being aged and is not available for sale.

Much of the next few chapters of the book stress the key accounting concepts. The cost concept of a minimum compliance objective of accounting appears frequently in these chapters.

OBJECTIVITY (AND VERIFIABILITY)

The thoughts underlying objectivity are credibility and avoidance of variation in accounting measurements. When a person has a minimum compliance approach to accounting, and wants to avoid needless debate, then the use of "original invoice cost" makes sense because third parties can agree about the amount of dollars that have been spent. The figure is believable; however, it may not be the figure that we need to form a particular judgment. We may have a different objective of accounting in mind. If so, *our* definition of objectivity could be much different than the one used for a "minimum compliance" objective.

What is "objective" to one person may be subjective to another. What one person would accept as "objective" in one situation, e.g., a mining engineer's estimate of the amount of gold in a rock and ore vein under ground, may be unacceptable in another situation, e.g., the same engineer's estimate of the amount of gold in a bank's vault. In the latter case, a bank inspector may want to know the exact number of ounces, and not an estimate by an expert in mining.

Objectivity is a continuum, as follows:

I ———————————————————— I
Full   Full
Objectivity   Subjectivity

Is any measurement that is *toward* the left side "objective", or must it be at the "full-objectivity" end? We must use our judgment with due regard to the particular circumstances; there is no "right" point on the continuum.

To illustrate, suppose that we look at one section of a balance sheet, which shows:

Long-lived assets, at cost:	
Building	$896,320
Accumulated depreciation	134,600
	$761,720

Which of the three figures is "objective"? Quite likely none are, if we adopt a "full objectivity" definition. The depreciation figure could be highly subjective, as we will see in future chapters. Therefore, the net figure of $761,720 has to be somewhat subjective. What about the $896,320? In the discussion of "cost", we noted where interest and certain other expenditures may be included as period expenses, or as an asset. Thus, variation could exist in all three figures. Yet, all three could appear on the balance sheet of a company that is following a minimum compliance objective of financial accounting; and, some accountants would regard these figures as "objective". In short, when we hear the word "objective", we need to ask the user for a definition.

MATCHING

Forms of accounting can be traced back for thousands of years. Double entry book-keeping has existed since the 1400s. Matching is largely a twentieth-century concept if we think in terms of full accrual accounting. The basic idea of matching expenses to revenues earned makes much sense if we desire to measure income. In practice, however, matching is difficult to attain.

There are several practical forms of matching:

1. Match on a year-by-year basis;
2. Match over the life of an asset, or contract, or lease; and
3. Match over the life of a company.

The shorter the time period, the harder it is to match.

At this point, we will look only at the year-to-year matching. Let us examine a typical income statement of a merchandising company:

Revenue		$1,000,000
Cost of goods sold		600,000
Gross profit		400,000
Expenses:		
Salaries	$100,000	
Commissions paid on sale	40,000	
Depreciation of equipment	30,000	
Interest expense	80,000	
Rent—store	60,000	
Office expense	35,000	
Advertising	20,000	
Other	15,000	380,000
Income before income taxes		$ 20,000

Which expenses can we match to the $1,000,000 revenue? We can try to match "the cost of the goods (that were) sold", i.e., $600,000. That is, we can try to set up a consistent pattern of identifying or tracing which inventory costs will be called "cost of goods sold". Also, we can avoid matching some costs to revenue simply by calling them "period costs", i.e., costs that attach to a period of time. Examples are salaries of sales personnel (who have to be in the store whether or not a sale takes place), and rent of the store. Other expenses, such as commissions paid to sales personnel, are easy to trace, or match, to revenue that has been recognized in a period.

What do we do with a long-lived asset such as equipment? Over its complete life of, say, ten years, we can match its cost to the revenue that it helps to generate. On a year-to-year basis, however, it is difficult to measure the cost that has expired in any one year.

The more long-lived assets that a company owns, the more difficult it is to apply the matching concept. Its income figure could be largely guesswork. Some accountants have therefore come to believe that the matching concept is no longer appropriate today. (Attempts by supporters of matching-to-buttress the concept, through various explanations, have jokingly been referred to as "patching the matching" concept.) If we abandon matching, however, what do we replace it with? Some accountants have suggested that matching is adequate only when it is restricted to those transactions that can be matched to revenue with reasonable accuracy. They suggest that the income statement be subdivided, somewhat as follows:

Revenue		$1,000,000
Cost of goods sold		600,000
Gross profit		400,000
Expenses:		
Salaries	$100,000	
Commissions paid on sales	40,000	
Interest expense	80,000	
Rent—store	60,000	
Office expense	35,000	
Advertising	20,000	
Other	15,000	350,000
Cash income before taxes		50,000
Allocated expense—depreciation of equipment		30,000
Income before income taxes		$ 20,000

The thinking is that such income statement disclosure clearly indicates which expenses, i.e., depreciation, are measured in a "softer" way than others.

Some accountants refer to depreciation as an *arbitrary allocation,* which does not merit inclusion with expenses measured in a "harder" way. What is hard and what is soft is subject to debate, as we have seen from previous discussions about the hardness of facts.

In summary, the matching concept has its supporters and its detractors. We will encounter matching's strengths and weaknesses many times in subsequent chapters. How we apply the concept has a major effect on income statements and balance sheets. For example, observe that a depreciation figure of $50,000 instead of $30,000 would reduce income before income taxes, in the foregoing example, to zero.

REVENUE RECOGNITION/REALIZATION

The previous chapter discussed revenue recognition in detail. Income is measured by commencing with revenue recognition, and then matching expenses to revenue. This process is the *opposite* to how businesses function. Usually, businesses incur costs first, e.g., buy inventory, and the revenue comes second. Why do accountants reverse the process? Under a minimum compliance objective (where expenses of accounting/bookkeeping are to be kept low through adherence to concepts such as objectivity), the reversal makes sense because it provides hindsight. That is, management decides to open a store because it anticipates the arrival of customers, and believes that it can make a profit. Accounting reports on the success of management's anticipations. Did the customers actually arrive? What did they buy? What did it cost to serve them? All these questions refer to the past and what actually happened.

Realization tends to be a broader term than revenue recognition. Realization refers to the increase or decrease in asset and liability *carrying values,* i.e., those figures recorded in the books of account, as a result of a transaction, or perhaps an event (such as a currency devaluation). Under the minimum compliance objective, "realization" combined with arm's length, cost, and objectivity put pressure on accountants to avoid any write ups of assets above cost figures. For example, we may buy land that increases in value because:

1. the location proves beneficial and buyers are willing to pay a high price for the land; or

2. general inflation in the country pushes up the prices of most assets. Would accountants record the value increase? Generally not, under the minimum compliance objective, because *no realization has occurred.* That is, the land has *not* been sold, and therefore there has not been any cash receipt or realization.

If the land had been sold, then realization would have occurred because cash or a receivable would exist. The sale would *not* result in revenue being recognized because the land is not an inventory item. The difference between cost and the proceeds of sale would be a "gain". Thus, *realization* is a broader concept than revenue recognition because realization includes all gains and losses, plus revenue recognition. The realization concept tends to be based on the same criteria that we used with revenue recognition, i.e., costs and proceeds of sales figures are known, and so forth.

Real estate companies, with large investments in revenue-producing office buildings and apartments, are particularly subject to the realization concept. Increasing values of their buildings would *not* appear as income until they actually sold the buildings and met the criteria that we used in the previous chapter. Thus, we have to interpret the financial statements of real estate companies very carefully.

CONSISTENCY/COMPARABILITY

Some people use these terms interchangeably. We use consistency to refer to the *same* company's use of an accounting policy over several accounting periods. For instance, our policy may be that "sales to the federal government are recorded as revenue when the goods are shipped from our warehouse". Year-to-year trends may be ascertainable if consistency of accounting exists. In contrast, comparability refers to *one* company's financial statements being "compared" to *another* company's for the same time period.

Some people seem to believe that a main goal of accounting ought to be to permit persons to compare the profits of two companies. Unfortunately, such a belief is often quite unrealistic. If three companies have the same objectives of accounting, and facts, and constraints, it would be ideal if they used the same accounting policies. This would aid us in comparing the companies, so that we might invest in one of them. How many companies have the same objectives-facts-constraints as their competitors, however?

Newspaper business-reporters often take the financial statements of two or more companies and compare them without paying due attention to fundamental differences in a company's operations. To illustrate, let us consider two banks. Bank A offers us a $10,000 loan at 14 percent interest per annum. Bank B offers us a $10,000 loan at 12 percent interest per annum, but we have to pay a $700 service fee immediately. Suppose that Bank B records the $700 as revenue as soon as the loan is granted and the customer signs the bank's note receivable. In the first three years of the loan, the revenue for each bank would be (assuming each bank grants the $10,000 loan):

	Bank A	Bank B
First year	$1,400	$1,200 plus $ 700
Second year	1,400	1,200
Third year	1,400	1,200

After one year, Bank B's income statement would look much better than A's. As long as B could find *additional* customers each year to pay the $700 "up front", the fact that its annual interest rate was 12 percent could be disguised for a few years. Once additional "up front" customers do not appear, however, and banks had to operate at 12 percent interest revenue, pressures could mount. This is because banks and similar institutions have to have a good "spread"—the interest rate difference between what it lends at and what it borrows at, e.g., the rate paid on savings accounts. Typically, this rate difference is about three or four percent. Hence, a two percent cut (from 14 to 12) could have a dramatic effect on income or loss because "gross profit", so to speak, would be cut in half—from four to two percent.

Other examples could be provided, but let us mention another bank example. Suppose that both Bank A and Bank B have made large loans to developing Third World countries. In the 1980s, the newspapers have printed many articles about the inability of these countries to repay their loans, and some of the interest on the loans. Bank A may therefore decide *not* to accrue interest revenue and also to make an allowance for bad loans by debiting bad debt expense. Bank B may decide to lend more money to these same countries so that they can pay interest on their previous loans. B, therefore, continues to record interest revenue and not to record an expense. Is the difference between the accounting by these two banks a matter of judgment? Or, is there a more significant difference? May accounting policies be making two so-called "like" situations appear as "unlikes"? Alternatively, is the accounting merely reflecting the business decisions—that B was paid interest in cash, and it is unimportant where the cash came from? In light of the array of ways of conducting business (such as noted for the banks), accounting becomes demanding. Comparing companies' financial statements may be a useful technique of analysis for *small* companies; but for larger companies, analysts must be careful.

Consistency means much more than using the same accounting policy, e.g., choosing the percentage of completion basis for contracts with minimal measurement risk, for several years. The important point is: What happens when we want to change to another accounting policy? How do we handle this to avoid losing one of the strengths of financial statements—the displaying of trends?

We can generalize at this point and state that there often are just two reasons for a change in accounting policies:

1. Facts change. This occurs when a business transaction is arranged a different way than before, or a new plant is built, or the type of work undertaken presents a new risk or some other change occurs. When facts change, a new accounting policy is selected for the *present* and *future* years. *No* alteration is made to financial statements of prior years. (Typically, companies prepare financial statements for the current year, and show last year's figures to aid readers who look for trends.) The statement format may be as follows:

| | Balance Sheet as at December 31 | |
	19—9	19—8
Current assets:		
Cash	$200,000	$ 5,000
Receivables	820,000	999,000

(Many larger companies present five and ten-year summaries of the more important figures in separate financial statements.)

2. Objectives of accounting change. Management may decide that another accounting policy better portrays a particular objective. As long as facts have not changed, GAAP accounting calls for *retroactive* treatment of the change.

That is, the financial statements of prior years would have to be recast to show what the figures would have looked like *assuming the new accounting policy had been used during that past time.* (As it is not possible to call back all financial statements that the company has issued in previous years, "recasting" or "restating" is restricted to making the changes in any financial statements that are to be issued in the future— and which contain two, five, or ten-year summaries of financial results of prior years. For example, suppose that we decided to make a change in one of our accounting policies effective with the 19—8 financial year. Suppose also that the policy change was the result of management's decision to alter its objective of accounting in some way. Typically, our 19—8 financial statement package or annual report would show the 19—7 financial statements side-by-side with our 19—8 figures. These 19—7 financial statements would have to be recast to use the new accounting policy that we adopted for 19—8. Similarly, if our 19—8 annual report contained a five-year annual summary, the figures for 19—7, 19—6, 19—5 and 19—4 would have to be restated to reflect the accounting policy that we adopted for 19—8.)

The retroactive method has limitations because it does not indicate what the current year would look like using the old principles. Despite auditors' objections, a company could possibly decide to switch from the percentage of completion to the completed contract basis in the year in which the contract is completed. If most of the eventual profit had already been reported in previous years, a "doubling-up" effect tends to occur.

To illustrate, suppose that the profit was $500,000 on a three-year contract, and that 40 percent of the work was done the first year, 50 percent in the second year, and 10 percent in the third year. The figures would appear as follows:

	Percentage of Completion	Completed Contract	Retroactive Change in Principle in 19—3	Income as Reported in Financial Statements Previously Issued★ and in 19—3
19—1	$200,000	—	—	$200,000
19—2	250,000	—	—	250,000
19—3	50,000	$500,000	$500,000	500,000
Total	$500,000	$500,000	$500,000	$950,000

★Percentage of completion used in 19—1 and 19—2. Completed contract used in 19—3.

With complete note disclosure (see Appendix 1-A), the change is unlikely to be misinterpreted by readers; they would deduct the $450,000 duplication from 19—3. Without complete disclosure, however, misinterpretations may arise.

CONTINUITY/GOING CONCERN

What is the logic underlying the expensing of an asset, such as a building, over its useful life? For instance, we may choose to depreciate over a forty-year period. To do this, we have to be assuming that the business will be in existence for that period of time, and that the asset will be used effectively for that length of time. Obviously, if our assumptions later prove to be unrealistic, we will have to alter the accounting policy. At the commencement of the depreciation process, however, we are being optimistic and assume continuity or a going-concern nature of the business. The continuity concept therefore tends to support the matching, cost, and other concepts of a minimum compliance objective.

What happens when we do not have going concern status? If the business is in bankruptcy, or is to be closed down tomorrow, GAAP accounting makes little sense. If the business is to be sold, or the assets are to be auctioned, cash liquidation figures ought to be used on any balance sheet.

We often have situations that fall somewhere between the going concern and bankruptcy/liquidation state. One example would be a mine that has been closed for a few years because metal prices (gold, silver, platinum) have been below the cost of mining and refining. We can continue to depreciate the buildings and show the assets at cost less depreciation as long as we believe that the company is viable. When does it cease to be a going concern, however? We cannot estimate, with any accuracy, what future metal prices will likely be. If we could predict accurately, we would be spending all our time investing. Metal selling prices may triple next month; who is to know?

A second example involves a company that has been struggling, and may be close to bankruptcy. Think what would happen if an accountant or auditor for the company decided to prepare a balance sheet that showed only liquidation values. No doubt the appearance of such a financial statement could be disastrous and may cause creditors to petition the court to declare the company bankrupt. The opposite side of the coin is a creditor's viewpoint. Might a creditor try to sue an auditor for giving a conventional audit report (see Appendix 1-A) that attests to the fairness within GAAP of the use of original cost figures—when the company went bankrupt two months later? In short, there are arguments on both sides of the issue. But, the accountant who follows the going-concern concept will always assume that the company will continue in existence, until strong evidence to the contrary appears.

DISCLOSURE VERSUS MEASUREMENT

GAAP accounting calls for the use of explanatory notes to accompany the financial statements (see Appendix 1-A). One group of these GAAP notes sets forth the important accounting policies that the company is following. Other note disclosure situations will be described later.

The difficult aspect of this disclosure/measurement concept is that there are three usual situations:

1. Where measurement (on the income statement and balance sheet) is the *only* appropriate accounting response;

2. Where disclosure (in the notes to the financial statements, or on the face of the balance sheet) is the *only* appropriate accounting response;

3. Where a combination of disclosure and measurement exist, or one may be substituted for the other.

Illustration 8-1 lists some common measurement-only and disclosure-only situations. Under a minimum compliance objective, the accountant would do whatever is necessary to comply with the law—whether it involves measurement or disclosure. For other objectives, or when there are multiple objectives of accounting, however, the disclosure/measurement issue becomes extremely important. For example, *note disclosure* about a difficult to measure circumstance (e.g., a vague note about the amount of bad debt expense needed by a bank that has loans that *may* not be repaid) would be *totally irrelevant* for a measurement situation.

A measurement only emphasis (such as a bonus or a restrictive covenant) occurs when a serious matter depends entirely upon balance sheet and income statement figures. And *notes* to financial statements simply *do not* affect the figures. The restrictive covenant may state that "no dividends may be declared unless retained earnings exceed $2 million after declaration and payment of the dividend". If we charge a large

ILLUSTRATION 8-1

Disclosure versus Measurement

Some Measurement Situations	*Some Disclosure Situations*
• Income taxes that are based on taxable income figures that may be close to accounting income in nature.	• GAAP requires a particular note to the financial statements, e.g., about accounting policies.
• Bonus plans that are based on an income statement figure.	• An explanatory note may be added to the financial statements to minimize the threat of a lawsuit by a shareholder or creditor.
• Selling prices of a company that are based in part on balance sheet or income statement figures.	• Where highly sophisticated investors are the only readers of financial statements, and they make their own interpretations and prefer the lengthy explanations of notes.
• Restrictive covenants, when they are based on balance sheet figures (e.g., no dividends unless retained earnings exceed a particular figure.)	

bad debt expense against revenue (thereby reducing retained earnings below $2 million), a note saying: "More than adequate provision has been made for possible bad debts" does not undo the problem. Retained earnings fell below $2 million; hence, no dividend could be declared. The rule is automatic.

A disclosure-only emphasis occurs when a secondary user of the financial statements is being accommodated. For example, the prime user may be the owners and managers who rely on the financial statements for profit sharing and bonus plans. Accordingly, the accounting measurement policies are selected with these objectives in mind. The secondary user may be a large group of creditors who want some information about unfilled sales orders on hand at the year end. The latter information *could* be included in notes to the financial statements, and would not affect measurements on the income statement or balance sheet.

A combination of measurement and disclosure occurs when a debit or credit entry is made (thereby affecting income statement and balance sheet figures), and additional explanation is provided in notes to the financial statements. For instance, revenue may be recognized during the period; and a note explains that the percentage of completion basis was used, and a particular formula method or approach was selected.

MATERIALITY

Professional judgment is an extremely important attribute that accountants, financial analysts, and others must acquire. We have advocated the objectives-facts-constraints framework as a starting point until we devise our own scheme on which to attach new ideas, and develop judgment.

Materiality can be defined in many ways. A common way states that an amount or disclosure is *material* if awareness of it would tend to alter a person's assessment or judgment. For example, suppose that a firm was being sued for $100,000. Is this *material*? Should it be disclosed in financial statements? If the firm's total assets were $500,000 and net income $50,000, the sum of $100,000 would seem material. If the firm's assets were $10 billion and net income $50 million, the $100,000 would not be material. What about amounts between $50,000 and $50 million of net income? We must apply our professional judgment.

What do we consider in exercising our professional judgment with respect to materiality? Our guiding criterion is users' decisions, particularly whether the users would be misled if they were not made aware of the sum or event. (Would awareness of the information have changed their decision? If so, the amount is material.) Accountants have tended to translate effects on users' judgments into effects on current and future net income, income trends, and effects on assets and liabilities. Because different accountants apply different materiality guidelines, it is not surprising to see a lack of uniformity in financial statements.

CONSERVATISM

Conservatism in accounting is sometimes explained as "anticipate no profit; provide for all known or estimable losses". Under the climate of the 1929 Stock Market Crash and the Depression, it is not surprising that such a concept gained acceptance. In its place, accompanied with uncertainty and conservative financial-statement users, it makes sense. What about its effect on other users, however?

Conservative accounting eventually reverses itself, and what may be called "ultra *un*conservative" accounting could result. For example, if management writes down its inventory of goods for resale, the current year's profit and retained earnings plus the asset "inventory" are "understated" compared to no writedown. But what happens next year, when the goods are sold? With a smaller cost of goods sold, net income is much higher.

	Conservative Accounting Inventory Written Down		No Inventory Write-Down	
	19—1	19—2	19—1	19—2
Revenue	$1,000	$1,000	$1,000	$1,000
Cost of goods sold	900*	500	700	700
Gross profit	100	500	300	300
Expenses	100	100	100	100
Income	$ 0	$ 400	$ 200	$ 200

*Comprised of $700 cost of goods sold plus $200 write down.

Have some readers been misled? In the above "Conservative Accounting" case, they have been misled because $200 was charged through cost of goods sold in 19—1, but selling prices did not decline in 19—2. The effect was $200 extra gross profit in 19—2. What conclusions may readers draw about the company's future profitability? In short, conservative accounting can be dangerous to some and beneficial to others. It is something that we must watch for when we perform financial statement analysis.

REVIEW

The foregoing list of concepts appears frequently in financial accounting, and in this book. From this point onward, we have to ask ourselves why accountants "do things the way that they do". In subsequent chapters, when we observe a particular accounting treatment, we must ask ourselves whether it can be explained by one of the foregoing concepts—or one of the ones that will be presented next. *There definitely are underlying foundations or concepts to what we see.* We should not memorize the treatment that we see without understanding the underlying concept. When we encounter a slightly different situation, we need to be able to deal adequately with it. Because business changes the way contracts are written, and the way commerce is conducted, "new" situations will continually appear. If we learn the underlying concepts now, future understanding will be easier. Problem solving will also be simplified.

A User-Based Objective

Chapter 6 devoted much space to some of the different objectives of financial accounting. The concepts that we just finished including under the minimum compliance objective came first, chronologically-speaking. They were initially developed at a time when accounting was trying to be all things to all people. Refinements have been made to those concepts over the past fifty years. Cost, objectivity, matching, and so forth, however, carry with them a particular viewpoint or bias of caution and verifiable figures, etc.

About twenty years ago, another approach to accounting began to catch the people's attention. This approach may be called the user-power set of objectives. Although its accompanying user-power concepts tend to apply to large public companies, they are not restricted to this category. For a country such as Canada, however, with its large number of private companies and resourced-based economy, we must be careful to accept the user-power concepts for only those places where they make sense. They are not "new truths" that will solve all of our problems.

To this point in the book, we have identified a few situations where users have power to demand particular accounting. It is time to give additional attention to a particular situation—where the parliamentarians decide to give users more power by enacting stronger legislation. Although this may not occur in Canada, we have to consider the situation because it exists in the U.S.A., and many of our larger companies are either

U.S. owned or have to borrow money in the U.S.A. Thus, they sometimes have to follow U.S. practices or the U.S. philosophy.

If we are a small shareholder in a large, public company, how much power or influence do we have? Virtually none. If we are the major banker to this same company, how much power do we have? Much more. What can be done to prevent the powerless small shareholder from being "kept in the dark"? To an important extent, the U.S. economy has been built on the idea that small amounts of funds obtained from a large number of private citizens can build huge corporations—and that these corporations can improve a person's lifestyle. This so-called "capital markets" system has to be protected. The markets require safeguards, and one of them in the U.S.A. is a national securities commission (called the S.E.C.—Securities & Exchange Commission). The S.E.C. and a private sector (i.e., non-government) group, called the Financial Accounting Standards Board (FASB), have been active in trying to protect the small investor. Between them, they have been pushing for more and different disclosure and measurement in corporate financial statements and annual reports.

In the early 1980s, the FASB published a series of "Concepts" booklets in which they addressed the objective of providing information to present and potential investors and creditors. The cornerstone of the material was the idea that accounting reports should help these people in assessing the "amounts, timing, and uncertainty of prospective cash receipts". *(Qualitative Characteristics of Accounting Information,* FASB: May 1980). A series of concepts was outlined by the FASB. Several of the important ones are:

1. Decision Usefulness

Under a user-power situation, it logically follows that we would choose the accounting policy (from a list of alternatives) that produces the most useful information for decisions—about the amounts, timing, and uncertainty of prospective cash receipts less cash disbursements. That is, we would like to forecast *how much* will appear in the future, *when* it will appear, and *what* likelihood exists that our forecast will be accurate.

The FASB readily acknowledges that the cost of collecting the information is important, and that the better or best alternative may not always be selected. For instance, it would be pointless to hire ten construction engineers to make a forecast of expected construction costs just to try to use percentage of completion revenue recognition—especially when we are not sure that the users would fully understand the accounting.

The FASB stresses that individual needs and objectives vary. Thus, what appears to be the best accounting policy for one group's decisions may not be best for another's. (It is possible that shareholders may be interested in longer-term effects whereas creditors may be most concerned about the company's ability to repay debt coming due in eighteen months.)

2. Relevance

This term follows up on the generalization of decision usefulness. (Relevant to whom, and for which decision?) Relevance has been defined by the FASB, in part, as: "...accounting information must be capable of making a difference in a decision by helping users to form predictions about the outcomes of past, present, and future events, or to confirm or correct expectations." (Page 21 of "Qualitative Characteristics".) That is, the information is relevant when it can cause us to stop to think about the alternative decisions that we may make—because the information clearly pertains to what we are pondering. For instance, both information on original cost and information on today's selling price of a company's land are relevant to its decision to sell or retain the land. Knowledge about each figure may cause it to sell instead of hold onto the land. The selling price tells it how much cash it is likely to receive. The original cost figure helps it to compute the income taxes that it will have to pay when the land is sold. (Income taxes are based on the profit—selling price less original cost.)

Should both original cost and selling price be reported on a company's *general purpose* financial statements? It is precisely this type of question that causes considerable difficulty for accountants. The "decision-usefulness" and "relevance" concepts are provided as guidance to keep accountants focussed on what they have to consider when choosing among accounting-policy alternatives. Who are the decision makers? What decisions are they trying to make? As we have noted before, what is relevant for one type of decision may not be relevant for another decision.

The FASB approach is in contrast to the concepts set forth under the minimum compliance (preparer power) objective of accounting. Cost and objectivity were regarded as important under preparer power, and the attitude was taken: Well, that is the way we do it; if you find the figures useful, then use them; if you do not find them useful, then that is unfortunate; we have complied with the laws of the land." In short, we see two different sets of concepts that make sense within their particular objectives of either preparer power or user power.

3. Reliability

The FASB has defined reliability in terms as follows: "Accounting information is reliable to the extent that users can depend on it to represent the economic conditions or events that it purports to represent." (Page 27 of "Qualitative Characteristics".) The distinction between relevance and reliability can be a fine or subtle one. Thus, the FASB has elaborated through two additional concepts:

A. *Representational Faithfulness*—"correspondence or agreement between a measure or description and the phenomenon it purports to represent": This concept is often referred to as validity. Is a particular examination a valid test of our knowledge of the subject and ability at applying what we have learned? If the test was administered in a hot, noisy room, the results would not faithfully represent our abilities. The same idea applies in accounting. When accountants say that the cost is $1 million, what does this mean? We saw in the discussions of the cost concept, earlier in this chapter, that variation exists in what accountants call "cost". The point is: Does a knowledgeable reader understand how we have arrived at "cost", and can she/he *rely on the figures to represent what we say that they represent?*

B. *Verifiability:* This concept pursues the idea that different, independent measurers would arrive at the same figures when they used the same measurement methods. When verifiability exists, there is assurance that the measurer avoided personal bias and followed the measurement procedure carefully.

The FASB material contains many concepts that build on the foundation concepts that we have just discussed. Some examples are materiality, neutrality, timeliness, consistency, and comparability.

RELATIONSHIP TO OBJECTIVES

What is important at this point is that we fully understand how important objectives of accounting are to what is measured, and how and what is disclosed. Once we choose objectives, certain concepts and accounting policies tend to flow logically from them. Thus, *cost* figures may make considerable sense for a minimum compliance objective. However, they could be less important for a cash flow prediction objective—(but they would still be relevant for computing the income tax effects).

The distinctions get foggy when we examine what would appear to be a preparer-power situation, such as bonus plans based on income figures. What figures ought to be used: original cost? market values? Much depends on the facts and circumstances. If the bonus is for a person who is investing our money in the stock market, an adequate reward would be based on what she/he earns for us, *after income taxes.* Thus, *both figures* are needed—as we saw in the case where we had to decide whether to buy or hold onto the land.

Suppose, however, that the bonus is for someone who is selling the house we have lived in for twenty years. (Any profits on the sale of such houses are not taxable.) Cost would not be relevant. Probably the bonus plan that makes the most sense is based on a percentage of selling price. Finally, suppose that we are a candy manufacturer, and the bonus is for the "gross profit" that our purchasing agent makes by buying sugar. Suppose that the agent is buying and selling contracts for future delivery of sugar nearly every day —and that the price of sugar is fluctuating widely. Might we prefer to use the concepts outlined under the "minimum compliance" objective— especially revenue recognition based on the four criteria that were outlined? This may avoid the measurement problems that could arise when prices are erratic. It may also minimize disputes between the owners of the business and the purchasing agent.

In brief, it is necessary to watch for amendments that we must make to what was said in earlier chapters. For example, the illustration involving the bonus plans shows how we can view the situation several different ways. Accounting is very much a function of objectives of accounting, facts, and legal constraints including GAAP.

Summary

In this book, we provide a variety of accounting approaches and methods, and thereby convey the basic theme that it is essential that we understand the *relativism* concept that applies in accounting. That is, accounting has to be tailored to the situation. A search for the one, all-purpose method of accounting is non-productive.

The first four chapters of this book provided the basic bookkeeping techniques so that we could see the entire bookkeeping cycle. Chapter 5 provided some insights into uses of accounting and served as a transition to tailoring accounting to fit the situation, i.e., to particular objectives and facts and constraints. Chapters 6, 7, and 8 have provided the foundations for understanding the relative nature of accounting. That is, this book attempts to steer between extremes in approaches to accounting.

We have to focus on the objectives, facts, and constraints that we face in each situation. To be able to interpret financial statements, we have to understand the criteria or concepts used by the preparer. For instance, what materiality level is being used? Did the accountant expense an amount because she/he thought that it was not material? Might other accountants have added the amount to the cost of inventory or land? If so, there is an effect on income and asset cost. Would this difference affect the conclusions that we reach from our review of the financial statements? It depends on our decision situation. If the accountant did a good job of anticipating our situation, the difference in accounting should not affect our decision. But, if he or she did not...

Much of the remainder of the book illustrates how accountants apply the ideas expressed in Chapters 6, 7, and 8. No doubt it will be to our benefit in subsequent chapters to come back to these three chapters. The relativism way of thinking has to be at the heart of our understanding.

APPENDIX 8-A
Another Problem Solving Illustration

Appendix 8-A is provided to give us an opportunity to develop our cognitive skills through practice. For best results, the problem should be attempted before the response that follows it is read.

INTRODUCTION

There is little doubt that our analytical and judgmental skills improve when we work through many different problem situations. To aid understanding, a short situation is presented in this appendix to provide an opportunity to use *some* of the material presented in this and earlier chapters, and in Appendix 7-A.

A caution is in order. Problem situations that encourage the development of diagnostic, analytical and judgmental skills are asking for *much more* than a display of memory skills. To try to fit a memorized format or technical point into a problem situation, when it just does not fit, is to miss the point. It displays a *lack* of judgment. The business world contains few right answers, and needs problem solvers instead of memorizers.

Accordingly, to obtain maximum benefit from this Appendix, try to resolve the situation that follows before looking at the response that accompanies it. Try to employ relevant portions of the problem solving format from Appendix 7-A and applicable portions of Chapter 8, and of earlier chapters.

ENLIGHT CORPORATION LIMITED

Enlight Corporation Limited (ECL) was incorporated under federal corporate legislation many years ago by Ms. M. Enlight. She was the sole owner-manager of ECL until three years ago, when she hired a general manager, Mr. Keen. Mr. Keen was given a salary plus a bonus of 10 percent of net income, and was placed in charge of the entire operations of ECL.

As a result of Mr. Keen's enthusiasm, ECL's revenue grew from $4 to $6 million. He expanded the business (which consists of publishing community newspapers and various types of advertising material) by borrowing from an industrial finance company, Wrestle Finance Limited (WFL). WFL placed a restrictive covenant on ECL's operations at the time of the loan. If ECL's net income dropped below $20,000 in any year, WFL's ten-year loan would become payable on demand, and the interest rate would rise from 10 to 15 percent per annum until the loan was called for payment by WFL, and paid off.

During the most recent year, 19—8, ECL undertook to commence the publication of two new weekly community newspapers. This increased the number of ECL's community newspapers to five, and they were the first new ones to be added in twenty years. The two new newspapers were published twice each in December 19—8, and were provided free in the hope of attracting subscribers. As of December 31, 19—8 (ECL's year end), the following receipts and expenditures, and expense/revenue accruals, for the two new newspapers were entered in a ledger account called "Two New Newspapers".

	Debit	Credit
Advertising revenue		$26,100
Cost of printing—paid to printer	$21,690	
Cost of distribution	2,940	
Advertising expense—circulars delivered to each house and apartment	4,200	
Purchase of additional office equipment	9,250	
Salaries and training manuals for people who are being trained to work on these two papers (reporters, writers, editor)	12,710	
Bank interest on loan obtained to start up the two new community papers	1,360	
Salary of Mr. Keen, (time spent on starting new newspapers)	10,000	
Articles purchased, for use in the papers in 19—9	19,200	
	$81,350	$26,100

Ms. Enlight and Mr. Keen were not able to reach an agreement on how the amounts in the "Two New Newspapers" ledger account should be handled in the 19—8 financial statements. They have hired you to make recommendations, and give your reasoning. After investigating the matter, you have learned that the net income of ECL in 19—8, *before* considering the "Two New Newspapers" ledger account, is $44,000. Much better results are expected for 19—9.

Required: Advise Ms. Enlight and Mr. Keen. Explain your response.

A RESPONSE TO ENLIGHT CORPORATION LIMITED

Technically, our report ought to be addressed directly to Ms. Enlight and Mr. Keen. We are using a discussion format, however.

We have to commence our analysis with the objectives of ECL. Both Ms. Enlight and Mr. Keen would like ECL to be as profitable as possible. Ms. Enlight would like to postpone income taxes as long as possible, however, by keeping taxable income as low as is compatible with Mr. Keen's bonus plan objective. Presumably, they have been able in the past to work out a sensible compromise to their conflicting personal objectives.

The year 19—8 presents a new challenge because the objectives of both persons are threatened if the restrictive covenant comes into effect. Both would likely be receptive to our suggestions if ECL can legitimately keep its net income above $20,000. Our basic approach therefore has to shift to searching for any constraints that prevent us from attaining the objective. Also, we have to clarify facts to learn where alternative accounting treatment is possible. (If the facts are clear, they would determine our accounting methods.) Finally, we have to support our recommendations with "key concepts", from Chapter 8, and with credible reasoning. In short, where can we legitimately capitalize some of the debits in the "Two New Newspapers" ledger account?

Our first consideration is whether the two new newspapers are in their "pre-operating" stage. That is, we may be building up an asset that is not yet ready to earn adequate revenue. (This is a variation of the ideas expressed under the "cost" concept in Chapter 8. Just because *some* "revenue" has been received does not mean that the two new newspapers are ready to be declared as operational. As we will see later in the book, the so-called "revenue" received prior to the commencement of *profitable* operations need only be deducted from asset costs, with the *net* figure being declared as the "new" asset. We may support this approach by selecting the matching and cost concepts. That is, if we had to match revenue and expenses in 19—8, a net loss would appear for an asset that is in its infancy.) When we declare the two new newspapers to be in the "pre-operating", or asset build-up stage, we still have to separate between assets and expenses, or period costs, that have been incurred. The latter category would include bank interest and Mr. Keen's salary. Also, we should separate out, i.e., place in a separate asset ledger account, the office equipment because its life span may differ from the capitalized pre-operating costs. The remaining figures, net of "revenue receipts" (which are therefore *not* "revenue, because revenue appears on the income statement) would be shown on the *balance* sheet under a title such as "Newspaper Development Costs".

If we decide that the two new newspapers have passed the "pre-operating" stage, however, we would have to look at each item in the ledger and investigate its potential to be called an asset. (The new newspapers would be beyond the pre-operating stage when we could no longer justify building up an asset—because we were not certain whether it would generate future benefits in excess of its cost.) Clearly, the office equipment is an asset. Also, the articles purchased for use in 19—9 could be regarded as assets—to be matched against 19—9 revenue.

Now comes the difficult part. We need a few more dollars to be capitalized as assets so that we do not drop below $20,000 of net income. The most likely item to be called an asset would be the "salaries and training manuals...". We could develop a reasonable set of logic to support calling this an asset for a short period of time, at least over the December 31, 19—8 year end—because these people will generate revenue in 19—9, after they have been trained. Once we capitalize this type of expenditure, however, we have to be *consistent*. (Because the previous magazine "start up" was twenty years ago, we can probably justify a new accounting policy in 19—8 —but we should follow it in the next five or so years.)

Are we being misleading? Have we intentionally violated the spirit of the covenant? No, because the person who thought of the restrictive covenant should have been aware of the adaptability of accounting *when facts are not clear.* A judgment has to be made. ECL seems to have a reasonable future. It is a going concern, until contrary evidence appears. We are merely trying to match revenue and expenses in an unclear situation.

Ours is *not* the only approach that could have been followed. What is important is that we set forth our reasoning, and thereby gain experience in judgmental and analytical skills—which are important skills for business people.

QUESTIONS

8-1 Your aunt owns shares in Canada Development Corporation, and owns a condominium that she rents to tenants for $1,200 per month. She also owns one-half of a retail store, and works part-time for a large company. How many entities exist in this situation? Why? How many sets of journals and ledgers exist? Why?

8-2 What effect does the unit of measure have on what is, and is not, accounted for?

8-3 Why does the income statement of an unincorporated business not include income taxes?

8-4 What is the effect on the reliability of the financial statements when an entity engages in many non-arm's length transactions?

8-5 A company sells 95 percent of its products to one customer. Is this information of sufficient importance that it ought to be reported on the company's financial statements? Consider different situations, and explain your response.

8-6 What are the benefits and the limitations of the cost concept?

8-7 What figures on a balance sheet are objectively measured? Explain.

8-8 What effect does the length of the time period have on the ease with which accountants can apply the matching concept?

8-9 What effect does the realization concept have on what is and is not accounted for?

8-10 Why is consistency one of the most important concepts of minimum compliance accounting?

8-11 Why do accountants avoid using liquidation values for assets and liabilities when a company is struggling financially but is not bankrupt?

8-12 Why is note disclosure inadequate or perhaps irrelevant in situations where bonus plans, or selling prices of a company, are based on income statement figures?

8-13 How does an accountant ascertain what transactions are material?

8-14 Of what relevance to an income tax objective of accounting is a financial statement that helps readers ascertain the amounts, timing and uncertainty of prospective cash receipts?

8-15 What is meant by the concept of relativism? Relate your explanation to the study of accounting.

EXERCISES

E8-1 The bookkeeper for George's Grocery (a proprietorship) prepared the following income statement:

Revenue		$520,000
Cost of goods sold		335,000
Gross Profit		185,000
Expenses:		
Heat, light, power	$ 1,850	
Wages paid to George	40,000	
Wages paid to others	62,350	
Rental paid to George	18,000	
Interest paid on loan by George	10,000	
Depreciation	6,500	
Other	15,000	153,700
		31,300
Income tax		15,000
Net income		$ 16,300

Required:

What key accounting concepts has the bookkeeper probably used in preparing the income statement? Explain fully. What key accounting concepts have been misapplied or not understood? Explain.

E8-2 Compute *cost* in each of the following situations. Explain your response.

1. Equipment is purchased from the U.S. for $285,000 Canadian. Delivery cost is $11,750; unloading costs are $750; installation costs are $2,290; and interest on a bank loan taken out to acquire the equipment is $4,850.
2. An automobile is purchased for $15,000. A licence for the automobile costs $200; driving lessons amount to $350; sales tax not included in the $15,000 amounts to $900; and insurance for one year is $1,400.
3. Inventory is purchased at a retail price of $10,000 less a 10 percent discount, plus delivery charges of $625.
4. Inventory is purchased at a payment of $2,000 per month for five months. The company chose to not pay cash of $9,400.

E8-3 Use the following coding system to indicate the degree of objectivity/subjectivity that exists in measuring the undernoted transactions or account balances:

  I = objective transaction with unrelated party.
  II = components partly objective and partly subjective.
  III = subjective measurement made by the accountant or management.

Transactions or account balance:

1. purchased equipment for $38,500 Canadian cash from the U.S.
2. recorded allowance for bad debts of $8,000.
3. net figure (cost less accumulated depreciation) for an automobile is $11,360.

4. collection of an account receivable.
5. recorded depreciation for the year.
6. payment of a warranty repair.
7. net figure for accounts receivable (after deducting allowance for bad debts) is $20,990.
8. revenue is recognized on a completed contract basis.
9. accounts receivable are invoiced to purchaser of building under construction.
10. revenue is recognized on a percentage of completion basis.

E8-4 For each of the undernoted situations indicate whether you believe that expenses have been matched to revenue in a satisfactory manner that permits preparation of a financial statement. Explain your response carefully.

1. cost of goods sold is recorded when revenue is recognized.
2. a salesperson's commission is expensed when revenue is recognized for that sale.
3. rent is expensed in the month in which it is paid.
4. depreciation on a salesperson's automobile is expensed on a straight line basis.
5. advertising charges are expensed in the period in which the advertisement appears in a magazine.
6. salaries of office employees are expensed in the month in which they work.
7. the year end allowance for bad debts is adjusted to reflect an estimate of which accounts will not be collected.
8. warranty repair expenses are recorded in the month in which they are paid.

E8-5 Indicate *when* realization would occur for each of the undernoted situations:

1. the market value of a company's building increases.
2. inventory is sold for cash.
3. a fire totally destroys one of the company's trucks, which is fully insured.
4. a fire totally destroys one of the company's buildings, which is *not* insured.
5. the market value of a company's land decreases.
6. a customer returns inventory that was previously sold for cash, and receives a full refund.
7. wheat in a farmer's field grows.
8. a fishing company catches a large quantity of fish.

E8-6 M. Woltersdorf Construction Corporation (WCC) had one large construction contract in the years 19—7, 19—8 and 19—9. The profits that could have been recorded under this contract are:

	Percentage of Completion	Completed Contract
19—7	$ 600,000	
19—8	700,000	
19—9	700,000	$2,000,000
	$2,000,000	$2,000,000

Assume that selling and administrative expenses in each of the years 19—7 to 19—9 would have amounted to $300,000.

Required:

How much income would WCC have reported in the years specified below under each of these stated independent assumptions:

1. income that would have been reported in 19—8 (assuming the completed contract method).
2. income reported in 19—9 (assuming a retroactive change from percentage of completion in 19—7 and 19—8 to the completed contract method).
3. income reported in 19—8 (assuming a retroactive change from percentage of completion in 19—7 to completed contract).
4. income reported in 19—9 (assuming that percentage of completion was used in 19—7 and 19—8, but that completed contract is to be used in 19—9 without retroactive application to 19—7 and 19—8).

E8-7 N. Wilson Corporation Ltd. (WCL) reported the following results in 19—8 and 19—9:

		Years ended December 31
	19—9	*19—8*
Revenue	$1,800,000	$1,750,000
Cost of goods sold	1,500,000	1,500,000
Gross profit	300,000	250,000
Expenses	130,000	120,000
Income before income taxes	$ 170,000	$ 130,000

Management of WCL had used a valuation of $650,000 for the inventory as of December 31, 19—8. At the time that they chose the $650,000 cost figure, the selling price of the inventory was about $750,000. However, by the time that the inventory was sold in 19—9, only $525,000 was received for it. Management receives a bonus of 10 percent of gross profit in a year.

Required:

A. Restate the income statements for 19—8 and 19—9 assuming that a year end valuation of $525,000, instead of $650,000, had been used for the December 31, 19—8 inventory.

B. What accounting concept would you have to use to support the $525,000 inventory figure? Why?

C. What are the shortcomings of WCL's bonus plan?

PROBLEMS

P8-1 J. Torcov owns 50 percent of Seneca Blue Sox Baseball Club Limited (SBCL). The other 50 percent is owned by a major league baseball team. The major league team supplies many of the players for the team, which plays in the Class A Central College League. Some of the players are owned by SBCL, which signed them to contracts.

Most of the players that are signed to contracts by SBCL are paid a small signing bonus plus an annual wage. The wage is negotiated on the basis of the player's skills and promise for rising to the major league level. Some of the players are not successful and are eventually released from their contracts. Players showing promise are promoted to Class

AA and AAA leagues. Their contracts are purchased by the teams in higher leagues. As a result, SBCL can sometimes make sizeable profit gains on sales of players' contracts.

Until recently, SBCL has expensed all payments to players. However, this year they have spent close to $2,000,000 signing several promising players. Management believes that it should be able to develop several of these players and sell their contracts to teams at higher levels. The president of SBCL has asked you whether he can record the signing bonuses as assets, and only expense the players' monthly wages. He believes that the players represent the major assets of a baseball team.

The president is willing to expense the capitalized signing bonuses whenever a player is released from the team. However, whenever a player's contract is sold, the proceeds of sale would be recorded as revenue. The capitalized cost would then be expensed.

Required:

A. Select some key accounting concepts that you could use to defend your opinion that the signing bonuses:
   1. should *not* be capitalized as assets
   2. should be capitalized, and expensed only when the player is released, or his contract is sold. Explain your reasoning.

B. If the signing bonuses are capitalized, and a player's contract is later sold, should revenue be credited? Explain.

P8-2 Nancy Arr wants to sell her florist shop, Nancy's Flowers. Nancy owns the building in which the florist shop is located. She also works in the store at a salary of $40,000 per year. During 19—8 she loaned the store $100,000 interest free even though a bank would have charged interest of $12,000. A clerk being paid $16,000 a year could perform the duties that Nancy undertakes each year.

Nancy does not want to sell the building. She is willing to rent the store space to the buyer of the florist shop for $15,000 per year. The owner of the flower shop would have to pay heat, light and utilities.

Some of the flowers that Nancy buys are at a discount of five percent below wholesale cost. In 19—8 Nancy paid $380,000 for flowers from a cousin who grows them. This discount would not be available to a buyer of the florist shop.

In the year ended December 31, 19—8, the income statement for the florist shop showed:

Revenue		$1,080,500
Cost of goods sold		790,500
Gross Profit		290,000
Expenses:		
Salary	$105,000	
Depreciation on building	12,500	
Heat, light and utilities	2,100	
Advertising	11,650	
Interest	5,150	
Office	24,600	
Other	9,000	170,000
Income		$ 120,000

Required:

A. Reconstruct the income statement for 19—8 as it would appear if someone bought the florist shop, and rented the store space from Nancy.

B. What effects on the income statement in A would occur if the buyer of the florist shop operated it as an incorporated company instead of a proprietorship?

P8-3 Kennedy Gardens Limited (KGL) is engaged in producing fresh vegetables for restaurants and smaller grocery stores in Saskatchewan and Manitoba. The company's year end is December 31. The common shares of KGL are owned by the three Kennedy brothers. Their sole objective of financial accounting is to minimize the payment of income taxes.

The crops (lettuce, beans, cucumbers, and similar) are planted in the spring of the year, and every few days thereafter to ensure that a fresh supply is continually available to customers over a several week period. Most of the crop planting and cultivation is performed by the Kennedy brothers. Some seasonal employees are hired to pick the crops and deliver them to customers.

In 19—9 the following costs were incurred in generating revenue of $1,620,000:

Seeds	$ 70,000
Fertilizer	241,600
Fuel	242,800
Sprays	69,900
Depreciation on equipment	22,200
Other	42,800
Wages	230,800
Property taxes and licenses	97,700
Rentals	115,500
Utilities	96,700
	$1,230,000

Most of the sales are on account. Customers pay in 60 to 120 days.

Required:

A. Prepare an income statement for KGL for 19—9.

B. What accounting policy should KGL adopt for its inventories of vegetables? Explain.

C. Which accounting concepts mentioned in this chapter are of *little* or no importance in preparing KGL's financial statements? Explain.

P8-4 You have been engaged by a provincial government to conduct a study of the logging industry in a small region of Canada. The government obtained the financial statements of two companies that it wanted you to compare. Both companies own approximately the same amount of timber cutting rights, which they acquired about 80 years ago. The cutting rights require them to reforest the land after they have cut the timber, so that the land will generate a perpetual forest yield. Annual cutting of timber is restricted to a particular volume. If that volume is not cut one year, it may be cut the next year. The two companies are H. Liebman Corporation Limited and V. Hanton Logging Limited. Their financial statements for the year ended December 31, 19—9 show:

H. LIEBMAN CORPORATION LIMITED
Income Statement
Year ended December 31, 19—9

Revenue		$2,560,000
Cost of logging operations	$1,960,000	
Reforestation	320,500	
Depreciation	210,000	
Interest	105,500	
Other	92,000	2,688,000
Loss for year		$ 128,000

V. HANTON LOGGING LIMITED
Income Statement
Year ended December 31, 19—9

Revenue		$12,650,000
Cost of logs sold		7,790,000
Gross profit		4,860,000
Expenses:		
Selling	$1,255,000	
Administrative	1,277,000	
Depreciation	890,000	
Interest	375,500	
Reforestation	105,000	
Other	67,000	3,970,000
Income before income tax		890,000
Income tax		430,000
Net income		$ 460,000

In 19—9, the North American economy was in a recession. Sales of logs and lumber were declining from prior years.

Required:

A. Compare the two income statements. In which respects are they the same, and in which are they different? Explain.

B. Why might the results of these two companies have differed in 19—9? Refer to key accounting concepts mentioned in the chapter to defend your response.

C. How useful are the 19—9 financial statements of H. Liebman for predicting the next year's income or loss? Explain.

P8-5 In October 1985, Canadian Pacific Air Lines Ltd. offered to buy the common shares of Nordair Inc. for $17.57 per Nordair share. The senior executives of Nordair held options to "buy 251,000 shares of Nordair at $9 each in the event of a takeover" of their company (the *Globe and Mail*, October 12, 1985, B3). That is, the remuneration of the executives included more than a salary plus a possible bonus based on some income statement figure.

If the takeover proceeded, the executives would be able to buy shares from Nordair at $9 each and immediately sell them to Canadian Pacific Air Lines for $17.57 each. The difference of $8.57 would not appear on Nordair's income statement as salary or bonus.

Required:

A. Use the concepts explained in this and the previous chapters to explain why the $8.57 would not appear as salary expense.

B. Would Canadian Pacific Air Lines record the $9 or the $17.57 in its ledgers? Explain.

EXPLORATION MATERIALS AND CASES

MC8-1 Brown Automotive Parts Limited (BAPL) was incorporated under federal legislation several years ago. BAPL is owned by the Brown family, who until this year, 19—8, managed BAPL. In January 19—8 a president and a vice-president of sales were hired by the Brown family, which wanted to devote its attention to another of its companies. The new executives agreed to accept a salary plus a bonus based on income before income taxes. The bonus is expected to be a large portion of their remuneration as executives.

After much discussion between the owners and the two new executives, they decided to engage you to help them choose accounting policies that would be appropriate for the new situation. Previously, the Brown family had chosen accounting policies and practices that helped to minimize the amount of income taxes that BAPL would have to pay. Now, they would have to seek a reasonable compromise between what is appropriate for the bonus plan and what would help to postpone the payment of income taxes.

You review the type of transactions that BAPL enters into, and discover the following:

1. About 60 percent of BAPL's sales of its manufactured parts are to large automobile manufacturers, which order in advance at fixed prices. Usually, they pay in 30 to 60 days of receipt of the parts.

2. The remainder of BAPL's sales of manufactured parts are to a variety of automotive parts distributors, auto dealers and repair garages. Some of these customers are slow in paying for parts, and tend to return a large number of parts that they do not sell or use.

3. BAPL's inventory has been costed at the lower of weighted average cost or net realizable value. Wherever possible, costs of the manufacturing plant have been expensed, instead of being included as part of the cost of manufactured inventory. For instance, depreciation on manufacturing equipment is included as an expense below the gross profit line of the income statement. Also, repairs of equipment are expensed wherever possible.

4. BAPL has tended to make a full allowance for bad debts on any receivables that have not been paid within six months of a sale.

Required:

Explain the issues that would be relevant to the owners and new executives of BAPL in trying to resolve their problem with accounting policies.

MC8-2 Four years ago, Garbage Disposal Corporation (GDC) and White City (WC) entered into a contract that requires GDC to collect garbage within the boundaries of WC for a period of five years, with an option by WC to renew for a further five years. The major terms of the contract specify that GDC is to be reimbursed for all "cash, out-of-pocket costs that are directly incurred in the process of carrying out the contract". In addition, GDC is to receive "reasonable administrative expense reimbursement, based on a fair allocation of the company's incurred cash costs as spread among its entire contract revenue". Finally, GDC is to receive 25 percent per annum as a return on its investment in all vehicles and equipment that are being used to carry out the contract" with WC. The term "investment" has been defined in the contract as a "simple average of replacement cost and original cost less accumulated depreciation, as determined by generally accepted accounting principles". The "investment" is to be an average of the beginning and end of year investment computations.

The contract provides for the appointment of an arbitrator, in case of disputes between GDC and WC. Each party to the contract is required to submit its position on items that are in dispute, and the arbitrator chooses *one* of the two, and gives reasons (that is, reasons which may prevent further disputes).

The contract became effective almost three years ago. The parties have not been able to agree on the final invoicing for the first two years of the contract. Your employer has been appointed arbitrator. He has assigned to you the task of reviewing the two written submissions from the parties, and preparing questions that ought to be asked at a one day hearing of the oral arguments of the dispute. He wants full explanations of your reasoning process.

Your review of WC's written submission to the arbitrator provides the following:

1. "Before we contracted to GDC, we handled our own garbage collection. We did not overhaul the trucks every year, and therefore did not incur a cost of $398,000, that GDC has charged as an out-of-pocket cost in the first year of the contract, and $412,500 in the second year of the contract. A more appropriate charge would be $100,000 in total for the two years."

2. "We sold GDC some of our trucks for $1,600,000. We believe that these trucks are being depreciated for income tax purposes at 30 percent per annum on a declining balance basis. However, GDC states that it has used only 10 percent straight-line depreciation, for the purposes of calculating its investment in trucks. We believe that the 30 percent figure should be used."

3. "GDC does not seem to have credited the contract costs for scrap received on disposal of spare parts for trucks that have been sold."

4. "Also, GDC does not seem to have credited the contract costs for proceeds on disposal of used tires."

5. "GDC has included losses on disposal of two trucks in the contract cost category. We disagree."

6. "In calculating investment, GDC has used replacement cost for a new truck, for about one-half of its trucks. We believe that replacement cost in used condition is appropriate."

7. "GDC has charged us overhead costs of invoicing us, plus interest on unpaid balances after 15 days."

8. "GDC appears to have divisionalized the operations of their company, and placed most of their assets into a 'Contract With WC' division. As a result we believe that they have overcharged us for administrative costs, such as the salary of the president of GDC, for computer time, and for office costs."

9. "GDC apparently has been able to convince some residents of WC to set aside newspapers and other salvageable items—which it picks up in separate (non-WC contract) trucks. We believe that the revenue from the sale of these items should be credited to the WC contract."

10. "We disagree with the way GDC has handled discounts on the purchase of new trucks."

Your review of GDC's written submission provides the following:

1. "We have tried to organize our company to separate the costs of servicing from our other operations. We have allocated costs in accordance with our best estimates of the amount of service provided."

2. "We would not be able to obtain fleet discounts if we had only the WC contract. Therefore, we have not reduced the cost of WC's investment for quantity discounts for volume purchases of new trucks."

3. "We maintain our trucks in a way that helps prevent breakdowns. We believe that the cost of overhauls is worth the effort in the long run."

4. "We base replacement costs on the cost of a new truck, unless the efficiency of our used truck is somehow impaired by age."

5. "We did not charge WC with the advertising costs of our 'non-pollution newspaper and scrap' recovery program."

6. "Some of our parts are transferred to non-WC contract trucks when WC contract trucks are scrapped."

Required:

Prepare the report for your employer.

CHAPTER 9

Cash, Receivables and Discounting

Chapter Themes

1. We may think that cash is cash. But, when we dig a little deeper, other issues arise: suppose that the cash is in U.S. dollars, or is temporarily invested in certificates that generate interest income. You may recall from Chapter 5 that cash is important because of its status as the most liquid asset, and its significance in avoiding bankruptcy. People who have internal control as a prime objective have to give special attention to cash because it is easily mishandled.

2. Accounts receivable are important assets in some companies and therefore merit attention. We will not devote much time to them, however, because accounting for them is a fairly simple application of what was discussed in chapters 6, 7, and 8. Under GAAP, receivables are recorded on the financial statements at their cash equivalency—called *net realizable value*—or what we will receive in cash shortly. The main issue is the determination of bad debt expense and the offsetting credit to allowance for doubtful accounts or allowance for bad debts. The allowance is deducted from the asset to arrive at net realizable value.

3. Discounting is another name for recognizing the difference in cost or value that arises when interest is paid or received on assets or liabilities. A sum of $100 that is to be received in one year (with no interest being due) is *not* the same as $100 received today. (The $100 received today can be invested to generate interest.) Recognizing this distinction is important, especially for cash flow prediction objectives. The *timing* of receipt of cash and its effects are important in other situations and for other objectives of accounting.

4. Chapter 9 focusses on the *application* of the material that is contained in Chapters 6, 7, and 8. The term "application" refers to the ability to use the knowledge in a setting different from the one where we first acquired it.

Cash

Cash can be on hand, in a chequing or savings account, or perhaps temporarily invested, e.g., for 24 hours, in some short-term investment certificates. If the cash is in a foreign currency at the balance sheet date, it would have to be *translated* to Canadian dollars, using the foreign exchange rates prevailing on the balance sheet date. Short-term investments of cash would not be included with cash, but would be current assets.

Cash on hand refers to petty cash funds, cash floats, and cash awaiting deposit in a bank. A petty cash fund, of say $100, is used to pay incidental charges—such as for messenger deliveries, extra newspapers purchased, taxi fares, and other small, unexpected expenditures requiring immediate cash payment. The word *imprest petty cash fund* is used when the balance remains fixed at, say, $100. This means that cash plus receipts in the fund would always total $100. When more cash is needed to replenish the fund, the journal entry would be:

Office expense	$50.30	
Delivery expense	36.70	
Other expense	5.10	
Cash (in bank)		$92.10

That is, a cheque is issued and the custodian of the imprest fund cashes it to replenish the petty cash fund to $100.

Although we have used the word cash to this point in the book, it is necessary in practice to be more precise. If we have two bank accounts and an imprest petty cash fund, we should be debiting and crediting "General Bank Account", "Payroll Bank Account", "Petty Cash" or whatever is affected.

Some types of businesses require large amounts of cash on hand to serve immediate needs. Some examples are: banks, trust companies, pawn shops, and so forth. A less obvious one is a department store, which has many small cash-floats spread throughout the store. The floats are needed by each cashier to make change for the first few customers in the day. The amount can add up to give a high cash on hand figure on the balance sheet.

BANK ACCOUNTS

The problems that businesses have with bank accounts are similar to those we have—do the bank's figures agree with what we show? If we have a bank's passbook that we keep up to date, our problems are fewer than when we receive a monthly statement. We still have differences between our records and the bank's, however, for the following types of reasons:

1. Someone has not cashed a cheque that we have written.

2. We wrote a cheque that the bank cashed, and we forgot to enter it in our cheque book.

3. A deposit that was sent to the bank was delayed in the mail, or in one of the automatic teller machines.

4. The bank charged us for something such as a service charge, or credited our account (account payable on their books) for interest earned; but, we have not recorded these in our cheque book.

5. The bank made a mistake on a deposit or service charge or cheque or interest.

For internal control purposes, i.e., trying to protect against error and fraud, it is wise to *reconcile* the bank's figures to ours once a month, after we receive our account statement. (Errors have to be caught quickly if they affect the bank account because consequences can be serious. For instance, the bank may refuse to correct their error because the records and documents are old and too difficult to locate.) Broadly-speaking, we have to distinguish *three* categories of differences between our books and those of the bank:

1. Legitimate charges or credits on the bank's statement that we have not yet made in our books—and journal entries are needed:
   A. Expenses—such as service charges for writing cheques:

Office expense	35	
Bank—chequing account		35

   B. Revenue—such as interest received on a deposit:

Bank—savings account	110	
Interest revenue		110

   As soon as we record the journal entries, the difference between our books and the bank's disappears, and we no longer have to be concerned about reconciling.

2. *Timing* differences between what the bank's balance is and what our books show as at a particular date:
   A. Cheques that we have written but which have not been cashed.
   B. Deposits (or receipts) entered in our books that did not get into the bank's records until later.

3. Errors by the bank, or us, that have to be corrected. *Our* corrections probably require journal entries, as in (1).

No journal entries are required for the timing differences in (2), because the passage of time eliminates the difference. For internal control purposes, however, a reconciliation should be prepared.

A *bank reconciliation* is a form of work sheet or working paper that accounts for the difference between our ledger figure and the bank statement figure. A simple one would appear as follows:

COMPANY NAME
Bank Reconciliation
November 30, 19—6

Balance per bank statement	$10,199.98
Add:	
Deposit recorded on company's books on November 30, but not credited by bank until December 3	2,962.44
	13,162.42
Deduct:	
Cheque issued, but not yet cashed	3,725.90
Balance per ledger	$ 9,436.52

The ledger account is correct in the above example. At the close of business on November 30, our balance per the bank's records differs from the ledger account in our books. But, the difference vanishes, as soon as the deposit of $2,962.44 is recorded by the bank and the person cashes the cheque for $3,725.90.

In doing bank reconciliations, the trick is to figure out into which of the preceding categories does the difference between our ledger account and the bank's balance fall.

PRACTICE PROBLEM—BANK RECONCILIATION

Bank reconciliations seem confusing at first, but, with practice, we come to understand the process. Make the necessary journal entries and do the bank reconciliation from the following information for Retco Ltd.:

Balance of ledger account - December 31, 19—7	$36,844.78 Debit
Balance per bank statement - December 31, 19—7	31,686.70 Credit

(Remember that the "credit" per the bank is per *their* books, and means that they owe us money; hence, we have an asset.)

Cheques written but not yet cashed	$ 5,231.74
Deposit recorded by company in December 19—7 but not entered by the bank until January 19—8	10,679.38
Bank service charges for December 19—7; not yet recorded by Retco	62.15
Bank records a cheque as $1,099.88 when it should have been for $1,088.99	10.89
Interest earned on a temporary investment made with the bank (i.e., Retco had excess cash and invested it with the bank); the sum was credited by the bank, but not recorded in Retco's journal and ledger	362.60

It is strongly recommended that you do the above practice problem before reading beyond this paragraph. Until you become quite familiar with bank reconciliations, it is important to set the data up as we did so as to avoid confusion between pluses and minuses.

Response:

The first step would be to adjust Retco's ledger account for legitimate transactions that the bank has recorded, but which have *not* been recorded in the company's ledger account. The journal entries are:

Bank service expenses	62.15	
Bank		62.15
Bank	362.60	
Interest revenue		362.60

These two journal entries adjust the ledger account:

Ledger, before adjustment	$36,844.78
Interest revenue	362.60
	$37,207.38
Service expenses	62.15
Ledger, after adjustment	$37,145.23

The point of the reconciliation at this stage is to start with the bank statement figure at December 31, 19—7 and amend it to what it *would have* looked like *if*:

1. All the deposits had been credited by the bank by the close of business on December 31, 19—7,

2. All the outstanding cheques had been cashed by December 31, 19—7, and

3. No bank errors had been made.

Balance per bank statement		$31,686.70
Add: Outstanding deposit	$10,679.38	
Bank error - cheque #99 cashed		
as $1,099.88 instead of $1,088.99	10.89	10,690.27
		$42,376.97
Deduct outstanding cheques		5,231.74
Balance per company's ledger		$37,145.23

Note that the $37,145.23 agrees with Retco's ledger for bank, after we adjusted it, i.e., posted the journal entries. If it did not agree, we would have to go back and check our work. Common errors are:

1. Addition or subtraction of columns;

2. Adding a number instead of subtracting it, or vice-versa; and

3. Picking up an incorrect number—such as $31,868.70 for the bank-statement balance instead of $31,686.70.

Additional problems may arise because we have not carefully compared the cheques and deposits in our cash journal against the bank statement. We may have missed a service charge or not noted that a cheque had *not* been cashed. Or, one of our deposits may not have cleared the other person's bank because she or he did not have sufficient funds on deposit. This is called an NSF cheque (not sufficient funds) and would be charged against us on the bank statement. What should we do if a customer's cheque is returned by our bank, stamped NSF? Is it a bank error? Timing difference? In need of a journal entry?

A journal entry is needed because our records are incorrect. They show a customer as having paid our receivable when the cheque "bounced". The entry is:

Accounts receivable	xxx	
Bank - chequing		xxx

The debit to accounts receivable re-establishes that an amount is due. If the bank also charged a service expense of $5, we would add this to the receivable.

When the bank reconciliation explains all of the differences between the bank statement and ledger balance, we can be confident that certain types of errors or frauds have not occurred. We say "certain types" because one of the employees may have written a cheque on Retco's bank account and recorded it in the books—but Retco did not receive whatever was paid for. To prevent other errors or frauds, we must introduce many internal-control steps. Some of these are touched on in the sections on auditing and accounting controls in succeeding chapters.

Temporary Investments

Managers of a company may decide that they will have excess cash for a short period of time. (A statement of expected cash receipts and disbursements may have been prepared for the next few months showing that a large amount of cash would exist for ninety to hundred days.) Investment dealers, banks, and others will invest these sums for as short as one day, if the amount is large.

What journal entry would we make under GAAP if $1 million were invested on April 1 for ninety-two days at 10 percent interest per annum? Perhaps we need to refresh our memories by referring to the concepts set forth in Chapter 8. Which should we use and why?

The prime concept that applies to the above transaction under GAAP is *cost*. That is, if we paid $500 to a broker to locate a reputable company in need of funds for ninety-two days, our journal entry would be:

Short term investment	1,000,500	
Bank		1,000,500

The *matching* concept would also apply when we accrued interest on the investment and credited it to the particular period in which the interest was earned:

April 30:   Accrued interest receivable   8,300
                    Interest income   8,300

If we wanted to be especially particular we could match the cost of brokerage to the $8,300, by treating the $500 as a prepaid expense (which it is *not*; it is a part of the cost of $1,000,500). We may make this entry:

April 30:   Interest income   160
                    Short term investment   160

This entry reduces both the short term investment and the interest income for the number of days (twenty-nine or thirty) in April for which the investment existed. At the end of ninety-two days, the reduced cost of the short term investment would be $1 million—which is precisely what the borrower would be repaying us. That is, the $500 is our *cost*, and not what the borrower received on April 1.

The short term investment account at the end of ninety-two days may look like this:

	Short term investment		
April 1:	1,000,500		
		April 30:	160
		May 31:	170
		June 30:	165
		July 2:	5
		July 2:	1,000,000

On July 2, we would receive our $1 million back in time to use it—or we could reinvest.

Most accountants would not be concerned with the $500 broker's fee because the sum is not *material*. (We thus have identified three concepts, listed in Chapter 8—cost, matching, and materiality—that apply to this one temporary investment transaction.) Those who invoke the materiality concept may make *one* of the following entries on *July 2*:

Cash	1,000,000	
Interest income	500	
Short term investment		1,000,500
OR		
Cash	1,000,000	
Loss on disposal of investment	500	
Short term investment		1,000,500

Where would the "interest income" or "loss on disposal of investment" appear on the income statement? If the amounts involved are minor, they *may* be grouped under an "other income" or "other expense" category, toward the bottom of the income statement. If the amounts are large, however, the company would have to be engaging in this type of investing quite frequently. As a result, the figures *could* appear near the top of the income statement:

Revenue:	Sales of company's products	$ xxx	
	Interest revenue	<u>xx</u>	$xxxx
Cost of sales			xxx

Notice that the words "may" and "could" were used. As we have repeatedly stressed, there are no "right" answers to such questions. We have to ask ourselves: Who are the users, and what do they need?, and Do the users have any power to demand the disclosure they seek? (Or, are the preparers in command? If so, will they do what they want?)

ACCRUED INTEREST AT THE DATE OF PURCHASE

Many short term investments, e.g., short term Government of Canada bonds, have interest accrued at the date on which we purchase the bonds. For example, the government may pay interest on a particular bond on March 1 and September 1. If we purchase the bond on June 1, we will have to pay the seller of the bond for the interest that has accrued between March 1 and June 1. The journal entry on June 1 may be:

June 1:	Government bond	10,000	
	Interest income	300	
	Cash		10,300

Observe that we have *debited* interest income. The reason is that on September 1, we will make the following journal entry when we receive the interest cheque:

September 1:	Cash	600
	Interest income	600

After the September 1 journal entry, interest income will have a credit balance of $300. This is precisely what we want in the account—to reflect interest earned from June 1 to September 1.

The concepts that we have illustrated for temporary investments also tend to apply to longer term investments, but there are some differences:

1. Short term investments are classified as current assets. Longer term investments are only shown as current assets in the year before they come due. For example, bonds investments (*not* liabilities) due on August 31, 19—7 are a current asset as of December 31, 19—6.

2. Interest rate complications may arise. More will be said about this later.

3. Some longer term investments may be in the form of common shares of other companies. This is a major topic that is covered much later in the book. (It is referred to as Intercorporate Investments.) Common share investments generate dividends instead of interest.

Receivables

Accounts receivable can arise for several reasons: (1) sales of merchandise or services, i.e., accounts receivable is the offsetting debit when revenue is credited; (2) sales of long-lived assets, i.e., offsetting debit when a gain/loss on disposal occurs; (3) sales of shares, i.e., offsetting debit when a credit is made to a balance sheet share capital account—as opposed to an income statement transaction; (4) loans are made to certain employees of the company, i.e., offsetting debit when cash is credited; and similar transactions.

Other types of receivables can exist if a customer or a buyer of long-lived assets promises to pay over a long period of time. Typically, if we agreed to allow someone to pay us over an extended period of two or more years, we would require them to sign a note receivable. This same procedure occurs when we borrow from a bank, and have to give them some collateral to support the loan and a note.

Under GAAP, receivables are shown on the balance sheet at today's cash-equivalent value, called *net realizable value.* When we use the word "today's", we really mean "today and within the next year". That is, we often ignore interest effects if the receivable is likely to be paid to us within one year (and the customer does not have to pay us any interest on the receivable). When the receivable is not due for eighteen months or so, however, we use a lower value to recognize the interest that is *lost* by not having the cash today. That is, *if* we had the cash today, we could invest it and earn interest. This is discussed in detail later in the chapter.

FINANCIAL STATEMENT LINKAGE

After we have progressed through two chapters (6 and 8) where few references were made to journal entries and the bookkeeping cycle, we will reinforce the double entry relationship in this chapter. Much of the remainder of the book examines the effects of alternative policies and methods of accounting and reporting on balance sheets, income statements, users' interpretations, and preparers' objectives. The same ideas appear over and over as we proceed through an examination of the various assets and liabilities. Consequently, we will now spend some time going through the basic thought process, and reinforce it from time to time in later chapters. But, it is essential to remember that the idea *applies to all situations* where a debit/credit is made to an asset/liability and the offsetting debit/credit is to an income statement account.

Suppose that you have obtained a summer job working for a labor union. You have been asked to assist the people who will be handling negotiations for various union bargaining-units. They have asked you to review the financial statements of *three companies* with which the union will enter into separate negotiations for wage increases and other benefits. You start with a look at cash and receivables, and note the following:

N Limited
Balance Sheet

Current assets:		
Cash		$ 5,600
Accounts receivable		927,400

N Limited
Income Statement

Sales		$10,642,000
Cost of goods sold		xx
Gross profit		xx
Expenses:		
Bad debts	$129,700	

O Limited
Balance Sheet

Current assets:	
Cash	$ 5,600
Accounts receivable, less allowance for doubtful accounts of $240,000	927,400

O Limited
Income Statement

Sales	$10,642,000

(There is no mention of bad debts or doubtful accounts expense.)

P Limited
Balance Sheet

Current assets:	
Cash	$ 5,600
Accounts receivable, at net realizable value	924,400
Inventory	xxx
Non-current assets:	
Accounts receivable	3,000

P Limited
Income Statement

Sales, less doubtful accounts	$10,512,300

In which respects are N, O, and P similar, and different? Is it possible that the three companies are *identical*, and that the only differences arise from *accounting presentation* on the financial statements? That is, we have seen (Chapter 6) how alternative accounting policies can affect the income figure as well as the valuation attached to assets and liabilities. Now we see that methods of financial statement presentation can give the *illusion of difference* when identical situations exist.

All three companies (N, O, and P) have identical cash figures. (We have arranged this deliberately so as to focus only on differences.) The figure of $5,600 is meaningless because it is at an instant of time. One day later, the figure could be much different. In total, the accounts receivable are $927,400 for each company. In P Limited, $3,000 has been shown as non-current whereas in the other two companies the $3,000 is a current asset. Quite possibly those who prepared the financial statements of N and O may have viewed the $3,000 as not being *material*. (The materiality concept is applied differently in N and O, than in P.) Companies N and O did not want a separate category for such a small amount, which they felt would have no effect on the decision-making of readers of the financial statements.

Company O's balance sheet tells us that $240,000 was deducted in order to arrive at the $927,400. Canadian GAAP does not require disclosure of the $240,000. Now that we know the amount, however, why does it differ from the $129,700 figure on the income statement of N Limited? And why is there no mention of bad debts on O Limited's income statement? (Again, the reason may be materiality; the $129,700 could be included in another expense account—such as selling expense—that we have not yet looked at.) Finally, in P Limited, why have the bad debts of $129,700 been deducted to arrive at a net sales figure of $10,512,300 ($10,642,000 – $129,700)?

Let us start with the last question. In practice, the debit for bad debts or doubtful accounts is usually classified as an expense. But, both theoretically and in reality, it is an *adjustment to revenue*. You thought that you would get $10,642,000 when you recognized or credited revenue. BUT, hindsight is showing that you likely will receive, in cash, closer to $10,512,300. Hence, there really would seem to be a revenue decrease. But, most often you will see the expense treatment in practice. Some consumer finance companies do use the same presentation as P Limited, perhaps because their bad debts can be large, and possibly because they do not wish to disclose the amount.

Canadian bank accounting and reporting tends to differ from policies that are followed by most other organizations. Therefore, banks provide us with another interesting illustration. Banks calculate their current loan losses in a somewhat mysterious manner. As we saw in earlier examples, banks are sometimes in the difficult position of keeping a troubled business afloat or sending it into bankruptcy—because of their willingness to extend a loan for a few months or require immediate payment, both of which may make a difference concerning the loan's eventual collectibility. (If a bank demands an immediate loan repayment, in all probability most troubled businesses would be forced into bankruptcy. However, when the bank grants additional funds, or allows more time for the business to repay a loan, this decision confuses the issue of whether a bad debt expense should be recorded—and *when*, and *for how much*. As a result, banks follow their own accounting methods, subject to directives from federal government bank inspectors. Consequently, when we read financial statements for a bank, we have to read carefully if we want to estimate what bad debt "expense" has been charged in arriving at net income.) In summary, we will see diversity of disclosure among companies. Although we have used banks as an illustration—because they have been in the news frequently in the 1980s—the same theme applies in other businesses.

Next, we should pursue the point about the debit being $129,700 and the allowance for doubtful accounts showing $240,000. This concept was noted in Chapters 3 and 4, and is the same concept as was used for depreciation expense (income statement account) and accumulated depreciation (balance sheet account). The $129,700 represents the amount that we chose to expense this year. The $240,000 is the amount that we believe will *reduce the gross or total amount of accounts receivable to the figure that we expect to collect in cash*—called the *net realizable value.*

The journal entries would be as follows:

(a)	Bad debt expense (or similar title)	129,700	
	Allowance for doubtful accounts		129,700
(b)	Allowance for doubtful accounts	105,000	
	Accounts receivable		105,000

Entry (a) is much like the depreciation expense journal entry. Entry (b) occurs when we give up hope of collecting the account receivable, and choose to *write it off*.

The ledger accounts would be as follows:

Bad Debt Expense		Allowance for Doubtful Accounts	
Opening 0			Opening 215,300
(a) 129,700			(a) 129,700
	Close to retained earnings 129,700	(b) 105,000	
			240,000
0			

The bad debt expense account would be closed out to the "income summary" or "retained earnings" at the end of the year—the same procedure as would be followed with all revenue and expense accounts. The workings of the "allowance for doubtful accounts" are a little more complicated. Note that at the *beginning* of the year, $215,300 had accumulated (much like retained earnings accumulates) to reduce the beginning balance of accounts receivable to net realizable value. In theory, what happens after that is:

1. A manager, or an accountant, looks over the accounts receivable and decides which ones should be written off as uncollectible. Journal entry (b) is therefore made for $105,000.

2. A credit manager and others examine the *remaining* accounts receivable (ending balance) and decide what figure seems necessary to reduce the *ending* receivables to estimated net realizable value. A figure of $240,000 was chosen.

3. The $129,700 therefore becomes the sum that is *needed to balance*, given that we know the $215,300, the $105,000, and the $240,000. In short, the $129,700 is the "plug figure".

In summary, what does the N, O, P example illustrate? It shows the workings of the basic accounts receivable/allowance for doubtful accounts/bad debts relationship. Above all, it shows how three companies with exactly the same transactions and net income effects can be made to look different simply by putting the figures in different locations on the balance sheet and income statement. Finally, it reinforces the theme that there is *not* a "right" way and a "wrong" way of reporting the figures. All the alternatives presented for N, O, and P make sense under particular circumstances.

Estimations are involved in arriving at the $240,000 and at some of the other figures. Given the lack of clarity about facts and the need for assumptions, objectives of accounting should be considered. For instance, someone wanting to keep income taxes as low as the law permits may use a figure of $250,000 or $260,000 instead of $240,000. The additional $10,000 or $20,000 would have to be supported by them in some way, or Revenue Canada would disallow it—meaning they would not accept the additional sum as an expense deduction in computing taxable income. When there is sufficient doubt, however, the additional amount may be accepted by Revenue Canada. If the same financial statements are being shown to a banker, she or he may wonder about the "large" figure of $260,000—and about management's abilities. Therefore, we have to consider the consequences of our accounting methods and policies, and rank the importance of our competing objectives of accounting. Who is more important, Revenue Canada or the banker?

CONTROL ACCOUNTS AND SUBSIDIARY LEDGERS

In the *N-O-P* illustration, we referred to having a person examine the accounts receivable and arrive at a figure, i.e., $240,000, needed to reduce the receivables to net realizable value. This step is easier than may appear because accountants make use of *subsidiary ledger* accounts. These subsidiary accounts exist in many places in accounting—for receivables, for payables, for different inventory items, for different long-lived assets.

For accounts receivable, the idea is to have a separate subsidiary ledger account for *each* customer. The system operates as follows:

1. When a sale is made on account or cash is collected on account, the debit or credit is made to the general ledger *control* (or master total) account called Accounts Receivable.

2. In addition, a *second* debit or credit is made to the subsidiary ledger account for the particular customer—Mr. A. Smith. (This sounds as though we have made two

debits or two credits, and therefore we would not be able to balance the trial balance. But, *only one* is being made to the *general ledger* account for accounts receivable.) Therefore, in the general ledger, the debits will still equal the credits. The *subsidiary* ledger is exactly what it says—a "back up" listing by customer of who owes what. The total of the subsidiary ledger will equal the total of the control account.

To illustrate, suppose that you have a younger brother or sister who just acquired a paper route (November 1). The newspaper gives him or her a "collection book"— a separate sheet of receipts for each of the customers on the route. This separate collection book is a *subsidiary ledger.* In total, the customers owe $5 each per month and there are eighty customers. The account receivable in the newspaper's general ledger *control* account would therefore show a $400 debit, (80 x $5). As he or she collects and issues each customer a receipt, the general ledger receivable would decrease:

Cash	380	
Accounts receivable		380
(Sums received from paper route)		

At this point (November 30), the general ledger control account shows $20 due, and the subsidiary ledger collection book would have amounts owing as follows:

Wanda Vance	(27 Main Street)	$ 5
John Holmes	(47 Main Street)	5
Donna Walker	(85 Main Street)	5
Les Filer	(99 Main Street)	5
		$20

The next month (December 1), another $400 would be added to the control account, raising the total to $420. Your brother/sister may decide on December 2 to stop delivering to Donna Walker and Les Filer and ask for a $10 credit from the newspaper publisher for *December*—thereby reducing the general ledger control account balance to $410. The subsidiary ledger account would now show seventy-six customers owing $5 each, and two (Wanda Vance and John Holmes) owing $10 each. Two not included in the seventy-eight are Ms. Walker and Mr. Filer, who are probably bad debts from November. Your young friend may have to pay the $10 to the newspaper. But, suppose that the newspaper does *not* charge the carriers for bad debts, and makes the following general ledger journal entries:

(a)	Bad debt expense	10	
	Allowance for bad debt		10
(b)	Allowance for bad debts	10	
	Accounts receivable		10
	To write off Ms. Walker and Mr. Filer re November's paper		

After recording these journal entries, the general ledger control account would show a $400 debit—representing $380 (76 customers @ $5 each) and $20 (each of Ms.

Vance and Mr. Holmes owe $10). The control account should always be in balance, with the subsidiary ledger details by customer totalling to the control balance debit or credit.

A review of each customer's subsidiary ledger account would help us decide whether an allowance for doubtful accounts is needed. For instance:

Mr. Warren Down

19—5		Feb: Returned
Jan: Purchase	6,200	some of
		January
		purchase 3,100
Apr: Purchase	6,350	
Balance		
Dec. 31:	9,450	

Notice that Mr. Down has not made a cash payment *at all*. Such precise information about an individual customer would not be readily available if only a general ledger control account were in use for accounts receivable.

SALES RETURNS AND ALLOWANCES

The subsidiary ledger account for Mr. Down shows a credit of $3,100 for goods that have been returned. What has been debited? Again, there is *not one* right answer—it depends on the facts, and who is using the information for which judgments/decisions. Suppose that we own a small company and salespersons are being paid a bonus based on dollar sales figures. Would we want to debit "sales revenue" for the $3,100? Or might we want to use a separate general ledger control account called "Sales returns and allowances"?

If we suspected that the salespersons would try to make fake sales to increase their bonus, we would want the bonus based on "sales revenue less any returns". (A phony sale would occur when a salesperson tells a customer to take five dresses home, and "return the four you do not want next week". Initially, the customer is debited for a receivable of five dresses, but would be credited for four returns the following week.) How could accounting help to discourage salespersons who are paid their bonus weekly and do not worry about the charge for returns next week, or next month, or next year?

One way is to use a separate "sales returns and allowances" general ledger control account—and to have two subsidiary ledgers for each salesperson. (One subsidiary ledger would be for sales and the other for sales returns and allowances.) A review of the subsidiary ledgers would quickly tell us who has excessive returns or allowances and requires some counselling. (Allowances are price reductions that are granted because the goods are slightly damaged, or the service is inferior in some respect.)

Is the cost of keeping subsidiary ledgers worth it? We have to compare the costs against benefits. Subsidiary ledgers are easily kept on microcomputers using a spreadsheet approach, such as Lotus 1-2-3 software. Thus, the costs are not as high as one may at first suspect.

If we have few or no uses for separate general ledger control accounts, however, the debit could go to sales instead of to "sales returns and allowances". We should avoid having subsidiary ledgers by salesperson if you want to keep bookkeeping costs low.

It is worth remembering that we *may* still show sales as one net figure on the income statement even though we may be using two general ledger control accounts—one for sales and the other for sales returns and allowances. The data by salesperson may be useful for our payroll (bonus) purposes. The financial statements could be for a different audience of users. This point has to be kept in mind throughout the study of accountancy. For instance, subsidiary ledgers may help in catching errors or frauds, and therefore be useful *internal control* devices. For financial statement presentation purposes only the total figure *may*, however, appear for net sales. We could use the following income statement presentation (if we felt that it were necessary):

Revenue:	Sales	$2,500,000
	Less returns and allowances	299,000
	Net sales	$2,201,000

Discounting

We know that one dollar received today is preferable to one dollar received one year from now when the purchasing power of the dollar is *constant*. ("Purchasing power of the dollar" refers to what the dollar will buy in food, clothing, shelter, and other commodities. During periods of inflation, a dollar loses purchasing power. During deflation a dollar gains purchasing power. That is, under deflation it is better to hold dollars than commodities, such as automobiles, because the price of commodities is dropping with deflation.) When we ignore the effects of purchasing power of the dollar, a dollar received today is preferable because it can be invested to generate interest income.

To illustrate, suppose that we were able to invest at 10 percent per annum. A sum of $100,000 invested today would accumulate to $110,000 in one year, i.e., $100,000 plus 10 percent of $100,000. In technical terms, the $110,000 received in one year has a *present value*, at a 10 percent interest rate, of $100,000. The ratio of $100,000 divided by $110,000 = 0.909. If we look at Appendix A (p. 592), we will find 0.9091 listed under the 10 percent column for one period hence. The decimals in the Appendix are merely conversions of many ratios, such as the $100,000 divided by the $110,000 equals 0.9091.

Similarly, a sum of $100,000 invested at 10 percent per annum for *two* years accumulates to $121,000, i.e., $110,000 plus 10 percent of $110,000. The *present value*, at 10 percent interest per annum, of $121,000 received two years hence is $100,000. The ratio of $100,000 divided by $121,000 = 0.8264. In Appendix A (p.592) the 0.8264 figure appears under the 10 percent column for two periods hence.

On page 597, a figure of 1.736 appears under the 10 percent column for two periods from 0 (now). The 1.736 is 0.9091 plus 0.8264 rounded out to three places after the decimal. Thus, the present value of $100,000 received at the end of one year and $100,000 received at the end of two years is $100,000 times 1.736 = $173,600. Alternatively, we can use the longer way:

$100,000 x 0.9091	$ 90,910
100,000 x 0.8264	82,640
	$173,550

The difference of $50 ($173,600 - $173,550) arises from our not employing several places of decimals.

The cumulative table is useful whenever the same amount, e.g., $100,000, will be received over several years. The cumulative figure, e.g., 1.736, helps to simplify arithmetic. This "same amount" idea is often referred to as an *annuity*.

SOME APPLICATIONS OF DISCOUNTING

To this point in the book, discounting could have been employed in several situations:

1. Cash Flow Prediction Objective

Chapters 6 and 8 refer to the idea of trying to ascertain the amount, *timing*, and uncertainty of cash flows. Which of the following investments would you pick?

Situation A: $300,000 to be received in three years? OR
Situation B: $90,627 to be received at the end of each of the next three years?

People interested in a cash flow prediction objective would try to follow the procedures outlined in Chapter 5 to ascertain the *time* when cash or funds from operations would appear. The foregoing situation already tells us the amounts and timing—$300,000 lump sum at the end of three years, or $90,627 each year. But, in order to make our choice, we have to know what interest rate applies. What can we invest the $90,627 for?

Suppose that we can invest any cash that we receive at 10 percent per annum. How much would we have accumulated at the end of three years?

	End of 3 Years
Situation A:	$300,000

Situation B:
    (i) $90,627 received at the end of the first year would be
        re-invested at 10 percent for 2 years:
        $90,627 × 10% = $9,063 interest.
        ($90,627 + $9,063) × 10% = $9,969 interest.

$90,627 plus $9,063 plus $9,969	$109,659

   (ii) $90,627 received at the end of the second year would be
        re-invested at 10 percent for 1 year:
        $90,627 × 10% = $9,063

$90,627 + $9,063	99,690
(iii) $90,627 received at the end of the third year	90,627
	$299,976
Rounding difference	24
	$300,000

At 10 percent interest, it would not matter which Situation (*A* or *B*) were selected. At the end of three years, the figure (called a *terminal value*) is the same, $300,000.

If we used present value techniques instead of terminal value, the answer would be the same because the interest rate is the same:

	Present Value
Situation A: $300,000 × 0.7513 (p. 592) =	$225,390
Situation B: $90,627 × 2.487 (p. 597) =	$225,390

If we switched to a 5 percent interest rate, however, we get a different response:

	Present Value
Situation A: $300,000 × 0.8638	$259,140
Situation B: $90,627 × 2.723	$246,777

Situation *A* is more favorable than *B*.

If we switched to a 15 percent interest rate, Situation B is a better choice than is A:

	Present Value
Situation A: $300,000 × 0.6575 (p. 593) =	$197,250
Situation B: $90,627 × 2.283 (p. 598) =	$206,901

In summary, interest rates are very important in investing, and can affect our choice of companies in which we may invest. Observe that we are discounting *cash flows*, and not accrual income figures. (See Chapter 5.) The *timing* of receipt of *cash* is vital. Sometimes we can approximate the amount of cash by using accrual accounting figures; other times we cannot.

We will now relate this interest and discounting concept to the ideas discussed in the previous three chapters. The following crucial point arises frequently: Which accounting policies and treatment best reflect the timing of cash flows (receipts less disbursements)? *If our main objective is cash flow prediction* (in our external financial statements), our goal has to be to choose the policies that best reflect the appearance of cash flows.

For example, the policy that we would want to adopt for revenue recognition with a major objective of cash flow prediction would be the one that keeps the accrual accounting figures close in time and amount to the cash figures. *But,* we can only do this *if the facts are supportive.* For instance, completed contract revenue recognition methods (see Chapter 7) bear little relationship to cash flows, i.e., such as monthly billing and related collections. Yet, we may use completed contract revenue recognition because the facts about expected profit are not clear—the *uncertainty* about profit is great. (Recall from Chapter 8 that amount, timing, *and uncertainty* of cash flows are important under a cash flow prediction objective.) Thus, sometimes facts are so strong that we are not able to pursue a particular objective of accounting. We choose the completed contract method and have to accept the consequences. One consequence is that the completed contract method makes computations more difficult for those who want to try to predict cash flows—and try to discount them to a present value. (Under completed contract accounting, most cash is received and paid out months in advance of the recording of earned revenue and the related computation of funds from operations. Thus, major discounting errors could occur because we discounted for, say, three years under completed contract accounting. Yet, most actual cash receipts and disbursements could have occurred, say, two years earlier.)

Generally speaking, those who wish to cash flow predict are usually trying to establish the present value of a company by discounting future cash flows. They want to answer the following type of question: What would I pay for a company today that generates $100,000 per year (at the end of the year) for a period of twelve years? If the $100,000 is cash, and they know the interest rate that they can re-invest the annual $100,000 at (say 10 percent), the calculation is easy:

Present Value =
$100,000 × 6.814 (10 percent for 12 years) (p. 597) = $681,400.

As a result, if someone offers to sell them the company for $650,000, in theory they would buy it because the $650,000 is *less than* the $681,400. That is, the $650,000 price is a bargain.

Similarly, someone may offer them 20 percent of the company's shares for $140,000. Twenty percent of $681,400 is $136,280. As the $140,000 is higher than the $136,280, the prospective investor/buyer may not want to acquire the shares.

There are situations more complex than we have just described. Accurate predictions of events that may happen tomorrow are difficult enough without having to look twelve years ahead. In addition, there is the problem of accrual accounting not always reflecting cash flows, e.g., the completed contract illustration. This is why some people are skeptical of the "ability" of general-purpose financial statements to provide much help to those who wish to predict. Nevertheless, some aspects of financial statements can be useful to forecasters. (This will become more apparent as we proceed in the book.)

Illustration 9-1 is a useful reminder of what general-purpose financial statements purport to do, and what is sought by those who wish to forecast corporate cash flows. On the surface, there seems to be a conflict. We must bear this in mind when we choose accounting policies and analyse financial statements.

ILLUSTRATION 9-1

	Financial Statements	What Forecasters Want
Time Period:	Primary focus on past and present	Primary focus on the future
Measurement:	Accrual basis accounting	Cash receipts and disbursements
Type of Report:	General-purpose, for the entire company	Special purpose, perhaps for detailed parts of the business

It is also worth recalling that it is frequently difficult, if not impossible, to serve many different types of readers of general-purpose financial statements. A general-purpose financial statement that is primarily set up to assist a forecaster of cash flows may result in the company having to pay more income taxes than would otherwise be the situation. Which objective ought to be catered to? The owners and management have to decide, based on which is more critical to the eventual success or failure of the company, i.e., lowering current taxes? *or* attracting more investors/forecasters who will furnish capital dollars to the company, thereby permitting expansion?

2. *Revenue Recognition and Receivables*

A second application of discounting could centre on situations where a buyer of long-lived assets (or inventory) chooses to pay over a period of several years. What would we record as revenue, and as a receivable, in the following situation?

• The buyer pays us $3,000 now, and promises to pay $5,000 at the end of the current year and again at the end of the following year for some land that we do not need.

• A bank charges us 12 percent interest per annum on all borrowings from them.

• Income tax effects can be ignored. (This applies to most of the illustrations in the early part of the book.)

The present value of the $3,000, $5,000, and $5,000 ought to be what we would sell the land for to a buyer who would pay *100 percent cash* today. (That is, we will assume that we would take the cash received today and give it to the bank to lower the amount of our loan with them—and "save" 12 percent interest per annum from what we would otherwise have to pay.) Thus, we should calculate a present value for the $3,000, $5,000, and $5,000 at 12 percent interest:

		Present Value
Received today		$ 3,000
Received one year hence $5,000 × 0.8929	=	4,465
Received two years hence $5,000 × 0.7972	=	3,986
		$11,451

The receivable and cash are therefore NOT $13,000, but total $11,451; and the journal entry is:

Cash	3,000	
Account receivable	8,451	
Land - at cost (assumed)		10,000
Gain on sale of land		1,451

What happens in the next two years? Two effects occur:

1. We will have to pay the bank interest on the $8,451 ($11,451 - $3,000) that we *were not able to* pay them because we did not sell today for 100 percent cash. (In the second year, the interest sum becomes less because we will repay $5,000 of principal and interest at the end of the first year.)

2. We will earn interest on the account receivable. (This is complex. The buyer will *not* actually be paying us interest. But, he will be paying us two sums of $5,000—which total $10,000. Yet, our account receivable shows $8,451. The difference of $1,549 is interest that we earn *because it is inherent in the discounting process*. That is, when we discounted, we split the $10,000 into a principal amount due and into interest due:

Principal due ($11,451 − $3,000)	$ 8,451
Interest on the $8,451 @ 12 percent	1,549
Total due over two years	$10,000

We can prove this as follows:

Principal due - beginning of first year	$8,451
Add interest at 12 percent for first year	1,014
	9,465
Sum paid at end of first year	5,000
Principal due - beginning of second year	4,465
Add interest at 12 percent for second year	535
	5,000
Sum paid at end of second year	5,000
Principal due - beginning of third year	0

As the journal entry stands at the date of sale, *no mention* is made of interest due. Typically, accountants record interest only when it accrues and none has accrued at the date of sale.)

At the end of the *first* year, the two effects are captured in the following journal entries:

1. Payment to bank for $8,451 not paid back:

Interest expense	1,014	
Cash		1,014

2. Accrual of interest, and cash receipt of $5,000:

A. Account receivable	1,014	
Interest revenue		1,014
B. Cash	5,000	
Account receivable		5,000

Note that (1) and (2A) tend to cancel each other—a debit to an expense and a credit to revenue. That is, although we did not sell for *100 percent cash,* we recorded revenue as though we had! We matched revenue and expense as best we could, and did *not* burden the two years after the sale of the land with interest on the bank loan *and* no offsetting interest revenue.

At the end of the first year, the account receivable ledger account looks like this:

Accounts Receivable	
8,451	
1,014	
9,465	
	5,000
4,465	

At the end of the *second* year, the journal entries are similar:

1. Payment of interest to bank for $4,465 still unpaid:

Interest expense	535	
Cash		535

2. Accrual of interest, and cash receipt of $5,000:

A. Account receivable	535	
Interest revenue		535
B. Cash	5,000	
Account receivable		5,000

At the end of the second year, the account receivable is zero. The net income figure for the second year is not really affected by the transaction that took place two years previously. (Interest expense is offset by interest revenue.)

Are there any additional messages that we should draw from this illustration and application? Yes, there are some important ones for statement analysis and objectives. In practice, some Canadian accountants do not appear to make full use of discounting, even though GAAP calls for discounting when sums are due beyond one year from the transaction date. The absence of discounting may be because the accountants learned their subject in a previous era, because they may not like the estimation involved in choosing a discount rate or because they cannot be bothered to alter what they regard as an "objective" figure of $13,000. An important point for those who use financial statements is that it may be vital to learn whether discounting has been used in measuring, and what rate has been chosen. If discounting has not been used, next year's income may suffer as a result of the benefit being given to the current year. For instance, by using $13,000 as the revenue figure, someone would be able to increase his bonus (based on net income) this year. Less of a bonus would be paid in succeeding years because interest expense would be incurred on the bank borrowing. But, by then the person may have left the company. If the person is still with the company, the present value of the bonuses will be higher when more dollars are received closer to today. (See the present value tables for proof.) Thus, discounting can be very important for some objectives of accounting.

3. Income Tax Postponement Objective

This point was illustrated at the beginning of Chapter 6. Postponing the payment of taxes saves interest on bank loans. Over time, this saved interest can add up.

4. Temporary Investments

These can take many different forms, and usually are acquired to earn interest on cash that is in excess of current needs. It would seem that the logical procedure would be to choose the investment that yields the highest interest rate in the period for which we have excess cash. Unfortunately, there is more to the matter than this—in particular the complication of *compound interest*, which is interest owing on the interest that we have already earned.

To illustrate, which of these two investments would we choose if we had $100,000 of capital or principal to invest for three months?

Investment *R:* Interest is 1 percent per month, is compounded monthly, and is paid at the end of three months, when we get back our $100,000 of principal.

Investment *S:* Interest is 3 percent for the three-month period, does not compound, and is paid at the end of the three months.

At the end of three months, Investment *R* would accumulate to:

Interest paid at the end of the 1st month	$ 1,000.00
Interest paid on the $1,000 interest, for the period of the 2nd month (i.e., compound interest)	10.00
Interest paid on the $100,000 of principal for the 2nd month	1,000.00
	2,010.00
Compound interest on the $2,010 for the 3rd month	20.10
Interest paid on the $100,000 of principal for the 3rd month	1,000.00
Total interest earned in the 3 months	3,030.10
Principal amount	100,000.00
Total received at the end of 3 months	$103,030.10

In contrast, Investment S would not earn compound interest and would accumulate to only $103,000 at the end of 3 months:

Interest at 3 percent on $100,000	$ 3,000.00
Principal amount	100,000.00
Total received at the end of 3 months	$103,000.00

Therefore, we would select Investment R because it accumulates to the higher figure.

Although the foregoing is fairly straightforward, other situations are not. If we go to a bank or trust company to invest, they may give us the following schedule of interest rates:

Annual rate	10.00 percent
Semi-annual rate	9.75 percent
Monthly rate	9.50 percent

That is, if we desire one payment of interest at the end of the year, we receive $100 annually for every $1,000 that we invest. But, if we desire our interest receipt every six months, they will pay us one-half of 9.75 percent every six months. Finally, if we desire our interest paid monthly, we will receive one twelfth of 9.50 percent every month. If it does not matter to us when we receive our interest, which one would we choose? Think out how you would answer before you read beyond this sentence.

The question is difficult to answer because it does not tell us all that we have to know. The key to our response is: at what interest rate am I able to re-invest the interest that I receive monthly or semi-annually? To keep the question from getting too cumbersome, suppose that our only alternative is to put the interest in a bank account that earns one half of one percent per month, *but* there is *no compounding on the bank account* interest. (This is a somewhat unrealistic assumption made to cut down the amount of arithmetic.)

At the end of a year the three accumulate to:

Annual payment: $1,000 plus 10 percent		<u>$1,100.00</u>
Semi-annual payment:		
Interest at the end of 6 months	$ 48.75	
Compound interest for next 6 months on		
$48.75 is $48.75 × 3 percent	1.46	
Interest for the second 6 months	48.75	
Principal	<u>1,000.00</u>	<u>$1,098.96</u>
Monthly payment:		
Interest for each of the 12 months, $7.92		
($1,000 × 0.007917) × 12	$ 95.04	
Bank interest ($7.92 × 11 months' interest;		
$7.92 × 10 months; $7.92 × 9 months;		
etc.)	2.61*	
Principal	<u>1,000.00</u>	<u>$1,097.25</u>

* one half percent on $95.04 for an average of 5.5 months

With the assumptions that we have made (i.e., no compounding on the *bank* account balance), the alternative that generates the highest terminal value is the annual payment at 10.00 percent interest. We have worked out an answer doing it the long way. (Tables are available to make the process easier.)

Summary

This chapter has *applied* several of the concepts and ideas and bookkeeping procedures, set forth in the previous eight chapters, to three assets: cash, investments, and receivables. It has also introduced the technique of discounting and noted the impact that it has on accounting figures, and perhaps on the judgments and decisions of some users of financial statements. Emphasis was placed on *applications* of discounting rather than on an exhaustive explanation of techniques having increasing complexity. This emphasis is consistent with major themes of the book—especially having us work toward the development of our *cognitive skills*. It is easy to try to develop only bookkeeping and memorization skills. When this happens, we are not able to transfer our memorized knowledge to situations that differ from the one in which the concepts were first learned. We study accounting for practical reasons: to learn how to use it to help us to form judgements and to make decisions.

Opinion differs on what skills should be included under the term "cognitive". For purposes of accounting, we may want to include application, judgment, evaluation, analysis, diagnosis, assessment, memory. All of these are needed by those who desire to be good users and preparers of financial accounting statements. The term "apply" has a special meaning here. We can "apply" a concept successfully only when we use it effectively in a situation that *differs* from the one in which the concept was initially learned. That is why we are varying the objectives of accounting, facts and assumptions, and legal constraints—to provide diverse situations to allow practice of our application skills. We also do not want to lock into a conception of accounting that is absurdly false, that is, a belief that one set of rules and procedures somehow fits all situations.

Application in accounting requires a grasp of general or generic problem solving steps and skills. This means that we have to learn how to diagnose problems, rank the relative importance of each, think about possible solutions, and the pros and cons of each possible solution, make a recommendation, and defend it. (See Appendices 7-A and 8-A.) In further chapters, we will combine accounting techniques and procedures with problem-solving steps in the hope of improving our application abilities.

QUESTIONS

9-1 Define net realizable value. In which situations is this figure used?

9-2 What does the term application mean in education?

9-3 What is an imprest petty cash fund? In which situations would it be used?

9-4 What is a bank reconciliation? What objective of accounting is served by it?

9-5 What is a temporary investment? What valuation basis is given to it? Why?

9-6 Explain the term intercorporate investment.

9-7 Suppose that a bank is paid $500,000 (for interest) on the day that a two-year loan is negotiated between the bank and a creditor, and interest was to be paid by the creditor over the two-year period. When may revenue be recorded as earned for the $500,000? Explain.

9-8 Explain the relationship between control accounts and subsidiary ledgers.

9-9 Should sales returns and allowances be placed in a separate account or be debited to sales revenue?

9-10 What are some important uses of the present value technique?

EXERCISES

E9-1 N. Wilson operates an imprest petty cash fund of $1,000. By November 20 the fund had less than $25 cash in it, and the following receipts:

Taxi charges	$329.60
Miscellaneous office expenses	292.75
Postage	177.55
Casual wages paid to part-time employees	130.00
Miscellaneous items	45.60
	$975.50

She decided that it was time to replenish the fund.

Required:

A. Give the journal entry to replenish the fund.

B. In which circumstances is an imprest petty cash fund useful?

E9-2

Accounts receivable — beginning balance	$ 39,855
Sales revenue for period (all sales are on account)	100,000
Unearned revenue —beginning balance	22,100
—closing balance	19,730
Allowance for doubtful accounts:	
—beginning balance	2,620
—closing balance	2,885
Bad debt expense for period	3,575
Cash collections:	
—unearned revenue	10,000
—accounts receivable	89,575

Required:

Compute "accounts receivable—closing balance" from the above information.

E9-3 Prepare a bank reconciliation for J. DeRooy at November 30, 19—9 from the following information:

Balance of ledger, November 30, 19—9	$19,377.35 Dr.
Balance of bank statement, November 30, 19—9	15,676.55 Cr.
Items on November bank statement, not recorded in ledger in November:	
Interest revenue	65.15
Bank service charges	32.70
Bank error—cheque cashed as $1,010 instead of correct sum of $1,001 shown in ledger.	
Cheques written but not cashed by November 30, 19—9	16,275.75
Deposit recorded in ledger November 30, but not credited by bank until December 2, 19—9	20,000.00

E9-4 Prepare a bank reconciliation for G. Baxter at October 31, 19—8 from the following information:

Balance of bank statement October 31, 19—8	$20,110.75 Cr.
Items on October 19—8 bank statement not recorded in the ledger in October:	
Bank service charges	67.90
Interest revenue	12.60
Accounts receivable due to G. Baxter, paid directly to bank	8,000.00
Cheques written, but not cashed by bank by October 31, 19—8	16,420.50
Deposit credited by bank on November 3, 19—8 but recorded by company in October 19—8	3,210.45
Balance of ledger, October 31, 19—8	?

E9-5 R. Lemoine purchased $20,000 of Government of Canada bonds that mature in 2001, and bear an interest rate of 12 percent per annum. At the date of purchase in July, Mr. Lemoine paid $20,350 for the bonds because $350 represented interest that was accrued at the date of purchase. Interest is paid every six months on June 1 and December 1. At the date of purchase, the current interest rate on Government bonds that mature in 2001 was 12 percent. As a result Mr. Lemoine had to pay $20,000 just for the bonds, excluding interest.

Required:

Provide the journal entries that Mr. Lemoine should make in July when the bonds were purchased, and in December when an interest payment is received.

E9-6 Vachon Enterprises Limited (VEL) had the following transactions and results for March 19—8:

Allowance for bad debts—February 28, 19—8	$22,900
Accounts receivable written off as uncollectable	14,250
Allowance for bad debts required as of March 31, 19—8	15,000

Required:

A. Prepare the journal entry needed for bad debts as of March 31, 19—8.

B. Suppose that the two accounts receivable written off were $8,500 for Donna Wanna-pay and $5,750 for Izzy Everhome. Illustrate the subsidiary ledger accounts for these two people for March 19—8.

E9-7 Suppose that a rich uncle has offered you one of the following alternative investments:
1. $10,000 today.
2. $4,225 per year at the end of each of the next three years.
3. $1,000 today, plus $5,000 received at the end of one year, plus $5,500 received two years from today.

Required:

Which alternative investment would you select if you were able to invest the money at:

A. 10% interest per annum?

B. 5% interest per annum?

C. 20% interest per annum?

PROBLEMS

P9-1 The bank reconciliation of Khalil Corporation (KC) at January 31, 19—8 showed:

Balance, per bank statement		$20,500.00
Add:		
Outstanding deposit	$10,000.00	
Bank error	9.00	10,009.00
		30,509.00
Deduct outstanding cheques		18,912.75
Balance, per general ledger		$11,596.25

During February 19—8, the following occurred:

	Bank General Ledger		Per Bank Statement	
	Debits	*Credits*	*Debits*	*Credits*
Error corrected				$ 9.00
Deposits recorded	$86,500.00			95,100.00
Interest revenue	—			102.50
Service charges		—	$ 29.90	
Cheques—issued		$65,990.00		
—cashed by bank			77,920.70	

Required:

Prepare the bank reconciliation for KC at February 28, 19—8.

P9-2

Accounts receivable—opening balance	?
—closing balance	120,900
Sales revenue for the period (all sales are on account, or from unearned revenue)	820,550
Unearned revenue —opening balance	16,255
—closing balance	14,970
Allowance for doubtful accounts: *Amount belonged to reduce AR*	
—opening balance *to netrecievable*	8,590
—closing balance	8,115
Accounts receivable written off in period	5,210
Bad debt expense for the period *— amount we choose to expense this year*	3,880
Cash receipts:	
—added to unearned revenue	5,000
—accounts receivable	801,770

Required:

Compute "accounts receivable—opening balance" from the above.

P9-3 Crandall Corporation (CC) bought a bond issued by an industrial company many years ago. The bond has a face value of $100,000, and pays $5,000 in interest every March 31 and September 30.

The bond was purchased on June 30, 19—8 for $98,500 plus accrued interest of $2,500. The bond expires on September 30, 19—9, at which time CC will receive the $100,000 face value of the bond plus interest of $5,000.

Required:

A. Provide journal entries to record:

1. the purchase of the bond in June 19—8.

2. receipt of the first interest cheque on September 30, 19—8.

B. How would you account for the $1,500 difference ($100,000 less $98,500)? What accounting concepts from Chapter 8 would you use to justify your accounting treatment? Is there more than one way of accounting for the $1,500? Explain.

P9-4 The owners of D. Hope Mining Limited (HML) are trying to ascertain the present worth of their company, which has only about three more years of ore left. The best estimates of the revenues and expenses over the next three years are:

	19—7	19—8	19—9
Revenue (cash receipts)	$720,000	$480,000	$240,000
Expenses:			
Cash	310,000	180,000	100,000
Depreciation	50,000	50,000	50,000
	360,000	230,000	150,000
Income before income tax	360,000	250,000	90,000
Income tax (cash)	110,000	80,000	20,000
Net income	$250,000	$170,000	$ 70,000

It is expected that the income will be earned on an even, monthly basis within each year. The mine will be closed down at the end of 19—9 and will cost $50,000 cash to wind down.

Required:

A. Use an interest rate of 10 percent per annum to approximate the present value or worth of HML at the beginning of 19—7. Explain your computations and reasoning process.

B. If the interest rate were five percent higher, or lower, than 10 percent, is there a material (see Chapter 8) effect on the present value that you calculated in (A)? Explain.

P9-5 French Appliances Limited (FAL) has traditionally sold its appliances on a no down payment basis. However, one twelfth of the amount owing has to be paid each month. For example, appliances may be sold on the basis that the customer has to pay $150 per month at the end of each of the next 12 months.

A customer has approached the manager of FAL and asked how much she would have to pay today if she paid all cash, instead of $150 per month at the end of each of the next 12 months.

Required:

A. What answer should the manager give to the customer if the manager has built the following interest rates into his computations of the $150 per month:

1. two percent per month

2. one percent per month

B. What revenue and expense recognition policies should the manager be using for customers who pay monthly? (Does this differ from how you would account for the transaction if all cash were received at the beginning of the twelve months?) Explain.

EXPLORATION MATERIALS AND CASES

MC9-1 Sam Johnson is the sole proprietor of a hardware store. He has conducted business at the location for the past twenty years and owns the building in which his store is located. The neighborhood surrounding his store is well established and since his is the only hardware store in the area, he tends to get all the neighborhood business.

Mr. Johnson started thinking about quitting when he received an offer from Mr. Galvin to buy his business for $225,000. Mr. Johnson had trouble understanding why Mr. Galvin's offer was so high because for the past few years the hardware business has lost money. The most recent income statement showed:

Sales revenue	$400,000
Cost of goods sold	320,000
Gross profit	80,000
Selling and administrative expense	81,000*
Loss	$ (1,000)

*This includes a $55,000 salary paid to Mr. Johnson, $12,000 rent for the building and $2,000 depreciation expense.

Mr. Johnson went to his banker to discuss the offer. He was curious to know what his business was worth. His banker said that the net realizable value of the assets minus liabilities was about $100,000. Upon discovering this Mr. Johnson decided that Mr. Galvin's offer was ideal. He would receive $50,000 now and the rest in three years.

Required:

Assume the role of Mr. Johnson's accounting advisor. What would you recommend? Explain your recommendation in a manner that would be understandable to Mr. Johnson given his limited knowledge of accounting.

MC9-2 Faultless Construction Co. Ltd. (FCCL) is owned by Mr. K. Rack. It was incorporated on January 1, 19—1 for the sole purpose of constructing four identical buildings on adjacent pieces of property. Mr. Rack borrowed $1,200,000 from his wife. This loan was at an interest rate of 10 percent compounded annually and paid semiannually. The principal is repayable on December 31, 19—3. The project took six months to complete and the total cash costs associated with the purchase of land and the construction of the buildings was as follows:

Land	$ 400,000
Materials	240,000
Labor	260,000
Interest (6 months' interest)	60,000
Other (includes equipment rental, land servicing, property taxes, etc.)	200,000
	$1,160,000

There were no other costs associated with the project. Based on these costs Mr. Rack determined the cost per property to be $290,000 since they were identical in every way including size and quality of land. He decided that he would like to make a 40 percent profit on each property and therefore began to seek buyers.

On July 1, 19—1 he found three buyers. The first buyer, Ms. S. Stewart, offered $500,000 cash for one of the properties and Mr. Rack accepted immediately. The second buyer, Mr. S. Ruid, offered $325,000 cash. Mr. Rack contemplated the offer and decided that, since he only wanted to make a 40 percent profit overall and the first property sold for $500,000, he would accept. The third buyer, Mr. B. Rowk, offered $450,000. The terms of his offer were $50,000 immediately and $100,000 payable on July 1 for each of the next four years. Mr. Rack quickly accepted this offer. For the next six months Mr. Rack was unsuccessful in his attempts to find a fourth buyer. His only cost during this period was interest on the loan from his wife. Since he needed a building, he decided to keep the fourth property as premises for FCCL.

Required:

A. Assume that you are the accountant for all four buyer individuals (organizations). At what cost would you record the property which was acquired?

   Explain your reasoning. How would you split the cost between land and building? How would you decide on a depreciation expense for each of the buildings?

B. Record in FCCL's books the first payment of $100,000 made on July 1, 19—2 by Mr. B. Rowk.

C. Assume that you are not the accountant for Ms. S. Stewart and that her accountant recorded the property purchased by Ms. Stewart at $500,000 on the company's books. Suppose Ms. Stewart's business went into bankruptcy in the first year and one of the investors who relied on the financial statements is suing the accountant for fraud. If you were an expert witness in the case what would you argue on behalf of the accountant? Why?

D. Based on your answers to (A), what conclusions about the comparability and objectivity of historic cost accounting financial statements can be made?

E. What recommendations for improving financial accounting do you have?

CHAPTER 10

Inventory Applications

Chapter Themes

1. In GAAP financial statements, inventory is shown on the balance sheet at "the lower of cost or market". There are many definitions of "cost", and of "market". We have to focus on which definition seems to be the most suitable for particular situations, with specific facts and objectives.

2. The term "inventory" tends to mean "goods held for resale", when we are referring to a merchandising company, e.g., a company that buys goods from a manufacturer, and sells them to a retailer or the general public. When we encounter non-merchandising businesses, however, it may be less clear what is inventory and what is a different type of asset (such as long-lived assets used in producing other assets). Whereas inventories and short term investments may be shown on GAAP financial statements at the lower of cost or market, a long-lived asset could be reported at "cost" or "cost less accumulated depreciation". Classifying the asset in one category instead of the other alters the current-income figure, and may affect the judgments of users of the financial statements, such as employees being paid a bonus based on income.

3. Accountants generally do not try to keep track of the cost of a single-inventory asset—by tracing its physical movements into and out of an organization. Instead, groupings of similar assets or commodities, e.g., all food or all clothing, occur, and accountants trace what they call a "costing flow", which represents a collection of assets costed at the same amount or in a similar way. This distinction is important. Accountants are not trying to measure a particular "truth" (which does not exist); instead, they are trying to be faithful to the system of measurement that they have

selected for an organization, which has particular objectives of accounting and environmental effects. This means that we have to understand *which* of the various possible measurement methods that a specific accountant is trying to be faithful to. Until we do this, it is too easy to misunderstand that company's financial statements.

4. Toward the end of the chapter, we will consider some non-GAAP applications. When evaluating a person's performance, it would not seem fair to count only the mistakes and ignore the successes. Yet, that is precisely what would occur if we chose only a *"lower* of cost or market" inventory-valuation approach. This does not keep track of current successes in which the market price of what we bought is well in excess of cost. Under GAAP revenue recognition policies, such a success would be recorded only when the inventory was regarded as sold on an arm's length (Chapter 8) basis. These non-GAAP applications tend to make sense for particular objectives of accounting and environmental facts.

5. More and more attention is given in this and succeeding chapters to the *process* that has to be followed to resolve accounting and statement interpretation issues. A series of problem-solving steps must be taken. Leaving out a step has the same important consequences as leaving out a step while performing a bank reconciliation.

What Is Inventory?

Suppose that you have an uncle and aunt who breed and race horses. The horses fall into the following categories: (a) those kept strictly for breeding, (b) those that will race when the horses attain age two or three, (c) those that are currently racing, and (d) those that are to be sold. Your aunt and uncle have learned that you are studying accounting, and they ask you: Which of the horses would be called "inventory"? After some discussion, you learn that some of the horses that are currently racing eventually will be used for breeding, or they may be purchased at any time because a condition of *some* horse races is that the horse can be bought ("claimed") by others.

Fortunately, at the time your aunt and uncle ask you, enough of the accounting course has been covered to enable you to answer promptly: "What do you want to use the financial statements for? It may make a big difference if the facts are not really clear, and I have several choices open to me." Your aunt and uncle tell you that, until now, they have used the financial statements only for income tax purposes. But a banker they have been talking to, in order to obtain a loan, wants to see their financial statements for the year that will end in a few weeks.

You explain to them that:

1. In some situations, income tax legislation allows them to use a different accounting policy or concept from the one that is used in their general-purpose report.

2. But, for *most* situations and transactions, Revenue Canada assesses income tax on the basis of accounting policies that are chosen for the general-purpose financial statements. (Revenue Canada is interested in *consistent* application of policies.) Therefore, if they now decide that they ought to have two objectives of accounting, instead of one, i.e., tax postponement, they ought to rank the relative importance of each. Any changes in accounting policy would have to be handled as described in Chapter 8 ("Consistency" and retroactive application).

Suppose that your aunt and uncle choose to give income tax postponement a low ranking because they believe that taxable income will be insignificant in the next few years. Suppose also that they want a general-purpose financial statement that will help the banker decide to give them a high loan. Thus, they again ask you: Should the horses be inventory or long-lived assets?

You commence the process of deciding what difference the categorization makes, and list the following points:

1. Except for assets such as land, accountants depreciate the cost of long-lived assets over their useful life. Thus, there can be a charge, e.g., depreciation expense, to the income statement over *several* years.

2. Inventory is charged to the income statement through cost of goods sold only when the goods are sold—according to the revenue recognition policy that you selected.

3. If the inventory is *not* to be offered for sale this year, then you would *not* call it a current asset. It would be in the non-current category along with long-lived assets, but still called "inventory of horses." (The owners of the horse may intend to run it only in "allowance" races, where it *cannot* be "claimed", or bought for the price specified as a condition of running horses in claiming races. The concept of "claiming" races exists to ensure that horses of equal calibre race together. If you run a $20,000 horse in a $5,000 claiming race, with horses worth $5,000, in the hope that your horse will win the prize money, you face the risk that someone will buy (claim) your horse for $5,000.)

4. Suddenly it hits you! What *cost* are we talking about? *If* all the horses that your aunt and uncle own have been bred at their farm, is there *any* cost? If you check their accounting records for several past years, you may discover that at one time your aunt and uncle had to buy the grandparents or great-grandparents of the horses, so to speak. (Therefore, some cost may be passed along to the current generation. This type of problem is discussed later in this and the next chapter.) But most of the cost of breeding and feeding the current group of horses would have been expensed in prior years. Thus, the balance sheet figure for horses, regardless of whether they are called inventory or a long-lived asset, would bear little relationship to what they may be sold for today. Net realizable value would be much higher than cost. The banker therefore would not find useful information in the figure for

"horses", but may find other parts of the financial statements, e.g., revenue or owners' common-share capital, informative for a lending decision.

Therefore, the problem that you initially tried to resolve did not turn out to be a serious issue once you:

1. Identified the *user* and *use* of the financial information.

2. Looked at the financial statement *presentation/disclosure* alternatives and the impact of each alternative on 1.

3. Gathered some facts about the costs (and revenues, if any) involved, and their effects on the magnitude of balance sheet and income statement *numbers*, and the likely effects on 1.

4. Thought out the implications of applicable accounting *concepts*, in this case, the "cost" and "revenue recognition" concepts.

These steps of thinking about users, uses, disclosure, magnitude of numbers, and concepts are common to many accounting preparation and interpretation issues and therefore require careful study.

In order to obtain additional practice with applications, let us return to the horses and *assume* that their classification *is* important. That is, we could assume that all the horses had just recently been purchased for large sums. The "inventory" classification would have to include the horses that are to be sold, i.e., category d., and probably those that are racing in "claiming" races, i.e., a portion of category c. The other horses probably could be included in the non-current asset category. Notice use of the word "probably". We cannot go to a rule book to find the "right answer". If we are preparers, we have to think out our objectives of accounting and the hardness/softness of the facts, i.e., "soft" means subject to much interpretation. Then we make our choice and try to be consistent or faithful to our selected accounting policies in the next several accounting periods.

INVENTORY COSTING METHODS

It is important to clarify whether we are referring to merchandising (retail or wholesale) or manufacturing organizations. Canada has a large number of oil and gas, mining, forest products, farming, fishing, hydro-electric and similar "natural resource" companies. Such companies tend to fall into the manufacturing category, for accounting purposes, and will be mentioned later. Our initial focus will be on merchandising concerns that buy manufactured goods and sell them at a later time.

How would we account for the following?

Purchases:	1 TV set @	$600
	1 TV set @	$620
	1 TV set @	$640
Sale:	1 TV set for	$850

How much gross profit have we made?

Method AA:	$850	– $600	= $250
Method BB:	$850	– $620	= $230
Method CC:	$850	– $640	= $210

Obviously, one of the methods is *not* the "truth" and the others "false". When we are dealing with TV sets, which have serial numbers, we could check to see which set the customer actually bought. Then, we could calculate the gross profit using the actual *physical flow* of TV sets into and out of the store. But, what do we do when the sets are *identical*, or there are no serial numbers or ways of telling them apart? We must have a different system of accounting, which accountants call a *costing flow*. *Some* costing flow techniques are referred to as:

1. FIFO (first in; first out). Method AA.

2. Weighted average ($600 + $620 + $640 = $1,860 divided by three TV sets, for an average of $620). Method BB.

3. LIFO (last in; first out). Method CC.

We must examine these three and another one (Specific Identification) in some detail because of the effects on income and asset costs, and their implications for readers of financial statements.

A. Specific Identification

This method can be useful when there are means of identifying the specific commodity, such as an automobile or a house. We can cost on the basis of the actual unit that was sold, by using serial or house numbers and individual cost records (subsidiary ledgers) for each item that is purchased. Specific identification is therefore a *physical flow* approach to accounting (and not a costing-flow method of accounting).

On the surface, specific identification sounds like an ideal approach to use for those who like to think of accounting as being "accurate". But, there are complications. Suppose that we own a car dealership that specializes in selling very expensive imported automobiles. At any time, we would have no more than ten automobiles of a particular model/manufacturer in our inventory. Purchasing costs vary, because foreign-exchange rates fluctuate daily between Canadian currency and the currency of the countries that we buy our automobiles from. Under these circumstances, how would we cost inventories and charge cost of goods sold—*when* the managers of our dealership receive a bonus based on the quarterly net income before income taxes of the dealership?

Specific identification would not be a good choice if the managers do not tend to stay with our company for more than a year or two. They probably would try to keep quarterly income as high as possible by convincing the customer to buy the identical unit that costs the least—and which generates the highest gross profit and bonus. Therefore, specific identification unfortunately has the serious disadvantage that it is too vulnerable to manipulation whenever inventory consists of units that cannot easily be distinguished from each other.

Specific identification is useful for inventory and cost-of-goods-sold accounting when large unique objects exist. A house builder may use specific identification because it is easy to ascertain which house was sold. (But, it may be difficult to keep track of costs of building the house, if tradesmen build several houses at the same time.)

Someone interested in a *minimum compliance* objective (Chapter 6), however, may not want to go to the trouble of keeping track of which specific item was sold. He would therefore look to one of the *cost flow* methods to ease bookkeeping.

B. Cost Flow Methods

Suppose that a new company purchases the following items of inventory:

February 15	4 items @	$10 each	$ 40.00
February 22	3 @	11	33.00
February 29	1 @	12	12.00
March 7	2 @	13	26.00
	10 items		$111.00
	Weighted Average = $111/10 =		$11.10 per unit

On March 10, six items are sold for $16 each. What is the cost of goods sold, and cost of closing inventory of four items?

In several chapters, but especially in Chapter 8, *consistency* was stressed. Somehow we have to choose an accounting policy that will cost inventory and goods sold on a consistent basis for several years. We have to anticipate likely facts, and choose an objective (or objectives) of financial accounting that meets the needs of the owners or managers (or both) of the company.

The three different methods produce the following effects:

	Cost of Goods Sold	Closing Inventory	Total Dollars
FIFO (first in; first out):			
Sold: 4 @ $10 plus 2 @ $11	$62		
Closing inventory: 1 @ $11;			
1 @ $12 and 2 @ $13		$49	$111
Weighted Average This method is weighted by the quantity of each item that is purchased):			
Sold: 6 @ $11.10	$66.60		
Closing inventory: 4 @ $11.10		$44.40	$111
LIFO (last in; first out):			
Sold: 2 @ $13; 1 @ $12;			
3 @ $11	$71		
Closing inventory: 4 @ $10		$40	$111

Note that the transactions (purchases and sale) were *identical*. Yet, a different gross profit and balance sheet could arise, *simply as a result of our choice of an accounting policy.*

	Income Statement		
	FIFO	*Weighted Average*	*LIFO*
Revenue	$96.00	$96.00	$96.00
Cost of goods sold	62.00	$66.60	71.00
Gross profit	34.00	29.40	25.00

In view of the fact that the income statement and balance sheet can change, perhaps materially, depending on which of the three methods that we select, we must look closely at each. When might we select each?

It is not possible to list all the possible situations where each may be sensibly applied. We can, however, think in terms of the objectives, facts, and concepts mentioned in chapters 6 to 8.

LIFO: Revenue Canada will *not* accept this method for the purpose of calculating income taxes. (They believe that it would reduce taxable income too much. U.S. tax authorities, in contrast, accept LIFO.) Thus, if we chose LIFO for our general-purpose financial statements, we would have to adjust our figures when we submitted our income tax forms to Revenue Canada. A typical "adjustment schedule" may appear as follows:

Net income per general-purpose financial statements	$ xxxx
Add adjustment to convert cost of goods sold from	
LIFO to weighted average costing	xx
Net income adjusted for inventory cost method	xxx
Other adjustments:	
Depreciation (etc.)	

For many companies this "adjustment" would be sufficiently discouraging that they would not want to use LIFO. That is, a considerable amount of work would be involved in keeping track of inventory and cost of goods sold on *both* a weighted average and a LIFO basis—so that the adjustment figure could be determined.

Nevertheless, LIFO may have offsetting advantages. The example we chose showed rising prices from February 15 to March 7. The use of LIFO *under these conditions* had the effect of *lowering income* (compared with FIFO) because it increased cost of goods sold (LIFO = $71 and FIFO = $62). LIFO also lowered the balance-sheet figure for inventory (LIFO = $40 and FIFO = $49).

One convenient way of thinking out the effect of so-called "increases" and "decreases" is to use a balancing scale:

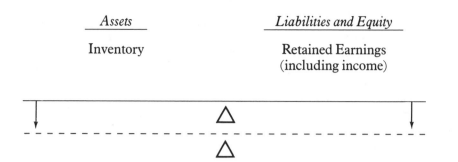

Assets	Liabilities and Equity
Inventory	Retained Earnings (including income)

The balance sheet *must* balance. Therefore, if inventory is lowered (from the black line to the dotted line), retained earnings *must* have been lowered. This means that *income was lowered*, i.e., inventory does not affect dividends, and dividends is the only other account that would tend to affect retained earnings. In the previous paragraph, a choice of LIFO instead of FIFO "lowered" inventory by $9 ($49 – $40) and retained earnings by $9. This means that income was "lowered" by $9 because an *expense*, (cost of goods sold) "increased" from $62 (FIFO) to $71 (LIFO).

Suppose that we do not think that "lowering" is a reasonable way to view the situation. We may, for example, believe that income should reflect the revenue received less what we have *sacrificed*, or given up. What is more representative of what we have given up? Would it not be what it would cost us to *replace* the inventory that we just sold? Although LIFO does *not* reflect current replacement cost, it would come closer to it than either FIFO or weighted average. That is, on March 10, replacement cost may be $14 each. The replacement cost of goods sold would therefore be $14 × 6 = $84, which is higher than $71 (LIFO) and $62 (FIFO).

LIFO would therefore be preferable to FIFO when replacement costs are rising, i.e., facts, and we have an objective of accounting requiring close attention to the income figure. An example would be a bonus plan in which managers receive a percentage of net income. If we owned the company, we probably would not want profits and bonuses being calculated on the oldest cost basis. (FIFO's cost flow assumption is that the oldest cost is charged first to cost of goods sold. LIFO's cost flow assumption is that the oldest cost is still in inventory. That is why some accountants, such as Professor George Sorter, jokingly refer to LIFO as FISH—first in; still here.) Replacement cost gross profit would be $96 − $84 = $12, whereas FIFO is $96 − $62 = $34. LIFO is a compromise, under these set of figures, at $96 − $71 = $25 gross profit.

From a company owner's point of view, an even worse situation occurs when a sales staff starts to think of making a profit of X percent of cost. This danger can be greater for LIFO than FIFO *when replacement costs are rising*. That is, someone may look at the LIFO inventory cost of $40 and decide to sell it for a 30 percent gross profit on cost, at $52. Yet, replacement cost would be $56 (4 x $14). The company would lose $4 *plus* any income taxes that may be payable on the inventory profit, i.e., $52 less costs acceptable for income tax purposes).

In summary, LIFO makes sense for some objectives/facts scenarios, but not for others. An "all-purpose" inventory costing method does not exist. Therefore, we have to decide, *given the facts and our best estimates of the future*, which objective of accounting we want to cater to. Sometimes we will be successful; at other times, our figures may be compromises. (Replacement cost accounting is not GAAP; LIFO may be the closest that we can come to replacement cost under a GAAP constraint.)

FIFO: Unlike for LIFO, Revenue Canada permits the use of FIFO in computing taxable income. Consequently, we see FIFO used in a number of companies in Canada. From the discussions of LIFO (in our illustration of rising replacement costs), we could observe that FIFO's cost figures gave a more current figure for the balance-sheet "inventory" than did LIFO and weighted average. Some accountants refer to FIFO as having a balance sheet orientation rather than an income statement emphasis, when prices are fluctuating. Thus, reliable FIFO applications would exist in those (*objectives*) situations where the focus is on the balance sheet rather than on the income statement *and* (the *facts* are that) inventory purchase costs are not stable.

Such FIFO applications are not plentiful; however, one possible situation might be when a creditor will loan money to a company, and accept as collateral (in case the loan is not repaid) the company's inventory. A bank, for instance, will loan money and accept accounts receivable as its prime collateral, and inventory as secondary collateral. Accounts receivable are the prime collateral because they are due from a known person and can legally be assigned to the bank. Inventory that is being offered for sale is not satisfactory collateral, from the bank's point of view, because its location and ownership could change. A FIFO *balance sheet* figure in a period of rising replacement costs would tend to be closer to replacement cost than would LIFO or weighted average. Thus, a less sophisticated creditor may find the FIFO data useful. *But*, a creditor tends to be more interested in cash coming into the company (net realizable value) than cash leaving it (replacement cost). With inventory, net realizable value usually is *above* cost by the amount of gross profit. Thus, even with its balance sheet orientation, FIFO is not as helpful to creditors as it may first appear to be.

Another possible application for FIFO could be in situations where there is a *restrictive covenant*. Such covenants exist in borrowing/lending documents drawn up by lawyers to protect the lender. For instance, the lender may not want the shareholders to receive dividends unless there is a "cushion" of owners' equity to cover any sudden losses. Therefore, the lawyers may put a clause (restrictive covenant) in the lending agreement to prevent the payment of dividends "unless retained earnings exceeds $1,000,000 after declaration of the dividend". Careful corporate lawyers try to recognize the variability that exists within GAAP, and may specify that "for the purposes of computing retained earnings under this agreement, the following accounting principles and policies will be followed:

1. "...inventory will be costed at the lower of cost or market, using FIFO methods...."

However, if the reference in the lending agreement merely refers to using "generally accepted accounting principles", and the replacement cost of inventory is rising, FIFO would make sense from the preparer's point of view.

Weighted Average: In performing the arithmetic for this method, particular attention has to be paid to the word "weighted". The "weights" being referred to are quantities bought and on hand at the date of sale. To illustrate, assume the following:

Purchases:	May 29	5 items	@	$30 each	$150
	May 30	3 items	@	$28 each	84
	June 1	4 items	@	$29 each	116
	June 3	5 items	@	$30 each	150
Sold:	May 31	4 items	@	$40 each	$160
	June 2	5 items	@	$40 each	200

Required: What is the cost of the inventory on hand at the close of business on May 31 and June 3?

In order to compute the cost of goods sold on May 31 and June 2, we have to assemble a *perpetual inventory* system, which is merely a "running balance" of the cost of inventory on hand. As mentioned in the previous chapter, a separate subsidiary ledger card could be kept for each type of inventory item. (Perpetual subsidiary ledgers would also be kept for FIFO and LIFO costs, if this is what the company is using. To save space, and enable us to spend our time on both interpretation as well as on bookkeeping, only one illustration is being given for weighted average costing, instead of providing a series of "running balances". But, the same general computation steps apply.)

Perpetual Inventory Card—Item xxx

	Purchased			Sold			Inventory on Hand		
Date	Price	Quantity	Total	Quantity	Weighted Average Price	Total	Quantity	Weighted Average Price	Cost
May 29	$30.00	5	$150.00				5		$150.00
30	28.00	3	84.00				8	$29.25	234.00
31				4	$29.25	$117.00	4	29.25	117.00
June 1	29.00	4	116.00				8	29.125	233.00
2				5	29.125	145.625	3	29.125	87.375
3	30.00	5	150.00				8	29.672	237.375

Observe that the "sold" column merely lists the weighted average price that exists at the date of sale. On May 31, the weighted average price was $29.25 per item. By June 2's sale, the weighted average price was $29.125—because the balance of 4 (Inventory on Hand—Quantity) combined with the 4 purchased on June 1 to produce a new weighted average of $29.125:

Inventory:	4 @ $29.25	=	$117.00	
June 1:	4 @ $29.00	=	116.00	
	8		$233.00	
	Weighted average	=	$233.00/8	= $29.125

In a sense, weighted average represents a compromise between FIFO and LIFO. The figure charged to cost of goods sold on the income statement would not equal replacement cost, except by coincidence. When prices are fluctuating, however, the weighted average cost may be as good as either of FIFO or LIFO. Weighted average may be a sensible choice when a company has multiple objectives of financial accounting, all of which are of similar importance. An example could be a company seeking income tax postponement that also has a restrictive covenant, and a bonus plan for managers that is tied to an income statement figure, such as income before income tax.

WHAT IS MARKET?

The term *market value* is not sufficiently descriptive for our purposes. It would be like referring to "they" or "people" when someone wants to know specifically which person he should talk to. Illustration 10-1 sets out the more common definitions of market for inventories.

ILLUSTRATION 10-1

Market Value Bases

Buying Market	Selling Market
Replacement cost	Net realizable value
Discounted cash disbursements	Discounted cash receipts

"Buying Market" in Illustration 10-1 refers to the place where we normally would buy our inventory. A grocer would buy from a wholesaler or farmer. "Selling Market" means the customer to whom we would normally sell our inventory, such as to a homemaker/consumer. For a grocer, the difference between buying market and selling market price is the gross profit.

The GAAP term "lower of cost or market" therefore means little unless the definitions of "cost" and of "market" are clearly specified. A more descriptive term would be "lower of weighted average cost or replacement cost", or "lower of FIFO cost or net realizable value".

The "discounted" references in Illustration 10-1 refer to situations where cash is disbursed or received in the future. For instance, we may have rented some land for $1,000 per month for five years. We were able to turn it into a parking lot and rent out the space on an hourly, daily or monthly basis. By discounting our expected receipts as well as our disbursements, we could calculate a net present value "profit".

There obviously can be a major effect on a company's balance sheet and income statement if it chooses replacement cost instead of net realizable value, or vice versa. Under GAAP, whatever policy it chooses ought to remain in place (for consistency purposes) for a few years. We therefore have to focus on when each of replacement cost and net realizable value would be sensible applications.

Suppose that we are managing a mine that primarily yields copper. When metal prices are high, we operate the mine at full capacity. When prices are low we may operate the mine only with a skeleton staff, or close it down. Which market definition (replacement cost or net realizable value) seems to make the most sense? Replacement cost may be trivial compared to net realizable value because it may have cost us very little to locate the ore and mine it. The cost of locating additional ore, however, may be totally unknown at this point in time. Our replacement cost of the ore that we presently have could primarily represent the wages of miners and some hauling costs. The same uncertainty may apply in fishing companies, logging, farming, oil and gas, and other resource industries. On any one day, the relation between selling prices and replacement costs could be negligible. Thus, net realizable value would be a likely choice for the definition of market.

In contrast, suppose that we operate a grocery store, where we are purchasing and selling the same types of products day after day. We intend to stay in business for a long time, and therefore have to look toward selling for more than our replacement cost. In this situation, with continuity and fairly stable relationships between replacement cost and selling price, we likely would choose replacement cost.

To illustrate, suppose that at the year end of the company the following data is available:

December 31, 19—8:

Cost	$48,000
Replacement cost	44,100
Net realizable value	46,750

As both replacement cost and net realizable value are below cost, under GAAP we would have to use one of the "market" figures. Suppose that we *chose net realizable value*. Also, suppose that replacement cost and net realizable value remained fairly stable in the next few months of the new year, 19—9. When the December 31, 19—8 inventory is sold in 19—9, the income statement would show:

Sales revenue	$46,750
Cost of goods sold	46,750
Gross profit	0

That is, zero gross profit appears in 19—9 when we reduce inventory at December 31, 19—8 to only net realizable value. A gross profit of $2,650 ($46,750 - $44,100) would result in 19—9 if replacement cost were used as the December 31, 19—8 closing inventory (and January 1, 19—9 opening inventory).

Which is the "right answer"? Obviously, there is *not* one, right answer. Accountants have differing views on which year will be favored. If we want a $2,650 gross profit in 19—9 it clearly means that 19—8 absorbs an additional expense (cost of goods sold) of $2,650. If we were a manager being paid a bonus based on gross profit, which method would we prefer? (Refer to Chapter 9 and discounting. The sooner we receive our bonus, the better it is—to earn interest.)

We have just looked at an objective of accounting, i.e., bonus plan. Let us consider a fact/assumption scenario. Suppose that there is a sudden drop in replacement costs and selling prices (perhaps because a government reduces a tariff), and stability in the market seems to be developing at this new cost/selling price level. Would it make sense to use net realizable value as our definition of "market"? These are fairly strong facts and would seem to be more powerful to most people (except for the managers on the bonus plan) than would the bonus objective. Thus, there are some "fact scenarios" where replacement cost is persuasive. In addition to objectives/facts, we have to look at concepts such as consistency and matching. The definition of market would be selected so that it could be used for several years. We would have to think hard about changing our accounting policy simply because a government reduced a tax. In short, when we resolve problems in accounting, we tend to refer to the material in chapters 6 to 8 inclusive to get us started.

One further complication of "market" merits comment. We can apply replacement cost or net realizable value to *each* item or category of items, *or* to the *entire* inventory. Suppose that on December 31, 19—7 the following inventory figures exist:

	Cost	Replacement Cost
Shoes	$ 52,000	$ 59,600
Dresses	167,220	168,400
Other (purses, etc.)	40,100	30,000
	$259,320	$258,000

In *total*, we could reduce the closing inventory by $1,320 ($259,320 - $258,000). If we applied the "lower of cost or market" on a group-by-group basis, however, we would get:

Shoes	$ 52,000
Dresses	167,220
Other	30,000
	$249,220

The reduction to market would now be $10,100 ($259,320 - $249,220.)

When may we use each? When the products tend to sell together, e.g., shoes and purses, and the profit on one can offset the loss on another, a total application, $259,320 vs. $258,000, makes sense. When the products are unrelated in price effect, e.g., logs used for making lumber vs. logs used only for making pulp and paper, application to each group seems wise.

On the balance sheet, the inventory may appear as follows:

Current assets:

.... $

    Inventory, at the lower of weighted average
      cost or replacement cost   249,220

MERCHANDISING COMPANY SUMMARY

This chapter has introduced a variety of inventory application issues. The alternative GAAP that we choose and how we apply it can have a major effect on the balance sheet and income statement figures. As a result, we have to turn much of our attention to the circumstances where each of the alternatives *seems* to make sense. When we do this, we have to keep telling ourselves that: *"there isn't a right answer,"* and "Let us pick the policy that seems *preferable to the others* under the specific situation that we are now facing."

Here is a list of some of the alternatives that we have encountered to this point in the chapter:

1. Is it inventory, or a long-lived asset? (The latter often is depreciated over a long period of time.)

2. Which cost (FIFO, LIFO, and so on) do we choose?

3. What is market?

4. Do we apply replacement cost or net realizable value to the total inventory or to each group?

In addition, we encountered a major point discussed in Chapter 8. What do we include in the cost figure? (See the discussion of "Cost".) All costs to the point where the product is available for sale, or only some of them? (Consider materiality.) Do we include interest and storage charges? What interest rate would we choose? (More will be said about this later.) With each chapter, more issues arise where judgment must be applied.

MANUFACTURING AND RESOURCE COMPANIES

Manufacturing and resource companies face the same types of inventory costing and valuation problems as do the merchandising companies. But, manufacturing companies can have great difficulty determining "what is cost".

Suppose that we have a farm that specializes in growing mushrooms and in producing chickens and eggs. We sell both eggs and chickens. We also use the chicken manure to help to grow the mushrooms. Our main costs are feed for the chickens, costs of maintaining the farm (property taxes, light, heat), and marketing/office expenditures. What does it cost us to produce one dozen eggs?

Our reaction should be: "Who wants to know the cost, and for what purpose?" Three main products are being sold: chickens, eggs, and mushrooms. They are interrelated. We have to know how much of the cost of chicken feed should be split among the three main products. In brief, the "cost of a dozen eggs" could range widely, depending on how we divide the costs among the three products.

Over the years, accountants have arrived at a few "conventions" (or practical approaches) for determining inventory cost *for purposes of preparing balance sheets and income statements.* Observe the stress placed on financial accounting and its balance sheets and income statements. This is important because in management accounting (which we only touch on in this book) many different costs exist, depending on the purpose or use of the information. A major theme of management accounting is the preparation of "different costs and different revenues for different management decisions". Thus, a cost figure that we use for evaluating the performance of people is quite different from the cost figure we use in determining how much to bid in order to try to win a construction contract. (The distinction is explained in advanced accounting books.) The important point is that the conventions for determining financial accounting cost are quite different from those used in management accounting.

In a manufacturing organization, costs are often classified this way:

1. Manufacturing — direct material
— direct labor
— variable manufacturing overhead
— fixed manufacturing overhead

2. Selling costs — variable
— fixed

3. Administrative costs — variable
— fixed

This classification and its effects are very complex; so, we will provide only a simplified version—enough to understand the basic issues. The first accounting convention is that costs of selling the product (2) as well as administrative/office costs (3) are viewed as *period costs,* to be expensed on the income statement in the year that they are incurred.

They are *not part of inventory cost,* and do not go on a balance sheet. One main reason for expensing is that it is too difficult to identify the costs with particular inventory production. For instance, a company may be manufacturing twenty different types of chairs and twelve different types of tables. A salesperson calls on a potential customer to sell the products, and incurs travel expenses, wages, and fringe-benefits expenses, etc. The potential customer may not buy any products on the first three or more calls. Thus, accountants feel that they cannot trace the salesperson's or office person's costs to a particular inventory product in an *objective* way.

As a result, all selling and administrative costs (fixed and variable) become expenses, and *not* inventory assets, under this convention. In general, variable expenses are ones that are incurred because *activity,* e.g., number of calls on customers, occurs. Fixed expenses tend to be ones incurred because of the passage of time, e.g., depreciation on the salesperson's automobile.

Costs of *manufacturing* a product such as a chair fall into one of four categories:

A. *Direct material* Broadly speaking, direct material includes wood, metal, fabric, and other parts of a chair that cost a significant (material) amount. They are costs that can be traced to the manufacturing of one or 100 or more chairs of a particular style/design. They become inventory assets.

B. *Direct labor*   Employees who work directly on the production of the style/design of chairs are called direct laborers. Their wages and fringe benefits, e.g., health plan and pension costs, become inventory assets.

C. *Variable manufacturing overhead*   This includes the costs of the manufacturing plant that vary with production activity. For example, glue and screws for the chairs, wages of foremen supervising the production of many different tables and chairs, and heat/light are gathered into a variable manufacturing ledger account. The total in the account is then split up among each type of table and chair in a somewhat approximate manner, i.e., much as accountants take the cost of a building and divide it over several years. This *allocated* sum usually becomes part of the inventory asset.

D. *Fixed manufacturing overhead*   This category includes costs such as depreciation on the manufacturing building, property taxes and insurance on the factory building, and depreciation on factory equipment that is used to make several different tables and chairs.

All accountants would follow a convention of including (A), (B) and (C) (direct material, direct labor, and variable manufacturing overhead) in the inventory asset cost. The total of (A), (B) and (C) is referred to as *variable costing,* or *direct costing.*

Those accountants who also include fixed manufacturing overhead as part of inventory cost are adhering to *absorption costing,* or *full costing.* They would have to *allocate* the total fixed manufacturing overhead in a somewhat approximate manner to each type of table and chair that was produced during the particular time period. Advocates of absorption costing believe that allocations of fixed manufacturing overhead are much less arbitrary than allocations of selling and administrative costs. Thus, they treat selling and administrative items as period costs, i.e., expenses, but fixed manufacturing overhead becomes an inventory cost.

Accountants who advocate variable or direct costing for ascertaining the inventory cost of manufactured goods will expense fixed manufacturing overhead. Which method of costing—variable, or absorption—would we use if we had an income tax postponement objective of financial accounting? The expensing of fixed manufacturing overhead, i.e., variable costing, would increase expenses and lower taxable income, and income taxes.

We need to note that variable or direct costing *is* acceptable for income tax purposes in Canada under specific conditions—such as when the company is new and uses direct costing from its inception, or is in an industry where fixed overhead cost allocation would be highly arbitrary. In Canada, variable costing is GAAP; but in the U.S.A., it is unclear. Most U.S. companies use absorption costing in their financial accounting statements.

In summary, the cost of manufactured inventory can vary depending on whether variable costing or absorption costing becomes the policy chosen to calculate inventory cost. Refer to Illustration 10-2.

ILLUSTRATION 10-2

Costing Manufactured Products

In practice, we face additional problems. Suppose that the president spends a large percentage of her/his time directly supervising the production of a new product. Normally, a president's salary and benefits would be an administrative cost. In this situation, however, should the president's salary be direct labor or variable manufacturing overhead? Our response affects the income figure and inventory-cost figure.

Another practical problem arises when companies use *standard costs* instead of actual costs of manufacturing. There are several definitions of standard cost, depending upon why we want to use them. That is, the standard cost that we use to evaluate new employees today may be a different standard to the one we use to bid for work—which will be performed when these employees become experienced and do the work in less time. Standard costs that are not *materially* different from actual costs are acceptable as GAAP. Once we choose to use standard costs, we have to be consistent in our application.

Overall, there is considerable freedom in choosing the financial accounting policies that we will apply to determine inventory cost on the balance sheet. What is not shown on the balance sheet becomes an expense. Inventory cost does not become an expense (cost of goods sold) until revenue is recognized—which could be several accounting periods later than when we expensed, say, fixed manufacturing overhead.

REVIEW PROBLEM—MANUFACTURING COMPANY

How many different inventory asset (balance sheet) costs per unit, that are acceptable per GAAP, can we calculate from the following?:

	Actual Cost	Standard Cost	Replacement Cost	Net Realizable Value
All Costs Are Per Unit of One Chair				
Direct material	$12.50	$12.00	$12.10	
Direct labor	4.00	4.20	4.10	
Variable manufacturing overhead	1.00	.80	.70	
Fixed manufacturing overhead	2.00	2.10	2.35	
Total	$19.50	$19.10	$19.25	$26.00
Selling costs	0.75	0.70		
Administrative costs	0.25	0.20		
	$20.50	$20.00		

The possibilities are:

1. If the company's inventory policy is the "lower of actual cost or net realizable value":

   A. Variable costing: $12.50 + $4.00 + $1.00   = $17.50

   B. Absorption costing: $17.50 + $2.00   = $19.50

2. If the company's inventory policy is the "lower of actual cost or replacement cost". Replacement cost is being applied in total:

   A. Variable costing: $12.10 + $4.10 + $0.70   = $16.90

   B. Absorption costing: $16.90 + $2.35   = $19.25

3. If the company's inventory policy is the "lower of standard cost or net realizable value":

   A. Variable costing: $12.00 + $4.20 + $0.80   = $17.00

   B. Absorption costing: $17.00 + $2.10   = $19.10

4. If the company's inventory policy is the "lower of standard cost or replacement cost":

   A. Variable costing: $12.10 + $4.10 + $0.70   = $16.90

   B. Absorption costing: $12.00 + $4.20 + $0.80 + $2.10   = $19.10

(Note that under variable costing, replacement cost is lower. Under absorption costing, however, the standard costs are lower.)

The range is from $16.90 to $19.50—which is $2.60, or over 15 percent of the $16.90 figure. The percentage impact on net income could be much greater. What is the message? When we now read the financial section of a newspaper, and it quotes company profit figures, *and compares them,* we realize that we have come a long way from when we started Chapter 1.

DISCOUNTS

Suppliers of inventory may offer discounts for paying promptly (cash discounts) or for buying in large volume (quantity discounts). If the volume or quantity discount is allowed at the time that we are invoiced, e.g., 10 percent discount, we merely pay the net figure, e.g., 90 percent. If the discount is given at a much later date, then we probably cannot trace the cost reduction back to specific purchases, and would be inclined to credit "other income" on the income statement. This would be below the gross profit line. An alternative would be to credit cost of goods sold.

Cash discounts may be journalized in two ways:

Transaction	*Gross Method*		*Net Method*	
January 10:				
Buy goods; 2%	Inventory	2,000	Inventory	1,960
cash discount	Accounts		Accounts	
if paid by	payable	2,000	payable	1,960
January 31				
January 31:				
If we pay by	Accounts		Accounts	
this date	payable	2,000	payable	1,960
	Cash	1,960	Cash	1,960
	Other			
	income	40		
February 15:				
If we pay after	Accounts		Accounts	
January 31	payable	2,000	payable	1,960
			Expense—	
			discount	
	Cash	2,000	lost	40
			Cash	2,000

The cost concept would support the net method—lowest cash cost. The net method provides a closer matching of revenue and cost of goods sold. But, the amounts may be trivial in relation to the other issues that have been discussed in this chapter.

Finally, the "discounts lost" account is an internal control mechanism that may help in identifying weaknesses in our accounts payable system, e.g., not operating efficiently enough to pay on time and thereby earn the discount. Over the years, business practice has changed from granting discounts for prompt payment to charging interest on overdue accounts, i.e., invoices not paid within thirty days. Nevertheless, some companies, such as a few utilities, still utilize a discount approach, and we may see the gross method in use.

PERPETUAL vs. PERIODIC INVENTORY ACCOUNTING

To this point in the book, the perpetual method of inventory bookkeeping has been used. That is, whenever we sold inventory, we debited cost of goods sold and credited the inventory account. To be able to do this, we had to be using a subsidiary ledger system for each inventory item or category; otherwise, we would not know how much to credit inventory when a sale occurred.

Many small businesses cannot afford to keep perpetual inventory records. Therefore, they resort to what is called a *periodic* system. Under a periodic system, cost of goods sold can be calculated only when inventory is counted—which is "periodically"—whenever "more accurate" income figures are needed. The computation operates this way:

Inventory at beginning of period	$ 60,800
Purchases of inventory during the period	192,990
Goods available for sale	253,790
Inventory at end of period—per count	70,000
Presumed cost of goods sold	$183,790

Whenever inventory is counted, and priced by looking at purchase invoices or other records, accountants call this a *physical inventory* count. A physical inventory count is needed from time to time to check the accuracy of perpetual records (subsidiary ledgers). By comparing the physical count to the perpetual record count, shortages (or overages) can be discovered. Perhaps someone is stealing inventory. We would not be able to discover this easily if we were using a periodic inventory system.

Illustration 10-3 provides journal entries to show the difference between bookkeeping under a periodic system and a perpetual system. The entry for $103,500 under the periodic method can be considered to be an adjusting entry. Note that under both bookkeeping methods, the credit to retained earnings is $26,499. The prime benefits of a perpetual system are: an ability to show any shortages or overages, and the availability of inventory figures to permit the preparation of financial statements whenever they are needed, which may be monthly.

ILLUSTRATION 10-3

Periodic vs. Perpetual Inventory Systems

Transaction	Periodic Method		Perpetual Method	
1. Opening inventory balance is $15,000	(This would be journalized in the previous financial period; debit balance in inventory account is $15,000.)			
2. Purchased $120,000 of inventory for cash	Inventory	$120,000	Inventory	$120,000
	Cash	$120,000	Cash	$120,000
3. Some purchased inventory is returned to the supplier, $8,000	Cash	$8,000	Cash	$8,000
	Inventory	$8,000	Inventory	$8,000
4. Inventory costing $100,000 is sold, $129,999	Accounts receivable	$129,999	Accounts receivable	$129,999
	Revenue	$129,999	Revenue	$129,999
	No entry		Cost of goods sold	$100,000
			Inventory	$100,000
5. A physical count shows $23,500 of inventory on hand; perpetual records show $27,000	Cost of goods sold	$103,500	Inventory shortage (expense)	$3,500
	Inventory	$103,500	Inventory	$3,500
6. Closing entry	Revenue	$129,999	Revenue	$129,999
	Cost of goods sold	103,500	Cost of goods sold	$100,000
	Income summary or retained earnings	26,499	Inventory shortage	3,500
			Income summary or retained earnings	26,499

RETAIL INVENTORY CONTROL

Many improvements have occurred in recent years in internal controls of retail stores by using computers connected to different types of cash registers. Standard product codes are printed on grocery items and other commodities. A scanning system can read the codes (lines of varying thicknesses) and convert them into a number, such as 55476-38801. The computer then prints out the price that we have to pay on our receipt from information in its memory about 55476-38801. But it also prepares a perpetual inventory record for each item that is sold. This helps the retailer know when to order more inventory because quantities are declining. When a physical count of inventory is taken, any shortages can be identified, and investigated. Slow-moving merchandise can be sold at lower prices to reduce the store's investment in inventory—and reduce the store's bank loan that finances the inventory.

Smaller retailers can obtain some control over inventory stocks by keeping a perpetual inventory based on *selling prices* (instead of cost). The system operates well when the relation between purchase cost and selling price is fairly *constant*. For example, suppose that we operate a store where inventory is *"marked up"* 50 percent *on cost* to arrive at retail price. That is, cost becomes 66.67 percent of retail price, e.g., cost = $100, retail price = $150. You then keep all of your inventory records at *retail* price. When a customer buys inventory, the *retail* price is subtracted from our inventory on hand, i.e., beginning/opening inventory plus purchases during the period less sales during the period. The retail price is easy to keep track of because that is what is entered into a cash register. Also, the inventory on hand is ticketed or labelled with retail prices. To arrive at cost of our closing inventory, we merely have to multiply the retail price of our closing inventory by our percentage markup on retail, i.e., 66.67 percent.

For example, assume the following:

	Cost	Retail Price
Opening inventory	$ 76,000	$110,000
Purchases	204,000	290,000
Inventory for sale	$280,000	400,000
(Cost = 70% of retail)		
Sales @ retail price		320,000
Closing inventory		$ 80,000

In this illustration, our closing inventory at *cost* (to comply with GAAP) would be 70 percent of $80,000 = $56,000. Observe that the 70 percent is a *weighted average* of the opening inventory plus purchases during the period. To arrive at the overall percentage of cost to retail, i.e., 70 percent, it is necessary that the percentage of cost to retail be kept on all purchases so that a weighted average may be determined. Complications arise when these cost-to-retail percentages—called markups and markdowns—change during the year. But this is just a matter of keeping a "good set of books".

To repeat, the essence of this method—called the retail inventory control method—is having a *stable* cost to retail percentage. If this does not exist, then several "departments" would have to be set up. For example, in a food supermarket, separate retail inventory-control computations may be needed for each of meat, produce, groceries, snack bar, and bakery.

Use of Replacement Cost

GAAP requires that inventory be recorded at the "lower of cost or market". We have seen that, although this appears to be a strong constraint, considerable freedom exists in choosing "cost" and "market". Nevertheless, those who desire to "evaluate overall management performance", or "predict cash flows" will find that lower of cost or market is restrictive.

During the 1970s and 1980s, considerable attention was directed by accountants and the business community toward alternatives to GAAP cost. Some Canadian companies provide supplementary financial statements based on such concepts as replacement cost. These supplementary figures may help to attain performance-evaluation and prediction objectives *if* the figures used are reasonable estimates of cash flows.

Suppose that we (as shareholders) wish to evaluate management's performance in (a) purchasing steel for the company's steel-warehousing operation, and (b) selling it. Figures for the year are:

	Lower of Cost or Market	Replacement Cost
Opening inventory (January 1, 19—8):		
2,000 tonnes @ $30	$ 60,000	
@ $34		$68,000
Purchases (during 19—9):		
60,000 tonnes @ $36	2,160,000	
	$2,220,000	

Sales were 37,000 tonnes at an average price of $45 per tonne. The company uses FIFO cost. The top portion of the GAAP income statement would appear as follows:

		GAAP
Revenue (37,000 tonnes @ $45)		$1,665,000
Cost of goods sold:		
2,000 tonnes @ $30	$ 60,000	
35,000 tonnes @ $36	1,260,000	1,320,000
Gross profit		$ 345,000

How successful has the company been in producing $345,000 of gross profit? It is important to remember that the $345,000 is the result of two accounting policies (see chapters 7 and 8):

1. Revenue recognition based on having contracts with other parties.

2. An inventory valuation concept of the lower of cost or market.

As stated previously, these concepts tend to have a preparer-power orientation, and not the user-power orientation of objectives of accounting such as cash flow prediction or evaluation of management by outsiders.

Suppose that we take the figures and recast them using replacement cost. To do this we need two additional pieces of information.

A. Replacement cost of the steel at the date
   that it was sold—average $38.00 per tonne

B. Replacement cost of the steel at the year
   end $40.00 per tonne

The top portion of the income statement would now look like this:

	Replacement Cost
Revenue (37,000 tonnes @ $45)	$1,665,000
Cost of goods sold (37,000 tonnes @ $38)	1,406,000
Gross profit	$ 259,000

On the surface, the company looks "worse off" under replacement cost than under GAAP ($345,000 versus $259,000 gross profit). We do not have the whole story, however, because the company has 25,000 tonnes of steel for which it paid $36.00 per tonne, on average. But, to replace this steel, $40.00 per tonne or more would have to be paid. The company therefore has what might be called an unrealized profit (using GAAP realization terminology per Chapter 8) on the inventory to be sold next year.

There are at least three ways of viewing the *difference* between the GAAP cost of closing inventory ($36.00 per tonne) and its replacement cost ($40.00 per tonne) under replacement cost thinking.

Method A:

The entire amount is a profit in the current year. (But, it may be called unrealized profit if we use GAAP concepts per the first portion of Chapter 8.)

Method B:

The entire amount is *not* profit, but is an addition to owners' equity, because profit can exist only after capital has been maintained. (See Chapters 1 to 3.) The thinking here is that additional capital (owners' equity) is needed to keep the company in business whenever replacement costs rise. For example, if we bought a house for $100,000, and over time the replacement cost of it rose to $150,000, would we have a profit? We have to live somewhere. An equivalent house may cost us $150,000 because the price of all shelter has risen. If we sold the house for $150,000 and bought another equivalent house for $150,000, would we really have made a profit? Thus, the thinking underlying Method B is that we have an increase in price of $50,000, but it will not be called profit. It will be called an increase in our equity—the increase needed to maintain our *equivalent* accommodation.

Method C:

This is a variation of Method B and defines a "normal" asset level—which we will say is 2,000 tonnes in our example. (That is, we may not need a house—a two-bedroom apartment may be adequate.) Any price change in the 2,000 tonnes is debited or credited directly to owners' equity. Any price change in the excess over 2,000 tonnes would be called a "holding gain" profit.

The journal entries for each of the three methods to *increase the figures from cost to replacement cost* would be:

	Method A		Method B		Method C	
19—8:						
Re Opening Inventory						
$68,000 - $60,000:						
Inventory (2,000 tonnes)	8,000		8,000		8,000	
Income statement		8,000		—		—
Owners' equity		—		8,000		8,000★
19—9:						
To increase the opening						
inventory from $34 to the						
$38 at the date of sale:						
Inventory (2,000 tonnes)	8,000		8,000		8,000	
Income statement		8,000		—		—
Owners' equity		—		8,000		8,000★
To increase purchases						
from $36 tonnes cost to $38 tonnes at						
the date of sale:						
Inventory (60,000 tonnes)	120,000		120,000		120,000	
Income statement		120,000		—		120,000
Owners' equity		—		120,000		—
To increase closing						
inventory from $38 per tonne						
to $40 per tonne:						
Inventory (25,000 tonnes)	50,000		50,000		50,000	
Income statement		50,000		—		46,000
Owners' equity		—		50,000		4,000★

★ Owners' equity is credited for 2,000 tonnes for every price increase, and debited for any price decrease.

The top portion of the income statement for each of the three methods for 19—9 would appear as follows:

	19—9		
	Method A	Method B	Method C
Revenue	$1,665,000	$1,665,000	$1,665,000
Cost of goods sold	1,406,000	1,406,000	1,406,000
Gross profit	259,000	259,000	259,000
Holding gains (increases of cost to replacement cost)	178,000	—	166,000
	$ 437,000	$ 259,000	$ 425,000

The inventory account under Method A would appear as follows:

Inventory

Opening inventory:			
Purchases @ $30	60,000		
Increase to $34 per tonne	8,000		
Increase to $38 per tonne	8,000		
	76,000		
Purchases:			
Cost @ $36	2,160,000		
Increase to $38 per tonne	120,000		
	2,356,000	Sold:	
		37,000 tonnes @ $38	1,406,000
	950,000		
Closing inventory			
Increase to $40 per tonne	50,000		
25,000 tonnes @ $40	1,000,000		

When we compare the $345,000 computed under GAAP to the figures under methods (A), (B) and (C) ($437,000 and $259,000 and $425,000), we receive a different impression about management's actions in 19—9. Methods (A) and (C) give credit to management for holding much more inventory than is normal (25,000 tonnes instead of 2,000)—during a time when replacement costs are rising. GAAP statements report the gain in the year in which revenue is recognized. Method (A) reports the "holding gain" *in the year that replacement costs rise.* Thus, in Method (A) someone interested in evaluating management receives two viewpoints:

Selling ability—gross profit	$259,000
Purchasing ability—holding gain	178,000
	$437,000

These viewpoints are not available in GAAP statements, and a mixture of the two are given at a later date—perhaps a year later when the goods are sold.

Method (B) provides a different perspective. It avoids describing all price rises as profits. It also focuses on cash outflows/disbursements—because any cash that has to be disbursed for inventory would be at replacement cost. Those who wish to predict cash flows have to ascertain both receipts and disbursements. Replacement cost gives only the disbursements, and therefore by itself is not adequate to permit a computation of future funds from operations, or cash receipts less cash disbursements. By having a replacement cost figure for cost of goods sold, those interested in cash flow prediction are better off than having to forecast from GAAP figures.

In summary, replacement cost inventory accounting has potential advantages over GAAP costing for those who choose to cash flow predict, or wish to evaluate management (see Chapter 6). The illustrations in this section of the chapter reinforce the theme that accounting has to be tailored to fit the circumstances, such as objectives, facts, and constraints. More will be said about replacement costs in later chapters.

Summary

Objectives of financial accounting, facts and estimates of the future, accounting concepts, and legal constraints are important factors that have to be brought together when selecting accounting policies and financial reporting. Inventory accounting is a good example of the existence of multiple alternatives. Preparers of financial statements must be careful to choose policies that can be followed for several future years; otherwise, credibility is lost when policies are frequently changed. Users of financial statements have to avoid jumping to conclusions about the meaning of accounting numbers.

The GAAP term "lower of cost or market" can be applied many different ways because there are several definitions of cost, and of market. Income and balance sheet figures are also affected by what is included in cost. Wide variety can exist in manufacturing companies about the definition of cost, such as actual cost versus standards, and the exclusion or inclusion of fixed manufacturing overhead.

GAAP accounting for inventories has serious limitations for those outsiders who desire to evaluate management or predict cash flows for a company. Replacement cost accounting can aid these users if the figure for replacement cost is a reasonable approximation of cash flows, and is not one person's unsupported estimates.

QUESTIONS

10-1 Why do GAAP financial statements report inventory at the lower of cost or market? Explain by reference to accounting concepts and objectives of accounting.

10-2 Provide several different definitions of cost and of market. Explain each.

10-3 Why do accountants have several different ways of costing inventory? What effect does this have on comparability?

10-4 Distinguish inventory from a long-lived asset. What differences in accounting exist when an asset is classified as inventory, rather than as long-lived?

10-5 How do accountants determine the cost of a herd of cattle that a rancher has bred over the past 30 years?

10-6 What are the strengths and limitations to the specific identification method of inventory costing?

10-7 Under what circumstances would FIFO be preferable to weighted average or LIFO costing of inventory?

10-8 Under what circumstances would net realizable value be preferable to replacement cost as a measure of market value?

10-9 What is direct costing? Is it GAAP in Canada?

10-10 What are the alternative ways of recording cash discounts on purchases of inventory?

10-11 What are the advantages of a perpetual inventory system?

10-12 Under what circumstances would the retail method of inventory be appropriate?

10-13 What are holding gains? Under what circumstances would the computation of these gains be useful? To whom?

10-14 Is the use of replacement cost for inventories GAAP? Under which circumstances?

EXERCISES

E10-1 Byrd Corporation (BC) recently commenced a retail business. It buys small appliances from the manufacturers and sells them to a variety of consumers. During the first month of operations BC purchased the following toaster-ovens:

February 2	100 purchased @ $40 each	$4,000
15	50	@ 42	2,100
22	40	@ 44	1,760

During February BC sold 160 toaster-ovens at an average price of $79.

Required:

A. Compute cost of goods sold for February for the toaster-ovens, assuming that the company costs its inventory on:

1. the FIFO basis.
2. the weighted average basis.
3. the LIFO basis.

Assume that cost of goods sold is determined at the end of each month.

B. Compute gross profit for each of the three inventory costing bases noted in (A).

E10-2 Termite Lumber Corporation (TLC) adopted the lower of cost or market basis of inventory valuation three years ago, when the company commenced operations. Since that time cost has always been below market value. At the company's most recent year end of December 31, 19—3 the following situation exists for the closing inventory:

Species	Cost	Replacement Cost	Net Realizable Value
Fir	$ 600,000	$ 640,000	$ 650,000
Hemlock	175,000	165,000	90,000
Spruce	420,000	445,000	430,000
Cedar	50,000	40,000	35,000
	$1,245,000	$1,290,000	$1,205,000

TLC is trying to decide what definition it should give to the term market: replacement cost, or net realizable value. Also, should the lower of cost or market be applied to each species or to the overall lumber inventory?

Required:

A. Compute the value of the closing inventory at December 31, 19—3, assuming market is defined as:

1. replacement cost, and is applied:
   a. to each species.
   b. to the total of all species.
2. net realizable value, and is applied:
   a. to each species.
   b. to the total of all species.

B. If the prices of lumber tend to vary considerably for each species, and in total, what definition would you give to market? Why? For which objectives of financial accounting?

E10-3 Super-Y Drug Stores Limited (SYS) utilizes the retail method of inventory costing in its stores. During March, the following occurred in its huge superstore:

	Cosmetics Department		Other Departments		Total	
	Cost	Retail	Cost	Retail	Cost	Retail
Inventory, February 28	$102,000	$ 240,000	$ 600,000	$ 850,000	$ 702,000	$1,090,000
Purchases during March	400,000	900,000	1,800,000	2,500,000	2,200,000	3,400,000
	502,000	1,140,000	2,400,000	3,350,000	2,902,000	4,490,000
Sales during March at retail		990,000		2,800,000		3,790,000
Inventory, March 31		$ 150,000		$ 550,000		$ 700,000

Required:

A. Compute the cost of inventory at March 31 on the following bases:

1. for the store in total (*not* for each department separately).
2. for each of the two departments separately. Then add the two departmental figures together to arrive at the total for the store.

B. Why do the figures for (A2) differ from (A1)? What does this result convey about the retail method of inventory costing, and where it can be sensibly applied?

C. Which of (A1) or (A2) would you apply in SYS? Explain.

E10-4 Compute the cost of closing inventory at March 31, 19—8 from the undernoted information, assuming that the company uses:
1. direct costing.
2. absorption costing.

Costs: direct material	$5,000
direct labor	8,000
variable manufacturing overhead	4,000
fixed manufacturing overhead	6,000
selling expenses	3,000
administrative expenses	2,000
Quantity of units produced in month	1,000
Inventory at beginning of month	Nil

Explain your answer.

E10-5 Prepare journal entries to record the undernoted information on the periodic inventory basis:

Opening inventory	$ 20,000
Purchases during the month	216,000
Purchases returned to suppliers	14,500
Inventory costing $180,000 is sold for $225,500	
A physical count of inventory at the end of the month amounts to	38,900

E10-6 The following information relates to Beechy Corporation (BC):

Opening inventory	10 units @ $20 per unit	$ 200
Purchases	60 units @ $22 per unit	1,320
Sold	55 units for $29 per unit when the replacement cost is $23 per unit	
Closing inventory	15 units. Replacement cost is $24 per unit	

Required:

Provide journal entries to record the above information for BC on each of the following methods:

Method A: Any increase in replacement cost is recorded as income for the year.

Method B: Any increase in replacement cost is recorded as an increase in owners' equity.

Method C: Any increase in replacement cost for the first 10 units is recorded as owners' equity, and any increase in excess of 10 is recorded as income.

PROBLEMS

P10-1 The following information is for Hanna Limited (HL).

Opening inventory	25 units @ $10 per unit.	$ 250
Purchase #1:	100 units @ $11 per unit.	1,100
Sale #1:	90 units sold at $20 per unit when replacement cost is $12 per unit.	
Purchase #2:	100 units @ $8 per unit.	800
Sale #2:	105 units sold at $9 per unit when replacement cost is $7 per unit.	
Closing inventory	30 units. Replacement cost is $6 per unit.	

Required:

Provide journal entries to record the above information for HL on each of the following methods:

Method A: Any increase or decrease in replacement cost is recorded as income or expense for the year.

Method B: Any increase or decrease in replacement cost is recorded as an increase or decrease in owners' equity.

Method C: Any increase or decrease in replacement cost for the first 25 units is recorded as owners' equity, and any increase or decrease in excess of 25 is recorded as income or expense.

P10-2 Eprile Manufacturing Corporation (EMC) had the following operating results in 19—7 and 19—8:

	Years ended December 31	
	19—7	*19—8*
Inventory, January 1, 19—7	Nil	
Units produced	100,000	70,000
Units sold @ $50 per unit	60,000	110,000
Costs incurred during year:		
Direct material	$ 600,000	$420,000
Direct labor	1,000,000	700,000
Variable manufacturing expense	500,000	350,000
Fixed manufacturing expense	700,000	700,000
Selling expense	395,000	417,500
Administrative expense	285,000	299,000

Required:

A. Prepare income statements for EMC for each of 19—7 and 19—8 assuming a FIFO costing method is used in conjunction with:
1. absorption costing.
2. direct costing, or variable costing.

B. Summarize the effect that each of the direct costing and absorption costing methods has on income when sales volume and production volume are changing.

C. If your sole objective of financial accounting was to postpone the payment of income taxes, would you choose absorption costing or direct costing? Why?

P10-3 Johnston Limited (JL) manufactures two products, A and B, on one machine:

	Products	
	A	*B*
Direct material	$5.00/unit	$10.00/unit
Direct labor	7.00/unit	3.50/unit
Variable manufacturing overhead	1.00/unit	.50/unit

Other data:

1. Annual depreciation of the machine is $20,000.
2. Annual rent of the manufacturing facilities is $12,000.
3. Sales for the year are 4,000 units of A and 6,000 units of B.
4. Production for the year is 6,000 units of A and 10,000 units of B.
5. Product A requires twice as much labor time as product B.
6. Opening inventory is nil, because JL is a new company.

Required:

A. Assuming that there are no other costs related to the manufacture of products A and B, determine the cost per unit of each of product A, and product B. State your objective of accounting in each situation, and justify your reasoning process.

B. Calculate the cost of goods sold and ending inventory for JL.

C. The controller of the company has informed you that management is giving serious consideration to costing inventory at direct material plus direct labor cost. As an advisor to the board of directors of JL, what is your opinion of management's idea? Explain.

P10-4 Lam Film Corporation (LFC) arranges for the production of films. It also distributes its own films plus those produced by others, and sells films outright to other distributors. The first year end of LFC is approaching, and the president is asking about the measurement and disclosure of the assets and related liabilities. His questions are:

1. Should the costs of developing and/or distributing a film be reported as inventory, or as long-lived assets?
2. Should the costs be reported as current assets, or non-current assets?
3. If some or all of the films are reported as long-lived assets, over what period of time should they be amortized?
4. When films are sold, should the proceeds be reported as revenue, or should only the gain or loss be reported on the income statement? Does it make any difference whether the film that has been sold has been used for a few years to generate revenue from movie theatres, or is new? Explain.

You have been engaged as an advisor to the president. Your analysis of the situation provides the following information:

1. Some films are produced only when a buyer is found for the film. Usually, the buyer is a distribution company, which rents the films to theatres, and receives a percentage of the revenue that the theatre receives from patrons. Sometimes, only a portion (e.g., 50 percent) of the film is sold to a distribution company, and LFC receives its percentage of revenue from the theatres.

2. Many of the films that were rented to theatres will be sold two or more years later to companies that sell the rights to television networks or stations.
3. LFC buys a few films from other film producers, and will distribute them to theatres for a few years. Eventually, the better films will be sold to television networks.
4. Some films turn out to be poorly received by the critics and theatre patrons.
5. Some films are produced on speculation, in the hope that theatre patrons will find them worthwhile. These films may be retained by LFC, or they may be sold.

Required:

Advise the president, giving thorough explanations.

P10-5 Nelson Corporation (NC) is owned by the three Nelson brothers. In May 19—8, a fire destroyed the company's distribution warehouse, and all of its inventory. Some of the purchase and sales invoices were destroyed in the fire, as was the perpetual inventory control system. NC's income statement for the first quarter ended March 31, 19—8 showed:

Revenue		$800,000
Cost of goods sold		560,000
Gross profit		240,000
Expenses:		
Selling	$100,000	
Administrative	80,000	180,000
Income before income taxes		60,000

The closing inventory at March 31, 19—8 was $220,000. It was recorded at the lower of cost or market.

In the period from March 31, 19—8 to the date of the fire, May 29, 19—8, the purchase and sales invoices showed:

Sales revenue—cash	$120,000
—on account	510,000
Purchases of inventory—on account	460,000
Purchases returned—on account	30,000

You have been engaged by NC's insurance company to calculate the probable cost of the inventory destroyed by fire. You have learned the following:

1. All of NC's products are similar, with a similar cost to selling price relationship.
2. Replacement costs of inventory have risen about 4 percent, as have selling prices, from the beginning of the year to the date of the fire.
3. Replacement costs rose another 3 percent in June, July, and August.

Required:

A. Compute the probable cost of the inventory that was destroyed by the fire. Explain your reasoning process.

B. Assume that it is now September 19—8. What sum would you recommend that the insurance company pay to NC for the inventory that was destroyed in the fire? Assume that the inventory was fully insured.

P10-6 Zin Corporation (ZC) commenced business in October 19—8. Its year end is December 31. The following purchases and sales occurred.

October 17:	Purchased 1,000	units of inventory @ $10/unit	$10,000
24:	Purchased 2,000	units of inventory @ $ 9/unit	$18,000
31:	Sold 1,800	units of inventory @ $15/unit	
November 10:	Purchased 3,000	units of inventory @ $11/unit	$33,000
24:	Sold 2,800	units of inventory @ $16/unit	
December 14:	Purchased 2,500	units of inventory @ $10/unit	$25,000
22:	Sold 2,400	units of inventory @ $14/unit	

At December 31, 19—8 the replacement cost of the inventory was $9.50 per unit and the likely selling price was $13.50 per unit. The president has decided to adopt GAAP, and the lower of cost or market for inventory costing purposes.

Required:

A. Compute revenue, cost of goods sold, and the closing inventory at December 31, 19—8, assuming:

1. A perpetual inventory system is in use, and ZC costed goods sold and closing inventory using:
   a. weighted average   b. FIFO   c. LIFO

2. Periodic inventory methods are in use, and ZC determines its cost of goods sold and closing inventory at the end of the year, after adding all purchases and sales volume together. Assume that ZC's costing method is:
   a. weighted average   b. FIFO   c. LIFO

B. What are the benefits of a perpetual inventory system for ZC if the prime objective of financial accounting is to provide quarterly reports to the board of directors, so that they can pay managers a bonus based on income before income tax?

EXPLORATION MATERIALS AND CASES

MC10-1 Below are three separate situations. In each situation, select the cost flow assumption that you feel is most appropriate. Be sure to indicate the aspects of the company's operations that were most significant in leading to your recommendation.

Situation 1:   Prentice Automobile Sales Ltd. is a car dealership. It sells both used and new automobiles and also provides parts and repair service.

Situation 2:   Edible Bits Ltd. is in the food processing business. Its operations consist of buying bulk commodities such as nuts and raisins in world markets, then cleaning and packaging them into units that can be marketed at retail, primarily through the major supermarket chains. The commodities involved lose freshness and deteriorate with the passage of time, so the production schedule uses the oldest goods first. Prices in the buying market are subject to the contingencies of crop conditions in various parts of the world and prices in the retail market are tied fairly closely to the annual world price situation.

Situation 3: Tanbar Limited operates a leather tannery, obtaining the hides that are its raw material from the various meatpacking houses, where hide production is a by-product of the slaughtering process. It sells the finished leather to a variety of markets, but the majority of sales are to footwear and luggage manufacturers.

Tanbar has little control over either the prices at which it buys hides or those at which it sells finished leather. On the selling side this is because the company's customers view Tanbar's price entitlement as composed of the current cost of hides (adjusted by standard factors for waste, etc.), plus a processing allowance for the tanning operation. On Tanbar's supply side, hides come on the market not because of any factors related to ultimate leather demand but because of the volume of cattle offerings and slaughter directed at meat production that take place at the packing houses. Hide prices can thus vary significantly depending on whether there is a surplus or deficiency of supply relative to ultimate leather demand. Because the processing of leather takes time and this is not allowed for by Tanbar's customers in the prices they offer, the company can find itself gaining or losing on its inventory depending on fluctuations in hide prices.

MC10-2 Fun Co. Limited (FCL) is incorporated under the *Canada Business Corporations Act.* All of its shareholders and major creditors are located in Canada. FCL consists of several retail stores that stock a particular line of citizen band radios.

The success of the company depends to a large extent upon sales in the car and truck industry and upon the disposable income of potential customers. Over the past three years FCL has experienced a dramatic increase in sales and in the current year, 19—5, just ended, sales were 10,000 units or $1,000,000 (i.e., average selling price was $100 per unit).

Much of the company's recent growth has caught it by surprise and it is uncertain whether it has adequate information to satisfy its needs. At present it is reviewing both its method of costing and controlling inventories and has accumulated the following data from its records:

Inventory, October 31, 19—4	2,000 units @ $90
19—5 purchases:	
January 15	1,000 units @ $80
April 18	2,000 units @ $75
June 22	2,000 units @ $70
September 18	1,000 units @ $70
October 15	6,000 units @ $60

FCL uses a periodic inventory system, and a physical inventory taken on October 31, 19—5 revealed that 3,500 units were on hand. The manufacturer from whom FCL usually makes its purchases quoted a price of $60 per unit on October 31, 19—5 for a lot of 1,000 units. Up until this time FCL had been content with the service that it received from its major supplier; however, as a matter of interest it decided to obtain prices from other suppliers. All suppliers surveyed indicated that their prices were above $60 per unit except for one small supplier who was just starting up in the business. This supplier's price was $55 per unit. Further investigation revealed that this supplier might not be successful and definitely would not be able to supply FCL's entire annual needs. FCL's expected resale price in 19—5 - 19—6 was $85 a unit.

The president of the company (who is not a shareholder) is particularly concerned about adopting a fair method of evaluating the company's inventory for the following reasons:

1. Managers of the retail stores receive a bonus based on profits.
2. During the year the company issued an income debenture (that is, the interest on the debenture is 5 percent of net income based upon generally accepted accounting principles).
3. The company's sales price of citizen band radios has declined significantly since the beginning of the year.

The president is aware that there are several acceptable methods of costing inventory and has asked you which is the fairest—FIFO, LIFO, or weighted average. He would also be interested in hearing your opinion about the company's present method of controlling inventory and on the accounting significance of the company's declining sales price.

Required:

What would you recommend? Why? Explain your answer clearly by stating the assumptions that you have made, the calculations you have used (hint: calculate cost of goods sold and inventory figures on a FIFO, LIFO, and weighted average basis), and the logic you have employed.

MC10-3 Apple Company (AC) was recently formed by a group of 32 independent apple-orchard owners in order to obtain better profits from their apple harvest. AC is required to buy all the apple output from each orchard owner at the prevailing fair market value. It then sells some fresh apples but also makes bottled apple cider, canned apple juice, and applesauce. According to the agreement signed by each of the 32 owners, 75 percent of annual net income of AC is to be distributed to the owners in cash within 90 days of the company's March 31 year end. The remaining 25 percent is to be retained for expansion of processing facilities. There are no provisions in the agreement for admitting new owners of AC. If an orchard owner sells his farm, the new owner automatically must become an owner of AC.

On commencement of the business each owner contributed $10,000 of which 80 percent consisted of a 10-year loan bearing interest at 9 percent per annum (the market rate at that time). Each owner also had to give a bank a personal guarantee of $40,000 so that short-term loans could be obtained as needed in order to finance inventories and receivables. No other sources of cash financing are used by the company.

AC leased a building for ten years. It also acquired about $400,000 of processing equipment, trucks, tools, and other necessary assets. Agreements were signed with several large national grocery chains to buy output at prevailing market price. Terms are cash payment within 60 days of delivery to each store. Prices of "finished" products per the agreement are to be a function of supply-demand at the date of sale. Because some inventory could be stored for up to two years, selling prices could be substantially higher or slightly lower than inventory cost (i.e., cost of the apples plus processing, packaging and storing). That is, the market prices are set by the combined action of all buyers and sellers; but AC makes its own decisions as to whether it will sell at prevailing prices, or store, or process fresh apples.

The company's first year end has just passed. The agreement among the owners does not give any guidance as to how net income is to be computed. In the rush to get the company started, officials have not yet paid much attention to the selection of accounting principles and policies. However, they recognize that the company was primarily formed to increase profits of the orchard owners. Also, they know that the owners will be anxious to have their dividend paid before June 30 because each owner's liquid assets will be nearing the low point for the year.

Required:

Assume the role of an accounting advisor to the company, and thoroughly explain which financial accounting policies and principles the company should adopt.

MC10-4 The president of S. Rink & Cloth Ltd., Ms. Lee, was disappointed to learn from her controller that the company had suffered a loss of $175,000 in its first year of operations. She was disturbed for the following three reasons:

1. She receives a bonus of 10 percent of profit.
2. The terms of sale to customers are set by contract. Each year on January 1 the selling price to customers is set at replacement cost plus 25 percent and regardless of any changes which occur in replacement cost subsequent to January 1, no change in selling price is permitted.
3. In anticipation of replacement cost increases Ms. Lee purposely purchased large quantities of inventory at the beginning of the year. As it turned out, during the year the cost of cloth did rise and she thought she should be rewarded for her astute management of company resources. The following data relate to the company's first year of operations:

Date	Purchases		Sales
	Units	*Unit Cost*	
1/1	600,000	$4.00	
3/15			200,000 (Replacement cost at the time of sale was $4.50/unit)
4/12	300,000	4.50	
5/8			400,000 (Replacement cost at the time of sale was $5.00/unit)
7/12	400,000	5.00	
8/20			300,000 (Replacement cost at the time of sale was $5.50/unit)
9/15	200,000	5.50	
10/2			500,000 (Replacement cost at the time of sale was $6.00/unit)
11/6	300,000	6.00	

During the year the company incurred operating costs of $125,000. A review of the year indicated that the cost per unit had increased dramatically. This was due to a severe shortage of supply which has now been remedied. At December 31, the company's year end, the replacement cost per unit was $6.40 and there was every indication that this cost would remain stable throughout the upcoming year. In addition customer demand is expected to be 1,500,000 units next year.

Required:

Assume the role of an accounting advisor. Evaluate the various alternative inventory costing methods available to the company (including replacement cost) and determine income under each method. Which do you recommend? Why?

CHAPTER 11

Long-Lived Asset Applications

Chapter Themes

1. Many of the themes of Chapter 10 continue in this chapter. But there is a major difference. Except for a few costs, such as depreciation on machinery and buildings, the sums included in *inventory* represent continual cash outflows. The cash flow for long-lived assets, such as buildings, occurs at the beginning of the asset's long life, and not throughout its life. Long-lived assets that have a limited life are depreciated, which does *not* involve a flow of cash or funds from operations. Depreciation expense is needed to compute accrual-based net income. Accrual-based net income that includes depreciation expense may not, however, be useful for some users of financial statements. Objectives such as income tax postponement, evaluation of management by outsiders, and cash flow prediction tend to require figures other than non-cash depreciation expense.

2. A second important difference between inventories and long-lived assets lies in the turnover of the asset into an expense. Inventory assets usually turn over quickly into cost of goods sold. Closing inventory of one period is opening inventory of another period. Thus, *two* years are affected by judgments applied to closing inventory. A few longer term effects of inventory can occur as a result of choosing particular accounting policies with respect to cost, e.g., FIFO vs. LIFO, and market. In contrast, depreciation methods and rates affect income over a *long* period of years. There are also a few situations where short term income can be affected, such as by including some types of costs as assets instead of expensing them, e.g., labor costs incurred to get a machine operating at top efficiency. Overall, accounting-policy choices for long-lived assets have a long-term effect on asset costing and income numbers. Industries that are capital-asset inten-

sive, e.g., steel makers or public utilities, have income numbers that are greatly affected by physical depreciation and accounting for depreciation.

3. Many methods and applications of depreciation exist. In recent years, research conducted into depreciation accounting and similar allocations has concluded that they are *arbitrary*—and any one method of depreciation cannot be defended as being superior to another method. As a result, we have to be very careful what credibility we give to depreciation figures. Assets such as buildings and equipment depreciate because of technological obsolescence, and wear and tear. Obsolescence occurs when new methods or equipment are developed that render older equipment more expensive to operate. At what rate or pace do wear and tear, and obsolescence, occur? Estimates are difficult to make; yet, they have to be made at the *beginning* of an asset's life, and may not be revised for several years.

4. The "arbitrariness of depreciation" theme continues when we look at "intangible assets". These are assets that do not have a physical presence that we can touch, but they exist and provide future benefit. A trade name (e.g., Coke) or a patent or a copyright produce revenue—but over what period of time?

5. The cost concept and recognition/realization concept of GAAP have an identifiable effect on what the income statement and balance sheet do, and do *not* show. A company may have spent $3 million to discover oil, which has a discounted present value of $40 million. The balance sheet reports an asset of $3 million, per GAAP. To predict cash receipts, we would have to (a) focus on the number of barrels of oil that will be produced at what date, and (b) multiply by our best estimate of the price that will be received at that time. Recent financial statements may help us to estimate only cash *disbursements*. But the $3 million itself may have limited usefulness. It tells us that $3 million was spent (and not $20 million). But it does not give any hint as to the $40 million.

Different Business Decisions

Supermarket A Ltd. borrowed $5 million from a mortgage company and bank to buy land and to construct ten new stores. An interest rate of 12 percent has to be paid on the outstanding principal balances, which initially total $5 million.

Supermarket B Ltd. decided to rent space in ten different shopping malls for a period of ten years. The space is considered equivalent to that being occupied by Supermarket A.

Five years later, the income statements for the ten stores of each of the two supermarkets show the following:

| | Year ended January 31, 19—8 | |
	Supermarket A	Supermarket B
Revenue	$11,000,000	$11,000,000
Cost of goods sold	8,910,000	8,910,000
Gross profit	2,090,000	2,090,000
Expenses:		
Selling and administrative	850,000	850,000
Rent on buildings	—	400,000
Depreciation—building	200,000	—
—other	50,000	50,000
Interest —building	460,000	—
—other	80,000	80,000
	1,640,000	1,380,000
Income before income taxes	$ 450,000	$ 710,000

Who made the best business decision? How much can we tell from looking at the income statement? What else would we need to know? (Form an opinion before reading the next few paragraphs.)

Supermarket A is really two businesses: a food retailer, and a real estate company. The cost concept of GAAP requires the use of "cost" or "cost less depreciation" for reporting *tangible* long-lived assets, e.g., buildings, and equipment. Thus, the major, missing piece of information is "What can the ten stores (land and building) be sold for today? Will an investor buy them from Supermarket A and rent them back to it for $400,000 per year?"

At the end of five years, Supermarket A's building would appear on its balance sheet as:

Building, at cost	$5,000,000
Accumulated depreciation	1,000,000
	$4,000,000

Suppose that the ten stores (land and building only) can be sold for exactly $4 million. If so, Supermarket B would have made the better decision because it has earned $710,000 (or so) for five years whereas Supermarket A has earned only $450,000 (or so).

If the buildings and land can be sold for, say, $7 or $8 million, however, then Supermarket A made the better decision—about real estate. The two stores are equal in their supermarket operations, i.e., same gross profit and same "interest-other" and "selling and administrative expense".

What is the "commercial message?" There are two. Many companies are engaged in more than one "line of business". Sometimes an income statement hides this fact.

Fortunately, in comparing supermarkets *A* and *B*, the income statements kept the real estate operations of *A*, and the rent paid by *B*, separate, i.e., rent, depreciation-building, and interest-building.

The second message is that much of GAAP accounting makes more sense for certain types of businesses than others. A supermarket buys groceries and meat and sells them, i.e., turns them over, fairly quickly for cash. Supermarkets encounter some of the inventory valuation problems mentioned in Chapter 10; but these tend to be less severe than when inventory turns over slowly, or is a huge (material) asset. Thus, accounting figures tend to have good credibility for supermarkets, and similar situations where cash and near cash assets are primarily involved.

When there are large investments in long-lived assets, such as buildings, research programs, and natural resources, however, concepts such as cost, matching, and revenue recognition produce less credible figures for *some* of the possible objectives of accounting. We have to go elsewhere than accounting and financial statements to gather relevant information for say bonus plans, cash flow prediction, and evaluation of management objectives.

Real estate companies that hold assets for many years, mainly to obtain gains on sale of the long-lived assets, are but one example of companies where the income statement does not "tell the whole story". Others are forest products companies, which may have large investments in growing timber, and oil and gas producers, mining companies, and possibly farming. What does an income statement of a wheat farmer look like in midsummer, before the crop is harvested and sold? (Under GAAP, there is merely an asset that mainly consists of the cost of seed and fertilizer—an inventory.)

Types of Long-Lived Assets

The long-lived asset category includes a variety of assets with quite different accounting treatment. Some long-lived assets do not depreciate in an accounting sense. An example is land on which a building is situated. Per GAAP, the land is recorded at cost. For long-lived assets, GAAP does *not* have a lower of cost or market rule. The value of land could drop somewhat because the district or general area could become "run down". Unless evidence could be gathered that the decline is likely to be other than temporary, the land would continue to be recorded, per GAAP, at cost. Thus, with our supermarket example, it is possible that the net book value of $4 million could be higher than what the asset can be sold for (net realizable value).

Tangible long-lived assets that have a limited life are *depreciated*. Examples are buildings and equipment. Intangible long-lived assets with a limited life are *amortized*. Exceptions to these two "rules" exist. For instance, office partitions and improvements to leased office-space may be called tangible assets. Yet, many accountants call the expensing of these "amortization". Some intangibles, e.g., copyrights, have a life that is specified by law. Other intangibles, e.g., goodwill, have a life that is restricted by GAAP.

Goodwill can be recorded under GAAP only when it is *purchased*. This usually occurs when we buy the operations of another company, and continue to sell or manufacture the same products or services. Such a purchase of the assets and liabilities of a continuing *(going concern)* company is called a *business combination.* We would buy the inventory, tangible assets, perhaps some other assets or liabilities, and the services of people/managers. When we buy these assets and liabilities (as opposed to buying the common shares, which would be an *intercorporate investment*), the journal entry may be:

Accounts receivable	28,000	
Inventory	65,500	
Equipment	170,000	
Goodwill	26,500	
Accounts payable		18,000
Cash		272,000

The figures that we would record are so-called "fair market values". Accounts receivable would be recorded at net realizable value. Inventory would be valued at the lower of cost or market—to allow for a profit when it is sold, at a later date. Equipment would be recorded at current replacement *cost*, because it will be used in the business, and not sold. Accounts payable would be credited at the cost of paying it. Cash is what was paid. This leaves goodwill as the balancing figure.

In effect, we probably would have paid $26,500 for management talent and experience. We hope that the management that we acquired will help us earn a reasonable return on our investment of $272,000. If it does, what do we do with goodwill? Some accountants believe that the goodwill should immediately be expensed because GAAP does not attach costs to people. (See "objectivity," Chapter 8.) (An exception to this would be a sports team that buys playing rights of individuals.) Other accountants believe that goodwill will last forever because "acquired" management probably will train new management and thereby replenish itself. Given the wide variation in opinion, and public complaints about some major controversial purchases of companies' assets and liabilities that occurred in the 1970s, GAAP was tightened. GAAP in Canada now calls for "systematic" amortization of purchased goodwill over a maximum of forty years. The term "systematic" usually means an annual straight-line basis of, say, 2.5 percent of the original cost (of $26,500 in this case). An amortization of 2.5 percent often tends to keep the effect on the income statement at the "immaterial" level.

Overall, the long-lived asset category includes a variety of assets with quite different GAAP treatment. Some assets such as land are usually not depreciated. An exception may be where the land is being used, such as an iron mine. Intangible assets are amortized over different periods of time. Tangible assets that have a limited life can be depreciated in different ways over varying periods of time. Thus, once again we have to be alert to the consequences of each method in different situations.

What Is Cost?

Suppose that we decide to build a new office building on land that currently contains an old house. We have to tear down the house, sell the scrap recovered on demolition, excavate the land to provide a foundation and parking space, construct the building, landscape the land surrounding the building. In order to finance construction, we arrange a mortgage on the building and borrow money from a bank. What is cost?

In effect, there are three different long-lived assets in the above situation: land, building, and land improvements. The cost of *land* includes the purchase price of the land and old house, *plus* the cost of demolition, and *less* any cash received on sale of materials recovered from the old house. The reason for calling these items a cost of land is that all are required to put the land in condition so that a building can be constructed. Legal costs of transferring title to the land to us could also be included in "land". (In practice, a lawyer may not separate the costs of transferring land from other costs associated with the mortgage and construction activity. Thus, a company with an income tax postponement objective may take advantage of this and include lawyers' fees under building, which can be depreciated and is called "capital cost allowance", for tax purposes.)

Building costs would include all payments to the company constructing our building (including excavation costs), plus such fees for building permits and various legal charges. Interest expense could be capitalized until the building is ready for occupancy. When is a building ready for occupancy? Often the building is completed on a floor-by-floor basis. Thus, there is some room for judgment; and, companies may capitalize interest until about one-half or more of the floors are occupied.

Land improvements include trees, shrubs, grass, and other landscaping items. These are assets with a limited life and are depreciated or amortized. Expenditures incurred to maintain the grass and landscaping are usually expensed, because they are matched to revenue (see Chapter 8).

Complications arise when we try to ascertain the cost of *machinery and equipment.* Often, machinery has to be installed and then debugged until it is operating efficiently. Debugging costs can be capitalized under GAAP by following the cost concept (dealt with in Chapter 8), because the machinery is not yet ready to earn revenue. The cost of moving the machinery a few years later, installing it a second time, and debugging it, however, usually is expensed under GAAP. (The thinking here is that we cannot increase the cost of an asset by moving it around. A legitimate cost would include only one installation, because at this point the asset is available to earn revenue.)

Sometimes, machinery and equipment has to be imported. Various import charges may be incurred, and payment would usually be in a foreign currency. The equivalent cost in Canadian currency, including any bank charges, would be capitalized as the asset.

TRADE-INS AND REPAIRS

When capitalizing a long-lived asset, careful attention has to be paid to sales "gimmickry", or deception.

Cost ($13,500) less accumulated depreciation ($7,200) of old automobile being used as a trade in	$ 6,300
Net realizable value of old automobile	5,000
Trade-in allowance granted by dealer	8,000
Cash needed, in addition to trade-in	11,500

What is the cost of the new automobile? To answer this question, we have to ask ourselves what we would pay if there were no trade-in, and "all cash" has to be paid? The trade-in is worth only $5,000 to the dealer if it is sold quickly—perhaps to another dealer. Thus, the $5,000 is a cash equivalent. By adding the $5,000 to the additional cash payment of $11,500, we arrive at the new cost of $16,500.

The journal entry would be:

Automobile (new)	$16,500	
Accumulated depreciation (old auto)	7,200	
Loss on disposal of old auto		
($6,300 - $5,000)	1,300	
Automobile (old)		
($7,200 + $6,300)		$13,500
Cash		11,500

Note that the $8,000 offered by the salesperson does not appear. He or she is just giving the illusion that the old car would generate a $1,700 ($8,000 - $6,300) profit on book value to entice the buyer. In reality, we have a loss of $1,300. The $1,300 is usually referred to as a *sunk cost*.

In ascertaining the cost of a new automobile, remember the cost concept, and the reference to "lowest cash cost". The only figure that counts is "the price that would be paid by someone who pays 100 percent cash".

Notice that we have debited the $1,300 to a loss/expense account. (*Losses* or *gains* arise on the disposal of long-lived assets that are used over a long period of time to help earn revenue.) If we had many automobiles, we may just debit accumulated depreciation for $8,500 ($7,200 + $1,300). The logic underlying this is that some automobiles will be sold at a loss and others at a gain. Over the longer term, the gains and losses should even out as long as our depreciation policy reflects obsolescence, wear and tear, and other similar causes of depreciation.

Repairs are usually expensed under GAAP. This because (1) the period of benefit is indefinite, and difficult to measure objectively, and (2) any repair costs related to new parts have already been capitalized once, when the asset was purchased. A second capitalization would increase the cost of the asset—unless the initial cost were removed. There are, however, situations where equipment may be repaired *and* improved. For example, we may decide, a few months after we buy our new automobile, to have it converted so that it will also operate on either propane or natural gas. We also decide to have some repairs completed, e.g., tune-up, oil change, new filters, while the car is being converted to a dual system.

The cost of the conversion would improve the automobile because it permits it to be operated on a cheaper fuel per kilometre. Therefore, we would capitalize the cost of the improvement. The repairs, such as the tune-up, would be expensed.

Depreciation Methods and Rates

How would we depreciate the automobile that we just bought? If we knew little about GAAP accounting, we would probably say: "I'd try to guess what it could be sold for at the end of one year, two years, and so on. I've read that an automobile has the greatest depreciation occur to it when we drive it 'off the lot' of the new car dealer. (Much of the initial "depreciation" represents the gross profit of the dealer.) As soon as the car is used, even a little bit, people will think that we are selling it because it's a 'lemon'...I may take 25 percent depreciation in the first month." In addition, you lose the dealer's gross profit as soon as you drive "off the lot". The dealer will only buy a car back for a sum that allows for another gross profit.

The depreciation approach implied in the above is "an attempt to use depreciation to approximate fair market value". (Cost less accumulated depreciation equals fair market value.) This approach would seem to be sensible if our objective of accounting is evaluation of management, and we were operating a limousine or taxi service. We would want to know what expenses were incurred in earning revenue—and one expense would be a decline in selling price of the automobile.

However, GAAP depreciation is *not* designed to approximate fair market value. Cost, continuity, matching, and objectivity (see Chapter 8) play a central role in GAAP depreciation, which is an *allocation* of the *cost* of the asset over its *useful life*. That is, with GAAP depreciation we are merely spreading out the cost, in an attempt to expense against revenue earned. Presumably, if our taxi earns roughly the same amount of revenue each year, we would think of using a straight-line system that charges the same amount of depreciation each year. Yet if the taxi earns more revenue in the early years, then we would try to match more depreciation expense to the higher revenue of the early years.

GAAP depreciation methods for long-lived assets tend to fall into three main categories:

1. **Straight-line depreciation**   The same amount is charged for wear and tear, and obsolescence each year, over the asset's useful life.

2. **Accelerated depreciation**   The highest expense is charged in the first year of an asset's life, and the amount declines each year thereafter.

3. **Annuity-type depreciation**   The first year of an asset's life bears the least depreciation expense, and the amount increases each year thereafter.

If we have a minimum compliance objective of accounting, straight-line depreciation may be appealing because it is easy to use. We do not have to guess at the expected revenue and cost pattern in the future—and we therefore can claim to be "objective", and to be matching as best we are able to, in an uncertain world with unpredictable events.

Accelerated depreciation may be used by a person who is *conservative* (per Chapter 8) and wants to expense the long-lived depreciable asset as soon as possible. Federal income tax legislation uses accelerated depreciation extensively. Therefore, we will see accelerated depreciation used by those companies that have *only* an income tax postponement objective of accounting. (That is, by selecting the income tax method and rate, only one method of depreciation need be used for both accounting and income tax purposes.)

Annuity-type depreciation methods qualify as GAAP only under very specific conditions. Broadly speaking, the conditions relate to an ability to estimate future revenues and the larger expenses with reasonable accuracy. Usually, this would occur only when an enforceable contract exists, such as when a long-term lease has been signed. (The criteria for usage are much like the ones we used in Chapter 7 for revenue recognition.) For instance, we may lease our building for thirty years under conditions where the user (*lessee*) pays for all operating expenses such as property taxes, insurance, heat and light, *and* agrees to pay a specified amount of revenue. Thus, we would know the future revenues and expenses. We may choose to use annuity depreciation under these conditions, to enable us to show a *constant* return on our investment in the building. That is, we would tend to choose whatever depreciation expense figure gives us the return on investment (income divided by investment) that exists in the contract. Under these conditions, the building is treated much like an interest-yielding investment—as we illustrated in Chapter 9, and will again illustrate shortly.

The specific method by which annuity depreciation is calculated is very complex and will not be discussed in this book. But it is important to *understand why* annuity depreciation has acquired a group of strong supporters, because we will find some Canadian companies using it, perhaps without adequate justification. That is, they do not really know what their future expenses and revenues will be. (They may not have any signed contracts but rent from month to month, or year to year.)

Annuity depreciation can have sensible applications in regulated utility companies, where a utility board of a government in effect guarantees a fairly constant return on investment in power plant or telephone assets. For years, in Canada, few applications existed outside of utilities and the long term contracts described in previous paragraphs. Then, about fifteen years ago, people became aware of the limitations of straight-line depreciation, and what it does to accrual income figures. Consequently, annuity depreciation began to be seen in Canada a little more frequently.

Suppose that we buy an investment certificate for $1,000 that results in our receiving $437.97 at the *end* of *each* of the next three years. How much does this *yield* us in a return on investment? If we divide $1,000 by $437.97, we get a figure of 2.28326. When we look at the table of present values (page 598) under the three periods' row, we find 2.283 at the "15%" column. Thus, our yield or return on investment is 15 percent.

What happens when we buy a $1,000 piece of equipment that lasts for three years, and has no value at the end of three years? Assume that someone leases it from us for the full three years at a price of $437.97 per year, to be paid at the *end* of each year? Assume that we do not have any expenses; therefore, our cash receipt is the same as for the investment certificate. We are earning 15 percent on our investment, if we ignore income tax. Under accrual accounting and straight-line depreciation, our income statement and balance sheet (in part) for each of the three years looks like this:

	Year 1	Year 2	Year 3	Total
Net cash revenue	$ 437.97	$437.97	$437.97	$1,313.91
Depreciation	333.33	333.34	333.33	1,000.00
Income before tax	$ 104.64	$104.63	$104.64	$ 313.91
Investment at beginning of year	$1,000.00	$666.67	$333.33	
Depreciation	333.33	333.34	333.33	
Investment at end of year	$ 666.67	$333.33	$ 0	

	Year 1	Year 2	Year 3	Total
Average investment (one half of beginning and ending)	$ 833.33	$500.00	$166.67	
Return on average investment (income before tax divided by investment)	12.6%	20.9%	62.8%	

We hinted, earlier in this chapter, that straight-line depreciation made sense when we could *not* forecast cash receipts and disbursements over the asset's life. But, once we look at the return on investment effect under *accrual accounting*—where the depreciation gets deducted from our initial investment (of $1,000)—we can see why people may dislike straight-line depreciation and favor an annuity method. Instead of having a return on investment that increases from 12.6 percent to 62.8 percent, we would get a constant rate over the three years when we used an annuity method. That is, income would decline as our average investment declined, through depreciation being increased per annuity depreciation accounting.

When readers of our financial statements are not sophisticated, we may have second thoughts about using straight-line depreciation. However, an annuity basis *cannot be used* unless we know beforehand what the constant yield will be. And, we can only *know* the yield when we have an enforceable contract that assures particular cash receipts and disbursements.

Notice that accelerated depreciation would give wider variation than straight-line depreciation. Net income would be lower in Year 1, making return on investment lower. As a result, what appears to be a conservative effect on the first year's income statement has an *un*conservative effect on the return on investment computation.

In short, none of the methods may appear to have strong underlying logic in situations where the future is difficult to predict. But, accountants have to select a method of depreciation.

At this point, it is worth compiling a list of alternatives in accounting and their likely effect on income figures, balance sheets, return on investment, unsophisticated readers, and similar factors. The list is not long, e.g., straight-line, declining balance, and annuity methods of depreciation, and FIFO vs. LIFO. It reinforces a major theme that we are *not* searching for the "one true way". We should focus on when each method (objectives, facts, constraints) *makes more sense than the others*.

The list ought to cover revenue recognition, accounts receivable, inventories, long-lived tangible assets, and all the other topics that have been discussed, and will be discussed. This does *not* make the subject more complicated than it is. Instead, it focusses on where our attention *has to be*—on relativism, or on where one method makes more sense than the possible alternatives. Bookkeeping appears to have right answers; accounting has many alternatives. Why? Because in some circumstances alternative "y" may make far more sense than "x", and "z". We have to concentrate on the strengths and weaknesses of each alternative in a series of specific situations. This search for the approach or accounting policy that makes more sense than others *in a specific situation* has to occur throughout our professional lives.

MECHANICS OF DEPRECIATION METHODS

The *straight-line* method of depreciation is based on the following formula:

$$\frac{\text{Depreciation}}{\text{for a period}} = \frac{\text{Cost less estimated scrap value (at end of asset's life)}}{\text{Number of periods of useful life}}$$

Perhaps a truck has a cost of $45,000, a useful life of five years, and a scrap value or net realizable value at the end of five years of $5,000. Annual depreciation would be:

$$\frac{\$45,000 - \$5,000}{5} = \underline{\$8,000}$$

If at the end of five years, the truck is sold for $5,000 scrap, the journal entry would be:

Cash	$ 5,000	
Accumulated depreciation	40,000	
Truck		$45,000

Observe that the $5,000 is our best estimate, made at the date of purchase, of the scrap value at the end of five years. It will likely differ from what actually happens. Therefore, a gain or loss will probably result unless the income effect is "grouped" with other trucks. This is done by debiting or crediting accumulated depreciation, and is called "group depreciation", and is covered in more detail later in this chapter.

What happens part way through the life of the asset if we obtain new information that leads us to believe that the truck's life will be eight years, instead of five? Suppose that this "new information" is learned after two years, when the net book value is:

Cost	$45,000
Accumulated depreciation	16,000
Net book value	$29,000

The important point in this example is that the information is new, and does not result from changing our mind. With new information, the $29,000 less $5,000 scrap value would be allocated over the *remaining* life of six years:

$$\frac{\$29,000 - \$5,000}{6} = \underline{\$4,000} \text{ per year}$$

(The accounting to be followed when we change our mind is noted under "consistency" in Chapter 8.)

There are many *declining balance* methods. The one that is most commonly seen in Canada applies a fixed percentage to a declining balance, and *ignores estimated scrap value*. For example, assume that we have acquired an automobile costing $10,000 and choose to use the same rate as would be acceptable, as a maximum, to Revenue Canada, i.e., 30 percent. The annual figures for depreciation expense, and capital cost allowance, would be:

Year	Cost, and beginning of year asset balance	Depreciation for year	Accumulated depreciation at end of year	End of year asset balance
1	$10,000	$3,000*	$3,000	$7,000*
2	7,000	2,100	5,100	4,900
3	4,900	1,470	6,570	3,430
4	3,430	1,029	7,599	2,401
5	2,401	720	8,319	1,681
6	1,681	504	8,823	1,177
7	1,177	353	9,176	824
8	824	247	9,423	577
9	577	173	9,596	404
10	404	121	9,717	283
11	283	85	9,802	198
12	198	59	9,861	139

*Ignores half rate in first year, as required by Revenue Canada.

Notice that a balance remains after twelve years ($139), and some amount will continue to exist until we close the asset and accumulated depreciation account. This is because we are applying a rate of 30 percent to a figure, always leaving 70 percent.

For income tax purposes, Revenue Canada furnishes taxpayers with a listing of asset characteristics, and assigns each asset to a grouping or "pool" of similar assets. For example, all automobiles fall into a class where the *maximum* rate is 30 percent. This means that we could choose any amount up to 30 percent to suit whatever taxable income made the most sense in the circumstances.

Using the automobile example, we may choose to do the following:

Year	Undepreciated capital cost at beginning of year	Capital cost allowance for year	Capital cost allowance claimed to date	Undepreciated capital cost at end of year
1	$10,000	$3,000	$3,000	$7,000
2	7,000	500	3,500	6,500
3	6,500	1,950	5,450	4,550

That is, we may elect to claim only $500 in year 2. As a result, in year 3, we can claim a maximum of $1,950, instead of the $1,470 shown in the previous example. Years 2 and 3 combined add to only $2,470 ($500 + $1,950), however, instead of the $3,570 ($2,100 + $1,470) that we could have claimed with maximum capital cost allowance.

Unless a company experiences losses for several years, it is usually wise to claim maximum capital cost allowance each year. This is because Canadian income tax law allows corporations to offset taxable income of one year against taxable losses of other years. For instance, assume that a corporation has a taxable loss, after claiming maximum capital cost allowance, of $250,000 in the year ended December 31, 19—3. This loss can be used to offset taxable income in the three previous years, and in the next seven, if necessary. Hence, if we had the following taxable income:

19—2	$100,000
19—1	75,000
19—0	25,000
	$200,000

and paid income taxes of $60,000 for these three years, we would receive a refund of the $60,000. Also, we have $50,000 ($250,000 − $200,000) of losses left to claim against any taxable income of 19—4, 19—5 through to 19—10.

If we decided *not* to claim any capital-cost allowance in 19—3, we may not get back the full $60,000 refund. We would therefore lose interest-income by not being able to invest the $60,000 (or a portion of it). Or, we would have to borrow from a bank and pay interest on the $60,000, or a portion thereof.

One other method of depreciation is *unit-of-production* depreciation, or *unit-of-activity* depreciation. It does not conveniently fit into the three categories previously mentioned (straight-line, declining balance or accelerated, and annuity) because it does not have an obvious obsolescence element to it. Unit-of-production depreciation tends to be based on the assumption that depreciation occurs only through wear and tear. That is, the asset would tend *not* to lose its usefulness because a better, less costly to operate, machine became available.

Unit-of-activity depreciation is based on this formula:

$$\text{Depreciation per unit of activity} = \frac{\text{Cost less salvage value}}{\text{Total number of units expected}}$$

Suppose that we bought some logging equipment for $250,000 that we felt could be used to haul out 22,860m³ of logs from forests. Depreciation per unit (cubic metre) would be:

$$\frac{250,000}{22,860} = \$10.94 \text{ m}^3$$

Actual logging activity would depend on weather conditions and the state of the economy, i.e., market price of logs and lumber. If we hauled 228.6 m³ in the first year of using the equipment, depreciation expense would be:

$$228.6 \text{ m}^3 \times 10.94 = \underline{\$2,500}$$

AN APPLICATION

One common application of the concepts underlying depreciation accounting is: Should I record depreciation during a labor strike? Our response has to be: Depreciation on what? If the depreciation is based on unit-of-activity, and there is no activity, then no depreciation need be expensed. When one of the other depreciation methods is in use, however, we have to be concerned about two factors:

1. the consistency concept, Chapter 8, which calls for consistent application of accounting policies, including a depreciation policy; and

2. the amount of obsolescence built into the depreciation formula.

Obsolescence does not vanish during a strike; therefore, it is necessary to record this obsolescence effect. If the depreciation formula for a company does not split out obsolescence from wear and tear, then consistency would seem to require recording depreciation in full. The reasoning is that *time* has passed during the strike, and the formula is based on the passage of time.

GROUP DEPRECIATION

For a large company that has many assets of a similar nature, e.g., microcomputers, word processors or automobiles, it is easier, from a bookkeeping point of view, if these assets are grouped. The basic idea underlying group depreciation was illustrated for the declining balance method, i.e., gains and losses are *not* recorded on the sale or disposal of an individual asset. For instance, suppose that one of several word processors costing $3,000, with accumulated depreciation of $800, is smashed in an accident. It is not insured and has to be *written-off*, meaning that the asset is credited to reduce it to zero. The journal entry under a group-depreciation application would be:

Accumulated depreciation—word processors	$3,000	
Word processors		$3,000

If only one asset existed, the journal entry would result in a *debit* to accumulated depreciation. But, when other assets exist in the *group*, a debit balance would be unlikely.

The journal entry for a disposal would also not show a gain or loss. Suppose that accumulated depreciation amounts to $950 when we sell for $2,400 one of the word processors costing $3,000.

Cash	$2,400	
Accumulated depreciation—word processor	600	
Word processor		$3,000

Eventually, the word processors may become fully depreciated, i.e., accumulated depreciation equals asset cost. This may occur when we have decided to replace the word processors with a different type of asset, such as microcomputers with word processing. If the word processors had originally cost $30,000 (10 @ $3,000 each), the journal entry to write off the word processors would be:

Accumulated depreciation—word processor	$30,000	
Word processor		$30,000

Just because the accounting ledgers no longer show the existence of a net cost, i.e., cost less accumulated depreciation, of the word processors does not mean that we have stopped using them. For internal control purposes, i.e., to minimize fraud and error, we can keep track of the assets' existence through subsidiary ledger cards, or some similar record.

ARBITRARY ALLOCATIONS

Under GAAP, depreciation and amortization are *allocations* of the original cost of the asset or group of assets. Many similar allocations exist in accounting. For instance, in Chapter 10 we saw that fixed manufacturing overhead may be allocated to several inventory products, such as different tables and chairs.

Some writers, notably Arthur L. Thomas [*The Allocation Problem in Financial Accounting Theory, 1969*, and *The Allocation Problem: Part Two (Sarasota: American Accounting Association, 1974)*] have conducted research into the logic underlying allocations, such as depreciation. Thomas' conclusions are that allocations are "incorrigible", meaning that they are "impossible to verify or falsify". That is, they are arbitrary; and one method of allocation (straight-line) is as arbitrary as another (declining balance).

But, as we have seen, effects on the balance sheet and income statement can be significant by choosing one method instead of another. Financial statements send out general "signals"—that the company is "generally healthy" or "generally in trouble". We cannot dismiss the broad impact that they may have on our thinking. To improve our decision making, we have to ensure that we are getting reliable figures. Yet, Thomas is warning us that we cannot place much faith in allocated figures.

With respect to objectives or purposes of financial accounting, Thomas states "no legitimate purpose for financial accounting that has been advanced to date is furthered by making allocations". [*The Allocation Problem: Part Two (p. 5)*]. This is a strong statement, and has been challenged by some, such as those who are using financial statements to share profits, e.g., partners, to determine bonuses or to compute whether a restrictive covenant is being adhered to. When financial statements are being used for these purposes, it is most important that both the preparer and user know which choice, e.g., straight-line or declining balance, is being used in measurements. There is likely to be less argument when the rules of measurement are set out in advance. This is the challenge for accountants and readers—to anticipate problems and head them off by giving clear accounting-policy statements in contracts and agreements; explain what measurement choices have to be applied consistently.

Notes to financial statements contain accounting policies. (See Appendix 1-A.) When a company tells us that straight-line depreciation is being used, it is helpful in estimating what may happen to accounting income (but *not* funds from operations or cash flow) next year. (Accounting income of next year may, however, bear little relation to the company's common-share price movements.) If a creditor's restrictive covenant is based on net income and retained earnings, then awareness of the policy helps us to form a conclusion about the likely existence of a covenant violation in the next few months or year.

Thomas' research has relevance for several objectives of accounting. For the cash flow prediction objective, depreciation is not relevant because it is *not* a cash flow. Income tax legislation specifies its own rules for claiming depreciation (capital cost allowance). In evaluating management, it probably makes sense to disregard depreciation on the income statement and use our own estimate of usage of the assets. Fortunately, this is easy to do because corporate law requires that depreciation and amortization be set out on a separate line on the financial statements. Unfortunately, however, we may not know about other allocations that have been made, e.g., allocating fixed manufacturing overhead.

Overall, we cannot ignore Thomas' warnings. We can take some steps to minimize any difficulties in interpreting financial statements by learning as much as possible about the methods that are in use and whether they have been applied consistently.

ANOTHER APPLICATION

Canada depends to an important extent on its ability to sell resources to other countries, especially sales of lumber, metals, wheat, natural gas, fish. Accounting for resource companies provides some interesting intellectual challenges because political and economic conditions have major effects on demand for these products.

Suppose that we have been requested to provide financial statements for a new mining company. A prospector found the mine site and was paid $2 million for his discovery. We expect to extract 40,000,000 tonnes of ore from the mine over an eight-year period. The amount of metal that will be recovered from each tonne of ore is expected to vary considerably. We have built a cookhouse, bunkhouses, a maintenance building, an office, and other structures at the mine site, which is in the far northern part of British Columbia, away from main roads and towns.

How would we depreciate the buildings, and amortize the $2 million cost? Before we can answer, we have to find out who is using the financial statements and for what purpose. If the sole use of the financial statements is for income tax purposes, we probably would use whatever method is prescribed by taxation law and regulations. If we had a minimum compliance objective of accounting, however, we could base depreciation and amortization on 40,000,000 tonnes. If we extracted 4,000,000 tonnes of ore in the first year, our journal entry for amortization might be:

Amortization of mineral deposits (expense)	$200,000	
Mineral deposits (asset)		$200,000

Even though the buildings may physically last for more than eight years, we would try to match their cost against the tonnage that is extracted. When all the ore is extracted, the buildings probably are worthless because they are in an isolated region.

A person who is interested in predicting or forecasting cash flows from the mine would ignore our depreciation method and focus on cash flows. The factor that is of greatest significance is the price of the metal that will be recovered from the ore. The financial statements do not tell us this information. Accounting data would be far less important, and would be useful primarily for determining cash production costs per tonne.

Research and Development Costs

In Chapter 8, a reservation was expressed that matching was becoming more and more difficult because companies were making longer-term investments in long-lived assets. During the 1970s, many situations arose where companies were capitalizing research and development expenditures in balance sheet accounts, and amortizing them slowly to expense. One example was expenditures on research for the transportation and space industries. After perhaps two or three years, companies were discovering that no longer was there a market for their products. Yet, they had not yet amortized well over one half of the expenditures that they had made on research or development or both.

GAAP was tightened in Canada at the end of the 1970s for both research and development. Typically, whenever there is a feeling that there have been abuses of judgment, accountants tend to impose one way of accounting. Although this approach may curtail one type of questionable accounting treatment, it can have the effect of making "unlikes look alike".

Broadly speaking, the accounting treatment advocated by the Canadian Institute of Chartered Accountants (CICA), which became GAAP in the 1980s, called for expensing research and development in the period in which it was spent, or incurred. An exception was permitted for some types of development costs that met five demanding criteria—to the effect that a marketable product would be completed and could be sold to a clearly defined market.

The effect of the CICA pronouncement is that research and development could be treated differently from other long-lived "depreciable" assets. We noted that there is no "lower-of-cost or market" rule for long-lived assets—unless a decline of net realizable value below cost is, in effect, permanent. Thus, the asset remains on the balance sheet until strong evidence exists that it is overvalued. In contrast, research and development tends to be expensed, unless strong evidence exists that there is an asset.

Some companies, such as those engaged in new product research—perhaps in the computer field—could be hit hard by the CICA's research and development pronouncement. A balance sheet for them could well understate their potential if some of their expensed development costs have resulted in a marketable product.

Appraisals

The reporting of appraisal values of long-lived assets in financial statements is discouraged under GAAP, but is not ruled out. Suppose that an asset costing $1 million with an accumulated depreciation of $300,000 is appraised (using replacement cost concepts or insurance values) as being worth $1.05 million in its *used* condition. That is, the $1.05 million is 50 percent higher than book value of $700,000 ($1,000,000 less $300,000). The journal entry to record the appraisal would be:

Asset—appraisal increase	$500,000	
Accumulated depreciation appraisal		
increase		$150,000
Appraisal increment		350,000

The "appraisal increment" would appear as a separate line in the owners'-equity section of the balance sheet.

Owners' equity:	
Common shares	1,000,000
Retained earnings	599,999
Appraisal excess on land and buildings	350,000

The $350,000 represents the portion of the $500,000 appraisal increment that reflects the remaining life of the asset (i.e., 70 percent).

	Appraisal	Original Cost	Difference	Percentage
Cost	$1,500,000	$1,000,000	$500,000	100
Accumulated depreciation	450,000	300,000	150,000	30
Net	$1,050,000	$ 700,000	$350,000	70

Canadian GAAP requires that the asset be described on the balance sheet or notes thereto as having been appraised. The amount of any write-up must be provided. Also, GAAP requires that depreciation expense be based on $1.5 million—and *not* on $1 million. Thus, we can record an appraisal under some conditions, i.e., primarily when the company is being reorganized and there is new ownership or facts change dramatically. But, there are consequences, especially to the depreciation expense charge on the income statement.

Replacement Cost

Supplementary financial statements based on replacement cost were briefly described in Chapter 10. When we apply replacement-cost thinking to depreciable assets additional complications arise. For instance, assume that an asset costing $500,000 with a life of two years has a replacement cost *new* as follows:

| | End of first year | $600,000 |
| | End of second year | $700,000 |

The figures would look like this, if replacement cost depreciation is taken on the year *end* balance:

	Cost		Replacement Cost	
Year	Depreciation for year	Accumulated depreciation	Depreciation for year	Accumulated depreciation
1	$250,000	$250,000	$300,000	$300,000
2	250,000	500,000	350,000	650,000

Observe that the $500,000 is $200,000 short of the $700,000 amount needed to replace the asset. This supports the point made earlier in the chapter that depreciation per GAAP is an allocation of original cost. It does not attempt to reduce net book value (cost less accumulated depreciation) to current replacement cost or net realizable value.

Note also that even the $650,000 is $50,000 short of the $700,000 replacement cost. This is because the $300,000 expensed in year 1 is $50,000 short of the $350,000 needed to represent one half of the new replacement cost of $700,000.

It is possible to "cure the problem" of the $50,000 shortage. But the explanation of the alternative methods is too lengthy at this level in financial accounting. Our reasons for mentioning the subject are that replacement-cost accounting has its weak points, as does any measurement system, including financial accounting. We are digging into GAAP in some depth in this book, and exposing its soft spots, because this is the method of accounting used in Canada in most, but not all, situations. When we analyse in depth, it is possible that we may find GAAP wanting. All systems, however, have their deficiencies as well as their strengths. We need information to make decisions; we have to use some measurement system. Therefore, we have to know its strengths and limitations.

Disclosed Basis of Accounting

Replacement cost financial statements can be prepared as *supplements* to GAAP financial statements. That is, both sets of financial statements could appear in the annual reports of companies. As was mentioned in Chapter 10, supplements such as replacement cost may better aid those outside the company who wish to forecast cash flows or evaluate management's overall performance.

There are also situations where a type of special-purpose report may serve readers better than GAAP financial statements. For instance, various appraisals and net realizable values may be useful for potential buyers of a company. When such non-GAAP financial statements are prepared it is important that readers know what system of measurement and accounting policies have been selected. Accounting policies would be described in notes to the financial statements. For example, a note might say that no depreciation has been recorded. Or, it might say that "valuation depreciation" has been recorded, which is the difference between net realizable value at the beginning and end of a year. Another note may describe a particular way of recognizing revenue. Sometimes it is possible to audit "disclosed basis" financial statements; sometimes it is not possible.

Accounting and Audit Relationships

Accounting and its relation to audit has been mentioned from place to place in the book. It seems worthwhile at this point to set forth a formalization of the relationship, per Illustration 11-1.

ILLUSTRATION 11-1

Organizational Objectives, Accounting, and Audit

Objectives, goals, pursuits of the organization

Factors critical to the success and failure of the organization

Objectives of financial accounting (See Chapter 6)

Accounting policies and practices

Financial statements

Audit of statements

Illustration 11-1 emphasizes that objectives of accounting have to be fitted to the goals, objectives, and vulnerabilities of the organization. Organizations can differ widely; therefore, their objectives and accounting policies can differ—and ought to be tailored to the needs of those in positions of power to decide the objectives. Auditors (see Appendix 1-A) audit financial statements that have been prepared by management and the board of directors of a company. In essence, the auditor attests to the belief that the financial statements are "fair per GAAP". The auditor would not choose depreciation policies or have the power to force a client to adopt another policy as long as the client was following a GAAP policy.

Summary

The long-lived asset category includes a variety of assets with quite different accounting treatment. Land, for instance, is not depreciated nor amortized unless there are special circumstances such as its being a gravel pit or an open-pit copper mine. Other long-lived assets such as buildings and equipment can be depreciated in one of several ways. Under GAAP, depreciation is an allocation of original cost and is *not* a valuation process. Research tends to support the viewpoint that allocations are arbitrary and cannot be defended. As a result, we have to be very careful how we interpret financial statements of companies, especially those in which a large percentage of their expenses represent depreciation and amortization, e.g., capital intensive companies such as steel mills.

Intangible assets such as goodwill, and research and development are subject to GAAP *constraints*, in which accounting for them is somewhat rigidly specified. More and more constraints appear as we commence our look into liabilities and owners' equity. Objectives of accounting tend to take on less importance when one, or a few, accounting treatments are specified regardless of objectives and specific facts.

Alternatives to GAAP exist. But, these are usually only seen in special-purpose reports, financial statements prepared for income tax purposes, and in supplementary statements to accompany GAAP. Alternatives to GAAP have particular strengths and limitations, and this chapter has outlined a few of these.

Chapters 10 and 11 continued to focus on interpreting financial statements under different situations. We have to work with interpretation and application as much as possible. One way that we can improve our analysis is by preparing a list of alternative accounting policies. Then we can note the effect of each on the balance sheet and income statement, and on probable interpretations by different users of the statements.

QUESTIONS

11-1 What is meant by the "arbitrariness of depreciation"?

11-2 What are the effects on financial statement *interpretation* when a company is engaged in more than one line of business, or is in two or more different industries?

11-3 What type of assets are "amortized"?

11-4 Illustrate why there can be several definitions of cost, and why cost is difficult to calculate.

11-5 What are land improvements? What is their usual accounting treatment? Why?

11-6 What is a sunk cost? What accounting treatment is given to it if you:

    a. are still using the asset?

    b. are selling or trading in the asset?

11-7 Why are repairs expensed? (Refer to the concepts in Chapter 8.)

11-8 What is the purpose of accounting depreciation? Is it likely that a long-lived asset will be sold for its original cost less accumulated depreciation? Explain.

11-9 Under what circumstances does annuity depreciation make sense?

11-10 For which depreciation methods should we take scrap value into account in setting annual depreciation? Explain.

11-11 Where might unit of production depreciation be sensibly applied? Why?

11-12 What is the purpose of group depreciation? Where may it be sensibly applied?

11-13 Does Canadian GAAP permit appraisal values on financial statements?

11-14 What is meant by a disclosed basis of accounting?

EXERCISES

E11-1 Feltham Corporation (FC) acquired three different assets costing $110,000 each and having an economic life of five years. At the end of five years each asset may be sold for $10,000.

Required:

Compute depreciation expense for each of the first two years of one asset's life, assuming:

1. straight-line depreciation over five years.

2. accelerated or declining balance depreciation at a 30 percent rate.

3. unit-of-production basis depreciation assuming that the asset will produce 50,000 units as follows:

First year	12,000
Second year	11,000
Third year	10,000
Fourth year	9,000
Fifth year	8,000
	50,000 units

E11-2 Stollar Company Limited (SCL) owned a truck costing $120,000 upon which $66,000 of depreciation had accumulated. SCL had been offered $35,000 for the used truck by two different companies. However, it decided to trade-in the truck on a new one that retailed for $165,000. The new truck dealer offered SCL $54,000 as a trade-in on the old vehicle, as long as SCL paid $111,000 in cash to the dealer. SCL agreed to the offer and paid the $111,000.

Required:

Give the journal entry to record the purchase of the new truck. Explain your journal entry.

E11-3 A. Compute the accounting return on average investment for each of years (1), (2) and (3) assuming:

1. an asset is purchased for $5,000 and has a life of three years with zero scrap value.
2. straight line depreciation is applied to each of the three years.
3. the asset generates a cash return (cash revenue less cash expenses to maintain the machine) of $2,189.91 at the *end* of each of the three years.

B. What overall return on investment does the machine generate in the three year period?

E11-4 Amernic Corporation (AC) purchased an asset costing $50,000 and having zero salvage value.

Required:

A. Compute depreciation expense in each of the first *three* years of the asset's life, assuming each of these independent situations:

1. a 30 percent rate of depreciation is applied to the declining asset balance (i.e., accelerated depreciation).
2. same as (1) except that only $4,000 of depreciation expense is recorded in the second year.
3. a 15 percent rate of accelerated depreciation is used in the first year of the asset's life, and a 30 percent accelerated rate is used thereafter.

B. Explain when each of the above situations (1), (2) and (3) might be utilized.

E11-5 Murphy Limited (ML) employs group depreciation methods for its fleet of 60 buses. The buses are depreciated at a rate of 20 percent on a declining balance (or accelerated) basis. At the beginning of 19—9 the ledger accounts for buses showed:

Cost	18,500,000
Accumulated depreciation	6,500,000

During the year, eight new buses were acquired for a total of $3,100,000. In addition, five older buses were sold for a total of $500,000. Their original cost was $1,700,000, and $1,420,000 of depreciation had accumulated to date.

ML records depreciation expense once per year on the last day of the business year.

Required:

Give journal entries to record:

A. the purchase of the new buses in 19—9.

B. the disposal of the five older buses.

C. depreciation expense for 19—9.

E11-6 Estrin Corporation (EC) is being reorganized prior to the admission of more shareholders, and expansion of its operations. The board of directors of EC decided to have the long-lived assets appraised, with the results being recorded in the ledgers.

At the date of appraisal, the ledgers showed the following:

Land		$ 200,000
Buildings and equipment	$2,500,000	
Accumulated depreciation	1,000,000	1,500,000

The appraisers have agreed on a figure of $500,000 for land, and $2,850,000 for the used buildings and equipment.

Required:

Provide journal entries:

A. to record the appraisals.

B. to record depreciation expense for the year.

Explain your journal entries.

E11-7 Archibald Corporation (AC) is considering the use of replacement cost valuations in a special purpose report. Replacement cost will be applied to land and building only.

In recent years, end-of-year replacement cost has been:

	19—5	*19—6*	*19—7*
Land	$ 500,000	$ 550,000	$ 605,000
Building	$6,000,000	$6,600,000	$7,260,000

AC has been recording depreciation at five percent straight-line since it purchased the building at the beginning of 19—5. The cost of the land and building on January 1, 19—5 was: land $500,000 and building $5,500,000.

Required:

A. Compute depreciation expense for each of 19—5, 19—6, and 19—7 on both a cost and a replacement cost basis. Use end-of-year replacement costs in computing annual replacement cost depreciation.

B. Compute accumulated depreciation on a replacement cost basis for each of 19—5, 19—6 and 19—7.

C. Comment upon the adequacy of the accumulated depreciation figure calculated in (B) for the end of 19—7. What does the figure convey to us?

PROBLEMS

P11-1 Ericksen Copper Mine Limited (ECML) decided to mine its northern property. The procedure consists of stripping off copper ore near the surface of the earth, instead of having to sink a shaft and mine underground.

ECML purchased used stripping and mining equipment and ore carriers for $2,600,000. This equipment can be sold at the end of the mining operations for perhaps $200,000. Various buildings had to be constructed at the mine site, at a cost of $650,000. These buildings should have a physical life of at least 20 years, but their salvage value would be zero because they would have to be abandoned at the site.

The mine contains about 1,000,000 tonnes of ore, which is likely to be stripped and sold as follows:

First year	150,000
Second year	300,000
Third year	300,000
Fourth year	150,000
Fifth year	100,000
	1,000,000

Weather conditions may delay the above production schedule. Also, the selling price of copper could increase or decrease, and thereby lead to a speed up or slow down in the production schedule.

Required:

A. Journalize the purchase of the equipment, and the buildings.

B. Compute depreciation expense for the first year and second year, assuming that the above production schedule was maintained.

C. Justify the depreciation methods that you chose in B.

D. What would you do in the third year if the mine were shut down because copper prices were too low?

P11-2 Friedlan Corporation (FC) (100 percent owned by J. Friedlan) acquired some apartment buildings two years ago at the following costs:

Building (1)	$ 6,500,000
(2)	7,900,000
(3)	8,400,000
	$22,800,000

Earlier this year, FC decided to sell building (1) to a new company, Sommers Limited (SL), which is 100 percent owned by the wife of J. Friedlan. The selling price was $19,600,000. At the end of the year SL sold building (1) back to FC for $21,000,000.

Required:

A. Provide the journal entries on the books of each of FC and SL to record the above transactions.

B. How should SL depreciate building (1)? Why?

C. Use the accounting concepts mentioned in Chapter 8 to both support and criticize the accounting treatment that you have given in (A).

D. Why might FC and SL have engaged in this transaction?

P11-3 Bolla Corporation (BC) is engaged in the business of constructing buildings for sale to various investors. Usually BC buys land that contains old buildings, and has to demolish them before a new building can be constructed. The following costs were incurred in 19—8 in constructing a small office building:

Cost of old building and land	$167,500
Cost of demolishing the old building	16,200
Proceeds received on sale of scrap	(2,100)
Construction costs	820,000
Interest on bank loan obtained to finance construction	41,600
Property taxes during construction	4,700
Costs of grass, trees and landscaping	12,900
Advertising incurred in trying to locate a buyer	4,000
Heat, light and power incurred to December 31, 19—8	820
Salaries of persons who are trying to sell the building	6,100
Security guard	2,550

Required:

Use the concepts in Chapters 6, 8 and 11 to provide guidance on how to account for each of the above items. Provide your accounting treatment of *each* item, including a description of the principal accounts that are to be debited or credited.

P11-4 Your company, Sunshine Corporation (SC), just paid $4,000,000 to acquired all of the common shares of Fogg Limited (FL). The assets and liabilities acquired, as a result of buying the common shares of SC, were:

	(in thousands of dollars)	
	Per books of FL	Estimated Replacement Cost
Cash	50	50
Receivables	450	450*
Inventory	900	1,000
Land	400	700
Building and equipment	2,500	2,600**
Accumulated depreciation	600	—
Accounts payable	400	
Bank loan payable	500	
Common shares	1,000	
Retained earnings	1,800	

*Net realizable value; not replacement cost.
**The $2,600,000 is net of accumulated depreciation.

Required:

A. Prepare a balance sheet for FL based on its original costs per its books.

B. Prepare a balance sheet for FL as it would look *if* $4,000,000 had been paid directly to FL to acquire its assets and liabilities (i.e., common shares were $4,000,000 and retained earnings were zero).

C. Compare the two financial statements. What objectives of accounting are being served by each? Why?

P11-5 Siamese Limited (SL) is a multiple division company. It has a large computer facility to service the needs of the departments. New computer hardware and software were recently purchased at a cost of $18,000,000. SL is hopeful that this computer facility will work at peak efficiency for six years or more. However, it believes that advances in technology may render the hardware somewhat inefficient in, perhaps, four years. The computer software may have to be revised every year or two.

The manager of the computer facility is supposed to charge each of the divisions for use of the computers at a sum that is sufficient to cover the $18,000,000 of equipment costs, plus operating expenses. Each division uses the computer, but some divisions may use it five to six times more than other departments. There are peak demand times when the equipment could become overloaded.

Required:

A. Select one or more depreciation policies for computer hardware (i.e., equipment) that would be suitable for financial accounting reports and may also prove useful in charging the various divisions for usage. Explain your reasoning.

B. Would your policy described in (A) also be suitable for computer software costs (i.e., for computer programs)? Why?

 P11-6 Thomas Toys (TT) was recently formed to manufacture and distribute some recent toy inventions of the founder, A. Thomas. Thomas invested a large sum of his own money to commence operations and borrowed about $100,000 from a bank to finance working capital needs.

A special machine, costing $40,000 to build, was needed to make one toy, "The Incorrigible". Thomas doubts if he can ever use that machine again for other toys, although some parts worth about $4,000 can be salvaged at any time over the next four years. Estimated production volumes, selling prices, and out-of-pocket costs (excluding depreciation) for "The Incorrigible" are:

	Production & Sales Volume	Selling Price Per Unit	Out-of-Pocket Production and Selling Costs
Year 1	100,000 units	$3.00	$0.40
2	100,000 units	2.00	0.40
3	100,000 units	1.00	0.40
4	100,000 units	.50	0.40
5	Zero	Zero	Zero

Thomas has been told that he ought to prepare a set of financial statements to attach to his income tax return, and for the banker. He has heard that he ought to consider a depreciation policy or method—especially for the machine which makes "The Incorrigible" toy. He has come to you for advice.

Required:

What detailed advice would you give Thomas on his accounting problem with the machine that makes "The Incorrigible"?

EXPLORATION MATERIALS AND CASES

MC11-1 On January 1, 19—7 Blazouske Co. Ltd. (BCL) was formed to acquire and operate a gold mining property at Red Lake in northwestern Ontario. A geological report on the property revealed that the ore would yield approximately 25 percent gold. The yield could not be exactly determined until the ore was processed. However, based on the geologist's reports the owners estimated that about 250,000 ounces of gold could be extracted from the mine.

Five engineers own BCL. None of the owners has taken an accounting course. The bank, from which they have borrowed substantial funds, has requested that a set of financial statements be prepared in accordance with generally accepted accounting principles. This request has the owners puzzled. They have kept accurate records of cash receipts and disbursements and even prepared a schedule of cash flows for the year. However, they are not sure whether this schedule will satisfy the bank's request.

For this reason they have come to you for advice and provide you with the following schedule:

Schedule of Cash Receipts and Disbursements
For Year Ending 19—7

Cash receipts:		
Sales of common shares		$ 7,500,000
Bank loan (Note 1)		7,500,000
Collections from gold sales		
(10,000 ounces sold at an average price of $200 per ounce)		2,000,000
Total receipts		17,000,000
Cash disbursements:		
Cost of mining properties (Note 2)	$10,000,000	
Building and structures (Note 3)	2,400,000	
Equipment (Note 4)	650,000	
Production costs (Note 5)	2,500,000	
Delivery expenses	75,000	
Administrative expenses	525,000	
Total disbursements		16,150,000
Cash on hand		$ 850,000

Note 1: The bank loan was received on January 1, 19—7. Interest at 12 percent is compounded and payable annually. The first interest payment is due January 1, 19—8.

Note 2: Includes the cost of land, roads, mine shafts, and other costs necessary to bring the property to a point of production.

Note 3: The buildings and structures have a useful life of 15 years.

Note 4: Equipment has a useful life of 5 years and a salvage value of $50,000.

Note 5: All production and operating costs incurred were paid during the year.

BCL's production records for 19—7 show the following breakdown in ounces of gold produced:

Sold, delivered and proceeds collected	10,000	ounces
Sold and delivered but proceeds not collected	20,000	ounces
Extracted and refined but not sold or delivered	10,000	ounces
Total production	40,000	ounces

Discussions with the owners indicate that the mining property is located in an area unsuitable for any alternative use and consequently the property has no residual value after the gold deposits are exhausted. In addition, the buildings and structures cannot be economically dismantled and moved to another location at the end of the mine's life. The owners inform you that the price of gold is determined by world supply and demand and at December 31, 19—7 the price of gold was at $240 per ounce.

Required:

Assume the role of an accounting advisor. What would you recommend? Thoroughly explain which accounting policies and principles the company should adopt.

MC11-2 Brooks Motor Company Limited (BMCL) is a public company that manufactures a number of lines of cars and trucks. Until recently the company had an excellent history of earnings. However, the crunch of inflation and unemployment has had a significant effect on this year's profit.

It is now October 19—9 and Mr. Furd, the president of BMCL, is very concerned. Unfortunately he sees no signs of recovery before December 31, the company's year end. This places him in an extremely embarrassing position because in the company's last annual report to shareholders he indicated that there would be an upturn in profits this year.

Therefore, he instructed his controller, Mr. Gibbins, to review the company's accounting principles and policies to ensure that the company's performance is reported in the best possible light. Upon his review, Mr. Gibbins discovered the following:

1. In February, some of the plant employees were idle. Therefore, the production manager decided to have them construct a small warehouse, to store old parts, behind the plant. The labor and material costs to build the warehouse amounted to $75,000 and $50,000 respectively. Unfortunately, one week after the work was completed one of the walls fell in and the company had to hire a construction company to restore the building for $30,000. All these costs were originally expensed. Since the building has future service value the controller decided to capitalize $155,000 now and depreciate it over 25 years.

2. In May, the plant employees rejected the company's wage offer and went on strike. As a result, the plant was shut down for one month. Depreciation on plant and equipment for May was $250,000. BMCL had originally expensed this amount. However, it did not make sense to the controller that there should be a depreciation charge when the plant and equipment were not used. Therefore he decided to reverse the depreciation charge (i.e., debit accumulated depreciation and credit depreciation expense).

3. In September the company commenced commercial production of a new line of sports cars. While reviewing the costs related to this new line the controller noticed that the design and testing costs had been inadvertently charged to cost

of goods manufactured. While detailed records were not kept for the design and testing of models he estimated that labor (including executive time), materials, and overhead amounted to $1,000,000. He felt these costs should be capitalized and not amortized until the new line begins to make a profit.

Required:

Assume the role of the company's auditor. Discuss the acceptability of the accounting treatment suggested by Mr. Gibbins. What would you recommend?

MC11-3 Carleton Emporium Limited (CEL) is owned by Harold Carleton, who incorporated the company many years ago under federal legislation. CEL's one-store operation is located in the downtown area of a large city. The company has two segments in its business, a "pawn" division and a "second-hand" division. Total sales revenue of both divisions is about $300,000.

The pawn division accepts merchandise from customers who are in need of funds. The customer has a certain number of days to buy the merchandise back from CEL; otherwise, the merchandise is offered for sale. Around 90 percent of the merchandise that is pawned at CEL is not reclaimed, but is transferred to the second-hand division. A customer who claims his/her pawned merchandise pays back the money received from CEL plus a "service charge" that really amounts to interest.

The pawn division is required by law to keep records of all merchandise that it buys (in case some has been stolen). Hence, the division has good inventory records, including serial numbers of some types of merchandise. However, profits of the division are difficult to ascertain because unclaimed merchandise is transferred to the second-hand division at cost (excluding any interest for the period since acquisition).

The second hand division has two types of merchandise: the somewhat more expensive items transferred from the pawn division (e.g., cameras, electronics goods) and inexpensive goods (such as golf clubs, some clothes). The latter are usually acquired in bulk as a result of a death, or when people move a great distance and want to sell nearly all of their belongings for a lump sum. Inventory records are therefore poor because it is hard to allocate costs to a particular item that is part of a bulk purchase.

The inventory turnover (i.e., inventory divided by cost of goods sold) in the second hand division is much higher for the more expensive items, and averages twice per year. The inexpensive items, on average, are in the store for over a year before they are sold. Some goods eventually have to be given to charities to make room in the overcrowded store.

Harold Carleton is nearing retirement and wants to sell the entire company. CEL owns the building in which the store is located. Two floors of apartments are located above the store, and each floor has four two-bedroom apartments that are usually occupied. Some tenants are slow at paying their rent, and a few have to be evicted. Rental revenue is about $50,000 per year.

A bookkeeper friend has always helped Harold prepare his income tax return. CEL has never used GAAP, but the bookkeeper has modified Harold's cash basis system— each division has its own cash register—to whatever Revenue Canada will accept.

The bookkeeper has told Harold that a lawyer would want to see better financial statements, perhaps prepared in accordance with generally accepted accounting principles. Harold has come to you for accounting and related advice.

Required:

Advise Harold.

MC11-4 X-L-N-T Limited (XL) is incorporated under federal corporate legislation and owned by four business persons. The company makes specialized components for the electronics industry. XL has financed its operations through retained earnings, bank loans, and the sale of debentures to life insurance companies. During the current year just ended, June 30, 19—2, the following transactions, among others, occurred:

1. A new sales office was opened in May 19—2. The following costs were incurred in getting the office ready for dealing with customers:

Moving expenses for new staff	$106,900
Rent, heat, light from March 1, 19—2 (the date the lease was signed)	63,600
Advertising the opening of the office	22,000
Hiring and training costs of new employees	69,900
Head office executive salaries—time spent at new office prior to its opening	60,000
Travel costs of above executives	16,440
Office partitions, carpets, paintings, furniture and fixtures	263,400

2. From time to time the company has sold components on the basis that additional revenue would be received if performance exceeded high levels over the shorter of five years or the life of the asset. In April 19—2 $180,000 was received on a contract written in 19—0 for which the component was delivered in February 19—1. Management of XL believes that similar performance bonuses should be received in each of the next four years.

3. One contract was signed in early 19—2 requiring the purchaser to provide a deposit of $1,000,000 by July 15, 19—2. In late April 19—2 the purchaser handed over a face value $1,000,000 90 day Government of Canada Treasury Bill, dated April 15, 19—2 and due 90 days later, to the treasurer of XL. On April 15, 19—2 the Treasury Bill was worth $960,000.

Required:

Assume the role of advisor to XL. What accounting and reporting treatment would you recommend? Why?

CHAPTER 12

Creditors and Liabilities

Chapter Themes

1. Accounting for long term liabilities is similar to accounting for long-term investments. However, under GAAP, one *major* difference does occur. Long-term investments are recorded at *cost*, unless net realizable value is materially lower for "other than a temporary" period of time. Liabilities are recorded at the *face amount* of the obligation, which is what the company eventually must pay the creditor, such as $1,000. Any premium or discount over what the bond is initially issued at, such as $980, is recorded in a separate account—in this case a "discount" ($20). The distinction between the treatment of the asset and the liability is not a trivial one. GAAP accounting tends to take a legalistic or "obligation" approach to liabilities, which means clear disclosure is given of what eventually must be paid, either on the face of the balance sheet, or in the notes to the financial statements. A legalistic approach is also taken toward owners' equity reporting.

2. As a result of the process of attempting to match revenue with expenses, a variety of credits arise that are somewhat difficult to classify. Most accountants loosely refer to them as liabilities, but some are not really obligations to pay in a legalistic sense. Generally speaking, understanding these credits, which relate to leases, pensions, and income taxes is difficult, at first. The explanations may have to be read carefully, and practice problems worked through slowly.

3. The relationship between debt (liabilities) and equity is very important for both liquidity and profitability. The accounting treatment of showing interest as an expense and dividends as a deduction from owners' equity has important implications in financial-statement analysis.

Debt Versus Equity

There have been many instances in recent years where the financial media and others have misunderstood the implications of changing a company's percentage of debt to equity. One example involved Air Canada and CN. Both companies had been showing large losses, mainly because they were paying interest on large sums of debt owing to the Government of Canada. The Government decided "with the stroke of a pen" to convert the debt into common-share equity. Suddenly, both companies were able to show a net income—because interest expense no longer existed.

Several articles appeared in the financial press suggesting that major, almost miraculous, improvements had occurred in both companies, and led to the turnaround from losses to profits. Although some improvements may have occurred, the major change was the disappearance of interest expense on the income statement.

Issuing debt can be attractive for two reasons. The first is that interest expense can be deducted from revenue for income tax purposes. Dividends cannot. Suppose that a company pays 10 percent interest per annum on its debt, and has an income tax rate of approximately 45 percent. The after-tax interest rate is therefore only $5.5 (10-4.5)$ percent. This leads to the second reason. If the funds that were borrowed can be invested to generate 8 percent after income taxes, the difference of $2.5 (8.0-5.5)$ percent flows to the common shareholders. Thus, the common shareholder is able to "lever" or "trade on equity" and increase her/his return on investment.

To illustrate, assume that a company makes an after tax profit of $8,000 on an investment of $100,000, i.e., 8 percent. It then decides to borrow $100,000 at an after income tax rate of 5.5 percent. The next year, the company earns 8 percent after taxes on the $200,000.

Income before interest ($200,000 @ 8%)	$16,000
Interest-after-tax effect ($100,000 @ 5.5%)	5,500
Balance accruing to common shareholders	$10,500

Return on common shareholders' equity:

$$\frac{\$\ 10,500}{100,000} = \underline{\underline{10.5\%}}$$

The existence of debt has increased the shareholders' return on equity to 10.5 percent from 8 percent. The debt therefore enables shareholders to "trade on equity" or "lever" their position.

The $100,000 debt to $100,000 equity is called a debt-to-equity ratio of 1:1. As this ratio increases to, say, 2:1, the debtholders carry two thirds of the risk instead of one half. The prime risk as a debtholder is the loss of $100,000 or $200,000 of principal plus any unpaid interest. To compensate for this additional risk, the debtholders may ask for a higher interest rate, additional collateral security (such as a mortgage on long-lived tangible assets), or tighter restrictive covenants. For instance, maybe "no dividends may be declared unless the debt-to-equity ratio is 1:1 after declaration and payment of the dividend". Perhaps the debtholders will refuse to lend above a 1:1 ratio. There are limits to how far debtholders will allow leverage.

Creditor Viewpoint

The main reason why interest rates can be lower than equity rates is that the creditor or debtholder often has a prior claim on the assets in the event of bankruptcy. (Chapter 5 outlines the different categories of creditors.) A secured creditor, for instance, could have a first mortgage on the company's building. If payments on the mortgage are not made for a few months, the property can be seized by the debtholder and sold at a public auction.

A creditor tries to vary a number of factors when a loan is being negotiated. Some of these are:

1. Interest rate to be charged;

2. When repayments of the principal and interest are to be made;

3. The amount and nature of collateral to be provided by the borrower;

4. The nature and type of any restrictive covenants that are required. For instance, a covenant may state that no more long-term debt may be issued until certain debt to equity ratios exist; and

5. The amount that will be loaned, given the collateral position of the borrower and any prior obligations that it has to repay debt.

A borrower will try to convince the lender to provide as much money as is feasible at a low interest rate with as little collateral as possible. A special purpose report showing expected cash flows may be assembled to try to convince the lender that the loan can be repaid. General-purpose financial statements may also be useful to the lender in helping to support the general assumptions about cash-and-funds flow that the special-purpose report contains.

The general-purpose report may or may not be audited. If the borrower is a small company, and does not already have audited financial statements, most lenders will not ask for an audit, unless the financial statements lack credibility. (They do not want the borrower to incur the cost and use up time needed to complete the audit.) Generally, the lender wants to learn the following from financial statements:

1. the type of assets the borrower owns or uses (*not* their valuation, because GAAP has limitations), and their availability as collateral;

2. the liabilities that exist and their likely effect on repayment of the contemplated loan; and

3. the funds from operations or cash flows that the company has generated recently.

Some lenders may hope that the financial statements will divulge more than is possible. As we have seen in the previous few chapters, there is considerable freedom in GAAP to tailor accounting to fit the situation, according to objectives, facts and constraints.

Debt Instruments and Their Significance

A company needs a solid base of owners' capital (common shares), or some other collateral, if it hopes to attract many creditors. Owners of small businesses typically have to pledge their personal assets, e.g., house and car, as collateral when they deal with commercial banks. Somewhat larger businesses try to rely on the amount of their common-share investment to attract creditors.

It is not possible to give some easy rule-of-thumb recommendation about the ratio of debt to equity that makes sense for all businesses. Much depends on the riskiness of the business, especially as it affects swings in earnings. A construction company, for example, is subject to wide variation in earnings because activity tends to be dependent on the state of the economy. Long-term creditors usually are not attracted to small and medium-sized construction companies because the risk of loss of their capital is too great when construction activity is slow for a period of three or more years. In contrast, for regulated utility companies, the risk of loss for a creditor tends to be negligible. A specified return on investment tends to be assured for regulated utilities because a utility board calculates and approves whatever revenue figure is needed to approximate the allowed return.

"Income" allowed ($100,000,000 x 12%)	$12,000,000
Add expected expenses	60,000,000
Needed revenue	$72,000,000

In the above example, the utility board would agree first to the capital ($100 million) that is required to operate the telephone or electricity utility. Then the board assesses the overall return on investment that seems to make sense—in this case, 12%. The so-called "income" (*not* accounting income) of $12 million would result. By adding the expected expenses of $60 million, we can arrive at $72 million of needed revenue. The number of customers are divided into $72 million and a cost per customer or customer/service is determined. The utility then informs each customer what her/his telephone or electricity charge per month, or per kilowatt hour, will be. The $12 million (or what actually happens a year later) is then allocated to creditors and shareholders. The creditors receive whatever interest rate is specified on their bonds. The shareholders receive the remainder.

It is also difficult to give easy rules-of-thumb about the percentage of debt that should be in current and in long-term categories. A bank or trust company has to be especially careful in matching the maturities of its assets and liabilities. It does not want to become illiquid and risk failure. If the trust company is able to have somebody purchase one of its five (or ten) year investment certificates, it can then lend the money for five (or ten) years on a mortgage. (This explains why trust companies are unwilling to cash a five-year investment certificate after we have held it for only one year. They cannot ask the person who received the mortgage money to pay it back after one year.)

Whenever possible, we try to ascertain what our so-called "permanent investment" is in long-lived assets *and working capital*. (That is, accounts receivable and inventory tend to be permanent assets *in total*, even though they are turning over on a current basis.) We would then try to finance these permanent assets through long-term debt or equity.

Short-term borrowings (often from a bank) are useful for financing cyclical or seasonal needs. A fish canner, for instance, needs large sums of money during the fishing season to buy and process the fish. As the fish is sold over, say, the fall and winter, the bank loan would be repaid. Banks usually ask the borrower to sign a note payable. Security for the loan tends to be accounts receivable and whatever else may be available as collateral.

Longer-term borrowings may take several different forms: (1) mortgage payable, (2) agreement for sale or other deferred payment plan, (3) bonds or debenture payable, (4) term loans from an industrial finance company or government agency, (5) debt that may be converted into equity, and (6) some combination of these. The mortgage payable and agreement for sale categories tend to be situations where the debt is secured only by a particular piece of real property (land, building) or a chattel, i.e., a movable item such as furniture or an automobile. The lender usually does not seek out the company's general-purpose financial statements. Hence, we need not be concerned about this category of lender becoming a powerful group that can demand additional or special reporting.

Lenders who choose to provide money under term loans, or bonds payable, or a similar debt instrument can be in a position of power. That is, if we do not provide them with what they seek, we may not receive the money. Or, we may receive it under tougher restrictions and at a higher interest rate. These groups can bring about a change in the objectives of financial accounting and reporting. For instance, they may want some demanding restrictive covenants before they provide the funds. Accounting policies may have to be spelled out clearly, so that the covenant can be calculated in a particular way.

For accounting purposes, it is important to distinguish between a *public offering* and a *private placement*. If we own all of the common shares, and have borrowed only under a private placement, our company is *private*. This means that we do *not* have to comply with provincial securities legislation. Private placements are usually arranged through brokers, or with insurance companies that are looking for places to invest policyholders' premiums that are in excess of current needs.

When a company borrows money from the public, through a bond issue, or sells them shares, the company is *public*. The buyers have to be given a *prospectus*, which is a document that has a description of the company, and contains the most recent five-years' income statements, retained earnings statements, and statements of changes in financial position. (The last item is discussed in a later chapter.) The prospectus also contains balance sheets for the most recent two years. These statements have to be prepared in accordance with the CICA Handbook. For some assets and liabilities this requirement becomes a tough constraint. However, the CICA Handbook is silent on many issues, and therefore does not become a constraint for these items. The degree of constraint is a function of the type of assets and liabilities that the company has, and the transactions that it enters into.

In summary, the existence of debt may or may not have an effect on financial-accounting policies and objectives of financial statements. Mortgage lenders, for instance, primarily focus their attention on the worth of the collateral that they receive. Lenders under a private placement may request special-purpose reports and some restrictive covenants. Public offerings are expensive, and may impose tougher constraints than for the other liabilities mentioned. The existence of public debt may have an effect on objectives of financial accounting and reporting. Overall, therefore, we have to assess the situation that we face, and account in accordance with the specific situation. We *cannot* assume that the existence of debt automatically gives the debtholder power to choose objectives of accounting. (See Chapter 6.)

Journal Entries

A. Demand Loans

When we obtain a bank loan, the banker will ask us to sign a note, payable to the bank. The journal entry on our books will be:

Cash	10,000	
Note payable		10,000

The note may be payable "on demand", or it may be a term loan lasting for a short period. The word "demand" means that the bank can ask for the money at any time, although the banks tend to exercise this right only when interest and required payments on the loan have not been made for a few months. That is, although the loan is payable on demand, the understanding between us and the bank may be to pay the principal over a two-year period. Interest probably is payable monthly:

| Interest expense | 100 | |
| Cash | | 100 |

When lump sum payments of principal are made, the entry is:

| Note payable | 1,000 | |
| Cash | | 1,000 |

The bank records our payment of the principal; we do *not* have to sign a new note for the remainder of $9,000 ($10,000 original loan less $1,000 payment).

B. *Mortgages*

Mortgages on our house, condominium, factory or office building and similar real property can be obtained from many sources. A "first mortgage" means that this lender has the first claim against the asset, in the event that it has to be seized, owing to non-payment of the monthly mortgage installment. There may be second, third or fourth mortgages on property if the lender feels secure in being behind others. For instance, land and building may be appraised at $800,000 and have the following mortgages registered against it:

First mortgage	@ 10% interest	$450,000
Second mortgage	@ 15% interest	200,000
Third mortgage	@ 24% interest	100,000
		$750,000

The holder of the third mortgage hopes that the property value does not drop below $750,000 and that the borrower continues to make monthly payments. If the borrower cannot make payments and the building is sold for only $710,000, after disposal costs, the holder of the *third* mortgage loses $40,000 ($750,000-$710,000). That is why the interest on the third mortgage is shown at 24 percent in the illustration, versus the 10 percent on the relatively secure first mortgage.

Mortgage payments tend to be a *blend* of principal and interest. That is, mortgage formulas and tables (or computer programs) exist to calculate what amount paid monthly will reduce the principal balance to zero after, say, twenty-five years. The twenty-five years is called an amortization period. The mortgage itself may be due in five years, which means that we have to pay the remaining principal balance at that time, or negotiate a new mortgage. In the 1980s, interest rates have fluctuated widely, and lenders often have not been willing to have lengthy due dates on most mortgages.

When payments are made on a mortgage, the sum is recorded this way:

Mortgage payable	52.10	
Interest expense	647.90	
Cash		700.00

As each month goes by, and we are able to reduce the principal balance, less interest expense is due and a greater portion of principal is paid:

Mortgage payable	170.60	
Interest expense	529.40	
Cash		700.00

C. Bonds Payable

Bonds have a face value, e.g., $1,000, and a coupon rate, e.g., 10 percent. The interest rate may be decided by the issuer of the bond to be a round, convenient figure. On the date that the bonds are to be sold, the interest rate that is prevailing in the market place for our company may be more or less than 10 percent. Thus, bonds payable are often issued at a premium or a discount.

A bond issued for its *face value* would be recorded as:

Cash	960,000	
Financing costs	40,000	
Bonds payable		1,000,000

The $40,000 may be lawyers' fees, cost of printing, and sales commissions. They would be amortized over the life of the bonds, which may be ten or twenty or twenty-five years. The amortization may be on a straight-line or yield basis, which is briefly described later.

A bond that is issued at a *discount* would be recorded as:

Cash	940,000	
Discount on bonds payable	20,000	
Financing costs	40,000	
Bonds payable		1,000,000

The discount could be handled like the financing costs, and would be amortized over the life of the bonds.

A bond that is issued at a premium would be recorded as:

Cash	975,000	
Financing costs	40,000	
Bonds payable		1,000,000
Premium on bonds payable		15,000

The premium and financing costs would be amortized over the life of the bonds, usually on a straight-line or yield basis.

Observe that original or initial sale of the bonds at a premium or discount changes the yield (or return on investment) that the buyer receives, and company pays. A bond bought for $98, which has a face value of $100, yields more than the 10 percent rate. This is because we receive the 10 percent interest payment plus $2 ($100 − $98) when the bond matures after ten or so years.

Balance-sheet presentation of discounts and premiums on bonds payable can vary. Occasionally, a net figure of $980,000 ($1,000,000 − $20,000) may be shown on the face of the balance sheet, with details provided in the notes to the financial statements. Usually, the balance-sheet presentation would be:

Bonds payable	1,000,000
Less discount on issuance	20,000
	980,000

or,

Bonds payable, less discount on issuance of $20,000	980,000

Bonds payable may be issued between interest dates; this slightly complicates the journal entries. For instance, bond interest may be paid semi-annually (March 1 and September 1) on the $1 million of 10 percent bonds. However, the bonds may not be sold until April 1. When this happens, the buyer would have to pay accrued interest of one month—say $8,333. If the bonds are sold at a discount ($98 on a face of $100) on April 1, the journal entry would be:

Cash	948,333	
Financing costs	40,000	
Discount on bonds payable	20,000	
Bonds payable		1,000,000
Interest expense		8,333

The credit balance in the interest expense account is eliminated on September 1, when the first interest payment is made.

Interest expense	50,000	
Cash		50,000

The debit balance in the interest expense account is now $41,667, which represents five-months' interest at 10 percent on $1 million.

Income Tax Effects

To this point in the book, we have tended to ignore income taxes. Unfortunately, income tax effects are nearly always *material* in their impact on profit-seeking enterprises. Major changes in income tax legislation have occurred in Canada in the 1970s and 1980s, as governments have struggled with the problem of large annual *deficits* (government expenditure less taxation revenue). Changes in legislation have been frequent as various ministers of finance have used the annual (or more frequent) budget to implement social change. Taxation is a very complex subject, and only brief comments can be made about its effects on financial accounting. But, we must *always* bear in mind that, in business, we do *not make any financial decisions* until we check the income and other *tax* cost and *implications*.

The word "deficit" seems to appear in the newspapers every day. Yet, few understand how it is really calculated. It is *not* calculated in accordance with GAAP. The joke is that "the federal deficit is calculated in accordance with accounting policies that are generally accepted by federal governments in Canada". Although the accounting policies change from time to time, the following broad thrust has applied to the computation of the annual deficit over the past ten to fifteen years:

1. Long-lived *assets* are "expensed" down to $1, i.e., all government buildings and similar investments, except those in government-owned Crown Corporations, are carried on the balance sheet at $1.

2. Except for minor accruals (say, due within thirty days), cash-basis accounting is employed for receivables and payables, e.g., taxation revenue is not accrued as a receivable.

3. Some loans to countries that have received "foreign aid" are shown as assets, even though there is little chance that they will be repaid. Even if they were repaid in forty or fifty years, their present value would be very small.

4. Natural resources, such as mineral rights in parks and government-owned land, are not shown as assets.

5. Investments in the education and health of Canadian citizens are not shown as assets.

6. Pensions to be granted to government employees are not really accrued as full expenses during the working life of the employee.

As a result of the foregoing policies, we cannot think of the government deficit in the same way that we would regard a net loss for a private corporation. Large "investments" in buildings, education, and health care are expensed by the Canadian government as though they would have no future benefit. Similarly, some items recorded as assets, e.g., aid to developing countries, would tend to be expensed under GAAP.

Are the federal government's accounting policies "wrong"? Wrong for what purpose? Most of the government's deficit is financed by issuing debt. One major, annual expenditure of the government would therefore be interest expense. Would creditors be interested in seeing financial statements, or are they more interested in other factors, such as the health of the Canadian economy? Let us consider who may use the government's financial statements.

Suppose that a $200 million government building complex constructed in 19—7 was financed entirely by twenty-five-year bonds bearing a 10 percent interest rate. Suppose, also, that the estimated useful life of the complex is forty years, and the $200 million does not include the cost of land. Under GAAP, two expenses would appear on an income statement for the first twenty-five years:

Interest expense	$20,000,000
Depreciation—assume straight-line with zero salvage value in 40 years	5,000,000

The depreciation expense reflects the *consumption of the capital asset.*

However, under federal government accounting the $5 million depreciation expense would not appear because the capitalized asset cost would be $1. The $200 million was *previously expensed;* and, $200 million was borrowed to finance the asset. The annual cash-effect of the building complex appears as interest expense. There is no annual capital-consumption expense. At the end of twenty-five years, the government would have to borrow again to repay the $200 million due at that time.

Which set of financial statements is closer to cash flow? It is the government's statements because their annual statement of receipts and expenditure shows the "expense" of $200 million when cash is needed to finance purchase of the asset. Which financial statement attempts to attach revenue and expenditures to particular years? GAAP clearly is preferable for annual matching.

Once again, we cannot give a recommendation about which method of accounting—Canadian federal government or GAAP—ought to be used for all situations. People who lend money to governments evaluate risk by looking into the government's ability to tax the people, and thereby repay whatever the government borrows. Are the people healthy? Are they educated enough to sell their products in a world market? What natural resources does the country have? What is the inflation rate and any effects of employment—and, therefore, the amount of tax that will be collected? GAAP financial statements, and depreciation accounting, would not help to answer the lender's/creditor's questions.

In contrast, lenders to companies may look more to accounting-related factors. They may investigate the assets of the enterprise as a clue in estimating future cash flows. Sometimes, the current years' funds from operations figures can assist lenders in forecasting cash flows. Replacement cost depreciation may indicate what asset or capital is currently being consumed, and may have to be replaced in the near future—thereby requiring a cash outflow. Company expenditures on capital assets might be more susceptible to being predicted than are those of governments, which are often influenced by political considerations.

This need to tailor accounting policies and practices to each specific situation is what makes accounting challenging and rewarding. The more we understand about people and how they make decisions, the easier it is to find a satisfactory accounting solution to complex problems.

GENERAL PURPOSE REPORTS vs. INCOME TAX RETURNS

Income-tax legislation and administrative practices are designed with several goals in mind. The federal minister of finance may want to decrease unemployment, decrease inflation, stimulate economic activity in certain regions of the country or work toward other objectives. To accomplish these objectives, different tax regulations apply in different situations. It is not surprising, therefore, that we find some important differences between GAAP accounting policies and the methods that have to be used for purposes of computing taxable income. The objectives of accounting mentioned in Chapter 6 are not fully compatible with the objectives of taxation policy.

Differences between GAAP and accounting policies acceptable for income tax purposes fall into two categories: (a) permanent differences and (b) timing differences. *Permanent* differences, as the name suggests, are situations where GAAP accounting requires a particular treatment, and taxation "rules" handle it in an entirely different way. This results in a permanent difference between long-term taxable income and GAAP income. For example, a company may pay an illegal bribe to a foreign official, and expense it. But for purposes of computing taxable income the bribe would not be allowed as an expense.

Timing differences are situations where a difference between taxable income and accounting income in one particular year will eventually reverse itself. The difference arises because financial statements are prepared annually or quarterly, and not for the life of the asset. For instance, the general-purpose financial statements may be based on straight-line depreciation whereas for income tax purposes declining balance depreciation is used. Eventually, the amount of cost less scrap value will be expensed for both purposes; although in any particular year, the amount of expense may differ between GAAP and taxable income. Another example of a timing difference occurs with warranties. Under GAAP accounting, an accrual entry may be made in an attempt to match revenue with expense:

| Warranty expense | xxx | |
| Estimated liability for warranty | | xxx |

However, for income tax purposes the expense would not be deductible until (a) the cash was spent to repair defective products, or (b) repairs had been made, and cash payment would follow shortly.

Accounting for timing differences is somewhat difficult, and a review of Chapter 5 may be useful, to focus on differences between cash and accrual accounting. After all, that is all we really have to watch out for in the next few pages—cash versus accrual accounting.

TAX ALLOCATION FOR TIMING DIFFERENCES

Suppose that our company has an income *before* depreciation expense and income tax expense of $30,000 in each of 19—1 and 19—2. Suppose also that it purchased an asset costing $25,000 at the beginning of 19—1. At the date of purchase, the asset was thought to have a life of two years with zero scrap value. Straight-line depreciation was selected. For income tax purposes, let us assume that the entire $25,000 could be claimed as capital cost allowance in 19—1. For simplicity, we will use an income tax rate of 40 percent.

The *income tax form* that our company would file in 19—1 and 19—2 would show:

	19—1	19—2
Income before depreciation and income tax	$30,000	$30,000
Capital cost allowance claimed	25,000	—
Taxable income	$ 5,000	$30,000
Tax @ 40%	$ 2,000	$12,000

(Note that this is *not* an income statement. It is a calculation of taxable income.)

The $2,000 and the $12,000 represent *cash outflows*. We have to keep this in mind *at all times* as we proceed.

If the company prepared income statements for 19—1 and 19—2 using the *cash basis of accounting for* income taxes, the figures would be:

	19—1	19—2	Total
Income before depreciation expense and income tax	$30,000	$30,000	$60,000
Depreciation expense	12,500	12,500	25,000
	17,500	17,500	35,000
Income tax expense	2,000	12,000	14,000
Net income	$15,500	$ 5,500	$21,000

That is, in spite of the fact that $30,000 of income before depreciation and income taxes arose in each of the two years, net income varied from $15,500 to $5,500. In the foregoing *income statements*, it is important to note that depreciation expense, not capital-cost allowance, is used.

Which objectives of accounting would be served by the foregoing income statement? Shareholders of small companies who share profits equally, or those employees who are being paid a bonus based on a percentage of net income, would be happy in 19—1 and upset in 19—2. Those outsiders who are trying to evaluate management may be misled by 19—1's results, and think that the same figures ought to appear in 19—2. Those who are trying to forecast cash flows or funds from operations using 19—1's results probably would use the $30,000 figure (to avoid non-cash depreciation and variable tax effects), and therefore may not care what happens below the $30,000 line.

In view of the belief that *some* users of financial statements may be misled by the *cash-basis* income tax expense figure, GAAP in Canada now calls for "accrual" accounting for income taxes. Quite possibly over the past thirty years, GAAP accounting for timing differences has been changed more than for any other accounting transaction. Accounting for timing differences are likely to undergo more changes, because the topic continues to be controversial. Also, it is not understood by many people.

Accrual accounting for timing differences departs from the cash flow approach by making a journal entry to accrue the tax effect in the amount of timing difference. For example, in 19—1 the amount of the timing difference is:

Capital-cost allowance claimed in 19—1	$25,000
Depreciation expense charged in 19—1	12,500
Timing difference (excess of capital-cost allowance)	$12,500
Tax effect @ 40%	$ 5,000

Accountants therefore make this additional accrual journal entry in 19—1:

Income tax expense	5,000	
Deferred (or accrued) income tax		5,000

It is *very important* to note that this is a *non-cash* journal entry made to measure *accounting* income.

In 19—2 the timing difference reverses itself in our example:

Depreciation expense charged in 19—2	$12,500
Capital cost allowance claimed in 19—2	—
Timing difference (excess of depreciation)	$12,500

As the timing difference is in the opposite direction, the journal entry is the opposite to 19—1. In 19—2 it is:

Deferred (or accrued) income tax	5,000	
Income tax expense		5,000

Under GAAP accrual accounting, the *income statements* would now appear as:

	19—1	19—2	Total
Income before depreciation			
expense and income tax	$30,000	$30,000	$60,000
Depreciation expense	12,500	12,500	25,000
	17,500	17,500	35,000
Income tax expense:			
Cash portion	2,000	12,000	14,000
Accrual or non-cash portion	5,000	(5,000)	—
	7,000	7,000	14,000
Net income	$10,500	$10,500	$21,000

Notice that the net incomes are the *same* in both years. This occurs because a tax effect is calculated on the timing difference. That is, it is *assumed* that tax is payable on accounting income, using straight-line depreciation. Since tax actually is payable on taxable income, and *not* on accounting income, the deferred/accrued journal entry is *artificial*. The non-cash entry has the effect of smoothing out swings in net income, which arise when tax legislation prescribes an accounting treatment different to GAAP. It is these swings in net income (as per our illustration) that accountants in Canada fear will be misinterpreted.

TAX ALLOCATION ASSESSED

We should remember Thomas' warning about the arbitrary nature of allocations. On the other hand, it is important to identify the needs of particular users of financial statements, e.g., persons who have to use the net income to share profits, pay bonuses, compute restrictive covenants, or who may in part be basing purchase/sale price of a business on accounting income. In addition, we have to think about the effect on the balance sheet.

If we did *not* record the deferral/accrual non-cash journal entry at the end of the first year (in our previous illustration), the balance sheet would show:

Asset, at cost	$25,000
Accumulated depreciation	12,500
Net	$12,500

This would tend to indicate that one half of the asset's life remained. (We could have a note to the financial statements saying that the balance sheet did not tell the whole story, although we are not sure how effective this would be.) *But, does one half remain?*

Once we allow income tax effects to enter into how we think about accounting, some fundamental re-alignment of how we view accounting has to occur. For example, with long-lived depreciable assets, we have to think in terms of its two parts:

Tax effect 40% (assumed tax rate) x $25,000 cost	=	$10,000
Our remainder ($25,000 – $10,000)		15,000
		$25,000

That is, we have a "partner" (the taxation authorities) who will give us back $10,000 as we claim capital-cost allowance. (On a present value basis, the $10,000 would be worth much less.)

When we view the situation on this "partnership" basis, what do we actually have *remaining* at the end of the first year?

	Remaining
Tax effect (is now all used up)	$ 0
Our remainder (one half used of $15,000)	7,500
Net	$7,500

Notice that when we compare the two "net" figures ($12,500 and $7,500), we arrive at the difference of $5,000, which is the income tax effect of the timing difference in the first year ($25,000 – $12,500) times 40 percent tax rate. *If* we used the "partner" approach in our balance sheet presentation, the figures would look like this at the end of the first year:

Asset, at cost		$25,000
Less: Accumulated depreciation	$12,500	
Tax benefit used	5,000	17,500
		7,500
OR, like this:		
Asset, at cost		$25,000
Less accumulated depreciation		12,500
Remainder		12,500
Less tax benefit already used on the remainder		5,000
		7,500

Some Canadian accountants believe that the foregoing two presentations on the balance sheet are awkward. They therefore have elected to follow this type of presentation:

Assets			Liabilities and Owners' Equity	
Current:			Current liabilities:	
Long-lived:			Deferred (or accrued)	
Asset, at cost	$25,000		income tax	$5,000*
Accumulated				
depreciation	12,500	12,500		

*In our example, this would be a current liability; but generally, reversal of timing differences may not occur for several years, and are therefore classified as non-current.

The net effect of $7,500 is the same. When the figures of $12,500 and $5,000 are separated, we have to remind ourselves to put the two together, which is possible when there is only one major timing difference. But when several timing differences exist it is difficult to ascertain what they belong to (depreciation, warranties or other differences). Yet, we know that at some time the differences will reverse.

This point about *when* the timing differences will reverse lies at the heart of a major controversy about tax allocation. One group believes that the reversal is usually many years away. Therefore, they do not want to record the tax effect of timing differences that are "unlikely" to reverse within three or so years. A second group states that accrual/deferral of the tax effect of the timing differences must be journalized because it is uncertain when the reversals might occur. (Over the past thirty years, this group has constituted the majority.) A third group wants to discount the effect of the reversal, and record only the discounted figure. For example, we noted in our illustration that our government partners "owned", so to speak, $10,000 of the $25,000 asset. In actuality, when 100 percent capital cost is not permitted as an expense in the first year, their share on a discounted basis would be much less than $10,000. This is because the capital cost allowance would have to be claimed over several years. The longer the period over which capital cost has to be claimed, and the higher the interest rate, the less is the present value.

When one method of accounting is chosen from three or more alternatives (all of which may have merit in a particular situation), controversy will continue to exist. What seems to lie at the base of the controversy is both *facts*, using our terminology, and *objectives* of accounting. When are the reversals likely to occur (fact/assumption)? Who is using the financial statements, and for which decisions (objectives)?

A PRACTICE PROBLEM

Suppose that a company had the following results and transactions in recent years:

	19—5	19—6	19—7
Income before depreciation and income tax expense	$100,000	$ 5,000	$200,000
Depreciation expense	30,000	30,000	30,000
Capital cost allowance	70,000	5,000	65,000
Income tax rate = 40%			

Required:

Give the journal entries in 19—5, 19—6, and 19—7 to record income tax effects.
The journal entries would be:

19—5:

Tax payable or credit to cash re tax:
$100,000 – $70,000 = $30,000 x 40% = <u>$12,000</u> Cr.

Timing difference: (Capital cost allowance
exceeds depreciation)
$70,000 – $30,000 = $40,000 x 40% = <u>$16,000</u> Cr.

Tax expense based on accounting income:
$100,000 – $30,000 = $70,000 x 40% = <u>$28,000</u> Dr.

Tax expense	28,000	
Cash		12,000
Deferred/accrued tax		16,000

The journal entry may be split into a cash and a non-cash portion:

A. Cash portion:

Tax expense	12,000	
Cash		12,000

B. Non-cash portion:

Tax expense	16,000	
Deferred/accrued tax		16,000

19—6:

Tax payable or credit to cash re tax:
$5,000 – $5,000 capital cost allowance = $ 0
Timing difference (Depreciation exceeds
capital cost allowance; therefore, the
amount is a debit):
$30,000 – $5,000 = $25,000 @ 40% = <u>10,000</u> Dr.

Tax expense: $30,000 – $5,000 = $25,000
@ 40% = <u>10,000</u> Cr.

Deferred/accrued tax (balance sheet)	10,000	
Income tax recovery (income statement)		10,000

Note that we are *crediting* the income statement for a tax recovery:

Income before depreciation and tax recovery	5,000
Depreciation expense	30,000
Loss before tax recovery	25,000
Income tax recovered (Note x)	10,000
Net loss	$15,000

(Note x could provide additional details.)

On the balance sheet, the "deferred/accrued tax" account would have a credit balance of $6,000 ($16,000 credit less $10,000 debit) at the end of 19—6.

19—7:

Tax payable or credit to cash re tax:
$200,000 – $65,000 = $135,000 @ 40% $54,000 Cr.

Timing difference (Capital cost allowance
exceeds depreciation expense; therefore, the
amount is a credit): $65,000 – $30,000 =
$35,000 @ 40%   = $14,000 Cr.

Tax expense: $200,000 – $30,000 = $170,000
@ 40%   = $68,000 Dr.

Income tax expense	68,000	
Income tax payable		54,000
Deferred/accrued tax		14,000

TAX-ALLOCATION TERMINOLOGY

Earlier in the book, we mentioned that GAAP differs from country to country. The foregoing journal entries use the term deferred/accrued tax because some countries use the deferral method, others use the accrual method, and still others use a combination of the two. The *accrual* method attempts to show the liability that is due in a legalistic sense. That is, if the tax rate increased from 40 percent to 50 percent, the accrual method would increase the credit to the current tax rate. The debit would go to the income statement. In contrast, the *deferred* method leaves the credit at the tax rate that existed in the year that the credit was made, e.g. 40 percent.

Canada has been moving toward the accrual method. In the 1950s, it adopted the deferral method for all situations. In the 1970s, the accrual method, in effect, was adopted for particular types of losses. Further changes are expected.

Politicians have used tax allocation, whenever it has suited their convenience. Some call deferred/accrued tax an "unpaid tax". (One political party referred to companies having deferred income taxes as "corporate welfare bums".) Given this situation, it is worth stressing that deferred/accrued tax arises from a *non-cash bookkeeping journal entry*. A company that does *not* follow GAAP (but uses the cash basis), and one that *does* follow GAAP (and sets up the deferral/accrual) could have *exactly the same* cash flow for income taxes. That is, both may claim maximum capital cost allowance.

The political issue is the adequacy of the capital cost allowance. If the rates are too generous, companies could postpone paying income tax by always claiming the maximum capital cost expense allowable under the law. Unfortunately, over the years, governments have frequently changed rates for some capital cost allowance categories in order to stimulate or delay new investment in capital assets. For example, at times rapid expensing has been allowed for buying pollution equipment or for building in certain high-unemployment regions.

Leases

Suppose that we are financial analysts for a life insurance company and are responsible for recommending companies in which the insurance company may invest dollars placed with it by policy holders. We look at the balance sheets of two companies and note:

		(in $ thousands)	
		R Limited	S Limited
Current assets		$20,000	$20,000
Long-lived:			
Land	$ 2,000		—
Buildings	5,000		—
Equipment	6,000		—
	13,000		
Accumulated depreciation	3,000	10,000	—
		$30,000	$20,000
Current liabilities		$ 3,500	$ 3,500
Deferred income tax		1,000	—
Mortgage payable		5,500	—
		10,000	3,500
Owner's equity:			
Common shares		12,000	10,000
Retained earnings		8,000	6,500
		20,000	16,500
		$30,000	$20,000

Here are some thoughts that ought to occur to us. Which company would be the *safest* investment for our insurance company employer? S Limited does not have any debt. Therefore, in the event of a downturn in the economy, and a decrease in S Limited's net income, the insurance company would have greater equity protection to cushion possible losses in this company. Or, would it?

Can we also assume that S Limited has fewer cash obligations? That is, would we be safe in assuming that interest does not have to be paid, and cash repayments of the principal amount of debt are not needed? Yes, we would, but there may be other cash obligations, and more to the story.

What business are the companies engaged in? Suppose that both are in manufacturing, which requires equipment, buildings, land, and similar assets. If so, where are these on S Limited's financial statements? We have to assume that they are being rented or leased. If so, is S Limited still the better investment choice? It does not have any long-lived assets that could serve as collateral for long-term debt. (However, much of R Limited's long-lived assets are mortgaged, and we may not want a cumbersome chattel mortgage on movable equipment, or a second mortgage on buildings.) Maybe the companies would buy new assets that could be assigned as collateral, however, if they obtained a loan from our employer.

We are making progress, but we have not arrived at a supported recommendation. Collateral is not the only point that a creditor has to consider. Does the cash flow exist to enable the companies to pay interest and repay principal? (We may look at *R* Limited's balance sheet and notes thereto to ascertain the interest rate and repayment date.) Where do we learn about the cash obligation for any leased-asset contracts?

At one time, GAAP in Canada did not require any worthwhile disclosure of lease obligations. Then, GAAP called for disclosure of lease payments due in the next five years. Next, GAAP called for (1) disclosure of required lease payments over a longer future term, *and* (2) capitalization (debit asset, credit liability) of leases that fitted into a category where the user, in effect, was assuming all of the risks of ownership, e.g., the user was required to pay for repairs, insurance, and similar expenses over much of the remaining useful life of the long-lived asset. In brief, GAAP has changed over the years to respond to demands from users of financial statements, such as us—as analysts for a life insurance company.

The note disclosure ought to help us to determine the cash lease obligations of *S* Limited. Then we can decide whether they are higher or lower than the interest and long-term debt repayment obligations of *R* Limited. We may calculate, for example, by how much income can decline and our employer still receive interest payments. That is, what is our safety margin?

Who, then, is served by capitalizing (debit asset, credit liability) some types of leases? Those who look at debt to equity ratios in judging safety margins may be puzzled by *S* Limited's balance sheet. They may think that the company does not have any interest and debt obligations. But, if this is what they are thinking, we have to question their understanding of the situation. Most of us would not assume that every automobile that we see being driven is fully owned by the driver. If the driver asked us for a loan, we would want to know what monthly payments he or she already had for furniture, credit cards, and similar purchases. If we saw their personal balance sheet, we would notice the *absence* of the leased furniture, automobile, and similar items. In brief, capitalization would not seem to be of great benefit to potential creditors who are entitled to ask questions before making a loan.

When we do not have the power to ask questions, capitalization may help us. For instance, we might be a minor owner of common shares in a large company. Capitalization tells us that a debt obligation exists, and that the company has contracted to face risk, much as if it had issued bonds. Also, when we lease, we may or may not be foregoing any gains from appreciation of the value of the asset. (Generally, users would not be foregoing appreciation because the type of leases that are capitalized under GAAP tend to allow the user to buy the asset for a nominal, minimal, sum on expiry of a long term lease period.) Thus, a few benefits of capitalization exist for *some* users.

LEASE BOOKKEEPING

The journal entries made for the user (lessee) of the long-lived leased asset differ from those of the legal owner (lessor) whenever the benefits and risks of ownership are transferred from the lessor to the lessee. (Ownership risks are transferred to a lessee when specified conditions are met, such as when the asset is leased for most of its remaining life or can be purchased at the end of the lease period for a nominal sum.)

To this stage in the chapter, we have been assuming the viewpoint of the *lessee*. Capitalization of the asset, and recording of the liability, would be the normal accounting treatment when the lessee assumes the benefits and risks of ownership. When the leased asset is capitalized, it is also depreciated as though it were fully owned by the lessee.

From the *lessor's point of view*, an asset that has been leased to someone who is assuming ownership benefits and risks really is a type of loan receivable. The lessor enters the transaction in the hope that she/he will make a reasonable return on investment on the "loan". (The lessor's behavior is like that of a banker who loans money to a borrower, who buys the asset.) Generally, the discounted present value of the lease-payments receivable would be shown on the balance sheet under a title such as:

Current assets:
....
Net investment in leases		50,000

Non-current assets:
Net investment in leases	800,000	
Less current portion	50,000	750,000

The interest rate that the lessor has built into the lease as a return on investment would be used as the discount rate—to arrive at the discounted present value of the receivable, "net investment in leases". (See discounting material in Chapter 9.)

For example, suppose that we bought an asset for $403,740 and leased it for its *entire* life of five years for $100,000 per year commencing with an annual payment at the *beginning* of the first year. This means that the discounting for beginning-of-year payments would be:

		Discount Period
Payment:	first year	None
	second year	1 Year
	third year	2 Years
	fourth year	3 Years
	fifth year	4 Years

We can ascertain the discount rate that we are seeking by dividing the $403,740 present value by the $100,000 annual payment, to get a figure of 4.0374, which is the cumulative present-value factor. Because the first payment has a present value of 1.0, we can subtract it and get 3.0374 for *four* payments—discounted for one, two, three, and four years respectively.

On page 598, for four periods, a figure that approximates 3.0374 is under the 12 percent column. Thus, the yield or return on investment to the lessor is 12 percent. Stating this another way, 12 percent equates a $403,740 present value with five $100,000 payments—four of which are due in one, two, three, and four years respectively.

How would the leased assets appear from the *lessee's or asset user's point of view?* In a non-complex example (with no scrap value or other complications), the lease could appear as follows at the *beginning* of the *first* year *before* the first $100,000 payment was made:

Long-lived assets:		
Machinery under capital lease		403,740
Liabilities:		
Current:		
Obligation under capital lease		100,000
Non-current:		
Obligation under capital lease	403,740	
Less current portion	100,000	303,740

As soon as the $100,000 lease payment is made, the asset side of the balance sheet remains at $403,740, but the liability side will have decreased to $303,740—because cash decreased by $100,000. Assume that the machinery is depreciated on a straight-line basis over five years with no scrap value. The balance sheet of the *lessee one year later, before* the second $100,000 payment is made, will show:

Long-lived assets:	
Machinery under capital lease	403,740
Less accumulated depreciation	80,748
	322,992
Liabilities:	
Current:	
Obligation under capital lease	100,000
Non-current:	
Obligation under capital lease	240,190

The interesting part of the "one year later" balance sheet is "where did the $240,190 come from"? This represents the $100,000 payments *now* due one, two, and three years hence at 12 percent. That is, at the *beginning* of the lease, the five relevant present-value factors were:

	Factor
Due today @ 12%	1.0000
Due in one year @ 12%	0.8929
Due in two years @ 12%	0.7972
Due in three years @ 12%	0.7118
Due in four years @ 12%	0.6355
	4.0374

One year later, *after* the second payment of $100,000 has been made, the relevant factors are:

	Factor
Due in one year @ 12%	0.8929
Due in two years @ 12%	0.7972
Due in three years @ 12%	0.7118
	2.4019

The *second* payment of $100,000 (at the beginning of the second year) appears as a $100,000 current liability on the balance sheet that is made up just prior to the $100,000 cash payment.

A second interesting part is "how do we account for the decline from a liability of $403,740 ($100,000 + $303,740) to a liability of $340,190 ($100,000 + $240,190) in the first year, i.e., just before the first payment to just before the second payment? This was briefly discussed in Chapter 9. During the year, interest expense accrues on the discounted liability. The sequence is:

Total obligation before first $100,000 payment	$403,740
Deduct first payment	100,000
	303,740
Interest @ 12% on $303,740	36,450
	340,190
Deduct second payment	100,000
Non-current liability at beginning of second year	$240,190

At the end of the first year, the journal entry on the lessee's books would be:

Interest expense	36,450	
Obligation under capital lease		36,450

By capitalizing and depreciating the long-term lease, the lessee produces a balance sheet similar to what appears when the asset has been purchased, and financed by a long-term loan. However, it is important to remember that only particular types of long-term leases are capitalized—ones that, in effect, transfer all of the risks and rewards of ownership to the lessee. Capitalizing such leases is controversial because only some users of the financial statements may be served. Capitalizing results in (1) an asset, (2) accumulated depreciation, (3) a current liability, (4) a long term liability, (5) depreciation expense, (6) interest expense, and (7) note disclosure of lease particulars and future payments due. When we do *not* capitalize we have:

1. Lease expense on the income statement, and
2. Note disclosure of obligations or cash payments due.

There could be situations where lease or rent expense would differ in amount from the combination of interest expense and depreciation expense. For instance, lease *expense* (from *not* capitalizing) could be unrelated to the revenue that is being earned by the leased asset. If so, matching per Chapter 8 is not achieved. But, capitalization and depreciation may *not* produce a better matching because the depreciation expense could be arbitrary. Once again, therefore, there is not an all-purpose method of accounting. Learning has to focus on the strengths and weaknesses of GAAP accounting for leases, and other alternatives.

Pension Accounting

Pension accounting probably will be evolving over the next twenty or more years. The average age of the Canadian population will continue to increase for the next several years, until the so-called "baby boomers" generation ceases to be the largest single age group. With an increasing percentage of the population reaching retirement age, Canadian citizens have to be confident that resources will exist to provide an adequate living standard for the elderly. We also have to be assured that corporations account for pension costs and expenses in ways that do not pass most of the burden of supporting the elderly to future generations.

For instance, wastage of resources, e.g., timber and fish, may occur because selling prices may be kept low as a result of management not having considered what is the *full* cost of production. When a company undertakes to pay pensions at some later date, an expense is being incurred. Presumably this expense should be absorbed by the person who consumes the goods that are being produced by the workers who *will get* pensions. But, is this happening? Are accounting policies for employees' wages and benefits charging expenses to the year in which they belong? Or, are the figures misleading management?

If the pension expense charge is being partially delayed until the persons retire, the consequences are by far the most serious they have ever been in the history of Canada—as a result of the aging population issue. That is, Canada may now appear to be an efficient producer in the world marketplace, based on costs that do *not* include full pension obligations. When these pension obligations have to be paid at a later date, what is to be debited—a previously accrued liability (because the expense was inadequately charged in a prior year) or current expense? If a current expense has to be incurred for people who have retired, production costs may be so high that they exceed revenue. At that time, Canada will not be an efficient producer, and the standard of living of Canadians will drop. There is more to the matter than what we have described, but the potential consequences of illogical accounting for pension costs are especially severe.

As with tax allocation and some other topics that we have discussed, it is vital in our discussions of pensions to separate cash from accrual accounting. Typically, *cash flows* occur in accordance with laws or labor contracts. That is, a company will pay so many dollars to a pension administrator (perhaps a trust company) who is responsible for investing the money. When the employee leaves the company, cash flows outward from the pension administrator to the retired worker.

There are two broad types of pension plans: (1) cost-based, and (2) benefit-based. Under a *cost-based* plan, the retired employee receives whatever the cash contributions made over the years on her/his behalf, plus interest, add up to. This type of plan is easy to account for—expense equals the amount of cash disbursed to the pension administrator.

The *benefit-based* plan guarantees a particular level of pension to the retired employee. For example, an employee aged sixty-five at the date of retirement may have a life expectancy of fifteen additional years. To keep the arithmetic simple, let us assume that the employee receives $20,000 a year at the end of each of the fifteen years. At an interest rate of 8 percent, a sum of $171,180 would have to be paid to the pension administrator at the employee's sixty-fifth birthday:

$$\$20,000 \times 8.559 \ = \ \underline{\$171,180}$$

The sum of $171,180 plus interest at 8 percent would provide an annuity of $20,000 per year at the end of each of fifteen years.

```
                                                $171,180
   |————————————————————————————————————————————|———($20,000)————————

   AGE                                          AGE                AGE
   25                                           65                  80
```

Pension accounting is challenging and complex for many reasons. We have been required to make *two assumptions:* the life expectancy of an employee (65 + 15), and the interest rate that will be earned by the pension administrator on the $171,180— during the employee's next fifteen years. In reality, a third assumption is needed for this period: Where does the $20,000 come from? In a benefit-based plan, the $20,000 may be "50 percent of the average annual earnings of the employee for five years"— usually the five years in which the employee receives the highest salary. When the employee is aged twenty-five or thirty and the three assumptions have to be made by the actuary, who advises the pension administrator, considerable room for measurement error exists.

Now we turn to the problems of how we accumulate the $171,180, which is called *funding,* and is the cash side of pensions, and expense the cost over the working life of the employee, which is the *accrual* accounting issue. In theory, the *funding* could be made: (1) at age sixty-five, called *terminal* funding of $171,180, or (2) at age twenty-five, called *initial* funding of X dollars that, with interest, will accumulate to $171,180 at age sixty-five, or (3) year by year. Terminal funding is not permitted under pension legislation. However, many other funding methods are permitted and have major consequences for when cash has to be disbursed by companies. Actuaries recommend funding methods based on the following assumptions: (a) employee turnover, (b) average working life of employees, (c) deaths and disabilities, (d) interest rates, (e) inflation rates. Cash funding could differ from year to year, and is dependent upon actuarial methods and the many assumptions.

The *accrual accounting* problem is one of spreading the $171,180 over the working life of the employee. Thus, it is another allocation problem, such as the one that we encountered with depreciation. Several expensing methods exist. Again, there is *not* one right way of spreading out the cost year by year. When we read financial statements we have to pay close attention to pension accounting because wide diversity exists in accounting treatment, and material effects (see Chapter 8) on income may occur.

Typical journal entries for a pension plan that is to be funded are:

A. *Accrual:*

Pension expense (including interest)	183,300	
Pension liability		183,300

B. *Funding:*

Pension liability	66,800	
Cash		66,800

The net figure for "pension liability" would appear on the balance sheet. Additional explanations may be in footnotes.

Estimated and Contingent Liabilities

It is important to distinguish (1) liabilities that exist at a balance sheet date, from (2) liabilities that might arise as a result of transactions and events that occurred up to, and including, the balance sheet date. For example, an accident could have occurred prior to that date. But, a liability may not exist until a court case is heard three years later. At the balance sheet date, the existence or not of a liability is contingent on the outcome of a future event (the court case). Accountants call this a *contingent* liability. GAAP calls for note disclosure of contingent liabilities, such as the court case example, that may or may not become liabilities.

In contrast, suppose that the accident occurred prior to the balance sheet date, and the company clearly is at fault for the first $1 million that is *not* covered by insurance. The future court case, which is concerned with establishing the total claim, will merely confirm that the loss exceeded $1 million. In this instance, the $1 million should be accrued as an expense and a liability when the accident occurs. That is, the amount may be estimated at the time of the accident, and the court case will merely confirm existence of the liability.

Subsequent Events

As the name suggests, a subsequent event is one that occurs after the balance sheet date but before the financial statements are finalized, which could be a few weeks or months after the company's year end. Subsequent events fall into two categories under GAAP:

1. Events that clarify a situation that existed at the balance sheet date, and
2. Events of significance that occurred *after* the balance sheet date.

Events that fall into category 1 require an adjustment to the financial statements. Category 2 events that have a material effect on assets and liabilities, and may materially affect future operations, are reported in notes to the financial statements.

Category 2 events tend to involve considerable difficulty. What is and is not reported is a matter of judgment that has to be related to objectives of accounting and facts/assumptions. For instance, if the *sole* use of the financial statements is to accompany an income tax return, then the subsequent event would not be material to (indeed would not affect) a prior year's taxable income. Similary, if the *sole* use of the statements is to calculate bonuses of the prior year, the subsequent event would not be relevant. However, when the uses of the financial statements are not known, or a user wishes to predict cash flows, many subsequent events could be material in their effect.

Many events that occur after the balance sheet date are really only normal business activities of the following year. For example, a salary increase to the president, the addition of a new product line to ten other products that are being manufactured, the construction of a new building, and similar activities are unlikely to be subsequent events.

Summary

The study of the liability section of the balance sheet is challenging. It reminds one of the story about the enthusiastic host who is trying hard to impress his visitor from another country:

Host: "In this country it takes trains five whole days to travel from one coast to the other."

Visitor: "Yeh. We have trains like that, too."

Tax allocation, leases, and pensions can be confusing unless the cash transactions are separated from the accrual entries. Deferred/accrued income taxes do not result from cash transactions. They arise from journal entries made to recognize that the "tax benefit" portion of a depreciable asset has been used up. Capitalized leases are recorded at the present value of future cash flows. Pension expense often is unrelated to cash flows. The figures that result from applying GAAP accounting have strengths for some users, but may not be informative for other users.

Long-term debt carries benefits, and risks. Debt interest is deductible for income tax purposes. This helps common shareholders to improve their return on investment because they are able to use debtholders' money to earn more than it costs in interest expense less income taxes. In a downturn of corporate success, however, interest expense may become a burden. When interest is not paid on long-term debt for several months, the debtholder may receive enough voting rights to be able to take over management of the company. Striking a sensible balance in the amount of debt-to-owners' equity is a continuing concern for management.

To this point in the book, much has been stated about the nature of accounting. A major theme is that there is *not* one, right answer. Large corporations engage in complex activities, in response to major changes in the world. It is unrealistic of users of financial statements to expect to see all of this complexity captured in a single income number, or an accurate figure for inventories, or liabilities. In accounting, our search is for the accounting treatment that makes the most sense under the circumstances.

APPENDIX 12-A

Payroll Accounting

Appendix 12-A explains the journal entries that are needed to account for employees' wages.

PAYROLL TRANSACTIONS

Although they present few conceptual considerations that have not already been dealt with, payroll expenses and the related payroll liabilities require some discussion. They are of concern to virtually all business and non-profit organizations, and are sometimes of major magnitude.

Accounting for payroll transactions is characterized by the facts that the wage or salary *expense* for an individual employee may be considerably greater than that indicated by his wage or salary rate, and the amount actually *paid* to the employee may be considerably less than that which would be indicated by his rate. The business firm must pay additional payroll charges such as Canada Pension Plan, Workers' Compensation, and Unemployment Insurance that are levied on the employer. Employers also must provide for fringe benefits in addition to regular wage and salary payments.

The employer must withhold from each employee's wages and salary the employee's share of income taxes, as well as amounts for other designated purposes. Amounts withheld from the employee ordinarily represent a liability of the employer; they must be remitted either to the government or to a specific fund, such as for pensions.

For example, an employee is paid at the rate of $2,000 per month. From her or his salary must be withheld (by law, union contract, or otherwise) the following: federal income tax—$350; provincial income tax (applies only in a few Canadian provinces)—nil; unemployment insurance—$20; Canada Pension Plan—$30; health and dental plan—$30; purchase of Canada Savings Bond by employee—$100; contribution to pension plan—$110; disability insurance—$15; and union dues—$20. As a consequence of the deductions, take-home pay of the employee would be $1,325.

This might be journalized as follows:

(1) Salary expense $2,000

Employee income tax deductions payable		$ 350
Unemployment insurance payable		20
Canada Pension Plan payable		30
Health and dental insurance payable		30
Canada Savings Bond payable		100
Pension plan payable		110
Disability insurance payable		15
Union dues payable		20
Salaries payable or cash		1,325

To record salary expense for the period.

The $350 represents the sum that employers have to deduct per the *Income Tax Act* and Regulations.

Some of the employee deductions noted above may represent only a portion of the cost of the benefit, e.g., health insurance. The other portion would be paid by the employer. On the assumption that the employer pays an additional sum representing 50 percent of the total cost (excluding the Canada Savings Bond and union dues deduction), the journal entry would be:

(2) Salary expense: $205

Unemployment insurance payable		$ 20
Canada Pension Plan payable		30
Health and dental insurance payable		30
Pension plan payable		110
Disability insurance payable		15

To record employer's share of joint costs.

In addition to the above two journal entries, a third would be needed to accrue those costs that are borne entirely by the employer. Two common ones in this category are workers' compensation insurance and vacation pay, although others such as health, dental, and disability insurance could be borne entirely by the employer. Workers' compensation does not apply to all positions or employment; it is primarily associated with occupations with greater risk of injury to workers (construction, for example). Vacation pay is an accrual, needed to cover the outlay that is required when the employee actually takes a vacation. Provincial law stipulates the minimum vacation-pay rate; some employers pay more than this.

In the following situation, workers' compensation is accrued at 2 percent and vacation pay is at 6 percent of gross salary. Based on the $2,000 salary, the journal entry would be:

(3) Salary expense $160

Workers'-compensation provision		$ 40
Provision for vacation pay		120

To recognize costs to be borne entirely by employer.

Eventually, the Workers' Compensation Board (or equivalent) would assess the company (usually based on a complex formula that recognizes the accident-prone nature of the company's employees and other factors) and seek payment. The journal entry would be:

(4) Workers' compensation provision $40
    Cash $40
  To record payment, based on assessment.

Similarly, when the employee goes on vacation, the entry would be:

(5) Provision for vacation pay $120
    Salaries payable $80
    Employee income tax deduction payable   25
    Other deductions (similar to the first journal entry—(1))   15

Some companies would accrue more than the $120 in the "Provision for vacation pay" account in order to cover the employer's share of the costs included in journal entry (2), plus the employer's share of other costs in entry (3), such as workers' compensation. That is, they would accrue all costs of a vacation at the time when the employee is fully working. Other companies do not bother with an accrual if employees are taking vacations at various times during the year, and vacation costs tend to be fairly evenly incurred.

QUESTIONS

12-1 Compare and contrast long-term liabilities and long-term assets. How are each valued, and reported on the financial statements?

12-2 What is meant by "trade on equity"? Provide an illustration.

12-3 What factors does a banker try to negotiate with a lender when a loan is being considered? Why?

12-4 Explain the process that a utility board might use in setting telephone charges that can be assessed against customers of the utility.

12-5 Should short-term debt, or long-term debt or equity, be used to finance the purchase of inventory, and the holding of accounts receivable?

12-6 Distinguish between a public offering of shares or debt, and a private placement. How might a public offering affect accounting?

12-7 What is a second mortgage?

12-8 What is a financing cost, and how is it accounted for in the case of long-term debt?

12-9 What accounting policies are used in the computation of the federal deficit? How do they differ from GAAP?

12-10 Compare and contrast timing differences and permanent differences with respect to accounting for income taxation.

12-11 What are the reasons for recording deferred or accrued income tax?

12-12 What effect does the existence of leases have on a company's balance sheet? What effect might the existence of many leases have on readers of financial statements who are not familiar with many accounting procedures?

12-13 What accounting issues and problems are created by the existence of pension plans?

12-14 Distinguish between a cost-based and a benefit-based pension plan.

12-15 What is a contingent liability?

12-16 What is a subsequent event, and how do accountants report it?

12-17 Why is an employer's cost for one employee far greater than the payroll cheque that is issued to the employee? Explain by citing several differences between cost to the employer and take-home pay.

12-18 How might accountants cost and account for vacation pay? What are the benefits of the method that you would recommend?

EXERCISES

E12-1 Dewhirst Corporation (DC) was recently incorporated with a common share investment of $500,000. The $500,000 was invested in a small office building, for which DC was able to obtain a one-half ownership. The building is being leased to a large corporation so that DC receives a 10 percent per annum rate of return on its $500,000 investment.

DC's income tax rate may be assumed to be 40 percent. It is considering the purchase of the other one-half interest in the office building. The purchase price would be $500,000 and the investment would generate 10 percent per annum—the same as for the initial investment.

DC believes that it should be able to borrow the $500,000 at 12 percent per annum before income tax. The lender would want a first mortgage on the office building.

Required:

A. Should DC purchase the other half of the office building?

B. What return on investment would DC receive if it borrowed the $500,000 and had a total of $1,000,000 invested in the office building?

E12-2 Provide journal entries to record each of the following *independent* situations (1, 2 and 3):

1. A. A bank loan of $50,000 is arranged, and the bank deposits the sum in our bank account.
   B. Interest of $428 is paid to the bank for the first 23 days of the loan.
2. A. A mortgage of $100,000 is arranged on a building that we are having constructed. The $100,000 is to be paid directly to the builder.

B. The first payment on the mortgage is for $1,378.26 of which $1,197.29 is for interest expense.

3. A. We issue a $1,000,000 bond payable for 98 percent of its face value. In addition we have to pay $55,000 in commissions, or financing cost to the seller.

B. The first interest payment is for $60,000.

E12-3 J. Hughes Limited (HL) purchased a new asset for $80,000, which has a life of two years and is to be depreciated on a straight line basis. HL's income tax rate is 40 percent of taxable income. For income tax purposes, the new asset may be claimed as an expense in full in the first year of its purchase.

Assume that HL's income before depreciation and income tax is $100,000 in each of the two years in which the new asset is used.

Required:

A. Compute the amount of *cash* that would have to be paid in income taxes on the taxable incomes of each of the two years in which the new asset is used.

B. Compute net income in each of the two years, assuming:
1. income tax expense equals the figure that must be paid in cash for income taxes.
2. income tax expense is computed on a deferral/accrual basis.

C. Which objectives of accounting are served by the method that you employed in (B) above, (1) and (2)? Explain.

E12-4 The balance sheet of Caterina Corporation (CC) just prior to a transaction involving a building shows:

Current assets	$1,500,000
Current liabilities	300,000
Owners' equity:	
Common shares	1,000,000
Retained earnings	200,000

The building and its land may be acquired as follows:

Land	$150,000
Building	600,000
	750,000
Mortgage on the property by CC	500,000
Cash payment by CC	$250,000

Alternatively, the building and land may be leased for 10 years for $3,000 per month plus payments for property taxes, utilities, insurance and similar operating expenses. At the end of 10 years, the land and building may be acquired by CC for a sum that would be regarded as a bargain.

Required:

Prepare a balance sheet for CC from the above information under each of these assumptions:

1. The building and land are purchased for $250,000 cash plus the mortgage.

2. The building and land are leased, and the lease is capitalized. State all of the assumptions that you make.

E12-5 Laimon Limited (LL) incurred the following wage expenses for November:

Cheques issued to employees	$410,015
Union dues deducted from employees	1,755
Unemployment insurance deducted from employees	3,990
Canada pension plan deductions from employees	3,960
Pension plan deductions from employees (private plan)	16,700
Life and disability insurance deductions from employees	3,200
Health insurance deductions from employees	2,970
Income tax deductions from employees	77,855
LL's share of costs and benefits:	
Unemployment insurance	3,990
Canada pension plan	3,960
Health and dental insurance	4,780
Private plan for employee pensions	16,700
Life and disability insurance	3,200

LL pays for 100 percent of dental insurance and pays 50 percent of most other employee benefits (except for items such as union dues).

Required:

Prepare journal entries to record the payroll information for November.

E12-6 McIntosh Corporation (MC) has just arranged a pension plan for the company's president. The president will retire at age 65 and receive a pension of $100,000 per year at the beginning of each year, commencing with his 65th birthday. Life expectancy of a person with the president's background is 14 years after age 65.

The president has just had his 55th birthday. The administrator of the president's pension fund would like the company to pay a constant annual sum, commencing immediately, that will accumulate to what is needed at age 65 to provide the necessary pension. The funds can be invested at eight percent for the foreseeable future.

Required:

A. How much is needed at age 65 to provide the president with the necessary pension?

B. How much cash has to be paid into the pension administrator's fund *each* year, commencing immediately, to accumulate to the amount needed at age 65?

C. Discuss how pension expense ought to be computed for the president from age 55 to 65.

PROBLEMS

P12-1 (Revenue Recognition Review) De Bono Corporation (DC) prepares computer software for a variety of clients. Its software packages are of two varieties: standard and specially prepared. The standard software packages have been tested extensively to ensure that they are effective under a variety of situations. The software that is specially prepared for clients often has to be de-bugged to make it fully operational.

DC tends to have two types of clients: medium-sized corporations that cannot afford their own computer specialists, and smaller clients who have special needs for computers and sometimes do not have sufficient cash to pay for software programs.

DC is a private company owned by the De Bono brothers. The company is managed by three senior officers (a president and two vice-presidents). As a result of recent negotiations, these officers are to be paid a salary plus a bonus based on income of DC before income tax. The De Bono brothers rarely become involved in the affairs of DC and are primarily interested in maximizing their income from DC, which includes keeping income taxes as low as possible.

The owners and senior officers of DC have engaged you to help them develop revenue recognition policies that are suitable for the company. They believe that the following revenue recognition points might prove sensible under different conditions:

1. on completion of the computer software program.
2. on sale of the program to a reliable customer.
3. on collection of the account receivable for (2).
4. when the warranty period expires, which is one year after the program is delivered to a customer.

Required:

A. What are the most likely goals or objectives of DC?

B. How would you rank the likely goals? What is the most important one? Why?

C. How would you rank the objectives of financial accounting?

D. Which is the most important? Why?

E. What are all of the different situations that the company faces with respect to collectibility of the receivable, and likely need to incur warranty expenses?

F. Which revenue recognition policy should be used for each of the situations described in (E)?

G. Explain how your recommended accounting policies noted in (F) support the company's goals and objectives, and have the intended consequences.

P12-2 (Review Problem: Chapters 6 to 12) Vibrand Film Corporation (VFC) is in the process of being sold. The buyer and seller have tentatively established a fixed portion of the buying/selling price of VFC's common shares, but are still trying to settle the variable portion. At the moment, the variable portion is to be based on the income before income taxes of the *next* three years. The seller will receive 10 percent of the amount by which income before income taxes exceeds $500,000 each year. Both the buyer and the seller have requested a postponement in negotiations until they have had a chance to assess the effects of this variable portion.

VFC produces films, or contracts with others to produce films. The buyers of its films fall into two categories:

1. those who buy films outright, for a fixed fee, or who buy large percentages of film ownership such as 80 percent.
2. those who provide financing to VFC so that the film may be made, and who are therefore permitted to purchase a portion of the film for a lower price than those in the first category.

The main steps in producing a film are: buy story rights from writers or distributors; obtain financing from investors to produce the film; hire actresses, actors, directors, and similar people; acquire insurance coverage in case an unforeseen event delays production of the film or causes costs to rise; arrange for a distributor to obtain theatres willing to show the film; and find buyers of the film either for immediate release or for later showings on television. Several months may be needed to arrange for all of these contracts.

The success or failure of a film is ultimately decided by the general public. Usually, success is determined in the first few months after the film is released and is shown in theatres. It is for this public response reason that the seller of VFC wants the 10 percent contingent price clause for the next three years.

At the date of purchase/sale of the common shares, several films will be in process, at different stages of arranging for financing, filming and other factors. Some films may not be produced because financing or other arrangements cannot be made.

VFC usually retains a portion of the ownership of a film. Accordingly, it is entitled to receive a share of profits from the films after all costs have been recovered. Most films, however, do not generate a profit or income. Companies invest in several films in the hope that a few will be very successful.

You have been engaged to comment on the buying/selling arrangement, especially the variable portion. You have been asked to give special attention to the recognition of revenue and the matching of expenses to revenue.

Required:

A. Explain in which respects the viewpoint or goals of the seller of the shares differs from that of the buyer.

B. What are the logical revenue recognition points? (e.g., when story rights are purchased?) Why?

C. What problems or consequences do you foresee for the *seller* if all of the shares of VFC are purchased by the buyer? (Hint: review Chapters 6 to 12.)

D. If you were engaged by the seller, what revenue recognition point for the films would you prefer? Why?

P12-3 The following information is for Hopkins Corporation (HC):

	19—1	*19—2*	*19—3*
Income before depreciation and income taxes	$100,000	$30,000	$50,000
Depreciation	40,000	40,000	40,000
Capital cost allowance	65,000	30,000	50,000
Income tax rate = 40%			

Required:

A. Prepare the journal entry for income tax in *each* of the years 19—1, 19—2, and 19—3.

B. Should HC have claimed more than $30,000 capital cost allowance in 19—2, assuming that it was eligible to claim more? Explain.

P12-4 The president of Beshara Enterprises Corporation (BEC) has been approached by the head of the labor union that organized BEC's hourly paid employees. The union head wants BEC to introduce an improved pension plan for employees. The basic line of reasoning that she provided to the president of BEC is that the union can claim a victory for its workers in the upcoming labor contract negotiations without forcing a strike at BEC. That is, instead of seeking a much higher wage rate, the union will seek a moderate wage plus the improved pension plan. The union head told the president that "the cash needed to pay for an improved plan can be provided over many years. However, when a wage increase is given, the entire amount of cash must be provided each year. Thus, the company will be better off by granting an improved pension in its upcoming negotiations with the union."

Required:

Do you agree with the head of the labor union? Why?

P12-5 Michael McKay is the director of a charity. The charity does not have to pay income taxes nor does it claim capital cost allowance on its depreciable assets.

In the next month Michael has to acquire new automobiles for the employees, so that they may visit the disabled recipients who are aided by the work of the charity. The automobiles are expected to last for three years. If they are bought, the cost in total would be $50,000. At the end of three years, the fair market value would be $10,000. In order to buy the automobiles, about $20,000 would have to be borrowed from a bank for about two years at 12 percent per annum.

Michael is also considering the possibility of leasing the automobiles. Payments of $7,000 per quarter would have to be paid at the end of each of the 12 quarters. On completion of the three year lease, the automobiles would be the property of the leasing company.

Required:

Which alternative should Michael choose? Explain your response thoroughly.

P12-6 Barber Limited (BL) has a June 30 year end. Usually, its financial statements are not finalized until mid September. Several events occurred in July, August and early September 19—8, and the accountant is wondering how they should be handled in the financial statements for the year ended June 30, 19—8:

1. In August 19—8, the president of BL was granted a substantial wage increase effective September 1, 19—8.
2. In late July 19—8, inventory that was recorded on the June 30, 19—8 balance sheet at net realizable value of $160,000 had to be sold for $105,000.
3. In early September 19—8 BL sold $1,000,000 of common shares.
4. In August 19—8, BL negotiated a new labor contract effective June 1, 19—8. Wage increases of 8 percent were granted.

Required

A. How would you handle each of the foregoing events in the financial statements for the year ended June 30, 19—8?
B. Would your response to (A) differ if BL were a private company, with income tax postponement and a bonus plan for senior executives as the only two objectives of accounting? Explain.

P12-7 Lau Corporation (LC) has no debt and $5,000,000 of owners' equity at December 31, 19—7. The entire sum is invested in leases that generate LC a return on investment of 10 percent after income taxes.

LC has an opportunity to borrow $3,000,000 at 12 percent interest per annum, using the leases as collateral. In actuality, LC would receive only $2,900,000; the other $100,000 would be a commission to the person who arranged the five year loan.

LC can invest the $2,900,000 in a five year lease that will generate 8 percent after income taxes. All costs of the lease will be borne by the lessee, and LC has no risks.

It can be assumed that LC pays income tax at a 40 percent rate.

Required:

A. Should LC borrow the $3,000,000 that is repayable at the end of five years? Why?

B. How should the $3,000,000 loan be recorded *if* it is borrowed? Give the journal entry and the balance sheet presentation.

C. How should the lease be reported *if* it is entered into? Clearly state the assumptions that you have made.

EXPLORATION MATERIALS AND CASES

MC12-1 Mark Enterprises Limited (MEL) was incorporated under federal legislation to acquire the assets and liabilities of a partnership, Mark and Partners. You have been asked to recommend accounting principles for MEL. Your investigations have disclosed the following:

1. MEL is an importer of cutlery from Korea, the U.K. and Europe. It sells to a variety of small stores in smaller towns in two Canadian provinces.
2. MEL's owners hope to double the size of the company in the next two years. They hope to borrow funds from friends.
3. Inventory has to be purchased well in advance of distribution to the store.
4. MEL leases office and warehouse space on 20 year leases. MEL has to pay for all utilities, insurance, property taxes and similar operating expenses.
5. MEL allows stores to return up to 20 percent of annual sales for full credit.
6. Approximately $20,000 was spent on leasehold improvements in the rented premises.
7. The sales personnel work on a commission basis with a small salary. Others are on a salary plus pension.

Required:

Advise the owners of MEL.

MC12-2 Johnstone Manufacturing Corporation (JMC) is federally incorporated and privately owned. It manufactures machine components for larger manufacturing companies.

Three years ago JMC entered into a contract with a U.S. manufacturer to supply 300 components at $100,000 each over a several year period. To its latest year ended December 31, 19—4 JMC supplied 100 components, 34 of which were produced and delivered during 19—4. The cost of these 100 components averaged $122,000 with the average in 19—4 being $118,000.

The reason for the high cost per component is that the components had to be modified several times. The U.S. manufacturer stated in 19—4 that some of the modifications were at its request, and tentatively agreed to pay for these changes. Other modifications were made by JMC. The balance of the unexpected costs were incurred because the learning effect did not commence until all the modifications were finalized, which was after 70 components had been completed. JMC's cost records do not show the cost of each modification, and who initiated it.

In 19—5, production is expected to be 80 components at a cost of $105,000 each. As a result of renegotiating the contract, revenue per component will be $118,000 effective for production completed after January 1, 19—5. The U.S. manufacturer will pay an additional amount if Canadian inflation exceeds 10 percent in 19—5.

The financial statements for 19—4 are now (late January 19—5) being finalized. The president of JMC had just been informed (January 25, 19—5) by letter that the U.S. manufacturer has agreed to pay $1,000,000 for modifications that were made on the first 70 components manufactured. Also, $200,000 is to be paid to JMC for the loss of its learning curve cost savings on the 300 components. Finally, interest of $25,000 will be paid to JMC by the U.S. manufacturer. The president of JMC has agreed to accept the $1,225,000 in full settlement.

The December 31, 19—4 balance sheet of JMC shows $600,000 of development costs incurred for the components, less $200,000 amortized to date. Another $235,000 less amortization of $35,000 has been shown as "deferred modification cost" for the components.

You have been hired by the management of JMC to advise them about the accounting and reporting treatment of the foregoing for 19—4 and 19—5.

Required:
Advise management.

MC12-3 A friend, J. David, who knows that you are knowledgeable about financial statements, has asked for some help in deciding on which of the following two companies to invest in:

Opening balance sheets, January 1, 19—5

A Ltd.		B Ltd.	
Total assets	$100,000	Total assets	$100,000
Long-term debt	$ 10,000	Long-term debt	$ 90,000
Shareholders' equity (9,000 common shares outstanding)	90,000	Shareholders' equity (1,000 common shares outstanding)	10,000
Total liabilities and shareholders' equity	$100,000		$100,000
Net income for 19—5	$ 19,000	Net income for 19—5	$ 11,000

Additional information:
1. Both companies began operations at the beginning of 19—5 with $100,000 cash.
2. On December 31, 19—5 both companies paid interest in the amount of 10 percent on the outstanding long-term debt.
3. On December 31, 19—5 both companies paid dividends of $1 per common share.
4. Both companies are in the same industry.

J. David believed that since both companies started with $100,000 at the beginning of the year, A Ltd. was the better company. Its net income of $19,000 represented a 19 percent return on investment whereas B Ltd. had only an 11 percent return. Given the higher return on investment, J. David felt that A Ltd. had more efficient management and better cash generating ability.

Required:
What advice would you give to J. David?

MC12-4 Wayne Company Limited was incorporated thirty years ago. Since that time it has been entirely owned by Mr. Wayne. Mr. Wayne is now sixty-five and has lost interest in taking an active role in the management of the company. He considered hiring a president and becoming a passive owner. However, he decided that it would be impossible for him to take an inactive role in his company. Since he wanted to retire, he decided the best thing to do would be to sell his company.

Mr. Kaiser, a next-door neighbor of Mr. Wayne has offered to purchase the company. This pleases Mr. Wayne because he knows that Mr. Kaiser has the interest and resources to successfully run Wayne Company Limited. They decide that the selling price of the company should be six times the income determined in accordance with generally accepted accounting principles.

You have been hired to prepare the financial statements in accordance with generally accepted accounting principles. In the past, the financial statements were prepared primarily for income tax purposes. Since there were no creditors and Mr. Wayne took an active role in the management of the company there were no other purposes of accounting. Upon reviewing the company's accounting principles you discover the following:

1. The company depreciates its building and equipment at rates permissible for income tax purposes.
2. The company has a benefit-based pension plan and it expenses its pension costs in the year of funding (i.e., when it pays into the pension plan).
3. The company leases some equipment. The lease agreement stipulates that the company is responsible for all maintenance and insurance costs. In addition, it has the option to buy the equipment at the end of the lease for a nominal sum. Presently the company records the lease payments as an expense when paid.
4. The company calculates its tax expense on the cash or taxes payable basis. Its tax rate is 50 percent. Since its income statement reflects taxable income it simply records 50 percent of income before taxes as a tax expense.
5. All other principles adopted by the company are in accordance with generally accepted accounting principles.

Required:

What would you recommend? Justify your position logically.

CHAPTER 13

Using Financial Statements

Chapter Themes

1. The term "application" may be given several definitions. The one most widely held is that application skills exist when a person is able to use concepts and techniques in situations that are different to the one in which the concept was initially learned. Canada is made up of many different profit-seeking, charitable, government, and other institutions. Accounting has to be fitted to the needs of these organizations. A study of accounting also has to be fitted to the needs of various persons—especially to those who use the end product—financial statements. Chapter 6 listed some users and uses, and subsequent chapters have attempted to show some effects of different objectives of accounting, and facts on assets, liabilities, revenue, and expenses. This chapter furthers our understanding in these areas.

2. Throughout the book, warnings have been issued about comparing the financial statements of two different companies—that may have different corporation act constraints, factual situations, and objectives of accounting. We should keep this in mind as we proceed to a discussion of using financial statements.

3. Accounting data is one of several inputs that are used by people who have to make decisions. Most accounting data is accrual-based, in aggregate form, i.e., several similar items are grouped into one line or category, and pertains to the past. As a result, accounting's main uses have to be in this context, and less so on helping in the prediction of cash flows for segments or divisions of the business.

Accounting Alternatives

A series of topics needs to be discussed before we cover how financial statements may be used. In taking an overview approach to looking at alternatives, Illustration 13-1 provides us with a useful starting point. The alternatives at the top of the illustration are:

1. Asset (has a future benefit), or
2. Expense (to be matched against revenue earned), or
3. Loss (no revenue and no anticipation of it).

Across the bottom, similar choices exist:

4. Liability (obligation to pay in future, or a deferral such as tax allocation), or
5. Revenue (recognition of benefit received or receivable), or
6. Gain (no expense and no anticipation of it).

For example, although a debit may reduce, (4), (5) or (6), the Illustration is primarily concerned with showing the choices that one has among an asset, or an expense, or a loss. Judgments have to be made—and once we decide a debit will not be included as an asset, the sum has to become either an expense or a loss. Similarly, a credit that is not revenue is either a gain or a liability. Gains and losses of a material amount often are shown on the income statement net of income taxes:

Gain on sale of land, net of income taxes
of $62,000 $180,000

ILLUSTRATION 13-1

Accounting Alternatives

Asset	Expense	Loss

Liability	Revenue	Gain

The expense category, under GAAP, is divided into three subcategories:

A. "Usual" items—such as cost of goods sold, revenue, and selling expenses; and

B. Unusual items—such as an infrequent write-down of a material dollar amount of inventory; and

C. Extraordinary items—transactions that are not typical of normal business activities and are not expected to occur regularly. (An example would be a gain or loss on disposal of a portion of the business.)

Unusual items and extraordinary items are usually given separate disclosure on the

income statement, by using a separate line. Unusual items are shown at their gross amount, whereas extraordinary items would be shown net of taxes (as noted previously, for the gain on sale of land).

Why would accountants want to have three subcategories of expenses? Chapters 5 and 6 help provide a reasonable response. If our sole objective of financial accounting was postponing income taxes, it would not be necessary to have three subcategories. Suppose, however, that we want to reward managers by giving them a bonus based on income. If the managers have no power to influence sales of land, and similar extraordinary items, then the bonus ought to be based on income *before* extraordinary items. Another possibility is that someone wishes to predict recurring cash flows—so that the flows may be discounted to a present value or worth of a company:

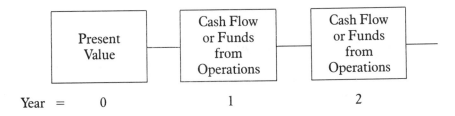

A separation of recurring from non-recurring would be useful in prediction. Usual items would probably recur, but extraordinary items probably would not. What about unusual items? They ought to be infrequent, but could repeat in "*X*" years. By having the three separate categories, a user is free to use the information in different ways.

Prior-Period Adjustments

Occasionally, events arise that indicate that a gain or loss should be attributed to a prior period. GAAP is very restrictive on this point, and limits prior period adjustments to those having *all four* of these characteristics (CICA Handbook, Section 3600):
1. "are specifically identified with and directly related to the business activities of particular prior periods"; *and*
2. "are not attributable to economic events, including obsolescence, occurring subsequent to the date of the financial statements for such prior periods"; *and*
3. "depend primarily on decisions or determinations by persons other than management or owners", *and*
4. "could not be reasonably estimated prior to such decisions or determinations."
Item 3 rules out consideration of prior period treatment for any change of objectives of accounting by management. Thus, management or the board of directors cannot easily attribute current losses to prior years.

When an event or transaction qualifies as a prior period adjustment, the treatment on the statement of retained earnings would be:

Statement of Retained Earnings

Year Ended December 31

	19—2	19—1
Retained earnings, beginning of year		
As previously reported	$109,000	$100,000
Adjustment of prior years' income taxes (Note 4)	7,500	6,000
As restated	101,500	94,000
Net income	14,200	12,500
	115,700	106,500
Dividends	5,000	5,000
Retained earnings, end of year	$110,700	$101,500

Observe that the retained earnings at the end of 19—1 ($101,500) ties into the "as restated" line in 19—2. The foregoing is saying that $6,000 of additional taxes pertains to *19—0 and earlier.* That is, $6,000 has to be deducted to arrive at *beginning of year 19—1* retained earnings. The remaining $1,500 ($7,500 − $6,000) pertains to *19—1.*

Segment Reporting

Large corporations may be engaged in several different industries, which have different profitability and risks. For example, Canadian Pacific, as a total company, has interests in real estate, timber, mining, oil and gas, airlines, hotels, trucking and rail transportation. Someone looking at the balance sheet and income statement for all these *combined* would not be in a good position to forecast cash flows, or evaluate management, because the figures are too aggregated.

Some corporation legislation (and the CICA Handbook) requires reporting of (1) industry and (2) geographic segments for public companies. This information would be in a separate schedule, or would be in notes to the financial statements. For instance, an *industry* segment for a utility company may appear as on page 413.

Observe that depreciation is set out separately, so that segment funds from operations may be calculated. In some companies, head office and certain other expenses may not be traceable to a segment. They therefore would be entered in the total column, as has been done with "income taxes". If a large percentage of the expenses are not shown under the segment columns, then segment information could be less useful to those who wish to predict cash flows.

Note that "total assets" for the segment are provided. This allows a reader to calculate a return on investment (income divided by total assets). Such a calculation may or may not be useful; much depends on what has been said throughout the book about the accounting policies that have been followed. Also, replacement costs may differ significantly from depreciated original cost.

Operating Segment (millions of dollars)	Electric		Natural Gas		Other		Total	
	19—8	19—7	19—8	19—7	19—8	19—7	19—8	19—7
Revenues:								
Outside	$305	$290	$810	$770	$ 50	$ 45	$1,165	$1,105
Between segments	2	2	6	5	(8)	(7)		
	307	292	816	775	42	38	1,165	1,105
Operating expenses:								
Between segments	1	1	3	3	(4)	(4)		
Operations	160	155	760	740	36	32	956	927
Depreciation	29	25	15	12	4	4	48	41
	190	181	778	755	36	32	1,004	968
Segment operating income	$117	$111	$38	$20	$6	$6	161	137
Income taxes							68	59
Net income							$93	$78
Total assets	$910	$870	$730	$690	$125	$115	$1,765	$1,675
Capital expenditures	$110	$80	$60	$55	$10	$15	$180	$150

Overall, segment figures can be useful in situations where it is possible to separate one segment from another. If considerable allocation of revenues must occur to set up segments, the figures are obviously less useful. Quite often management has the power to decide what is a segment; although, some GAAP rules exist to limit management's decision.

Quarterly Reports

Both stock exchange and securities legislation call for more frequent reporting than annually, when companies come under their jurisdiction. The frequency of reporting is likely to increase over the next few decades as computers speed up communication and facilitate the solution of computational problems.

Some companies prepare a full set of unaudited, quarterly financial statements for their shareholders. However, many tend to delete the balance sheet, and just provide operating results (income statement, statement of retained earnings, and statement of changes in financial position—to be discussed in Chapter 16).

The difficulties that we see in trying to match on an annual basis become magnified when quarterly reports have to be prepared. Allocations such as depreciation still exist and can be more difficult to handle. But they are accompanied by additional issues, such as income taxes and annual bonuses. A company like Air Canada traditionally has heavy losses in its first quarter, which is the Canadian winter. Most department stores also have huge first quarter losses. For the entire year, however, these companies hope to make profits—Air Canada from high summer traffic and the department stores from Christmas sales.

Given the circumstances, how do we account for such items as income tax and annual bonuses to management in the *first* quarter's report? Do we show a negative figure (given the losses) or simply show zero effect? Once more, how we respond can have a significant effect on the financial statements, and *possibly* on users' interpretations.

Investor Sophistication

By their nature of being *general* purpose, such financial statements cannot cater to several groups of users with differing objectives of reporting, and different decision needs. Choices have to be made when preparing general-purpose statements. Under such circumstances, what group may be favored, or receive more attention, than others? Preparers of financial statements probably would be *most* concerned with those who might sue the company because they felt that the financial statements showed a falsely "rosy" picture. Concepts such as objectivity, cost, and conservatism (Chapter 8) are designed to minimize the likelihood of showing "too rosy" a picture. Sufficient flexibility does exist, in choosing accounting policies for those who may want to inflate the income figure. Overall, although they are general purpose, such financial statements may be directed toward the less sophisticated, to head off lawsuits.

In the previous chapter, we encountered capitalization of leases and tax allocation, both of which seem, on the surface, to be procedures designed to cater to less sophisticated users. That is, the information *could* have been placed in notes to the financial statements. However, it has been reported on the balance sheet for those who prefer to see a calculation done for them. We may hope that this balance sheet reporting will serve their needs; but it may not. Such balance-sheet calculations obviously can be performed only after making some assumptions, e.g., interest rate for capitalization. The assumptions may differ from what a particular reader believes. In addition, a group of readers may not want the calculation performed because it requires them to "undo" or reverse it. In short, we cannot hope to find an all-purpose answer. Tax allocation and lease capitalization may be useful in performing a restrictive-covenant calculation, but be annoying to someone interested in evaluating management, or in predicting cash flows.

The previous two chapters serve as a reminder that we have to contend both with differing and perhaps multiple objectives of accounting, *and* with variations in the level of sophistication of readers of financial statements. There is more. For *public companies*, we have to pay attention to the behavior of the *market* place. If a large number of investors are closely watching a particular company, and are seeking information from many sources (not just accounting), we get a much different effect from that when only one creditor sees a private company's financial statements. The latter may be misled by the financial statements and lose money to the company. In contrast, in the public-company situation, an unsophisticated investor could lose money to a sophisticated investor, e.g., common shares have been sold to the sophis-

ticated investor for "too low" a value. Nevertheless, if the public company's financial statements were thought to be materially misleading, both the preparer company and its auditors (and perhaps the purchaser of the shares) may be sued.

It is very important that we distinguish sophistication of *people* from sophistication of the *market place*, such as the stock market, in which people act as a *group*. In the past twenty years, considerable research has been conducted into such matters as the efficiency of stock markets, whether participants in the market use accounting information, and what impact accounting has on share prices. This type of research is difficult to perform, and it is not reasonable to expect conclusive answers for a variety of market situations. Nevertheless, there is some evidence that *some* markets are what are called "efficient" in a "semistrong" form. Although the *market* may be efficient in this form, there could be naive or unsophisticated investors engaged in this market alongside sophisticated investors. The former could become the losers in an exchange of money, as a result of buying and selling common shares of companies. Market efficiency would tend to arise from having many sophisticated investors buying and selling shares in certain public companies.

What does "efficient in a semistrong form" mean? A more common name is the "semistrong form of the efficient market hypothesis". It has these general characteristics or implications:

1. Information that is made available to the *public* (such as in annual financial statements) is assessed for its information content or relevance by investors. When relevant, it is incorporated into share prices in an unbiased fashion within hours or a few days of its release.

2. Information that is *not* publicly available is guessed at, and guesses or anticipated results will tend to be captured in share prices; the guesses are revised as better information becomes available.

3. Knowledgeable and sophisticated investors with moderate or large amounts of money will tend to make share trading in a particular company efficient in the semistrong form because they will follow and assess all public releases of information, and through buying or selling adjust share prices accordingly.

4. Avoidance of guesswork about accounting figures can only occur when accountants explain the dollar effect of choosing different accounting policies or principles, and not just the one that was used to measure income and assets. (Suppose that a company is using FIFO accounting for inventories and cost of goods sold. During periods of inflation, analyst readers will want to know what cost of goods sold figure would exist if replacement costs had been chosen. Accountants typically do not provide replacement costs in general-purpose reports. Readers must therefore "guess". Guesswork errors may be reduced by providing replacement cost figures that the analysts believe have been professionally assembled.)

5. Share prices, under the semistrong form, will not necessarily reflect a "true value", whatever that may mean. This "imperfection" occurs because we do not have perfect information about the company and its prospects. Therefore, guesswork is occurring.

The foregoing has some important implications; and, a few cautions are worth remembering:

A. Note that the term "hypothesis" has been used in the title. That is, some people have set out this semistrong form as their *theory* of behavior—and have tried to test whether it actually applies, in practice. We are not talking about a proven fact.

B. Some markets may be efficient in the semistrong form, and others will *not* be. Thus, this is not a universal concept. The chances of a particular market being efficient in the semi-strong form will likely increase when there are many sophisticated investors with large sums of money to buy and sell shares. But, this is just a generalization about what may cause efficiency, and cannot be accepted as conclusive evidence.

C. When the market is efficient in the semistrong form (in which we are discussing *publicly available* information, and *not* information known only to a few insiders, such as the president and vice-presidents), the prime implications for accounting concern *location* of disclosure as well as the quantity/quality of information provided. This concerns the objectives of accounting and measurement versus disclosure situations, discussed earlier in the book.

One frequently discussed implication of the hypothesis is whether information can be in footnotes instead of being directly incorporated into measurements on the income statement and balance sheet. Both alternatives provide publicly available information. Therefore, in an efficient market (in the semistrong sense), the location should not matter—the data will be assessed for relevance and incorporated, where applicable, into stock prices.

Note that location of disclosure would *not* be a concern to a person having all of these "characteristics": (1) sophisticated investor, (2) operating in an efficient market in the semistrong form, (3) who also has an objective of accounting of cash flow prediction or evaluation of management. That person would use the information regardless of its location. *However,* location of disclosure is *extremely* important in the following *measurement* situations:

1. Tax postponement. Income tax is based on taxable income, and not on what is included in a note to the financial statements.

2. Bonuses based on income figures. Location could be extremely important when a bonus can be based on any one of: (a) gross profit, or (b) operating income before income taxes and extraordinary items, or (c) net income, or even (d) income less dividends.

3. Partners sharing income before taxes. This is a variation of (2), but is important to partners whose income depends upon the income statement figure and not on what is in a note to the financial statements.

4. Restrictive covenants. When a covenant is based on a quantified figure on the financial statements, measurement and location have to be important whereas note-disclosure is *not* relevant.

5. Purchase and sale of a company is based in part on financial-statement figures.

Again, note-disclosure would not affect the purchase price whereas an adjustment to any asset, liability, revenue or expense may do so.

D. Some portions of the financial statements (such as disclosure of interest rates for bonds, and lease payments required) provide information about the future. Much is based on accrual accounting of the past. It is not realistic to expect that accounting data will have a major impact on share prices. Investors anticipate the future and move stock prices accordingly. However, accounting ought to serve as a *check* on people's anticipations and guesses—*if* they believe what the financial statements tell them.

E. The semistrong form of the efficient-market hypothesis is certainly *not* telling us that accounting is irrelevant, and that people can guess at the figures, or acquire them from press conferences or press releases.

In summary, the efficient-market hypothesis has implications for accounting in those situations where the market is efficient in the semistrong form—with respect to *publicly available* information. That is, in the semistrong situation the form and location of disclosure of accounting data could be far less important than accountants may think. There are many other situations, such as with bonus plans, however, where measurement and location are important in *general*-purpose financial statements. Improvements have to be made in accounting and in tailoring it to specific situations. Some words communicate better than others. As users, we have to ascertain what objectives and facts the accountants and management had in mind when the figures were prepared.

Financial Statement Ratios

We have previously discussed ratios such as debt to equity. But, we have also warned that ratios may not be informative because accounting figures can vary significantly from company to company. Officers or a board of directors usually are free to choose one accounting policy over another. A major theme of the book is that accounting policies are selected after consideration is given to who has the *power* to choose and rank objectives of accounting. Constraints, such as corporate law, may or may not be restrictive. When they are *not* restrictive, greater emphasis is placed on facts/estimates and objectives. Two companies in the same line of business may show quite different accounting results from having engaged in identical transactions, because their objectives of accounting differ, the "facts" have been interpreted differently, and they face different constraints. (See "consistency" and "comparability" in Chapter 8.)

Ratios have other limitations because of their mathematical composition. A numerator divided by a denominator equals the ratio. If *either* figure is suspect for any reason (arbitrary allocation, accounting policy of questionable relevance for a user's objective), the ratio is of doubtful use. Also, magnitude is a problem because one divided by ten and one million divided by ten million give the same ratio.

Where might ratios be applied sensibly? The differences in objectives, facts, and constraints from company to company are eliminated when the *same company's* results are compared year to year. Thus, trends in ratios can be easily seen:

	19—1	19—2	19—3	19—4
Return on investment (income divided by owners' equity)	0.12 to 1	0.11 to 1	0.1 to 1	0.09 to 1
Expressed as a percentage	12	11	10	9

Ratios can prove useful in comparing two or more stores in the *same chain* (e.g., Canadian Tire or Shoppers Drug Mart):

	Store *A*	Store *B*	Store *C*	Store *D*
Gross profit to sales	0.38 to 1	0.4 to 1	0.36 to 1	0.31 to 1

What is the problem with Store *D*?

Ratios *may* be useful in analysis when two different companies are being compared, *and* the assets of both are essentially liquid (and therefore comparable because accounting policy differences are minimal). For example, a retail store may lease all or most of the long-lived assets that it uses. If the store "turns over," i.e., sells quickly, the inventory several times per year, and sells only for cash, the assets "tend" to be cash equivalents. That is, differences between FIFO and weighted average are of minor importance when the inventory is virtually measured at replacement cost. The gross profits to sales and a few other ratios may be usefully compared when two retail stores are operating on a cash-equivalent basis, as described above.

To this point in the "Financial Statement Ratios" section of this chapter, emphasis has been placed on being careful how we use ratios. The reason for this is that it is not unusual to see meaningless ratios being compiled by people who do not understand that they are comparing "apples and oranges". In view of this situation, only a few ratios will be mentioned.

1. Working capital (Current Assets to Current Liabilities): The ratio is:

$$\frac{\text{Current Assets}}{\text{Current Liabilities}}$$

At the beginning of this century, this ratio was viewed as a measure of financial liquidity. That is, current assets were more liquid than long-lived assets. The usefulness of the ratio decreased, however, as people came to recognize that an asset such as inventory is really a "permanent" financial investment. Although the inventory, physically, is being sold, it has to be replaced. Thus, the *financial* investment is somewhat permanent.

Another limitation of the working capital ratio is that the composition of current assets is a mixture of items at different valuations and states of liquidity. Inventory is at cost whereas accounts receivable is at net realizable value. Accounts receivable is one step removed from cash, i.e., the collection of the receivable. Inventory is usually two steps removed from cash, i.e., the sale of the inventory on account, and then collection of the receivable.

The working capital ratio can vary dramatically from industry to industry. A retail store, for instance, would have a large quantity of inventory in its current asset category. As a result, the ratio may be 2:1 or 3:1. But, a hotel or a utility would have its saleable commodity (rooms, or electricity) in the long-lived category. As a result, a "normal" working capital ratio may be 0.9 or 0.8 to 1.

2. *Income to Sales:*   This type of ratio is watched closely in some industries, such as retailing, where management needs high volume to compensate for the low income made on each sales dollar. It is not uncommon to see the following analysis, expressed as a percentage:

	January	February	March	April
Gross profit to sales	28.1%	28.4%	29.1%	27.6%
Income to sales	3.2%	2.9%	2.8%	3.1%

The trend lines (if any) can point to problem areas within a store.

The ratios are often much less useful for comparing departments within a larger store. This is because the markups on cost to arrive at retail price can vary significantly with different types of merchandise. Jewellery markups can be exceptionally high, whereas grocery markups are much lower.

3. *Inventory Turnover:*   This ratio is:

$$\frac{\text{cost of goods sold}}{\text{average inventory (opening and closing)}}$$

The investment in inventory can be costly because storage, interest, and insurance expense have to be incurred. Most businesses try to strike a balance between having so little inventory that sales are lost and having so much that carrying costs are higher than possible gross profits. The inventory turnover ratio can be monitored from month to month to watch for trends, e.g., obsolete or slow-moving goods.

Ratios are only informative when there is some basis for comparison. A comparison with a prior month may not be worthwhile because conditions may have changed. We must always ask ourselves: What are we comparing the ratio to?

4. *Receivables Collection Period:*   This ratio is:

$$\frac{\text{current accounts receivable}}{\substack{\text{sales on account for the previous year} \\ \text{(or a similar period)}}}$$

For example, accounts receivable may amount to $400,000 and sales on account for the previous year could be $1.2 million. *If* sales are roughly equal per month, i.e., $100,000 per month, four months of sales on account are uncollected. This *could* indicate that the credit department or collection staff are being too casual, or that extended credit terms are being given, or that some major customers are in financial difficulty. The ratio is only informative when we have a worthwhile basis for comparison. As many businesses have seasonal or cyclical sales patterns, ratios based on receivables, and perhaps, inventories, have to be interpreted carefully.

5. *Expenses to Some Base, Such as Sales Dollars:* This ratio and the previous four are primarily of benefit to managers and owners of small businesses. That is, management of the business may be aided by keeping track of trends or variations. Some expenses are "fixed" with time, e.g., property taxes, insurance, and the president's salary. That is, they continue whether or not a sale is made. Other expenses may vary with sales volume. If a base upon which expenses (or revenues) tend to vary is ascertainable, the following ratios or percentages can be computed:

A. Selling expenses to sales, and

B. Advertising expenses to sales, and

C. Sales returns to sales.

Creditors and investors tend to look at the following types of ratios or percentages:

1. Debt to equity (long term liabilities divided by owners' equity, or total liabilities divided by owners' equity.)
2. Income to owners' equity (or return on investment).
3. Times bond interest is earned.
4. Earnings per common share.
5. Price-earnings ratio.

The first two have been discussed before. The last two are mentioned in the next chapter. "Times bond interest is earned" tends to be reported in prospectuses, i.e., documents that are made available to persons who may want to buy shares or bonds in a company. In a sense, it is a measure of safety for the bondholders. Suppose that income *before* income taxes and bond interest is $1 million and that bond interest is $200,000. The interest is therefore earned *five* times ($1,000,000 divided by $200,000). Note that the figures have to be comparable—*before* income tax and *before* interest.

In summary, ratios and percentages can prove useful in situations where some reasonable basis for comparison exists, and the figures are compiled from period to period on a consistent basis. Often, this occurs in small businesses, in chain or franchise operations, and when the assets are essentially liquid. In many other situations, ratios have to be interpreted with care, or viewed with skepticism.

Interpretation Examples

Example 1

A headline in the *Toronto Star* (March 19, 1983, p. D8) reads: *Hudson's Bay has huge loss following accounting change*. The article describes how the merchandising profit dropped from $107 million in 1981 to $22.1 million in the year ended January 31, 1983. The total loss for 1983 amounted to $122.2 million, over 50 percent of which was from an accounting change affecting tax losses. What accounted for the difference between a $22.1 million merchandising profit and a loss before the accounting change of about $25 million? That is, which figures tend to fall into the income statement between merchandising profit and net loss?

The article does not give us an answer. Interest and income taxes, however, may provide a clue. Has some interest expense been deducted in arriving at the $22.1 million? The Bay paid $261.3 million in interest in 1983. It was caught, along with many other businesses, in the early 1980s with a high debt, much of it at high interest rates. If this debt had been equity, the loss would vanish.

The accounting change consisted of *not* reducing the loss for taxes that *may* be recovered in future years. Federal tax law allows a company with a "taxable loss" to reduce income taxes for the previous three and the next seven years. Thus, no income taxes would be payable if the Bay had taxable income (before the loss claim of $122.2 million) of, say, $120 million in 1984 through to 1990. A tax "saving" of say $55 or $60 million in 1984 through 1990 would represent a dramatic turn around.

This is a good example of where conservative accounting *may* reverse itself in the future. As an article by Lee Berton (*The Wall Street Journal*, April 26, 1984), joked: "Did you hear the one about the accountant who is asked the color of a particular horse? His answer: Brown on this side."

Example 2

The Globe and Mail (May 17, 1984), p. B1, carried the following headline: *Burned Airliner Becomes $6 Million Profit For* PWA. Fortunately, the article explains the headline: "But the profit is largely illusory because the Calgary-based airline will have to spend about $20 million to replace the Boeing 737 that burned on the runway in Calgary...in March. No one was killed in the accident." The writer goes on to say: "This accounting practice, which disguises disaster as income, made the difference between a profit and a loss at Air Canada in 1983." (Air Canada's 1983 net income was $3.8 million.) The financial statements show an $18.5 million "gain on disposal of property and equipment". The gain is not called an extraordinary item, presumably because disposals of equipment occur each year. *The Globe and Mail* writer quotes a source as estimating that Air Canada had "a gain of as much as $10 million from the settlement" on one accident in the U.S.A. in 1983, in which a DC9 was destroyed.

What do we learn from this example? We have to know something about industry accounting practices *or* we have to be familiar with the company. Then we can check to see how they chose to account for particularly important transactions.

Example 3

Accounting Change May Have Averted Huge Canadair Loss is a headline in *The Globe and Mail* (June 8, 1983, p. B15). The article says: "Canadair Ltd...could have avoided last year's sudden billion-dollar write-off if it had been more cautious in capitalizing the costs of its Challenger jet development program...." This example tends to be the opposite situation to Example 1.

The article explains: "Canadair 'treated all costs which were in any way related to the Challenger program as costs of the program.' All such costs showed up on the balance sheet as work-in-progress inventory."

In brief, for some years, Canadair's balance sheet showed an asset that turned out to be an expense. Hudson's Bay is *not* showing an item on the 1983 balance sheet that may turn out to be a major asset.

Example 4:

Examine the income statement that follows, and record as much useful information and analysis as possible before reading the paragraphs that follow it.

Income Statement
For the Year 19—8

Sales		$150,000
Expenses:		
Wages and benefits	$95,750	
Rent	14,000	
Utilities	2,250	
Supplies	1,420	
Office expense	700	
Depreciation	860	
Other	330	115,310
Income		$ 34,690

In interpreting financial statements, it is useful to have a list of questions to ask ourselves. For example:

1. In which types or lines of business is the company engaged?

2. Is the business incorporated?

3. What accounting policies are being followed?

4. Can we ascertain the likely objectives of financial accounting?

5. Is the company following GAAP? If so, are there other constraints, such as securities or company legislation. (Note that a company is incorporated under *one* Companies Act, but could be subject to more than one securities act, because securities legislation is provincial, and the company may wish to sell its securities in more than one province.)

6. Is the business owner-managed?

These points are examples only. They are relevant, however, for the following reasons:

1. Different fact and business situations are encountered with different lines and types of business. Accounting for revenue and expenses could differ among construction, real estate, mining, and other resource companies. All these are higher risk businesses, and are unlike a grocery chain, bank or insurance company. Observe that the income statement does not have a cost of goods sold. Maybe it is a service business—such as a hair salon or barbershop.

2. The absence of income tax suggests that the business is unincorporated. For income tax purposes, the income figure of $34,960 would be taxable in the hands of the proprietor, or partners.

3. We would have to read the notes to the financial statements, and the balance sheet, in order to learn which accounting policies are in use. With no inventory, and minimal depreciation ($860), however, the accounting policies may not be significant in the computation of income. That is, the business may largely be on a cash basis.

4. If the business is a barbershop, for instance, probably the only use of the financial statements would be for income tax purposes. The premises are rented; thus, there would be few assets to pledge to a bank as collateral for a loan. The proprietor or partners would have to guarantee any bank loan personally. General-purpose financial statements of the barber shop are not likely to be required by a banker.

5. A small company with sales of $150,000 is not likely to prepare GAAP financial statements. The company is private and would not have to be concerned about securities legislation. As we concluded previously, the prime use of the statements would be for income tax. Depreciation probably would equal the capital cost allowance on chairs and equipment.

6. If the business is *not* owner-managed, there may be an incentive plan for the managers, and it *may* be based on an income statement figure. If so, there would be a second objective of accounting that could be in conflict with the income tax postponement objective. But, with an uncomplicated barbershop example, we do not have to be concerned about conflicting objectives—especially if the two largest items (sales and wages) are based on cash receipts and disbursements.

The foregoing is "speculation"—not found in the income statement. As we practise reading financial statements, and preparing a list of questions to ask ourselves, we learn to "speculate". As we will see in the next chapter, it is *not* always clear what business an organization is engaged in, and what are its objectives.

Example 5:

Whose *condensed* financial statements are these, for the year ended December 31, 1984?:

	(in millions)
Working capital	$1,848
Investments and other long-term assets	511
Property, plant, and equipment at cost less accumulated depreciation and amortization	4,974
	$7,333
Long-term debt	$1,184
Deferred income taxes	1,544
Capital stock	1,324
Retained earnings	3,281
	$7,333

Revenues:		(in millions)
Crude oil		$ 690
Natural gas		185
Petroleum products		6,366
Chemicals		753
Other operating		454
Interest and investment		167
		8,615
Expenses:		
Exploration	$ 63	
Purchases of crude oil and products	3,909	
Extracting, processing and manufacturing	1,068	
Marketing and administration	879	
Interest	126	
Depreciation and amortization	260	6,305
		2,310
Taxes and levies		1,777
Net income		$ 533

This chapter has mentioned the importance of knowing what we are comparing matters to when we make judgments. We have stressed that comparing the financial statements of two companies has serious potential danger. Who has the power and whose objectives of accounting have prevailed (Chapter 6)? Are the facts and legal constraints the same? How do the accounting policies differ?

When we try to figure out whose financial statements the foregoing are, we are forcing ourselves to think in terms of comparisons. We must read critically, seeking out the important clues—the same types of clues that we have to look for when we are reading a financial statement for an identified company.

What stands out?

1. The words oil, and gas, and chemicals. Who would have over 70 percent of its revenue from petroleum products?

2. Who would be purchasing $3.9 billion dollars of crude oil? Paying $1.777 billion in various taxes?

3. Who would have close to $5 billion in plant and equipment? Deferred income taxes of $1.5 billion? A debt to equity ratio of about 1:4 ($1.184 debt versus equity of $1.324 plus $3.281)?

4. Who may have a return on accounting investment of about 12 percent ($533 million versus $1.324 and $3.281 billion)?

To interpret financial statements, we have to combine statement analysis with our general knowledge, and awareness of Canadian business operations will help us.

All of us pass gas stations every day. Which are the "big" ones—in terms of number of stations? Which is mentioned frequently in the newspapers as having huge investments in refineries? Our company is Imperial Oil Limited, or Esso.

How has it performed? We can look at 1983's figures (net income was $290 million in a recession year). We can ascertain which accounting policies the company is following, and what effect they may have on income. But largely, as investors (if this is our orientation), we have to focus on what will happen to the price of petroleum products and how they will be taxed by the Canadian government. The future for Imperial Oil lies in exploration, and in receiving an "adequate" or better return on its assets. Additionally, as investors, our concern may also be whether accounting will reflect what is happening in the business, or (through its choice of accounting policies) may delay recording the effect. If the market is efficient in the semistrong form, *and* additional credible sources of information are available, we may not have to be concerned what the financial statements show. (A company such as Imperial Oil is likely to be watched closely by informed investors. Other companies whose financial statements are analysed, however, may present us with a quite different situation.)

In total, this section of the chapter commenced with some examples of what the financial press may look at when it interprets financial statements. We saw the contrast of Hudson's Bay's having an unrecorded tax claim that *may* become an asset, and Canadair's having to expense development costs that they previously thought were assets. Canadair was more optimistic than the Bay. We also saw how Air Canada and Pacific Western Airlines treated insurance claims for burned airplanes, and how the financial writer could claim "this accounting practice...disguises disaster as income..." The message is that we cannot read financial statements as they appear to be, but must draw on all the information that we have discussed in this book.

Next, we switched to some interpretation strategies to stress the importance of a company's environment on our judgments and conclusions. We have to deliberately look for certain features in financial statements. To do this, we often find that a list of questions (checklists) is helpful to proceed through—much as a pilot goes through a list before "takeoff", or much as a doctor questions a patient in trying to diagnose a disease.

Summary

This chapter reinforces the diagnostic, analytical, and application approach that we have been working toward throughout the book. The product or end result of accounting usually is the financial statement. (Exceptions exist for objectives of accounting such as internal control.) Preparers build their personality and preferences into the figures (Hudson's Bay versus Canadair example). There are no clear choices but there are indicators. Some are subtle, such as the extraordinary expense versus a usual expense that we saw in the PWA example.

One chapter cannot really be singled out as *the* statement analysis chapter. The process of interpreting financial statements is an ongoing challenge.

QUESTIONS

13-1 What are extraordinary items, and what is their significance to different objectives of accounting?

13-2 What are unusual items, and how are they reported? Why?

13-3 What is a prior period adjustment? Why is the sum not included in the current period's income?

13-4 How are prior period adjustments reported under GAAP? Why?

13-5 What are the likely uses of segment information?

13-6 Why does GAAP for public companies require both the reporting of geographic and industry segments?

13-7 For which objectives of financial accounting would quarterly reporting make sense?

13-8 Define and explain what is meant by the semi-strong form of the efficient market hypothesis.

13-9 In general, what are the benefits and limitations of ratio analysis?

13-10 Why might a hotel have a working capital ratio of less than 1 to 1?

EXERCISES

E13-1 Indicate whether the undernoted transactions or items are likely to be (1) usual, *or* (2) unusual, *or* (3) extraordinary *or* (4) not applicable, for *each* of the following two independent business organizations:

A. a retail department store that owns its land and store buildings.

B. a real estate organization that has a primary objective of selling its buildings in later years at large gains, but is currently renting the space to various tenants.

Transaction or item:

a. obsolete inventory is written down to zero, and the amount is material.

b. land that was held to construct a building was eventually sold at a material gain.

c. interest costs on a large bank loan.

d. a material amount of accounts receivable that appear to be uncollectible are written off.

e. land and building are sold at a large loss.

f. fire destroys a building that is only partially insured, thereby leading to a loss for the company.

E13-2 Illustrate the statement of retained earnings for Paton Limited (PL) for the years 19—8 and 19—9, from the undernoted information:

Before adjustment:

Retained earnings, January 1, 19—8	$820,000
Net income for 19—8	220,500
Dividends in 19—8	100,000
Retained earnings, December 31, 19—8	940,500
Net income for 19—9	266,700
Dividends in 19—9	100,000

During 19—9 a major error in accounting for income tax was discovered. A total of $100,900 relates to 19—7 and prior years, and a further $80,400 applies to 19—8. None relates to 19—9. All dollar figures are amounts owing to Revenue Canada for income taxes that were eventually paid in late 19—9.

E13-3 The following financial statements are for Curnew Corporation (CC):

Balance Sheets
December 31

	(in thousands of dollars)		
Assets	19—8	19—7	19—6
Current:			
Cash	$ 10	$ 15	$ 20
Accounts receivable	5,755	3,495	1,635
Inventory	6,230	3,795	2,020
Prepaid expenses	270	120	75
	12,265	7,425	3,750
Long-lived:			
Land	1,000	1,000	1,000
Building and equipment	9,925	9,460	9,145
	10,925	10,460	10,145
Accumulated depreciation	4,380	3,455	2,620
	6,545	7,005	7,525
	$18,810	$14,430	$11,275
Liabilities and Owners' Equity			
Current liabilities:			
Accounts payable	$ 1,680	$ 1,175	$ 960
Income tax payable	300	280	290
Bank loan	980	800	500
	2,960	2,255	1,750
Long-term debt, 14%	7,000	4,000	2,000
Owners' equity:			
Common shares	4,000	4,000	4,000
Retained earnings	4,850	4,175	3,525
	8,850	8,175	7,525
	$18,810	$14,430	$11,275

Income Statement

Years ended December 31

	(in thousands of dollars)		
	19—8	*19—7*	*19—6*
Sales revenue	$29,795	$25,670	$20,200
Cost of goods sold	21,715	18,380	13,700
Gross profit	8,080	7,290	6,500
Expenses:			
Selling	2,415	2,295	2,070
Administrative	1,225	1,200	1,165
Depreciation	980	870	735
Interest	1,160	650	330
	5,780	5,015	4,300
Income before income taxes	2,300	2,275	2,200
Income taxes	1,025	1,025	1,000
Net income	$ 1,275	$ 1,250	$ 1,200

Statement of Retained Earnings

Years ended December 31

	(in thousands of dollars)		
	19—8	*19—7*	*19—6*
Balance, beginning of year	$ 4,175	$ 3,525	$ 2,925
Net income	1,275	1,250	1,200
	5,450	4,775	4,125
Dividends	600	600	600
Balance, end of year	$ 4,850	$ 4,175	$ 3,525

Required:

A. Compute the following ratios for each of the three years:
1. Working capital
2. Income to sales
3. Inventory turnover
4. Receivables collection period
5. Selling expenses to sales revenue
6. Long-term debt to owners' equity
7. Income to owners' equity
8. Gross profit to sales revenue

B. Explain what information each of the ratios in (A) is designed to convey to creditors and/or owners of CC.

C. Which of the ratios is particularly significant or informative in CC? Why? What advice would you give to the company?

E13-4 Prepare a segment report for the following situation, and interpret the financial statement for a potential owner of the company:

| | (in thousands of dollars) | |
	19—9	19—8
Revenue:		
Manufacturing	$5,670	$ 5,375
Wholesaling	3,890	4,020
Retailing	4,980	4,600
Cost of goods sold:		
Manufacturing	3,170	2,980
Wholesaling	1,970	1,965
Retailing	2,625	2,410
Operating expenses:		
Manufacturing	1,235	1,180
Wholesaling	1,560	1,500
Retailing	1,060	1,015
Depreciation:		
Manufacturing	860	850
Wholesaling	775	765
Retailing	525	510

Some of the inventory sold by the wholesaling and retailing divisions of the company have been purchased from the manufacturing division.

E13-5 Segovia Corporation (SC) is considering the introduction of a bonus system for its new senior officers. During the most recent year, the following income statement transactions, among others, occurred:

Gain on sale of land	$198,550
Bad debts expense	566,230
Write-down of inventory to net	
realizable value	301,770

SC expects similar transactions to the above to occur in the next few years. Previous management had made a series of decisions three years ago that proved to be unsuccessful. It will take some months to withdraw one unsuccessful product line, and cease dealing with some customers who have poor credit ratings.

The board of directors of SC has asked you to recommend the figure on the income statement on which the bonus should be based. The board is considering using the net income figure, income before extaordinary items, income before unusual items, or gross profit. The new senior officers are in charge of *all* aspects of SC's operations.

Required:

Which figure(s) would you recommend to the board of directors for calculating the amount due under the bonus plan? Why?

E13-6 The income statements for D. Charron Limited (DCL) for 19—7 and 19—8 are:

	(in thousands of dollars)	
	19—8	*19—7*
Sales revenue	$9,285	$7,710
Cost of goods sold	5,975	4,760
Gross profit	3,310	2,950
Expenses:		
Selling	765	885
·Administrative	975	755
Depreciation	320	415
Interest	400	295
	2,460	2,350
Operating income before extraordinary item	850	600
Loss on disposal of equipment, net of income taxes of $100,000	—	300
Income before income taxes	850	300
Income taxes	400	250
Net income	$ 450	$ 50

Required:

Compute the following ratios for 19—7 and 19—8 and explain the ones that indicate a significant effect, or important change from year to year:

A. Gross profit to sales revenue

B. Selling expenses to sales revenue

C. Administrative expenses to sales revenue

D. Interest expense to sales revenue

E. Net income to sales revenue

F. Income before income taxes to sales revenue

PROBLEMS

P13-1 Indicate which of the undernoted companies/industries probably would have a working capital ratio of less than one to one. Explain your reasoning process. (Hint: Consider inventory and receivables less payables.)

1. Grocery chain
2. Hotel
3. Airline
4. Textbook publisher
5. Chicken farmer
6. Real estate—owner of shopping centres

P13-2 Indicate which of the undernoted companies/industries probably would have a low (less than 1 to 2) long-term debt to equity ratio. Explain your reasoning process. (Hint: Would you want to be a creditor of a company in that industry?)

1. Telephone company
2. Construction company specializing in northern exploration
3. Bank
4. Mining company
5. Oil and gas exploration company
6. Computer software developer
7. Real estate—owner of large office buildings
8. Wheat farmer

P13-3 Blazouske Corporation (BC) has a working capital ratio and a long-term debt to equity ratio of 1 to 1 prior to the undernoted transactions. Indicate whether the transactions that follow *increase*, *decrease* or have *no effect* on each of the ratios. Explain your reasoning. Treat each transaction as being *independent* of the others.

1. BC issues long-term debt.
2. Inventory is purchased on account.
3. A building is acquired by paying 10 percent cash and by signing a twenty year mortgage.
4. A dividend on common shares is declared and paid in cash.
5. Depreciation is recorded.
6. Inventory is sold on account, at a profit.
7. Obsolete inventory is expensed.
8. Receivables are collected in cash.
9. Long-term debtholders exchange their debt for new common shares of BC.
10. Long-term debt is retired or redeemed by paying cash.

P13-4 Assume that each of the undernoted companies has a December 31 year end. Indicate which probably would have a first quarter income statement that would *not* be indicative of their actual *annual* income. Explain your response.

1. A fishing company.
2. A department store.
3. A bank.
4. A Canadian airline.
5. A travel agency.
6. A major league baseball team.
7. A television station.
8. A natural gas distribution company.

P13-5 You have just been hired as an investment analyst for a large underwriting house, Good Fundy Limited. Your first assignment is to evaluate two companies in the same industry and to recommend which is the best buy. You have been provided with the following data:

1. Both companies have total assets of $5,000,000 and liabilities of $3,000,000;

2. The companies have the following income statements:

	Company A	Company B
Sales	$500,000	$500,000
Cost of goods sold	300,000	200,000
Gross margin	200,000	300,000
Selling and administrative expenses	75,000	125,000
Income before tax	$125,000	$175,000

3. Both companies are engaged in the manufacture of chemicals.

Required:

Which company is the best buy? Identify the information that you would require, together with the reasons for needing the additional information, in order to decide which company is the best investment.

P13-6 The Canadian government ordered that the *Canadian Commerical Bank* be placed in liquidation as of September 1985. In an October 1985 report to the Senate Committee on Banking, Trade and Commerce, the two external auditors of the bank gave the following explanation (in part) of why they had given a standard form or normal audit report on the financial statements of CCB at October 31, 1984. (See a typical audit report in Appendix 1-A.)

> One of the fundamental concepts underlying the preparation of financial statements of a bank (or of any other enterprise) is that it will be able to realize its assets and discharge its liabilities in the normal course of business for the foreseeable future. This is commonly referred to as the "going concern" assumption. In the past, banks have experienced liquidity problems or incurred operating losses but, nevertheless, continued operating in an orderly manner. The 1984 annual financial statements of CCB were prepared using the going concern concept because management was of the opinion, with which we concurred, that the Bank would continue as a going concern. Had such a conclusion not been reached it would have been necessary to prepare the financial statements on a liquidation basis, valuing all assets at forced sale basis values, thereby ensuring the failure of the Bank.
>
> Under both the going concern and liquidation bases, generally accepted principles would require that loans should be written off when they are *known* to be uncollectible and a provision made for shortfalls where it is *probable* that loans will not be collected in their entirety. It should be noted that no provision is required if it is *possible* that a loss may be incurred: rather, such loss must be probable, that is, likely to occur.

Required:

A. What do the auditors mean by "… thereby ensuring the failure of the Bank"?

B. Given that auditors usually tend to accept the going concern basis of valuation (instead of values that would be received if liquidation or auctions were necessary) what effect does this have on ratio analysis—especially of current or liquidity ratios?

C. Do you agree with the viewpoint of the auditors of CCB?

EXPLORATION MATERIALS AND CASES

MC13-1 (Review) Newton Corporation Limited (NCL) was incorporated under the *Canada Business Corporations Act* in January 19—5. NCL is owned by three wealthy businesspersons, who hired a president and a vice-president of sales to manage their company.

A bookkeeper was hired to record NCL's transactions during 19—5. However, she has not been consistent with her journal entries, and the accounting journals and ledgers are difficult to understand and not what the company thinks that it needs.

You have been hired to help the owners and president of NCL choose suitable accounting policies and procedures for NCL. The owners of NCL would like to keep the company's income taxes as low as possible, through keeping the company's income as low as is reasonable. The company wants to have its financial statements prepared in accordance with generally accepted accounting principles. The owners also recognize that the president and the vice-president are important to NCL, and that they are being paid, in part, through a bonus system. The bonus is 10 percent of NCL's income before income taxes.

You have been able to investigate the operations of NCL and have learned the following:

1. The company has three products: (a) distribution of computer hardware manufactured by a company with a well-recognized name; (b) sale of computer software programs, many of which are prepared by NCL, and (c) distribution of computer books.

2. The computer hardware is purchased from the manufacturer and sold to various customers, most of whom pay cash or use a credit card. A few customers are permitted to buy on credit, and one bad debt has arisen to this point (December 19—5).

3. The computer software programs carry a warranty for two years, and NCL provides services at the customer's office free of charge.

4. The distribution of books involves selling to the public and to bookstores. The latter are allowed to return up to 50 percent of their purchases made in the previous six months. The former pay by cash or credit card. NCL has exclusive Canadian rights to some types of computer books.

5. To early December 19—5 invoices rendered to customers for the three products amount to:

Hardware	$18,629,420
Software	5,500,200
Books	899,600

Servicing costs to date on the software amount to $310,000. Books returned to date amount to $101,200 at retail price.

6. The purchase prices of the hardware and book inventory vary with each purchase. The cost of particular titles of books is always rising whereas the cost of purchases of computer hardware fluctuates by five to twenty percent with each purchase order.

7. NCL bought its own building, which includes a warehouse, sales offices, and administrative offices. The building is about five years old, and should have a life of thirty or more years. It is centrally located, which makes the land a good investment. In total, NCL paid $1,690,000 for the land and building. A mortgage of $1,000,000 was arranged, and the balance was paid in cash.

Required:

A. List up to three alternative policies or methods of accounting (e.g., depreciation methods) for long-lived assets, inventories, receivables, liabilities, and revenue that would be appropriate for NCL's circumstances. Explain your reasoning.

B. Which of the policies that you have mentioned in (A) would likely be chosen by the president and vice-president of sales to meet their personal objectives? Why? What would be the likely consequences to NCL if the accounting policies favored by the president and vice-president were selected for accounting for the next five years?

C. Would the owners agree with the accounting policies that you chose in (B)? Why?

D. What accounting policies would you recommend, given your role of reporting to the owners and the president and vice-president? How would you explain your choice to the interested parties?

MC13-2 (Review) DeBono Corporation (DC) prepares computer software for a variety of clients. Its software packages are of two varieties: standard and specially prepared. The standard software packages have been tested extensively to ensure that they are effective under a variety of situations. The software that is specially prepared for clients often has to be debugged to make it fully operational.

DC tends to have two types of clients: medium-sized corporations that cannot afford their own computer specialists, and smaller clients who have special needs for computers and sometimes do not have sufficient cash to pay immediately for software programs.

DC is a private company owned by the DeBono brothers. The company is managed by three senior officers (a president and two vice-presidents). As a result of recent negotiations, these officers are to be paid a salary plus a bonus based on income of DC before income tax. The DeBono brothers rarely become involved in the affairs of DC and are primarily interested in maximizing their income from DC, which includes keeping income taxes as low as possible.

The owners and senior officers of DC have engaged you to help them develop revenue recognition policies that are suitable for the company. They believe that the following revenue recognition points might prove sensible under different conditions:

1. on completion of the computer software program
2. on sale of the program to a reliable customer
3. on collection of the account receivable for (2)
4. when the warranty period expires, which is one year after program is delivered to a customer.

Required:

A. What are the most likely goals or objectives of DC?

B. How would you rank the likely goals? What is the most important one? Why?

C. How would you rank the company's objectives of financial accounting? What criteria would you use?

D. Which is the most important objective? Why?

E. What are all of the different situations that the company faces with respect to collectibility of the receivable, and likely need to incur warranty expenses?

F. Which revenue recognition policy should be used for each of the situations described in **E**?

G. Explain how your recommended accounting policies noted in (F) support the company's goals and objectives, and have the intended consequences.

H. How would your recommended accounting policies in **G** differ if DC were:
i) a public company, and
ii) obtained most of its necessary funds from a bank?
Explain in detail.

MC13-3 Hardwood Furniture Company (HFC) is a public company that has been in the furniture-making business for a number of years. As a result of its emphasis on manufacturing a quality product at a reasonable price, it has been able to develop a wide customer base. Consequently, it has never been seriously affected by changes in consumer tastes or incomes. Until recently, it has been able to operate on its fine reputation, and shareholders have become accustomed to receiving healthy dividends.

However, early in 19—6, other companies began to offer a similar quality product to that of HFC at a lower price. This competition had an immediate effect on HFC's sales and it became evident to HFC's president and major shareholder, Mr. Marshall, that the company would have to reevaluate its strategy.

After a careful review of market conditions, Mr. Marshall decided that the key to HFC's survival would be a major modernization of its equipment. With this in mind during 19—6 the company:

1. Disposed of equipment that had an original cost of $100,000 and accumulated depreciation of $80,000 (i.e., a net book value of $20,000) for $30,000 cash. (Note: Assume no tax is applied to this transation.)

2. Acquired new equipment for $400,000 cash.
According to Mr. Marshall the $400,000 of new additions is only a beginning. He estimates that an additional $500,000 of new equipment is required to restore HFC's competitive edge in the industry.

In order to buy this additional equipment, HFC needs cash and therefore Mr. Marshall has come to you requesting a $500,000 loan. He would like to borrow this money for a five-year term at a 15 percent rate of interest (i.e., the going rate of interest for a medium-risk loan). He has left the following financial statements for your review and would like to have your decision concerning the loan as soon as possible.

HARDWOOD FURNITURE LIMITED
Balance Sheet

	October 31	
Assets	*19—6*	*19—5*
Cash	$ —	$ 50,000
Marketable securities at cost (market: 19—6 — $75,000, 19—5 — $60,000)	60,000	60,000
Accounts receivable, net	300,000	300,000
Inventories (Note 1)	500,000	350,000
Total current assets	860,000	760,000
Property, plant, and equipment, at cost (Note 2)	1,200,000	900,000
Less accumulated depreciation	410,000	400,000
	790,000	500,000
Organization costs (Note 1)	20,000	30,000
	$1,670,000	$1,290,000

Liabilities

Bank indebtedness	$ 240,000	$ —
Accounts payable and accrued liabilities	350,000	300,000
Dividends payable	50,000	—
Income taxes payable	2,000	80,000
Total current liabilities	642,000	380,000
Long-term debt:		
10% note payable due November 1, 19—8	300,000	300,000
12% note payable due November 1, 19—9	100,000	—
	400,000	300,000
Deferred income taxes	48,000	40,000

Shareholders' Equity

Common shares (Note 3)
Authorized:
  1,000,000 common shares, no par value
Issued:

120,000 common shares	150,000	120,000
Retained earnings	430,000	450,000
Total shareholders' equity	580,000	570,000
	$1,670,000	$1,290,000

HARDWOOD FURNITURE LIMITED
Income Statement

	For the Years Ended October 31,	
	19—6	19—5
Revenue:		
Sales	$1,000,000	$1,500,000
Costs:		
Cost of goods sold	800,000	1,000,000
Marketing and distribution	10,000	50,000
Administrative and general	90,000	60,000
Interest	60,000	30,000
	960,000	1,140,000
	40,000	360,000
Income taxes:		
Current	12,000	170,000
Deferred	8,000	10,000
	20,000	180,000
Net income before extraordinary item	20,000	180,000
Gain on sale of property, plant, and equipment, net of taxes	10,000	—
Net income	30,000	180,000
Retained earnings, opening	450,000	320,000
	480,000	500,000
Less dividends	50,000	50,000
Retained earnings, closing	$ 430,000	$ 450,000

HARDWOOD FURNITURE LIMITED
Notes to Financial Statements

1. Summary of significant accounting policies:

   Inventories:

   Inventories are stated at the lower of LIFO cost or net realizable value.

   Property, Plant and Equipment:

   Depreciation is recorded on the straight-line basis over the estimated service lives of the assets.

   Organization Costs:

   Organization costs are amortized on a straight-line basis of $10,000 per year. This policy was commenced in 19—5.

   Income Taxes:

   Income taxes are accounted for on the tax allocation basis for all timing differences between accounting and taxable income.

2. Property, Plant and Equipment:

	19—6		19—5	
	Cost	Accumulated Depreciation	Cost	Accumulated Depreciation
Land	$ 100,000	$ —	$100,000	$ —
Buildings	600,000	270,000	600,000	240,000
Machinery	500,000	140,000	200,000	160,000
	$1,200,000	$410,000	$900,000	$400,000

   Total depreciation for 19—6 was $90,000 ($50,000 in 19—5). The long-term debt is secured by the company's property, plant and equipment.

3. Common shares:

   During the year the company issued an additional 20,000 shares for cash at a value of $1.50 per share.

4. Contingent Liabilities:

   The company is a defendant in an action brought in the Supreme Court of Ontario for damages in the amount of $200,000 for an alleged breach of contract. Legal counsel is of the opinion that there is no reason to concede any liability or to assume that the result of the action will adversely affect the financial position of the company.

   Required:

   Assume the role of a potential creditor.

A. Indicate whether you would loan Hardwood Furniture Company the $500,000 that they have requested. Explain your position clearly by stating the assumptions that you have made, the financial statement analysis that you have performed and the logic that you have employed.

B. What additional information would you require to ease your decision?

MC13-4 Three years ago your uncle, Mr. Galvin, was forced to sell his business because of poor health. He realized $500,000 on the sale of his business which he invested in government bonds yielding 8 percent per annum.

The other night, January 31, 19—8, your uncle was over for dinner. During a lull in the conversation, he expressed a keen desire to get back into business. He had completely recovered and over the past two months had been investigating numerous private companies.

He was anxious to use his $500,000 to purchase a business in the same industry in which he had spent his last 20 years. He had narrowed his choice down to two companies, Sugar Ltd. and Butter Ltd., which generally satisfied his requirements. He was under the impression from some of the stories that you had told him about your accounting course that you were a sharp interpreter of financial statements. He therefore wanted you to assist him in his decision.

Sugar Ltd. is wholly owned by Mr. Sugar; Mr. Sugar and his wife are directors of the company. Mr. Sugar is retiring shortly and will sell all of his common shares for $500,000. Mr. Sugar desires to retain his preferred shares as a source of retirement income. Butter Ltd. is wholly owned by Mr. Butter, his wife and their son. Mr. and Mrs. Butter are the directors of the company. Mrs. Butter is not active in the company's operations and is not drawing any salary. The Butters wish to sell all of their common and preferred shares for $500,000. Both sets of prospective vendors require cash for their shares.

He left you with a summary of financial data for the last four years. He has also determined that the accounting practices of the two companies are similar and both companies operated at approximately 70 percent capacity during 19—7.

Required:

Analyze the facts and financial data presented to you in the attached financial statements. Prepare a summary of the comments that you would discuss with your uncle at your next meeting, together with your recommendation. State all assumptions that you feel are required to make your recommendation. (Ignore any tax implications.)

Statement of Income and Retained Earnings (in thousands of dollars)

	Sugar Ltd.				Butter Ltd.			
	Years Ended June 30				Years Ended November 30			
	19—7	19—6	19—5	19—4	19—7	19—6	19—5	19—4
Sales	$900	$810	$792	$774	$495	$330	$480	$405
Cost of sales	578	513	505	505	157	112	150	135
Gross profit	322	297	287	269	338	218	330	270
Selling and variable operating expenses	37	30	25	24	22	18	18	15
Depreciation and other fixed expenses (Notes 1 and 2)	181	177	174	161	210	214	222	219
	218	207	199	185	232	232	240	234
Income (loss) before income taxes	104	90	88	84	106	(14)	90	36
Income taxes	52	45	44	42	36	—	35	8
Net income (loss) for the year	52	45	44	42	70	(14)	55	28
Retained earnings at beginning of year	241	226	212	200	211	246	227	220
	293	271	256	242	281	232	282	248

		Sugar Ltd.				Butter Ltd.		
Deduct dividends on								
—Preferred shares	15	15	15	15	14	14	14	14
—Common shares	15	15	15	15	32	7	22	7
	30	30	30	30	46	21	36	21
Retained earnings at end of year	$263	$241	$226	$212	$235	$211	$246	$227

Notes: (1) Fixed expenses include directors' remuneration ($30,000 per year for Sugar Ltd. and $50,000 per year for Butter Ltd.)

(2) For Butter Ltd. only, fixed expenses also include lease payments of $100,000 per year. Butter Ltd. leases its premises under a 15-year lease that commenced in 19—5.

Balance Sheets (in thousands of dollars)

	Sugar Ltd.				*Butter Ltd.*			
	as at June 30				*as at November 30*			
	19—7	*19—6*	*19—5*	*19—4*	*19—7*	*19—6*	*19—5*	*19—4*
Assets								
Current assets								
Cash	$ 10	$ 12	$ 5	$ 9	$ 50	$ 40	$ 35	$ 30
Accounts receivable	92	80	80	70	262	237	208	185
Inventories—at lower of cost or net realizable value	215	197	188	176	203	190	166	148
Prepaid expenses	8	6	7	5	5	8	6	8
	325	295	280	260	520	475	415	371
Fixed assets								
Land, building and equipment at cost (Sugar Ltd.)	1,638	1,571	1,510	1,443				
Equipment and leasehold improvements, at cost (Butter Ltd.)					375	331	277	288
Less accumulated depreciation	630	525	424	326	177	144	116	87
	1,008	1,046	1,086	1,117	198	187	161	201
Other assets								
Goodwill, at cost	50	50	50	50	—	—	—	—
	$1,383	$1,391	$1,416	$1,427	$718	$662	$576	$572

Liabilities

Current liabilities

Bank loan	—	—	—	$ 15	$100	$100	—	—
Accounts payable and accrued liabilities	$ 211	$ 193	$ 185	147	88	76	$ 51	$ 63
Income taxes payable	9	7	5	3	20	—	4	7
Instalments due within one year on long-term debt	50	50	50	50	—	—	—	—
	270	250	240	215	208	176	55	70
Long-term debt (8%), non-current portion	400	450	500	550	—	—	—	—
Shareholders' equity:								
Share capital:								
Preferred—5% (Sugar Ltd.)	300	300	300	300	—	—	—	—
Preferred—7% Butter Ltd.)	—	—	—	—	200	200	200	200
Common	150	150	150	150	75	75	75	75
Retained earnings	263	241	226	212	235	211	246	227
	$1,383	$1,391	$1,416	$1,427	$718	$662	$576	$572

CHAPTER 14

Owners' Equity

Chapter Themes

1. Considerable attention was given to objectives of accounting and facts or estimates in the early chapters. Chapter 12 mentioned that various constraints, such as restrictive GAAP, exist with liabilities and equities. This chapter is primarily concerned with legal constraints, especially the separation of legal capital/shares from income. Incorporated companies are granted limited liability for their shareholders. In exchange for this benefit, legislators have placed some limitations on how companies may operate.

2. If we were going into business for ourselves, how would we structure our company? There are income tax, administrative, and business reasons for selecting one form of organization, e.g., proprietorship versus limited company, over another.

3. Larger corporations become involved with many methods of financing—including preferred shares, warrants, options, convertibles, and a variety of methods and sales presentations. These matters are covered briefly, instead of in depth, because their relative popularity is strongly tied to income tax implications.

4. Dividends may be in the form of cash, shares or assets. Again, only brief comments are made because taxation law influences dividend rates and the form that dividends take. Federal budgets tend to change taxation effects frequently.

Forms of Organization

It is possible to incorporate a small limited liability company in most Canadian provinces and regions for under $1,000. A person can be a 100-percent shareholder or nearly 100-percent shareholder if she or he wishes. What benefit does this have over operating as an unincorporated proprietorship, or as a partnership? We have to look at the "paperwork" effect, taxation implications, relations with creditors, and similar matters.

When we wish to incorporate a company, a lawyer (the usual person involved) will want to know:

1. What we want to call our company?

2. What are the objects or purposes of the company?

3. How do we wish to operate the company? Who votes?

The answers to these and similar questions have to be provided before we may apply to a registrar of companies (or equivalent) for a certificate of incorporation (or equivalent). We use "equivalent" because there are differences among the provinces and regions, and the federal *Canada Business Corporations Act*. We incorporate under *one* of these corporations acts, but may operate in other regions by complying with the laws of that province, or region.

When we pick a name for the company, it has to be sufficiently different from other names to avoid possible confusion. It is not unusual to have to pick several alternative names before one is eventually accepted by the registrar of companies. To avoid this problem, some owners incorporate numbered companies, such as 123456 Ontario Limited. The number is chosen by the registrar of companies. Detective programs or shows tend to give a mysterious connotation to numbered companies. But, such a reference is undeserved.

A company is incorporated with particular objects or purposes: to import and sell goods, to be a consulting firm, to be an investment firm. Most people want the objects of their company to be sufficiently broad that they may legally enter into different activities to make a profit. *But*, we would not want the objects so broad that Revenue Canada would tax all of our activities at regular taxation rates. That is, Canadian taxation law has a category called *capital gains* and only *one half* of these gains is taxed. A capital gain arises from an infrequent transaction, which would be beyond the usual objects of the company. We would not want to confuse any *negotiations* with Revenue Canada by having objects that make everything appear to be regular income, which would be taxed in full. (A capital gain may arise by selling land that we bought many years ago.)

Many corporations acts draw a distinction between large companies and small ones, in terms of the amounts of their revenue and assets. For instance, the *Canada Business Corporations Act* uses figures of $10 million of revenue *or* fixed assets of $5 million to separate large from small. When our company exceeds either figure our company is "large". Other acts may have smaller numbers than the $10 and $5 million. Large corporations usually have to file financial statements with the government, and have to have an audit, unless this is waived by the government. The auditor would require financial statements to be prepared in accordance with GAAP.

The second distinction that has to be drawn is whether a company is private or public. A company incorporated under the *Canada Business Corporations Act* and having less than $10 million of revenue and less than $5 million of fixed assets *may* be a public company. That is, debt or shares could have been sold to the general public. Public companies have to comply with securities acts of the provinces or regions in which shares or debt are sold. An audit and GAAP would apply for public companies.

Large, public companies tend to produce much of Canada's goods and services. The vast majority of Canadian companies are *private* and *below* what is called the "size test", i.e., below $10 million of revenue or $5 million of fixed assets. As a result, they need not follow GAAP nor have an audit. They tend to have income tax postponement as their sole objective of financial accounting, or as an important objective. Bankers tend to *not* ask for audits in the smaller private companies owing to the cost. Usually, bankers are more interested in collateral security for their loan than in an audit.

A small private company can therefore operate without much of the red tape encountered by large companies from corporation or securities legislation. However, the small private company has to file an annual tax return, and make monthly payments to Revenue Canada for: payroll items (Canada Pension Plan, Unemployment Insurance, Income taxes deducted from employees), and installment payments for estimated annual income taxes payable by the company. That is, corporations must make monthly tax payments the same as we do when we work for an employer. Other paperwork for governments is necessary, but it is not a major nuisance.

What, then, are the prime costs and benefits of a private company? On the surface, the "corporate shell", or incorporation, grants limited liability to shareholders. This means that the shareholders cannot lose more than the amount that they have agreed to pay for the common shares. *But,* in practice, the owners of small private companies usually have to guarantee personally any loans made to their company, because creditors are unwilling to accept the limited liability concept. Therefore, by a process of elimination, the *main* benefit of a private company usually turns out to be freedom to plan income tax effects. An owner may (1) pay herself or himself a salary (which is taxed at personal income tax rates), or (2) leave the sum in the company (which results in taxation as income at corporate rates; but, these rates *may* be lower in small private companies than in large public companies), or (3) pay herself or himself a dividend (which may be eligible for a tax *reduction* because corporate tax has already been paid on taxable income of the corporation).

This situation with a private company is therefore quite different from a proprietorship or partnership. The full taxable income of a proprietorship/partnership, before salaries to the owner(s), is taxed at personal tax rates, which may be much higher than corporate tax rates for a small private company. Given this situation, why would anybody want to operate a business as a proprietorship or partnership? The main reasons *may* be:

1. Ignorance of income tax effects.

2. Ethics and public perceptions. Doctors, lawyers, and accountants operate as proprietorships or partnerships because patients and clients are likely to distrust a

professional who hides behind limited liability, granted through incorporation. Some professional legislation and rules of conduct discourage incorporation by professionals.

3. Fear of small amounts of paperwork.

4. Sometimes, in special situations (including for tax reasons) a proprietor/partner form makes sense.

Proprietorships and Partnerships

Corporations legislation requires that common share capital be segregated from retained earnings, so that creditors can easily determine the amount of share capital that has been placed in the company. Dividends become payable by debiting retained earnings. The source of dividends has to be disclosed under corporate law to help minimize frauds that could occur by paying shareholders out of share capital, and calling the amount a "dividend".

Such a segregation does *not* have to occur with proprietorships and partnerships because:

1. There is no limited liability in proprietorships and in *most* partnerships. (Partnership law allows for a limited partner category, but a limited or silent partner cannot be active in the business.) Proprietors and partners usually have to guarantee debt, from their personal assets (house, car). Therefore, a segregation of capital from retained earnings is not informative.

2. Partnership law is silent on most accounting matters, and does not refer to owners' equity financial reporting.

3. The prime users of partnership and proprietorship financial statements are the owners, and not an outside group (except Revenue Canada). The owners do not need a segregation of capital from retained income.

When we form a partnership with one or more persons, we ought to have a partnership agreement that sets out the following types of matters:

1. How much each partner should contribute as capital.

2. How income and losses are to be shared.

3. Whether salaries are to be paid; and, if so, how much.

4. Whether interest is to be paid on any loans or capital; and, if so, how much.

When the partners do *not* specify how income and similar items are to be shared, partnership legislation calls for it to be divided *equally*.

Proprietorship and partnership accounting is best illustrated by choosing a typical set of facts. Suppose that the following occurs:

1. Roger and Hedda Kassall each contribute $20,000 to commence their partnership, "Fresh Veggies Company", which operates a retail store in Pinetree Mall. (Note that they may use the word "company" in the title, but cannot use "limited", "incorporated", "ltd.", "inc.", "corporation", or similar words that signify that the business is a limited liability company.)

2. The partners buy various assets and incur liabilities. (These would be recorded as described in chapters 2 to 4.)

3. Income for the first year, before a salary of $16,000 to Hedda, who works at the store, amounts to $37,000. The partners agree to share income equally. Hedda withdraws her $16,000 in cash, treating it as a salary expense.

4. Each partner chooses to withdraw in cash $5,000 as a share of income.
   The journal entries to record the foregoing are:

1. Cash	40,000	
Capital, Roger Kassall		20,000
Capital, Hedda Kassall		20,000
3A. Expense	16,000	
Cash		16,000
3B. Revenues (various accounts)	xxx	
Expenses (various accounts)		xxx
Capital, Roger Kassall		10,500
Capital, Hedda Kassall		10,500

To share the income after salary of $21,000
($37,000—$16,000).

4. Withdrawal, Roger Kassall	5,000	
Withdrawal, Hedda Kassall	5,000	
Cash		10,000

The withdrawal account need not be used. It could be closed to capital at the end of the financial year:

Capital, Roger Kassall	5,000	
Capital, Hedda Kassall	5,000	
Withdrawal, Roger Kassall		5,000
Withdrawal, Hedda Kassall		5,000

The ledger accounts for each partner would show:

Roger Kassall			Hedda Kassall	
	20,000			20,000
	10,500			10,500
5,000			5,000	
	25,500			25,500

The "owners' equity" section of the balance sheet at the *end* of the period would show:

Partners' capital:
Roger Kassall	$25,500	
Hedda Kassall	25,500	$51,000

The details would be backed up by a "Statement of Partners' Capital", which is much like a statement of retained earnings.

FRESH VEGGIES COMPANY
Statement of Partners' Capital
(Period of Time)

	Roger Kassall	Hedda Kassall	Total
Opening balance	$20,000	$20,000	$40,000
Share of income	10,500	10,500	21,000
	30,500	30,500	61,000
Withdrawals	5,000	5,000	10,000
Closing balance	$25,500	$25,500	$51,000

The statement of partners' capital has been prepared on the assumption that the income statement contains a line within the expense category:

Salary to an owner   16,000

That is, the income being divided is $21,000, and not $37,000.

If the $16,000 is not on the income statement, it would appear under Hedda Kassall's column in the statement of partners' capital. The $10,500 would become $26,500 and the $5,000 would become $21,000. The opening and closing balance would remain the same.

Private Corporations vs. Partnerships

Chapter 8 described some accounting concepts that are used extensively by accountants to reason through situations that they have not encountered before. Disclosure and arm's-length status concepts are important in proprietorships/partnerships. A proprietor cannot negotiate an arm's-length salary with himself. Therefore, accountants use separate disclosure on the financial statements, such as the one that we just described, "Salary to an owner".

Surprisingly, the same type of non-arm's-length disclosure treatment is not always carried through in small private corporations. A one-owner private corporation may show a salary figure on its income statement, and yet some of this amount could have been paid to the owner. What effect would this have on someone who is thinking about buying the private corporation? An attempt to ascertain a discounted worth for the company by looking to recurring cash flows would prove troublesome or perhaps impossible.

Earlier in the book (Chapter 6), we indicated that a private company may choose accounting policies that help to keep taxable income as low as possible. We also stressed that a set of financial statements for a private company having an income tax postponement objective could be misinterpreted by a creditor, who may believe that the company is unprofitable. This chapter has pointed out that owners of small private companies tend to vary salary/no salary and dividends/no dividends alternatives to keep their personal taxes as low as possible. In short, before we reach any conclusions from private-company financial statements, we have to ask questions about:

1. The accounting policies that are being used, and what their effect is on asset and income figures.

2. How have non-arm's-length transactions been handled, e.g., salary, interest, loans due from owners?

3. What is the recurring cash flow before non-arm's-length transactions?

4. What is the fair market value of services being provided by the owners? (That is, if someone had to be hired to perform the work of the owners, what sum would have to be paid? This ought to be deducted from 3.)

5. How has income tax expense been affected by salaries paid or not paid to owners? (What would income tax expense be if the company were being managed by non-owners?)

The financial statements of a private company have to be recast to the point of view of the user. For example, if we wanted to buy the company, everything (salary, dividends, loans, etc.) would have to be viewed from our perspective and personal tax side. Similarly, if we wanted to buy a business operated as a proprietorship, we would have to look at income tax effects—especially whether we should incorporate the proprietorship.

To illustrate, suppose that three business *entities* (proprietorship/partnership, co-operative/limited company, and a public corporation) have *identical* transactions for gross profit, and selling and administrative expenses. The income statements could differ, as a result of choosing different accounting policies. In this situation, however, we will use the same general accounting policies. Nevertheless, income differs because of salary, income tax, bonuses, interest, and non-arm's-length transactions:

	Proprietorship/ Partnership	One or Two Owner Private Corporation	Public Corporation
Revenue	$1,000,000	$1,000,000	$1,000,000
Cost of goods sold	600,000	600,000	600,000
Gross profit	400,000	400,000	400,000
Expenses:			
Selling	100,000	100,000	100,000
Administrative	80,000	80,000	80,000
Salary to owner/partner	40,000	—	—
Bonus to owner/partner	30,000	30,000	—
Interest on loan by owner/partner	20,000	20,000	—
Rental on building owned by shareholder	—	10,000	—
	270,000	240,000	180,000
Income before tax	$ 130,000	160,000	220,000
Income taxes		40,000	55,000
Net income		$ 120,000	$ 165,000

The income statements are merely showing how the $220,000 ($400,000 less $100,000 less $80,000) is being "distributed" among the owners. In the proprietorship/partnership situation, the entire $220,000 is taxable in the hands of the owners. The private company owner may choose whatever combination of bonus, dividend or other return, e.g., interest and rental, that helps to *minimize* (as opposed to postpone) income taxes. (The owner of the private company may also choose accounting *policies* that help postpone income taxes.) The public company would have to engage in arm's-length transactions, or transactions where arm's-length values, e.g., market prices, are in use.

Special Incorporations

Not all business corporations/limited companies are incorporated under a corporations act of a province or the federal government. Banks, trust companies, insurance companies, and some government owned Crown corporations are a few examples of companies that may be regulated by separate legislation. Financial institutions may have to follow accounting policies, in reporting to federal or provincial government agencies, that differ from what shareholders would want. For instance, *liquidity* is important in banks, trust companies, and insurance companies. As most long-lived assets are somewhat illiquid, an inspector of trust companies may give these long-lived assets a zero value. A *special-purpose* balance sheet prepared for the inspector would have to charge these "written off" assets against retained earnings—producing quite a different balance sheet from what has been discussed in much of this book.

Readers of financial statements should always look over the notes to the financial statements and the auditor's report very carefully in case some constraint has a major impact on accounting or provides additional information. For example, the February 15, 1985 auditors' report on the 1984 financial statements of Air Canada states:

> We further report that, in our opinion, the transactions of the Corporation and of its subsidiaries that have come to our notice in the course of our examination of the financial statements were in accordance with Part XII of the Financial Administration Act, its regulations, the Air Canada Act and its By-laws.

The auditors have therefore worked with the company in ensuring that the various pieces of legislation that affect the company have been complied with. Air Canada is a Crown Corporation and is therefore subject to more regulations than many companies.

Types of Shares

Shares may be categorized in several ways: (1) whether they rank first, second or perhaps last in the event of liquidation of the company, (2) whether they have a vote under normal circumstances, (3) whether they are entitled to an annual dividend, (4) whether they carry restrictive covenants, (5) whether they are convertible into another class of shares. As a general rule, shares contain whatever features are felt to be necessary in order to sell them. (The procedures followed in selling shares are much like the steps that are carried out to sell any commodity, such as houses or automobiles. They have to be made attractive to a potential buyer.)

COMMON SHARES

The most basic share is the common share. The holder of the common share is the "residual claimant" in a company. In the event of liquidation of a company, everybody else would have to be paid *before* the common shareholder would receive anything. As mentioned in Chapter 5 and elsewhere, the order of payment in liquidation would tend to be: secured creditors, e.g., bondholders, preferred creditors, e.g., government, unsecured creditors, e.g., accounts payable, preferred shareholders, and lastly common shareholders. The same approach tends to apply to interest/dividend payments. Bondholders would have restrictive covenants in their purchase/sale agreements (often called bond indentures) that do not permit dividends to be paid until any bond interest that is due has been paid. Similarly, most types of preferred shares would contain provisions preventing payment of common share dividends unless the preferred shareholder has been paid whatever dividends are due to her or him.

The attractiveness of one type of share over another, and the relative attractiveness of bonds versus shares is often decided by the current wording of income tax legislation. In the past twenty years in Canada, many significant changes in taxation law have occurred. Also, wide swings in interest rates, combined with taxation policies, create important effects on how buyers view shares and bonds. Consequently, we may only generalize about situations because they can change dramatically with taxation alterations and interest rate swings.

PREFERRED SHARES

Taxation law has caused the appearance of many "strange" types of preferred shares in the past ten years. At one time, the typical preferred share was cumulative and redeemable, and carried a fixed dividend rate. "Cumulative" means that the dividends accumulate as a "form of debt" if they are not paid when due. For instance, an 8-percent preferred share may call for 2-percent dividend payments four times per year—perhaps January 10, April 10, July 10, and October 10. Suppose that the dividend payments due on January 10, April 10, and July 10 are not paid. The unpaid dividends would accumulate, not as a liability but as an obligation that would have to be paid before common shareholders receive a dividend. In a strict sense—and this is very important—dividends become a liability only when the board of directors of the company declare a dividend, i.e., vote upon and pass an official resolution, at their legally constituted board of directors meeting. The unpaid dividends (called *dividends in arrears*) would be reported as a note to the financial statements until they have been declared—at which time they become a liability. If the board of directors decided to declare a dividend of 4 percent payable on October 10, this would represent the January 10 and April 10 payments—and those of July 10 and October 10 would still be in arrears.

"Redeemable" means that the board of directors could call the shares for redemption and pay the preferred shareholders whatever is owing to them. For example, the preferred shares may have been sold for $100 each but have to be redeemed for $102 *if* they are called for redemption within 10 or so years. If $4 is unpaid in dividends, the journal entry would be:

Preferred shares	100	
Retained earnings—dividend	4	
Retained earnings—premium on redemption	2	
Cash		106

Observe that the $2 is not charged to the income statement because it is a *capital transaction*. That is, preferred shares are a part of owners' equity, and any transactions affecting owners' equity are capital—not an income statement transaction.

"Fixed dividend rate" means that the preferred shares are sold at a rate that does not change over the life of the preferred shares. Bonds and debentures are issued for specified periods of time—often twenty or twenty-five years. Conventional preferred shares are issued without redemption dates, and therefore may be outstanding for well beyond twenty-five years. The combination of long terms and fixed dividend rates may make preferred shares unattractive at times—especially when taxation of preferred dividends may change, and interest rates are fluctuating. These two factors plus other corporate-taxation policies have led to the appearance of many unconventional preferred-share issues. By "unconventional" we mean shorter terms, variable rates, and special-taxation consequences.

Preferred shares (as well as bonds) often have to be sold with what are called "sweeteners", i.e., to make the shares more attractive to potential buyers. One of the original sweeteners was convertibility into common shares. This feature would be attractive to those who like the relative security of a preferred dividend rate for several years *and* a chance to get a higher dividend rate on common shares—if the company does well, and they choose to exchange their preferred shares for common.

The market price of preferred shares with fixed dividend rates will fluctuate with the prime rate of interest, i.e., the rate supposedly charged by the Bank of Canada to commercial banks. Hence, an 8-percent preferred share with an unlimited life and original face value of $100 will sell for $80 when the current rate for a similar type of share, i.e., same risk of loss of equity capital, is 10 percent. That is, the preferred share will generate $8 per year. To yield the current rate of 10 percent, the preferred share would have to sell for $80 ($8 divided by $80 = 10 percent).

Preferred shareholders who have convertible shares may be able to lessen the effect of the interest rate swings on the market price of their shares—from $100 down to $80, and perhaps up to $133.33. (If interest rates drop to 6 percent, an $8 fixed dividend share yields 6 percent interest at a price of $133.33 per share—$133.33 × 6% = $8.00.) That is, a preferred share that is convertible into common shares would *not* be treated as a pure fixed rate security by the market place. Therefore, swings in interest rates would often not affect the market price of the convertible preferred shares as much as they would the market price of preferred shares that are not convertible. When market price of the common shares rose significantly (and higher than an 8-percent dividend would be received if the shareholder held common, instead of preferred, shares), the preferred shareholders would "convert"—or trade their preferred shares for common. (Once we have converted, we cannot convert back to preferred.)

However, when the common shares are doing poorly on the market place, such as a stock exchange, the holder of a convertible preferred share would have to rely on the 8 percent (or whatever) dividend for cash income. Then, she/he would still be treated the same as someone with preferred shares that do *not* convert, and would be subject to swings in the market price of the preferred shares.

WARRANTS

A warrant is a document that entitles the holder to acquire (usually) common shares at fixed prices. The warrant may be issued as part of a unit of one common share and one warrant. For example, the warrant may be issued in 19—0 when the common share market price is $10. The warrant may entitle the holder to acquire one common share for $12 until the end of 19—2 and for $15 from 19—3 until the end of 19—6. The hope is that the common share price will increase to $16, or $20 or more by 19—5 or 19—6.

If a warrant or two is attached to an issue of non-convertible preferred shares to make them attractive, the acquisition price for the warrants may be set at, say, $11 per common share that may be acquired, instead of $12, and $13 instead of $15. The warrant therefore becomes an alternative to issuing convertible preferred shares. When exercised, the warrants help to bring additional equity into the business in future years—to provide a base of equity to allow for more debt to be sold.

Some complicated accounting problems can arise when common or preferred shares are issued with warrants attached, or when convertible preferred shares are issued. To illustrate, suppose that a company probably would be able to sell "straight" (non-convertible, and without warrants) preferred shares at a 12 percent dividend rate. However, it decides to sell a package for $100 that consists of a *convertible* preferred share, having two warrants to buy common shares for the next ten years. But, the preferred share dividend rate is *only 8 percent*. What is the most sensible journal entry? Should the entire amount be shown as:

Cash	100	
Preferred shares		100

Or, should a credit be made to a "share warrant" account? This complex subject is not further discussed; it is pointed out to show that so-called sweeteners, such as warrants, cause complex problems. (The warrants and convertibility must have some value; otherwise, the dividend rate could not have been reduced from 12 to 8 percent.)

RIGHTS

A *right* is similar to a warrant, but tends to have a much shorter life. Banks tend to issue rights to holders of their common shares in order to entice them to buy additional common shares. A right may be granted for 120 days, enabling the holder to buy one common share at 90 percent of market value as of the date on which the right was issued. The added equity-base enables the bank to increase its lending power.

Rights tend to acquire a market value and can be actively traded on stock exchanges or through investment dealers. Shares, warrants, and rights not traded through a stock exchange are usually traded "over-the-counter", i.e., through brokers and dealers. This means that as a buyer or seller, we do not have the additional protection of the stock-exchange rules. Brokers and underwriters, however, are actively supervised by securities commissions, and usually tend to be a safe way of conducting business.

A CAUTION

Newcomers to business must be careful to clarify in their minds the difference between buying shares from the company and buying through a stock exchange. When we buy shares from a company, the journal entry is:

Cash	100	
Common shares		100

If the province or region in which the company is incorporated permits the use of "par-value" shares, the journal entry may be:

Cash	100	
Common shares		80 (or so)
Contributed surplus		20 (or so)

(Par-value shares were in extensive use in Canada several years ago; but, because the term "par value" became somewhat meaningless, these shares have been eliminated in many jurisdictions today. Contributed surplus would appear in the owners' equity section of a balance sheet just above "retained earnings".)

However, when we buy shares through a stock exchange from a broker/dealer, we are *usually* buying from another person. No journal entry would appear on the books of the company for trades between two people (new shareholder and former shareholder). The company maintains a record of who the owners of the shares are, to permit it to send out notices, dividend cheques, and the annual and quarterly reports. The new name would be listed to replace that of the person who sold the shares. But, *no entry is made to common or preferred shares.*

Companies usually sell shares through broker/dealer/underwriters. These are called *primary* issues, and the *company* receives the money after paying commissions. Any notice that we receive from the broker would clearly indicate that the issue is new. Securities law requires that we be provided with a document called a prospectus when we buy a new issue of shares. As mentioned previously, wherever possible, the prospectus includes statements of income, retained earnings and changes in financial position (Chapter 16) for the previous five years, plus balance sheets of the two recent years. The prospectus also describes the company in ways permitted or required by securities law. Thus, it can be a thick document. Once these new securities have been issued to a primary buyer, however, no further entries occur on the company's accounting statements for trades between buyers and sellers.

OPTIONS

The term *options* has taken on a variety of meanings in the past ten years as stock exchanges generate new ways of speculating (as opposed to investing). We will concern ourselves with only one type of option—the type granted to the officers (president and other managers) of the company. Options of this type are granted as incentives to encourage the officers to work harder at increasing the market value of the common shares (presumably by increasing the profits of the company).

Options are arranged somewhat like warrants. That is, the holder may buy common shares, usually at only one set price, for a long period of time. Options may be granted for, say, 95 percent of the current market price because income tax law allows minor discounts to avoid taxation. A president may therefore be granted the right to buy a specified number of shares at $9.50 per share when the market price is $10 per share. The president does not have to give any money to the company until the date when the options are exercised—which could be five or more years later. When the option is exercised, the journal entry would be:

| Cash | 9.50 | |
| Common shares | | 9.50 |

But, the market price of the shares may be $20 or $30 at the date on which options are exercised.

The holder of the option clearly obtains a benefit of, say, $10.50 ($20 − $9.50). If this were a salary being paid to the president, the sum would be expensed. Under Canadian GAAP, however, the $10.50 appears only indirectly—as a reduction of the credit to common shares. We *do not* make the following journal entry:

Salary expense	10.50	
Cash	9.50	
Common shares		20.00

Therefore, when options exist, the income statement tends to understate salaries and benefits to corporate executives. Why do Canadian accountants not record the $10.50 as an expense? Chapter 8 provides the clues. How does a person *objectively match* on a year-to-year basis—especially when the market price of the common shares is fluctuating? Also, how *material* in amount is the $10.50 or equivalent? Canadian taxation law has affected options in different ways over the years, and the extent of popularity of them is directly traceable to taxation consequences.

Recording and Reporting

The previous section of the chapter discussed several transactions. Journal-entry illustrations usually help to clarify what has happened.

1. Bond conversions

When bonds are convertible into common shares, the journal entry on conversion would be:

Bonds payable	100,000	
Common shares		98,000
Discount on bonds payable		2,000

The $2,000 represents a discount on sale of the bonds that has not yet been expensed. The net figure for the bonds, $98,000 ($100,000 − $2,000), is credited to common shares on the assumption that only *no par value* shares may be issued by the company. (That is, the act under which the company is incorporated does *not* permit the issuance of par value shares. Legislation to eliminate par value shares was enacted in part because some people believed that par value meant something significant. However, at one time, many years ago, par value caused problems because the credit may have been split into two parts:

| Common shares (10,000 shares @ $5) | 50,000 | |
| Contributed surplus | 48,000 | |

Common shares would be credited for whatever the par value was—in this case, we have assumed it to be $5. The remainder would go to a contributed-surplus account—and could be paid back to the shareholders. (Some shareholders may think that the sum paid to them was a dividend instead of the portion of their capital investment that had been credited to contributed surplus.)

2. Preferred-share conversion

The journal entry is essentially the same idea:

Preferred shares	100,000	
Common shares		100,000

One type of share is being replaced by another. Again, the journal entry assumes the existence of only no-par-value shares.

3. Warrants, rights, and options

When warrants, rights, and options have been issued at no cost, there is nothing to debit when they are exchanged for common shares—except the *cash* that has to be paid by the prospective shareholder. The journal entry is therefore:

Cash	19.75	
Common shares		19.75

4. Reporting

The owners' equity section of the balance sheet (or accompanying notes) is required by corporate legislation to include some details about (a) the shares that the registrar of companies will permit the company to issue, ("authorized shares"), *and* (b) how many shares have been issued to date, *and* (c) how many shares were issued during the latest year, *and* similar particulars. Thus, the owners'-equity section of the balance sheet may appear as follows (also see the Fiberglas Canada Inc. financial statements in Appendix 1-A—especially Note 6):

Shareholders' equity:

Preferred shares. Authorized 100,000 shares of no-par-value. Cumulative, redeemable, with a 10% dividend rate. Issued 60,000 shares	$6,000,000	
Common shares without par value. Authorized 1,000,000 shares. Issued 400,000 shares	4,000,000	
Retained earnings per statement	5,678,000	
Appraisal increment on land (Note x)	2,000,000	17,678,000

The appraisal increment was discussed in Chapter 11. It is a part of owners' equity but is not "retained earnings" until the land is sold and the cash is realized—and the gain is determined. Note x would have to describe who computed the figures for the appraisal, and when. The asset "land" would be carried at appraised value, and not cost, on the asset side of the balance sheet.

Owners' Equity Ratios and Analysis

Chapter 13 provided some ratios that we tend to see in practice. Three more are: (1) book value per share, (2) earnings per share, and (3) price-earnings ratio.

Book Value

We saw the term *book value* in discussions of long-lived assets—cost less accumulated depreciation equalled book value. Book value per share means something quite different, and refers to owners' equity. In the foregoing shareholders' equity illustration, the total owners' equity amounted to $17,678,000. But, not all of this "belongs to" the common shareholder. We have to subtract the $6 million of preferred shares. We therefore have two book values per share:

Preferred:

$$\frac{\$6,000,000}{60,000 \text{ shares issued}} = \$100 \text{ per preferred share}$$

Common:

$$\frac{\$11,678,000}{400,000 \text{ shares issued}} = \$29.19 \text{ per common share}$$

If, for example, preferred shares had to be redeemed at $104 per share, their book value would increase to $104 per preferred share. The $240,000 ($4 x 60,000 shares) would be subtracted from $11,678,000 to arrive at a book value per common share of:

$$\frac{\$11,678,000 - \$240,000}{400,000 \text{ shares}} = \$28.59 \text{ per common share}$$

What does book value per common share mean? Often, it means little because the figures for assets are at cost, and not market price, and the company's choice of accounting policies affects what is included in retained earnings. Yet, some financial analysts refer to the figure as though it conveys something significant. When we see book value per share quoted, we should question it. When all the assets and liabilities are liquid, it may mean something.

This figure is often quoted in an attempt to convey how much net income attaches to a particular common share. Suppose that 100,000 common shares have been issued, and net income is $550,000. But, suppose that a dividend of $150,000 has to be paid to the preferred shareholders—who have priority over the common shareholders. This leaves $400,000 for the common shareholder:

$$\frac{\$400,000}{100,000 \text{ shares}} = \$4 \text{ per common share}$$

When the company's earnings pattern is fairly stable and no additional common shares are being issued, the $4 tells us the amount of net income that attaches to one common share this year, and perhaps next year. But, when either the numerator or denominator are increasing or decreasing, earnings per share is not much of a *predictor.* Yet, some financial analysts tend to use earnings per share in a futuristic or predictive context.

It is important to observe that some equity transactions *may dilute* the $4 that we calculated. Convertible preferred shares, when converted to common, would increase the denominator, or number of common shares outstanding. The numerator would increase because the preferred dividend would no longer have to be paid. When we recalculate the earnings per common share the figure could be higher or lower than $4 per share.

Rights and options to acquire common shares are more complicated to handle when we try to compute earnings per share. Rights and options bring in additional cash, whereas a conversion of debt or preferred shares does not bring in cash to the company. How much will the new cash earn—more or less than $4? This matter is not discussed further; it is mentioned to indicate that earnings per share is not easy to calculate and contains many assumptions that may limit its usefulness.

Price-Earnings Ratio

Like the previous two, this is another "rough-and-ready" figure that usually has to be treated with skepticism. Suppose that the current market price of a common share is $28 and the earnings per share is $4. The price-earnings ratio would be 7 to 1. More commonly, the term "seven times earnings" is used.

The idea underlying the price-earnings ratio is that we are paying, in this example, seven years of *current* earnings when we pay $28 to buy a share. We say that the concept is "rough and ready" because:

1. It is highly unlikely that $4 per share will be earned in each of the next seven years;

2. The $4 is an accrual figure, and not cash; and

3. A figure of $4 per year to be "received" over seven years does *not* have a present value of $28, i.e., $4 x 7 years.

When we value a company in an ideal state, we are discounting the future cash flows:

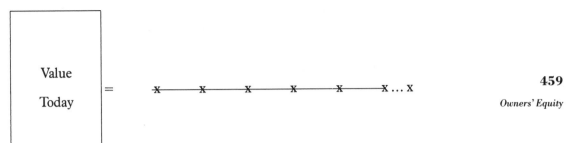

Future Cash Flows From Operations

Overall, therefore, the relationship between a *discounted* cash flow approach and a price-earnings ratio is remote. Nevertheless, analysts use the figure of price-earnings in a *valuation* context. As a result, we have to be cautious when we see the price-earnings figure because it is not a sophisticated measure.

Share Dividends and Share Splits

Share or stock dividends are popular in Canada only when taxation law gives reasonable treatment to them, compared to the usual dividend, which is paid in cash. A share dividend gives us additional common shares in the company instead of cash. *If* we have to pay tax on these share dividends, when we are not receiving cash, the share dividend is not attractive. Over the past thirty years, the taxation of stock dividends has varied widely as ministers of finance have used taxation to stimulate the economy or dampen price inflation.

The basic journal entry for a share or stock dividend is:

Retained earnings	1,000	
Common shares		1,000

For taxation reasons, the number of shares received may be a percentage (say 95 percent) of the recent, average fair market value. We may receive a "fractional" number of shares as a result, e.g., 0.51234.

From the company's point of view, the stock dividend saves cash that may be needed in the operations of the company. Also, the owners' equity in total is left unchanged because retained earnings is converted to so-called permanent share capital. Various brokerage or underwriting fees are avoided when the company does not have to issue a prospectus to sell more common shares.

To obtain benefits that are similar to those that arise under stock dividends, several Canadian companies have introduced "dividend reinvestment" plans. These may not be very popular, however, when the ever-changing income tax laws tax the dividends as though they are cash dividends. Companies tend to offer shareholders the alternative of receiving cash or of receiving more common shares. When the shareholder elects to receive more shares, the price that she or he pays would tend to be a slight (say 5 percent) discount from market value of the shares. This discount is usually not taxed as an income benefit, but would qualify as a capital gain, to be taxed at a reduced (or perhaps zero) tax rate when the shares are sold. The dividend is merely "reinvested" in the company. For tax purposes, the reinvested dividend is treated as a cash dividend to the recipient, and is subject to tax in the year of receipt. In view of the frequent changes in income tax law, it is useful to check with tax specialists before planning an investment portfolio

A *stock split* does not involve a journal entry. The company merely changes the number of shares that are outstanding. For instance, in a two-for-one stock split, 2 million shares would become issued instead of 1 million. This would have the effect of reducing book value per share to 50 percent of what it previously had been. (The total dollar value attached to common shares remains unchanged.)

The split is primarily designed to reduce the market value of shares that have increased in value because the company has become quite successful. A share selling for over $50 or $100 *could* be a candidate for a split—although some companies allow their shares to sell for over $100 for extended periods of time. The idea underlying a split is to make more shares available, perhaps at a price that psychologically appeals to some investors.

Retained Earnings

This account is constrained by corporate legislation, but not to the same degree as are the different classes of shares. Retained earnings is the only account on most company balance sheets that has its own financial statement. This is because the *continuity* in the account has to be shown per corporate law. We have delved into the history of this on previous occasions. It centres on ensuring that shareholders know when they are receiving a return *of* (repayment of) their capital, or a return *on* capital, i.e., income. A second reason for the continuity is to keep track of charges/credits to retained earnings that arise from other than income and dividends. Examples would be corrections of errors, prior-period adjustments, and retroactive changes in accounting principles/policies. Analysts examine these three items carefully, to ensure that they should not be included in current income—especially if they are debits.

The law is strict for retained earnings because abuses have existed in the past. Twenty or so years ago, companies were able to include *losses* on sales of some types of long-lived assets in retained earnings. Now, these losses are called extraordinary items and are part of net income/net loss. Meanwhile, gains would have appeared in income twenty years ago. As explained in Chapter 12, GAAP has also restricted the use of prior-period adjustments. Auditors in Canada have tended to be tough in recent years on companies that want to make retroactive changes in accounting that charge debits to a prior year. (Retroactive means changing the policy as far back as it is feasible to go. This has the effect of changing the income figures from what were previously reported. Companies do not, however, issue revised financial statements unless prior years' statements contained material errors. Therefore, income effects of prior years are adjusted through opening retained earnings.)

Business and accounting practices have also changed over the past ten or more years for what are called "appropriations of retained earnings". *At one time* the following journal entry was made:

Retained earnings	1,000,000	
Reserve for contingencies (or for some other reason)		1,000,000

The idea behind this entry was to alert shareholders to management's belief that $1 million was not available to be debited for dividends—because some type of loss may occur. Yet this type of accounting lacked credibility because few companies were willing to eliminate most of their retained earnings by paying dividends. Thus, the $1 million was a somewhat meaningless signal to shareholders—especially if it remained on the balance sheet (as a portion of retained earnings) for a few years.

Now, some conclusive evidence has to exist before contingencies may be recorded as liabilities under GAAP. Where there is doubt, note disclosure could be chosen by preparers to convey their message.

Summary

The liability and owners' equity items on balance sheets tend to have more *Corporations' Act, Securities' Act,* CICA-Handbook, and GAAP *constraints* than do most of the assets. Most of the owners'-equity legislative "rules and regulations" that exist today are the result of frauds of some years ago, especially those where perpetrators have purposely tried to confuse capital with income. GAAP constraints tend to exist because some preparers of financial statements have tried to manipulate income by accruing or not accruing losses, possible losses, and various non-recurring events.

Early in the book, we drew major distinctions in how we have to account, as a direct result of the existence of objectives of financial accounting, clarity of circumstances (facts versus assumptions), and constraints. Objectives of accounting are often closely related to the size of the business and how it is structured, such as by way of a proprietorship/partnership or private limited company. At this point in the book, we begin to understand how the various aspects of accounting and reporting fit together. (For example, a tax postponement objective of accounting is likely to be very important in a small, private company.)

Considerable judgment is required in assembling financial statements. The choice of one alternative over another affects revenue, expense, income, assets, liabilities, equity, footnotes—*and* the judgment of some users of the statements. For example, which accounting policies would *you* select if *you* were president of a public company, and knew that a large number of your shareholders had limited understanding of accounting methods and practices?

The next three chapters build on our coverage of the accounting cycle, financial statements, and user/preparer viewpoints. The first two give necessary information for understanding GAAP. Chapter 17 looks at alternatives to original cost, and some of the concepts introduced in the first portion of Chapter 8.

QUESTIONS

14-1 What are the three *or* four usual forms of organization for a business?

14-2 What effect does the size of a company have on accounting and auditing?

14-3 What effect does being a public company (instead of a private company) have on accounting and auditing?

14-4 Why might a business operate as a proprietorship or partnership, instead of as a limited company?

14-5 How might the income statement of a proprietorship differ from that of a private limited company?

14-6 What is a special incorporation?

14-7 List several characteristics that distinguish one type of share from another.

14-8 What are common shares?

14-9 What characteristics of preferred shares distinguish them from common shares?

14-10 Describe a warrant. What is its purpose?

14-11 Describe a right. What is its purpose?

14-12 Why would a company issue a share option?

14-13 Illustrate how book value per share would be calculated.

14-14 What is the significance of earnings per share?

14-15 Distinguish a share or stock dividend from a share split. How is each accounted for?

EXERCISES

E14-1 Ms. Green and Ms. White share income from their partnership in the ratio of 60 percent to Ms. Green and 40 percent to Ms. White. In arriving at income a deduction has to be made as follows:

Salary to Ms. White	$ 30,000
Interest at 12 percent on $100,000 loan to the partnership by Ms. Green	12,000

At the beginning of the year the partners' capital accounts showed:

Ms. Green	300,000
Ms. White	200,000

During the year the results were:

Income of partnership before salary to Ms. White and interest on loan by Ms. Green	192,000
Withdrawals:	
Ms. Green	32,000
Ms. White	18,000

Required:

Prepare the Statement of Partners' Capital for Ms. Green and Ms. White for the year just ended.

E14-2 Provide journal entries for 19—8 to record each of the undernoted *independent* transactions. Explain your response to each situation.
1. The owner of a proprietorship invests $100,000 in the business.
2. The three owners of a partnership (Ms. Smith, Mr. Jones, Mrs. Ferguson) each invest $35,000 in their business.
3. The owner of a private, limited company invests another $100,000 in no par value common shares of the company.
4. The proprietor withdraws $10,000 in cash from the business.
5. Each owner of the partnership in (2) withdraws $3,000 in cash from the business.
6. A dividend of $10,000 is paid by the company in (3).
7. The company in (3) splits its shares by issuing three new ones for one old one.

E14-3 Prepare journal entries for A. Coish Limited (ACL) for each of the undernoted transactions. Explain your response.
1. ACL sells 10,000 common shares, which are without a par value, for $85,000.
2. The company sells 20,000 of its preferred shares, with a par value of $10 each, for $204,000.
3. The board of directors grants an option to the president of ACL allowing him to pur-

chase 1,000 common shares of ACL for $9.00 per share at any time in the next three years.

4. Bonds that had previously been sold for $200,000 were converted by their owners into 20,000 common shares of ACL.

5. The president exercised a portion of the option in (3) by paying $4,500 for 500 common shares of ACL.

6. The president sold the 500 common shares of ACL to a friend, and received $5,500.

E14-4 Prepare the owners' equity section of the balance sheet of J. Hilton Limited (JHL) at July 31, 19—9 from the following information:

Common shares without par value 1,000,000 authorized; 560,000 issued	5,600,000
Options granted to management to buy 10,000 common shares at $12 per share; no options have been exercised to date	120,000
Retained earnings	1,234,500
Appraisal increment on land	1,200,000
Preferred shares of a par value of $50 each. Authorized 100,000 shares; issued 60,000 shares at $54 each. Dividend rate is 12 percent.	3,240,000
Warrants were issued when the preferred shares were sold. They enable the preferred shareholders to acquire one common share at $14 per share for every preferred share that they purchased.	840,000

E14-5 Prepare the following ratios for L. Gallway Corporation (LGC) from the undernoted information:

Ratios:

1. Book value per preferred share
2. Book value per common share
3. Earnings per common share
4. Price-earnings ratio for common shares

Net income for the year	$1,000,000
Bond interest expense for the year	100,000
Preferred share dividend for the year	50,000
Common share dividend for the year	100,000
Preferred shares outstanding throughout the year; 25,000 shares issued for $20 per share	500,000
Common shares outstanding throughout the year; 500,000 shares issued at $2 per share	1,000,000
Market price of common shares	$9 per share
Retained earnings at end of year	3,000,000

E14-6 Prepare journal entries to record the following activities of A. Laughlan Limited (ALL) during the year:

1. A stock dividend of $200,000 is declared and issued during the year.

2. ALL splits its common shares three for one, so that 6,000,000 common shares are now outstanding.at $5 per share.

3. A cash dividend of $100,000 is declared and paid.

4. An option is granted to a senior manager to purchase 5,000 common shares of ALL at $10 per share.

5. Preferred shares shown in ALL's ledgers at $600,000 are converted into common shares by their owners.

6. The preferred shares were originally issued with warrants attached to them. The warrants were exercised so that 6,000 common shares of ALL were issued for $8 per share.

7. Bonds with a face value of $1,000,000 were issued earlier in the year for $1,020,000. A few months later, all of the bonds were converted into common shares.

PROBLEMS

P14-1 Beef Limited (BL) obtained mineral rights to a region in northern Ontario several years ago. The company was dormant until January of this year (19—5), when plans were made to develop a mine at the site of the ore. By December 31 of this year, the following cash receipts and disbursements had occurred:

Disbursements:

Clearing the land for a campsite	$ 62,950
Building the main shaft to the 5,000 metre level below surface	2,655,110
Cost of a portable concentrator, plus installation	897,985
Bunkhouse, cookhouse and office building	684,300
Operating and miscellaneous expenditures	152,120

Receipts:

Sale of ore concentrates (obtained during the building of the main shaft)	320,000
Sale of timber (from clearing the campsite land)	60,000
Sale of common shares to friends	4,000,000

The mine is not expected to be fully constructed and operational until May 19—6. Financial statements are to be prepared as of December 31, 19—5. You have been hired by the board of directors to advise them about appropriate accounting for BL for 19—5.

In addition to the above cash transactions, common shares valued at $500,000 were issued to the prospector who discovered the ore.

Required:

Advise the board of directors, giving full explanations.

P14-2 Match the accounting treatment described under column 1 with the *most appropriate* description in column 2 of facts, objectives of accounting and related matters. Set out your response as follows:

$$
\begin{array}{cc}
1 & Z \\
2 & Y
\end{array}
$$

If more than one letter applies to a number, explain your response.

Column 1	Column 2
1. Net realizable value is used as the definition of market for its inventory.	A. Replacement costs of inventory are rising and the company has a sole objective of postponing income tax.
2. FIFO is used as the cost of inventory.	
3. Replacement cost is used as the definition of market value.	B. Replacement costs of inventory are rising, and the company has two objectives of accounting that are of equal importance—tax postponement, and a bonus plan based on income before the bonus.
4. Common shares are issued for the replacement cost of a building that was just acquired.	
5. Depreciation is based on a fixed rate applied to undepreciated cost.	C. The company has a minimum compliance objective of accounting as its prime objective, and it mines gold that is sold as soon as possible.
6. Weighted average is used as the cost of inventory, and market is defined as replacement cost.	D. The company's prime objective of accounting is minimum compliance, and it has been incurring a loss in recent years.
7. Straight line depreciation is used.	
8. All assets and liabilities are shown on the financial statements at net realizable value.	E. The company is bankrupt and is in the process of being liquidated.
9. Revenue is recognized when cash is collected.	F. Replacement costs of inventory are rising, and the company's prime objective of accounting is evaluation of management by outsiders. But, the outsiders are naive and can be fooled by the figures.
10. The definition of net realizable value of inventory is compared to cost of individual items and not to the inventory as a whole.	
	G. The building is to be used to manufacture various products for several future years; however, its use will be uneven over the next few years.
	H. The company has a steady market for its products, and most items are sold on a cost plus basis.
	I. The company's prime objective of accounting is income tax postponement, and long-lived assets become obsolete quickly.

J. The company has a cash flow objective of accounting and the cost and selling prices of its individual products seem to fluctuate widely.

K. The company has several objectives of accounting, but its customers are permitted to return its products at any time up to 12 months after delivery, for a full refund.

L. The company has an income tax postponement objective of accounting, with a product that can incur substantial warranty costs.

P14-3 The income statement of Sylvester Corporation (SC), a small private limited company, is as follows for 19—9:

Revenue		$720,000
Expenses:		
Wages and employee benefits	$405,500	
Travel	26,200	
Salary to owner (of SC)	60,000	
Office	37,950	
Interest on loan from owner of SC	17,660	
Heat, light, power	6,220	
Rent paid to owner of SC	18,000	
Other	37,825	609,355
Income before income tax		110,645
Income tax		28,000
Net income		$ 82,645

Required:

A. Prepare the income statement for SC assuming that the company was a proprietorship instead of a private company.

B. Explain why your income statement in (A) differs from that prepared for SC. (See the concepts in Chapter 8.)

C. Explain why ratio analysis could be of very limited benefit when ratios for a proprietorship are compared to those for a private company, and a public company.

P14-4 Although Mr. Zap is a major partner, he has less than a 50 percent interest (i.e., proportion of owners' equity) of Ex Co., a partnership. Ex Co. discovers during the year that it requires an audit for credit purposes.

The controller informs Mr. Zap that in order to comply with generally accepted accounting principles, partners' salaries and interest on loans must be reported separately in the financial statements and not hidden in the income statement figures, as is presently being done. On hearing the controller's comment, Mr. Zap becomes very upset and gives the controller the following arguments as to why he does not favor separate disclosure:

1. Separate disclosure is only necessary when salary and interest are not at fair values of services provided or at current interest rates.
2. The banker is not interested in "earnings" and if he were, he could get this information easily from Mr. Zap over the telephone.
3. Materiality should be considered. In some years, Mr. Zap has taken only a small withdrawal in salary and interest, and in other years none at all. In these years, Mr. Zap argues that no disclosure is necessary.
4. Separate disclosure would not be required if Ex Co. were incorporated.
5. Such salary and interest payments are "objective" because they are negotiated by several partners dealing with each other at arm's length.
6. Such disclosure is an annoying constraint which does not suit the facts at hand nor the objectives of Ex Co.'s financial statements. Mr. Zap argues that neither he nor his partners benefit from this kind of information.

Required:

Assume the role of the controller and give a reply to Mr. Zap concerning each of the arguments raised.

P14-5 Several years ago two brothers, Dave and Gord, decided to go into business manufacturing popular brands of soft drinks and selling them directly to customers, using their rented warehouse as a retail outlet.

Business has flourished and the two brothers have decided to incorporate their business, and take advantage of limited liability and the lower corporate tax rate (25 percent for small business).

An excerpt from the most recent balance sheet of Soda Shoppes Co. is as follows:

SODA SHOPPES CO.
Balance Sheet
December 31, 19—7

Assets

Current assets:		
Accounts receivable, less doubtful accounts		$ 24,000
Inventories of raw materials		66,000
Total current assets		90,000
Long-term assets:		
Equipment, at cost	$42,000	
Less accumulated depreciation	10,000	32,000
		$122,000

Liabilities and Partners' Capital

Current liabilities:		
Accounts payable		$ 31,000
Loan by Gord, at 12% per annum		15,000
Partners' capital:		
Dave	$38,000	
Gord	38,000	76,000
		$122,000

The two partners have always kept their capital accounts in a ratio of 1:1. Any excess above this ratio would be credited to a partner loan account, at 12 percent per annum.

The partners agree that assets are not being carried on the books at fair values. Specifically, they note that:

1. According to a court-appointed trustee, an account receivable of $1,000 (previously written off) is now collectible in full.

2. Included in inventories is $5,000 of slow-moving stock that will have to be scrapped. The replacement cost of saleable inventory is $70,000.

3. The replacement cost of the used equipment is estimated to be $50,000.

4. There is unrecorded goodwill, due to the location of the warehouse and customer loyalty. As evidence of this, they point out that they were recently offered $150,000 for their business by Non-Cola Ltd. They declined the offer.

The partners agree that each should be issued 50 percent of the voting share capital of their new corporation, Soda Shoppes Ltd. However, they are unsure how to settle Gord's partnership loan account. They want to convert this to some form of equity or senior debt to facilitate later bank borrowing. Some suggestions by their lawyers are:

1. Unsecured debentures yielding 12 percent per annum.

2. Cumulative preferred shares (par value $100) having a dividend rate of $15 per share. (Assume legislation permits the issue of par value preferred shares.)

3. Non-voting common shares. Soda Shoppes Ltd. will pay common share dividends using a fixed payout rate of 40 percent of net income. The partners feel a growth rate of 20 percent per annum in the market value of common share equity is possible.

Required:

A. Prepare journal entries to wind up the partnership's books and to record the opening of Soda Shoppes Ltd. Also, prepare the opening balance sheet (December 31, 19—7) of Soda Shoppes Ltd. Carefully explain your decisions regarding valuation of partnership assets. Assume that the partnership loan is converted to non-voting common share equity.

B. Write a letter to the partners containing your thoughts, analyses, and recommendations regarding the form of equity or debt to be issued to Gord in exchange for his loan to the partnership. Consider the needs of the company in addition to those of Gord, and state any assumptions that you make. (Ignore personal tax implications for Gord.)

P14-6 Commencement Company Limited (CCL) is a federally incorporated company owned entirely by Mr. Gunn, who is the president. Business over the past few years has been extremely good and the company has been operating at full capacity. There is every likelihood that the demand for CCL's product will increase in the future. Rather than turn down orders in the future, Mr. Gunn has decided that it would be an appropriate time for the company to expand its operations. In this way the company could benefit more fully from the increased demand for its product.

Mr. Gunn realizes that expansion requires funds for investment in a larger plant, new equipment and higher receivable and inventory levels, because of higher sales. He has reviewed a number of alternative ways to finance the company's expansion program and has decided to sell shares to the general public.

He understands from the company's controller, Ms. Briscoll, that:

1. The company recognizes revenue on long-term contracts on a "completed con-

tract" basis. This is because the completed contract basis is acceptable for tax purposes and thus minimizes the company's tax payments.

2. The company depreciates its fixed assets in accordance with the rates stipulated in the *Income Tax Act*. Since there are no other major uses of the financial statements, the company has found it easy to maintain one set of books, for tax purposes only.

3. The company values its inventory of raw materials at the lower of FIFO cost or net realizable value. It has considerable work in process representing the work performed on long-term projects.

4. The company expenses supplies in the years that they are purchased.

5. All other accounting treatments are in accordance with generally accepted accounting principles.

Required:

Assume the role of an accounting advisor to Mr. Gunn. Prepare a report addressed to the president outlining the accounting implications to the company of selling shares to the public. Include in your report all relevant considerations such as possible changes in accounting principles, additional information that would be required and the accounting treatment that you would recommend for the issue of shares.

EXPLORATION MATERIALS AND CASES

MC14-1 Canada Book Corporation (CBC) was incorporated under federal corporate legislation several years ago. This year (19—8) all of the ownership shares were purchased by three businesspersons. Prior to the recent purchase of CBC, all of the company's assets were financed by owners' equity and short term debt. The new owners of CBC hope to expand the company, and have arranged to obtain longer term debt financing. A large lending institution has agreed to loan CBC two dollars for every dollar of owners' equity (common shares plus retained earnings) of CBC. As a result the new owners of CBC are re-thinking the company's present methods of accounting as well as its objectives of accounting. Until 19—8, the financial statements have been prepared so as to postpone the payment of income tax.

You have been engaged by the new owners to review their business practices and present methods of accounting, and recommend appropriate changes in accounting policies and methods. You learn the following about practices and policies in 19—7 and earlier years:

1. CBC has always sold two types of books: special editions and regular stock. Special editions are sold on a "no return; final sale" basis. However, customers are allowed to return 50 percent, at retail price, of the regular stock that they have purchased in the previous 10 months.

2. The company has three different types of customers: individuals, who have to pay cash or use credit cards; book stores, which buy on extended credit terms; and groups that operate special courses that use CBC's books. These groups tend to pay for their purchases several weeks after shipment by CBC.

3. CBC has always depreciated its building and equipment using income tax methods and rates. Maximum rates and amounts have always been claimed, which has resulted in a larger accumulated depreciation figure than if straight-line depreciation had been used.

4. Inventory has always been costed on a weighted average basis. In recent years the cost of printing books has risen steadily at 5 to 10 percent per year. CBC tries to keep its inventory low by not printing a large number of its books. It therefore has to have popular books reprinted each year to keep up with demand. Generally, CBC has written off slow-moving inventory as soon as it could, to postpone income taxes.

5. CBC has always recognized revenue as late as it could, in order to postpone income tax payments. Wherever possible, bad debt allowances have been kept high.

Required:

Recommend appropriate changes in accounting policies and methods to the owners. Explain your reasoning.

MC14-2 (Review) Denham Stables Corporation (DSC) was incorporated under federal legislation several years ago. The company is involved in breeding and racing horses. Earlier this year, all of the voting shares of DSC were purchased by the daughter of the founder of DSC. You have been engaged by the daughter to review the accounting policies being followed by the company, and to suggest appropriate changes.

The new owner's father is wealthy, and never had to be concerned about financing a project or DSC. His prime objective of financial accounting for DSC was the postponement of income tax. The daughter, however, has considerably less wealth at the present time, and has to be alert to possible demands from creditors and lenders for financial information.

DSC buys some horses (at yearling sales) when they are young, to use for racing, and for breeding purposes later. The company also breeds horses extensively, and sells many of its young horses at the yearling sales. The horses that race might be entered in either races where they might be purchased by others (claiming races) or races where they cannot be purchased (allowance or handicap races). Horses may commence a season in one type of race, and switch to the other type if their performance improves or declines. DSC relies heavily on the revenue that is received if a horse places in the top three or four of a race.

The father tended to expense as quickly as feasible, and where possible, to record revenue only on receipt of cash. However, bad debt expense was negligible.

The company incurs significant operating costs each year, for salaries and wages, cost of jockeys, feed, depreciation and similar expenditures. The racing season for DSC tends to be about eight months per year. The financial year end of DSC is December 31, when there is no racing.

The new owner's banker is somewhat cautious about accounting and financial statements, and prefers to see a "strong" balance sheet and income statement. Therefore, you have been asked by the daughter to give greater attention to the desires of the banker. The financial statements are to be in accordance with generally accepted accounting principles.

In addition to the foregoing, you have been able to learn that DSC has employed the following accounting policies:

1. Depreciation on buildings, equipment and automobiles has always been recorded on a basis that is acceptable to Revenue Canada. Thus, a rate of 10, 20 or 30 percent was applied to the undepreciated balance in the ledger accounts for each grouping of similar assets.

2. Inventories of feed and straw for horses were usually expensed when they were purchased.

3. Sales of manure to fertilizer distributors were for cash, and amounts received were minimal.

4. Interest on short term investments was accrued.

5. One figure appeared on the balance sheet for "Investment in Horses". The amount included the cost of any horses that were purchased, less the cost of those that were sold. Since most of its horses were bred by DSC, the "Investment in Horses" account represents only a small fraction of the current worth of the horses.

6. Costs of maintaining the farm where most of the horses are kept are usually expensed. Typical costs are property taxes, wages, insurance, maintenance, electricity, water, and depreciation.

Required:

Suggest appropriate changes to accounting policies to the daughter. Provide full reasons.

MC14-3 Hunter Corporation (HC) was incorporated under federal corporate legislation 20 years ago. About 12 years ago HC issued some preferred shares to the general public, and became a public company. It also issued a few common shares to the public through a brokerage firm. These common shares were traded on an over-the-counter basis (i.e., they were not listed on a stock exchange).

Last year (19—4), HC commenced the process of buying back its preferred shares whenever it had available cash. In 19—4 the principal common shareholders decided to buy the shares that were being offered over the counter. By early 19—5, all of HC's outstanding common shares had been acquired by the six shareholders who had incorporated the company 20 years ago. In September 19—5 the last block of preferred shares of HC that were held by the public were purchased by the company, and cancelled. HC therefore became a private company once again.

You have been engaged by the common shareholders to re-examine the accounting policies being followed by HC in 19—5 and, where necessary, to make them suitable for a private company. Senior management of HC had been granted options to purchase common shares. These options were acquired by the common shareholders, in order to permit 100 percent ownership of HC by the six investors. When the options were acquired, the shareholders promised to introduce a bonus plan based on either operating income or net income of HC.

You review the operations of HC, and the accounting policies, and learn the following:

1. The six shareholders are wealthy, and spend little time managing HC. They gather twice per year at meetings of the board of directors, and delegate operating decisions to senior management.

2. HC is a real estate company that buys farm land, holds onto it for several years, and then develops it into shopping centres, office towers, and housing projects. Some

of the developments are sold, whereas others are kept as cash-generating investments.

3. Most of the cash-generating investments are leased at fixed rates. However, the leases at the shopping centres are based on a small fixed monthly charge plus a percentage of monthly sales made by the tenant of the store/boutique. Until now, HC's management has always accrued expected rental revenues on percentage-of-sales clauses. Often, the cash for percentage-of-sales clauses is not collected for several months after the accrual has been made.

4. Management of HC has never recorded depreciation on the properties held for resale. It has used a straight-line depreciation rate of two percent per year on cash-generating investments.

5. Where possible, management of HC has tried to capitalize all expenditures made in the process of readying a project for sale or occupancy. As a result, advertising, costs of constructing a rental office, wages and commissions of salespersons, and similar expenditures have been treated as assets.

6. On projects that were built with the purpose of selling them, management has always capitalized interest on mortgages on the project until the building has been sold. A similar procedure has been used on cash-generating investments until they are about 60 percent occupied.

Required:

Review HC's accounting policies and recommend appropriate changes. Provide your reasoning.

CHAPTER 15

Intercorporate Investments and Business Combinations

Chapter Themes

1. Many financial statements that we see in Canada are labelled "*consolidated* balance sheet" and "*consolidated* income statement". (See Appendix 1-A, for example.) The term "consolidated" refers to the fact that the financial statements of two or more limited companies have been grouped together—because one owns over 50 percent of the *common shares* of another. That is, the owner of the common shares holds an *intercorporate investment*. Canadian GAAP calls for a particular way of "grouping" or "consolidating", and the results of this procedure could affect the judgments of readers of financial statements.

2. One company may have a less than 50 percent intercorporate investment (in common shares) of another company, and follow what is called "equity basis reporting". Equity basis *reporting* does not provide as much grouping as does a consolidation—but it does result in the *same* net income as if we had consolidated.

3. Besides consolidation, and equity basis reporting and disclosure, there are situations where investments may be recorded at *cost*, (so-called "portfolio investment"), or where a *portion* of the investment in another company is "sort of" consolidated (called "proportionate consolidation"). This latter GAAP method is a little complex, and differs from full consolidation and equity reporting.

4. Canadian income tax law assesses income taxes on a *separate* corporate-entity basis—meaning that each incorporated company has to keep its own set of ledgers for income tax purposes, and prepare separate company financial statements. Consolidated financial statements are therefore *not* helpful for the income tax postponement objective. They are also *not* overly useful for those who wish to predict cash flows and need information on different product segments of the company. In some situations, consolidated statements give an overview for management-evaluation purposes. Mainly, however, consolidated statements are prepared to comply with the law and GAAP. As with the material in Chapter 14, the current state of corporate law and GAAP affecting intercorporate investments have been heavily influenced by the frauds and manipulations of prior decades.

5. Income tax effects are usually the prime financial consideration when one limited company (the "acquirer") is considering the acquisition of another limited company. The acquirer may buy the other company's common shares directly from its shareholders, or it may buy newly issued shares. This would be called an *intercorporate investment* by the acquirer in the acquiree. Alternatively, given the income tax situation, the acquirer may choose to buy individual assets and liabilities *directly from* the acquiree company. This *may* result in what is called a *business combination*. (We should add that the purchase of over 50 percent of the common shares may also be a business combination in addition to its having the status of an intercorporate investment.) In short, the subject is complex and requires some illustrations to sort out the different situations and how they affect financial statements. Consolidations are an example of a situation where there are many rules. We will try to avoid the rules and adhere to the implications—but some detail is necessary to illustrate contrasts, and convey essential messages.

Consolidated Balance Sheet

BASIC SITUATION

Suppose that Horse Limited buys 100 percent of the common shares of Radish Limited, paying $100,000. One moment after the purchase, Horse Limited's *unconsolidated* balance sheet appears as in Illustration 15-1. On the date of purchase by Horse Limited, Radish's balance sheet is as shown in Illustration 15-2.

ILLUSTRATION 15-1

HORSE LIMITED
Balance Sheet
January 2, 19—8

Assets		*Liabilities and Owners' Equity*		
Current	$230,000	Current liabilities		$120,000
Investment in Radish		Long-term debt		
Limited	100,000			150,000
Land	80,000	Owners' equity:		
Building	350,000	Common		
		shares	$200,000	
Accumulated depreciation	(110,000)	Retained		
		earnings	180,000	380,000
	$650,000			$650,000

ILLUSTRATION 15-2

RADISH LIMITED
Balance Sheet
January 2, 19—8

Assets		*Liabilities and Owners' Equity*		
Current	$ 75,000	Current liabilities		$ 60,000
Land	25,000	Owners' equity:		
Building	100,000	Common		
		shares	$80,000	
Accumulated depreciation	(40,000)	Retained		
		earnings	20,000	100,000
	$160,000			$160,000

The idea behind a consolidation is fairly simple. We are merely *replacing* the "Investment in Radish Limited......$100,000" line in Illustration 15-1 *with the individual asset less liabilities of Radish Limited* (in Illustration 15-2). The balance sheet equation tells us that assets minus liabilities equal owners' equity. Horse's $100,000 investment in Radish is really represented by the owners' equity of $100,000. But, because owners' equity equals assets less liabilities, we can use the latter to provide *more details about what Horse actually bought*. We can make the following "elimination" journal entry on a work sheet (*not* in a ledger, because there is no ledger for a consolidated company; each company keeps its own, separate set of books):

Common shares (Radish's balance sheet)	80,000	
Retained earnings (Radish's balance sheet)	20,000	
Investment in Radish Limited (Horse's balance sheet)		100,000

The consolidated balance sheet is arrived at by *adding* what is left after the "elimination entry" is made. (See Illustration 15-3.) Note that the remaining common shares and retained earnings are those of Horse Limited *only*.

ILLUSTRATION 15-3

Current assets:	$230,000 + $ 75,000	$305,000
Land:	$ 80,000 + $ 25,000	105,000
Building:	$350,000 + $100,000	450,000
Accumulated depreciation:	$110,000 + $40,000	(150,000)
		$710,000
Current liabilities: $120,000 + $60,000		$180,000
Long-term debt		150,000
Common shares		200,000
Retained earnings		180,000
		$710,000

On a consolidated basis of management, Horse Limited is able to exercise control over the entire asset-and-liability situation. That is, it owns over 50 percent of the shares and would be able to elect a majority of members to the board of directors of Radish. The majority could vote to transfer some assets from Radish (the *subsidiary* company) to Horse (the *parent* company). Thus, given the integration that is possible in managing Horse-Radish, a consolidated balance sheet makes sense. It tells the shareholders of Horse the type and amount of their assets and liabilities.

A set of consolidated general-purpose financial statements would be prepared when a *parent* company such as Horse owns over 50 percent of the voting common shares of another company. When the ownership is less than 50 percent, or other special conditions exist, consolidation could be inappropriate under a GAAP constraint.

FAIR VALUE SITUATION

In the previous example, we purposely set up a situation where Horse paid precisely the *same* amount as the book value of Radish's common shares and retained earnings. We also *assumed*, without saying so, that the fair market value (mostly replacement cost, but also net realizable value for some assets) of Radish's assets and liabilities equalled the book value of $100,000.

GAAP requires that the buyer use *fair market values* of the assets and liabilities of the company that has been purchased whenever consolidated financial statements are prepared. The fair market values would be established at the *date of acquisition* of the acquiree company (Radish); and become *cost* to the acquirer (Horse). The reason for this procedure is that the use of the book value figures (as shown on Radish's books) permits too much manipulation. For instance, Horse could buy a company that has fully depreciated long-lived assets, i.e., book value is zero. The day after purchasing the company, many of these assets could be sold for their net realizable value, which could be a material amount and the amount would be shown as income. Actually, *cost* to Horse is what Horse had to pay Radish, and *not* what is shown on Radish's books.

In illustrating the "fair value" situation, we will use the *same* facts as in illustrations 15-1 and 15-2 *except* that Horse pays $120,000 for all of Radish's common shares. This means that the current assets of Horse would now be $210,000—because we will assume that they paid the additional $20,000 in cash.

What are the fair market values of Radish's assets and liabilities at the date of the acquisition of Radish's common shares by Horse? We will assume the following:

Current assets	$ 80,000
Land	32,000
Building (in used condition)	67,000
	179,000
Current liabilities	59,000
Price paid by Horse	$120,000

(Note that, although Horse bought Radish's common shares, we have to focus on the fair market value of *each* asset *and liability.* As we saw in previous chapters, liabilities may change in amount because interest rates change, or because we over/under estimate an amount owing.)

As far as the shareholders of Horse are concerned, their cost is what they paid for the assets and liabilities, which is $120,000. Their consolidated balance sheet is prepared on a *cost* basis using the concepts in Chapter 8. (See Illustration 15-4.) The accumulated depreciation on Radish's books is usually *not* carried forward to Horse because the figure is not relevant to Horse's shareholders. (Note that we also could have subtracted $40,000 from both the building and accumulated depreciation in Illustration 15-3.)

When we compare Illustration 15-4 to Illustration 15-3, we may note some differences. The most obvious is the disappearance of Radish's accumulated depreciation in Illustration 15-4. There are other differences for the fair market value effect, however. (The differences between book value per Radish and fair market value are often called *fair value increments.*)

We should again stress that there is no such physical object as a consolidated set of journals and ledgers. Work sheets or computers are used to perform and assemble a consolidation. The work sheet that would be used is similar to the one shown in Appendix 4-B.

ILLUSTRATION 15-4

Current assets:	$210,000 + $80,000	$290,000
Land:	$ 80,000 + $32,000	112,000
Building:	$350,000 + $67,000	417,000
Accumulated depreciation		(110,000)
		$709,000
Current liabilities: $120,000 + $59,000		$179,000
Long term debt		150,000
Common shares		200,000
Retained earnings		180,000
		$709,000

Another point worth stressing is that it is the *cost* to Horse—for the inventory (included in current assets) and building of Radish—that is expensed in the years after the acquisition. Thus, the 19—8 income figure on Radish's books will *not* be the same as what Horse calculates Radish's net income to be. Through the eyes of Horse's shareholders, income will be less in 19—8 than what is on Radish's books, because more was paid for inventory and building *by Horse*, than was paid by Radish when it originally bought.

GOODWILL SITUATION

The purpose of providing these separate situations is to work toward a comprehensive example that illustrates all the usual situations that we will encounter when we read Canadian corporate financial statements.

The goodwill situation is a minor modification of the fair-value situation. To illustrate it, we need only assume that Horse paid $128,000 for all of Radish's common shares (and not the $120,000 in the fair-value situation). This means that Horse's current assets drop to $202,000 (from the $210,000 in the fair-value situation).

The fair value of the assets less liabilities of Radish is $120,000. Yet, Horse paid $128,000. What was the additional $8,000 paid for? It presumably would *not* have been paid for any of the assets and liabilities that were fair valued. (They are fair valued *net* of their income tax consequences—so we can also ignore income tax effects in most situations.) Therefore, the $8,000 must have been paid for assets that, for objectivity reasons (Chapter 8), accountants do not record—such as people.

Illustration 15-5 sets forth the composition of the consolidated balance sheet. Goodwill would have to be amortized, under GAAP, on a systematic basis over a period of up to forty years. This is a significant point. Fair market values are estimates, and can vary, depending upon our choice of appraiser. If we had just acquired a company, and the facts about fair value were somewhat vague, we may prefer to record a sum in dispute as goodwill, rather than equipment or inventory. Goodwill would be expensed over forty years whereas equipment may be expensed over five years, and inventory in one year. (In our example, *if* we were unsure of the $80,000 figure for current assets, we may reduce the amount to $75,000 and increase goodwill to $13,000. The total figure for assets less liabilities would still be $128,000.)

ILLUSTRATION 15-5

Current assets:	$202,000 + $80,000	$282,000
Land:	$ 80,000 + $32,000	112,000
Building:	$350,000 + $67,000	417,000
Accumulated depreciation		(110,000)
Goodwill		8,000
		$709,000
Current liabilities: $120,000 + $59,000		$179,000
Long-term debt		150,000
Common shares		200,000
Retained earnings		180,000
		$709,000

MINORITY INTEREST SITUATION

If we look at Appendix 1-A, the financial statements of Fiberglas Canada Inc., we will notice that they do not have "goodwill" or "minority interest". Their financial statements consolidate subsidiaries that are wholly owned. Quite likely they did not buy their subsidiaries from another company, but started them up. (Hence, there is no goodwill.) Their consolidated financial statements are therefore unlike most of the ones that we will encounter.

Minority interest arises when the acquirer (Horse) purchases less than 100 percent of the common shares of the acquiree (Radish). It can also arise when the acquiree has issued preferred shares, and the acquirer does not purchase the preferred shares from the shareholders.

To keep the situation clear, we will return to the basic situation, and illustrations 15-1 and 15-2. Suppose that 80 percent of the common shares of Radish are acquired from its shareholders, and $80,000 is paid. Also, assume that the fair market values on the date of acquisition are exactly the same as those that appear in Illustration 15-2.

Under GAAP, a consolidation includes 100 percent of Radish's cost for the assets and liabilities—and not 80 percent. The entire 100 percent is included because the board of directors of Horse has complete control over Radish's assets and liabilities, and not just over 80 percent. As we are including the entire 100 percent, we have to set up some form of credit balance for the 20 percent that Horse does not own. This credit is called "minority interest", which is a shorter name for the 20 percent of *common shares and retained earnings* of the acquiree that Horse did not buy.

If we think ahead to what happens on the income statement, we can recognize that 20 percent of what Radish earns after the acquisition by Horse will belong to the "minority shareholders" of Radish. To be consistent with accounting used on the balance sheet, the consolidated income statement will include 100 percent of Radish's sales revenue, cost of goods sold, and various expenses. But, the consolidated income statement will have to include a *deduction* for minority interest, because only 80 percent of Radish's net income belongs to Horse. Since Horse has included 100 percent of Radish's income in the consolidated figures, the other 20 percent belonging to the minority shareholders would have to be *subtracted*, to arrive at the majority shareholders' share of consolidated income:

Revenue	$100
Cost of goods sold	60
Gross profit	40
Expenses	25
Operating income	15
Minority interest share	2
Income	$ 13

In the above illustration, we have assumed that $10 of the $15 of operating income is from the subsidiary company. Twenty percent ($2) would therefore be subtracted. The $13 is therefore made up of:

Parent, or acquirer's operating income excluding the subsidiary's figures ($15 − $10)	=	$ 5
Plus 80 percent of the acquiree's operating income ($10 @ 80%)		8
		$13

(We have also assumed, in using the $10 figure, that the book value and fair value of Radish's assets and liabilities were *identical* on the date of Horse's acquisition of Radish. Otherwise, Horse could not have used the $10 figure in calculating its share of Radish's income.) (See "Fair Value Situation".)

Illustration 15-6 shows the consolidated balance sheet figures. As Horse paid $80,000 and not $100,000, the current assets of Horse would be $250,000, and not the $230,000 shown in Illustration 15-1.

The minority interest would usually appear on the balance sheet between the long-term debt and shareholders' equity sections. Under Canadian GAAP, minority

ILLUSTRATION 15-6

Current assets:	$250,000 + $ 75,000	$325,000
Land:	$ 80,000 + $ 25,000	105,000
Building:	$350,000 + $100,000	450,000
Accumulated depreciation: $110,000 + $40,000		(150,000)
		$730,000
Current liabilities: $120,000 + $60,000		$180,000
Long-term debt		150,000
Minority interest: 20% of ($80,000 + $20,000)		20,000
Common shares		200,000
Retained earnings		180,000
		$730,000

interest is the percentage of common shares and retained earnings (and other sums attributed to the common shareholders, such as appraisal increments) that the acquirer did *not* buy from the subsidiary's shareholders.

MINORITY INTEREST AND GOODWILL

The "usual" situation occurs when the acquirer buys less than 100 percent of the voting common shares and pays more than fair market value of the recorded assets less liabilities of the acquiree. This situation may be illustrated by using the basic facts for the "goodwill situation". Instead of paying $128,000 for 100 percent, we will assume that Horse paid $102,400 for 80 percent. Current assets of Horse would therefore be $227,600 ($202,000 plus the difference between $128,000 and $102,400).

This situation is quite complex. Canadian GAAP has adopted one of several possible ways of consolidating. The "rules" under Canadian GAAP are:

1. Include in the consolidated figures *100* percent of the amounts recorded on the *acquiree's books* for each asset and liability.

2. Include in the consolidated figures only *80* percent (or whatever percentage was acquired) of the *increase/decrease* between what the acquiree's books show and what is being used as fair market value for each asset or liability.

3. Include in the consolidated figures only the percentage of *goodwill* that corresponds to what we bought, i.e., in this case, it is 80 percent. That is, we do *not* write up the goodwill to 100 percent and credit minority interest for the 20 percent needed to balance the accounts.

For instance, in the goodwill situation, the current assets of Radish showed:

Fair market value	$80,000
Balance per Radish's books	75,000
Difference	$ 5,000
80% share	$ 4,000

The consolidated balance sheet would have the following GAAP figure for current assets:

Book value per Radish's books	$ 75,000
Horse's balance	227,600
80% of difference between book value and fair market value	4,000
	$306,600

Some of the thinking underlying this approach is that the *cost* to Horse is for only the 80 percent that was purchased—*and* that the price that would have to be paid for 100 percent may *not* be proportionate to what was paid for 80 percent. That is, it does not necessarily follow in logic that because we paid $80 for 80 percent that we would pay $100 for 100 percent. Some shareholders may ask for more, or less, than others when they offer their shares to us. Also, a "control block" of shares, such as 51 percent, may be worth more per share than a smaller amount because the control block allows the owner to make all of the important decisions, i.e., the control block can outvote the others because it has 51 percent of the votes.

Illustration 15-7 shows the consolidated balance sheet figures. We can prove these amounts by doing the following:

Price paid for shares	$102,400
80% share of Radish's common shares and retained earnings—80% × ($80,000 + $20,000)	80,000
Difference	$ 22,400

Difference accounted for as follows:

Current assets: 80% × ($80,000 − $75,000)	$ 4,000
Land: 80% × ($32,000 − $25,000)	5,600
Building less accumulated depreciation: 80% × ($67,000 − $60,000)	5,600
Current liabilities: 80% × ($60,000 − $59,000)	800*
Goodwill: (In the "Fair Value Situation", the fair market value of 100 percent of Radish is $120,000. Eighty percent of $120,000 is $96,000. Goodwill is the difference between the price paid, $102,400, and the percentage of fair market value, $96,000.)	6,400
	$ 22,400

*Note that this figure is a debit or positive number because fair market value of the liability is *less* than book value, and therefore *reduces* the liability.

ILLUSTRATION 15-7

Current assets:	$227,600 + $75,000 + $4,000	$306,600
Land:	$ 80,000 + $25,000 + $5,600	110,600
Building:	$350,000 + $60,000 + $5,600	415,600
Accumulated depreciation		(110,000)
Goodwill		6,400
		$729,200
Current liabilities: $120,000 + $60,000 − $800		$179,200 ★
Long-term debt		150,000
Minority interest		20,000
Common shares		200,000
Retained earnings		180,000
		$729,200

★In this situation, we have deducted the $800 because the $60,000 figure for liabilities of Radish has been used, instead of $59,000.

NEGATIVE PURCHASE DISCREPANCY

One more situation merits some attention. This occurs when the so-called goodwill figure is a credit balance. In real situations, we may encounter a circumstance where we have to retain particular unproductive people, or encounter losses, for a short period of time. Negative (credit balance) goodwill is rare in Canada because GAAP focusses on *allocating* the total purchase price to the assets and liabilities that were acquired. This is in accordance with the cost concept explained in Chapter 8. The credit balance therefore gets absorbed into some assets.

The negative purchase discrepancy situation may be explained by modifying the illustration used for "Minority Interest and Goodwill". Suppose that Horse paid $93,500 for 80 percent of the common shares of Radish:

$120,000 fair market value of Radish @ 80%	$96,000
Price paid	93,500
Negative purchase discrepancy	$ 2,500

The $2,500 would be credited to "tangible non-monetary assets" under GAAP. Tangible assets in the case of Radish would be inventory and land and buildings. The term *non-monetary* is described in Chapter 17, and would coincide with inventory, land, and buildings in our example. GAAP is flexible about which of the three assets the $2,500 could be credited to. We may credit some of it to each asset. Note, however, what effect this would have on subsequent years' income.

If the entire $2,500 is credited to land, the land would have to be sold before any "gain" would appear on the income statement. At the other extreme, $2,500 credited to inventory would quickly appear in income as reduced cost of goods sold. If the $2,500 is credited to buildings, the income effect would be spread out over several years. This is because the increment between book value and fair market value would be depreciated over the *remaining* life of the asset. In summary, when facts are unclear, preparers have several ways open to them in accounting for negative purchase discrepancy.

DISCLOSURE

Consolidated financial statements are titled with just the name of the parent:

HORSE LIMITED
Consolidated Balance Sheet
Date

The names and percentage ownership in subsidiaries could be provided in a footnote.

Consolidated Income Statement

BASIC SITUATION

The basic approach to the income statement was briefly explained under the "Minority Interest Situation" heading in the previous main section of this chapter. The figures for the two companies, Horse and Radish, are added together, and a deduction is made if the subsidiary is less than 100-percent owned.

As we may suspect, there is more to consolidated income statements than what has been described so far. Earlier in the chapter, we mentioned that consolidations gained in importance as a result of legal constraints and a tightening of GAAP, because manipulation of accounting figures was too easy when neither consolidations nor equity accounting were required in certain types of situations. Income "manipulation" or variation can occur as a result of these types of activities:

1. Allocating negative purchase discrepancy to one asset instead of another.

2. Selecting a particular period of amortization (instead of another) for goodwill, and increments between fair market value and book value of assets and liabilities.

3. Not eliminating profits on sales between a parent (Horse) and its subsidiary (Radish), or vice-versa, when goods have yet to be sold to unrelated third parties.

4. Intercompany transactions similar to 3, e.g., one company provides services to another at prices in excess of cost—or, one company buys bonds payable issued by another, and pays a price that differs from what is shown on the issuer's books.

We have already mentioned the potential income effects of negative purchase discrepancy. The period of amortization of goodwill and the amortization of the fair value increments is a similar situation to what has been described earlier in the book—in commentary about allocations, such as depreciation. The basic idea underlying items 3 and 4 may be illustrated by choosing one example of intercompany inventory transactions.

Suppose that a person owns two companies, and decides to account for them on a basis other than GAAP. For instance, maybe a naive creditor wishes to see the financial statements of one of the companies (Company *A*), and the owner wants to increase the net income quickly. By ignoring the arm's-length concept (Chapter 8), the owner could sell inventory to the other company (Company *B*, owned by him) at amounts well in excess of cost:

Price charged to Company *B*	$1,000,000
Purchase cost of Company *A*	600,000
"Profit"	$ 400,000

The $400,000, less income taxes thereon, would appear on Company *A*'s income statement. Perhaps the creditor would be deceived about Company *A*'s profitability.

A more sophisticated creditor would ask for collateral security for any loan from *all* companies owned by the borrower. Also, GAAP-based consolidated financial statements may be requested. If so, the $400,000 would be *eliminated* as a profit *unless* Company *B* had been able to sell the inventory to an independent third party for a *sum in excess* of $1,000,000.

The elimination of unrealized intercompany profits is a main strength of consolidated financial statements. Profits are *un*realized when a third party has *not* acquired the goods or services at a sum in excess of cost to the related company buyer. That is, the profits remain in the inventory of the buyer when the goods are not yet sold.

STATEMENT INTERPRETATION

When companies that are related in ownership deal with each other on a frequent basis, GAAP-based consolidated statements would be essential for understanding the *net effect* of the intercompany transactions. Consolidated statements therefore seem to meet the "minimum compliance" and "evaluation of management by outsiders" objectives mentioned in Chapter 6. The statements definitely provide the information required for an overall picture.

Canada had several alleged frauds during the 1960s that would have been far more difficult to perpetrate if consolidated financial statements had been requested by creditors and *customers* of the companies. Unrealized intercompany profits were not being eliminated in these companies. Thus, consolidations clearly would have served a useful purpose. Consolidated statements also have their disadvantages, however, especially because the figures are grouped or aggregated.

Any time that figures are aggregated, something is gained and something is lost. What is gained is (1) an overall picture, (2) the elimination of intercompany profits, and (3) the amortization/depreciation of the fair value increments and goodwill. What is lost is details about how well or poorly each company in the group is performing. A consolidation may hide the fact that two or three companies in the consolidated group may be on the verge of bankruptcy. Which of the companies made a profit? What we really need to determine the profitability of each company is the statements for each, adjusted for unrealized profits.

If we were a creditor of one of the subsidiary companies, which financial statements would we want to see—the consolidated ones? Not unless the entire group of companies guaranteed the loan or debt. A banker for one of the subsidiary companies, where there are no guarantees by the other companies, wants to see only the financial statements of the subsidiary that previously received the loan from her or him. Any other financial statement is not relevant to the situation. If the profit of the subsidiary that we loaned money to is being overstated by intercompany sales, this would be misleading. Nevertheless, as long as the buyer of the goods (a sister company) is able to pay for the purchases, the seller is legally entitled to payment.

This topic about the strengths and weaknesses of consolidated statements is complex, and is much like walking through a mine field. We have to keep asking ourselves: Consolidations versus what? Much of the foregoing discussion compared consolidated statements to unconsolidated statements of the separate companies. But, there are other possible comparisons—for example, to equity *reporting*.

Equity Reporting

Equity reporting has some of the advantages of consolidations, and does *not* have some of consolidation reporting's disadvantages. As with most accounting, however, a mixture of weaknesses and strengths exist. In short, equity reporting consists of:

1. On the Balance Sheet—one line would exist in the non-current-asset section of the balance sheet of Horse Limited:

   Equity in Radish Limited $ xxx

2. On Horse's Income Statement—one (or perhaps two if extraordinary items exist in Radish) line would show Horse's share of the net income of Radish:

   Income of Radish Limited $ xx

The income figure that would be reported above would *not* be a simple percentage ownership by Horse times the income figure on Radish's book. Instead, it would be a percentage ownership of Radish's income *adjusted* for various items that are needed to compute Radish's income as seen through the eyes of Horse Limited. For instance, the following adjustments may exist, assuming that Horse bought *40 percent* of Radish:

Unadjusted income of Radish ($50,000);	
Horse's 40 percent share	$20,000
Deduct:	
Intercompany profit not realized, on sale of inventory from Radish to Horse—40 percent share	(2,000)
Depreciation on fair value increment	(1,500)
Amortization of goodwill	(800)
Adjusted income of Radish	$15,700

The adjustments would be brought about by the following:

1. Intercompany profit. Radish could have sold Horse some inventory that cost Radish $11,000. Horse paid $16,000, which means that there was $5,000 of unrealized intercompany profit, assuming that Horse has *not* sold this inventory to third parties by the end of its year. Without this sale, Radish's unadjusted income would be $45,000 ($50,000-$5,000). Horse owns 40 percent of the common shares; thus, 40 percent of $45,000 would be $18,000. We therefore have to subtract 40 percent of $5,000, i.e., $2,000, from the $20,000 to arrive at $18,000.

2. Depreciation on fair value increment. Suppose that when Horse bought Radish, the fair market value (replacement cost) of some equipment was $50,000 whereas Radish's ledger showed a net book value of $35,000. Horse would have paid an additional $6,000 for its 40 percent of the $15,000 difference ($50,000 - $35,000). Assuming that this equipment had a *remaining* life of four years at the date of acquisition, $1,500 per year (one-fourth of $6,000) would have to be subtracted from Radish's income for each of the next four years.

3. Amortization of goodwill. Suppose that Horse paid $8,000 in excess of its 40 percent share of the fair market value of Radish's assets and liabilities. Horse then chose to amortize this over 10 years at $800 per year.

The $15,700 supposedly represents what the 40 percent share of income of Radish *would have been if* Radish's accounting was based on *cost* per what Horse paid—not on what Radish's shareholders actually paid. When we use equity reporting we have to look at everything from another point of view—that of Horse's shareholders.

This is a good example of why Chapter 1 stressed the adaptable nature of accounting, and why there is *not* one right answer. When accounting is looked at from a different point of view, the figures may change.

BALANCE SHEET

Where does the figure "Equity in Radish Limited", on the balance sheet of Horse, come from? To illustrate, we will choose a different example—where Elephant Limited buys 40 percent of Mouse Limited's common shares. Suppose that $100,000 is paid for the shares. In the first year after being purchased (in part) by Elephant, Mouse has a net income of $30,000. Elephant's 40 percent share would be $12,000. But, after adjusting for unrealized intercompany profits, amortization/depreciation of fair value increments, and amortization of goodwill, Elephant's share of adjusted income becomes $10,200. Mouse declares a dividend of $10,000 and Elephant receives $4,000 of this.

The ledger account in Elephant's books probably would be kept at *cost* of $100,000:

Investment in Mouse Limited

100,000	

The reason for this is to keep what are called the *corporate accounts* (meaning unconsolidated) on a basis that helps to simplify the computation of *taxable income*, and the filing of required unconsolidated financial statements. A dividend from Mouse to Elephant is *not* taxable, *nor* is the adjusted income of $10,200.

The *work sheet* "ledger accounts", however, (which are kept for preparing Elephant's reports to shareholders, and are *not* the official books of the company) would show the following:

Equity in Mouse Limited

Initial investment	100,000		
Share of income	10,200	Dividend	4,000
Balance at end of first year	106,200		

The $106,200 would be reported on Elephant's balance sheet (which would *not* be called a consolidated balance unless there was a subsidiary) as "Equity in Mouse Limited".

The *work sheet* journal entries (see Appendix 4-B) that could be "posted" to adjust the *actual* ledger balance from $100,000 to $106,200 would be:

1. Equity in Mouse Limited   10,200
    Income of Mouse Limited   10,200

2. Cash   4,000
    Equity in Mouse Limited   4,000

Notice that the credit of $10,200 would appear on the income statement of Elephant. Entry 2 is strictly a switch between two balance sheet accounts and may not be shown separately except on the Statement of Changes in Financial Position (Chapter 16).

TERMINOLOGY

The following listing may help to clarify some terms that could be encountered while looking at intercorporate investment data on financial statements:

Buyer	Company Bought (maybe in part)
Acquirer	Acquiree
Parent	Subsidiary
Investor	Investee

The terms "investor" and "investee" are universal terms that could be applied in any situation. The parent/subsidiary terminology should be used only when the investor buys over 50 percent of the voting shares of the investee. Acquirer/acquiree is used widely by non-accountants. We have to be careful, however, in using the term "acquirer" when we are discussing business combinations. It has a special significance, to be explained shortly.

Joint Ventures

Joint ventures are popular in the oil and gas, real estate, construction and in a sense, insurance, industries in Canada. Usually, joint ventures are used when risks of loss of capital are high, and/or when huge sums of money are needed to explore for oil or build tar-sands projects. The *venturers* decide how much money and management talent is needed to commence the venture and who will supply each in which proportions. We may see 50:50 ownership in construction joint ventures, but all sorts of odd numbers in oil and gas or real estate ventures, e.g., 30:30:20:10:5:5 percentages.

When a business conducts only a portion of its entire business operations through joint ventures, it would tend to use equity reporting of its interest in the joint venture:

Equity in joint venture $ xxx

However, when the entire business consists of joint ventures—as exists for a few real estate companies—a procedure called "proportionate consolidation" may be chosen.

Suppose that we use the basic information in illustrations 15-1 and 15-2, and assume that Horse and other venturers bought Radish as a joint venture. Assume also that Radish's book figures were exactly equal to replacement costs (and net realizable value in the case of accounts receivable and payable)—except "building" would be at a net figure of $60,000. If Horse had a 30-percent interest in the joint venture (having paid $30,000), and under GAAP qualified for proportionate consolidation treatment, the balance sheet would appear as follows:

Current assets:	$300,000 + (30% × $75,000)	$322,500
Land:	$ 80,000 + (30% × $25,000)	87,500
Building:	$350,000 + (30% × $60,000)	368,000
Accumulated depreciation		(110,000)
		$668,000

Current liabilities: $120,000 + (30% × $60,000)	$138,000
Long term debt	150,000
Common shares	200,000
Retained earnings	180,000
	$668,000

Current assets of Horse would be $300,000 because only $30,000 was spent, and not the $100,000 shown in Illustration 15-1 [$230,000 plus ($100,000 − $30,000)].

Proportionate consolidation would also exist on the income statement. The method gives shareholders of Horse a better idea what the composition of the assets and liabilities are. For example, how much is in long-term debt? in long-lived assets? and, are the two in balance, or is there a severe liquidity problem? (See Chapter 5.)

Proportionate consolidation has weaknesses, however. Horse is just a 30-percent owner, and others may combine their votes so that Horse has to compromise its management philosophy. The main control idea behind full consolidation of 100 percent of assets and liabilities may not apply when ownership is only 30 percent.

On the income statement, the usual intercompany profit eliminations would be made—and only the net effect shown. Amortizations of fair value increments and goodwill would not exist if the joint venture were commenced by the venturers from a cash only starting point.

Some Comparisons

None of the methods (consolidation, equity reporting, proportionate consolidation) would be able to satisfy all possible users of financial statements. Creditors of the parent company probably would prefer to see consolidated statements and would base restrictive covenants on the consolidated figures. Those who wish to predict cash flows would want segment information by product and region.

Equity reporting is accrual based. Those wishing to predict may be far more interested in the cash dividend than in Elephant's share of Mouse's adjusted income.

In recent years, GAAP has been moving to greater note-disclosure to compensate for the limitations of having to use one number on financial statements, such as on the balance sheet and income statement.

The alternative to consolidation and equity reporting is *cost basis*. This method was in use twenty to fifty years ago, and led to manipulation of income. Under cost basis accounting, income of an investee/subsidiary would only be recognized when a *dividend* was declared. Thus, a parent company could increase or decrease its income substantially by altering the amount of any year's dividend declared by the investee. The parent controls the board of directors of the investee and can do whatever it wants.

A typical journal entry under cost basis accounting would be:

| Cash | xx | |
| Dividend income | | xx |

In unconsolidated financial statements, the dividend income figure would appear on the income statement. When we have to consolidate, we would have to *eliminate* the amount of the dividend income. Otherwise, we would be *double counting* the dividend and our share of the subsidiary's adjusted net income. (See the "Equity Reporting" discussion earlier in this chapter.) (The "elimination" work sheet journal entry would cancel out the dividend income on the investor's books against the dividend account, or charge to retained earnings, on the investee's books.)

Consolidation and equity reporting seem to be complex. The alternative is cost based reporting of investees. Under cost based reporting, unrealized intercompany profits would *not* have to be eliminated. Manipulation through investee dividends could be significant. Is the cure (consolidations, equity reporting) worse than the ailment (cost basis manipulation)?

Before we attempt to respond to this question, it is important to remember that "preparer power" tends to exist in Canada. This means that the preparer decides what ranking to give to objectives of accounting and which accounting policies to pick. The consolidation/equity reporting "rules" restrict or constrain what the preparer may do. As a result, the rules reduce income manipulation.

Given the variety of different users of financial statements, it is not realistic to expect complete agreement on the question of cure versus ailment. For instance, the income tax postponement objective is well catered to by cost basis reporting. People who want to predict probably would not be happy with either cost basis or consolidations/equity reporting. They desire segmented data on a cash basis. Those who are concerned about manipulation naturally prefer an extensive number of rules.

Business Combinations

"Business combination" is a technical term that refers to one company buying *either* (1) over 50 percent of the voting common shares of another company, or (2) the assets and liabilities of a division or more of an *operating* company. A purchase of a collection of assets and liabilities, e.g., building, truck, equipment, that are used for another purpose, e.g., to produce other than the same product or service, is *not* a business combination. A purchase of assets and liabilities that is not material (see Chapter 8) in dollar amount is *not* a business combination. When two companies that are owned by the same persons enter into a purchase/sale of assets and liabilities, this is *not* a business combination. Why? Because it is *not* an arm's-length transaction. (See Chapter 8.) In summary, the purchase of assets and liabilities must be a *material* amount of a *going concern* and be at *arm's length*.

FAIR VALUING

Generally speaking, a business combination situation requires that the assets and liabilities be fair valued. (There are exceptions, however, called pooling-of-interests, to be discussed shortly.) When common shares are acquired, the fair valuing does *not* affect the tax status of the company. In practice, when shares are acquired from selling shareholders, the fair valuing of assets and liabilities has to be net of tax effects, because the fair value increment is *not* deductible as an expense. (Income taxes are assessed on the individual company accounts, not on consolidated results, and this does not change because there are new owners of common shares.) However, when assets and liabilities are acquired, the full amount of the fair value (except for goodwill, which is taxed at one half of its value, and land, which is *not* deductible) may be claimed for tax purposes.

Fair valuing merits a brief explanation. Suppose that the acquiree company's books show:

Machine, at cost	$100,000
Accumulated depreciation, and amount previously claimed as tax depreciation (capital cost allowance)	30,000
Net book value	$ 70,000

Suppose that the machine is acquired along with other assets and liabilities in a business combination. A fair value of $105,000, i.e., replacement cost, is placed on the machine. For income tax purposes, the purchase of assets and liabilities is like any other arm's-length transaction. The buyer can claim capital-cost allowance for tax purposes on the $105,000 figure.

But, when common shares are acquired, nothing changes from a tax point of view. (The owners change, but the company's ledgers do not.) Capital cost may be claimed on only the $70,000. The fair value increment *appears* to be $35,000 ($105,000 − $70,000), but it is *not* that much. If the income tax rate were 40 percent, a sum of $14,000 (40% × $35,000) would *not* be received from Revenue Canada. Capital cost allowance is usually claimed over many years, and when discounted to a present value would not be worth $14,000. If we ignore discounting, however, the fair value increment would be $21,000 ($35,000 − $14,000) when common shares are bought by the acquirer.

In summary, the same asset could have these different valuations:

1. On the ledgers of the acquiree—net figure of $ 70,000

2. On the books of the acquirer, if assets and liabilities are purchased $105,000

3. On the consolidated financial statements, if common shares are purchased: $70,000 + $21,000 $ 91,000

PURCHASE OF ASSETS AND LIABILITIES

When assets and liabilities are purchased, an entry is made directly on the acquirer's books. For example:

Accounts receivable	xxx	
Inventory	xxxx	
Land	xxx	
Building	xxxx	
Equipment	xxx	
Accounts payable		xxx
Cash (amount paid to acquiree)		xxxxx

Under GAAP, this information has to be disclosed somewhere in the financial statements, often in a note. Alternatively, the figures could be reported in the Statement of Changes in Financial Position (Chapter 16).

Someone interested in cash flow prediction would be quite interested in these figures because they ought to have an effect on future operations. How profitable will be the products that are to be manufactured from these assets? This is what the forecaster must ascertain.

POOLING-OF-INTERESTS

In the early 1970s, and during much of the 1960s, pooling-of-interests accounting was used for many Canadian business combinations. Many people felt that pooling-of-interests constituted manipulation—and was leading to business combinations that were not economic, but "looked good" from an accounting point of view. GAAP was changed just before the middle of the 1970s to make pooling-of-interests accounting applicable to only a limited number of situations.

In essence, pooling-of-interests accounting allows two companies to add the book values of their assets together. Neither one has to have fair values reported for its assets and liabilities. Therefore, there is no need to amortize/depreciate the fair value increments in future years, nor would there be any goodwill that has to be amortized. Pooling-of-interests would show a higher consolidated or combined income than would its alternative, which is called "purchase accounting", and which requires fair valuing and subsequent amortization/depreciation of the fair value increments.

The general nature of the difference between *purchase accounting* and *pooling-of-interests accounting,* from an asset and liability perspective, can be quickly seen by comparing Illustration 15-3 with Illustration 15-5. Illustration 15-5 constitutes purchase accounting, when the acquirer (Horse) buys shares for cash. Illustration 15-3 is not quite pooling-of-interests accounting because a "pooling" is usually carried out by issuing (to Radish's shareholders) shares of Horse in exchange for shares of Radish. The typical pooling-of-interests balance sheet would be per Illustration 15-8.

In Illustration 15-8, current assets of Horse would be $330,000 because $128,000 (see Illustration 15-5) would *not* have been paid out in cash. Common shares of Horse with a *market value* of $128,000 could have been issued to shareholders of Radish. This $28,000 difference ($128,000 − $100,000) results in having to use a deduction in the shareholders' equity section of the balance sheet, "Value of shares issued in excess of assets less liabilities pooled", or "Value of shares in excess of net assets pooled". Note that retained earnings would become the balancing figure—and is not necessarily the $180,000 retained earnings of Horse. In some poolings, a portion of Radish's retained earnings could be included in the pooled retained earnings.

Purchase accounting could still be required in Canada under GAAP even when shares (instead of cash) of Horse are issued to the shareholders of Radish. This would increase both the current assets and common shares, under the purchase accounting column in Illustration 15-8, by $128,000.

The major effect of a pooling-of-interests, however, is on subsequent income statements, which do not have to include fair values and amortization of the increments and goodwill. Unsophisticated investors may incorrectly believe the pooled income

to the income statement, because the $1.40 has been ignored. If the $1.40 rate is used, however, up to $200,000 may be credited to income as a gain in the period when the exchange rate moved from $1.30 to $1.40.

If we were a manager or company president, and knew that the consolidated financial statements were being used to judge our performance, would we want to see the $1.30 or the $1.40 used? With accounts receivable, the $1.40 makes sense because the receivable will soon be collected in cash. But, with the land anything could happen to the currency exchange rate between now and when the land is sold. Thus, GAAP has elected to have different rules for different types of assets and liabilities.

The situation gets complicated because most foreign subsidiaries will remain in the foreign country for many years. No doubt wide swings in foreign currency rates of exchange could occur over this period of time. When we use current exchange rates for translating foreign balance sheets, we are "sort of" suggesting that some of the assets will be physically sent to Canada very soon. In the case of cash, this makes sense. But, for longer-term investments in receivables and cash operating funds (both of which are needed to keep the business functioning) use of the current exchange rate is questionable.

Overall, the matter is complex. As readers of financial statements, we do have to ascertain what the company has done in translating its foreign subsidiaries to Canadian dollars. The impact on the income statement could be *significant*. In the 1980s, GAAP rules have been tightened. However, room still exists to make some judgments that affect income.

Summary

The chapter has outlined some of the complexities of intercorporate investments, business combinations, and foreign currency translation. Emphasis has been placed on the uses and limitations of the figures for different objectives of accounting. Our conclusions are that it is not possible to have one accounting treatment that satisfies all the main readers of financial statements. Therefore, we have to ascertain which policies a company has chosen, and note what effect this has on the income statement and balance sheet. Will the figures help us for the decisions that we wish to make?

QUESTIONS

15-1 What is an intercorporate investment?

15-2 What is equity basis reporting?

15-3 What is a business combination? List the two main types, and the criteria that have to be met for a business combination to exist.

15-4 What is goodwill?

15-5 Suppose that P Ltd. buys 100 percent of the voting shares of S Ltd. at a cost in excess of the owners' equity of S Ltd. Why would the net income figure of S Ltd. for the year that follows the date of acquisition *not* be regarded *by* P Ltd. as its share of the subsequent income of S Ltd.?

15-6 What is minority interest?

15-7 On whose set of journals and ledgers are consolidation elimination entries recorded?

15-8 What is negative purchase discrepancy?

15-9 What is meant by equity reporting of an intercorporate investment? What advantages and disadvantages does it have compared to consolidated financial statements for the various objectives of accounting mentioned in Chapter 6?

15-10 Explain the logic (see concepts in Chapter 8) of eliminating profits on inventory sales between an investor and investee whenever the purchaser has *not* sold the inventory to a third party.

15-11 Explain proportionate consolidation. Under what conditions would it be appropriate accounting (i.e., under which factual situation and which objective of accounting)?

15-12 Explain the logic of fair valuing the assets and liabilities of the investor when a business combination occurs.

15-13 Compare and contrast purchase accounting with pooling-of-interests accounting.

15-14 What are the principal accounting issues and controversies that exist in foreign currency translation?

EXERCISES

E15-1 Octopus Limited (OL) purchased 80 percent of the common shares of Shark Corporation (SC) on January 1, 19—8 for $1,000,000. At that date, the balance sheet of SC was as follows:

Current assets:			Current liabilities:		
Cash	$ 140,000		Accounts payable	$ 598,000	
Accounts receivables	425,500		Income tax payable	40,400	
Inventory	527,400		Other liabilities	281,600	
Prepaid expenses	32,100			920,000	
	1,125,000				
Long-lived:			Owners' equity:		
Land	350,000		Common shares	1,000,000	
Buildings and equipment	960,000		Retained earnings	250,000	
Accumulated				1,250,000	
depreciation	(265,000)				
	1,045,000				
	$2,170,000			$2,170,000	

On January 1, 19—8 OL's balance sheet showed:

Current assets:			Current liabilities:		
Cash	$ 62,300		Accounts payable	$ 1,970,000	
Accounts receivable	2,994,600		Income tax payable	210,200	
Inventory	2,650,700		Bank loan payable	1,200,000	
Prepaid expenses	220,600		Other liabilities	215,200	
	5,928,200			3,595,400	
Investment in Shark			Owners' equity:		
Corporation	1,000,000		Common shares	5,000,000	
Equipment	5,952,800		Retained earnings	2,660,700	
Accumulated				7,660,700	
depreciation	(1,624,900)				
	4,327,900				
	$11,256,100			$11,256,100	

On January 1, 19—8 the fair market values of SC's assets and liabilities were the same as the recorded book values as reported on SC's balance sheet. The common shares of SC were purchased from a variety of shareholders.

Required:
Prepare a consolidated balance sheet of OL as of January 1, 19—8.

E15-2 Refer to the facts in **E15-1.** Assume that OL paid $1,100,000 for 80 percent of SC's common shares (thereby reducing its cash balance to $40,000). Also, assume that the fair market value of SC's land was $425,000 (and not the $350,000 mentioned in **E15-1**).

Required:
Prepare a consolidated balance sheet of OL as of January 1, 19—8.

E15-3 Conrod Corporation (CC) acquired 90 percent of the common shares of R. Chesley Limited (RCL) on June 30, 19—9 for $2,375,000. On this date, the fair market values of RCL's assets and liabilities were the same as book values except for the following:

	Fair Market Value
Inventory	$840,000
Long term debt	520,000

The balance sheets of CC and RCL are as follows:

CONROD CORPORATION
Balance Sheet
June 30, 19—9

Assets		*Liabilities and Owners' Equity*	
Current assets:		Current liabilities:	
Cash	$ 35,000	Accounts payable	$1,127,720
Accounts receivable	1,137,440	Bank loan payable	650,000
Inventory	1,189,900	Other current liabilities	213,120
Prepaid expenses	196,310		1,990,840
	2,558,650		
Investment in			
R. Chesley Ltd.	2,375,000		
Long-lived assets:		Owners' equity:	
Land	500,000	Common shares	3,000,000
Building and		Retained earnings	2,658,110
equipment	3,275,000		5,658,110
Accumulated			
depreciation	(1,059,700)		
	2,715,300		
	$7,648,950		$7,648,950

R. CHESLEY LIMITED
Balance Sheet
June 30, 19—9

Assets		*Liabilities and Owners' Equity*	
Current assets:		Current liabilities:	
Cash	$ 130,800	Accounts payable	$ 502,600
Accounts receivable	1,514,400	Income tax payable	142,100
Inventory	810,000	Other current liabilities	277,600
	2,455,200		922,300
Long-lived assets:		Long term debt, 14%	500,000
Land	600,000	Owners' equity:	
Building and		Common shares	1,500,000
equipment	2,010,500	Retained earnings	1,400,000
Accumulated			2,900,000
depreciation	(863,400)		
	1,747,100		
Patent, less amortization	120,000		
	$4,322,300		$4,322,300

Required:

A. Prepare a consolidated balance sheet of CC as of June 30, 19—9.

B. What use may be made of the consolidated financial statement that you prepared in (A)? (Consider objectives of accounting and different users.)

E15-4 Elephant Limited (EL) acquired 40 percent of the common shares of Mouse Corporation (MC) on January 1, 19—8 for $2,000,000. On this date the book value of MC's assets and liabilities equalled the fair value, except for a building. EL also paid for goodwill. As a result, EL paid the following sums in excess of its 40 percent share of the book value of MC:

Building	$160,000
Goodwill	400,000

The $160,000 for the building will be depreciated over 10 years, and the $400,000 for goodwill will be depreciated over 40 years—both on a straight-line basis.

In the year ended December 31, 19—8, MC sold inventory that cost it $200,000 to EL for $320,000. At December 31, 19—8, EL had not sold any of the inventory.

According to MC's income statement it had a net income of $500,000 for the year ended December 31, 19—8. EL intends to report its investment in MC on the equity basis.

Required:

What figure should EL report on its financial statements for the year ended December 31, 19—8 for its:

A. investment in MC?

B. income from MC?

Show all calculations.

E15-5 Refer to the information in **E15-1**. Suppose that OL purchased 40 percent of SC for $500,000 instead of 80 percent for $1,000,000. (As a result, on OL's balance sheet the investment in Shark Corporation would be $500,000 and the cash figure would be $562,300.) SC is to be accounted for as a joint venture of OL, with the proportionate consolidation method being used.

Required:

Prepare the balance sheet of OL as of January 1, 19—8, reporting SC on the proportionate consolidation basis.

E15-6 Atkinson Limited (AL) acquired 100 percent of the common shares of Parker Corporation (PC) on March 1, 19—7 for several million dollars. On PC's books, *one* asset was recorded as follows:

Building	$900,000
Accumulated depreciation	270,000
Net book value	630,000

An appraiser, with little knowledge of income tax effects, appraised the value of the building in used condition at $945,000, net value after accumulated depreciation, and ignoring income tax. For convenience, it may be assumed that PC has an income tax rate of 40 percent.

Ignoring discounting, roughly what net amount ought to be used on the consolidated balance sheet of AL at March 31, 19—7 for its investment in the building owned by PC? Explain your calculation.

PROBLEMS

P15-1 (Review of Chapter 5, in preparation for Chapter 16.) Compute funds from operations for Adams Corporation (AC) from the following information:

Gross profit	$987,650
Gain on sale of land	100,200
Income tax expense—payable	21,700
—deferred	70,000
Depreciation	125,620
Selling and administrative expense	560,250
Dividends paid	50,000
Dividend received from subsidiary company	18,600

State your assumptions!

P15-2 A senior Canadian banker made the following remarks to a meeting of professional accountants:

Consolidated statements are always somewhat of a problem to analyze. Would it be possible to specifically list all the companies included and the percentage ownership of each? The perfect solution would be a consolidating statement (i.e., the consolidation work sheet, showing the combining and adjustments) but these seem rare in Canada.

Required:

A. Explain why the banker appears to be somewhat frustrated with consolidated financial statements.

B. Do you agree with the banker's "perfect solution"?

P15-3 Will Limited (WL) acquired 50 percent of the common shares of Knot Corporation (KC) in a joint venture arrangement in which Scout Corporation (SC) acquired the other 50 percent of KC. At the date of acquisition of KC, January 1, 19—9, the net book value and fair market values of KC were:

	Book Value on KC's ledgers	Fair Market Value
Current assets	$ 6,700,000	$ 7,600,000
Land	500,000	1,000,000
Building, net of accumulated depreciation	3,200,000	4,000,000
Equipment, net of accumulated depreciation	3,600,000	4,200,000
	$14,000,000	$16,800,000
Current liabilities	$ 1,800,000	$ 1,800,000
Common shares	10,000,000	
Retained earnings	2,200,000	
	$14,000,000	

On January 1, 19—9 the balance sheet of WL was:

Current assets	$11,500,000
Investment in KC	8,000,000
	$19,500,000
Common shares	$15,000,000
Retained earnings	4,500,000
	$19,500,000

Required:

A. Prepare a balance sheet of WL as of January 1, 19—9 for each of the following:
1. proportionate consolidation of KC is chosen.
2. WL consolidates KC (which would not be GAAP).
3. equity reporting is chosen.

B. Refer to Chapters 6 and 15. Explain which of the reporting methods noted in (A) appears to be suitable for one or more of the objectives of accounting. Why?

P15-4 Refer to the facts in **P15-3.** For the year ended December 31, 19—9 KC prepared the following income statement:

Sales revenue		$9,300,000
Cost of goods sold		5,150,000
Gross profit		4,150,000
Expenses:		
Selling and administrative	$1,500,000	
Depreciation	850,000	2,350,000
Income before income taxes		1,800,000
Income tax		800,000
Net income		$1,000,000

WL has chosen to amortize the differences between fair market value and book value as follows:

Current assets	during 19—7
Building	over 20 years
Equipment	over 10 years
Goodwill	over 40 years

A straight line basis of amortization will be used.

Required:

A. Compute the amount of income or loss from KC that WL ought to report in 19—9. Explain your computation. (Assume, for convenience, that income tax expense of KC remains at $800,000.)

B. Explain why full amortization of the current asset increment of $900,000 ($7,600,000 less $6,700,000) could logically occur in 19—9.

P15-5 Refer to the facts in **P15-3.** Suppose that WL acquired 100 percent of the common shares of KC for $16,000,000 (which means that its current assets would then be $3,500,000).

Required:

A. Prepare January 1, 19—9 financial statements of WL that combine the balance sheet of KC:
   1. on a consolidated basis that includes fair-valuing of KC's assets and liabilities (i.e., so-called purchase accounting).
   2. on a pooling-of-interests basis.

B. If you were a prospective shareholder of WL/KC would you prefer the financial statement that you prepared in (A1) or in (A2)? Why?

P15-6 Refer to the facts in **P15-5** and **P15-4.** That is, assume that WL acquired 100 percent of KC for $16,000,000, and the results in **P15-4** occurred during the first year after acquisition of KC.

During 19—9 WL's income statement showed:

Sales revenue		$15,000,000
Cost of goods sold		9,000,000
Gross profit		6,000,000
Expenses:		
Selling and administrative	$1,650,000	
Interest	150,000	1,800,000
Income before income tax		4,200,000
Income tax		1,950,000
Net income		$ 2,250,000

Required:

A. Prepare the income statement of WL and KC assuming that:
   1. WL consolidates KC on a purchase accounting basis, which fair values the assets and liabilities of KC.
   2. WL's and KC's income figures are reported on a pooling-of-interests basis.

B. Compare the two income statements that you prepared in (A1) and (A2). Do they help explain why the management of some companies prefer pooling-of-interests to purchase accounting? Provide your reasoning.

P15-7 Refer to the information in **P15-6**. What would the effect be on the income statements that would be prepared for 19—9 if KC had paid a $2,000,000 dividend to WL, and WL had credited the $2,000,000 to selling and administrative expense in 19—9? Explain your reasoning, and state your assumptions.

EXPLORATION MATERIALS AND CASES

MC15-1 Lemoine Limited (LL) was incorporated under federal legislation four years ago. Prior to that, LL operated as a sole proprietorship, under the name R. Lemoine.

The founder of LL, R. Lemoine, hoped that his daughter might become interested in taking over the business of LL, which operates two antique stores five miles outside of two large cities. Unfortunately for the founder, the daughter does not want to own or operate LL. Hence, it will be offered for sale.

You have been hired by Mr. Lemoine to "prepare modern financial statements to show to prospective investors", who would be interested in buying all of the shares in LL. After some preliminary checking you ascertain the following:

1. Mr. Lemoine has always prepared the financial statements of LL, and filed the income tax returns.

2. The founder maintains perpetual inventory cards on all items that cost him over $250 each, and would usually sell for over $500 each. He has tended to keep the inventory valuation low to minimize income taxes. That is, he shows some antiques at zero cost if they have not sold after two years.

3. LL owns both of the buildings in which the stores are located. The building housing Store A is almost fully depreciated; yet, being of stone, it could last for 50 or more years. The land on which the building is located cost LL about $5,000 and presently is worth around $200,000. The building could be sold for $150,000 or more.

4. The land for Store B cost $10,000 and is currently worth $120,000 or more. The building for Store B was rebuilt four years ago, and two-thirds of the space has been leased for 20 years to the provincial government for a district office.

5. About 10 percent of LL's sales volume is from charitable organizations that sell "raffle tickets" in order to raise funds for charitable purposes. The prizes tend to be gold and silver antique objects that are very expensive. Although the charitable organizations always pay their bills, LL has always recognized revenue when cash is received.

6. LL holds some common and preferred share investments in larger publicly-traded

companies. They are carried on the balance sheet at cost of $62,000. Annual dividend income is around $4,000. The current market value of these shares is about $28,000.

7. Store B has been separately incorporated under the name Richard Corporation (RC), and all of its common shares are held by LL. The main assets of RC are inventory and store fixtures.

Required:

Advise Mr. Lemoine.

MC15-2 Quirin Limited (QL) is incorporated under federal legislation. It is owned by two larger companies, both of which are privately owned and incorporated under federal legislation.

You have been the accounting adviser for QL for many years, and have also provided income tax advice to the company. You are currently completing your review for the year ended June 30, 19—2 and have encountered the following:

1. QL received a loan of $1,000,000, carrying an interest rate of eight percent per annum, from a provincial government. This loan was due for repayment in December 19—2 but was paid in full in January 19—2 when the provincial government offered a 10 percent discount for early repayment. QL was able to repay the $900,000 by negotiating a ten year debenture issue with an insurance company. The interest rate on the debenture is fixed at 16 percent, which was one-half percent above the prime rate charged by chartered banks at that time.

2. QL's division in the U.S. devoted about one-third of the year to seeking out common share investments in other companies. Primarily, the U.S. division was looking for small U.S. companies that could be totally acquired, and was not interested in acquisitions of less than 100 percent of the shares. During 19—2 about $85,000 in U.S. dollars was spent on research materials required to learn more about certain industries. Also about $200,000 U.S. in executive time, and $55,000 U.S. in travel expenses were incurred in seeking possible investments in U.S. companies. By July 19—2 no offers had been made to acquire these other companies.

3. In the year ended June 30, 19—1 QL accounted for its investment in a joint venture (incorporated Canadian company) by the equity method. This year, 19—2, QL would like to use the proportionate consolidation method for its 40 percent interest, which amounts to $3,200,000 (using equity accounting).

4. In January 19—2 QL ceased insuring for losses below $500,000. Previously it had always been fully insured. A saving in insurance premiums of $10,000 resulted.

Required:

Advise management about accounting and related matters.

MC15-3 Linder Corporation (LC) was incorporated under federal legislation many years ago. The company has been privately owned by one, large family since incorporation. LC's main operations consist of constructing and leasing shopping centres and office buildings. Virtually all of the actual construction activity is contracted out to general contracting companies.

LC incorporated a subsidiary company, Richardson Incorporated (RI), two years ago to hold the assets and liabilities of one combined shopping-office complex called

Richardson Heights. As of the latest year end, December 31, 19—2, of both LC and RI, LC had guaranteed $6,000,000 of the first mortgage on the Richardson Heights property. The $6,000,000 figure is the maximum that LC agreed to guarantee.

Currently it is December 19—3. You are the newly-hired controller of both LC and RI and have learned of the following as you prepare for the 19—3 financial statements:

1. As of December 31, 19—2 RI had capitalized the following:

A. Cost of leasing building and stores	$ 222,500
B. Interest and property taxes	1,674,800
C. Grass, shrubs and land-improvements	162,000
D. Land	1,080,750
E. Building, excluding items shown above	14,525,250

2. The first tenants of Richardson Heights began occupying the shopping and office complex in February 19—3, as construction was being completed. By December 19—3 approximately 60 percent of the rental space, by value, had been leased.

3. During 19—3 (to November 30) the following net costs had been incurred by RI, and were capitalized:

A. Advertising	$ 317,900
B. Portion of overhead charged by LC to RI	300,000
C. Interest and property taxes	720,700
D. Payment to contractor	1,095,000
E. Rental revenues to May 31	(62,900)
F. Insurance on property	292,000

4. As of June 30, 19—3 the agreed maximum mortgage on Richardson Heights had been reached at $11,000,000. (The mortgage holder, an insurance company, had made all of its advances to the general contractor by June 19—3.)

5. A general recession in 19—3 prevented RI from reaching its projected cash flows. By November 19—3 RI was four months behind in meeting its principal and interest payments on the mortgage. RI was also three months overdue on payments for a $1,200,000 bank loan.

6. An appraisal, based on discounted cash flows, placed the value of the Richardson Heights property at $17,000,000 as of March 19—3. Net realizable value is about $16,000,000 today.

7. The salaries of the president and senior executives of RI (including you) are guaranteed by LC. In total, the annual sum guaranteed is roughly $300,000. All of these executives are employed part-time, and work for other subsidiaries of LC.

8. LC's owners' equity is approximately $20 million.

Required:

Advise the president of LC and RI how you believe that the above should be handled on the 19—3 financial statements. (If sensible alternatives exist for management, explain your reasoning.)

CHAPTER 16

Statement of Changes in Financial Position

Chapter Themes

1. The Statement of Changes in Financial Position (SCFP) has existed since the turn of this century. But the design or format of the statement has changed to accommodate different users and uses. Most of these changes have occurred in the past thirty years, as financial accounting has been evolving toward providing more information to those external users who hope to predict cash flows and evaluate the performance of management. As both of these objectives of accounting (Chapter 6) assume the existence of "user power", accounting practice has tended to vary—with the most extensive disclosure being in those situations where the users have been able to convince management and the board of directors to provide sought-after disclosure.

2. For many years, the SCFP was built around changes in working capital (current assets less current liabilities) during a financial period. One of the reasons for this is that working capital tends to be somewhat compatible with accrual accounting. (See Chapter 5.)

3. People have difficulty with the SCFP if they have not fully grasped the differences between cash and accrual accounting. (See Chapters 4 and 5.)

4. The SCFP is an *operating* statement—like the income statement. That is, it portrays activities that have occurred during a designated financial period. But, which activities? The income statement concentrates on income activities. What is left? Liquidity transactions, such as cash receipts and disbursements, are one possibility. (See Chapter 5.) Another possibility is changes in the non-liquid sections of the balance sheet. For example, changes in long-term debt could be important in conveying information about the nature of the obligations *and* the company's borrowing ability. Yet, a comparison of the opening and closing balance sheets tell us the *net*

change only. We would not know whether certain non-current assets and liabilities could have decreased substantially during the period, and then increased before the period ended. Sometimes this information about increases and decreases is important; sometimes it is not. Sometimes the information is available in footnotes. In short, we have to tailor the SCFP to fit the circumstances about objectives and facts. There are situations where changes in liquidity are important; and there are situations where changes in non-current accounts are important.

5. The SCFP is not income-based and therefore is not intended to be useful for the income tax postponement objective. The SCFP would tend to have limited, if any, usefulness for income-based bonus-plan objectives.

The Basic Situation

Before we illustrate the SCFP in full, it is necessary that we spend *much time* clarifying two different concepts: (1) funds, and (2) funds from operations. Suppose that a company's beginning-of-year balance sheet is as follows:

Cash	$100,000	Common shares	$100,000

During the year, the following occurs:

1. Inventory of $60,000 is bought on account.

2. The entire inventory is sold on account for $89,999.

3. Expenses of $12,500 are paid in cash.

4. Land costing $80,000 is purchased for cash.

The end-of-year balance sheet would appear as in Illustration 16-1.

ILLUSTRATION 16-1

Cash	$ 7,500	Accounts payable	$ 60,000
Accounts receivable	89,999	Common shares	100,000
Land	80,000	Retained earnings	17,499
	$177,499		$177,499

The income statement would show:

Revenue	$ 89,999
Cost of goods sold	60,000
Gross profit	29,999
Expenses	12,500
Net income and retained earnings	$ 17,499

It is important at this point to study the foregoing transactions carefully to ensure that the path of each debit and credit has been followed. Cash transactions have to be separated from accrual effects on receivables and payables because of their different effects on *funds from operations*.

The year's non-income-related activities may be presented in *at least* three different ways. That is, the *funds* that are being tracked or traced by the SCFP may include at least the following:

1. Changes in cash. Why did it *decrease* from $100,000 to $7,500?

2. Changes in working capital:

	Beginning of Year	End of Year	Decrease in Working Capital
Cash	$100,000	$ 7,500	
Accounts receivable	—	89,999*	
	100,000	97,499	
Accounts payable	—	60,000*	
Working capital	$100,000	$37,499	$62,501

*Note that an increase in accounts receivable is an increase in working capital, and an increase in accounts payable decreases working capital, because it is a net figure.

3. Changes in a non-current asset or liability, such as land.

Many transactions that a company engages in during a period affect the working-capital (current asset minus current liability) accounts. Consequently, accountants have tended to group these transactions together, as "funds from operations". (We have to be careful not to confuse "funds" with "funds from operations".) In this example, because *all* the transactions on the income statement are offset by working capital accounts (cash, receivables, and payables), "funds from operations" is the *same as* net income. This is unusual.

WORKING CAPITAL STYLE OF STATEMENT

An SCFP based on *working capital* "funds" may be set up as in Illustration 16-2. What does this financial statement tell us? It says that we financed the purchase of the land by using working capital on hand at the beginning of the year, plus funds generated by operations, i.e., the regular operations of the company, such as buying and selling inventory. Mostly, though, we used up working capital from the beginning of the year, and will not have $62,501 from this source to use next year, for possible spending on some other long-lived asset.

ILLUSTRATION 16-2

COMPANY NAME
SCFP
Period of Time

Uses of working capital funds:		
Purchase of land	$80,000	
Sources of working capital funds:		
Funds from operations (accrual basis)	17,499	
Decrease in working capital funds	$62,501	

By focussing on funds from operations as an accrual unit, we do not have our mind distracted by the effect of each purchase and sale of inventory, and each transaction in payables and receivables. Thus, there is merit to computing funds from operations *as an accrual unit,* and we have to keep this in mind as we proceed through this chapter, looking at alternatives.

Illustration 16-3 summarizes the "accrual funds from operations" transactions:

ILLUSTRATION 16-3

Income Statement Item		Offsetting Debit (Credit)	Effect on Working Capital	
			Increase	Decrease
Revenue	$89,999	Cash or receivables	$89,999	
Cost of goods sold	60,000	(Inventory)		$60,000
Expenses	12,500	(Cash; accounts payable; prepaid expenses)		12,500
			$89,999 72,500	$72,500
			$17,499	

Note in Illustration 16-3 that each of revenue, cost of goods sold, and expenses is offset by a debit or credit to a working capital account. Consequently, a transaction affecting these income statement items tends to increase or decrease funds from operations—whenever funds from operations is defined as referring to *accrual* accounting. (We do *not* get the same result when *cash* is chosen as our definition, in place of accrual accounting. This is explained shortly.)

Notice, also, that we would have to alter our computation of funds from operations *if* the income statement included an expense for depreciation, *or* included income tax expense that was offset by a credit to *non-current* "deferred income tax". For instance, suppose that the income statement looked like this:

Revenue		$89,999
Cost of goods sold		60,000
Gross profit		29,999
Expenses		
Cash-type or accrual	$12,500	
Depreciation	6,200	18,700
Income		$11,299

Funds from operations (on an accrual basis) would still be $17,499. It could still be calculated as in Illustration 16-3. Or, it could be calculated as follows:

Income	$11,299
Add transactions that have affected income but have not affected funds from operations:	
Depreciation	6,200
Funds from operations	$17,499

In recent years, the popularity of working capital funds for the SCFP has declined. A main reason why the decline commenced was the severe recession of the early 1980s. Companies found themselves short of cash after having paid high interest rates during the rapid inflationary period that preceded the recession. Many unusual SCFP designs have appeared in the 1980s as preparers have wrestled with combinations of

ILLUSTRATION 16-4

Two Different Concepts: Funds From Operations, and Funds

1. The computation of funds from operations:
    - A. Accrual based, i.e., receivables, payables, and similar; and
    - B. Cash based, i.e., cash only.

2. The balancing figure that is being explained (or, what is "funds"):
    - A. Changes in working capital;
    - B. Changes in cash; and
    - C. Changes in some other asset or liability.

two of the main components of the SCFP: (1) the definition of funds from operations and (2) what figure the SCFP balances to (or, the definition of "funds"). These are shown in Illustration 16-4.

To this point in the chapter, funds from operations has been calculated on an accrual basis (1A in Illustration 16-4). The principal reason for this choice is that the accrual figure is less susceptible to "hard-to-interpret" change. Stating the point another way, the other choice, cash (1B in Illustration 16-4) can vary considerably from moment to moment because a payable (cash disbursement) or receivable (cash receipt) is delayed an hour, or a day, into the next financial period.

Nevertheless, some people choose to calculate funds from operations on a *cash basis*. If we did this using the figures from Illustration 16-1, we would arrive at a *negative* of $12,500, because expenses are the *only cash item* on the income statement. The $12,500 may be presented in at least two different ways on the SCFP:

1. Uses of funds:
   Cash applied to operations $ 12,500

2. Uses of funds:
   Cash applied to operations:
     Income $(17,499)★
     Deduct items affecting income
     but not affecting cash:
       Accounts receivable $89,999
       Less accounts payable   60,000   29,999
                                                                   $ 12,500

★The income figure is negative because we have shown the "cash applied to operations" under the uses section of the SCFP. The $17,499 would be a positive figure if it were shown under the sources section, as in Illustration 16-2.

A summary to this point is in order because the SCFP can be confusing. The point of this first section of the chapter is to keep separate in our minds the distinction between "funds" (which the SCFP revolves around), and "funds from operations", which is how the income statement transactions that have a funds effect may be reported. A company may design an SCFP on any one of these bases, *or more*:

A. Funds equals working capital, and funds from operations is computed on an *accrual* basis. (Illustration 16-2);

B. Funds equals working capital, and funds from operations is calculated on a *cash* basis. (Illustration 16-5);

C. Funds equals cash, and funds from operations is calculated on an accrual basis. (Illustration 16-6); and

D. Funds equals cash, and funds from operations is calculated on a cash basis. (Illustration 16-7).

ILLUSTRATION 16-5

COMPANY NAME

SCFP

Period of Time

Uses of working-capital funds:		
Purchase of land		$80,000
Sources of working-capital funds:		
Cash applied to operations	($12,500)★	
Effect on operations from non-cash current assets and liabilities:		
Increase in receivables	89,999★	
Less increase in payables	(60,000)★	17,499
Decrease in working-capital funds		$62,501

★It is important to note that the location determines whether the number is positive or negative. Something that is a source of funds should be a positive number when it is included under a "sources of working capital funds" heading. For example, an increase in receivables should be a positive figure, because it increases working capital. But, in Illustration 16-5, sources are being subtracted from uses; therefore, we have reversed the signs simply because we are subtracting from the $80,000.

What does Illustration 16-5 tell us? The design is complex. We have mixed working capital, which includes receivables and payables and inventories and other items that tend to be part of accrual accounting, with a cash basis of computing funds from operations. As a result, we end up having to "plug" in the changes during the period in receivables and payables, *just to balance.*

In short, the combination of working capital "funds" and "cash from operations" could be a waste of time. However, for completeness, and to stress the point, Illustration 16-5 was necessary. To this point, we have established that working capital funds and accrual based funds from operations can be compatible. It is time to switch, and to look at cash funds—or changes during the period in the cash figure (between two balance sheet dates).

FUNDS DEFINED AS CASH

As mentioned earlier, cash gained greater attention for the SCFP as a result of the serious inflation and recession problems of the early 1980s. Working capital has never been a particularly satisfying focal point for the SCFP, and has relied on its nearness to accrual accounting to maintain its credibility, i.e., many debits and credits to the income statement are offset by debits or credits to working capital accounts—debit inventory, credit accounts payable being examples. Working capital's deficiencies are:

1. Measurement incompatibilities. Cash and receivables and payables tend to be measured on a cash-equivalent basis. Inventory is at cost, however, which differs from a cash equivalency by the amount of gross profit.

2. Time differences. Cash is a "today's figure". Receivables may not be collected in cash for another sixty or ninety days. Inventory may have to be turned into receivables before it can become cash.

ILLUSTRATION 16-6

COMPANY NAME
SCFP
Period of Time

Uses of cash funds:		
Purchase of land		$80,000
Increase in accounts receivable		89,999
		169,999
Sources of cash funds:		
Increase in accounts payable	$60,000	
Funds from operations (i.e., accrual basis)	17,499	77,499
Decrease in cash		92,500*
Cash balance, beginning of period		100,000
Cash balance, end of period		$ 7,500

*This figure could be placed in brackets to signify that it is a subtraction from the $100,000, to arrive at the $7,500.

What does Illustration 16-6 tell us? It is a little confusing, but not as puzzling as Illustration 16-5. As we are dealing with cash funds, changes in all of the *other* accounts that make up working capital have to be accounted for—or we just will not balance our SCFP. Land has been purchased for cash. Also, accounts receivable has *not* been collected in cash yet. Therefore, at this point, the increase in accounts receivable represents a use of cash funds. These two uses of funds total $169,999. Where did the money come from?

Illustration 16-6 tells us that the cash came from two sources:

1. Regular operations of the business, which, on an accrual basis, generated $17,499, and

2. "Postponement" in paying accounts payable of $60,000.

Obviously, a few moments after the period end, the cash position of the company probably would have changed, and the effects may have changed. For instance, the receivables may have been collected and the payables may have been paid.

The SCFP reports on the *past* financial period, however, and therefore has all of the strengths and weaknesses of such financial statements. It is an historical record much like the details kept by official scorers of baseball and hockey games. Interesting trends may be revealed—especially if comparisons are conducted into which assets have been acquired, and how they have been financed. It is possible that the method used to finance the acquisitions could be expensive over the longer term. For example, preferred shares may have been issued, which require the payment of a dividend out of *after tax* net income. (If bonds had been selected as the vehicle for financing, interest would be deductible for income tax purposes. The company may, however, have had too much debt outstanding and therefore would not want to issue more.) The SCFP helps people to focus on *recent* changes to the balance sheet, which are not obvious by looking at just the end-of-period balance sheet.

The statement design shown in Illustration 16-7 has gained in popularity in the 1980s, because it focusses on cash. However, it may not be as commonly seen over the next few years as will Illustration 16-8. Illustration 16-7 provides what is called "articulation" with the income statement, by commencing with net income and adding (subtracting) whatever is necessary to convert funds from operations to a cash basis.

Illustration 16-8 is a *condensed* version of what may be seen in practice, because our

---

ILLUSTRATION 16-7

COMPANY NAME
SCFP
Period of Time

Uses of cash funds:		
Purchase of land		$80,000
Applied to operations:		
Funds from operations	$(17,499)★	
Add (deduct) items affecting		
income but not affecting cash:		
Accounts receivable	89,999	
Accounts payable	(60,000)	12,500
Decrease in cash		92,500
Cash balance, beginning of period		100,000
Cash balance, end of period		$ 7,500

★See page 512.

ILLUSTRATION 16-8

COMPANY NAME
SCFP
Period of Time

Uses of cash funds:	
Purchase of land	$80,000
Applied to operations (see Footnote x)★	12,500
	92,500
Cash position, beginning of period	100,000
Cash position, end of period	$ 7,500

★The footnote would give the details that are provided in Illustration 16-7.

sample situation has been kept to basics and does not include other sources of funds. (See Appendix 1-A.) The design of Illustration 16-8 clearly shows what caused cash to drop from $100,000 to $7,500, and this is important in monitoring *liquidity* and trends. Chapter 5 stressed the dual problem areas of liquidity and profitability, especially for small businesses. Illustration 16-8 focusses on the most liquid item of all, cash.

REVIEW

Some people find the SCFP difficult to comprehend—even some businesspersons and accountants. Note the title SCFP; not long ago, the statement was called a "Source and Uses of Funds Statement". This latter title conveyed a "flow of funds" approach. The statement's purpose and design has changed many times in the 1900s in a process of evolution. The designs illustrated so far in this chapter are based on a liquidity theme. But they need not be, and may centre on changes in, for example, land. (See Illustration 16-4, item 2C.)

We have intentionally illustrated several designs or formats because: (1) several different ones will be seen in practice, and (2) adaptability, and the *downplaying* of a "one truth"/"right-wrong" philosophy, is a prime theme of this book. We have shown that some designs are confusing and carry little information value. Their cost may exceed any possible benefits, and this point can be made only when we show impractical designs, and contrast them with more efficient formats.

We have to compare the alternatives. Which design makes the most sense under particular sets of facts and objectives of accounting? The SCFP is much less constrained by GAAP and legislation than are the income statement and balance sheet. *Flexibility* is the key to success for the SCFP.

OBJECTIVES OF ACCOUNTING

We have mentioned that the SCFP is not designed for the income tax postponement objective of accounting, nor would it be important for incentive plans, where bonuses are based on an income measurement. It is possible, however, that a restrictive covenant could be drafted by a lawyer to refer to "funds from operations" (cash basis or accrual basis), and the need to keep it above a certain level before dividends may be declared. (The restrictive covenant may be in a clause in a bond-payable agreement.)

Which objectives of accounting are served by the SCFP? Corporate law requires an SCFP, but does not give much guidance about how it ought to be designed. Nevertheless, a statement *is* required and the "minimum compliance" objective exists. When this is the *prime* objective, a preparer could "go through the motions" and merely recast what is already available from the income statement. Usually this means that *net* figures would be shown on the SCFP, *instead of* "gross ups", such as:

Bank borrowings negotiated	$1,000,000
Less repayments from cash flows	895,000
Net increase in bank loan	105,000

The gross up gives a powerful message about (1) the borrowing power of the company, i.e., a bank is willing to lend it $1,000,000, and (2) the ability of the company to repay most of the loan from cash flows, perhaps from operations.

For readers to be in a position to obtain the foregoing gross-ups and additional information, "user power" must exist in some form. The preparers *may* be willing to provide the information—especially if the company wishes to obtain capital (debt or equity)from the marketplace—and thereby grant some power to the users. Alternatively, the shareholders may request a more comprehensive SCFP. Or, a debt instrument may call for the disclosure.

Investor sophistication and market efficiency have to be considered in designing the SCFP under so-called "user power" situations. Sophisticated investors seek *new* information that is not available elsewhere in the financial statements when they read the SCFP. If the SCFP merely recasts what is available elsewhere in the financial statement package (including the notes), then it is worthless. For instance, the SCFP may show only the *net* change in non-current accounts, e.g., land or debt. This is something that the reader may obtain by subtracting the opening from the closing balance sheet. Who needs the SCFP just to do subtractions?

NEW INFORMATION

Three types of transactions may be shown on a different design of SCFP, and all three may provide *new* information to thereby enhance the importance of the SCFP:

1. *Flows each way,* (or increases as well as decreases). This can be especially important for the accounts, particularly the non-current assets and liabilities.

2. *Barter transactions,* (or non-cash transactions). For example, land and building may be acquired by assuming an existing mortgage and other debt. There are at least two methods of reporting this on the SCFP:

Method 1:
    Uses of cash:
        Purchase of land and buildings $100,000

Method 2:
    Uses of cash:

Acquisition of land	$200,000	
Acquisition of building	700,000	
	900,000	
First mortgage liability assumed	580,000	
	320,000	
Second mortgage liability	220,000	$100,000

Method 2 tells us much more than Method 1 about what really happened. Some-one wishing to predict funds flows, or cash flows, would want to ascertain what cash is likely to be generated by the land and buildings. Maybe they will replace other facilities that had to be rented, and the computation of cash savings will therefore be easy. Maybe the land and buildings have to be rented to others, how-ever, and some guesswork about the rental revenue will be necessary. In addition, costs of financing will have to be subtracted from any savings or rental revenue. A second mortgage for $220,000 likely will be very expensive when only $100,000 of down payment exists. An interest rate of 20 percent may apply on the second mortgage. Overall, Method 2 could help in interpreting balance sheet changes, and in permitting forecasters to focus on changes that will affect future funds flow.

3. *Liability rollovers and conversions:* Corporate law requires that changes in owners' equity accounts, especially in shares, be reported in the financial state-ments. Therefore, the SCFP may *not* be providing new information when it reports conversions of preferred shares into common shares:

Issues of common shares	$500,000	
Less conversion of preferred shares	500,000	0

But, when one type of debt is exchanged for another, the balance sheet may not show any change, and the footnotes may not give the full implications of what hap-pened with respect to covenants, repayment dates, and other terms. Thus, some new information could be available through the SCFP and its accompanying notes. This is especially important in real estate enterprises where there is a tendency to have "bridge financing" during a construction period, and to replace the tempo-rary or bridge financing with longer-term mortgages.

It is the disclosure or reporting of the above three, and similar types of transac-tions, that gave rise to the SCFP's getting the name "Statement of Changes in Financial Position" in place of its old name, "Statement of Sources and Uses of Funds". The latter is primarily concerned with liquidity flows. The former focusses on what are called *financing and investing* activities. For example, we *invested* in land and build-ings, and *financed* them mainly by way of mortgages.

The details about flows each way, and other new information, make the SCFP useful. Users would have to have some power to allow the SCFP to attain its potential as a statement of disclosure. Otherwise, preparers may report only what is required by law.

Common Situations

A small business probably would use an SCFP that defines funds as "cash". Quite likely, "funds from operations" would be based on accrual accounting. This combination (see Illustration 16-6) helps to focus on liquidity, especially the expenditure of cash and changes in the near-cash accounts such as payables and receivables. The importance of balancing liquidity and profitability was stressed in Chapter 5.

A cash definition of funds is *not* universally useful. It presents difficulties for the reporting of pure barter transactions, where no cash is involved, and for rollovers of liabilities, where no cash is involved.

Some accountants split barters into *two* transactions such as: (1) the redemption of the old liability for cash (use of cash), and (2) the issuance of the new liability for cash (source of cash). However, this is misleading because it suggests that *two*, unrelated cash transactions with third parties have occurred. But, there may have been only one transaction—acquisition of building and assumption of debt—and fair market value may *not* have been received. Some major lawsuits have occurred in Canada as a result of shareholders not believing that fair value was received in barter-type transactions. Thus, it is dangerous to imply that two unrelated cash transactions occurred, when they did not.

Concerning SCFP, we tend to have the most difficulty with the computation of funds from operations. Several topics have been illustrated in Chapters 6 through 15 that have important implications in computing funds from operations. We will illustrate a few just to ensure that the funds effect is clear:

1. Gain or loss on disposal of long-lived asset;
2. Accrued/deferred income tax increase/decrease;
3. Amortization of bond premium or discount;
4. Use of equity reporting; and
5. An entity that experiences a loss.

REVIEW

Funds from operations may be computed the "forward" way, or the "backward" way. To illustrate, suppose that the income statement of a company looks like this:

Revenue		$100,000
Cost of goods sold		65,000
Gross profit		35,000
Expenses:		
Cash-type	$16,000	
Depreciation	12,500	28,500
Income		$ 6,500

The revenue, cost of goods sold, and cash-type expenses are offset to the working-capital accounts—respectively, (1) cash, or unearned revenue, or receivables; (2) inventory; and (3) cash, payables, and prepaid expenses, respectively. Thus, on an *accrual* basis, funds from operations would be calculated on a "forward" basis (i.e., the direct way, because these are the transactions that affect funds) as follows:

Revenue	$ +. 100,000
Cost of goods sold	− 65,000
Cash-type expenses (e.g., cash, payables)	− 16,000
Funds from operations (accrual basis)	$ + 19,000

We can also compute funds from operations on the accrual basis, however, by the so-called "backward" method:

Income	$ 6,500
Depreciation	12,500
	$19,000

The backward method uses the figures on the income statement that were *not* used in the forward calculation. That is, we have an equation:

Accrual Revenue − Cash-Type Expenses − Non-Cash Expenses = Income

OR, by transposing the non-cash expenses:

Accrual Revenue − Cash-Type Expenses = Income + Non-Cash Expenses

$100,000 − ($65,000 + $16,000) = $ 6,500 + $12,500
$19,000 = $19,000

DISPOSAL OF LONG-LIVED ASSET

A disposal of a long-lived asset is complex from a funds-flow point of view because there are two effects: (1) any proceeds received on disposal of the asset would be a source of cash or of funds (cash or receivable); and (2) the gain or loss has an effect much like depreciation.

Suppose that some equipment with a cost of $100,000 and accumulated depreciation of $65,000 is sold for $20,000 cash. The journal entry is:

Cash	$20,000	
Accumulated depreciation	65,000	
Loss on sale	15,000	
Equipment		100,000

The cash received on sale of $20,000 is a *source* of funds, and the loss on sale has *lowered income*, but has *NOT affected funds*. On the surface, the latter is hard to understand until we split the journal entry into its parts:

A. Cash	20,000	
Equipment		20,000
B. Accumulated depreciation	65,000	
Equipment		65,000
C. Loss on sale of equipment	15,000	
Equipment		15,000

Only entry (A) affects cash, or a working capital account. Entry (B) is the journal entry that we make when we write off a fully depreciated asset. Entry (C) is much like depreciation—the credit is to a non-cash or non-working capital account and the debit is an expense that lowers income. An SCFP based on cash funds and accrual funds from operations would show:

Source of funds:
Proceeds on disposal of equipment		$20,000
From operations:		
Net income	$ xxx	
Add (subtract) items affecting income but not cash:		
Depreciation	xxx	
Loss on sale of equipment	15,000	

We may show a "gain" by using the same example, but by assuming that the cash proceeds are $45,000:

Cash	45,000	
Accumulated depreciation	65,000	
Equipment		100,000
Gain on sale		10,000

The gain of $10,000 would *increase* income, but would *not* affect funds. The SCFP presentation would therefore be:

Source of funds:
Proceeds on sale of equipment		$45,000
From operations: (i.e., accrual basis)		
Net income	xxx	
Add (subtract) items affecting income but not cash:		
Depreciation	xxx	
Gain on sale of equipment	(10,000)	

The journal entry split into its parts would show:

A. Cash	45,000	
Equipment		45,000
B. Accumulated depreciation	65,000	
Equipment		65,000
C. Equipment	10,000	
Gain on sale		10,000

Notice that we have to *debit* equipment in (C), because we overcredited it in (A) and (B).

ACCRUED/DEFERRED INCOME TAX

When capital cost allowance *exceeds* depreciation (or expenses that have been claimed for tax purposes exceed expenses reported on the income statement), the journal entry for tax is:

1. Tax expense	1,000	
Deferred/accrued tax		400
Taxes payable or cash		600

When depreciation exceeds capital cost allowance, the opposite effect occurs:

2. Tax expense	1,000	
Deferred/accrued tax	400	
Taxes payable or cash		1,400

Entry (1) is much like the loss on sale of equipment, and entry (2) has the same effect as a gain on sale of equipment. Entry (1) can be split into the two components of cash, and non-cash.

1A. <u>Cash Portion:</u>

Tax expense	600	
Cash or tax payable		600

1B. <u>Non-Cash Portion:</u>

Tax expense	400	
Deferred/accrued tax		400

The tax expense of $400 would lower income but *not* affect cash or working capital. When funds from operations are computed on the accrual basis, and the backward method is used, the SCFP may look like:

Source of funds:	
From Operations:	
Net income	$ xxx
Add item lowering income but not affecting cash or working capital	
Accrued/deferred income tax	400

Entry (2) would be split into:

2A. <u>Cash Portion:</u>

Tax expense	1,400	
Cash or tax payable		1,400

2B. <u>Non-Cash Portion:</u>

Deferred/accrued tax	400	
Tax expense		400

Observe that (2B) is *crediting* the tax *expense*, and is therefore reducing it. This is much like having a gain on sale of equipment, and would be treated in the same way, i.e., *deducted* from net income when the backward method of computing accrual funds from operations is used:

BOND PAYABLE—PREMIUM/DISCOUNT

When a bond payable is sold at a discount, the journal entry is:

Cash	980	
Discount on bond payable (non-current item)	20	
Bond payable		1,000

When the bond discount is amortized, the journal entry is:

Interest expense	2	
Discount on bond payable		2

The latter entry is much like depreciation: An expense has been debited and the credit is to a *non-current* account (like accumulated depreciation).

When a bond payable is sold at a premium, the journal entry is:

Cash	1,015	
Bond payable		1,000
Premium on bond payable (non-current item)		15

When the bond premium (premium on bond payable) is amortized, the journal entry is:

Premium on bond payable	3	
Interest expense		3

The credit to interest expense is just like the credit to income tax expense in the accrued/deferred tax example. The sum of $3 would be *deducted* from net income to arrive at *accrual* funds from operations, when the "backward" method of computing funds from operations is in use.

EQUITY REPORTING

When equity basis reporting of an intercorporate investment is in use, the journal entry to record income is:

Investment in *X* Limited	10,000	
Income of *X* Limited		10,000

The credit to "income" increases the investor's income for the period, but does *not* increase either cash or working capital funds. The debit is to a non-current "investment" account.

The computation of funds from operations would be the same as was used for bond premium amortization, and a "draw down" of accrued/deferred income taxes (i.e., when depreciation expense exceeds capital cost allowance)—*with one possible exception*. That is, some of the income may be paid in cash as a dividend. If so, the journal entry is:

Cash	4,000	
Investment in *X* Limited		4,000

This journal entry credits a non-current account, and therefore would generally be regarded as a *source of funds*. *But*, it is unlike typical sources, such as:

• Sale of bonds or shares, and
• Sale of long-lived assets, and
• From operations.

It really is turning over *cash from operations* of the *investee* to the investor.

As a result, the typical presentation of the income and dividend of the investee on the SCFP of the *investor* would be (when accrual funds from operations is being selected, and the backward method of computing funds from operations is in use):

Source of funds:
From operations:
Net income xxx
Add (deduct) items affecting
income but not affecting cash
or near cash★ accounts:
Income of investee .... (10,000)

xxx
Add dividend from investee 4,000
Total from operations xxx

★includes accrual effects to receivables, payables, and prepaid/unearned accounts

In effect, the dividend is treated as a separate portion of funds from operations. A net of $6,000 ($10,000 less $4,000) of income of the investee has *not* been included in funds from operations of the investor.

OPERATIONS AND NEGATIVE FUNDS EFFECT

The examples to this point have tended to look at situations where the company has a net income. There obviously are other possibilities, however. For example, consider the following:

Situation A:

Revenue		$200,000
Cost of goods sold		120,000
Gross profit		80,000
Expenses		
Cash-type	$38,000	
Depreciation	40,000	
Interest—bond discount amortized	5,000	83,000
Loss		$ 3,000

The depreciation charge and bond-discount amortization have "caused" the loss, in a sense. Funds from operations (accrual) is $42,000, made up of:

Depreciation	$40,000
Bond-discount amortized	5,000
	45,000
Less loss	3,000
	$42,000

The presentation on the SCFP has to treat the additions and subtractions in the *opposite* way when there is a net loss:

Source of cash:
  From operations:
    Net loss $(3,000)
    Add (deduct) items causing loss
      but not affecting funds:
        Depreciation   40,000
        Bond amortization   5,000
                                                          $42,000

That is, depreciation is *not added* to the net loss (as it was with net income), but is subtracted from it.

Situation B: This is a very serious scenario, where the company is generating negative funds from operations (and is bleeding to death by staying in business):

Revenue		$200,000
Cost of goods sold		180,000
Gross profit		20,000
Expenses:		
Cash-type	$38,000	
Depreciation	40,000	
Interest—bond amortization	5,000	83,000
Loss		$63,000

The SCFP based on accrual funds from operations would show:

Use of cash:
  From operations:
    Net loss $63,000
    Add (deduct) items increasing
      loss but not affecting funds
        Depreciation $(40,000)
        Bond amortization   (5,000)   (45,000)
    Funds used in operations $18,000

Observe that we have changed the signs surrounding depreciation and bond amortization, because the starting point is a loss, and the net effect is a *use* of funds. Note that operations is included under the heading "*use* of cash".

In summary, it is advisable to avoid memorizing the signs. Think out the *effect on funds:* Is it a source or a use? If a "use", it goes under the use heading, and has to be handled as just described.

Problem Situation

Here we use the material in Chapter 5 on funds from operations and the ideas in this chapter together by working through an integrative problem situation. Suppose that the financial statements of a company show the following:

ROBIN BANKS LIMITED
Balance Sheets
December 31

Assets

	19—8	19—7
Current assets:		
Cash	$ 2,000	$ 1,000
Accounts receivable	22,000	20,000
Inventory	56,000	55,000
	80,000	76,000
Long-lived assets:		
Land	70,000	110,000
Building and equipment	377,100	300,000
Accumulated depreciation	137,000	125,000
	240,100	175,000
Goodwill, less amortization	8,000	10,000
	$398,100	$371,000

Liabilities and Owners' Equity

	19—8	19—7
Current liabilities:		
Accounts payable	$ 40,000	$ 58,000
Income tax payable	3,000	2,000
	43,000	60,000
Owners' equity:		
Common shares (Note 1)	220,000	200,000
Retained earnings	135,100	111,000
	355,100	311,000
	$398,100	$371,000

Note 1: During the year, $20,000 of common shares were issued directly in exchange for equipment.

ROBIN BANKS LIMITED
Statement of Retained Earnings
Years ended December 31

	19—8	19—7
Balance, beginning of year	$111,000	$ 97,500
Add net income	30,100	18,500
	141,100	116,000
Deduct dividends	6,000	5,000
Balance, end of year	$135,100	111,000

ROBIN BANKS LIMITED
Income Statement
Years ended December 31

	19—8	19—7
Revenue	$220,000	$200,000
Cost of goods sold	120,000	115,000
Gross profit	100,000	85,000
Expenses:		
Selling and administrative (cash-type)	46,000	41,000
Depreciation	12,000	12,500
Amortization	2,000	2,000
Gain on sale of land	(4,200)	—
	55,800	55,500
Income before income taxes	44,200	29,500
Income tax	14,100	11,000
Net income	$ 30,100	$ 18,500

WORKING CAPITAL FUNDS

We will start with working capital funds and accrual funds from operations. Note that, in this problem, accrual per the income statement and accrual funds from operations differ because of:

> Depreciation, and
> Amortization, and
> Gain on sale of land.

The technique we will describe is the "*T* account method", which is consistent with the philosophy of the book in trying to blend together procedural and conceptual material with different user and preparer objectives of accounting. The *T* account method consists of setting up T accounts, or ledger accounts, for changes that have occurred during the year, and then reconstructing in ledger account form and journal entries what happened during the year.

Step 1: Set up ledger accounts for:

1. Funds (in this case, working capital, or current assets less current liabilities);

2. Funds from operations (to cover the income statement); and

3. For all other accounts, which are the balance sheet accounts other than funds.

Step 2: In the top half of the ledger account, enter the *net* change during the year. (This would not apply to the "funds from operations" account.) First, however, we have to calculate the change during the period in working capital:

Working capital computation:

	Beginning	*Ending*	*Change*
Cash	$ 1,000	$ 2,000	$ + 1,000
Accounts receivable	20,000	22,000	+ 2,000
Inventory	55,000	56,000	+ 1,000
	76,000	80,000	
Accounts payable	58,000	40,000	+18,000*
Income tax payable	2,000	3,000	− 1,000
	60,000	43,000	
	$16,000	$37,000	$ +21,000

*Note that a decrease in accounts payable increases working capital because it lowers the amount that has to be subtracted from current assets.

The changes in the other ledger accounts are easier to calculate. We merely have to subtract the opening from the closing balance sheet figures. We enter the difference above the double line in the ledger account.

Working Capital		Funds from Operations (Backward)	
Change 21,000			
============================			

Land		Building and Equipment	
	Change 40,000	Change 77,100	
============================		============================	

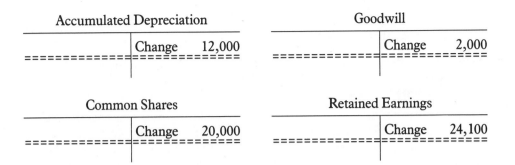

Accumulated Depreciation		Goodwill	
	Change 12,000		Change 2,000

Common Shares		Retained Earnings	
	Change 20,000		Change 24,100

Step 3: Prepare a trial balance to ensure that the debits in the change row equal the credits:

Working capital	21,000	
Land		40,000
Building and equipment	77,100	
Accumulated depreciation		12,000
Goodwill		2,000
Common shares		20,000
Retained earnings		24,100
	98,100	98,100

Step 4: Reconstruct the journal entries (of overall effects) that occurred during the year. First, as we are using the backward method of computing funds from operations, *we should start with the closing* journal entry, which closes the income accounts to retained earnings. All the other reconstructed entries are *original* transaction entries. (See Chapters 3 and 4.) *Second*, we move on to entries where there is some description of an event, such as the barter transaction involving shares, and the gain on sale of land. Certain logical assumptions on our part are often needed. We have to say to ourselves: What was the *most likely* transaction? *Third*, we continue the process with all accounts until the figures below the double line equal the sum above the double line.

The most likely journal entries are:

1. Funds from operations	30,100	
Retained earnings		30,100

Note that the debit is to funds from operations, because this one ledger account represents *all* income statement accounts. Any debit or credit affecting an income statement account would *always* be posted to funds from operations. (The credit to retained earnings signifies that the year generated a net income.)

To simplify the process of figuring out likely journal entries, each journal entry ought to be posted as we proceed. This would take up too many pages in a book, however; so we will do the posting at the end.

2. Building and equipment   20,000
    Common shares   20,000

3. Working capital (cash)   44,200
    Land   40,000
    Gain on sale of land   4,200

In this entry, we have to assume (as we are not told anything else) that the $40,000 decrease in land represents what was sold. We know the gain; hence, the total of $44,200 equals the proceeds. Any current account would be posted to working capital. Any income statement account, i.e., gain, would go to funds from operations.

4. Building and equipment   57,100
    Working capital   57,100

Presumably the figure needed to balance the "building and equipment" account arises from a purchase of more equipment/building.

5. Funds from operations   12,000
    Accumulated depreciation   12,000

This is the depreciation entry during the year. (If a sale of a depreciable asset occurred, we would have to bear in mind the resulting debit to accumulated depreciation that would be in the ledger account.)

6. Funds from operations   2,000
    Goodwill   2,000

This is the amortization of goodwill.

7. Retained earnings   6,000
    Working capital   6,000

This is the dividend for the year.
The posted ledger accounts would look like:

Working Capital				Funds from Operations		
	21,000			1.	30,100	
3.	44,200	4.	57,100			3.	4,200
		7.	6,000	5.	12,000	
				6.	2,000	
				44,100		4,200

Land				Building and Equipment		
			40,000		77,100	
		3.	40,000	2.	20,000	
				4.	57,100	

Accumulated Depreciation	
	12,000
	5. 12,000

Goodwill	
	2,000
	6. 2,000

Common Shares	
	20,000
	2. 20,000 (Barter)

Retained Earnings	
	24,100
7. 6,000	1. 30,100

Step 5: At this point, we can note that the "working capital" ledger account does not balance (below and above the double line) *until* we close out the "funds from operations" account to it by this entry:

Working capital	39,900	
Funds from operations		39,900

The $39,900 is, therefore, funds from operations.

Step 6: Prepare the SCFP *by looking at just the two ledger accounts:* "Working Capital" and "Funds From Operations", *and* any notes that we kept on unusual transactions, such as a barter.

ROBIN BANKS LIMITED
Statement of Changes in Financial Position
Year ended December 31, 19–8

Sources of working capital:		
Sale of land		$44,200
From Operations:		
Net income	$30,100	
Add (deduct) items not affecting funds:		
Depreciation	12,000	
Amortization	2,000	
Gain on sale of land	(4,200)	39,900
		84,100
Uses of working capital:		
Purchase of building and equipment	57,100	
Dividend on common shares	6,000	63,100
Increase in working capital		$21,000

Some companies append a note to their financial statements explaining the composition of the $21,000. Others may add the barter transaction to the SCFP, as follows:

Uses of working capital:
Purchase of building and
equipment $57,100
Dividend on common
shares 6,000
63,100
Purchase of equipment $20,000
Less shares issued 20,000 — 63,100

As we have stressed throughout the chapter and book, "there is *not* one, right answer".
In a formal financial statement, we avoid abbreviations. Note that the term SCFP has
not been used. The full title is given, as is a definition of funds ("working capital").

CASH FUNDS

A similar *T* account procedure could be used when funds is defined as cash. Instead
of having one "working capital" ledger account, there would be one for *each* current
asset and *each* current liability. The journal entries mentioned in Step 4 under
"Working Capital Funds" would be posted to the respective current account. The
SCFP would then be constructed primarily by using the "cash" and "funds from
operations" ledger accounts.

The SCFP may look like the following (as long as accrual funds from operations
applies):

ROBIN BANKS LIMITED
Statement of Changes in Financial Position
Year ended December 31, 19—8

Sources of cash:
Sale of land $44,200
From operations:
Net income $30,100
Add (deduct) items not affecting cash and
near cash:
Depreciation 12,000
Amortization 2,000
Gain on sale of land (4,200) 39,900
84,100
Uses of cash:
Purchase of building and equipment 57,100
Dividends 6,000
Decrease in accounts and income taxes
payable 17,000
Increase in inventory 1,000
Increase in accounts receivable 2,000 83,100
Increase in cash 1,000
Cash at beginning of year 1,000
Cash at end of year $ 2,000

To prepare the cash-funds statement, we merely broke down the working capital sum into its components of payables, receivables, and inventory. As stated earlier, sometimes showing the net increase or decrease is *not* informative, and a gross up would make sense. If so, the presentation might be:

Inventory purchased	122,000
Less inventory sold	120,000
Increase in inventory	2,000

(In this situation, the inventory figures are obvious, hence, there is no need for the gross up.)

CASH FROM OPERATIONS

If cash from operations is to be used for Robin Banks Limited, the presentation in Illustration 16-9 could be used. The caption "net change in non-cash working capital balances related to operations" includes payables, receivables, and inventory.

ILLUSTRATION 16-9

ROBIN BANKS LIMITED
Statement of Changes in Financial Position
Year ended December 31, 19—8

Sources of cash:		
Sale of land		$44,200
From operations:		
Net income	$30,100	
Add charges (deduct credits) to operations not requiring a current cash payment:		
Depreciation	12,000	
Amortization	2,000	
Gain on sale of land	(4,200)	
	39,900	
Net change in non-cash working capital balances related to operations	(20,000)	19,900
		64,100
Uses of cash:		
Purchase of building and equipment	$57,100	
Dividends	6,000	63,100
Increase in cash		1,000
Cash position at beginning of year		1,000
Cash position at end of year		$ 2,000

Summary

The SCFP is a flexible statement that may be used to convey changes in liquidity, e.g., cash definition of funds, or to report important financial activities that are not available from the other financial statements, e.g., barters or wide swings in current account balances such as bank loans. The SCFP may be skimpy or informative; much is dependent on objectives of accounting and who has the power to choose objectives. When the SCFP merely conveys what is available elsewhere, it becomes a somewhat useless financial statement. The design of the statement has to be geared to objectives of accounting, and facts or assumptions about user behavior.

To understand the SCFP, it is important to distinguish "funds" from "funds from operations". The latter is usually less subject to fluctuation and manipulation when it is prepared on an accrual basis. Funds from operations helps to tell us what we may finance internally, and what has to be borrowed from creditors or acquired from prospective equity or share owners. The SCFP has the potential to be an important part of the financial statement package.

QUESTIONS

16-1 Distinguish between "funds" and "funds from operations". What is the significance of the distinction?

16-2 What are the uses and limitations of a working capital definition of funds?

16-3 Distinguish between "accrual funds from operations" and "cash funds from operations".

16-4 What are the uses and limitations of a cash definition of funds?

16-5 What objectives of financial accounting are served by a Statement of Changes in Financial Position? Explain.

16-6 What is a barter transaction, and how might knowledge of it affect various users of financial statements? How should a barter transaction be reported to avoid misinterpretation?

16-7 What is a liability rollover? Why might it be of importance to potential investors?

16-8 What is a conversion? Why might a potential creditor be interested in the effects of a conversion?

16-9 What are financing and investing activities, and why might they be of interest to the creditors and investors of a company?

16-10 What effect does depreciation have on funds from operations?

16-11 What is the significance of negative funds from operations, when it is calculated on an accrual basis?

16-12 Comment on this quotation: "The SCFP is a flexible financial statement that ought to be designed to accommodate an organization's objectives of accounting."

EXERCISES

E16-1 Indicate the impact that each of the following transactions will have on the working capital position of the company. Specify whether it would increase (I), decrease (D), or have no effect (NE) on working capital.

1. Declaration of a $150,000 stock dividend.
2. Declaration of a $150,000 cash dividend.
3. Purchase of marketable securities for $12,000.
4. Sale, for $15,000, of marketable securities that had initially cost $12,000.
5. Declaration of $8,000 in dividends by a firm in which the company has a 5 percent interest.
6. Declaration of $8,000 in dividends by a firm in which the company has a 40 percent interest.
7. Write-off of an uncollectible account of $3,000 against the allowance provided.
8. Acquisition of another company in exchange for $1 million in long-term notes.
9. Sale for $600 of merchandise that had cost $400.

E16-2 Described below are several transactions in which Feltham Ltd. engaged in 19—7:

1. Sold merchandise, on account, for $6,000. Cost of the goods sold, which had been included in inventory, was $5,000.
2. Collected $3,200 of the amount owed by customers.
3. Purchased additional inventory for $1,700 (on account).
4. Paid $1,500 of the amount owed to suppliers.
5. Purchased marketable securities for $700.
6. Sold the marketable securities for $500.
7. Recorded one month's interest on notes payable, $50.
8. Paid one month's interest on the notes payable, $50.
9. Recorded one month's rent due from tenant, $200.
10. Received payment of one month's rent from tenant.

Required:
A. Indicate whether the transactions would increase (I), decrease (D), or have no effect (NE) on the working capital of the corporation.
B. Indicate whether the transactions would increase (I), decrease (D), or have no effect (NE) on the cash balance of the corporation.

E16-3 Compute *accrual* funds from operations from the undernoted income statement information, and explain your response:

Sales revenue		$865,700
Cost of goods sold		610,300
Gross profit		255,400
Expenses:		
Selling	$165,660	
Administrative	82,700	
Interest	39,770	
Depreciation and amortization	52,300	340,430
Net loss		$ 85,030

E16-4 Compute *cash* funds from operations from the undernoted financial information, and explain your response:

Sales revenue		$1,220,670
Cost of goods sold		805,510
Gross profit		415,160
Expenses:		
Selling	$185,600	
Administrative	102,430	
Interest	22,790	
Depreciation and amortization	55,620	366,440
Net income		$ 48,720

The above income statement is for the first year of operations of the company. All of the above transactions are for cash, except for:

1. Depreciation and amortization.
2. $298,645 of sales revenue is included in accounts receivable as of the end of the year.
3. $20,970 of selling expenses are included in accounts payable as of the end of the year.
4. $20,000 has been prepaid for administrative expenses for next year.
5. Inventory that was sold was replenished except that $15,760 was not yet paid for in cash of the end of the year.

E16-5 Prepare a Statement of Changes in Financial Position using an accrual definition of funds from operations, and a cash definition of funds, from the undernoted data. Explain what the statement tells readers.

EPRILE CORPORATION
Income Statement
from the date of incorporation, January 5, 19—8,
to December 31, 19—8

Sales revenue		$3,695,750
Cost of lumber sold		2,488,960
Gross profit		1,206,790
Expenses:		
Selling	$302,170	
Administrative	275,100	
Interest	122,230	
Depreciation and amortization	65,710	765,210
Income before income taxes		441,580
Income taxes		200,000
Net income		$ 241,580

EPRILE CORPORATION
Balance Sheet
December 31, 19—8

Assets

Current:

Cash		$ 65,710
Accounts receivable		1,026,725
Inventories		810,300
Prepaid expenses		26,950
		1,929,685

Long-lived

Land		200,000
Building and equipment	$1,725,640	
Accumulated depreciation	65,710	1,659,930
		1,859,930
		$3,789,615

Liabilities and Owners' Equity

Current liabilities:

Accounts payable		$ 565,710
Bank loan payable		400,000
Income tax payable		200,000
Other liabilities		90,200
		1,255,910

Long-term debt payable on building, 12%		392,125

Owners' equity:

Common shares	$2,000,000	
Retained earnings	141,580	2,141,580
		$3,789,615

EPRILE CORPORATION
Statement of Retained Earnings
from the date of incorporation, January 5, 19—8,
to December 31,19—8

Net income for the year	$241,580
Deduct dividends	100,000
Balance, December 31, 19—8	$141,580

E16-6 Use the information in **E16-5** to prepare a Statement of Changes in Financial Position that has a cash definition of funds, and compute funds from operations on a cash basis. What does the statement tell us?

E16-7 Explain how each of the undernoted transactions would be reported on *each* of the following three different types of SCFP, which compute funds from operations on an accrual basis, and define "funds" as:

A. SCFP: Cash

B. SCFP: Working capital

C. SCFP: Changes in building and equipment

Transactions:

1. A building is acquired by paying cash of $200,000 and signing a mortgage for $600,000.

2. Bonds payable are converted into common shares.

3. Equipment is sold for cash, but a loss is incurred.

4. Inventory is purchased on account.

5. Depreciation of $260,000 is recorded.

6. A dividend is declared and paid.

7. Equipment is purchased by issuing common shares to the seller of the equipment.

8. A bank loan is obtained, and the cash is deposited in the company's account.

9. Common shares are issued in exchange for a mining claim, and some buildings on the mine site.

10. Equipment is written off.

PROBLEMS

P16-1 Ripstein Ltd. began operations in 19—9. Its income statement and balance sheet for its first year of operations are indicated below:

RIPSTEIN LTD.
Statement of Income
Year ended December 31, 19—9

Sales		$94,000
Less: Cost of goods sold	$48,000	
Depreciation	3,000	
Amortization of organizational costs	2,000	
Taxes	7,000	
Interest	1,000	
Other expenses	20,000	81,000
Net income		$13,000

Balance Sheet
As of December 31, 19—9

Assets		
Current assets		$ 37,000
Plant and equipment	53,000	
Less: accumulated depreciation	3,000	50,000
Land		20,000
Organizational costs		8,000
Total assets		$115,000
Equities		
Current liabilities		$ 19,000
Income taxes deferred until future years		2,000
Note payable	$40,000	
Less: Discount	6,000	34,000
Common shares		50,000
Retained earnings		10,000
Total liabilities and shareholders' equity		$115,000

Note: The reported interest expense of $1,000 represents, in its entirety, amortization of discount on note payable.

Required:

A. Reconstruct the transaction journal entries which probably occurred during the year.

B. Employ the T-account method illustrated in the chapter to prepare a Statement of Changes of Financial Position using a working capital definition of funds.

C. Assume the role of a creditor (i.e., the holder of the company's note payable). Explain how you would use the Statement of Changes in Financial Position.

D. What dangers exist in using a Statement of Changes in Financial Position based on a working capital definition of funds for assessing the liquidity of a company?

BALANCE SHEET DATA

	December 31	
	19—7	19—6
Cash	$ 63,500	$ 64,000
Accounts receivable (net)	47,000	42,000
Inventory	44,000	46,000
Long-term investments	21,500	36,000
Fixed assets	128,000	110,000
Total debits	$304,000	$298,000
Accumulated depreciation	$ 69,000	$ 78,000
Accounts payable	42,000	49,000
Bonds payable	60,000	40,000
Common shares, no par	95,000	80,000
Retained earnings	38,000	51,000
Total credits	$304,000	$298,000

Additional data for the period January 1, 19—7 through December 31, 19—7:

1. Sales on account, $100,000.
2. Purchases on account, $70,000.
3. Expenses paid in cash, $39,000.
4. Decrease in inventory, $2,000.
5. Sold fixed assets for $6,000 cash; cost $21,000 and two-thirds depreciated (assume loss or gain is an extraordinary item).
6. Purchased fixed assets by issuing bonds payable of $30,000 and the remainder in cash.
7. Sold the long-term investments for $40,000 cash (assume this is not an extraordinary item).
8. Purchased long-term investments for cash, $21,500.
9. Retired bonds payable by issuing common shares, $10,000.
10. Collections on accounts receivable, $95,000.
11. Payments on accounts payable, $77,000.
12. Sold unissued common shares for cash, $5,000.

Required:

A. Prepare a Statement of Changes in Financial Position based on a cash concept of funds.

B. Prepare a Statement of Changes in Financial Position based on a working capital concept of funds.

C. Which Statement of Changes in Financial Position format would you recommend for Fleming Ltd.? Explain thoroughly.

P16-3 The accountant for Steel Ltd., Mr. F. Hintenberger, is having some difficulty deciding on the most meaningful Statement of Changes in Financial Position design for the company's financial statement readers. He has asked for your help and has provided you with the following comparative balance sheet and additional information:

Balance Sheet
December 31
(in thousands of dollars)

	19—5	19—4
Cash	$ 800	$ 1,500
Receivables	2,900	800
Inventories	1,650	1,600
Building and equipment	7,900	7,000
Accumulated depreciation	(1,800)	(2,400)
Land	4,500	3,000
Goodwill	450	500
	$16,400	$12,000
Accounts payable	$ 805	$ 800
Bank loan payable	3,000	900
Bonds payable	6,000	4,000
Preferred shares	500	2,000
Common shares	5,500	3,000
Retained earnings	595	1,300
	$16,400	$12,000

Additional information:

1. During the year the company negotiated a bank loan for $3,500, which it used in full temporarily and repaid some of it by December 31, 19—5.

2. In February 19—5 the company acquired an operating division ("X") of another company, recording it as follows:

Land	$ 700
Building and equipment	3,300
Goodwill	1,000
	$5,000

Consideration paid, at fair value	
Bonds payable	$4,000
Common shares	1,000
	$5,000

3. $1,500 par value of preferred shares were converted by holders into common shares.

4. Building and equipment costing $2,400 upon which $1,300 depreciation had accumulated was sold for $1,350.

5. Net loss for the year was $280, yet dividends of $125 were paid on the preferred shares, and $300 were paid on the common shares.

6. $2,000 face value of bonds payable were redeemed during the year for $1,880.

Required:

A. Identify the transactions that would be excluded from a Statement of Changes in Financial Position that discloses only the changes in working capital.

B. Prepare a Statement of Changes in Financial Position based on a working capital definition of funds.

C. Prepare a Statement of Changes in Financial Position based on a cash definition of funds.

D. Which statement (B or C) would you recommend for the company?

544

Accounting:
A Decision
Approach

P16-4 Doug's Software (DS) has been in operation for several years. In January this year, 19—8, the owner decided to incorporate the proprietorship. The name Doug's Software Corporation (DSC) was accepted by the registrar of companies.

Doug had been working on one particular software package for many years. He experienced a series of difficulties with the package, but suddenly made a breakthrough, and managed to finalize the project in March 19—8. He decided that the project was worth $10-20 million in sales, and turned it over to DSC, of which he was a 95 percent owner, for common shares of $5,000,000.

At the end of 19—8, DSC's accountant prepared a SCFP that showed the following:

Sources of working capital:		
Sale of common shares		$5,000,000*
Funds from operations:		
Net income	$ xxx	
Add amortization of		
software package	500,000	

*All other figures on the SCFP are for less than one million dollars.

Required: (Hint: Refer to the concepts in Chapters 8 and 16)

A. In what respects could the SCFP presentation be called materially misleading? Explain. (Suppose that you were a potential investor in DSC.)

B. How would you recast the SCFP or change the definition of funds to minimize the misleading presentation? Why?

P16-5 (Review): *The Globe and Mail* on December 5, 1985 carried the following headline on page B1: "Heavy trading precedes TCPL write-off". Some excerpts from the article are:

About an hour before the market closed and 90 minutes before Transcanada Pipelines Ltd. announced a massive write-off, some investors were acting as though they had heard the news already....

After the market closed, the Calgary-based company announced writedowns totalling more than $180 million, resulting from accounting changes and revaluations of investments...

After-tax profit will be reduced by about $70-million this year. In the nine months ended September 30, profit was $209-million. The company reported profit of $252.5 million for all of 1984...

TCPL also said profit for 1982-84 will be reduced by $40-million. That and the $70-million cut are the result of a change in the method of accounting for oil and gas properties...

Changes in the valuation of assets or investments could add another $44-million to the damage...

Montreal-based Bell Canada Enterprises Inc., (BCE) Transcanada's major shareholder, said the move would not affect the carrying value of its investment in Transcanada or its contribution to BCE profit.

Required:

A. How would each of the write-off and the valuation change be recorded on an SCFP based on (1) a working capital, and (2) a cash, definition of funds? State the assumptions that you make when responding to the question.

B. Explain BCE's reaction to the write-off, as it is noted in the last paragraph of the above excerpts from the article. (See Chapter 15.)

C. What are the implications for financial accounting and reporting if investors act in advance of public disclosure of corporate decisions?

D. According to the article, the price of the common shares dropped $1 per share to $22, perhaps as a result of the accounting procedure that was adopted by TCPL. Would you regard this as strong evidence that accounting policies affect share prices? Explain.

P16-6 The following information is for McCharles Limited (MCL) for its first year of operations:

Income Statement
From the date of incorporation, July 6, 19—8, to June 30, 19—9

Sales revenue		$4,000,000
Cost of goods sold		2,700,000
Gross profit		1,300,000
Expenses:		
Selling	$510,500	
Administrative	222,100	
Interest	55,220	
Income of Smith Limited	80,000	
Depreciation	260,600	1,128,420
Income before income tax		171,580
Income tax		40,000
Net income		$ 131,580

Balance Sheet
June 30, 19—9
Assets

Current:		
Cash		$ 22,200
Accounts receivable		821,650
Inventory		399,200
		1,243,050
Investment in Smith Limited, on equity basis		1,010,000
Long-lived:		
Land		240,000
Building and equipment	$1,696,500	
Accumulated depreciation	260,600	1,435,900
		$3,928,950

Liabilities and Owners' Equity

Current liabilities		
Accounts payable		$ 597,370
Bank loan		200,000
Income tax payable		5,000
Other liabilities		160,000
		962,370
Income tax deferred		35,000
Mortgage payable, 14%		800,000
Owners' equity:		
Common shares	$2,000,000	
Retained earnings	131,580	2,131,580
		$3,928,950

Required:

State any important assumptions that you make. Prepare a Statement of Changes in Financial Position from the above on each of the undernoted bases. Explain what each tells readers.

A. Funds is defined as working capital and funds from operations is on the accrual basis.

B. Funds is defined as cash and funds from operations is on the accrual basis.

C. Funds is defined as cash and funds from operations is on the cash basis.

P16-7 In a submission to a professional accounting group, a Canadian banker stated:

> "Cash flow lending is currently succeeding asset lending so requests for projections are becoming increasingly common. The variety of these is infinite with many difficult, if not impossible to analyze or relate to, year-end statements. A standard form would be useful."

Required:

A. Might a Statement of Changes in Financial Position help the banker quoted above? Why?

B. Comment on the banker's request for a "standard form".

EXPLORATION MATERIALS AND CASES

MC16-1 Knotty Pine Limited (KPL) is a small closely held company. The owners do not take an active part in the management of the company. Instead, they rely heavily on the financial statements of the company as an indicator of KPL's performance. All operating decisions are made by Mr. Langdon, the president of the company.

KPL manufactures pine furniture and has a history of good profits. Until recently, the owners of KPL were very pleased with Mr. Langdon's performance. Now, however, some of the owners suspect Mr. Langdon is senile. This suspicion is not based on his age, since Mr. Langdon is thirty-one. Nor is it based on his background, since he has successfully completed an introductory accounting course and appears to be able to select accounting procedures to fit the situation. Their suspicions are based entirely on the following comments which Mr. Langdon made at a recent Board of Directors meeting:

1. The cash dividend to shareholders should be reduced.
2. Inflation is making it harder for the company to operate.
3. The company requires additional capital investment from the owners to continue to survive and compete in the furniture market.

The owners find these statements hard to accept especially since the company is profitable and in fact just completed one of its best years with net income of $120,000. They admit that the equipment is old but as long as the company is profitable they see no reason to replace it. In their opinion Mr. Langdon is jealous of the dividend they are receiving and is over-reacting to the problems of inflation. You have been hired by the owners of KPL to act as an accounting advisor. They want you to investigate the proposals made by Mr. Langdon. One of the owners heard about a Statement of Changes in Financial Position at a recent cocktail party and wondered if it would be of any use to KPL. The following data have been provided for you:

Balance Sheet Data

Debits

	19—8	19—7
Cash	—	$20,000
Accounts receivable	$ 200,000	100,000
Inventory	300,000	150,000
Long-term investments	—	50,000
Land	50,000	75,000
Fixed assets	500,000	530,000
Patents	8,000	10,000
Total debits	$1,058,000	$935,000

Credits

	19—8	19—7
Accounts payable	$ 80,000	$ 40,000
Notes payable—short-term (non-trade)	20,000	10,000
Accrued wages	40,000	—
Accumulated depreciation	380,000	400,000
Notes payable—long-term	130,000	150,000
Common shares	300,000	250,000
Retained earnings	108,000	85,000
Total credits	$1,058,000	$935,000

Additional data for 19—8:

1. Net income for the year was $120,000.
2. Depreciation recorded on the fixed assets was $25,000.
3. Purchased equipment costing $30,000 by issuing long-term notes payable.
4. Sold old machinery for $26,000 that originally cost $60,000.
5. Sold long-term investments for $85,000 cash.
6. Sales of $800,000 were on account.
7. Collections on accounts receivable were $700,000.
8. Retired $50,000 on long-term notes payable by issuing common shares.
9. Sold land for $45,000 cash.

Required:

Assume the role of an accounting advisor to the company. How might a Statement of Changes in Financial Position assist the owners of KPL? Prepare a Statement of Changes in Financial Position using a concept of funds and disclosure which you feel would be most informative to the owners of the company. Justify your response.

MC16-2 Finney Limited (FL) is a small, closely held retail store chain which sells shoes. Its five stores are located in shopping centers in a large Canadian city.

The company requires annual financial statements for the bank and must file an annual income tax return; otherwise, it has no special need for accounting. Cash and inventory control are facilitated by a cash register which provides data for direct feeding to a computer (owned by a financial institution). Reports of sales, purchases, and inventory levels are provided monthly for each store for a small fee by the computer owner. A public accountant prepares audited, annual financial statements and the company's income tax return.

The following conversation occurred recently between the present of FL and the company's public accountant:

PRESIDENT: What do you mean that your fee will increase 30 percent this year? I can't increase shoe prices 30 percent. If I did I wouldn't have any customers! I only need the financial statements to keep the bank happy—and the banker doesn't even want an audit; just statements.

PUBLIC ACCOUNTANT: The banker wouldn't be very happy with unaudited statements. She wouldn't lend you as much money, I guess—and you need a high loan in the autumn and spring when your inventory is high…. Besides, you wouldn't save that much having only unaudited statements. By the time we prepare unaudited ones we've had to do a large amount of verification. The additional cost is minor.

PRESIDENT: Let's get back to the 30 percent increase.

PUBLIC ACCOUNTANT: Our costs are up. Your tax return is costlier to prepare because the regulations and legislation are more complex. In addition, we prepared a Statement of Changes in Financial Position for you this year.

PRESIDENT: Why did you do that? Our financial position didn't change during the year.

PUBLIC ACCOUNTANT: The Statement of Changes in Financial Position is a new type of statement. Public accountants across the country are introducing it to clients to improve financial reporting.

PRESIDENT: I don't want something if it costs too much and doesn't tell me anything. What good does it do?

The following statements were prepared by the public accountant:

FINNEY LIMITED
Balance Sheet
January 31, 19—2

(with comparative figures for 19—1)

	19—2	19—1
Assets		
Current:		
Cash	$ 22,750	$ 1,800
Accounts receivable	76,200	29,600
Inventory	361,600	420,600
Prepaid expense	5,450	3,000
	466,000	455,000
Leasehold improvements and fixtures	162,000	160,000
Less accumulated amortization	128,000	124,000
	34,000	36,000
Deferred charges	19,000	22,000
	$519,000	$513,000
Liabilities and Equities		
Current		
Bank loan	$160,000	$200,000
Accounts payable	114,700	86,900
Income tax payable	16,000	17,000
Other current	26,300	2,950
	317,000	306,850
Deferred income tax	5,000	4,000
Debt payable—12% due 19—2	—	120,000
Due to owners	23,850	20,000
Debt payable—14% due 19—9	100,000	—
Owners' equity:		
Common shares	40,000	40,000
Contributed surplus	10,000	10,000
Retained earnings	23,150	12,150
	73,150	62,150
	$519,000	$513,000

FINNEY LIMITED
Income Statement
Year ended January 31, 19—2
(with comparative figures for 19—1)

	19—2	19—1
Revenue	$1,200,000	$1,100,000
Cost of goods sold	800,000	714,800
Gross profit	400,000	385,200
Expenses		
Depreciation	4,000	4,000
Selling and administrative	265,000	246,000
	269,000	250,000
Income before income tax	131,000	135,200
Income tax (deferred: 19—2 and 19—1 $1,000)	60,000	50,000
Net income	$ 71,000	$ 85,200

FINNEY LIMITED
Statement of Retained Earnings
Year ended January 31, 19—2
(with comparative figures for 19—1)

	19—2	19—1
Beginning of year	$ 12,150	$ 6,950
Net income	71,000	85,200
	83,150	92,150
Dividends	60,000	80,000
End of year	$ 23,150	$ 12,150

FINNEY LIMITED
Statement of Changes in Financial Position
Year ended Jauary 31, 19—2

Sources:		
From operations:		
Net income		$ 71,000
Add: Leasehold amortization	$4,000	
Deferred charges	3,000	
Deferred income tax	1,000	8,000
		79,000
Debt payable		100,000
From owners		3,850
		182,850

Uses:

Leasehold improvements	2,000
Dividend	60,000
Repay debt	120,000
	182,000
Increase in working capital	$ 850

Required:

A. Analyze and comment upon the strengths and weaknesses of the Statement of Changes in Financial Position (SCFP) prepared by the public accountant for Finney Limited.

B. Revise the SCFP as best you can to make it more informative to the president of FL.

C. Explain the purpose or uses of the SCFP that you prepared in (B) in language that the president of FL will likely understand.

MC16-3 In January 19—2 Chan Ltd. purchased an apartment building for $100,000. The company paid $10,000 in cash and gave a 10-year note for the balance. The company was required to pay only interest on the note at 6 percent per annum on December 31 for the first five years. Commencing in 19—7, principal payments of $18,000 per year are required for five years.

In 19—2 the income statement of the company appeared as follows:

Revenues from rents		$20,000
Less: Depreciation	$9,000	
Interest	5,400	
Other expenses	6,000	20,400
Net loss		$ 400

Depreciation is based on 9 percent declining balance rate.

The president of the company, upon learning of the $400 loss, instructed his accountant to use the cash basis of reporting. In his opinion conventionally computed operating income was misleading in his company's situation and did not adequately measure the performance of real estate companies.

The accountant refused to adjust the statement. He told the president that the accounting profession required financial statements to be prepared on an accrual basis and that noncash as well as cash charges had to be matched against revenues in determining income.

The president could not understand how accountants could report a loss for a company which was successful. If this was the logic on which rules were based then he was obviously in the wrong business.

Required:

A. Do you believe the cash basis of accounting is a better measure for Chan Ltd.? Are there other ways to measure the performance of the company? How?

B. Why do you think the accounting profession generally adheres to matching and the accrual basis of accounting?

C. How might you help the president of Chan Ltd. and still adhere to generally accepted accounting principles?

CHAPTER 17

Current Cost Accounting and General Price-Level Restatements

Chapter Themes

1. When users have the power to demand information, they may request figures about the replacement cost of assets and liabilities. One of the main topics of this chapter is an illustration of how such a system may operate, and whether it could prove useful for different types of decisions.

2. It is important to contrast current cost accounting with general price-level restatements. They are two, different responses to quite different limitations of GAAP accounting.

Throughout the book, we have noted the strengths and weaknesses of a few measurements for the different, and sometimes conflicting, objectives or purposes of financial accounting. Mainly, though, we have focussed upon traditional historic cost accounting and GAAP. We have observed that additional disclosure directly on the financial statements, or in the notes thereto, can supplement the historic cost measurements, and perhaps help to meet the differing needs of users/readers. We have seen some GAAP attempts to reduce diversity of accounting methods so as to move toward a (probably unattainable) goal of having one method of accounting for one set of objectives-facts-constraints. We have also recognized the importance of judgment in choosing measurements and disclosure, because considerable choice still exists in the process of selecting "suitable" accounting principles. Above all, we can now better understand the comments made earlier in the book about the dynamic nature of financial accounting *and* the need for accounting to change—to meet changing environmental conditions and information needs of users of financial statements.

A considerable amount of information about a company may be gleaned from notes to financial statements; notes are not restricted to one main system of measurement—historic costs, one of the members of the current value family, or something else. An overall impression that we may be seeking about the financial strength and trends of a company, however, may still be observed by utilizing *one* system of measurement or financial statements with their accompanying notes.

This chapter examines two alternative measurement systems to the basic historic cost system used by many Canadian companies, and illustrated in the previous chapters. Each of these alternatives with accompanying notes could be viewed by some people as able to stand alone. However, the current thrust in most countries is toward reporting only *some* of the figures that these other measurement systems generate. The reporting would be *supplementary* information to the basic historic cost system. Our approach will be to illustrate the mechanics of each system in its entirety. If the resulting information is then considered useful, in whole or in part, it can be reported in whatever way seems informative to users.

Some Basics

Before proceeding to the techniques or how-to-do-it, some broader observations are in order. Important distinctions exist between a reporting format that must stand alone and one that is designed to supplement another system. Reporting a supplementary figure requires greater benefit-cost justification on the part of the preparer. This is because accountants often are subject to pressure from owners and higher management to avoid needless costs. Preparers usually ensure that a supplementary figure is provided *only when it conveys new, otherwise unavailable, information*, and the user has power to demand the information.

Although the foregoing cost-benefit point may seem obvious to some, it certainly does not appear to have been obvious to many others. During the second half of the 1970s, Canadian accountants spent considerable time debating the merits of alternative, *supplementary* measurements to a historic cost system. One of these alternatives, called a general price-level restatement of historic cost (to be described shortly), duplicates much (but not all) of the information included in a historic cost financial statement package.

Why would some accountants advocate such duplication? Many reasons could exist, a few of which are:

1. Prestige of the accounting profession in Canada;

2. Attempts, through duplication and contrast, to influence the federal and provincial governments of Canada so that they may allow greater recognition in the income tax system for the effects of inflation (tax postponement objective); and

3. Misunderstanding.

The prestige of accountants in Canada is at stake when the U.S.A. and other countries, such as the U.K. and Australia, attempt to respond to the effects of changing prices on accounting reports, whereas Canada may be viewed as moving cautiously. Some accountants want to choose a simple approach—perhaps one that is "too simple" and lacking in credibility.

Some company officials, such as those with huge investments in long-lived depreciable assets that are subject to rising replacement costs, may believe that they are overtaxed. They want greater relief from the effects of inflation than income tax legislation currently provides. They reason that an alternative-measurement system to historic cost may influence the governments, and in time provide relief from income taxation.

With reference to the misunderstanding issue, we can eliminate its distracting effects only by further education. Clearly, different people have different objectives of accounting in mind. If a historic cost system with its accompanying notes does not meet their needs, they will favor an alternative. When several alternatives are available, it is not surprising that different preparer and user groups may elect different alternatives. One group may favor replacement cost, another net realizable value, whereas another will want both figures.

Some people resist change. They will go to great lengths to criticize something new, often because the new system has not proven itself yet. How a new system can prove itself without being given a chance is a point overlooked by these critics.

In this chapter, we intend to investigate some alternatives to historic cost both from a "how-to-do-it" and "why-to-do-it" perspective. We will attempt to fit the material into the objectives-facts-constraints framework simply for analytical purposes. It would not be wise to assume that we are seeking the *best* measurement system under all circumstances. Rather, we are seeking to identify the specific circumstances where each system seems sensible and where it does not. For example, would a small owner-managed company need a complex system based on both buying market (replacement costs) and selling market (net realizable value) prices? Not likely. Do the costs of preparing the data exceed benefits in decision-making? If the small business does not need the different system, which companies may?

ALTERNATIVES COMPARED

The two alternatives to historic cost that have received the most attention in Canada in recent years are:

1. A general price level restatement of historic cost financial statements (GPL); and

2. A form of current value accounting (CVA)—either buying or selling market prices or some combination thereof.

Other alternatives exist, but we have space to deal with only the two above.

GPL accounting restates the traditional historic cost financial statements by employing a price index that measures *general* inflation (general or average price changes) in Canada. The federal government department in Canada that is charged with preparing such a price index is Statistics Canada. Of the many indexes that it prepares, the closest to the needs for accounting purposes is called the Gross National Expenditure Implicit Price Deflator (GNE deflator). It measures price changes in many, but not all, goods and services on which a *dollar* is spent in Canada. Price movements in the GNE deflator often are similar to those for the Consumer Price Index (CPI), which measures price changes in food, clothing, shelter, health care, transportation, and other items on which people spend their disposable income. To simplify discussions in this chapter, we will use the CPI, even though it is second best, because it is easier for people to identify with. *It is important to remember, however, that the only conceptually sound index for GPL is the GNE deflator. It is the only one that is broad enough to track changes in the purchasing power of the Canadian dollar. Less broad prices indexes are likely to be useful for CVA, not for GPL.*

555

*Current Cost
Accounting and
General
Price-Level
Restatements*

In one very crude sense, inflation is the result of having larger increases in the money supply than in the output of goods and services. (In this book, we will not discuss why the increases in money supply occur. Economics courses explain inflation, international trade implications, and other important factors.) As a result, more dollars are "chasing" the goods, and selling prices of food, clothing or other goods are forced upward by those possessing the dollars. This means that, on the average during a period of inflation, the dollar buys less than it did a few months or years ago. That is, the average *purchasing power* of the *dollar* has dropped.

Accounting figures on historic cost financial statements do not reflect current *general* or overall average purchasing power. (We already know that most figures on historic cost financial statements do not reflect current *specific* purchasing power for that particular asset or liability. By specific purchasing power, we mean current buying or current selling market prices of an asset or liability.) Some accountants believe that the accounting figures should reflect *purchasing power*, and that *it*, not dollars, should be the yardstick used in measuring financial statements. (See Chapter 8.)

Suppose that we bought a house on January 1, 19—1 for $50,000, when the Consumer Price Index (CPI) was 150. On January 1, 19—9 the CPI was 225. The selling price of the house on January 1, 19—9 was $80,000. Balance sheets prepared on different measurement scales as of January 1, 19—9 would show:

Historic cost $50,000

General price level restatement of historic cost (GPL):

$$\$50,000 \times \frac{225}{150} \qquad \underline{\underline{\$75,000}}$$

Selling market price $80,000

The GPL restatement follows the same accounting principles and concepts (see Chapter 8) as the historic cost system, even including "lower of cost or market". For instance, if the selling market price were $65,000 instead of $80,000, the GPL restatement would have to be reduced to $65,000 from $75,000. (Under these facts, GPL and current value are equal with regard to "objectivity" of the measurements.)

The basic technique of GPL is quite simple:

$$\text{Historic cost} \quad \times \quad \frac{\text{General price index at date of financial statements}}{\text{General price index on date the house was purchased}} \quad = \quad \text{GPL restatement}$$

Only through coincidence would the GPL figure represent buying or selling market price.

Illustration 17-1 provides another way of contrasting GPL with one of the current value measures—buying market price or selling market price—during a period of inflation.

The GPL line theoretically represents the weighted *average* price change for all goods and services exchanged in Canada. Some goods would obviously increase more, while others would increase less, than the average. When we are referring to the current prices of specific or individual commodities, we are referring to current-value accounting. The *average* price change for *all* goods and services in the economy is inflation or deflation, which can be accounted for by general price level accounting (GPL).

CAPITAL MAINTENANCE

The pricing or valuation of assets and liabilities is only half the picture. We must also specify what we wish our *capital* (owners' equity, roughly speaking) to be. *Then, and only then, can we compute an income figure.* Under the historic *cost* concept, we implicitly assumed that capital was maintained (capital maintenance) at the money or dollar (not purchasing power) contributions of owners, plus retained earnings.

Suppose that we sold the aforementioned house for $80,000. How much would be our income or profit? Here are three possibilities:

	(1)	(2)	(3)
Asset valuation basis chosen:	Historic cost	GPL	Selling price
Capital maintenance:	Historic money	GPL	Selling price (physical capacity)
Revenue	$80,000	$80,000	$80,000
Cost of house sold	50,000	75,000	80,000
Income	$30,000	$ 5,000	$ —

ILLUSTRATION 17-1

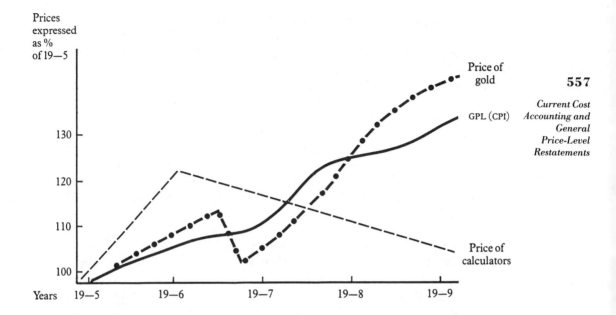

Prices
expressed
as % of 19—5

Price of gold

GPL (CPI)

Price of calculators

Years   19—5   19—6   19—7   19—8   19—9

557

*Current Cost
Accounting and
General
Price-Level
Restatements*

The rationale for using historic *money*-capital maintenance, (1)—the basis implied in traditional financial statements—could simply be that this accomplishes the minimum compliance objective of accounting. It is inexpensive to compute from a bookkeeping standpoint, and if no one demands anything else, why not select it if one of the three has to be chosen?

Category (2) assumes that people invest in a business in the hope of receiving a return on their investment that enables them to be "better off tomorrow". Specifically, category (2) suggests that when people invest, they in effect postpone consumption of *general* goods, or some composite of *all* goods and services in Canada. Do they? This would mean machinery, equipment, all imports, and exports, if we use the GNE deflator. Alternatively, using the CPI assumes that investors postpone the consumption of consumer goods. The CPI may make sense if we performed the GPL restatement for the original owner of the business, who may well have postponed the consumption of consumer, as opposed to all, goods. Few larger businesses, however, operate for several years with the same owners. Thus, a GPL restatement of the money investment of the original owner could be of little interest to someone who buys ownership at a later date, when the GPL index has shifted.

The use of "selling price" capital maintenance (or one of the other current value measures) is tied to a *continuity* assumption about the company. We have previously explained continuity in connection with a house example as meaning that if the occupant needed another place to live, then capital maintenance probably should be thought of in terms of a physical item, a house. Generally, we do not refer to selling price capital maintenance but to *physical* or *operating* capacity.

No *one* of the alternative capital-maintenance concepts is always the "best". Each makes sense under some identifiable circumstances. Mostly, we need more than one measure to draw informative conclusions about the operations of a complex organization. For example, should transit fares within a town or city be based on the original cost of the buses and other equipment, or on the replacement cost? If we choose original cost, Why? How would we defend it? Identifiable assumptions are present in our choice. We will try to identify some.

Suppose that a transit company owned by a city bases its fares on cost of operation, less a subsidy from the city's general property tax receipts. The transit company bought a new fleet of buses early in 19—0, which would operate for ten years, after which time they would have to be replaced. Annual operating costs for 19—0 to 19—9 are expected to be:

Wages, and all costs except depreciation	$ 8,000,000
Depreciation on original cost of buses	2,000,000
	10,000,000
Less subsidy	3,000,000
Net cost	$ 7,000,000
Expected number of riders	14,000,000
Ticket price	50¢ each

Assume that the buses, costing a total $20 million, were paid for in cash in 19—0. The funds were obtained from the city, on a long-term basis. Assume also that wages and related costs were constant from 19—0 to 19—9, and that fares remained at fifty cents each for the 14 million riders per year. Finally, assume that at the end of 19—9 the cost of replacing the buses is $55 million. (Normally, the price rise from $20 million would occur over ten years. To keep the example simple, we are ignoring reality somewhat. Suppose that the rise to $55 million from $20 million occurs early in year 19—0.)

Where will the $35 million ($55 million − $20 million) come from to acquire the new buses at the end of 19—9 (or beginning of 19—10)? Maybe it could be borrowed for a ten-year period and interest expense charged to riders from 19—0 to 19—19. (If so, we are treating the riders in 19—0 to 19—9—the first ten-year period—differently from those who rode in 19—10 to 19—19—the second ten-year period—, and did not pay interest on $20 million capital provided by the city.) Maybe we should charge the riders in the first ten-year period sufficiently to pay for the replacement cost of what they are using up each year.

What should the fare be for the second period, assuming that wages and other costs remain at $8 million, the subsidy is still $3 million, and 14 million riders per year use the service?

Wages, and all costs except depreciation	$ 8,000,000	
Depreciation on new buses	5,500,000	
	13,500,000	
Less subsidy	3,000,000	
Net cost	$10,500,000	
Expected number of riders	14,000,000	
Ticket price	75¢ each	

559

*Current Cost
Accounting and
General
Price-Level
Restatements*

If we charge a seventy-five-cent fare for the first ten-year period, this will generate enough cash to replace the buses at the beginning of the second period.

Per year:		
	Revenue: 14 million × 75¢	$10,500,000
	Costs, less subsidy ($8,000,000 − $3,000,000)	5,000,000
	Net cash received	$ 5,500,000
	Times 10 years	$55,000,000

If we charge a fifty-cent fare, however, we will generate twenty-five cents [(75¢ - 50¢) × 14,000,000 × 10 years] or $35 million *less*.

Which fare should we choose for 19—0 to 19—9—the first period? If our choice is fifty cents, then we are assuming that the additional $35 million would be "borrowed" from someone and that any "borrowing" cost (interest most likely, or dividends) would be charged to riders in the second ten-year period. We are also assuming that riders *in the first period* should benefit in this period from the company managers' having been able to purchase buses below the then replacement cost of $55 million.

In contrast, if we choose seventy-five-cent fares in the first period, we are favoring a continuity approach whereby the bus company is to be in business forever (or at least until the end of the second period when the replacement buses wear out). That is, our capital maintenance is a physical concept—a fleet of buses capable of handling 14 million passengers per year. We are also assuming that the current user ought to pay for what is used up year-by-year on a replacement-cost basis, and that the date of purchase of an asset and its original cost are not relevant in such a decision on fares.

The points noted are only a few of those that may be considered. Which fare would we pick: seventy-five cents or fifty cents for the first ten-year period? Why? If the company were to cease operations at the end of the second ten-year period, what fare would we choose for that period?

General Price Level Accounting

More could be said about the strengths and weaknesses of the alternatives to historic cost, but it is useful to illustrate the "how-to-do-it" first, in order to aid understanding of the "why". General price level accounting has existed in books since the 1930s, and perhaps before. Variations have been practised in countries with high inflation rates such as those in South America.

The steps in restating from historic cost dollars to dollars of general purchasing power are as follows:

Step 1: Separate what are called the "monetary" from the "non-monetary" assets and liabilities on the balance sheet. These two differ from current assets and current liabilities. An item is *monetary*, roughly speaking, when it is fixed in amount by some type of contract (although the definition of "monetary" can differ under a current value accounting system). A dollar bill is fixed by law; what it buys in purchasing power varies, but the amount—$1—remains unchanged over time. Accounts receivable is fixed (usually); the company receives a specified number of dollars from the debtor. Accounts payable and bonds payable are similarly fixed (usually) and, consequently, are monetary items: the company pays the creditors a specified amount of money, not an unchanging amount of general purchasing power.

Non-monetary items are free to float with inflation (or deflation). Inventory that is not yet sold may rise in price with inflation. It is not important for purposes of the non-monetary definition that the amount of price rise be the same as inflation, which is an average. Land, plant, equipment, goodwill, and other long-lived assets are non-monetary because their price is not fixed by a contract.

Some variations may occur. Rent may (at some future time if inflation persisted) be indexed to the CPI. If so, rent receivable that is indexed to correspond to inflation rate increases becomes, by definition, a non-monetary asset because it floats in price.

Step 2: The non-monetary items are restated by the formula:

$$\text{Historic cost} \times \frac{\text{General price index at balance sheet date}}{\text{General price index when asset was acquired}} = \text{GPL restatement.}$$

The numerator (top) index is as of the balance sheet date simply because this is the date closest to when the financial statements are being read. (Economists would use some *past* base year if they were restating a series occurring over time.)

Step 3: The income statement accounts are similarly restated. Depreciation expense would be restated as in Step 2 because depreciation is an allocation of original cost. Selling expense, in contrast, would be restated to the year end (numerator) from the date when cash (or a monetary item) were expended.

Step 4: A gain or loss on general purchasing power is computed and credited or charged (generally) to the income statement. This gain or loss item arises because net monetary assets (which signify a loss) or net monetary liabilities (which signify a gain) are held by a company during inflation. Being fixed by contract, the assets lose general purchasing power. Receivables, for instance, may be received in cash three months after a sale. If the receivable were for $1,000 and the CPI rose 5 percent during this time, a loss of fifty dollars (measured in end-of-period dollars) would result:

$1,000 + 5\%$ =	$1,050
Received	1,000
Loss of purchasing power	$ 50

561

*Current Cost
Accounting and
General
Price-Level
Restatements*

That is, at the end of three months, we require $1,050 to buy general goods that we could have bought for $1,000 three months ago. The debtor gained fifty dollars over the three months by paying us in dollars of *less* purchasing power.

We see this same concept at work every day in Canada. Someone buys a house with a huge mortgage. The house asset is non-monetary and its price tends to rise over time with inflation—sometimes more, sometimes less, dependent upon its location. The mortgage is a monetary liability, and as the years pass the home buyer pays it off with dollars of diminished purchasing power. The home buyer gains purchasing power on the mortgage payable. The mortgage company probably breaks even on inflation because it borrowed the money from others to lend to the home buyer. The mortgage company gains interest revenue, which exceeds interest expense, and tries to avoid being caught by inflation. (The mortgage company may gain from inflation if it, in effect, borrows for longer periods than it lends during inflation. This may occur if cash payments are due to it monthly but it repays in a lump sum to lenders at the *end* of five years.)

The restatement process can be illustrated by two examples. We will commence with a simple one. Suppose that a company opens for business on January 1, 19—1 with $100,000 cash. At midyear, it buys some land costing $60,000, paying cash of $40,000, and agreeing to pay the remainder one year later. With no other transactions, the company's historic cost balance sheet at December 31, 19—1 shows:

Cash	$ 60,000
Land	60,000
	$120,000
Accounts payable	$ 20,000
Capital	100,000
	$120,000

During this one-year period, however, the price index (CPI) rose as follows:

January 1, 19—1	100
Mid year, 19—1	105
December 31, 19—1	110

When we GPL restate the historic cost balance sheet to *dollars of general purchasing power* at December 31, 19—1, we obtain the following:

$$\text{Cash (a monetary asset) } \$60,000 \times \frac{110}{110} = \qquad \$\ 60,000$$

$$\text{Land (a non-monetary asset) } \$60,000 \times \frac{110}{105} = \qquad \underline{62,857}$$

$$\underline{\$122,857}$$

$$\text{Accounts payable (a monetary liability) } \$20,000 \times \frac{110}{110} = \qquad \$\ 20,000$$

$$\text{Capital (a non-monetary equity) } \$100,000 \times \frac{110}{100} = \qquad 110,000$$

$$\text{Deficit (figure needed to balance)} \qquad \underline{(7,143)}$$

$$\underline{\$122,857}$$

No restatement is necessary for year *end* monetary items because they already are stated in dollars of general purchasing power at December 31, 19—1—meaning in numerator 110.

Where did the $7,143 come from? It is the net loss in general purchasing power (measured in December 31, 19—1 dollars of general purchasing power) that arose from two factors:

1. The holding of a monetary asset (in this case cash) while the general price index rose, which incurs a purchasing power loss; and

2. A purchasing power gain resulted from holding a monetary liability while the price index rose.

Net Loss

Cash:

a. $100,000 was held from January 1 to midyear. This resulted in a loss measured at midyear in dollars of general purchasing power at midyear of:

$$\left(\$100,000 \times \frac{105}{100}\right) - \$100,000 \qquad = \qquad \underline{\underline{\$5,000}}$$

[Midyear − Beginning of year]

This $5,000 is measured in numerator index of 105, whereas we want it measured in numerator 110 (year-end dollars). Hence,

$$\$5,000 \times \frac{110}{105} = \qquad \$5,238$$

b. $60,000 was held from midyear until year end. The loss measured in index 110 is therefore

$$(\$60,000 \times \frac{110}{105}) - \$60,000 \qquad \underline{2,857}$$
$$8,095$$

Accounts payable:
The gain from midyear until year end is

$$(\$20,000 \times \frac{110}{105}) - \$20,000 \qquad \underline{952}$$

Net loss in general purchasing power measured in index 110 dollars $\qquad \underline{\underline{\$7,143}}$

563

*Current Cost
Accounting and
General
Price-Level
Restatements*

ANOTHER EXAMPLE

Illustration 17-2 provides a slightly more complex example to bring out the difficulties that arise when transactions are occurring regularly throughout the year. The object is to restate the historic cost financial statements in Illustration 17-2 to dollars of general purchasing power at December 31, 19—4.

ILLUSTRATION 17-2

DOUGLAS LIMITED
Balance Sheets

	19—4	December 31 19—3
Cash	$ 1,000	$ 800
Accounts receivable	4,100	3,200
Inventory	4,900	4,600
	10,000	8,600
Building and equipment	6,000	6,000
Less accumulated depreciation	1,800	1,200
	4,200	4,800
	$14,200	$13,400
Accounts payable	$ 4,650	$ 4,200
Owners' equity:		
Capital	8,000	8,000
Retained earnings	1,550	1,200
	$14,200	$13,400

Income Statement
Year ended December 31, 19—4

Revenue		$14,000
Cost of goods sold		11,050
Gross profit		2,950
Expenses:		
Selling and administration	$2,000	
Depreciation	600	2,600
Net income (income tax is ignored)		$ 350

Retained Earnings Statement
Year ended December 31, 19—4

Opening balance	$ 1,200
Add net income	350
Closing balance	$ 1,550

Additional information:

1. Consumer Price Index (CPI):

January 1, 19—1 (when business commenced)	150
January 1, 19—2 (when $6,000 of building and equipment acquired)	160
When $4,600 of inventory on hand at January 1, 19—4 was acquired	175
When $11,350 of inventory was acquired; $4,900 of which is on hand at December 31, 19—4	185
January 1, 19—4	180
December 31, 19—4	200

2. The selling and administrative expenses were paid in cash over the year, when the CPI averaged 190. Similarly, revenue arose evenly during the year and the CPI on average was 190.

3. Inventory acquisitions (reflected in accounts payable) were paid as follows:
   a. $4,200 payable at December 31, 19—3 was paid when the CPI stood at   185

b. The $6,450 that was paid from the $11,350 purchase that
   occurred when the CPI was   190

Restatement Process:

The simplest starting point is with the *closing* balance sheet. The object of the exercise is to restate the comparative balance sheets and the income statements to CPI 200 (dollars of general purchasing power at December 31, 19—4).

565

*Current Cost
Accounting and
General
Price-Level
Restatements*

		CPI Index 200
Cash	$1,000 × $\dfrac{200}{200}$	$ 1,000
Accounts receivable	$4,100 × $\dfrac{200}{200}$	4,100
Inventory (non-monetary)	$4,900 × $\dfrac{200}{185}$	5,297
Building (non-monetary)	$6,000 × $\dfrac{200}{160}$	7,500
Accumulated depreciation (non-monetary)	$1,800 × $\dfrac{200}{160}$	(2,250)
		$15,647
Accounts payable	$4,650 × $\dfrac{200}{200}$	$ 4,650
Capital (non-monetary)	$8,000 × $\dfrac{200}{150}$	10,667
Retained earnings (balancing figure)		330
		$15,647

Next, we restate the opening balance sheet. This can be done in two steps or through a one-step shortcut. We will handle this the longer way, which involves:

1. Restating the balance sheet to dollars of general purchasing power as of the *beginning* of the period (Index 180).

2. Moving the restated balance sheet from Index 180 to Index 200. First, the restatement to Index 180:

Cash	$\$\ 800 \times \dfrac{180}{180}$	$\$\ \ \ \ 800$
Receivables	$\$3,200 \times \dfrac{180}{180}$	$3,200$
Inventory (non-monetary)	$\$4,600 \times \dfrac{180}{175}$	$4,731$
Building and equipment (non-monetary)	$\$6,000 \times \dfrac{180}{160}$	$6,750$
Accumulated depreciation (non-monetary)	$\$1,200 \times \dfrac{180}{160}$	$\dfrac{(1,350)}{\$14,131}$
Accounts payable	$\$4,200 \times \dfrac{180}{180}$	$4,200$
Capital	$\$8,000 \times \dfrac{180}{150}$	$9,600$
Retained earnings (balancing figure)		$\dfrac{331}{\$14,131}$

Second, the entire balance sheet is rolled forward to Index 200 from 180:

		CPI Index 200
Cash	$\$\ 800 \times \dfrac{200}{180}$	$\$\ \ \ \ 889$
Receivables	$3,200 \times \dfrac{200}{180}$	$3,556$
Inventory	$4,731 \times \dfrac{200}{180}$	$5,257$
Building and equipment	$6,750 \times \dfrac{200}{180}$	$7,500$
Accumulated depreciation	$(1,350) \times \dfrac{200}{180}$	$\dfrac{(1,500)}{\$15,702}$
Accounts payable	$4,200 \times \dfrac{200}{180}$	$\$\ 4,667$

Capital	$9,600 \times \dfrac{200}{180}$		10,667
Retained earnings	$331 \times \dfrac{200}{180}$		368
			$15,702

Restatement of the income statement is more difficult. No dividends were declared; hence, the restated net income (in Index 200) has to be:

Opening retained earnings	$368
Closing retained earnings	330
Loss for the period	$ 38

The difficult parts are:

1. Computation of cost of goods sold, and

2. Computation of the loss in general purchasing power.

			CPI Index 200
Revenue	$14,000 \times \dfrac{200}{190}$		$14,737
Cost of goods sold:			
Opening inventory	$4,600 \times \dfrac{200}{175}$	$ 5,257	
Purchases	$11,350 \times \dfrac{200}{185}$	12,270	
		17,527	
Closing inventory	$(4,900) \times \dfrac{200}{185}$	(5,297)	12,230
	11,050		
Gross profit			2,507
Expenses:			
Selling and administration	$2,000 \times \dfrac{200}{190}$		2,105
Depreciation	$600 \times \dfrac{200}{160}$		750
			2,855
Net loss before gain of general purchasing power			348
Gain of general purchasing power			310
Net loss (income taxes are ignored)			$ 38

The gain of general purchasing power during 19—4, measured in dollars of general purchasing power as of December 31, 19—4, is computed as follows:

Monetary assets—monetary liabilities during 19—4 (at historic cost):

	Index	+	−	Net Asset (liability)
Opening balance (cash + receivables—payables)	180			$ (200)
Payables paid (no net effect)	185	$ 4,200	$ 4,200	(200)
Inventory acquired (credit to payables)	185		11,350	(11,550)
Revenue less selling and administration	190	14,000	2,000	450
Payment of payables (no net effect)	190	6,450	6,450	450
End of period	200			450

Components of the overall gain are:

a. $200 of net liabilities held while the Index rose from 180 to 185:

$$(\$200 \times \frac{185}{180}) \quad - \$200 = \quad \underline{\underline{\$ \ 6}}$$

b. $11,550 of net liabilities held while the Index rose from 185 to 190:

$$(\$11,500 \times \frac{190}{185}) \quad - \$11,5\underline{00} \qquad \underline{\underline{\$ 312}}$$

c. $450 of net assets held while the Index rose from 190 to 200:

$$(\$450 \times \frac{200}{190}) \quad - \$450 = \quad \underline{\underline{\$(24)}}$$

Restating them to Index 200 (dollars of general purchasing power as of December 31, 19—4):

	Gain in Index 200

a. $(\$6 \times \frac{200}{185})$ $ 6

b. $(\$312 \times \frac{200}{190})$ 328

c. (already at Index 200) (24)

Overall gain for the period $310

Note that we have computed the gain or loss whenever there is a *change* in the index number. In practice, this computation may occur monthly or quarterly.

GPL INTERPRETED

If the GPL financial statements are accompanied by the usual footnotes, what do the GPL financial statements tell users? How much is repetition of historic-cost financial statements? How much is new information?

As with historic cost, there is a danger that "unlike" companies could be made to look "alike". For example, two companies may have bought $1 million worth of land in 1930. Today, one piece may have a net realizable value of $100 million (in the centre of a large city) but the other may have a net realizable value of $40 million. A general price level restatement, however, may show $32 million for both parcels of land. The balance sheet figures derived under GPL usually do not represent a current buying or selling market price; yet, people may not interpret them that way. GPL figures are especially vulnerable to misinterpretation.

The GPL income statement shows a new piece of information: gain or loss of general purchasing power. Some accountants do not agree with showing the entire gain or loss on the income statement. By itself, the sum does not mean much; however, it may be compared to other effects. For example, a bank may incur a general purchasing power loss of $10 million; yet, it may have an interest revenue increase of well over $10 million. In brief, the bank raised interest rates on its loans receivable (a monetary item) to compensate for purchasing power losses owing to inflation.

Purchasing power gains can be increased by having huge amounts of debt outstanding. Huge amounts of debt, however, can be risky, and in poor years for a company may hasten bankruptcy. (See Chapter 5.) A balance between profitability and liquidity has to be struck.

Given the above somewhat inconclusive merits to GPL why do people advocate it? Some possible (yet questionable) reasons are:

1. It is not difficult to apply, and makes few alterations in the historic-cost system. As such, it is easier to audit than, say, a current buying or selling market value system; and

2. For some companies (not having huge amounts of monetary debt), income is lowered by GPL restatements. Perhaps, managers of these companies reason, if many companies report on a GPL basis, the governments may at some future date use GPL as a basis for assessing income taxes. Although the total tax revenue required by government may not change, some companies may pay less (and others would have to pay more, or individuals would have to pay more).

Some other reasons were noted earlier.

The main merits of the GPL concept may lie in comparing its balances with other figures. For instance, we may have invested in land costing $100,000. The land may have a GPL restatement of $180,000 and a net realizable value of $205,000. The comparison of the $205,000 with the $180,000 tells us that by investing in land, we did

$25,000 ($205,000 − $180,000) better than general inflation. We could sell the land and buy more general goods than we could have bought with the $100,000 investment (or postponed consumption).

Another possibility is to GPL restate current value figures of previous years to make them somewhat comparative.

Current Cost or Current Value

The term "current value", like "market value", lacks precision. Current value is a broad term that may mean any one of the following:

> Buying market price:
> > Reproduction cost (cost today of an *identical* item)
> > Replacement cost
> > Perhaps, discounted future cash costs

> Selling market price:
> > Net realizable value
> > Discounted future cash receipts

These terms tend to apply to the valuation or pricing of assets and liabilities. When equity is to be measured (or capital maintained) on a "current-value" basis, it is usually called physical or operating capacity/capability.

From time to time, we have stressed the need for two or more pieces of information in order to form judgments. Someone, such as a potential creditor, who is interested in management evaluation, may desire to separate and assess management's behavior into at least two functions: *buying*, or purchasing, goods, and *selling* goods. How is this separation accomplished in the following situation?

> January 1: Commenced business with $3,000,000.
> January 2: Bought 10,000 tonnes of raw sugar at $300 per tonne.
> May 1:   Processed the 10,000 tonnes of raw sugar; replacement cost is now $400 per tonne.
> June 30:   (Year end of company) Sold the 10,000 tonnes of processed sugar for $500 per tonne. Processing costs are $60 per tonne. Replacement cost is still $400 per tonne.

An income statement prepared under the traditional historic cost basis would show:

Revenue:		
10,000 tonnes @ $500		$5,000,000
Cost of goods sold:		
Purchased sugar:		
10,000 tonnes @ $300	$3,000,000	
Processing cost	600,000	3,600,000
Gross profit		$1,400,000

571

*Current Cost
Accounting and
General
Price-Level
Restatements*

Has management performed well? We may compare the $1.4 million to last year's figure of, say, $400,000, and assume that management's "ability" is improving. But is it? Maybe during this last year raw sugar prices were constant.

If we charge cost of goods sold at replacement cost of $400 per tonne, cost of goods sold becomes $4.6 million ($400 times 10,000 tonnes, plus $600,000) and gross profit would be $400,000—the same as last year. This means that from a *selling* (as opposed to buying) viewpoint management's behavior is constant. (Note that the two figures that we used for our comparison were net realizable value revenue and replacement cost of goods sold.)

From a *buying* standpoint, however, the company *may* be better off by $1 million ($400 less $300/tonne, times 10,000 tonnes) owing to buying practices. Why do we say *may*? In order to respond, we must turn to considering our "capital maintenance" concept. If capital is defined as original money capital, the $1 million would appear in income. Income equals revenue less historic cost of goods sold under the money-capital maintenance concept. If management were simply lucky by buying when they did, the appearance of the $1 million on the income statement makes them look better than they probably are. If the buying at $300 per tonne were the result of careful planning, then the appearance of $1 million in income is justified—*from an evaluation of management point of view.* (See Chapter 6.) But from a *cash flow prediction* point of view, misleading results may occur unless the $1 million is reported on a separate line. Then, those interested in prediction could exclude the $1 million from their thinking if it is not thought to be a recurring item.

Suppose, instead, that prices of raw sugar are expected to rise for some years, and that the company needs a basic tonnage of raw sugar, somewhere around the 10,000 tonnes level, in order to ensure its continuity. Under such circumstances, a physical-capacity capital maintenance concept and a replacement-cost asset price basis could provide useful information. Income would be $400,000 because replacement cost of goods sold would be $4 million (not $3 million), excluding processing costs. That is, the write-up of inventory to replacement cost would occur with this journal entry:

Inventory	$1,000,000	
Capital maintenance increment		$1,000,000

To write up 1,000 of inventory from $300/tonne to $400/tonne

(Unless the company's journals and ledgers were maintained on a replacement cost/physical capacity basis, the entry would be made on work sheets.)

A company applying the replacement cost (asset valuation) and physical capacity (capital maintenance) combination would show the following (partial) financial statements:

Income Statement:

Revenue		$5,000,000
Cost of goods sold:		
Materials purchased and used	$4,000,000	
Processing expenses	600,000	4,600,000
Gross profit		$ 400,000

Balance sheet:

Cash ($5,000,000 less $600,000)	$4,400,000
Owners' equity:	
Original capital	$3,000,000
Capital maintenance increment	1,000,000
Retained earnings (assuming no other expenses or income tax exist)	400,000
	$4,400,000

If detailed changes in the "capital maintenance increment" account are reported from year to year, this could assist those who wish to predict and maybe those who wish to evaluate management (Chapter 6). We state "maybe" because readers must be able to sort good luck from good management if they want to form a sound assessment. Such a sorting may be very difficult, or impossible. (Note that the capital-maintenance increment and inventory write-up represent the difference between the two figures: historic cost and replacement cost. In a more sophisticated system, the difference could be between replacement cost and possibly general price level restated historic cost.)

HUMAN BEHAVIOR

By changing the asset valuation basis and capital maintenance concept away from historic cost, not only do we alter income from year to year and over the life of the company, but *we may easily change people's behavior.* People can be amazingly flexible, and may adjust to new rules when they know that their performance is being evaluated on a new, different basis. They may first have to be educated to understand how to process the new information in their minds and convert it into actions, however.

Suppose that salespersons are paid a commission that is a percentage of gross profit (revenue less historic cost of goods sold). Suppose further that the company involved buys steel in bulk from the various Canadian steel mills and distributes it in small quantities to a variety of construction companies. When the economy is booming, the steel mills may not have adequate production volumes to satisfy demand, and prices of steel could rise. The opposite can occur during an economic slowdown.

If the salespersons receive a commission based on historic cost gross profit, they could cause problems for the company. When steel prices are rising, historic cost will lag behind replacement cost. Hence, the following could occur:

	Historic Cost Asset Pricing	Replacement Cost Asset Pricing
Revenue	$25,000	$25,000
Cost of goods sold	21,000	24,500
Gross profit	4,000	500
Income tax @45% (The income tax legislation taxes on historic profit)	1,800	1,800
Income (ignoring selling expense)	$ 2,200	Loss $(1,300)

In the mid 1970s in Canada, this was not an uncommon situation—to be selling at a loss based on replacement cost. Once we deduct the salesperson's commission, the loss based on replacement cost of goods sold would be even higher than the $1,300. In summary, the commission system *motivated* salespersons to cause losses.

When steel prices are declining in general, historic cost (unless written down to replacement cost—something that is not likely to occur daily or weekly in practice in a historic cost financial accounting system) likely exceeds replacement cost. How does this affect sales personnel? Unless they have permission to sell at a loss based on historic cost, and are rewarded by other than commissions based on historic cost, sales may cease. More likely, though, sales will cease on those items with huge drops in replacement cost. This is because salespersons will exert more effort toward selling items that provide them with a commission, i.e., products where replacement and historic cost are similar.

How may the behavior of people be changed? A *management* accounting system may be set up to separate the purchasing and selling functions of a business. When the system is operational for management purposes, it could be extended to external or financial accounting. In theory, using the foregoing wholesaling illustration, salespersons would receive a commission based on replacement cost gross profit. Buyers of commodities such as steel would be judged primarily on their performance in ordering the required quantity at the desired price. Thus, if a government removed a manufacturing tax and the replacement cost fell, salespersons would *not* be required to sell at the historic cost including tax. Any differences between historic cost and replacement cost would be charged or credited to whoever requested the commodity.

In practice, facts may differ. In this book, we have occasionally mentioned the discounted present value concept of valuation. Yet we know that we give this concept little attention when we make most of our major personal purchases. In business, we have to give the concept more attention than for our personal purchases; but how much more? A replacement cost system has similar soft spots. If, when replacement costs are rising, a competitor continues to base selling prices on historic cost, we are not going to sell much if our selling prices are considerably higher. We may have to strike a balance between holding onto inventory and selling it at less than we would like to obtain.

What do we do in practice? We may want to pay salespersons on some combination of gross profit based on historic cost plus gross profit based on replacement cost. Somehow, we must use the accounting system to motivate people in the ways felt necessary to achieve corporate and personal success.

ETHICS

From time to time, we have touched upon but not adequately dealt with a troublesome consideration—ethics. Do accounting reports and financial statements *manipulate people?* If so, should they?

Accounting information is not neutral; it is full of judgments. These judgments are made by preparers who bring their life-long experiences, knowledge, biases, and even prejudices to their judgments. The task of an auditor is to identify these biases and try to neutralize or disclose them; but how successful auditors are in this duty is unknown. Evidence of negotiations between client and auditor is not publicly available, and is hard, if not impossible, to gather. Essentially, auditors really just check on whether a client's financial statements are prepared in accordance with GAAP.

A change from an historic cost to a current cost system will not alter the potential for manipulation, which can be defined as causing people to behave in a way desired by the preparer. One of the prime reasons for choosing another measurement system is to provide a different point of view. However, some people will worry about multiple measures. "Which is the correct number?" Others will appreciate the different views being presented and be able to sort out the measurement biases a little better. The more information that is reported (a costly choice), the harder it can become to manipulate people.

Successful analysts are those who can understand, albeit only broadly, the personality of the preparer. Some preparers are cautious; others overly optimistic. Some may manipulate intentionally, others unintentionally. Analysts must be aware.

REPLACEMENT COST EXAMPLE

A two-year example may help to pull together some of the *net asset value* (basis of pricing assets and liabilities) and *capital maintenance* (basis of pricing long-term equity) concepts mentioned in the book. We intend to use historic cost or replacement cost for net asset values. Capital maintenance will be either historic money capital or physical capacity. In practice, companies may use more than one basis of net asset valuation in supplementary reports provided to shareholders.

Suppose that a company engages in the following transactions:

1. The business commences January 1, 19—1 with $3,000 of cash and capital.

2. Next day, 30 tonnes of inventory are bought for $100 per tonne.

3. No other transactions occur until December 31, 19—1, at which time the replacement cost of inventory is $115 per tonne.

4. On December 31, 19—1 (the year end of the company) 20 tonnes are sold for $140 per tonne.

5. On January 2, 19—2, 25 tonnes are bought for $115 per tonne.

6. No other transactions occur until December 30, 19—2, at which time the replacement cost of inventory is $90 per tonne.

7. On December 31, 19—2, 25 tonnes are sold for $102 per tonne.

We will show the results on *four* different bases:

Net Asset Valuation	Capital Maintenance
1. Historic cost (HC)	Money Historic Capital (MHC)
2. Replacement cost (RC)	Money Historic Capital (MHC)
3. Replacement cost (RC)	Operating Capability—method 1 (OC1)
4. Replacement cost (RC)	Operating Capability—method 2 (OC2)

Other bases could be used, such as general price level restated owners' equity (capital maintenance).

Illustrations 17-3 and 17-4 provide a response. We have split the computations into 19—1 and 19—2 for reasons that become obvious later. Income taxes and other expenses are ignored in the illustration.

ILLUSTRATION 17-3

19—1:

	1.	2.	3.	4.
Net asset valuation	HC	RC	RC	RC
Capital maintenance	MHC	MHC	OC1	OC2
Income Statements:				
Revenue	$2,800	$2,800	$2,800	$2,800
Cost of goods sold	2,000	2,300	2,300	2,300
Gross profit	800	500	500	500
Holding gain: 30 tonnes @ $15 ($115 − $100)		450		
Income	$ 800	$ 950	$ 500	$ 500
Balance Sheets: (end of year)				
Cash	$2,800	$2,800	$2,800	$2,800
Inventory	1,000	1,150	1,150	1,150
	$3,800	$3,950	$3,950	$3,950
Original capital	$3,000	$3,000	$3,000	$3,000
Capital maintenance increment	—	—	450	450
Retained earnings	800	950	500	500
	$3,800	$3,950	$3,950	$3,950

Illustration 17-3 requires some explanation. A holding gain arises in (2) for the entire thirty tonnes because this tonnage was held all year. The holding gain in (2) is replacement cost less historic cost money capital. Some people may split the $450 into two parts: (a) $300 representing the 20 tonnes that were *sold* @ $15 (sometimes called "realized" holding gain); and (b) $150 representing the *unsold* tonnage (sometimes called "unrealized holding gain"). Columns (3) and (4) credit the "holding" effect to capital maintenance increment. Both show $3,450 of equity ($3,000 plus $450), which represents thirty tonnes of inventory @ $115.

Illustration 17-4 portrays 19—2. In 19—2, replacement prices drop, and holding losses, or capital maintenance debits, occur. A distinction can be drawn between columns OC1 and OC2. OC1's definition of capital is tied to thirty tonnes of steel. That is, management believes that in order to stay in business for a long time, capital must be maintained at thirty tonnes times current replacement cost. OC2's definition of capital "floats" and represents the tonnage quantity on hand at any time. (In 19—1, thirty tonnes are on hand for most of the year, whereas in most of 19—2, thirty-five tonnes are on hand.) OC2 is more practical for businesses that are continually expanding and contracting.

ILLUSTRATION 17-4

19—2:

	1.	2.	3.	4.
Net asset valuation	HC	RC	RC	RC
Capital maintenance	MHC	MHC	OC1	OC2
Income Statements:				
Revenue	$2,550	$2,550	$2,550	$2,550
Cost of goods sold (FIFO)	2,725	2,250	2,250	2,250
Gross profit (loss)	(175)	300	300	300
Holding loss on 35 tonnes		(875)		
Write-down of closing inventory to replacement cost	(250)			
Loss on 5 tonnes in excess of 30 tonnes			125	
Income (loss)	$ (425)	$ (575)	$ 175	$ 300
Balance Sheets: (end of year)				
Cash	$2,475	$2,475	$2,475	$2,475
Inventory	900	900	900	900
	$3,375	$3,375	$3,375	$3,375
Capital—original	$3,000	$3,000	$3,000	$3,000
Capital maintenance (debit) increment	—	—	(300)	(425)
Retained earnings	375	375	675	800
	$3,375	$3,375	$3,375	$3,375

Illustration 17-4 requires careful study. We start with the balance sheet. The cash figure represents sales in years 19—1 and 19—2 less purchases of twenty-five tonnes @ $115. In all four cases, the inventory has to be written down to replacement cost. (Column (1), we will assume, employs lower of FIFO cost or replacement cost.) The capital maintenance debit in column (3) is the sum required to represent, together with original capital of $3,000, thirty tonnes at the current replacement cost of $90 per tonne ($2,700). Column (4) is a little more difficult because under the floating capital maintenance system, thirty-five tonnes existed in the year 19—2. Hence, 35 tonnes @ $25 ($115 less $90), or $875, is *debited* to capital maintenance. This lowers the $450 credit at the end of 19—1 to a net debit of $425 at the end of 19—2.

Turning to the income statement of Illustration 17-4, we note that the inventory write-down in column (1) is shown below the gross profit line; it could be part of cost of goods sold. The $875 holding loss in column (2) could be split into realized and unrealized portions. In column (3), which we have defined as a company with a physical-capacity capital maintenance of thirty tonnes, a write-down to *income* is needed because we held thirty-five tonnes—five tonnes over normal—during a period when replacement cost dropped $25 per tonne. In column (4) price changes go through the capital maintenance account.

RESULTS INTERPRETED

Who could fruitfully use financial statements based on columns (2), (3) or (4)? In a major sense, much of column (2) is already in use in Canada by open-end mutual fund companies. Such companies hold shares of other companies as their principal assets. Corporate law (constraints) requires that capital be based or maintained on a form of historic money capital. Yet, the common shares of these funds are bought and sold on the basis of a current value (often plus a salesperson's commission on the purchase side). Shareholders are interested in seeing the net assets valued at a current value, not at original cost. The actual (in practice) income statements of open-end mutual funds differ from those in illustrations 17-3 and 17-4 in that separation of holding gains between items that are sold and unsold is provided.

Column (3) can aid evaluation of management by outsiders. If management bought an extra five tonnes above its normal of thirty tonnes—presumably in the hope of making additional profits—the effects of this decision are income or loss items (not capital). In contrast, column (4) obscures the effect of the purchase of additional tonnage.

None of the four columns by itself gives a complete picture of several of the possible objectives or purposes of financial accounting. Someone interested in prediction would like to know both cash receipts (net realizable value) and cash payments (replacement cost) for all assets for many years into the future. This requires not only multiple measures but forecasting. On the other hand, owners of a small business with rapid turnover of assets may be well served by historic cost accounting.

The subject is more complex than we have described; but, the basic ideas are in place except for the effects of debt. Capital maintenance concepts change somewhat when a business finances with long-term debt.

Summary

Two types of alternatives to the historic cost measurement system—general price level restatements (GPL), and current value accounting (CVA)—have been introduced and explained briefly in this chapter. In some circumstances, where individual commodity prices are changing rapidly, or a general inflationary trend is occurring, these "alternatives" may provide an additional helpful perspective. GPL could apply for the latter (inflation) situation and CVA for the former. Viewing disclosure in cost-benefit terms, we note that these additional measures likely would be reported only when they provide otherwise unavailable information, or help accomplish an objective that is not well served under present accounting. Some people may hope that extensive use of GPL will serve as a lobby to the Federal Government, and encourage more recognition of inflationary effects in the income tax system.

GPL restatements of historic cost are an accounting response to general inflationary trends only, and make no attempt to reflect individual changes in asset and liability prices. Many people question whether they provide any information that cannot be approximated from historic cost financial statements. The income statement based on GPL may show a gain or loss on general purchasing power that arises from holding net monetary liabilities or assets. This may be useful information for analysts of banks and other companies with huge monetary balances. It must be used with care, however. By its nature of choosing one general price index for restatements, GPL may make unlike situations look alike to a partially informed reader.

CVA financial statements can take many forms and are dependent upon which bases are chosen for net asset valuation and capital maintenance. When used in management accounting systems, the CVA alternatives can help motivate managers in ways that differ from the effects of historic cost. Replacement cost net asset values, for instance, may help separate purchasing from selling functions of a (wholesaling or manufacturing) business that buys well in advance of selling its inventory. This separation may assist those who wish to assess judgments by senior management. Two or more current value figures may aid in prediction. Return on current investment requires both net asset and capital maintenance measures, and different combinations may aid investors in judging the relative profitability of businesses.

CVA has drawbacks, which have been mentioned from place to place in the book. CVA requires greater estimation than, say, historic cost accounting. At the present time in Canada, the concepts are not well understood by a large group of preparers and users. For those who believe in one of the efficient market hypotheses, CVA may not be adding information that is not already known to some investors. Many investors have sources outside of financial statements.

The theme that may be drawn from this chapter is that each of the different measures has its place. Our role as preparers or users is to apply and interpret the measurement system where it makes sense. Historic cost figures clearly have limitations when the purchasing power of the dollar (inflation) is dropping and prices of individual commodities are fluctuating. No single alternative will meet the approval of all preparers or users.

Notes

1. The accounting profession in Canada has produced some material for public review starting with a CICA study in 1972: L.S. Rosen, *Current Value Accounting and Price Level Restatements* (Toronto: CICA), some guidance on general price level accounting in 1974, and position papers on current value accounting in 1976 and 1979. The CICA *Handbook* also has an "optional" disclosure section for a form of replacement cost. Also worth noting are two important publications of The Society of Management Accountants of Canada: J.R. Hanna, *Accounting Income Models: An Application and Evaluation* (Hamilton, 1974); and S. Basu and J.R. Hanna, *Inflation Accounting: Alternatives, Implementation Issues and Some Empirical Evidence* (Hamilton, 1975).

QUESTIONS

17-1 Define and give an illustration of a general price level restatement of historic cost.

17-2 What is meant by current value accounting? What is its purpose?

17-3 What is the GNE deflator? Is it needed to perform current cost or current value accounting? Why?

17-4 What is meant by capital maintenance?

17-5 What is the rationale for choosing historic money capital maintenance?

17-6 What is a nonmonetary item?

17-7 What is a monetary item?

17-8 What objectives of accounting are served by a general price level restatement of historic cost?

17-9 Why might a general price level restatement make unlike situations look alike?

17-10 Distinguish reproduction cost from replacement cost.

17-11 How might current cost or replacement cost accounting assist persons who are trying to evaluate management?

17-12 What effects might replacement cost accounting have on human behavior?

17-13 What is a realized holding gain? Which objective of accounting (if any) is served by separating holding gains into realized and unrealized?

17-14 Which users of financial statements might benefit from having a company use replacement cost as its net asset valuation method, and historic money capital as its capital maintenance measure?

EXERCISES

E17-1 Indicate whether each of the following items should be considered a monetary (M) or a nonmonetary (N) item:
1. Cash on hand
2. Cash in bank
3. Marketable securities (e.g., shares)
4. Accounts and notes receivable
5. Inventories
6. Refundable deposits
7. Property, plant and equipment
8. Accumulated depreciation
9. Goodwill
10. Patents, trademarks, licences
11. Accounts and notes payable
12. Dividends payable
13. Bonds payable
14. Common shares
15. Retained earnings

E17-2 In 19—2, a certain grade of lumber sold for $115 per 1,000 board feet. In 19—7, the same grade of lumber sold for $165 per 1,000 board feet. In 19—2 the Consumer Price Index was at 135; in 19—7 it was 188. By how much did the price of lumber actually increase, after taking into account the decline in the overall value of the dollar? Express your answer in terms of 19—7 dollars.

E17-3 The only asset of Equipment Rental Co. Ltd. is equipment that is on lease to outsiders. As of January 1, 19—1, the terms of existing lease contracts provide for payments to the company of $10,000 at the end of each of the next five years.

On December 31, 19—1, and on December 31, 19—2, the company received $10,000 in rentals. It immediately distributed the same amount to shareholders in the form of both a dividend and a return of their invested capital. Moreover, on December 31, 19—2, the firm was able to renegotiate the terms of outstanding leases so as to increase rentals for the remaining three years to $12,000 per year.

Required:
A. Determine the value of the enterprise as of January 1, 19—1, 19—2 and 19—3. Value is to be defined as the present value of anticipated cash receipts discounted at a rate of 8 percent.
B. Determine income for 19—1 and 19—2. Income is to be defined as the amount of cash distributed to shareholders less the change in the value of the enterprise.
C. What are the problems with using a discounted cash flow basis of valuing assets (e.g., equipment) of a manufacturing company?

E17-4 As of the beginning of 19—7 an investor had $200,000 in cash. On the first day of the year he placed $100,000 in a savings bank and purchased, for $50 per share, 2,000 common shares (a nonmonetary asset) of a well-known company. In the course of the year, the investor earned interest of $6,000 on the money placed in the savings account. He earned dividends of $3,000 on the common shares which he held. At year end, he sold the 2,000 common shares at a price of $52 per share.

The Consumer Price Index at the start of 19—7 was at a level of 159. On average during the year it was at 170, and at year end it was at 178.

Required:

A. Determine income for the year on a conventional historic cost basis.

B. Determine the gain or loss in purchasing power for the year.

C. Determine the gain or loss, on a price level adjusted basis, on the sale of the common shares.

D. Determine price level adjusted earnings for the year, including the gains or losses in purchasing power on the sale of common shares.

E. Reconcile, on a price level adjusted basis, the equity of the investor at the start of the year with that at the end.

E17-5 Knight Limited is a steel distributor. The company commenced business on January 1, 19—8 with $150 that it used to buy 5 tons of steel at $30 per ton.

No transactions occurred until December 31, 19—8 when the replacement cost rose to $45 per ton and one ton was sold for $65. During 19—8 general prices rose 10 percent.

Required:

Prepare an Income Statement for the year ended December 31, 19—8 for the following situations:

Case (1) Net asset value   = general price level restated historic cost
         Capital maintenance   = general price level restated historic cost
                                       (purchasing power)

Case (2) Net asset value   = replacement cost
         Capital maintenance   = money capital

Case (3) Net asset value   = replacement cost
         Capital maintenance   = replacement cost (operating capacity)

Case (4) Net asset value   = replacement cost
         Capital maintenance   = general price level restatement of historic cost

E17-6 M. Hilton Limited commenced business on January 1, 19—9 with $2,000 which it used to buy 10 units of inventory at $200 each. No transactions occurred until December, 19—9. On December 31, 19—9 the company sold 5 units for $300 each and purchased two more units for $250 each. During the year the general price rose 10 percent.

Required:

A. Prepare an Income Statement for the year ended December 31, 19—9 under each of the following assumptions:

| Case (1) | Net asset value | = | historic cost |
| | Capital maintenance | = | operating or physical capacity (i.e., replacement cost) |

| Case (2) | Net asset value | = | replacement cost |
| | Capital maintenance | = | operating or physical capacity (i.e., replacement cost) |

| Case (3) | Net asset value | = | replacement cost |
| | Capital maintenance | = | general price level restated historic cost |

B. Explain where each of Cases (1), (2) and (3) would "make sense".

C. Indicate some of the problems in implementing the system described in Case (2) above.

PROBLEMS

P17-1 As of December 31, 19—8, a company reported a balance in its truck account of $106,000 and a balance of $62,800 in the related accumulated depreciation account. Supporting documentation reveals the following:

Year	Number of trucks acquired	Cost per truck	Balance in truck account	Balance in accumulated depreciation account
19—5	3	$12,000	$ 36,000	$28,800
19—6	2	15,000	30,000	18,000
19—7	2	20,000	40,000	16,000
19—8	0	—	—	—
			$106,000	$62,800

Depreciation is recorded on a straight-line basis. The useful life of a truck is assumed to be five years; salvage value is considered to be zero.

For the years 19—5 to 19—8, the Consumer Price Index was at the following levels:

19—5	148
19—6	159
19—7	178
19—8	188

Required:

A. Determine depreciation charges for 19—8 on both a conventional and a general price level restated basis.

B. Suppose that on December 31, 19—8, after 19—8 depreciation has been recorded, one of the trucks acquired in 19—5 was sold for $3,000. Determine the gain or loss to be recognized under both conventional and general price level restated basis of accounting. (State your assumptions.)

583

*Current Cost
Accounting and
General
Price-Level
Restatements*

P17-2 The balance sheet of the Byrd Flying Service Co. Ltd. as of December 31, 19—6, appears as follows:

BYRD FLYING SERVICE CO. LTD.
Balance Sheet as of December 31, 19—6

Assets

Cash		$ 5,000
Accounts receivable		6,000
Inventories		9,000
Planes and equipment	$320,000	
Less: Accumulated depreciation	80,000	240,000
Total assets		$260,000

Liabilities and Shareholders' Equity

Accounts payable	$ 7,000
Wages payable	2,000
Tickets sold for trips not yet taken	1,000
Notes payable	150,000
Common shares	40,000
Retained earnings	60,000
Total liabilities and shareholders' equity	$260,000

The inventory was acquired throughout 19—6. The average Consumer Price Index for 19—6 was 170.

The planes and equipment were acquired in 19—2 at a time when the Consumer Price Index was at 135.

Accounts receivable, accounts payable, wages payable, and tickets sold for trips not yet taken arose from transactions that took place during the third and fourth quarters of 19—6. The average Consumer Price Index for those quarters was 175.

The notes payable were issued in connection with the purchase of the planes and equipment in 19—2. (Consumer Price Index, 135.)

The common shares were sold in 19—1 when the Consumer Price Index was at 128.

The Consumer Price Index as of December 31, 19—6 was at 178.

Required:

Prepare a general price level restated balance sheet expressed in terms of year end 19—6 dollars.

P17-3 Two companies, firm A and firm B, are in different industries. Both, however, are of the same size and do the same volume of business. The 19—5 income statements and balance sheets for the two firms are presented below:

Income Statements
For the Year Ending December 31, 19—5

	Firm A	*Firm B*
Sales	$1,000,000	$1,000,000
Cost of goods sold (excluding depreciation)	700,000	850,000
Depreciation	200,000	50,000
	900,000	900,000
Net income	$ 100,000	$ 100,000

Balance Sheets
as of December 31, 19—5

	Firm A	*Firm B*
Inventory	$ 200,000	$ 800,000
Fixed assets	800,000	200,000
Total assets	$1,000,000	$1,000,000
Owners' equity	$1,000,000	$1,000,000

The fixed assets of both firms were acquired in 19—1 at a time when the Consumer Price Index was at 144.

Ending inventory was acquired in the fourth quarter of 19—5 at a time when the Consumer Price Index was at 178.

Sales and all merchandise may be assumed to have been made and purchased evenly throughout 19—5. The average for 19—5 was 170.

Required:

A. Prepare general price level restated income statements for each of the two companies.

B. Comment on the reason for the differences in general price level restated earnings.

P17-4 Presented below are the 19—7 comparative balance sheet and income statement for Crunch Limited.

Balance Sheet
As of December 31

	19—7	19—6
Cash	$ 225,000	$ 152,000
Receivables	300,000	250,000
Inventory	535,000	518,000
Plant—Net	860,000	900,000
	$1,920,000	$1,820,000
Accounts payable	$ 143,200	$ 220,000
Bonds	860,000	800,000
Common shares	400,000	400,000
Retained earnings	516,800	400,000
	$1,920,000	$1,820,000

Income Statement
Year Ended December 31, 19—7

Sales		$1,400,000
Cost of goods sold	$900,000	
Depreciation	140,000	
Interest	60,000	
Other expenses	30,000	1,130,000
Income from operations		270,000
Taxes		135,000
Net income		$ 135,000

Additional Information:

1. Dividends paid during 19—7 were $18,200. The dividends were paid during the third quarter of 19—7.

2. Purchases during 19—7 were $917,000.

3. On January 1, 19—7, Crunch acquired a fixed asset for $40,000 cash and $60,000 of bonds. The asset is to be depreciated over five years on a straight-line basis with a full year's depreciation to be recorded in 19—7.

4. The Consumer Price Index was as follows:

   100 at date of issue of common shares
   110 at date of issue of bonds outstanding at December 31, 19—6
      and acquisition of fixed assets
   190 when the 19—6 year end inventory was acquired
   200 at January 1, 19—7
   210 average for 19—7
   217.5 when the 19—7 year end inventory was acquired; and
   220 at December 31, 19—7.

Required:

A. Prepare a general price level restated historic cost comparative balance sheet at December 31, 19—7 and a statement of income and retained earnings for 19—7.

B. How might the price level restated historic cost income statement be used to persuade the government that they are over-taxing companies?

P17-5 The following data relate to Progress Co. Ltd.:

	Balance Sheet December 31	
	19—6	19—7
Monetary assets	$ 5,000	$ 2,000
Inventory	4,000	8,000
Plant and equipment	20,000	30,000
Accumulated depreciation	(9,000)	(12,000)
	$20,000	$28,000
Current liabilities	$ 2,000	$ 6,000
Long-term debt	7,000	7,000
Common shares	9,000	9,000
Retained earnings	2,000	6,000
	$20,000	$28,000

	Income Statement *Year Ended December 31, 19—7*
Sales (net)	$20,000
Cost of goods sold	12,000
Gross profit	8,000
Expenses	4,000
Net income	$ 4,000

Additional Information:

1. Plant and equipment were acquired on the following dates:

January 1, 19—1	$10,000
January 1, 19—4	$10,000
January 1, 19—7	$10,000

Depreciation on plant and equipment is 10 percent straight-line per annum.

2. The inventory at December 31, 19—6 was acquired when the general price index was 80. Additional purchases of inventory in 19—7 amounted to $16,000 and were made evenly throughout the year.

3. The common shares of the business were issued on January 1, 19—1.

4. The general price indexes were as follows:

January 1, 19—1	25
January 1, 19—4	75
December 31, 19—6	100
Average for 19—7	125
Average for last 6 months of 19—7	137
December 31, 19—7	150

Required:

A. Prepare a comparative balance sheet at December 31, 19—7 and an income statement for the year ended December 31, 19—7 in dollars of general purchasing power as of December 31, 19—7.

B. Clearly explain the uses and limitations of the financial statements which you prepared in (A) above.

P17-6 Crandall Limited commences business on January 1, 19—8 with $1,000 cash credited to capital. On January 2, 19—8 100 items of inventory are bought at $10 each. On January 15, 19—8 60 items are sold at $20 each. Current replacement cost of each unit of inventory on January 15, 19—8 is $13. The current replacement cost and the selling price of each unit of inventory on January 31, 19—8 are $16 and $25 respectively.

The remaining 40 items are sold on February 15, 19—8 at $30 each. The current replacement cost of each unit of inventory on February 15, 19—8 was $20.

587

*Current Cost
Accounting and
General
Price-Level
Restatements*

Required:

A. Prepare income statements and balance sheets for January and February using the following valuation bases:
   1. historic cost
   2. current entry price (current replacement cost)
   3. current exit price (current selling price)

B. Given the general price indexes for 19—8 were as follows:

January 1	100	February 15	120
January 15	100	February 28	140
January 31	100		

Prepare a revised income statement and balance sheet for February using a general price level restated historic cost basis of valuation.

C. Evaluate the difficulties of implementing a current entry price basis of valuation for Crandall Limited.

D. What additional problems would be encountered in implementing a current value basis of valuation if Crandall had fixed assets?

E. Evaluate the usefulness of the statements that you prepared in (A).

P17-7 Two companies, the FIFO Co. Ltd. and the LIFO Co. Ltd. engage in operations in an identical manner. The former, however, maintains its inventory on a FIFO basis and the latter on a LIFO basis.

As of the start of 19—4 each firm had 5,000 units of production on hand. The units of the LIFO Co. were assumed to have been acquired in 19—1 and were carried on the books of the company at a value of $170,000 ($34 per unit). Those of the FIFO Co. were assumed to have been acquired in 19—3 and were carried on the books at a value of $250,000 ($50 per unit).

In 19—4 each company purchased 24,000 units of product as follows:

1st quarter	6,000	units @ $51	=	$ 306,000
2nd quarter	6,000	units @ 52	=	312,000
3rd quarter	6,000	units @ 54	=	324,000
4th quarter	6,000	units @ 56	=	336,000
	24,000			$1,278,000

At the end of the year each company sold 21,000 units for $1,470,000; at year end each had 8,000 units remaining in inventory.

Relevant values for the general price level index are:

19—1 111 (when LIFO Co. acquired its opening inventory)
19—3 159 (when FIFO Co. acquired its opening inventory)
19—4 1st quarter   164
      2nd quarter   167
      3rd quarter   172
      4th quarter   178

Required:

A. Determine cost of goods sold and year-end 19—4 inventory for each of the two firms on a historical cost basis. Calculate income for the two companies.

B. Determine cost of goods sold and year-end 19—4 inventory for each of the two firms on a price level adjusted basis. Calculate income for the two companies.

C. Assume that the replacement cost of inventory was $50 per unit at the beginning of 19—4 and $58 at the end of 19—4 (when the company sold 21,000 units). If a replacement cost basis of valuing inventory is used to determine cost of goods sold and year-end 19—4 inventory for each of the two firms. Calculate income for the two companies.

D. Which net asset valuation basis would you recommend? Be sure to indicate the use you intend to make of the information in order to justify your response.

E. If the stock markets are "efficient" and the method of inventory valuation is disclosed, then how would investors interpret the difference in income of the two firms calculated in (A)?

EXPLORATION MATERIALS AND CASES

MC17-1 Canadian Steel Limited (CSL) is federally incorporated. Its common shares and debentures are held by the general public. CSL is a steel wholesaler engaged essentially in buying large volumes of steel at a discount, storing it and selling it in smaller units to customers.

Recently CSL increased its selling price of steel. Almost immediately articles appeared in the newspapers criticizing the price increase. The fact that the company reported earnings of $5.00 per share and had a 15 percent return on shareholders' equity received a lot of attention in the newspapers.

Management has decided to embark on a publicity campaign in order to explain to the public and their customers that the price increase was justified and that their return on investment before the price increase was inadequate.

In addition, the president of the company would like to improve the performance evaluation and motivation of managers. Specifically he would like an accounting system which:

1. Immediately motivates managers to raise the selling price when the replacement cost of steel changes.

2. Motivates managers to sell in bulk to customers if selling prices exceed replacement cost.

3. Gives credit to the purchasing department for bulk buying before prices increase.

4. Separates the efficiency of the selling departments from the buying and storing functions of the company.

Required:

What would you recommend? Consider potential implementation problems such as the availability of the information that you intend to use and the reaction of the company's auditors.

MC17-2 At a cocktail party, you happen to overhear the following conversation between a businessman and an accountant:

BUSINESSMAN: If my business is to be ongoing, I must generate enough money for the replacement of equipment when the equipment wears out or becomes obsolete. I don't see why accountants don't provide for this in their determination of profits.

ACCOUNTANT: Accountants cannot provide for future costs. Their job is to account for past costs. For instance, we record the actual cost of your equipment on your company's books, estimate for how long it will be useful and what its salvage value might be and then match the original cost, through depreciation, to revenue that the equipment generates. In this way, we derive an objective and useful income figure.

BUSINESSMAN (*slightly annoyed*): Your depreciation formula may be enshrined in professional standards, law and other impressive documents but it seems to me that the exercise is useless. It does not accurately reflect an important cost of doing business. I would say that the neat symmetrical depreciation charge that you so laboriously calculate distorts the performance of a company. In addition, your judgments about the useful life, the salvage value and the likely revenue stream are all subjective. Therefore, how can you stand there and tell me the income figure you derive is objective? In my opinion it is subjective and useless.

ACCOUNTANT (*fidgeting somewhat*): You have been talking about how to account for equipment from your own point of view. However, other people such as creditors, tax authorities, and so forth use your financial statments. The *Income Tax Act* defines cost as the price paid at the acquisition date, not the replacement date. Therefore, it is important to keep track of original cost.

In addition, creditors often compare your financial statements to those of other companies when making a lending decision. This comparability aspect is aided by historic cost accounting. While I admit some subjectivity does exist, at least we are dealing with one known amount—the original cost of an asset. Actually, I think the income figure would be even more useful to creditors if only one depreciation method was allowed.

BUSINESSMAN (*muttering while walking way*): These accountants are so righteous about their accounting methods. If only they would wake up one day and realize the books are not the business!

Required:

Evaluate the arguments of both the businessman and the accountant. How would you have dealt with the businessman's concerns?

MC17-3 Russell Electric Company Limited (RECL) is a public utility company. It is subject to regulation by a commission which established rates such as the RECL is permitted to earn a return of 7 percent on total invested capital. A condensed balance sheet and income statement of RECL for the year ending December 31, 19—1, the first year of its operations, appears as follows:

Balance Sheet

As of December 31, 19—1

Assets

Cash and accounts receivable		$ 1,500,000
Inventories and supplies		200,000
Plant and equipment	$12,000,000	
Less: Accumulated depreciation	850,000	11,150,000
Total assets		$12,850,000

Equities

Current liabilities	$ 300,000
Long-term debt (at 10% interest)	9,000,000
Shareholders' equity	3,550,000
Total equities	$12,850,000

Statement of Income

For the Year Ending December 31, 19—1

Revenue		$5,149,500
Operating expenses	$ 2,500,000	
Depreciation	850,000	
Interest	900,000	4,250,000
Net income before taxes		$ 899,500

Return on investment is defined as net income before taxes divided by total assets. Thus $899,500/$12,850,000 equals 7 percent.

All assets except for plant and equipment represent fair market value, that is, the cash and accounts receivable reflect cash the company either has or will receive in the near future and the book value of inventories and supplies equals the replacement cost of these items at December 31, 19—1. The plant and equipment consists of the following items:

	Historic Cost	Replacement cost at December 31, 19—1
Land	$ 500,000	$ 600,000
Building (depreciated on a straight-line basis over 25 years)	5,000,000	6,100,000
Equipment (depreciated on a straight-line basis over 10 years)	6,500,000	7,500,000
	$12,000,000	$14,200,000

The long-term debt and common shares were issued when the general price index was at 140. The fixed assets were acquired when the general price index was at the same level.

Revenues, operating expenses, and interest were incurred evenly throughout 19—1. The average general price index for 19—1 was 146.

The company paid dividends in 19—1 of $400,000. They may be assumed to have been paid evenly throughout the year.

At the start of 19—1 the company received $12,050,500 cash from the debt issue and the issue of common shares and paid $12,000,000 cash for the plant and equipment.

Inventories and supplies were acquired at year end. The general price index at year end was 152.

Required:

A. Determine the actual rate of return for 19—1 on a general price level restated basis and on a current value basis.

B. Which base do you think the regulatory commission should use? Why?

Appendix A Present Value Tables

TABLE 1 PRESENT VALUE FACTORS

Periods Hence	1%	2%	3%	4%	5%	6%	7%	8%	9%	10%
1	.9901	.9804	.9709	.9615	.9524	.9434	.9346	.9259	.9174	.9091
2	.9803	.9612	.9426	.9246	.9070	.8900	.8734	.8573	.8417	.8264
3	.9706	.9423	.9151	.8890	.8638	.8396	.8163	.7938	.7722	.7513
4	.9610	.9238	.8885	.8548	.8227	.7921	.7629	.7350	.7084	.6830
5	.9515	.9057	.8626	.8219	.7835	.7473	.7130	.6806	.6499	.6209
6	.9420	.8880	.8375	.7903	.7462	.7050	.6663	.6302	.5963	.5645
7	.9327	.8706	.8131	.7599	.7107	.6651	.6227	.5835	.5470	.5132
8	.9235	.8535	.7894	.7307	.6768	.6274	.5820	.5403	.5019	.4665
9	.9143	.8368	.7664	.7026	.6446	.5919	.5439	.5002	.4604	.4241
10	.9053	.8203	.7441	.6756	.6139	.5584	.5083	.4632	.4224	.3855
11	.8963	.8043	.7224	.6496	.5847	.5268	.4751	.4289	.3875	.3505
12	.8874	.7885	.7014	.6246	.5568	.4970	.4440	.3971	.3555	.3186
13	.8787	.7730	.6810	.6006	.5303	.4688	.4150	.3677	.3262	.2897
14	.8700	.7579	.6611	.5775	.5051	.4423	.3878	.3405	.2992	.2633
15	.8613	.7430	.6419	.5553	.4810	.4173	.3624	.3152	.2745	.2394
16	.8528	.7284	.6232	.5339	.4581	.3936	.3387	.2919	.2519	.2176
17	.8444	.7142	.6050	.5134	.4363	.3714	.3166	.2703	.2311	.1978
18	.8360	.7002	.5874	.4936	.4155	.3503	.2959	.2502	.2120	.1799
19	.8277	.6864	.5703	.4746	.3957	.3305	.2765	.2317	.1945	.1635
20	.8195	.6730	.5537	.4564	.3769	.3118	.2584	.2145	.1784	.1486
21	.8114	.6598	.5375	.4388	.3589	.2942	.2415	.1987	.1637	.1351
22	.8034	.6468	.5219	.4220	.3418	.2775	.2257	.1839	.1502	.1228
23	.7954	.6342	.5067	.4057	.3256	.2618	.2109	.1703	.1378	.1117
24	.7876	.6217	.4919	.3901	.3101	.2470	.1971	.1577	.1264	.1015
25	.7798	.6095	.4776	.3751	.2953	.2330	.1842	.1460	.1160	.0923
26	.7720	.5976	.4637	.3607	.2812	.2198	.1722	.1352	.1064	.0839
27	.7644	.5859	.4502	.3468	.2678	.2074	.1609	.1252	.0976	.0763
28	.7568	.5744	.4371	.3335	.2551	.1956	.1504	.1159	.0895	.0693
29	.7493	.5631	.4243	.3207	.2429	.1846	.1406	.1073	.0822	.0630
30	.7419	.5521	.4120	.3083	.2314	.1741	.1314	.0994	.0754	.0573
31	.7346	.5412	.4000	.2965	.2204	.1643	.1228	.0920	.0691	.0521
32	.7273	.5306	.3883	.2851	.2099	.1550	.1147	.0852	.0634	.0474
33	.7201	.5202	.3770	.2741	.1999	.1462	.1072	.0789	.0582	.0431
34	.7130	.5100	.3660	.2636	.1904	.1379	.1002	.0730	.0534	.0391
35	.7059	.5000	.3554	.2534	.1813	.1301	.0937	.0676	.0490	.0356
36	.6989	.4902	.3450	.2437	.1727	.1227	.0875	.0626	.0449	.0323
37	.6920	.4806	.3350	.2343	.1644	.1158	.0818	.0580	.0412	.0294
38	.6852	.4712	.3252	.2253	.1566	.1092	.0765	.0537	.0378	.0267
39	.6784	.4619	.3158	.2166	.1491	.1031	.0715	.0497	.0347	.0243
40	.6717	.4529	.3066	.2083	.1420	.0972	.0668	.0460	.0318	.0221
41	.6650	.4440	.2976	.2003	.1353	.0917	.0624	.0426	.0292	.0201
42	.6584	.4353	.2890	.1926	.1288	.0865	.0583	.0395	.0268	.0183
43	.6519	.4268	.2805	.1852	.1227	.0816	.0545	.0365	.0246	.0166
44	.6454	.4184	.2724	.1780	.1169	.0770	.0509	.0338	.0226	.0151
45	.6391	.4102	.2644	.1712	.1113	.0727	.0476	.0313	.0207	.0137
46	.6327	.4022	.2567	.1646	.1060	.0685	.0445	.0290	.0190	.0125
47	.6265	.3943	.2493	.1583	.1009	.0647	.0416	.0269	.0174	.0113
48	.6203	.3865	.2420	.1522	.0961	.0610	.0389	.0249	.0160	.0103
49	.6141	.3790	.2350	.1463	.0916	.0575	.0363	.0230	.0147	.0094
50	.6080	.3715	.2281	.1407	.0872	.0543	.0339	.0213	.0134	.0085

TABLE 1   PRESENT VALUE FACTORS

Periods Hence	11%	12%	13%	14%	15%	16%	17%	18%	19%	20%
1	.9009	.8929	.8850	.8772	.8696	.8621	.8547	.8475	.8403	.8333
2	.8116	.7972	.7831	.7695	.7561	.7432	.7305	.7182	.7062	.6944
3	.7312	.7118	.6931	.6750	.6575	.6407	.6244	.6086	.5934	.5787
4	.6587	.6355	.6133	.5921	.5718	.5523	.5337	.5158	.4987	.4823
5	.5935	.5674	.5428	.5194	.4972	.4761	.4561	.4371	.4190	.4019
6	.5346	.5066	.4803	.4556	.4323	.4104	.3898	.3704	.3521	.3349
7	.4817	.4523	.4251	.3996	.3759	.3538	.3332	.3139	.2959	.2791
8	.4339	.4039	.3762	.3506	.3269	.3050	.2848	.2660	.2487	.2326
9	.3909	.3606	.3329	.3075	.2843	.2630	.2434	.2255	.2090	.1938
10	.3522	.3220	.2946	.2697	.2472	.2267	.2080	1911	.1756	.1615
11	.3173	.2875	.2607	.2366	.2149	.1954	.1778	.1619	.1476	.1346
12	.2858	.2567	.2307	.2076	.1869	.1685	.1520	.1372	.1240	.1122
13	.2575	.2292	.2042	.1821	.1625	.1452	.1299	.1163	.1042	.0935
14	.2320	.2046	.1807	.1597	.1413	.1252	.1110	.0985	.0876	.0779
15	.2090	.1827	.1599	.1401	.1229	.1079	.0949	.0835	.0736	.0649
16	.1883	.1631	.1415	.1229	.1069	.0930	.0818	.0708	.0618	.0541
17	.1696	.1456	.1252	.1078	.0929	.0802	.0693	.0600	.0520	.0451
18	1528	.1300	.1108	.0946	.0808	.0691	.0592	.0508	.0437	.0376
19	.1377	.1161	.0981	.0829	.0703	.0596	.0506	.0431	.0367	.0313
20	.1240	.1037	.0868	.0728	.0611	.0514	.0433	.0365	.0303	.0261
21	.1117	.0926	.0768	.0638	.0531	.0443	.0370	.0309	.0259	.0217
22	.1007	.0826	.0680	.0560	.0462	.0382	.0316	.0262	.0218	.0181
23	.0907	.0738	.0601	.0491	.0402	.0329	.0270	.0222	.0183	.0151
24	.0817	.0659	.0532	.0431	.0349	.0284	.0231	.0188	.0154	.0126
25	.0736	.0588	.0471	.0378	.0304	.0245	.0197	.0160	.0129	.0105
26	.0663	.0525	.0417	.0331	.0264	.0211	.0169	.0135	.0109	.0087
27	.0597	.0469	.0369	.0291	.0230	.0182	.0144	.0115	.0091	.0073
28	.0538	.0419	.0326	.0255	.0200	.0157	.0123	.0097	.0077	.0061
29	.0485	.0374	.0289	.0224	.0174	.0135	.0105	.0082	.0064	.0051
30	.0437	.0334	.0256	.0196	.0151	.0116	.0090	.0070	.0054	.0042
31	.0394	.0298	.0226	.0172	.0131	.0100	.0077	.0059	.0046	.0035
32	.0355	.0266	.0200	.0151	.0114	.0087	.0066	.0050	.0038	.0029
33	.0319	.0238	.0177	.0132	.0099	.0075	.0056	.0042	.0032	.0024
34	.0288	.0212	.0157	.0116	.0086	.0064	.0048	.0036	.0027	.0020
35	.0259	.0189	.0139	.0102	.0075	.0055	.0041	.0030	.0023	.0017
36	.0234	.0169	.0123	.0089	.0065	.0048	.0035	.0026	.0019	.0014
37	.0210	.0151	.0109	.0078	.0057	.0041	.0030	.0022	.0016	.0012
38	.0190	.0135	.0096	.0069	.0049	.0036	.0026	.0019	.0013	.0010
39	.0171	.0120	.0085	.0060	.0043	.0031	.0022	.0016	.0011	.0008
40	.0154	.0107	.0075	.0053	.0037	.0026	.0019	.0013	.0010	.0007
41	.0139	.0096	.0067	.0046	.0032	.0023	.0016	.0011	.0008	.0006
42	.0125	.0086	.0059	.0041	.0028	.0020	.0014	.0010	.0007	.0005
43	.0112	.0076	.0052	.0036	.0025	.0017	.0012	.0008	.0006	.0004
44	.0101	.0068	.0046	.0031	.0021	.0015	.0010	.0007	.0005	.0003
45	.0091	.0061	.0041	.0027	.0019	.0013	.0009	.0006	.0004	.0003
46	.0082	.0054	.0036	.0024	.0016	.0011	.0007	.0005	.0003	.0002
47	.0074	.0049	.0032	.0021	.0014	.0009	.0006	.0004	.0003	.0002
48	.0067	.0043	.0028	.0019	.0012	.0008	.0005	.0004	.0002	.0002
49	.0060	.0039	.0025	.0016	.0011	.0007	.0005	.0003	.0002	.0001
50	.0054	.0035	.0022	.0014	.0009	.0006	.0004	.0003	.0002	.0001

TABLE 1 PRESENT VALUE FACTORS

Periods Hence	21%	22%	23%	24%	25%	26%	27%	28%	29%	30%
1	.8264	.8197	.8130	.8065	.8000	.7937	.7874	.7813	.7752	.7692
2	.6830	.6719	.6610	.6504	.6400	.6299	.6200	.6104	.6009	.5917
3	.5645	.5507	.5374	.5245	.5120	.4999	.4882	.4768	.4658	.4552
4	.4665	.4514	.4369	.4230	.4096	.3968	.3844	.3725	.3611	.3501
5	.3855	.3700	.3552	.3411	.3277	.3149	.3027	.2910	.2799	.2693
6	.3186	.3033	.2888	.2751	.2621	.2499	.2383	.2274	.2170	.2072
7	.2633	.2486	.2348	.2218	.2096	.1983	.1877	.1776	.1682	.1594
8	.2176	.2038	.1909	.1789	.1678	.1574	.1478	.1388	.1304	.1226
9	.1799	.1670	.1552	.1443	.1342	.1249	.1164	.1084	.1011	.0943
10	.1486	.1369	.1262	.1164	.1074	.0992	.0916	.0847	.0784	.0725
11	.1228	.1122	.1026	.0938	.0859	.0787	.0721	.0662	.0607	.0558
12	.1015	.0920	.0834	.0757	.0687	.0625	.0568	.0517	.0471	.0429
13	.0839	.0754	.0678	.0610	.0550	.0496	.0447	.0404	.0365	.0330
14	.0693	.0618	.0551	.0492	.0440	.0393	.0352	.0316	.0283	.0254
15	.0573	.0507	.0448	.0397	.0352	.0312	.0277	.0247	.0219	.0195
16	.0474	.0415	.0364	.0320	.0281	.0248	.0218	.0193	.0170	.0150
17	.0391	.0340	.0296	.0258	.0225	.0197	.0172	.0150	.0132	.0116
18	.0323	.0279	.0241	.0208	.0180	.0156	.0135	.0118	.0102	.0089
19	.0267	.0229	.0196	.0168	.0144	.0124	.0107	.0092	.0079	.0068
20	.0221	.0187	.0159	.0135	.0115	.0098	.0084	.0072	.0061	.0053
21	.0183	.0154	.0129	.0109	.0092	.0078	.0066	.0056	.0048	.0040
22	.0151	.0126	.0105	.0088	.0074	.0062	.0052	.0044	.0037	.0031
23	.0125	.0103	.0086	.0071	.0059	.0049	.0041	.0034	.0029	.0024
24	.0103	.0085	.0070	.0057	.0047	.0039	.0032	.0027	.0022	.0018
25	.0085	.0069	.0057	.0046	.0038	.0031	.0025	.0021	.0017	.0014
26	.0070	.0057	.0046	.0037	.0030	.0025	.0020	.0016	.0013	.0011
27	.0058	.0047	.0037	.0030	.0024	.0019	.0016	.0013	.0010	.0008
28	.0048	.0038	.0030	.0024	.0019	.0015	.0012	.0010	.0008	.0006
29	.0040	.0031	.0025	.0020	.0015	.0012	.0010	.0008	.0006	.0005
30	.0033	.0026	.0020	.0016	.0012	.0010	.0008	.0006	.0005	.0004
31	.0027	.0021	.0016	.0013	.0010	.0008	.0006	.0005	.0004	.0003
32	.0022	.0017	.0013	.0010	.0008	.0006	.0005	.0004	.0003	.0002
33	.0019	.0014	.0011	.0008	.0006	.0005	.0004	.0003	.0002	.0002
34	.0015	.0012	.0009	.0007	.0005	.0004	.0003	.0002	.0002	.0001
35	.0013	.0009	.0007	.0005	.0004	.0003	.0002	.0002	.0001	.0001
36	.0010	.0008	.0006	.0004	.0003	.0002	.0002	.0001	.0001	.0001
37	.0009	.0006	.0005	.0003	.0003	.0002	.0001	.0001	.0001	.0001
38	.0007	.0005	.0004	.0003	.0002	.0002	.0001	.0001	.0001I	.0000
39	.0006	.0004	.0003	.0002	.0002	.0001	.0001	.0001	.0000	
40	.0005	.0004	.0003	.0002	.0001	.0001	.0001	.0001		
41	.0004	.0003	.0002	.0001	.0001	.0001	.0001	.0000		
42	.0003	.0002	.0002	.0001	.0001	.0001	.0000			
43	.0003	.0002	.0001	.0001	.0001	.0000				
44	.0002	.0002	.0001	.0001	.0001					
45	.0002	.0001	.0001	.0001	.0000					
46	.0002	.0001	.0001	.0001						
47	.0001	.0001	.0001	.0000						
48	.0001	.0001	.0000							
49	.0001	.0001								
50	.0001	.0000								

TABLE 1 PRESENT VALUE FACTORS

Periods Hence	31%	32%	33%	34%	35%	36%	37%	38%	39%	40%
1	.7634	.7576	.7519	.7463	.7407	.7353	.7299	.7246	.7194	.7143
2	.5827	.5739	.5653	.5569	.5487	.5407	.5328	.5251	.5176	.5102
3	.4448	.4348	.4251	.4156	.4064	.3975	.3889	.3805	.3724	.3644
4	.3396	.3294	.3196	.3102	.3011	.2923	.2839	.2757	.2679	.2603
5	.2592	.2495	.2403	.2315	.2230	.2149	.2072	.1998	.1927	.1859
6	.1979	.1890	.1807	.1727	.1652	.1580	.1512	.1448	.1386	.1328
7	.1510	.1432	.1358	.1289	.1224	.1162	.1104	.1049	.0997	.0949
8	.1153	.1085	.1021	.0962	.0906	.0854	.0806	.0760	.0718	.0678
9	.0880	.0822	.0768	.0718	.0671	.0628	.0588	.0551	.0516	.0484
10	.0672	.0623	.0577	.0536	.0497	.0462	.0429	.0399	.0371	.0346
11	.0513	.0472	.0434	.0400	.0368	.0340	.0313	.0289	.0267	.0247
12	.0392	.0357	.0326	.0298	.0273	.0250	.0229	.0210	.0192	.0176
13	.0299	.0271	.0245	.0223	.0202	.0184	.0167	.0152	.0138	.0126
14	.0228	.0205	.0185	.0166	.0150	.0135	.0122	.0110	.0099	.0090
15	.0174	.0155	.0139	.0124	.0111	.0099	.0089	.0080	.0072	.0064
16	.0133	.0118	.0104	.0093	.0082	.0073	.0065	.0058	.0051	.0046
17	.0101	.0089	.0078	.0069	.0061	.0054	.0047	.0042	.0037	.0033
18	.0077	.0068	.0059	.0052	.0045	.0039	.0035	.0030	.0027	.0023
19	.0059	.0051	.0044	.0038	.0033	.0029	.0025	.0022	.0019	.0017
20	.0045	.0039	.0033	.0029	.0025	.0021	.0018	.0016	.0014	.0012
21	.0034	.0029	.0025	.0021	.0018	.0016	.0013	.0012	.0010	.0009
22	.0026	.0022	.0019	.0016	.0014	.0012	.0010	.0008	.0007	.0006
23	.0020	.0017	.0014	.0012	.0010	.0008	.0007	.0006	.0005	.0004
24	.0015	.0013	.0011	.0009	.0007	.0006	.0005	.0004	.0004	.0003
25	.0012	.0010	.0008	.0007	.0006	.0005	.0004	.0003	.0003	.0002
26	.0009	.0007	.0006	.0005	.0004	.0003	.0003	.0002	.0002	.0002
27	.0007	.0006	.0005	.0004	.0003	.0002	.0002	.0002	.0001	.0001
28	.0005	.0004	.0003	.0003	.0002	.0002	.0001	.0001	.0001	.0001
29	.0004	.0003	.0003	.0002	.0002	.0001	.0001	.0001	.0001	.0001
30	.0003	.0002	.0002	.0002	.0001	.0001	.0001	.0001	.0001	.0000
31	.0002	.0002	.0001	.0001	.0001	.0001	.0001	.0000	.0000	
32	.0002	.0001	.0001	.0001	.0001	.0001	.0000			
33	.0001	.0001	.0001	.0001	.0001	.0000				
34	.0001	.0001	.0001	.0000	.0000					
35	.0001	.0001	.0000							
36	.0001	.0000	.0000							
37	.0000									

TABLE 1   PRESENT VALUE FACTORS

Periods Hence	41%	42%	43%	44%	45%	46%	47%	48%	49%	50%
1	.7092	.7042	.6993	.6944	.6897	.6849	.6803	.6757	.6711	.6667
2	.5030	.4959	.4890	.4823	.4756	.4691	.4628	.4565	.4504	.4444
3	.3567	.3492	.3420	.3349	.3280	.3213	.3148	.3085	.3023	.2963
4	.2530	.2459	.2391	.2326	.2262	.2201	.2142	.2084	.2029	.1975
5	.1794	.1732	.1672	.1615	.1560	.1507	.1457	.1408	.1362	.1317
6	.1273	.1220	.1169	.1122	.1076	.1032	.0991	.0952	.0914	.0878
7	.0903	.0859	.0818	.0779	.0742	.0707	.0674	.0643	.0613	.0585
8	.0640	.0605	.0572	.0541	.0512	.0484	.0459	.0434	.0412	.0390
9	.0454	.0426	.0400	.0376	.0353	.0332	.0312	.0294	.0276	.0260
10	.0322	.0300	.0280	.0261	.0243	.0227	.0212	.0198	.0185	.0173
11	.0228	.0211	.0196	.0181	.0168	.0156	.0144	.0134	.0125	.0116
12	.0162	.0149	.0137	.0126	.0116	.0107	.0098	.0091	.0084	.0077
13	.0115	.0105	.0096	.0087	.0080	.0073	.0067	.0061	.0056	.0051
14	.0081	.0074	.0067	.0061	.0055	.0050	.0045	.0041	.0038	.0034
15	.0058	.0052	.0047	.0042	.0038	.0034	.0031	.0028	.0025	.0023
16	.0041	.0037	.0033	.0029	.0026	.0023	.0021	.0019	.0017	.0015
17	.0029	.0026	.0023	.0020	.0018	.0016	.0014	.0013	.0011	.0010
18	.0021	.0018	.0016	.0014	.0012	.0011	.0010	.0009	.0008	.0007
19	.0015	.0013	.0011	.0010	.0009	.0008	.0007	.0006	.0005	.0005
20	.0010	.0009	.0008	.0007	.0006	.0005	.0005	.0004	.0003	.0003
21	.0007	.0006	.0005	.0005	.0004	.0004	.0003	.0003	.0002	.0002
22	.0005	.0004	.0004	.0003	.0003	.0002	.0002	.0002	.0002	.0001
23	.0004	.0003	.0003	.0002	.0002	.0002	.0001	.0001	.0001	.0001
24	.0003	.0002	.0002	.0002	.0001	.0001	.0001	.0001	.0001	.0001
25	.0002	.0002	.0001	.0001	.0001	.0001	.0001	.0001	.0000	.0000
26	.0001	.0001	.0001	.0001	.0001	.0001	.0000	.0000		
27	.0001	.0001	.0001	.0001	.0000	.0000				
28	.0001	.0001	.0000	.0000						
29	.0000	.0000								

TABLE 2 CUMULATIVE PRESENT VALUE FACTORS

Periods 0 to:	1%	2%	3%	4%	5%	6%	7%	8%	9%	10%
1	.990	.980	.971	.962	.952	.943	.935	.926	.917	.909
2	1.970	1.942	1.913	1.886	1.859	1.833	1.808	1.783	1.759	1.736
3	2.941	2.884	2.829	2.775	2.723	2.673	2.624	2.577	2.531	2.487
4	3.902	3.808	3.717	3.630	3.546	3.465	3.387	3.312	3.240	3.170
5	4.853	4.713	4.580	4.452	4.329	4.212	4.100	3.993	3.890	3.791
6	5.795	5.601	5.417	5.242	5.076	4.917	4.767	4.623	4.486	4.355
7	6.728	6.472	6.230	6.002	5.786	5.582	5.389	5.206	5.033	4.868
8	7.652	7.325	7.020	6.733	6.463	6.210	5.971	5.747	5.535	5.335
9	8.566	8.162	7.786	7.435	7.108	6.802	6.515	6.247	5.995	5.759
10	9.471	8.983	8.530	8.111	7.722	7.360	7.024	6.710	6.418	6.145
11	10.378	9.787	9.253	8.760	8.306	7.887	7.499	7.139	6.805	6.495
12	11.255	10.575	9.954	9.385	8.863	8.384	7.943	7.536	7.161	6.814
13	12.134	11.348	10.635	9.986	9.394	8.853	8.358	7.904	7.487	7.103
14	13.004	12.106	11.296	10.563	9.899	9.295	8.745	8.244	7.786	7.367
15	13.865	12.849	11.938	11.118	10.380	9.712	9.108	8.559	8.061	7.606
16	14.718	13.578	12.561	11.652	10.838	10.106	9.447	8.851	8.313	7.824
17	15.562	14.292	13.166	12.166	11.274	10.477	9.763	9.122	8.544	8.022
18	16.398	14.992	13.754	12.659	11.690	10.828	10.059	9.372	8.756	8.201
19	17.226	15.678	14.324	13.134	12.085	11.158	10.336	9.604	8.950	8.365
20	18.046	16.351	14.877	13.590	12.462	11.470	10.594	9.818	9.129	8.514
21	18.857	17.011	15.415	14.029	12.821	11.764	10.836	10.017	9.292	8.649
22	19.660	17.658	15.937	14.451	13.163	12.042	11.061	10.201	9.442	8.772
23	20.456	18.292	16.444	14.857	13.489	12.303	11.272	10.371	9.580	8.883
24	21.243	18.914	16.936	15.247	13.799	12.550	11.469	10.529	9.707	8.985
25	22.023	19.523	17.413	15.622	14.094	12.783	11.654	10.675	9.823	9.077
26	22.795	20.121	17.877	15.983	14.375	13.003	11.826	10.810	9.929	9.161
27	23.560	20.707	18.327	16.330	14.643	13.211	11.987	10.935	10.027	9.237
28	24.316	21.281	18.764	16.663	14.898	13.406	12.137	11.051	10.116	9.307
29	25.066	21.844	19.188	16.984	15.141	13.591	12.278	11.158	10.198	9.370
30	25.808	22.396	19.600	17.292	15.372	13.765	12.409	11.258	10.274	9.427
31	26.542	22.938	20.000	17.588	15.593	13.929	12.532	11.350	10.343	9.479
32	27.270	23.468	20.389	17.874	15.803	14.084	12.647	11.435	10.406	9.526
33	27.990	23.989	20.766	18.148	16.003	14.230	12.754	11.514	10.464	9.569
34	28.703	24.499	21.132	18.411	16.193	14.368	12.854	11.587	10.518	9.609
35	29.409	24.999	21.487	18.665	16.374	14.498	12.948	11.655	10.567	9.644
36	30.108	25.489	21.832	18.908	16.547	14.621	13.035	11.717	10.612	9.677
37	30.780	25.969	22.167	19.143	16.711	14.737	13.117	11.775	10.653	9.706
38	31.485	26.441	22.492	19.368	16.868	14.846	13.193	11.829	10.691	9.733
39	32.163	26.903	22.808	19.584	17.017	14.949	13.265	11.879	10.726	9.757
40	32.835	27.355	23.115	19.793	17.159	15.046	13.332	11.925	10.757	9.779

TABLE 2   CUMULATIVE PRESENT VALUE FACTORS

Periods 0 to:	11%	12%	13%	14%	15%	16%	17%	18%	19%	20%
1	.901	.893	.885	.877	.870	.862	.855	.848	.840	.833
2	1.712	1.690	1.668	1.647	1.626	1.605	1.585	1.566	1.546	1.528
3	2.444	2.402	2.361	2.322	2.283	2.246	2.210	2.174	2.140	2.106
4	3.102	3.037	2.974	2.914	2.855	2.798	2.743	2.690	2.639	2.589
5	3.696	3.605	3.517	3.433	3.352	3.274	3.199	3.127	3.058	2.991
6	4.230	4.111	3.998	3.889	3.784	3.685	3.589	3.498	3.410	3.326
7	4.712	4.564	4.423	4.288	4.160	4.039	3.922	3.812	3.706	3.605
8	5.146	4.968	4.799	4.639	4.487	4.344	4.207	4.078	3.954	3.837
9	5.537	5.328	5.132	4.946	4.772	4.607	4.451	4.303	4.163	4.031
10	5.889	5.650	5.426	5.216	5.019	4.833	4.659	4.494	4.339	4.192
11	6.206	5.938	5.687	5.453	5.234	5.029	4.836	4.656	4.486	4.327
12	6.492	6.194	5.918	5.660	5.420	5.197	4.988	4.793.	4.610	4.439
13	6.750	6.424	6.122	5.842	5.583	5.342	5.118	4.910	4.715	4.533
14	6.982	6.628	6.303	6.002	5.724	5.468	5.229	5.008	4.802	4.611
15	7.191	6.811	6.463	6.142	5.847	5.576	5.324	5.092	4.876	4.676
16	7.379	6.974	6.604	6.265	5.954	5.668	5.405	5.162	4.938	4.730
17	7.549	7.120	6.729	6.373	6.047	5.749	5.475	5.222	4.990	4.775
18	7.702	7.250	6.840	6.468	6.128	5.818	5.534	5.273	5.033	4.812
19	7.839	7.366	6.938	6.550	6.198	5.877	5.584	5.316	5.070	4.844
20	7.963	7.469	7.025	6.623	6.259	5.929	5.628	5.353	5.101	4.870
21	8.075	7.562	7.102	6.687	6.312	5.973	5.665	5.384	5.127	4.892
22	8.176	7.645	7.170	6.743	6.358	6.011	5.696	5.410	5.149	4.910
23	8.266	7.718	7.230	6.792	6.399	6.044	5.723	5.432	5.167	4.925
24	8.348	7.784	7.283	6.835	6.434	6.073	5.746	5.451	5.182	4.937
25	8.422	7.843	7.330	6.873	6.464	6.097	5.766	5.467	5.195	4.948
26	8.488	7.896	7.372	6.906	6.490	6.118	5.783	5.480	5.206	4.956
27	8.548	7.942	7.409	6.935	6.513	6.136	5.797	5.492	5.215	4.964
28	8.601	7.984	7.441	6.961	6.533	6.152	5.810	5.502	5.223	4.970
29	8.650	8.022	7.470	6.983	6.551	6.166	5.820	5.510	5.229	4.975
30	8.694	8.055	7.496	7.003	6.566	6.177	5.829	5.517	5.235	4.979
31	8.733	8.085	7.518	7.020	6.579	6.187	5.837	5.523	5.239	4.983
32	8.768	8.112	7.538	7.035	6.590	6.196	5.844	5.528	5.243	4.986
33	8.800	8.135	7.556	7.048	6.600	6.203	5.849	5.532	5.246	4.988
34	8.829	8.157	7.572	7.060	6.609	6.210	5.854	5.535	5.249	4.990
35	8.855	8.176	7.586	7.070	6.616	6.215	5.858	5.538	5.251	4.992
36	8.878	8.192	7.598	7.079	6.623	6.220	5.862	5.541	5.253	4.993
37	8.900	8.208	7.609	7.087	6.629	6.224	5.864	5.543	5.255	4.994
38	8.918	8.221	7.619	7.094	6.634	6.228	5.867	5.545	5.256	4.995
39	8.936	8.233	7.627	7.100	6.638	6.231	5.869	5.547	5.257	4.996
40	8.951	8.244	7.635	7.105	6.642	6.234	5.871	5.548	5.258	4.997

TABLE 2 CUMULATIVE PRESENT VALUE FACTORS

Periods 0 to:	21%	22%	23%	24%	25%	26%	27%	28%	29%	30%
1	.826	.820	.813	.806	.800	.794	.787	.781	.775	.769
2	1.509	1.492	1.474	1.457	1.440	1.424	1.407	1.392	1.376	1.361
3	2.074	2.042	2.011	1.981	1.952	1.924	1.896	1.868	1.842	1.816
4	2.540	2.494	2.448	2.404	2.362	2.320	2.280	2.241	2.203	2.166
5	2.926	2.864	2.804	2.746	2.689	2.635	2.583	2.532	2.483	2.436
6	3.244	3.167	3.092	3.021	2.951	2.885	2.821	2.759	2.670	2.643
7	3.508	3.416	3.327	3.242	3.161	3.083	3.009	2.937	2.868	2.802
8	3.725	3.619	3.518	3.421	3.329	3.241	3.156	3.076	2.998	2.925
9	3.905	3.786	3.673	3.566	3.463	3.366	3.273	3.184	3.100	3.019
10	4.054	3.923	3.799	3.682	3.570	3.465	3.364	3.269	3.178	3.092
11	4.177	4.036	3.902	3.776	3.656	3.544	3.437	3.335	3.239	3.147
12	4.278	4.128	3.985	3.852	3.725	3.606	3.493	3.387	3.286	3.190
13	4.362	4.203	4.053	3.912	3.780	3.656	3.538	3.427	3.322	3.223
14	4.431	4.265	4.108	3.962	3.824	3.695	3.573	3.459	3.351	3.249
15	4.489	4.315	4.153	4.001	3.859	3.726	3.601	3.483	3.372	3.268
16	4.536	4.357	4.190	4.033	3.887	3.751	3.623	3.503	3.390	3.283
17	4.575	4.391	4.219	4.059	3.910	3.771	3.640	3.518	3.403	3.295
18	4.608	4.419	4.243	4.080	3.928	3.786	3.654	3.530	3.413	3.304
19	4.634	4.442	4.263	4.097	3.942	3.799	3.664	3.539	3.421	3.310
20	4.656	4.460	4.279	4.110	3.954	3.808	3.673	3.546	3.427	3.316
21	4.675	4.476	4.292	4.121	3.963	3.816	3.679	3.552	3.432	3.320
22	4.690	4.488	4.302	4.130	3.970	3.822	3.684	3.556	3.435	3.323
23	4.702	4.499	4.311	4.137	3.976	3.827	3.688	3.559	3.438	3.325
24	4.712	4.507	4.318	4.143	3.981	3.831	3.692	3.562	3.440	3.327
25	4.721	4.514	4.323	4.147	3.985	3.834	3.694	3.564	3.442	3.328
26	4.728	4.520	4.328	4.151	3.988	3.837	3.696	3.566	3.443	3.329
27	4.734	4.524	4.332	4.154	3.990	3.839	3.698	3.567	3.444	3.330
28	4.739	4.528	4.335	4.156	3.992	3.840	3.699	3.568	3.445	3.331
29	4.743	4.531	4.337	4.158	3.994	3.841	3.700	3.569	3.446	3.331
30	4.746	4.534	4.339	4.160	3.995	3.842	3.701	3.570	3.446	3.332
31	4.749	4.536	4.341	4.161	3.996	3.843	3.701	3.570	3.447	3.332
32	4.751	4.538	4.342	4.162	3.997	3.844	3.702	3.571	3.447	3.332
33	4.753	4.539	4.343	4.163	3.997	3.844	3.702	3.571	3.447	3.332
34	4.754	4.540	4.344	4.164	3.998	3.845	3.703	3.571	3.448	3.333
35	4.756	4.541	4.345	4.164	3.998	3.845	3.703	3.571	3.448	3.333
36	4.756	4.542	4.345	4.165	3.998	3.845	3.703	3.571	3.448	3.333
37	4.757	4.543	4.346	4.165	3.999	3.846	3.703	3.571	3.448	3.333
38	4.758	4.543	4.346	4.165	3.999	3.846	3.703	3.571	3.448	3.333
39	4.759	4.544	4.347	4.166	3.999	3.846	3.703	3.571	3.448	3.333
40	4.759	4.544	4.347	4.166	3.999	3.846	3.703	3.572	3.448	3.333

TABLE 2   CUMULATIVE PRESENT VALUE FACTORS

Periods 0 to:	31%	32%	33%	34%	35%	36%	37%	38%	39%	40%
1	.763	.758	.752	.746	.741	.735	.730	.725	.719	.714
2	1.346	1.332	1.317	1.303	1.289	1.276	1.263	1.250	1.237	1.224
3	1.791	1.766	1.742	1.719	1.696	1.674	1.652	1.630	1.609	1.589
4	2.130	2.096	2.062	2.029	1.997	1.966	1.936	1.906	1.877	1.849
5	2.390	2.345	2.302	2.260	2.220	2.181	2.143	2.106	2.070	2.035
6	2.588	2.534	2.483	2.433	2.385	2.339	2.294	2.250	2.209	2.168
7	2.739	2.677	2.619	2.562	2.508	2.455	2.404	2.355	2.308	2.263
8	2.845	2.786	2.721	2.658	2.598	2.540	2.485	2.431	2.380	2.331
9	2.942	2.868	2.798	2.730	2.665	2.603	2.544	2.486	2.432	2.379
10	3.009	2.930	2.855	2.784	2.715	2.649	2.587	2.526	2.469	2.414
11	3.060	2.978	2.899	2.824	2.752	2.683	2.618	2.555	2.496	2.438
12	3.100	3.013	2.931	2.854	2.779	2.708	2.641	2.576	2.515	2.456
13	3.130	3.040	2.956	2.876	2.799	2.727	2.658	2.592	2.528	2.468
14	3.152	3.061	2.974	2.892	2.814	2.740	2.670	2.602	2.538	2.478
15	3.170	3.076	2.988	2.905	2.825	2.750	2.679	2.610	2.546	2.484
16	3.183	3.088	2.999	2.914	2.834	2.757	2.685	2.616	2.551	2.488
17	3.193	3.097	3.006	2.921	2.840	2.763	2.690	2.620	2.554	2.492
18	3.201	3.104	3.012	2.926	2.844	2.767	2.693	2.624	2.557	2.494
19	3.207	3.109	3.017	2.930	2.847	2.770	2.696	2.626	2.559	2.496
20	3.211	3.113	3.020	2.933	2.850	2.772	2.698	2.627	2.560	2.497
21	3.215	3.116	3.022	2.935	2.852	2.773	2.699	2.628	2.561	2.498
22	3.217	3.118	3.024	2.937	2.853	2.774	2.700	2.629	2.562	2.498
23	3.219	3.120	3.026	2.938	2.854	2.775	2.701	2.630	2.563	2.499
24	3.221	3.121	3.027	2.939	2.855	2.776	2.701	2.630	2.563	2.499
25	3.222	3.122	3.028	2.939	2.855	2.776	2.702	2.631	2.563	2.499
26	3.223	3.123	3.028	2.940	2.856	2.777	2.702	2.631	2.564	2.500
27	3.224	3.123	3.029	2.940	2.856	2.777	2.702			
28	3.224	3.124	3.029	2.941	2.856	2.777	2.702			
29	3.224	3.124	3.029	2.941	2.856	2.777	2.702			
30	3.225	3.124	3.030	2.941	2.857	2.777	2.702	2.631	2.564	2.500
31	3.225	3.124	3.030	2.941	2.857	2.778	2.703			
32	3.225	3.124								
33	3.225	3.125								
34	3.225	3.125								
35	3.225	3.125	3.030	2.941	2.857	2.778	2.703			
36	3.226	3.125								
37	3.226									
38	3.226									
39	3.226									
40	3.226	3.125								

TABLE 2   CUMULATIVE PRESENT VALUE FACTORS

Periods 0 to:	41%	42%	43%	44%	45%	46%	47%	48%	49%	50%
1	.709	.704	.699	.694	.690	.685	.680	.676	.671	.667
2	1.212	1.200	1.188	1.177	1.165	1.154	1.143	1.132	1.122	1.111
3	1.569	1.549	1.530	1.512	1.493	1.475	1.458	1.441	1.424	1.407
4	1.822	1.795	1.769	1.744	1.720	1.695	1.672	1.649	1.627	1.605
5	2.001	1.968	1.937	1.906	1.876	1.846	1.818	1.790	1.763	1.737
6	2.129	2.090	2.054	2.018	1.983	1.949	1.917	1.885	1.854	1.824
7	2.219	2.176	2.135	2.096	2.057	2.020	1.984	1.949	1.916	1.883
8	2.283	2.237	2.192	2.150	2.108	2.068	2.030	1.993	1.957	1.922
9	2.328	2.279	2.232	2.188	2.144	2.102	2.061	2.022	1.984	1.948
10	2.360	2.309	2.260	2.214	2.168	2.124	2.083	2.042	2.003	1.965
11	2.383	2.330	2.280	2.232	2.185	2.140	2.097	2.055	2.015	1.977
12	2.400	2.345	2.294	2.244	2.196	2.151	2.107	2.064	2.024	1.984
13	2.411	2.356	2.303	2.253	2.204	2.158	2.114	2.071	2.029	1.990
14	2.419	2.363	2.310	2.259	2.210	2.163	2.118	2.075	2.033	1.993
15	2.425	2.368	2.315	2.263	2.214	2.166	2.121	2.078	2.036	1.995
16	2.429	2.372	2.318	2.266	2.216	2.169	2.123	2.079	2.037	1.996
17	2.432	2.375	2.320	2.268	2.218	2.170	2.125	2.081	2.038	1.998
18	2.434	2.377	2.322	2.270	2.219	2.171	2.126	2.082	2.039	1.998
19	2.436	2.378	2.323	2.271	2.220	2.172	2.126	2.082	2.040	1.999
20	2.437	2.379	2.324	2.271	2.221	2.173	2.127	2.083	2.040	1.999
21	2.437	2.379	2.324	2.272	2.221	2.173	2.127	2.083	2.040	2.000
22	2.438	2.380	2.325	2.272	2.222	2.173	2.127			
23	2.438	2.380	2.325	2.272	2.222	2.173	1.127			
24	2.438	2.380	2.325	2.273	2.222	2.174	2.128			
25	2.439	2.380	2.325	2.273	2.222	2.174	2.128	2.083	2.040	2.000
26	2.439	2.381	2.326	2.273	2.222	2.174	2.128			
27										
28										
29										
30	2.439	2.381	2.326	2.273	2.222	2.174	2.128			

Glossary

Note: A glossary is informative when it is tailored to the current technical level of a learner. The wording that is suitable after having read Chapters 1 and 2 may be too elementary when the student has covered ten chapters of the book. This glossary has been kept brief and at an introductory level in order to assist students who are new to the subject. Greater depth of explanation can be obtained by referring to the discussions in the book, which can be located by using the Index on page 606.

Absorption costing   Includes fixed manufacturing overhead, as well as variable manufacturing overhead and direct material plus direct labor, in the asset cost of manufactured inventory.

Accountability   Reporting results and efforts expended to the person or group which delegated responsibility to us to perform general or specific tasks. (Being accountable means having a responsibility to report results or efforts to your "employer").

Accounts receivable   Amounts owing to us from customers of our business; usually these sums are not secured by other collateral.

Accrual accounting   Amounts owed to us, or owing by us, and similar non-cash revenue and expense sums are employed to measure income; contrasts with cash basis accounting.

Acquiree company   The company that is purchased, as opposed to the acquirer company that buys the acquiree.

Amortization   An accrual accounting technique that charges income for the usage, or expiration of the life of intangible assets.

Appraisals   An estimate of the current cost, or selling price, or other value of an asset; under some situations an appraisal value may be used as a figure according to generally accepted accounting principles.

Auditor   A person who attests that the financial statements are fair according to generally accepted accounting principles.

Barter transactions   Occur when cash is not involved, and the parties exchange assets or assets and liabilities; sometimes accountants record the assets received at fair market value, and sometimes the cost of the asset given up is used in reporting.

Board of directors   Persons appointed by the owners of the company to oversee the operations, and to hire management that will handle day-to-day activities; ultimately, the board of directors is responsible for the selection of accounting policies and financial statement presentation.

Bond conversions   Some types of bonds are sold on the basis of their convertibility into shares, usually at the desire of the holder; at the time of conversion, a non-cash transaction occurs.

Book value   Has several meanings; it could mean cost less accumulated depreciation of a long-lived asset; or, it could mean common share amounts plus retained earnings; or, it could be applied to preferred shares.

Business combination   Acquisition of either the voting shares or the assets and liabilities of a going concern company that is acquired on an arm's length basis.

Capital   Has several meanings; capital usually refers to the common or preferred shares or both, but some people may also include retained earnings. The term "capital asset" refers to long-lived assets.

Capital cost allowance   The amount of depreciation expense that is permitted by the *Income Tax Act* and Regulations.

Capital gains   Proceeds less net cost for income tax purposes; only one-half of such gains or losses are normally subject to income tax.

Capital transactions   Those transactions that do not affect the income statement but involve changes in the share equity of an organization.

Cash from operations   Cash generated by those transactions that normally appear on the income statement.

Collateral   Assets that are pledged or assigned to creditors as security for a loan (e.g., accounts receivable may be assigned to a bank).

Comparability concept   Refers to comparisons among companies.

Constraints   Laws or regulations that confine or limit accounting choices, often recommending one or few methods.

Cost of goods sold   Cost of the inventory that was sold.

Critical success factors   Functions or activities of a business (e.g., advertising, or customer service) that, if performed well, help the company to be successful.

Currency translation   Determining the (Canadian) dollar equivalent of the amount of a foreign currency.

Debt   May include all liabilities, but usually refers to long term or non-current liabilities, such as bonds or debentures.

Deficit   May refer to the excess of cash disbursements over cash receipts (government accounting) or the negative balance of retained earnings.

Demand loan   A loan that is due whenever the lender requests repayment.

Direct costing   Only variable manufacturing costs are included in inventory cost.

Disclosed basis of accounting   A basis of accounting other than GAAP, whereby the accounting policies that are being followed are set forth in notes to the financial statements.

Dividends   Cash or asset payments to holders of common or preferred shares; usually the sum reduces the retained earnings balance.

Equity   Ownership interest in assets, after deducting liabilities.

Equity basis reporting   A method of reporting an intercorporate investment that gives the same net income effect as would occur when the investment was consolidated.

Fair value increments   The difference (at the date of purchase) between a current market figure, such as replacement cost, and the cost or book value shown on the financial statements of the intercorporate investment that was purchased.

Fixed manufacturing overhead   Expenses, such as depreciation on a manufacturing building, that are incurred regardless of whether any inventory is produced in the financial period.

Generally accepted accounting principles   Accounting principles that tend to be followed at the current time; these are not available from any one source; very few are listed in the CICA Handbook.

General purpose report   The one financial statement per financial period that is provided to owners to comply with corporate law.

Goodwill   The difference between the sum paid to acquire the net assets (assets less liabilities) or shares of another company and the fair market value of the net assets; usually goodwill represents the assets that accountants do not measure (e.g., worth of people).

Illiquid state   Occurs when the company has few cash assets, accounts receivable and other near-cash assets; might cause a creditor to try to place the company in bankruptcy.

Intercompany transactions   Usually this refers to transactions between related companies, such as between a subsidiary and its parent company.

Internal control   A system designed to minimize fraud and error.

Investor sophistication   Refers to the level of understanding of financial statements that is possessed by an individual, as opposed to the market place as a unit. Unsophisticated investors might easily misinterpret financial information, and make unwise investment decisions.

Invoices   Commonly called "bills", which others send to us for payment, for services that they rendered (e.g., telephone bill, or invoice).

Judgment   An important ingredient in the accounting process; preparers of financial statements must choose criteria to use in ranking the relative important of information, and must form opinions based on a variety of data. (Judgment is used extensively in accounting.)

Liability rollovers   Occurs when a liability comes due for payment and is replaced with another liability; or, a rollover occurs when the liability is exchanged for shares.

Limited liability   The liability of shareholders for debts of a company is usually restricted to the sum that they agree to pay for shares when they purchase common or preferred shares in their company.

Management accounting   Concerned with providing information so that the managers of a company (as opposed to the shareholders and creditors) can make better decisions about people, selling prices of the company's products, production, financing and similar matters.

Materiality concept   Refers to the use of judgment by preparers of financial statements; some effects on financial statements are not taken into account because the preparer does not believe that they are important to the persons who use financial statements.

Naive investor   Tends to believe accounting figures, instead of interpreting them, given that alternative accounting treatments exist.

Objectives of accounting   Become very important when constraints are minimal and facts can be interpreted in different ways, or are not clear. See Chapter 6.

Obsolete   An asset becomes obsolete when a more efficient one exists, and it would be less expensive or more economical to acquire and use the new one.

Pension funding   Refers to providing cash to a pension administrator who invests the cash so that pensions may eventually be paid; should be contrasted with pension expense.

Period cost   An expense that is charged to the income statement instead of being part of the inventory asset.

Pooling-of-interests   A business combination that is not accounted for by assigning fair market values to the acquiree, but instead uses the book figures of the combining companies.

Private company   The most common form of business organization in Canada; occurs when ownership is in the hands of one or more people who tend to know each other; the general public cannot be invited to buy shares in the company.

Private placement   When bonds or shares are sold to other than the general public; often, bonds may be purchased by insurance companies.

Proceeds   Usually refers to the cash that is received on sale of an asset.

Prospectus   A document that has to be given to the general public when debt or shares in a public company are offered for sale; financial statements and other descriptions of the company are contained in the document.

Quarterly reports Major stock exchanges require that companies having listings (i.e., registration on the exchange) provide timely disclosure of important transactions and events. Shareholders, therefore, have to be sent certain financial statements for each of the first three quarters of the year.

Rate of return May be calculated in several different ways. Discounted cash flow is one method. Another is income divided by investment.

Related party transactions Transactions among parties who do not deal with each other at arm's length. Usually, parties that exercise control or significant influence over financial and operating decisions of a company cannot deal with the company at arm's length.

Replacement cost The cost to replace productive or operative capacity; as opposed to reproduction cost, which refers to replacing the identical asset.

Restrictive convenants Restrictions placed on the activities of a company by a lender, who is concerned that he/she be repaid what has been loaned. Often, these restrictions pertain to liquidity of the company, and dividend payments.

Segment reporting Income and asset data that is compiled for particular product lines of the company, instead of for the entire company.

Special incorporation Some companies are not incorporated under either the Federal Companies Act, or its provincial counterpart. There may be constraints in the legislation that could have an effect on accounting.

Special purpose report Includes a wide range of possibilities. Several special purpose reports may be prepared each financial period. However, only one general purpose report may be prepared per financial period.

Standard cost A variety of standards might be used in management accounting. The standards may or may not approximate actual cost. Standard costs that are materially different from actual cost are not GAAP.

Stewardship reporting A virtually meaningless phrase today, because it is used in so many different ways. Broadly speaking, it refers to the obligation of managers or stewards of the company to report to owners.

Subsequent event Refers to events that occur after the date of the financial statements but before the preparers finalize them several weeks later. Some subsequent events are disclosed in the financial statements.

Tax allocation A controversial issue, which tend to be under frequent re-examination by accountants. It involves non-cash increases or decreases to the income statement and balance sheet, to recognize timing differences between accounting and income tax treatment.

Users of financial statements This includes a wide variety of persons and groups, some of which have the power to demand information in financial statements. However, many of the users are virtually powerless and have to rely on government legislation and administrative practices (through Securities Commissions) to require measurement and disclosure by public companies.

Variable expense An expense that decreases or increases with the level of activity. For example, expenses that are directly incurred to manufacture inventory (such as wood or metal materials) would be variable expenses.

Working capital Current assets less current liabilities. This sum or ratio varies considerably from industry to industry. Industries with little or no inventory, and minor amounts of receivables might have negative working capital.

Index